Prisoners of
WAR

PATSY ADAM-SMITH is one of Australia's best-known and best-loved authors. She was awarded the OBE in 1980 for services to literature and the Order of Australia in 1994 for services to recording oral history. *Prisoners of War* received the prestigious triennial Order of Australia Association Book Prize in 1993. Said Professor Geoffrey Blainey, a member of the judging panel: 'No book has previously been written on this wide theme, partly because of the immensity of the task. *Prisoners of War* is written with clarity and vivacity and compassion. It tells of import-ant, moving and sometimes humiliating episodes in Australia's history'.

Tim Hitchin

April 1997

Prisoners of
WAR

From Gallipoli to Korea

Patsy Adam-Smith

Penguin Books

Penguin Books Australia Ltd
487 Maroondah Highway, PO Box 257
Ringwood, Victoria 3134, Australia
Penguin Books Ltd
Harmondsworth, Middlesex, England
Viking Penguin, A Division of Penguin Books USA Inc.
375 Hudson Street, New York, New York 10014, USA
Penguin Books Canada Limited
10 Alcorn Avenue, Toronto, Ontario, Canada M4V 3B2
Penguin Books (N.Z.) Ltd
Cnr Rosedale and Airborne Roads, Albany, Auckland, New Zealand

First published by Penguin Books Australia Ltd 1992
This edition published 1997

10 9 8 7 6 5 4 3 2 1

Typeset in Sabon by Midland Typesetters, Maryborough, Victoria
Printed in Australia by Australian Print Group, Maryborough, Victoria

National Library of Australia
Cataloguing-in-Publication data

Adam-Smith, Patsy, 1926– .
  Prisoners of war : from Gallipoli to Korea.

  Bibliography.
  Includes index.
  ISBN 0 14 026143 5.

  1. Prisoners of war – Australia. 2. World War, 1914–18 – Prisoners
  and prisons. 3. World War, 1939–45 – Prisoners and prisons. 4.
  Korean War, 1950–53 – Prisoners and prisons. I. Title.

355.1296

Front cover photograph: The guards were old, the soldiers young. Bertie Giles is third from left.
Back cover photograph: Australian nurses (civilian and army) after being held POW for almost three-and-a-half years by the Japanese. Seventeen women had been captured at Rabaul and one at Kavieng early in 1942. They were taken to Yokohama and kept there until 1943, when they were transferred to a camp at Totsuki.

Publisher's note: Many measurements are given in imperial units, which were those in use in Australia at the time of the wars. Prisoners of the Japanese frequently used both metric and imperial terms, and many ex-prisoners also used both systems when recalling their experiences.
  The spelling of place names has, in general, followed the style in use at the time of the wars. Some variations of spelling of geographical names occur in various quoted documents and these have not been altered.

Contents

Introduction:
Preserving the Essentials

'My subject is War, and the pity of War.
The pity is in the poetry.'

Preface to poems, Wilfred Owen, introduced by Siegfried Sassoon.
Published by Chatto and Windus, 1920.
(Owen, a soldier, died in 1918)

'THINGS THAT SEEM COMPLETELY forgotten are present somehow and somewhere,' Sigmund Freud wrote. 'All the essentials are preserved.'

How the troops perceive war is no more foolish or inaccurate as are the assumptions of generals who write far from the terror and tumult of battle. For the real war surely is of 'the men', those who stand face to face with the enemy.

I have not attempted to give the history of the three wars where numbers of Australians were taken prisoner, nor of the battles or the service groups that fought in those wars. Most of the battalions, companies, divisions, squadrons, ships, have written their own history in detail, as have many individual men and women. As C.E.W. Bean said of his official history of the 1914–18 war, 'A complete book could have been written on each of the topics to which a chapter is here allotted. There had to be condensation. Sometimes a phrase which might have admitted of interesting expansion, has had to be left with perhaps a hint that there is more to be said.'

Neither have I attempted to represent all or any such groups, as volume would inhibit this.

The men and women in the book were chosen to represent all, to give a sample of what made a prisoner, cheered or dismayed them, crippled or ennobled them. The book has not

1

been written for ex-prisoners: they know the homesickness of exile, the tyranny of bondage; it was written for those people of today who know little (and that often wrong) of the experiences of men and women prisoners, their courage, endurance and pain. And it is written for the generations to come.

As the ex-prisoners of three wars have told me the truth as they saw it, these, our children's children, will know all of them. There are no tales of glory, no boasts of valour. They are men who once were hungry, thirsty, 'our souls fainting within us' as Private Donald Stuart, 2/4th Machine Gun Battalion, quoted. 'No man came to retrieve my soul from where it lay in the dust.' They themselves did that.

The people who tell their stories here have the toughness, wisdom and reticence of survivors who have seen more than any man or woman should do. Their stories add to the routine atrocities of history, but each atrocity throughout history becomes a thing of the remote past to the next generation. The lessons we have learned in every war we have sent our sons to were destined to be forgotten. But memories do live, they are deeply rooted in the soil of their own land, they remain in the psyche, in the nerve that never sleeps.

The men themselves forget nothing; no matter how long time goes on they see, hear, smell and silently recite like a litany what they know, and there are some things they can never tell. Some suffered torment and can no longer find their place in the world. Faith in humanity – cracked by the first slap across the face – can never be recovered.

These things I learnt as we went on many journeys together back to the lands where these Australians were seized, and later confined, to old camps and labour sites in Yugoslavia, Poland, Czechoslovakia, East and West Germany, Russia, Austria, France, Italy, Switzerland, Turkey, Egypt, Libya, Tunisia, Syria, Jordan, Iraq. Your memory leapt ahead and behind, and sometimes you remained silent, and sometimes eloquently profane. We travelled to Thailand, Japan, Malaya, Burma, Singapore, Borneo, Java, Sumatra, New Britain, New Guinea, on the Atlantic, Pacific, Mediterranean, the North Sea,

the Sea of Marmora, the Indian Ocean and almost every water-
way in the world, including both the Suez Canal and the Straits
of Magellan.

Wives talk, for they have walked with their menfolk through
the trials by fire that never leave a prisoner. All these women
are heroes in their own right. I do thank all my travelling companions, men and women, for the fun we had, the laughter
and the refusal to permit sentimental distortions and sympathetic historians to subvert what you knew to be the truth. The
tears you shed while telling of your lost years, lost mates did
not diminish your story, instead, it ennobled you.

I know much of your background, the battles you fought
'on land, sea and air'; I know that panicked instant in time
when you were captured, the bewilderment, frustration, the
anger when you realised your position; the gathering together
of your various energies – physical, emotional and
intellectual – to survive.

Donald Stuart put it well: 'It might be alright for some
nations to say it was more honourable to die, take your own
life rather than be taken prisoner. We thought it more honourable to live, as men were born to do, and we did our
damnedest to do just that.' But at a cost. Prisoners speak little
of that inward pain that has no name; tears alone tell of the
bottomless depth of it, one's heart aches for things we can
never be part of.

The story of your capture, imprisonment and return home
is, to many of you, deeply painful. To speak of those lost years,
of things held secret to prevent the pain of remembrance, often
brought tears. Sometimes the tears tumbled down on to our
hands, yours and mine. Those tears are the strength, manliness
and humanity in your spirit. Some of you felt bewildered anger
at being abandoned, followed by years of wondering what
Australians back home thought of your 'defeat'. Your pride
and dignity which cannot be equalled by those who have not
suffered as you have is unsurpassed. You have withstood the
slurs of the young and the criticism of those who were not
there and so attempt to discredit your achievements.

Perhaps this has not been too hard for you, because you know the secret of survival, and know that everyone who has not learnt this knowledge is the lesser for it. The journey you have travelled is unknown to those who have no scar on the body, the heart or the head.

In part, your humour helped you to survive, as did your particular Australian manner of telling a story that others may see as tragic. You may well be the last generations of Australians who have that gift. This is one of the reasons for your recovery; for you have recovered, not to the man you may have been had you not lost the years of your youth in the macabre world in which you were thrust, but you are certainly a man who has forced himself, through laughter, to cope.

You had one passion during your enslavement and you still have it: survival. You are now aging, tired, but you are living examples of successful adjustment to whatever life deals you. The rest of mankind needs to know of this because it will give them strength – and courage.

Some of you spoke of the depths of melancholy, of the anguished longing for time to slip back to before *that* time that only you know; to hear the voices as they had once been, chiakking, laughing, bawdy, gentle. The bane of a man or woman who has seen too much is that none but they know the whole terrible – or glorious – thing it was.

Your stubborn courage and determination to survive has uplifted all who know you and has become part of the nation's lore.

I have written twenty-eight books about our country. This, the last non-fiction book I will write, I dedicate to you.

Patsy Adam-Smith 1992

A Heart and Conscience Free

'Let's give today a burl. Let tomorrow do what it damned well likes.'

Private Donald Stuart, 2/4th Machine Gun Battalion

THERE WAS A TIME in Australia's history when our people were the most widely travelled in the world. Women and men – and their children – had journeyed for 12,000 miles in cramped, sometimes unseaworthy ships to get here to freedom, and here we stopped. We didn't travel again for over a hundred years. The distance to anywhere else was so great, the dangers so real, and our love for our new land kept us here. It wasn't until World War I that 'the masses' travelled, when over 300,000 of our young people sailed overseas. During that first Great War, hundreds of thousands of men, and a few women, went to over forty distant countries. Some fought, and some died, and after four years those first of the travelling Australians returned the long distance to their southern land; they brought a whiff of other lands home with them and stories of other people, nations, places so different from, but *never* as good as, their own land.

As well as light-hearted descriptions of their time away and an all-too-obvious concealment of the times no serviceman will speak easily about, there were those among these travellers who had greater difficulty, some an impossibility, to speak at all of their experiences.

And among those men and women were some who had been captives, 'taken into cruel slavery' as Othello had cried four hundred years ago. Their story may be seen as being more tragic than that of Shakespeare's 'Moor', their tenacity and courage in the face of adversity have as much merit and their attempts – and often successes – at escape were of the spine-chilling stuff of which films are made today.

5

The captives of World War I were mostly scattered in very small groups and, in some cases, alone in an alien land. They were the first to return, not as conquering heroes, but as vanquished slaves now freed, and marked in a way different from all others. They had, in the main, been put to work in a way no Australian had known since the harsh settlement period ended.

No soldier relishes the thought of being 'in the Bag', a captive of his country's enemy. There was, of course, a time when prisoners taken in war were not even kept as slaves but were put to death, often in barbarous ways as a sport for the delectation and satisfaction of troops or the populace.

Since time immemorial men captured on battlefields have been badly treated by their captors. Long before the birth of Christ, the King of Judah had thrown 2000 captive Edomites to their deaths from the heights of Umm el Bujara, a great cliff near Petra, Jordan. To walk beneath this cliff today is to hear the death cries of the young men whose only crime was to do what their countrymen had sent them to do.

Winston Churchill, once a prisoner during the Boer War, wrote that being a prisoner of war was a melancholy state: 'You are in the power of the enemy. You owe your life to his humanity, your daily bread to his compassion. You must obey his orders, await his pleasure, possess your soul in patience. The days are long, hours crawl like paralytic centipedes. Moreover, the whole atmosphere of prison is odious. You feel a constant humiliation in being fenced in by wire, watched by armed men, and webbed about by a tangle of regulations and restrictions.'

Shakespeare's adage that 'Every man thinks meanly of himself for not being a soldier' would not necessarily apply to a soldier who had become a prisoner of war. 'For a soldier to suddenly – always suddenly – become a prisoner of war, there is a nostalgia that has no equal, a languishing, longing, for the days when you were free to do what you left home to do, to fight for your country,' says Private Tommy Taylor, 14th Battalion, who was captured in France (World War I) and escaped from imprisonment by walking to Russia during the 1917 Revolution. Being captured was 'the bottom of the barrel'. Taylor had no option, he was surrounded, in a trench, and disarmed. But 'You don't join up to surrender or to run away or anything else. You go to war to see it out and no one but a POW knows the soul-searching he does. You think of your mates still back in the trenches, what do they think of you? Oh, you know they don't doubt you – some even saw what happened, but you still remember you are a soldier and that is what makes it hard because you can no longer fight for the cause you left home for.

'Being taken prisoner by the enemy demands a kind of soldiering that brings discipline from within rather than the army style of blind obedience from without. The most lasting of the painful effects of war on men is that which leaves a feeling of disquiet they can never resolve, the knowledge that they lay down their arms, under whatever condition, usually by order of their superior officers or, cornered, facing certain death. It makes no difference. In a prisoner of war camp each man gets to know himself, know the kind of man he is, probably for the first time in his life.' This realisation is a thing that men at home need rarely face in their lifetime. But, 'soldiers are citizens of death's grey land, drawing no dividend from times tomorrows', wrote English poet Siegfried Sassoon, and no soldier knows this more surely than the soldier taken prisoner, whether in World War I, World War II or Korea.

'For one day,' said a World War II prisoner, Private Donald Stuart, 'I wondered if there would be tomorrows. No, that's wrong, I thought would there even be all of today? And that made me think, "Well, bugger it, let's give today a burl, and let tomorrow do what it damned well likes".' He said, 'I'm an atheist, but I once heard the Catholic nuns up in Beagle Bay, north-west Australia, singing "Faith of our Fathers" and I never forgot the words they sang:

Our fathers chained in prisons dark
Were still in heart and conscience free ...

   And I thought, "and I bloody well am too".'

World War I
1914–1918

The Fledgling Navy

To the memory of Chief Petty Officer Barcoe, Petty Officer J. Gilbert, Able
Seaman W. Knaggs, and Stoker W. Williams, four of the crew of the AE2,
who died as prisoners of war.

From the diary of A.B. John Wheat, an Australian submariner of World War I

WORLD WAR I 'BROKE OUT' as the saying went – intimating
that it was comparable to a dangerous bull that had at long
last smashed down the reinforced fences built around it and
was now free to devastate all and sundry if it were not quickly
recaptured and returned to its corral.

The buzz of excitement began on 5 August 1914 when
word spread 'it's on', and didn't diminish until the casualty
lists were nailed up outside newspaper offices in 1915. In the
meantime, Australia's Prime Minister, Andrew Fisher, promised the motherland, England, that Australia 'would give to
her last man, to her last shilling'. And she did this, as row
upon row upon row of white crosses bear witness across the
face of the globe.

In 1901 before Federation, some men had left this land to
go to the distant skirmishes whenever they heard the drum
beat and the trumpet call or saw the pennants flutter, but
World War I was different: this country was going to war as
a new nation. It was a small nation but unlike Britain's other
dominions it had its own navy and air force and its army
would be going into battle under its own officers, beneath its
own new starry flag.

The navy, being the Senior Service, takes precedence over
the two other services and Australian mariners and submariners are part of that tradition.

The infant Australian navy was the first owned, maintained
and manned (as far as possible) by a British Dominion. The

Royal Australian Navy was unique in this throughout World War I.

Prior to 1901 when all Australian States resigned their colonial status and joined the Commonwealth of Australia, each had the odd naval vessel and some naval forces of its own. The visit in 1908 of the United States Fleet on its round-the-world voyage was seen by some as being an opportunity to tempt Australia to look for support in the future from America. But the Australians were too independent for that: they determined to have their own fleet.

On 1 January 1892, when Australia was still a colony, the Admiralty (in London) sanctioned the adoption of a system of recruiting in Australia for the Imperial Navy. 'It is announced that the intention is that recruits shall undergo a special training in gunnery in England and then return to the colonies to serve there.' But within the next decade, no longer a colony, Australia set off to found its own navy.

At Rose Bay, Sydney, HMAS *Tingira* was commissioned and used as a training ship for boys, many of whom later served in both world wars that followed. The Naval College was opened, fleet building begun, the building yards at Cockatoo Dock had been taken over by the Commonwealth, enlistment began, and boys around the nation were joining naval training brigades. 'Wireless experts', as they were termed, were being trained to use cypher for official messages whereas non-official messages had to be sent in plain language.

During the visit of the American fleet Prime Minister Alfred Deakin had stated: 'But for the British Navy there would be no Australia ... this does not mean that Australia should sit under the shelter of the British Navy. We live in hope that from our own shores a fleet will go out not unworthy to be compared with the quality, if not the numbers, of this magnificent fleet now in Australian waters.' His hopes were fulfilled when the first flag ship of the Royal Australian Navy, the battle cruiser HMAS *Australia*, steamed through the Heads into Sydney Harbour in October 1913. Within a year she was in action in the Pacific and shortly after led the starboard line

of the Grand Fleet on her arrival in English waters. At 10 a.m.
on 5 August 1914, when that first world war formally began,
the flag ship, along with nine other vessels of the newly formed
Royal Australian Navy, were already steaming into position
across the Pacific, the immediate concern being the German
naval squadron spread from the west of Australia to China and
down through the Pacific islands. Little was known about these
German ships except that the warships *Gneisenau, Scharnhorst,
Emden, Kormoran, Nürnberg, Leipzig* and the *Geier,* along with
colliers for their coal-burning ships, were in the Pacific.

Back in Australian waters the little ship *Protector* was bus-
tling up from Port Phillip to Port Jackson where she was to
become parent ship to the submarines AE1 and AE2 which
were both ready to sail on the 10th of the month. There are
many unsung heroes in every war but few as heroic, and forgotten, as were these submariners of World War I. John Wheat
from Woy Woy (NSW) sailed on the AE2.* He was with the
submarine from the time of its building in Barrow-in-Furness
until it was sunk in the Sea of Marmora, Turkey. The first part
of her crew had left Portsmouth in November 1913 to 'stand
by the boat' as naval parlance has it, the rest of the crew joined
them on arrival in Sydney.

These little craft were extremely crude, and now we gasp at
the courage of men who went beneath the sea in such fragile
boxes driven by the next-to-cart-and-horse machinery. One of
the theories for the disappearance in September 1914 of AE1
(the first Australian submarine) is that because these vessels
could not trim reliably, she 'fell into a hole' and her fragile
hull was crushed inwards by underwater pressure. John Wheat
only knew that the loss caused great gloom. 'All of us in AE2
had friends in AE1. We had been the only two submarines in
southern waters.'

---

* First letter for nation, in this case Australia, second letter for class of
vessel, then number of the type of craft registered in Admiralty records.
Only two submarines were commissioned by the Australian navy during
World War I.

The AE2 set off on 31 December 1914 with the second convoy of Australian troops to Egypt. Early in 1915 they made their base at Lemnos Island, the jumping-off point for the attack on the Gallipoli peninsula. The role given to AE2 was to attempt to navigate through the Dardanelles. Before she left on her history-making voyage, Admiral Sir Roger Keyes, Chief of Staff of the Eastern Mediterranean Fleet, had given Captain Stoker his orders, including the comment that if the wee vessel got safely through the Dardanelles and reached Chanak in the Straits, Stoker should have her 'run amok generally' causing confusion and fear in the armed services and citizenry and thus, if possible, deflect some of Turkey's arms away from the Gallipoli peninsula. No such vessel had, up to this time, been though the Dardanelles. 'We didn't know what dangers awaited us in the way of mines and submarine nets etc.,' Able-Bodied Seaman John Wheat wrote in his diary. 'A French submarine had indeed been sunk in the Passage and a British submarine lost in April. AE2 would be the third to make an attempt.'

Although Australians for over seventy years have used the name Gallipoli for the peninsula on which our men fought and endured for eight months in 1915, the actual town Gallipoli was never seen by these warriors. This town (Gelibolu on the Turkish maps) was on the other side of the peninsula to where the landing and the fighting took place. It was to Gelibolu/Gallipoli on the opposite shore near the Sea of Marmora that the men of AE2 referred in their diaries.

At 1.30 a.m. on 25 April, three hours before the Anzacs were to land on the opposite side of the Gallipoli peninsula, AE2 got under way to attempt the Dardanelles. Six miles inside the entrance she was fired on; searchlights were active so she dived immediately. She went along well until she came to the first minefields and the crew could hear the moorings of the mines scraping on the outside of their submarine.

'Shortly after we passed the minefield we came to the surface and showed our periscope to take observations before entering the Narrows. It was now 5.15 and the Anzacs a few miles

across the Gallipoli peninsula had been ashore for forty-seven
minutes.' Just prior to daylight, at 4.27 a.m., the submariners
had plainly heard the big guns firing, the moment of the
Anzacs landing. Soon guns began firing on the submariners'
side of the peninsula: Turkish fortifications had sighted AE2.

'The water was a sheet of glass, we were about 150 yards
off the European shore and the main forts noticed the wash
from our periscope and began to fire on us, so we soon got
down to 90 feet again on a different course. We passed
through the second minefield just below Chanak and surfaced
at 6 a.m. and saw a battleship laying at anchor and a gunboat
under way, so we immediately prepared to attack; but the forts
lower down had reported our submarine approaching so a
number of small craft, torpedo boats, launches etc. were
dashing about trying to ram our periscope whenever we
showed it.

'However, the foremost torpedo was brought up ready to
have a shot at the battleship but at the critical moment a
gunboat crossed in front of her. We immediately then went
down to 60 feet and a heavy concussion shook the submarine
and we knew that we'd secured a hit.' At this point they were
alarmed to hear a grating sound and knew the submarine was
aground. Ten minutes later she was grounded again. Lying at
an angle, down by the bows, there was only 8 feet of water
showing in the diving gauge which meant that the afterpart of
the boat and the top of the bridge were showing above water.
'We could hear the shells striking the water and bursting
outside. Captain Stoker told us to remain cool and all would
go well. He raised the periscope again, saw we were being fired
on from all sides, lowered the periscope and ordered full speed
ahead and soon we were moving off into deep water. During
this time the captain was extremely cool, all depended on him
at this stage and I believe it is due to his coolness that I am
alive. Nobody knows what a terrible strain it is on the nerves
to undergo anything like what we were going through now,
especially the captain.'

There was not sufficient electricity for the batteries to take her into the Sea of Marmora. 'We lay on the bottom and waited until night when we could come to the surface and charge our batteries. The watchkeeper was told off to watch the diving gauge and report any noises from outside the boat. The remainder of us were told to sleep as we were very tired, having been up all of this night.'

At 2 p.m. hands were called and put to diving stations. 'We tried to surface to see what was going on, but when we moved our screws we realised we must have been lying on the edge of a bank, and now the boat sank down to great depths.' This was exceedingly dangerous, as the thin skin of a submarine was only built to withstand a certain pressure of water and the diving gauge only made to register to 100 feet. 'But our gauge was now hard over, the gauge needle bending so we don't know what depth we went to. We thought this is what happened to AE1. It was a very close call, however we had sufficient air pressure in our ballast tanks to spill water and this worked against the pressure on the outside (at 100 feet there was a pressure of 45 pounds to the square inch, we tried not to think what it would be at 400 feet plus). We shifted a little nearer the shore, thinking it best to lay on the bottom and we tried to sleep again.' (Submariners were encouraged to lay down and sleep to conserve oxygen.)

'An hour later we heard a steamer passing over us. Everyone of us sat up. As the sound of the screws died away in the distance we slowly settled down again. In twenty minutes time we were awakened by sounds and this time she seemed to circle around us twice, sweeping for us with an explosive sweep, a grapnel with gun-cotton charge attached to blow up whatever the grapnel caught on.

'We didn't move. Regularly, every twenty minutes, the vessel passed over us, sometimes circling around us. Once something struck the outside of the boat making a loud report, but nothing happened. We didn't need smelling salts to keep us awake!'

When darkness fell the AE2 rose to the surface. 'Immediately the conning tower lid was opened a thick white mist rose off everything owing to the bad air, for we had been submerged for eighteen hours. We started our engines to charge our batteries. It was delightful to breathe fresh air again and have a smoke after eighteen hours. We were not allowed to smoke on the bridge as the smallest light would give us away to the enemy, we had to smoke inside the boat at the bottom of the conning tower. Forward of the conning tower the air was so bad that a match wouldn't burn for a fraction of a second.' During this time she lay close to the Asiatic coast. At 3.30 a.m. they prepared to dive and sail through into the Sea of Marmora. But in the meantime there was a gunboat and a battle ship coming towards the submarine and they fired a torpedo. And missed. The AE2 dived to 70 feet. 'We proceeded to the Sea of Marmora, entering it at 9.40 a.m.'

There was no time to celebrate. The Turks were now aware a submarine had come through the Dardanelles and had warned all shipping and fortifications. Forts outside Gelibolu fired on her periscope, two troop ships making for the battle area fired on her, so she submerged after firing a torpedo at the second ship – and missed. Another steamer had travelled around in circles to prevent her getting a shot at it. When this frenetic activity passed the submarine came to the surface to charge her batteries again.

Remembering the order to 'run amok' the AE2 steamed very close to a pilot boat 'with our White Ensign flying to show them what we were. [The Royal Australian Navy ships then sailed under the White Ensign of the British navy – a white flag with the St George cross and a small Union Jack in the top left corner.] The occupants seemed greatly alarmed, holding up their hands and crossing themselves.

'That night we lay on the bottom, certain we'd all have a good night's sleep after what we'd gone through. In the morning we came to the surface and sighted a big transport escorted by two destroyers. We immediately prepared to attack, the foremost torpedo was cocked, fired, but luck seemed against us and the torpedo didn't "run". Everybody was very disheartened with so many failures with the torpedoes. After this we came to the surface and spent the day slowly steaming around close to Marmora Island.

'We sighted a tug towing three lighters, all full of soldiers. We could do nothing but watch them, we were longing to have a three-pounder gun mounted.' In fact, the submarine had no small arms and carried only six torpedoes (and these appear to have been defective). 'Every time we showed our periscope we were seen and shot at.'

If to cause confusion amongst the enemy was their mission, they were certainly going the right way about it. The Turks must have thought a flotilla of submarines had got through the Dardanelles. The AE2 fired another torpedo at a transport and destroyers coming to harbour but the torpedo again did not run true. The AE2 turned and fired the stern torpedo, then had to immediately go down out of sight as the destroyers tried to ram her. Five minutes later she showed her periscope again but again had to dive swiftly as the destroyers were following her wake.

By now, when she dived, her batteries were very low and soon she must steam on the surface with her gas engine, at the same time charging her batteries. The AE2 been under way half an hour when she sighted six destroyers escorting three small transports from Constantinople (Istanbul). 'With only one torpedo left and as these were only small transports, we decided to keep this for something larger, but to show our-selves as much as possible so as to frighten them. We were all put at diving stations to be ready to go under at a moment's notice. The enemy fired, one shot fell 100 yards off our star-board bow, one just over us. We immediately dived down to 40 feet. One destroyer rushed over us at full speed hoping to ram us. When we came to the surface again, the destroyers were clear of us so we started our engines and steamed towards Marmora Island.'

She was only under way ten minutes when her crew sighted E14, an English submarine, who, like themselves had just come to the surface. 'This was indeed a delightful sight for us as it meant company. We ran up close and exchanged greetings. She had come through the Straits of the Dardanelles two days after us, on 27 April. [It was now 29 April.] We made a rendezvous for the following day and parted, and spent the night on the bottom.'

Next day the AE2 got under way and rose to the surface at 8 a.m. Nothing was in sight so she sailed on her way to meet E14. 'On the way we sighted a torpedo boat and gunboat coming from Gelibolu. The torpedo boat came full speed towards us, we immediately dived but just as quickly knew something was wrong. In trying to rectify this we surfaced, and the torpedo boat fired on us, putting two shots through the engine room. The water was pouring in, we had no gun and we couldn't fire our remaining torpedo. The torpedo boat fired two torpedoes at us and the gun boat one. All missed.'

The submarine was lying at an angle, down by the bows and sinking slowly; the torpedo boat came close and threw out life belts and a small dinghy. Just as everyone was clear, AE2 sank beneath the surface at 12.15 p.m. on 30 April 1915.

All men of the AE2 were safe and once aboard the torpedo boat they took off their wet clothes and hung them up to dry; the Germans treated them well and gave them clothes and tobacco. The ship went full speed to Gelibolu and put along-side a hospital ship which was full of wounded Turkish soldiers who had been brought around from Anzac Cove. The Australians were a great novelty.

Even the famous German General Liman von Sanders and his staff came to the waterfront to inspect the crew of the AE2, the men who had made history.

And so began three years of deprivation for A.B. Wheat and the captain and crew of AE2. They were taken to Constantinople, 'Quarters dirty, food not fit for a pig', and then to Afion Kara Hissar in the Taurus Mountains. At first the submariners were put to work stone-breaking for the roads and digging with picks and shovels, and working on farms during the harvesting season. The food continued to be bad and sparse, until Mr Phillips, attaché to the American Embassy in Constantinople, arrived with his guard and servants and gave each of the men a Turkish pound (worth eighteen shillings in English) and provisions, and said that if they were still there at Christmas he would bring Christmas puddings (which he did). He also arranged a regular supply of provisions and money. 'After living on practically nothing but dried bread we had a meal of bacon and eggs and sausage and felt the benefit of it.' Also they were given new work suits and the officers from AE2 sent them 100 piastres to buy a football so they played football every day after work.

By now there were prisoners from another two English submarines along with the Australian AE2 and three French submarines, as well as Australian, English and French soldiers taken prisoner at Gallipoli.

On 7 January 1916 there was great rejoicing by the Turkish wardens, flags were flying, bands were playing, there were processions galore. 'The explanation was given that the English had been driven off the Dardanelles.' That, of course, included the Australian troops.

Early in 1916 three naval officers escaped, including Captain Stoker, late of the AE2. They were away for seventeen days and almost reached the coast, but unfortunately fell in with a Turkish police guard, were arrested, and sent back to the military prison for officers in Constantinople where conditions were 'almost unbearably vile'. Many times they were asked for their parole and were told they could have liberty and comfort if they gave their word not to try to escape. They resisted such inducements for many months until through physical weakness 'and other refined methods of cruelty', they at last agreed and were sent back to Afion, but when they recovered some of their health they at once recalled their parole. They were then moved back to the military prison.

Wheat kept an accurate, minute account of his prison life in Turkey, particularly when working on the Taurus Mountains' section of the Baghdad railway. The prisoners' work helped to make it possible for travellers to board a train at Calais and go by rail to the Upper Nile with only one break in the journey, at the Bosporus-Scutari ferry. 'This extension of the Baghdad

railway is one of the few good results to the Allies of the work
of their prisoners and like the convict roads in Tasmania and
other parts of Australia, future generations reaped the benefit
of their forced labour', Wheat wrote.

'This narrow gauge railway was 12 miles long, and of the
twelve tunnels the longest was 3 miles, which is twice the
length of the Hawkesbury tunnel in NSW. Because of the
terrain the train clings precariously to the sides of the towering
Taurus Mountains, majestic, inaccessible peaks and deep dark
gorges.' These mountains reminded Wheat of Mt Owen on the
west coast of Tasmania, and he says the scenery was just as
wild as that isolated coast; 'the trees had been cut down and
used for timbering up the tunnels and fuel for the engines'.

Wheat hated every day of his time in captivity. He twice
tried to escape but was unsuccessful. Fever broke out in the
camps and he was 'a constant subject' and his slight figure
never fitted him for the heavy navvying work on the mountains. 'We climbed the mountains and were without any cover
at night and only when the Turkish officers' horses knocked
up through bad roads and severe conditions did they decide to
call a day's rest.' It was still well below freezing point during
the day and the men were 'lumped' into a very small living
space, twenty men, some sick, in a room 9 feet by 9 feet. 'In
this space we had to eat and sleep for a week, the only liberty
we had was one hour per day for those well enough to take
it. By the end of the week things were almost insufferable, all
were goaded to desperation. I have often been in cramped
spaces in submarines where you could cut the air with a knife
but never did I experience the nausea I suffered in that putrid
hole and it must have been worse for the sick and weak.'

The men worked from Gulekbasar on the Baghdad side of
the Taurus Mountains, passing through the twelve tunnels
until the line reached Belemedek on the other side. Until this
section was finished, all munitions, produce, etc. had to be
unloaded and reloaded at these two stopping places, changing
from broad to narrow gauge.

The work was very hard, the hours long. 'The prisoners

were divided into three shifts so that the work never stopped; many, especially the weak and wounded, preferred the night shift in the tunnels because there were no fleas and, as well, they escaped the intense heat of day. Those who refused to work in the tunnels were sent to Bazanti, a punishment camp where work was even harder and hours were longer. A number of men died here. One of my shipmates, Williams, a stoker on AE2, succumbed to this cruelty.'

On 4 May 1916 a party was sent to work on the mouth of the last tunnel through the mountains where food and accommodation and work conditions were even more extreme. When they learnt they were only 45 miles from the coast, Wheat and his friend Nicholls decided on an escape bid. 'We left on 12 August 1916. Our friends who were "in the know" wished us all sorts of luck as we went off with our packs at 8 p.m. while three men kept the old sentry occupied in conversation. The country here was so rough we had to keep resting, wet through with perspiration.' They climbed vertical precipices, 'hanging on by toes and fingertips, and at night lay down to sleep with the jackals howling all around'. They fell, they stumbled, their packs were broken open as they tumbled down cliffsides, they lost some of their bread and tobacco. Their line of travel was going up and down, travel was slow; when they tried to get water out of old wells, they'd haul up and find it was dirty and full of white maggots, but 'we had to drink it'.

After many days of climbing they reached the coast. With their 12-inch saws they had stolen back at the work camp they got some saplings together into bundles to make a raft and quietly took it down to the water, for they were very close to small towns and had seen Turkish soldiers, 'one having a bath, the other praying'. They launched the raft, named it 'Success', read the service from a prayer-book they carried, sprinkled water on it, but when the two of them got on it barely floated. It certainly wasn't good enough to put to sea in.

Wheat and Nicholls decided to return and wait for another opportunity to escape, but after travelling to within half a mile from the camp they were challenged and seized by a sentry who took them before the commandant. Their arms were bound behind their backs with rope. 'We thought we were in for a severe flogging.' But later the ropes were taken off and they were locked for some days in a room infested with mice. They were then marched 10 miles and brought before a Lieutenant-Commander from the Turkish navy who had kindly feelings towards the English, having served under English admirals. 'Nicholls had a bad attack of malaria and he collapsed in a faint, and the commandant was very much upset by this.' But Wheat was unrepentant. 'I told the oafish colonel who was with us at that time that it was our duty as Britishers to escape from our country's enemies if possible.' It was the end of that particular escape bid; it had lasted three weeks and Wheat was determined to try again.

New prisoners from a typhus-infested area brought the dreaded scourge into the camp and within days of their arrival fifteen were stricken, including Wheat. They were put on donkeys without saddles or bridles and sent away with the typhus victims to a 'crude' military hospital where they lay delirious. After three weeks and five days Wheat and others were ordered back to the camp, to work, without any convalescence. They walked the 9 miles back, 'staggering along like drunken men through sheer weakness'.

Private Beechie, a Queenslander of the 15th Battalion, set off with Wheat in the Christmas of 1917 on two days' leave of absence to visit old friends at Belemedek; a sentry went with them. On returning, a heavy fall of snow on the tunnels delayed them a day over their time.

'The commandant behaved like a maniac, waving, stamping, cursing in the way in which German sergeant majors are so well known and dreaded by the privates. I wandered away and had scarcely gone a few steps when they smashed Beechie on the head with a stick. His head was cut badly, blood was running down his face. I took him before the German doctor who attended to his wounds and reported the case. But by this time the sergeant major had laid a complaint against us and said we threatened him with violence. We were sentenced to five days solitary, with bread and water. It was a poor finish to our Christmas holidays, and I again decided to escape.'

They were persecuted for nearly five months and all this time they were collecting material for a collapsible boat, hiding their escape necessities in a cave they had dug. They thought that 'death in any shape was better than continuance of the slavery and degradation of the last five months, and there seemed to be no end to the war'. Indeed, it seemed to be getting further away. 'It was attempt to escape or die of fever if we remained in camp. We volunteered for working parties where we would be able to steal the required material to construct a canvas boat not far from the sea.' At this time a party of thirty prisoners, including Wheat, were sent to Gelebek, only 35 miles from the coast.

'I made friends with some Greeks and Armenians and got all the information I could. There were now three of us in the party, Stoker James Cullen AE2, Private F. Samson 9th Battalion and myself, and we worked for three months procuring the material for a fine little collapsible canvas boat, 12 feet long, 4 feet 6 inches wide, 2 feet 3 inches deep. The heaviest part was the canvas (painted with stolen Stockholm tar) and it would be one man's full load when we made our break-out. We buried parts of the boat so it couldn't be found. We had practised economy all this time and had saved biscuits and money, and procured a small German pocket compass. We left on the night of 29 April 1918 and got clear of the camp and hid in some low bushes.'

The rain fell in torrents and they got bogged in fields and spent time taking refuge to conceal themselves. After four days climbing and falling in the rain-lashed mountains they got down towards the coast where there were not even wet trees to shelter them: they had 13 miles to go over craggy, slippery ground and then, if they made the coast, the voyage in the little boat would take five hard days rowing along an unfriendly coast, and one of them, Cullen, had malaria. Another fierce storm broke, they were like drowned rats, down to their last few biscuits, which were wet. They couldn't possibly succeed. They ate the remaining biscuits and decided to start back to camp before they became too sick to walk. None knew when they would be stricken with malaria as they had been wet to the skin and almost sleepless for four days. 'One of the things given us before we left was a bottle of chlorodine in case of dysentery. We took twenty to thirty drops of this each night and found it warmed us up wonderfully', Wheat wrote. But on return to their camp the escapees were put in a terrible black hole, it was dark and two Turks were put in and after that six Kurds. 'There were eleven of us in this awful place swarming with lice and fleas. It was sweltering hot, and that, combined with the awful smell from this filthy pit was unbearable. We used to strip to the waist to enable us better to keep off attacks from vermin. Sometimes I think it was only a horrible dream but when I think it over I know it actually happened. We endured this for fourteen days. Then, on one of our five minutes daily outside, I saw one of our chaps in the distance. I took a risk and shouted to him to see Captain Clifford and ask him to get us out.

'The following day we were sent for. Captain Clifford, a wonderful English doctor, was in the commandant's office. He pleaded for us, saying if we remained where we were we would die. He said he'd stand bail for us, told the commandant we wouldn't go away again.

'Captain Clifford took us with him to the hospital where we had a good bath, a change of clothing and a good meal. Many a time since I've thanked him for that act of kindness, it was probably the means of saving our lives.' Wheat remained at the hospital for three days with a bad attack of malaria. The following day he was sent for and despatched with some wounded and sick who had come through from Palestine en route to Afion. Here he saw a newspaper and knew that Turkey must be in a state of collapse. Many trainloads of retreating German and Turkish soldiers came by from the front, trying to sell their arms and when they couldn't they threw them away. 'They couldn't fight any longer for a lost cause.'

Each prisoner had individual experiences. Stoker Herbert Brown was a veteran submariner and he too kept a handwritten diary recording the sea trials of his 'pride and joy' (AE2), the announcement of war in August 1914, and subsequent events until his departure from a Turkish POW camp at the end of hostilities.

After capture, Brown had met with Russian, French and British submarine crews while breaking stones and blasting rocks for road building. 'For two months we worked from 6.45 a.m. until 5.45 p.m. on bread and water alone.' Then, while some prisoners were taken into the countryside to work, Brown was kept behind with a few other Australians to put reaping machines together ready for harvesting. 'The machines had been made in Australia!' he records.

After the death of the chief stoker of the AE2, Chief Petty Officer Charles Barcoe, Brown, by rank, became chief stoker. Diseases were rife in the camp, every man had malarial fever, some also had yellow jaundice, ague and cholera. Men working in the tunnels often lost their sight 'and others had their brains affected'. On 4 August 1916, Brown writes, 'Up to this date two sailors and three soldiers have died and been buried'. By 26 August another AE2 man, Petty Officer Gilbert, died of a 'very high fever' and was buried, 'all available prisoners following him to the grave'. 'Fever very bad, hardly anyone who hasn't had a touch of it. Several Russians have died here and were buried with the English and French in the Christians' graveyard at Belemedek.' Another submariner, A. Coates, died of yellow jaundice, and on 9 October another AE2 man, Able Seaman Knaggs, died of fever followed by Stoker Williams, who died from acute dysentery.

'The sickness about now is terrible, there have sometimes been as many as five or six Russians dying in one day; they estimated that over the last six months there have been 800 deaths of all nationalities, some dying before reaching hospital. The submariners from the English E7 are dying from fever. A German nurse died from typhus. Some of the Australian army men are dying, particularly with the typhus raging.' In the twelve months between February 1916 and 1917, more progress on the railway was made than in the previous five years and early in 1917 eight trains per day came in from different fighting fronts.

Stoker Brown received regular letters from his mother, wife, mother-in-law, daughter and brother-in-law. He constantly received postcards and parcels from the British Red Cross as well as from the Australian Red Cross. Much of the Australian Red Cross material was coming in through the Dutch Embassy in Constantinople, which also doled out money to the men and sent them clothing. In his parcels were 'sugar, tea, milk, boiled beef, hashed mutton, stewed steak, salmon, tins of sardines, army and navy rations, cocoa, tin of veal and peas and a tin of roast mutton, and bovril and quinine'. His mother sent him 'aspirin, laxative pills, tea, coffee, milk etc.'

Herbert Brown saw the end of the war out and returned to his family. A strange pride remained in him that he 'saw, on the line completed, the first train coming through between Stamboul and Aleppo'.

John Wheat had already left. Towards the end of October 1918 the news had come through that 1000 men were to be exchanged for enemy prisoners. After medical inspection the most unfit men were selected, and Wheat was amongst them. They were sent off by train. At Smyrna they were fumigated. 'Mr McLoughlin of the American College threw the magnificent building open for the prisoners of war. Imagine our joy at living in a place like this after the hovels we'd been in for three and a half years.

'And then we saw the Australian hospital ship *Kanowna* sail into the harbour. It did us such a lot of good to see the bright, smiling faces of the nursing sisters on board, to see British women after three and a half years.'

Australian Boys Are We!

One! Two! Three! Australian boys are we!
Four! Five! Six! We've got the Germans in a fix,
Seven! Eight! Nine! We'll beat them every time
There'll be a great time in the old town tonight.

World War I Australian Soldiers' song. Anon.

AUSTRALIA HAD ONLY A 'home service' army but she regarded this army seriously. The early Labor leaders, Fisher, Pearce and Hughes, were responsible for the needs of defence and believed that Australia would some day have to fight for her existence. They encouraged the establishment of a citizens army and by 1909 had brought in compulsory service. Yet, in line with her outspoken independence Australia retained the right to exercise her own free decision as to whether or not to participate in any war.

But the moment of truth came suddenly and Australians realised that though they were 12,000 miles away from the guns of Europe, if Britain fell so too would Australia. And above all there was an old family loyalty. Corporal J.D. Burns, 21st Battalion (who was later killed on Gallipoli), wrote what became a much quoted verse:

The Banners of England unfurled across the sea,
Floating out upon the wind were beckoning to me.
Storm-rent and battle torn, smoke stained and grey;
The Banners of England – and how could I stay.

The free decision of Australians to go to war was never in doubt. They filled ships as their bodies would later fill trenches and graves, with the legend *Known only unto God* as their epitaph. By the morning of 5 August 1914 when war was

27

declared, young men were already lined up to enlist and the queue grew longer and longer as the months went by. As they enlisted the men were warned of the dangers abroad, from nits in the hair to venereal disease, but no one told them about death or of being captured and taken to an enemy camp – or worse.

By 10 August the British government had announced it had 'gratefully' received offers from Australia of 20,000 men as well as offers from the Royal Australian Navy. (The air corps were attached to the army.) And this was only the first trickle of Dominion forces that were to flow into the madness that ironically enough became known as The Great World War. No one could envisage the monstrous numbers of young men that would be used 'as cattle', as Wilfred Owen wrote.

The new Australian army (first titled a Division) was raised by Major-General Sir William Bridges KCB, CMG (who was later killed on Gallipoli on 18 May 1915). The Australian Imperial Force (AIF) was made up partly of youngsters in their 20th year and upwards, and partly of men who had been in the militia or fought in South Africa or other wars. In this way, Australia went to war and, like soldiers from time immemorial, men were taken prisoner.

They expected to be fighting in Europe 'getting the Germans in a fix' as their song went, but, instead, they were sent to the Gallipoli peninsula in Turkey. Private Jim Bryant, 8th Battalion, heard an aggrieved infantryman on the ship going into what became known as Anzac Cove say, 'No one never told me nothing about no Turks!' But Turks there were.

None of the men had heard of Gallipoli. It was not marked on school maps, nor even on some more detailed maps, and when diligent Australians found the name on reliable cartographic displays it was noted as Gelibolu. This Gelibolu was on the shores of the Sea of Marmora on the route to Constantinople. But this was not the shore where the Anzacs were soon to win fame as they died: they were put ashore on the other side of the peninsula which, in their language, was Gallipoli. It was an unpopulated, scrub-covered area of high cliffs and deep defiles where the invading Australians were pinned down for eight months to a small area backing on to the beach. Their opponents were Turks who rushed down to the peninsula to defend their homeland.

There has never been an authoritative figure given for Australian soldiers taken prisoner on Gallipoli: all unaccounted for are merely listed with the missing or dead. Jim Bryant: 'When darkness fell on 25 April 1915, the day of the landing on Gallipoli, of the hundreds of wounded men who lay out on the exposed battlegrounds only one man survived in Turkish hands. None other was heard of again'.

The Anzac men, believing that no wounded man would be left alive by the enemy as a prisoner, performed herculean feats, often under fire, to carry their wounded out with them from seemingly impossible positions over long, exposed distances. There are many recorded examples such as the following: on 28 June 1915 the Australian 5th Light Horse Regiment was ordered to retreat from a point named Balkan Pits as the enemy in strength was upon them and their position exposed. The Light Horse troopers determined to bring in all their wounded – making for slow and dangerously exposed movement. One trooper brought a seriously wounded man down a precipitous washaway by pulling him on to his own chest and then sliding on his back head-foremost down the slope, turning himself into a sledge on which he carried his mate. The official report states that the country was so rough and the heat so intense that all men were exhausted. 'Yet they were as deliberate in retirement as they had been swift in advance.

'To onlookers who anxiously waited for them to come in the men appeared to be deliberately dawdling. The men of the small rear-guard could still be seen conversing and firing occasional shots as the Turks crept up to them.' Twenty-nine men had been killed, ninety-nine wounded and one man taken prisoner. This man, Sergeant M. Delpratt, 5th Light Horse Regiment, was captured in an odd, unfortunate manner. He had been sent to take a message to the troops to retire from their impossible position – but when he arrived he found the troops had already got away – and an Australian Machine Gun Company, mistaking Delpratt for an enemy soldier, was firing at him thereby cutting off his retreat and enabling two Turks and a German sergeant to creep up and capture him.

By the second day after the landing much of the fighting at Anzac Cove was centred on Quinn's Post, a garrison where men could only survive by keeping their heads down. For a month this fearsome battle continued. Both sides fought bravely, both lost heavily. Battles were constant but the mere strain of holding the post was equivalent to that endured in battle. There at Quinn's Post on 28 May, Captain J. Hill MC, 15th Battalion, had heard 'plaintive cries' from the 'bomb-proof' tunnels. He gamely pushed his way into the tunnel, dark, devoid of sunlight. At the same moment two Australian privates entered at the other end, with bayonets fixed and eyes peering into the darkness. Crowded against the wall, shrinking from the bayonets with which the two Australians fresh from the sunlight were unconsciously prodding them, were seventeen Turkish soldiers. The officer who had accompanied them had some time before attempted to make his way back to the Turkish trenches, and had not returned. Bombs had exploded among them – twenty-three of their dead lay in the trenches and the bomb-proof tunnel, of which the floor, walls and roof were scattered with the torn remains of their comrades. The wretched survivors were terror-stricken, 'apprehending the fate too often reserved by their own people for any wounded enemy who fell into their hands,' as the *Official History*, Volume 1, states. They rushed to kiss their captors, threw their arms around them and cheered lustily. This extraordinary demonstration was later found to be an attempt by the Turkish prisoners to ensure kindly treatment from their captors. The waiting Australians slapped them on the back and offered them cigarettes as they marched them down the hill into captivity and a far greater assurance of life than if they had remained as front-line soldiers.

The Australians took some hundreds of Turks prisoner on Gallipoli. With the New Zealanders and Australians pinned

down to a narrow strip of beach already crowded with reinforcements and supplies, space for prisoners was at a premium.
They were held in barbed-wire enclosures until one of the
many ships shuttling backwards and forwards to Lemnos
Island or Egypt took them on board, usually the day after
capture. Their food and drink was as bad as was that given
the Anzacs, no worse, no better. As an example, over fifty were
taken at Sari Bair and on 8 August 1915 during the bloodiest
battle, Lone Pine, seventy Turks were captured in the underground tunnels in which much of this battle was fought. Few
of the wounded Anzacs left with the Turks survived. In
Volume 1 of the *Official History* C.E.W. Bean wrote: 'Some
were shot or bayoneted. A German officer, seeing the Turkish
soldiers kicking a number of wounded men and preparing to
roll them over a cliff on the hillside stepped in and saved their
lives'. Later, after he had been transported to Turkey as a prisoner, Lieutenant Luscombe, one of the few survivors, replied
to a request for information about Private J. O'Connor, 14th
Battalion: 'He had lost a leg in the battle on 8 August and was
badly injured through having been hit on the head with a large
stone by a Turk who found him wounded.'

A paragraph in the *Official History* tells of the battle down
the ridges adjacent to Lone Pine on Gallipoli. 'Many of that
brave band upon Pine Ridge were never heard of again. Sergeant G. Bennett, 6th Battalion, a boy of twenty years was one
of these. He was commanding a small party who was last seen
surrounded by Turks.' The Turkish version was given a month
later: The Australians were said to have shammed death and
later fired on the Turks. 'We were forced to kill all those', the
Turkish version stated. All that was certain was that none of
Bennett's men remained prisoner in Turkish hands, they were
never heard of again until their remains were found by the
Australian Historical Mission which visited Gallipoli in 1919.
'Skeletons of men in the rags of Australian uniform lay scattered in threes and fours down the length of Pine Ridge, the
red and violet of the 6th Battalion still discernible on their
sleeves.' Many of the bodies were in ridges near Lone Pine, as

if the wounded had crawled there for shelter hoping to escape death.

Lieutenant Luscombe was captured on 8 August during this battle. Later, in an official 'Statement made by Repatriated Prisoners of War' taken in London on 9 December 1918, Luscombe told of what he had seen near Hill 971 Gallipoli. When reporting on these few days in August, Luscombe stated that at first 'there appeared to be little or no organised resistance to our advance. A number of Turkish prisoners were taken and sent to the rear.' But the Australians did have 'casualties' and many men had fallen around Luscombe. At 0250 on 8 August so many 14th Battalion men, including their OC, Captain A. Groom, had been killed that when Lieutenant Warren was 'severely wounded', young Luscombe was next in line of command.

'Lieutenant Warren called out to me to go straight on. The enemy evacuated the first two positions as we advanced. At about 0500 I found myself with a party of about ten or twelve men in a small gully behind the second ridge. There was a store of ammunition, a field telephone etc. In this gully we took prisoners, three Turks (one of whom appeared to be an officer) and sent them to the rear.

'The slope in front of us was covered with low bushes. I sent one man a short distance ahead and others to either flank. I took Lieutenant Curlewis with me to a small rock to obtain a better view; the Turks appeared 80 yards from us and Lieutenant Curlewis was severely wounded by machine-gun fire and died soon afterwards.

'At 0535 I sent back a volunteer from the 15th Battalion with a note asking for reinforcements but he was killed by shrapnel while crossing the ridge behind us. By 0545 the Turks started to advance in a counter-attack along the gully. We built a barricade with boxes of ammunition and held them back for some little time. At about 0600 we found we were surrounded by Turks who now were closing in on us on all sides. The majority of our party had been killed or wounded and I had slight concussion from a bullet splitting on a bayonet alongside my head.

There were thirteen of us still alive, most wounded, when the Turks took us prisoners. Two 14th Battalion men, Privates W. Warne and M. Hennessy, died of wounds after capture. There were now eight wounded left and two unwounded taken prisoner with me. When the Turks took us prisoner they treated us fair.' The survivors were taken by carts to Constantinople, a journey of seven days, and from thence to Afion Kara Hissar where they remained until the end of the war.

On 31 December 1916 Lieutenant Luscombe, in a letter to Mr A. Sharp of Red Cross in London, mentioned four ORs of the 14th Battalion who were then prisoners in Turkey – Boyle, Lightfoot, Williams and Dowell, along with Foster of the 15th Battalion and Rose, 9th Light Horse. Luscombe then writes: 'The total number in our Australian employment here is about 75 all told'. This would include naval men, airmen who were shot down and ground crew of the flying services who were captured by the Turks in Mesopotamia. It is an exceedingly small roll-call when one considers the columns of 'missing' printed in newspapers back home.

Australians fought and were captured by Turks not only on Gallipoli but also in the Middle East.

The Australian Light Horse had been founded as the mounted arm of the Commonwealth military forces. Its members did not wield lance or sword but relied on their rifles, using their horses as a means of greater mobility.

These men were not so much recruited as voluntarily rushed 'to the colours' when war was declared; they came from the furthermost outposts of the Australian nation: stockmen, squatters, farmers, settlers who had worked their 'runs' since the earliest days of settlement. Many brought their own horses with them, some from Broome, Darwin and Northern Queensland, paying their own fare on coastal steamers to get to recruiting centres 1200 miles away. By 1915 they and their horses were shipped off to Egypt, which was a great clearing house in those early years of war.

The Turkish army of the old Ottoman Empire was under

the total sway of Germany, and German leaders saw an opportunity to divert British troops from the war being fought in
Europe: and so, Turkey invaded Egypt and the British,
including Australians, were their adversaries and, as elsewhere,
Australians were taken prisoners.

Leslie Duncan Richardson, a signaller in the 1st Light Horse
Regiment, left Australia on 13 October 1915, trained in Egypt
and was 'engaged in various skirmishes with the Turks'. He
tells of his last battle quite simply. 'On 3 August 1916, the
Turks advanced to the Suez Canal and attacked at 11 p.m.;
we were outnumbered and after severe fighting the order was
given for the brigade to retire. It was 7 a.m. During this retirement I was cut off from my regiment.'

In all wars 'the Turk' has upset military calculations and
sprung surprises upon his foe. 'It was just twelve months since
we met at Lone Pine on Gallipoli, and now the Turk repeated
that bravery, and surprise attack. With the traditional battle-
cry of "Allah! Allah!" they charged through the night. "Finish
Australia! Finish Australia!" Eventually they did. Many of the
enemy had crossed the desert on camels, our men had crossed
on horses. Now dismounted, we fired in the darkness at the
flash of each side's rifles. Then they charged with fixed bayonets. Two huge Turks with fixed bayonets prodded me in the
ribs. That informed me I was a prisoner of war. Three miles
behind their firing line their German General von Greff began
a series of questions regarding the numbers and positions of
our troops. I pleaded ignorance, stating I was a new reinforce-
ment, "having arrived the night before". I was cursed, spat on
by the General and ordered to be taken to the Turkish lines
some miles further back. An Arab gave me a drink of salt
water, a Turkish officer confiscated knives, photo, watch,
wallet, cigarettes, pay book, articles of clothing and my spurs.

'During the day other prisoners arrived at the camp from
various regiments, 119 of us there altogether. That night we
began a tedious 10-mile march across the Sinai Desert. Our
escorts then heard that our troops were pushing the Turks
back rapidly and they were much worried about this and

began digging a hole: an escort could not be spared to take us further so it was decided to shoot and bury us to save any inconvenience. The firing party was brought around us ready for the execution; at that point a German officer was riding by and we appealed to him. He'd been decorated twice with the Iron Cross and spoke fluent English. We stated we were prisoners of war and asked him to treat us as such and not allow these Turks to shoot us like dogs. He dismounted, thrashed the Turkish officer in charge – this is the usual German method of treating any Turkish soldier responsible for a breach of rules and regulations. We were handed over to a group of German artillery men who gave us food and coffee and kept us out of danger for twenty-four hours before handing us over to the Turks again.

'We were now tied together in pairs, with rope, and ordered to march. It was impossible, walking on one another's heels, causing us to fall over. Each time one fell he was struck on the back with a rifle butt for this carelessness. In this predicament we were marched from camp to camp for exhibition. After six days we received our second meal since capture.

'Our first march was 25 miles, taking ten hours, with the thermometer registering 120°[F] in the shade, without a drop of water. We were suffering from burnt feet, hunger, exposure and dehydration to such an extent we decided we would be shot rather than carry on. This refusal led us to being supplied with camels and these welcome ships of the desert carried us to the railhead at El Ordya where we had the first wash since being captured.

'We were hurried off to Damascus, into a tiny room, extremely filthy and full of vermin. Eighteen of us here were guarded by as many soldiers, who robbed us of our food and kept us petrified for three days. Then to Aleppo and thrown into barracks with a number of deserters from the Turkish army. We were in chains here, these quarters were even more verminous and filthy than the room at Damascus but we did get a bath. Again we moved, this time to a farm where we were housed in donkey sheds.

'Eventually we got on a train to the Taurus Mountains and then marched for 27 miles to Pozanti. This march will live in our memories forever; we were given no food before starting and being exhausted from the constant marching and lack of nourishment and no rest we all began to tire and were all punished with the butt of Turkish rifles. We rose in rebellion but were powerless and because of this uprising we were made to run instead of march. Most of the men contracted malarial fever and one man died. Ten days later when we arrived at our destination in the Gulf of Ismidt we found money sent from the Red Cross at Constantinople had been appropriated by the commandant of the camp for his own use. Money sent to prisoners was never allowed to pass him and he frequently sold the contents of parcels. We often found articles with soldiers' names on them in the town and could do nothing to prevent it, and several of the prisoners were severely thrashed for drawing attention to this fact.'

On 1 October 1916, 100, prisoners, including the Light Horseman, were taken 20 miles out to help lay railway lines. Suffering again with malarial fever and dysentery he was allowed to live in a tent and then a hospital for fourteen days. It was bitterly cold, snow fell and the men suffered in the small mud houses. As well, they had to walk 5 miles to and from work 'on one pound of black bread a day'.

'The vermin in the house was beyond what I can describe and the majority of us got typhus. At one time 90 per cent were in hospital, I amongst them, being unconscious for fifteen days. They told me I had a temperature reaching 103.2°. An Englishman in this ward looked after me with medicine and food and I would certainly not have lived had he not done so because the Turks stole the food and medicine as well as the few poor rags of clothing I possessed and sold them. When I was discharged from hospital I was almost without clothes. By the end of May 1917 I was declared fit for work but malaria again attacked me, and then I had rheumatic fever.' Later he rejoined the working gang in the Gulf of Ismidt, 60 miles from Constantinople, woodcutting and charcoal-making.

'Conditions here were a considerable improvement, the hours being only from 6.30a.m. to 5.30p.m. and an hour off for lunch at midday, but food just the same, wheat and bread. Later the Red Cross Society sent money to us and we now were able to buy food.' In this way Leslie Richardson lived to return home in 1918.

At Afion Kara Hissar in the Taurus Mountains area, Luscombe took on the huge task of acting as agent for the Red Cross. The lives of the ORs in this area were dependent to a great degree on the food parcels sent by a circuitous route from London. Luscombe kept the receipt books and had a vast correspondence with Mr A.T. Sharp, the Assistant Superintendent for Red Cross in London, listing parcels and letters arrived or reporting when food and mail had not got through to him. He had a surprising amount of mail to reply to, varied and always interesting: 'I and others here were very pleased indeed to hear of Captain Jacka's further success. Trust he is still well.' Jacka had been awarded the VC.

Other letters were not so happy: 'Re copy of Mrs A. Wallis's letter that you enclosed – I deeply regret to say that her son Private L.O. Wallis is not a Prisoner of War. I remember him very well, but I have no knowledge of what happened to him. Would you please write to Mrs Wallis conveying this information with my deepest sympathy. I regret that I cannot convey different news to her. The other son, Corporal T.S. Wallis was killed. He was with me on Gallipoli. I have already sent a postcard to Mrs Wallis.'

Another prisoner who had been at the landing on 25 April was Lieutenant William Elston, 16th Battalion. His platoon stayed on the beach until dark when ordered to reinforce the firing line. 'When we arrived we found about 100 men without officers were holding on to the edge of a steep ridge. I took a private with me towards the direction of the enemy and when pushing through a clump of rough, thick scrub was surrounded and captured by about thirty Turks. At the same time Captain D. McDonald, our adjutant came up and was taken as was Private R. Lushington.' The Australians were taken back to a rise.

'It was dark, we were unable to see much but judged there to be about 300 Turks grouped under the shelter. Another body of 500 or more were close by.' These Australians were treated well by their captors and 'after being marched off towards the Dardanelles' they met General Essad Pasha, the commandant of the Turkish Forces at Anzac, as had other prisoners. 'He spoke to us and promised to send word through of our capture, and said he would see we were well treated.'

The men were marched to Constantinople and from thence to Afion Kara Hissar. 'We were not robbed of anything except overcoat and haversack.' As an officer he was 'fairly well treated according to Turkish ideas and was not employed in any manner. The Germans we met were friendly. We were allowed our men for cooks and orderlies.'

Elston continued to speak well of the Turks. 'Taken as a body the peasants, especially the older ones were friendly to us.' (He praises the Red Cross but was surprised to see when the war was over and he was free, 'there were 20,000 parcels still awaiting delivery in Constantinople'.)

Sergeant Stanley Jordan, 9th Battalion, who enlisted on his 20th birthday, was an accountant in civilian life and his Statement of Treatment whilst prisoner of war in Turkey is neat and explicit. 'On the 27th June 1915 I was detailed by the CO of my Battalion to take my platoon and attack a place known as the redoubt which was situated about 400 yards from the front. This was at 12.45 p.m.

'I was told that I had, if possible, to take the enemy's trenches and hold them till nightfall and then retire. My platoon was at this time approximately thirty-five strong. Unfortunately the communication trench from which we were to leave was in full view of the Gaba Tepe and "A" Ridge to the seaward ... before we had left the trench the enemy had opened shrapnel fire upon us. I had a further order to advance "half left" diagonally across our front and get into the shelter of a place named the Razor Back and if I had enough men make a final charge on the enemy's trenches.' Jordan decided that, as it was downhill, he would make a 'quick rush' to try to gain the shelter of Razor Back. His pathway would be across low scrub which hid the terrain. 'I gave the order to advance.'

The young accountant had almost gained the shelter of the high rise when he fell 'headlong' into a washaway and lay stunned for 'half a minute'. At first he couldn't realise what had happened but when his head cleared he looked around for his platoon. 'The whole of the reverse side of the Razor was in view but none of my platoon had gained it.

'Recognising the impossibility of charging a redoubt alone', he set off to regain his trench. Further down the washaway he came on one of his platoon wounded through the leg. 'I tied his wounds as well as I could as I had been shot through the right arm on the advance and had lost a fair amount of blood.' He continues his report in this matter-of-fact manner: 'We then, together, crawled along the washaway and came across another of our platoon, this man having had his arm shattered by a bullet.

'We lay here waiting for darkness as we were not more than 90 yards from the enemy trenches, but after two hours the Turks sent out a party of twelve men to capture us as they had seen me crawling around to see if any of my men were in sight.'

As well as the two men with Jordan the Turks found two other wounded men amongst the scrub-covered ground. They blindfolded them, took money from their pockets and escorted them to the Turkish trenches. Here, when the blindfolds were removed from his eyes, Jordan was taken to General Essad Pasha. 'He asked no military questions. He was merely interested in the Australians and Australia. He had no conception of the distance we Anzac had travelled to reach Gallipoli.' Later, he found his gaolers were just as bewildered. 'No hostility was shown, only curiosity – I could not tell them often enough that I was "Australia".'

Jordan was transported to Afion Kara Hissar where he stayed for the whole of his captivity. His time as a prisoner was not arduous. He, like other officers, had 'servants' (orderlies) who shopped for them, cooked and cleaned for them. He shared a house with forty-nine officers including twelve Merchant Navy Russians and two French prisoners. In March 1916 after three officers escaped, Jordan and his house party were taken to an Armenian church with sixty Russian Mercantile marine officers and locked up for eight weeks. There were 120 officers with their servant orderlies here, but on release they were permitted to live again in houses.

Although all officer prisoners of war were relatively well off under the Turks, the Australian officers were aware of the very different life ORs were forced to live. 'We were not allowed any contact with them till near the end. They suffered considerable privations and of the five who were captured with me only one came out alive,' Jordan wrote.

As the enemy, the terrain, and the manner of fighting battles were different in each location, so too was the treatment of prisoners. Those men taken prisoner by the Turks faced an enemy who themselves suffered from appalling treatment by their own NCOs and officers: it was therefore most unlikely that such down-trodden men would show sympathy or care for prisoners taken in battle far from the civilising effects of towns or supervision. Turkish soldiers had traditionally been considered barbarous in comparison to German servicemen. The experiences of Sapper Leslie Barry, First Field Company Engineers, who was captured at Ypres, Belgium, 1916, by the Germans and imprisoned at Düsseldorf are an indication of these differences. But then Sapper Barry was a man to notice girls and this set him in good stead. Especially did it aid him in his escape bids.

Barry's particular friend at this time was Private Wesley Choate, 32nd Battalion, who had been captured at Fromelles on 19 July 1916. 'Our visits to our friends were frequent, two or three nights a week, and our progress in the "romancing direction" was by no means backward. The ladies were particularly fond of our tea and English cigarettes from the Red Cross parcels. Occasionally a bottle of choice wine would be awaiting us and we always had tea with fresh goat's milk served with our supper, a real treat as it was the only milk other than condensed I'd tasted in Germany. Saying "goodbye" to our friends at about half past four in the mornings, we would reluctantly make our way back in the dark to the barracks the way we came out and managed to get in about an hour's sleep before being called.'

There were four girls, two single, two married with husbands away. Sapper Barry had assiduously sought the company of these girls: romance was all very well, on the side, but he was after maps and information about routes to Holland. He and the girls devised a means by which they could exchange letters through a hole in the wall of the prison. It was not a simple thing to visit these girls. In the flat on one side of them the occupants had reported the visit of an earlier batch of prisoners, so the girls were 'just a little touchy and they carried on their conversations in whispers'. This didn't inhibit Barry. He says it was a glorious feeling to be entertained in a comfortable drawing room in women's company after the isolation and discomfort of his imprisonment.

One of the greatest problems in the escape plans was the getting ready of civilian clothes for the journey. 'They had to be made out of our prison clothes and it was only during the few hours of night that we could do the work without fear of being disturbed.' They had bribed a civilian at the camp with biscuits and a loaf of bread to buy for them collars, ties and headgear, items hard to come by in camp yet apt to raise suspicion if not precisely what the locals wore.

'Before leaving we were given supper of biscuits and fruit by the girls. This kindness touched us deeply, we knew the hard conditions and the little meat they obtained with their coupons, and high prices for luxuries such as tea, coffee, cocoa, butter which was smuggled in through Holland.' The men made their break in two parties of three each. They had only one compass; Barry had a chart of the skies he had found in a magazine and could pick up the North Star as a guide. They were well prepared but it was still summer nights on the continent with, at the most, six hours of darkness.

They left Düsseldorf six months after their arrival, 'in pretty fair condition thanks to our Red Cross parcels. We had accumulated a good supply of biscuits, chocolate and dried fruit. We six colonials broke out of camp successfully because during the past few months we'd become proficient at getting out to visit the girls. Our lady friends had given us the time and instructions on how to catch the train that left shortly after midnight from Düsseldorf. Choate, one Canadian and myself were in the last party to leave the barracks. The first three got away but we were a few minutes behind time and when we arrived the train had gone. We spent the night on the ground in a spare allotment and at three in the morning we made our way back to the station, not being too sanguine as to our improved civilian clothes passing the censor in the daylight. However, Choate got the rail tickets all right and we got on a platform to find our train wouldn't start until 7 a.m., which was very risky because by this time our escape from camp would have been reported. If the corporal in charge of the station had been sharp he would have stopped us.'

Then the journey started. 'We waited anxiously to hear the rumble of the wheels over the Rhine Bridge because then we would know we were on the right train and the biggest barrier had been passed; but unfortunately, the train switched off in a different direction. We got off and set out to walk the 20 kilometres which hadn't been included in the plans we'd set ourselves.' They were rounded up by a policeman but escaped by claiming to be Belgian workers.

'We reached a swamp and dug in as we'd learnt our lesson as regards walking in the daytime, and set off again at dusk, and astonished the villagers at one town when they found us washing ourselves at the village pump.' They had many alarms, including a pheasant shoot when the guns were going off over their heads and they were sure the shooters would see them and collect from the German government 30 marks per head, the amount given for capture of each escaping POW. Before daybreak they saw the lights of Holland, 'And at the same time heard the command, Halt! We were not across the border, we were still a little way on the wrong side. The Canadian with us was taken away and given some kind of third degree and let the cat out of the bag, so they learnt we were English prisoners of war.' They were lodged in the town gaol at Kaidenkirchen. 'We asked the sentry how far we were from the promised land and he said Holland was only ten minutes easy walk.'

The gaol again was disgusting, 'with lice, no sanitary arrangements and all three of us with dysentery'. Whenever they were moved around from gaol to gaol there was no food at all given them. Every alternate day in gaol they were given dry bread and a 'vile' soup. Sometimes other prisoners bribed the sentry to take in English food because the 'old stagers' in the camp knew what 'clink' diet was like. They were in a large cellar for four weeks awaiting trial 'for not getting to Holland', as Barry put it. At this trial they talked to other prisoners awaiting sentence and learnt that their three companions had reached Holland safely. In the dock they were asked, 'Why did you attempt to escape?' To this Barry replied, 'Because it was our duty'. They were sentenced to fourteen days solitary on bread and water.

Eventually they were taken to the lager at Münster. Astonishing graft went on at this camp and Barry and his companions again managed to get compasses, civilian clothes, maps, everything needed in the escaping line, even some civilian money. A French prisoner who worked by day in a jeweller's shop in the city of Münster manufactured compasses, stole the necessary glass and metal and had a steel needle magnetised from the dynamo that drove the camp picture show. A couple of tins of meat, dripping or jam from Red Cross parcels would always 'work the oracle' in bribery. The Russian camp tailors cobbled up civilian clothes for them, but just before the time to go for the 'hop over', the Germans decided to move everyone in the camp back to Düsseldorf because of so many British attempting to escape over the Dutch border. Barry managed to get his escaping gear away with him when he moved, he rolled civilian money into cigarettes and his precious compass into a piece of soap so that he was better equipped for his next escape – which had to be very soon because winter was coming on. They got in touch again with their 'lady friends' and exchanged notes per medium of a length of cotton reaching from one of the top windows to the street below and although unable to visit the girls again arranged to get another detailed map and more particulars of train travel.

'To prepare for our next attempt I needed "sick time" so I poisoned my left hand by rubbing rust into a blister which through the swelling necessitated being lanced by the doctor. This piece of swindling got me a fortnight in the barracks.' His mates working on the outside smuggled in a length of stout wire as well as food parcels to be hidden.

They observed everything, such as the break before teatime, realising they would have twenty minutes start if they went at that time. But their map was discovered and two of their group were arrested and sentenced to fourteen days solitary: the remainder decided they must go immediately, and left on 12 December 1916 in the continental winter, mud, rain, snow and sleet.

Because of having to leave so hastily, they had only a limited supply of foodstuffs 'and no cigarettes', but they still had the wire that had been smuggled in to lower themselves 20 feet down to another roof.

'Six of us made the attempt, each of us "old hands" taking a man in tow who had not attempted escape before. My pal on this attempt was an Englishman somewhat thick in the vicinity of the belt and he had trouble getting through the bars of the windows which were 10 inches apart. After several gymnastic contortions and a good push from one of those who stayed behind he got through and joined me on the roof. Choate and Pitts got through the window, shook hands with me and by the time we hit the street they were out of sight. Within an hour and a half we were on the train. We left it at the first station across the Rhine, walked into the frozen fields and lay down in the ditch among winter-stricken trees. We were covered by snow in a few hours and took turns at the one and only pipe in our possession. At about three o'clock an elderly civilian gathering firewood walked on top of us. We lay low on the off chance that the old man would not raise the alarm. An hour passed without interruption and we were beginning to think we were safe when two armed soldiers charged in on our position, taking us in front and rear and we were once again prisoners, after some twenty hours of liberty.

'Back to Münster to do two months in the cell in solitary confinement.' As he was marched in Barry saw a number of familiar faces, men who had made attempts at other times with him, and learned that only Pitts and Choate had been successful in escaping over the border.

As soon as he was released Barry began to get his escape gear together including another compass and some clothing, ready for his next attempt. But all that was in vain as he was sent away to another camp where he remained until war's end, far from the helpful lady friends of Düsseldorf.

An anonymous piece of doggerel was circulated throughout the lagers.

I am a Kriegsgefangener
I wish that I were dead
It's all through drinking sauerkraut
And eating mouldy bread.

My bed is in the corner,
I sleep upon the floor
My back is nearly broken
My ribs are very sore.

And when the war is over
And I settle down to rest,
If ever I meet a squarehead,
I'll smash his bloody chest.

Private John Albert Giles, 53rd Battalion, was also captured in Belgium in July 1916 and remained a prisoner until the finish of the war. Young Giles had earlier written to his father: 'Mediterranean 26 June 1916. We have left the desert with no regrets. I am on my way to France where we shall see a lot of sights. Before too long we will be at the front in the trenches, and I fancy it won't be long after we land before we are right amongst the thick of it and I am rather anxious to have a smack at them. I sincerely trust I have the good luck to come through and get back again to you all.' On 2 July 1916 he wrote from Flanders, 'With fond regards to all at Marshall Street from your fond son Bertie.' He was moving in to the battle of Fromelles, where over 80 per cent of the men were casualties.

The usual telegram sent to next-of-kin arrived in Australia. 'To Mr J.C. Giles, Regret to inform you that Private J.A. Giles, 53rd (late 1st) Battalion is officially reported missing 19th July. Should any further particulars be received, you will be informed immediately.' In September 1916, 'We have to inform you that Private J.A. Giles, previously reported missing now officially reported prisoner of war Germany'.

Friends wrote to his father. 'Dear Mr Giles, How glad I was to get your note today and hear dear old Bertie's safe even if a prisoner. Any news is better than the terrible uncertainty of these last weeks. I never knew so much dread and horror could be held in this one word "missing" and I know what you have gone through. We had a letter from him last week but as it was dated 26 July, I would not let anyone tell you as I knew it would surely only mean added pain.' In fact Bertie's letter, from its date, must have been one allowed to men about to go into battle; it also tells us how swiftly the army processed such information as the telegram to the father arrived within a few weeks of the battle.

He was in a Gefangenerlager (a German POW camp) at Dulmen, Westphalia. Through Red Cross in London various people adopted a prisoner and the Society sent food parcels in his or her name. In Giles's case a Mr Winston Hockmeyer paid for a weekly parcel for him and by 3 December 1916 he had

already received three of them. Clothes and boots had been
sent by the Red Cross Committee. Prisoners spoke of 'mucking
in', meaning they would make a group and throw their parcels
in together so everything became common property enabling
those who didn't receive a parcel to share. But it was never an
easy life. Prison camp photos taken at Schneidermull camp
bear the legend: 'When the prisoners of war had no barracks
to go to, they had to dig holes in the ground and put straw
in. The result was that typhus broke out.'

Private Claude Benson, 13th Battalion, gives us a brief moment
of his soldiering life before he surrendered. There was snow
on the ground at 4 a.m. the morning of 11 April 1917 when
orders were given to advance over the Hindenburg Line near
Riencourt. 'We were immediately exposed to heavy machine-
gun fire, several of the men in the section I was commanding
were hit making it necessary to take cover in a shellhole for a
short time. It wasn't the first occasion on which tanks went
into action with our division, with the one in front getting a
direct hit which put it out of action. Orders had been given
not to proceed beyond the tanks which were leading the attack
and upon being asked what to do when this tank in front of
us was out of action, we had directions "to go forward and
improve position and capture the frontline trenches of the
enemy". And we did this.'

Meanwhile the enemy started to counter-attack and bomb
the communication trench. Orders were given to clear the
trench, and the men went in fighting. Then, instructions came
to hand over their small arms and ammunition to the machine
gunners.

'Bombs (grenades) were passed around and we set off to
counter a heavy attack on our right. In a short time I found it
necessary to lead the remnant of my section to cover in a shellhole. Some of the men were hit by exposing themselves to the
enemy's fire while running instead of crawling to a place of
safety. We remained here for a long time, trying to keep a part
of the trench clear.'

They were surrounded by the Germans who told them to stop firing. 'Instead of sacrificing more lives we surrendered and were taken to a village 10 miles behind the German lines where the wounded were tended by German medical people.'

That battle was over for Claude, and another was beginning. After some hours he and others were removed by motor wagon to a little village. 'Two guards who took charge of us gave me little chance of escaping en route. We were taken to a church with some of our officers and for two nights most of us had to sleep on chairs. I found a very interesting place under the altar.'

Soon they were removed by train to a collecting station at Lille and here he experienced the same warmth from the French as did every other Australian prisoner passing through Lille. 'The German guard waiting to meet us there delighted in showing us to their own people, with the helpless French civilians looking on during our march from the railway station through the main streets of this captured town. The poor people were compelled to live under this so-called Prussianism but were not crushed. One French girl threw a biscuit to us from a window whereupon a German military policeman shook his fist at her and took the number of her house. I often thought of that poor woman and wondered what punishment she endured for her kindness to us. Shortly after a Frenchman threw his cap to one of our men who was without a covering to his head, and suddenly, military police seized him, took him into custody and marched him off. By this time our blood was up and it was hard to watch this sort of treatment without doing something to help these poor people. They stood outside, wet through in a rainstorm, just to give us courage as we went by. Many French girls bravely faced the risk of severe punishment in giving a slice of bread to us.

'We were taken to the French prison, placed thirteen to a cell, the door locked on us and we were told we were to be ready to go to work on the roads at 6 a.m. No sanitary arrangements, a wooden floor without blankets or straw, one loaf of bread for three men and one soup a day of barley and sometimes sauerkraut and if you were lucky you might score a bit of meat the size of a finger.

'As time went on our condition got worse, we were taken off the road work and put on to ammunition dumps, all the while being under the shellfire from our own army. We were building shelter sheds for German troops but we were not allowed to take shelter. We were shown a printed declaration to the effect that Germany had requested Great Britain to withdraw all prisoners of war not less than 30 kilometres from the front line and that Great Britain had failed to reply. Therefore, we Kriegsgefangeners were considered prisoners of respite who would be badly treated, get hard work, bad food and have to work beside the Hun guns; no straw to lie on, no blankets, long hours to work, no soap, no pay and were requested to write to our people or any authority in England and tell them how badly we were being treated "and surely Great Britain would do as Germany requests, then you will be sent to a camp in Germany where you will get good treatment".

'I made up my mind to try and make the best of things until I could escape or was released. We were very hungry and on the way to work the men would pick up cigar or cigarette butts from the street and smoke them just to try and satisfy the craving for food. Very often the French civilians would place bread on the road for us to pick up but they had to be very careful not to let a German officer see them do it. I have seen German guards, when food is placed this way, kick it into the gutter so the prisoners wouldn't get it. One poor Frenchman, noticing one of us without a cap, took the risk of placing a cap in a little boy's hand, directing him to give it to us; the German guard deliberately snatched it from the boy and threw it into the canal.

'On returning to our cells after a long day's hard work, very hungry, we'd lie down and wait for our mangle soup (a root vegetable fed to cattle) to be dished up and often the German guard would offer us half a loaf of bread for a watch and I have seen gold watches and rings go for less than half a loaf of bread, anything to satisfy hunger.

'We were becoming so weak from want of food that whenever we got the chance to gather nettles, we'd take them to the
prison, make a fire as best we could from sticks gathered from
our various jobs which we had concealed under our coats, we
then boiled the nettles and mixed them with our watery soup
which we drank from tins we'd collected by the roadside.
Those who weren't fortunate enough to possess a tin had to
use their steel helmets. When English shells fell in our vicinity,
they would often kill birds and we were very glad to eat those
that had died by concussion.'

Fantastic schemes for escape ran through the prisoners'
minds. 'One day I was walking near a German aerodrome and
got within 12 yards of a Taube flying machine when the
engines were going while waiting for the pilot. Seeing nobody
near, I was trying to judge how the thing worked and my heart
started to throb as I really thought for a moment I might be
able to escape, but not knowing anything about the machine
I had to give up the idea.

'After some months of hard treatment, we were sent to yet
another camp in France. We were marched off, many fainted
through weakness and in many cases the guards would kick
those who fell and shout at them to get up. I saw one of the
guards using his bayonet on a poor French woman who had
given one of our party a biscuit. She stuck on her feet, put her
hands to her face and went limping and crying into her house.
I thought I would rather die from starvation than see this
woman so ill-treated. I wished the poor creatures would not
try and help us. I never admired a woman's pluck and spirit
more than that of the French woman of about twenty-two
years of age who noticed us coming and ran back to her house
and returned, running towards us with a bag of biscuits and
as she came near the road she shouted, "English, sweeties".
The German guard rushed to intercept her and lifted his rifle
to hit her when she raised the bag of biscuits and let it fall
with all her force on his head. He was about to give her a
swing with his rifle. We all rushed in and wrenched it from
his hand and threw it away. My heart was in my mouth and

I wondered what would happen next but some Germans in charge of transport shouted out to the guard, he mumbled something in German, picked up his rifle and left her.

'The French population could only stand on the footpath, smile at us, touch their caps or nod their heads. Towns having suffered severe bombardment at the beginning of the war, were full of roof-less walls with holes in them, reminding me of an ancient city crumbling to ruins.'

At their new camp near Montaigu they were put to work from 11 a.m. to 8 p.m. and at night laid down on beds of wood shavings without blankets. 'We were marched out every day to work on barges and sandhills. Four men from the barge threw the sand by shovels to the first platform built of planks and two men would throw it from the platform to the wharf. It would be taken away in small trucks by three prisoners. I often jumped on to a barge from the wharf for bread offered by the barge people.

'The hardest part was when a man was too ill to keep working because it disorganised the whole system, and the guard would stand over weak men, knowing they were exhausted and knock a prisoner down for not being able to keep up with the others. I very often advised the boys when they were sick or too weak to work just to lie down and stand a few kicks as the guards willingly kicked the men who were down, but if unable to frighten the men to work they generally left them to lay there.'

Soon the men began to die of dysentery. After each death the Germans allowed the French to send in some greens or a few biscuits, just enough to make them wish for more. The only treatment given for dysentery by the Germans was to order the patient off food for twenty-four hours. 'This was ridiculous as the men were already starving. The French took great risks to help us keep alive. I shall never forget a little French girl in Montaigu, our village; I had managed to climb the fence just as the guard was enjoying a smoke and the wind was rustling the trees which prevented my movements being heard. On the other side I came upon this little French girl who brought me some bread immediately and told me to come again. Before I left she gave me her photo and on it wrote, "My pa has been a prisoner for three years. All I give you is from heart".' It was this courageous kindness of the French and their own outrageous sense of humour which kept the prisoners alive.

'Our clothes were covered in vermin and we found delight in picking them off ourselves and flicking them on to German officers. The German guards tried to frighten us by opening and closing the bolt of their rifles and pointing them at us. It made them very angry when we laughed at them.'

In December 1917 they were taken to Friedrichsfeld in Germany with a 'small bit of bread and two soups in three days'. In this new camp they were given eating bowls, towels, blankets, overcoats, etc. and were examined by a doctor who ordered them to bed for ten days. But after two days the whole of the barrack was punished because 'by accident one poor fellow had been just outside the barrack door when he was seen by one of the officers. We all had to stand on a square of ice and snow for five hours.' But this was the most sanitary camp Claude had been in, the only objection to it being severe discipline.

One of his tasks in hospital, when he was on crutches (after an accident while attempting to escape), was to sit and wait for men to die and then sort their gear to be distributed to those who had none. After he recovered he was put in a cell and left for seven days in total darkness. At the end of this time he was taken back to hospital for three days.

He went to an exchange barracks where there were men who'd been transferred from various hospitals awaiting a change-over with German prisoners held in Britain. 'Poor fellows with gunshot wounds were in terrible condition, some of the wounds hadn't been dressed for five days, so I went to the inspector of the hospital and he said I could look after these men. I found the British wounded were placed in the same beds that had been used by the Russians suffering from consumption and all sorts of infectious diseases. I washed the place out and thoroughly disinfected it, separated the contagious patients and gave them strict orders to keep themselves clean.'

The next thing was to get the men washed and dressed. He had to wash the bed-ridden himself and because there was no bath he had to take the patient, lay him on the table, wash him with hot water drawn from the cookhouse in a bucket and available only at 5 a.m. or 4 p.m. (He found it difficult to keep a basin or bucket as the Russians used to pilfer them and sell them.)

'One poor fellow who'd been wounded in three different places had his kneecap blown off and his leg in a splint. His wound was discharging more than it should and I discovered a piece of bone projecting from the side. Once inside this barracks men belonged to the transport office, to be sent to Aix La Chapelle, England or Switzerland, therefore the hospital didn't want to have any more to do with them and it was hard to get advice from a doctor, but I managed to get this man to hospital and they removed a piece of bone two and a half inches long. He was sent back to me feeling much better and finally reached England. I learnt that after arrival there his leg had been amputated with good results.'

Germany was hard pressed and supplies were needed for 'the front'. Claude saw only paper bandages and instead of wadding, a wood-wool for use on wounds where plugging was essential, or for large wounds. It would become saturated with pus and become very stiff and any movement of the body or limbs would cause the plugging to come out. The German medicines were only half strength and they were very short of implements, and it was common for British patients 'to wait sometimes for weeks before an operation could be performed because of the lack of instruments'.

He had as many as eighty patients to look after at one time and had great trouble in procuring dressing material and often was given orders by the Germans not to use so much dressing for wounds. 'I received some from the British Red Cross and was able to keep the patients' wounds clean until they were sent to England. I think 50 per cent of these boys would have died otherwise.' He performed minor operations on patients awaiting the exchange. 'The majority of these men didn't want to see a doctor because it may delay their exchange and they begged me to fix it up myself. I'd treat an abcess or splinter of bone not far from the surface. I would only operate when I was sure that by taking the risk the patient would not miss his exchange and perhaps wait for months before getting away.' Repatriated patients sent back to England spread word of Claude's work and the British Red Cross sent a case of surgical instruments to him. 'To remove the most serious cases to hospital where better treatment was available was enough to kill a sick man.

'Straw would be thrown into the four-wheeled army trans-port wagons for the patients to lie on and when it was full the remainder were allowed stretchers. They were given a portion of bread, taken to the railway station and placed on the hard wooden seats of third-class compartments without even a blanket. Sometimes they went for more than two days with their wounds not being dressed, a distance sometimes 500 miles from Hamburg, Bremen and Cologne. I asked at these stations for the necessary dressings for the patients but I was refused outright.'

'The hopelessness of it all' distressed Claude Benson. He was asked to see an Italian who'd cut his throat, as several Italians had done, and after dressing it he was removing the man's clothes when he discovered that he'd also tried to disembowel himself. 'Men were in despair. We had a thin rope in the hos-pital with which a Russian prisoner hung himself.'

Claude now planned a means of escape different from his earlier attempts. 'I got coat and trousers, cap, compass and a map from merchant seamen who had been captured and taken on board the raider *Wolf*. When it was time for me to dress the wounds of the men going on the next transport to England I placed 350 marks between the wadding on one man's head, the cap was placed on another man who I said had a bed sore on his head, and the trousers were placed in a similar way on another man. The overcoat was put under a young stretcher case who had a fractured leg and arm. Some of my fellow NCOs in the camp helped get the wounded to the station, mainly big Warrant Officer Kennedy who had also been taken aboard the raider *Wolf*. Now he was senior NCO in the prison camp. They all wished me luck, knowing I was determined to escape.'

At one point he was 500 yards from the Dutch border and had his feet on the footboard to jump off the train, but then he thought that if he left the wounded prisoners they would have a 'terrible time' from the guards when it was discovered he had escaped with their help. 'I decided to stick it out until they were safely in the hospital.' But in the hospital there were guards on every landing, even at the front door and the yard at the rear.

Several times he had been caught attempting to escape, once a German officer said, 'Ah, going for a promenade?' Eventually he draped his civilian overcoat over the shoulder of a young Australian who had a fractured arm in a sling and told him to go to the bottom of the stairs and wait near the door until Claude came down. 'Giving him time, I followed, dressed in POW garb, and found the way clear, snatched the civilian overcoat, stepped outside with a Belgian who was making the break with me, climbed an 8-feet high iron fence, got to the top of a hill outside Aix La Chapelle, threw my POW cap away, donned a cloth cap I had in my pocket and put on the civilian trousers I had worn under POW trousers. The Belgian ripped the POW braid off his trousers, we looked at our map to get our bearings and discovered we were going into Belgium instead of Holland. Being near a tram running into Aix La Chapelle, we went into town and got a tram running towards Vals, which was near the border.'

They walked on the dark side of the road, past sentries but were not challenged; they met a guard right in the middle of the road and turned into a field and through some barbed wire and came on cabbage patches which they crawled through. They thought they must be near the border. 'As we crawled we noticed a little villa on our left and something like a guard-box on our right.' They heard a dog's low growl; but they kept on climbing, came to another tangle of barbed wire and cut through this; then noticed electric torches flashing 100 yards away, got around this, passed through a hedge and, 'We were free. We'd done it!'

An English soldier, Private W. (Bill) Harrison, 18th Welsh Regiment, was captured at Fleur Baix on 9 April 1918. He speaks of his admiration of the Australian prisoners. 'The first Australians I ever saw was when I came on them there lying on the ground, wounded, prisoners of the Germans. There was no food to speak of. We found a horse, freshly dead, and boiled it in an old tin. The next day we were given some sauerkraut and black bread and, more dead than alive, the Jerries marched us through the streets of Lille. As always, the French women tried to give us food but as always they were bashed by the guards. One day they took us out to work and a woman gave an Australian a loaf of bread. He ran back and shoved it into my shirt. The Australians were good at getting food. I saw one grab a horse by its nostrils and twist its head around and the men killed it and we ate it.'

Many prisoners in Germany heard of, some met, an Australian Private with the most extraordinary background – even before he enlisted in the 13th Battalion and was taken prisoner in France. In 1881, when 2 years of age, Douglas Grant, an Aborigine, had been 'adopted' by a zoologist, Robert Grant and his wife, from his tribal home on the Atherton Tableland (Qld). The Grants had wandered into the midst of a retribution by black and white troopers against the natives who had killed several white traders and they saved the wee boy who was about to be killed.

As Douglas Grant he grew up in Sydney, acquired a fine education as well as the thickly burred Scottish dialect of his foster-father. He joined the AIF soon after war was declared and was captured in France in 1916 by the Germans. In a prison camp outside Berlin he was given 'considerable freedom' because he was 'such an unmistakable figure', a

German scientist, Dr Leonard Adam, wrote. 'He was appointed by his fellow prisoners, because of his honesty, his quick mind and because he was so aggressively Australian, to be in charge of the receipt of the Red Cross parcels that made their drab lives tolerable.'

Douglas's work was primarily with the British Help Committee supervising the distribution of comforts to the POW camp, Halbmondlager Wunstorf Zossen, Berlin. His records show the wide range of organisations attempting to alleviate the hardship of life in such a camp where there were Indian merchant seamen and others who didn't come under any other umbrella. Letters telling of the needs of prisoners poured into Grant's office. 'This morn not receiving any parcels about from us two months. Please see if you have any parcels of the above name, Ismail Babakhot, kindly send and oblige. My best compliment to all our Indians and oblige. Rangoouidala.' Another wrote saying: 'It is a long time since received any parcels and the people would indeed be thankful if he gets some provisions sent down to us, we are indeed in great need now in this few weeks before harvest. We also receiving less bread now and if some biscuits could be sent down to us it would be very kind on your part. We are working regularly and no complaints whatsoever.'

There is a letter from October 1918 referring to eight members of the SS *Clan McTavish* who had died in captivity and Douglas Grant 'need no longer send parcels'. The Merchant Seamen's Help Society had as secretary the Englishwoman Beatrix Neeld. Of the *Clan McTavish* members she wrote: 'We would be very glad indeed if you would give us your advice and help as to anything else that's wanted.'

There was the Invalid Comforts Fund for Prisoners and it sent things such as glucose, malted milk, Oxo, oats, adhesive plaster, boric ointment, powder, soap, toilet paper, kidney pills, rhubarb pills, quinine and tooth essence, as well as soda ginger and soda mints. Grant also sent tins of curry powder and parcels of books to the Indians and found time to record everything in and out of his office.

The Boy from the Gippsland Hills

When he learnt I was writing about prisoners of war, my father, an old bushman said, 'There was a mate of mine, Tommy Taylor, we were at school together at Neerim South; he got caught, escaped and walked to Moscow when the revolution was on.' And he had.

In 1970 Tommy remembered every step of his odyssey and the time leading up to it. He had written a book about it in the Depression, 'hoping to make ends meet', *Peregrinations of an Australian soldier in Germany and Bolshevik Russia, by Private T.E. Taylor, late of 14th Battalion, AIF*. In case any doubted him, Tommy had a reproduction in the front of his book of the 'safe pass' provided to him in Moscow.

In the introduction to his book he wrote, 'I was the only Australian who escaped by way of Russia, and, I believe, the only one who had first-hand knowledge of the real condition of affairs during the heart of the Bolshevik regime.'

Remembering that he had little money to finance his writing so must keep the book short, he set off right at the point of capture. 'Bullecourt, April 11th, 1917! What Digger will ever forget it? The dawn that saw us "hop over" was bitterly cold and cheerless. Snow had fallen during the night and no-man's-land was hidden beneath a white mantle as we silently crept forward on our mission to the Hindenburg Line.'

Tommy was wounded, and with another wounded man lay in the snow, cold and miserable. They then tried to reach their own lines. 'Our "bolt" for the trenches occupied but a few minutes. They were sniping and machine-gunning and killing our boys by the score. It was more like a nightmare than anything real.' He and his companion were caught, and taken prisoner.

'Passing back over the scene of the conflict we saw a good number of our comrades dead and many lying badly wounded and the Germans allowed them to be carried behind the lines.' Tommy himself helped twelve men in, and gathered ground sheets off the dead and covered the living from the snow.

When darkness fell, the Germans corralled all their prisoners and sent them off through the snow to Lille where they were put in a stone dungeon in a fort, without light, a barrel in a corner to serve as 'a convenience'. They were given 'one very small slice' of bread and some coffee each day, used their helmets to eat from, wash in when they were allowed water, and at night for a pillow.

'To men used to the open-air life and wide open spaces of dear old Aussie, it was a terrible time, as night followed day almost unnoticed, our tempers were set on edge. It all helped to produce an effect evidently intended by the Hun. When we were at last released from that living hell, we had been reduced to a state of sullen, resentful, semi-submission.'

When they were eventually brought out into the sunshine, the light at first blinded them. 'But it was a relief to get out of that black hole.' They were marched to the railway station and the French population of Lille lined the streets as they did whenever prisoners were coming through. 'The womenfolk had parcels of bread and various kinds of food which they endeavoured to stealthily pass to us as we marched by. The German sentries knocked the parcels from their hands, even brutally knocking down with their rifles some of the would-be donors themselves. I had often heard some women spoken of as angels, but I had never realised how angelic women can appear to a man until I got on that side of the line. The French and Belgian women on the German-occupied territory – even the little children and the old men – were ministering angels to the prisoners; not in one place only, but right through the many places in France and Belgium where I was marched. Time after time I have seen little children hovering around where we happened to be working, and around our camps, apparently empty-handed, but just waiting a favourable oppor-tunity to evade the vigilance of the guards, and leave food for us. The majority of those French people and Belgians invari-ably carried some little luxury about with them when near a prison camp for any prisoners they might meet. We would speak to them, or they to us, and they never failed us in our

extremity – either food or money would be left in our possession. Their stealthy visitations, and the parcels of food they
managed to smuggle to us, were the one bright spot in the
prisoner's life.

'Out of Arras we were put to work digging graves and
burying the German dead. Nothing would have pleased us
more at that time than to bury half the German forces.' Later
he worked at Douai loading shells on to lorries on the way to
the battlefront 'to deal out death and destruction to our own
comrades'. When they were moved on after a few months they
were 'skin and bone. My companion who had weighed 14
stone could barely turn the scale at 9 stone.'

This move took them to a veterinary hospital for sick and
wounded horses. Here Tommy saw upwards of nine diseased
horses put down every week. They were then cleaned, dressed
and the carcasses sent off for human consumption. 'Every
disease known to veterinary science was here and we worked
amongst these horses for months, and ate their lights (the rest
of the carcass was for German consumption). I eventually sick-
ened from the same disease that killed the horses.

'They proposed to make short work of my complaint by
removing my infected arm. I strenuously objected, and at
length prevailed upon one doctor, who could speak excellent
English to try an operation on my hand. They lost no time
over it; I was bundled on to an operating table, and without
an anaesthetic of any kind they opened my hand right up from
fingers almost to wrist. The shock was severe, but I saved my
arm.'

In the hospital, dysentery was carrying off the invalids in
scores, especially the Russians. 'I counted as many as 150
deaths in the Russian quarter in one week. Their ward was in
an upper floor of the building and each man as he died was
taken by the legs or an arm and dragged down the stairs and
thrown into one huge common grave. Even now I can hear the
dull thuds and bumps of those lifeless bodies. Several English
died at the same hospital while I was there, but they were
treated with more respect, and were carried out decently and

buried in separate graves, not like the Russians in pits.'

When Tommy recovered sufficiently, he was marched back to the stables. 'Our boots had seen the best of their days; we had had months of wear out of them, and had done many a long march in them, and they were not in a fit state to see out the 30 odd miles we had to face. By the time we had covered half the distance our feet were blistered and raw, and when we reached Tournai [Belgium] it was agony to put our feet to the ground. When nearing Orchies a number of French peasant women were working in a field of turnips and they quickly gathered bundles of swede turnips and carried them to the roadside. We were alowed to pick them up as we passed, and we ate them until our gums were sore. But, gee! didn't we relish those turnips.'

Prisoners were constantly moved to areas where a work force was needed. It was at Heilsburglager in Germany that Tommy received his first mail from home since he was captured. 'Letters from home! Who can imagine what it meant to us? For fifteen weary months we had been forced by starvation and hardship to submit to humiliation and indignities, allowed barely sufficient food to keep body and soul together, and forced to gather weeds and herbs for sustenance; gaunt, unwashed, unshaven, and devoured by vermin; knowing practically nothing of what was going on beyond our barbed-wire enclosures; seemingly dead to the world, and, for all we knew, mourned as dead; would we ever see our loved ones again? We dreaded to contemplate the future, and yet life seemed one long-drawn-out query, How long? Oh! how much longer? And at last to see the old familiar handwriting; to be brought into touch with the outer world. At sight of those letters I broke down completely. For hours I sat there, every attempt to read them bringing the tears to my eyes, try as I would to keep them back. Oh! it was grand to get those letters from my mother, and to hear that all were well, every line seeming to breathe to me the old motherly love. I cannot explain my feelings – they were heavenly. I seemed to take a fresh grip on life.

'Those letters brightened us all up wonderfully, and soon
after that our Red Cross parcels arrived. The scene will ever
be a memorable one to me. As we opened parcel after parcel
and delved into their contents, every now and then bringing
forth something to specially gladden the heart, we were all
behaving like children. It reminded me of the good old days
when we wakened on Christmas mornings to gleefully examine
our "stockings" to see what "Father Christmas" had left. You
Red Cross workers, could you have witnessed the joy they
brought us I am sure you would feel amply rewarded for all
the loving patience, time and care you bestowed on them. It is
not exaggerating in the slightest degree to say that the contents
of your parcels saved many a prisoner's life.

'The arrival of our parcels certainly set the German people
thinking and asking us questions. They had been led to believe
that England was starving, that the German submarines had
cut her off completely from her sources of supplies and that it
was only a matter of time before Germany emerged from the
war victorious. They could not understand how a country in
such straits as described to them could manage to be so liberal
to her imprisoned soldiers.'

Now the greatest drama of Tommy Taylor's life was about
to begin. 'We were distributed among the various farmers
around. I found myself on a farm with two Russian prisoners,
the three of us working for a woman whose husband and two
sons were at the war. Because I was so young she used to make
sure I wrote to my mother to tell her I was safe, and she fed
me in her kitchen. She didn't worry at all about the Russians.

'This was 1917 and we didn't know anything much about
Russian affairs and neither did the Russian prisoners for that
matter. But we did know a lot about the state of things in
Germany because thousands of women and children were sent
away to country districts to work on farms for their food. We
were working amongst a number of children from Berlin and
learnt about the terribly hard conditions the Germans had
imposed on them just to keep the war going. They told us that
food riots were frequently occurring in the capital, always

ending in conflicts with the soldiers who used machine guns on the rioters, killing them in scores.'

To make matters worse, the 'Spanish' flu was raging, killing men, women and children. It was severe at Heilsburg and Tommy had it badly and for two weeks lay close to death, with no medical attention at all, none having the courage to contact him except his companions – after working hours. 'One of them in particular, a Russian, did more to help me than all the others and to him I owe my recovery.' Now, knowing very little of the Russian language, the boy from Gippsland moved into another realm. He knew he had no hope of fighting his way back through the German lines and crossing no-man's-land to the Australian lines, but for some considerable time he had been thinking seriously of making a bid for freedom. One Russian prisoner on the farm had secured a compass, another had a map. 'From information we got from another Russian who had escaped and been recaptured and wanted to try again, we decided that our best course was to make for Minsk, on the border of Poland and Russia. Our German guards had at times told us contradictory tales of the outer world, and had even told us that the Russians had deserted their Allies, and that the country was in a state of chaos; but we did not believe anything. Especially did we disbelieve their statements about Russia, as that was our nearest way of escape, and they of course knew it. So we went in ignorance.

'We figured it to be well over 400 miles to Minsk, and so had to stint ourselves and save enough food to see the journey out. The Red Cross parcels helped with bully beef and biscuits. Every week I put something by, and in a few months I had quite a store.

'We chose a Sunday night for the venture, the third of November 1918, and four of us set out – three Russians and myself. We started off in the evening for the Polish border, 8 miles east, marked by a high barbed-wire fence, patrolled by Prussian cavalry.' They managed to get through and over these barriers and crossed the border into Poland, always on the

alert for treachery and German patrols. As their stock of provisions ran out they were forced to beg for food. 'It went very
much against my grain this cadging, but beggars cannot be
choosers. Bread was scarce in Poland and Germany and what
was available was almost unfit for human consumption.'

All bridgeheads were closely guarded and they must cross
the Niemen River in an old and decrepit boat. It filled up the
first time the escapees put it in the water, but they put their
faith in the planks swelling 'once the boat got used to being
in the water', and declared it seaworthy, cut down some
stunted trees for paddles, and decided to 'give it a fly'. They
stripped – 'and it was cold! Dinkum!' – and pushed off and
with as many adventures as Mark Twain could write about,
reached the other side.

The flight continued in Huckleberry Finn fashion, including
jamming logs in Canadian lumber-jack style to cross another
river while German guards were lunching in a secluded dell
nearby. To cross another bridge over a moat into a village they
must pass through they had a woman volunteer go ahead of
them and return if it were safe. 'I felt as if I was sitting on a
keg of gun-powder or a live bomb', Tommy Taylor said. 'I
was all nerves.'

And then, a little time after they had successfully negotiated
the narrow streets of this water-encircled town (whose name
they never knew), they realised they were near Minsk, their
first goal, when suddenly 'a command from the darkness ahead
halted us'. In their alarm they didn't recognise the language,
they took for granted it was German. But, on the next
command, they realised that it was a Russian soldier. 'We had
evaded the German outposts, had crossed the 20 miles of no-
man's-land, or neutral territory, without knowing it. We had
crossed just to the left of Minsk railway station, but did not
know at the time it was the goal we were making for. The
compass and map had served us faithfully and well. Germany,
with all its horrors, and Poland, with its haunting and hidden
dangers, were behind us, Russia and freedom (as I thought)
were before us.' They completed the journey that night to the

railhead, arriving in the early hours of the morning where they boarded a train of cattle-trucks.

Tommy was at a disadvantage in Russia, not being fluent in the language. 'Two of the Russians had left us and gone in another direction when we entered the country, so I decided to trust my lone comrade and let him do the bargaining. He had been my workmate in Germany, we had been companions in distress and I had often shared the contents of my food parcels with him so I had not the slightest misgiving when I handed over my money. The following morning he had completely vanished.

'Well, I was up against it properly, not much language, no money whatever, no friends; a stranger in a strange land. The outlook fairly appalled me. But I just had to stick it out. I decided to make use of my railway pass [an old POW transit document], continue my journey and chance what fate had in store for me.' He reached Smolensk, not having eaten for four days and on the verge of collapse, but was rescued by a clerk in the military depot who took him to his own home, where his wife fed him, and gave him a parcel of food to eat on his journey.

'One thought predominated: I was nearing Moscow and once there I expected a quick return to "Old Blighty", Australia and home. Alas for all my hopes!' On arrival in Moscow a Russian doctor befriended him and helped him to the home of the Reverend Mr North, an Anglican clergyman. 'I was so overjoyed and excited that I began mixing up French and German in an unintelligible tangle.' He had his first bath for two years, shaved off his whiskers and slept in a bed with 'sheets!'

'But what if I dirtied them?' he fretted, forgetting he had had a bath and was free of vermin. That first evening he had been treated as one of the household, and as it was his hosts' wedding anniversary, 'had a most sumptuous repast' and luxuriated in a comfortable chair before a warm fire. 'I thought I had been transported to another realm. Whether it was the nice bath, the good meal or the clean sheets that caused it, but

I dreamt that night of home, sweet home.'

Next day he learnt there was no longer a British Embassy in Moscow. The Russians were out of the international war and the revolution was raging; the Danish Consul had been entrusted with the welfare of all British subjects. Tommy shared a room in the Danish Consulate with two runaway sailors who had 'bolted' from their ship at Murmansk and been arrested by the Bolsheviks as suspected spies. After serving a term in prison, they had been released and were then 'marooned' as was Tommy. The three worked together cutting and carting wood amicably, until the sailors disappeared and so did Tommy's clothes and bedding he had spent his hard-won earnings to buy. Tommy later learnt the two absconders had now joined the Bolshevik army. 'From then on during the bitter Russian winter I had to sleep on a bed devoid of any bedclothing and owned no warm clothing.

'Well, I had knocked about Moscow a good deal and had, by then, picked up enough of the Russian language to rub along by myself, so I cut loose to paddle my own canoe and raise enough money to get away out of the country, as quickly as I could.' He knew that to throw himself into that vortex of starvation and misery of the Russian people was a momentous undertaking.

One of Moscow's chief attractions for him was the market square and he decided there was a living to be made by dealing. He made his bare room at the Danish Consulate his headquarters (here he slept *beneath* a mattress left behind by looters) and undertook various jobs and so earned a tidy bit of capital. 'At length I secured a stall in the market and went in for dealing in anything and everything. I had only to buy anything at all in the way of household commodities and hold it for a day or two, when I could sell at a profit, often realising as much as 50 per cent on my outlay.'

All over Europe soap was in demand, some people hadn't seen it since the war began as all fats and oils were needed for the war effort. Tommy heard of a man who was said to be secretly manufacturing it and disposing of it himself. 'I

located him many miles out of the city. He had been manager
of a paint factory, now closed down by the Bolsheviks, and
by boiling the oil left when the paint-making ceased and
mixing it with caustic soda, he made a reasonable enough
soap.' But by retailing it himself he ran a great risk, and
when Tommy offered him 10 roubles per half kilogram he
'jumped' at the offer. 'He assured me of a regular supply
while the oil lasted.'

The young Australian set up in the market square (near what
we now know as Red Square). He made a stand, as did other
vendors from piling up snow and flattening the top which then
set as ice. There were others selling soap, and old ladies came
up and sampled the newcomer's product. 'They smelled it,
tried to break or crumble the bar and eventually bit it and
tasted it. And they bought it.'

But money wasn't coming in fast enough as he wanted to
get away as soon as winter ended and the ports opened for
shipping. So he took up gambling, playing pontoon in the
clubs and the servants' quarters at the consulate. 'The first
night I slipped on to a stool at a table where I'd seen a regular
player go broke and leave, I was so nervy I felt sick. First I
thought they would knife me for edging into a private game,
then I thought I might lose!' He rarely lost. The money piled
up, what with the soap stall doing well in the daytime and the
gambling at night.

Moscow in 1918 was 'a reign of terror, soldiers were a
law unto themselves with rifle, revolver and sword; the hue
and cry of a chase and promiscuous shootings in the streets
went on day and night. A soldier was judge, jury and exe-
cutioner and many times I have seen a man running for his
life along the streets with soldiers in pursuit blazing away
with revolvers regardless of what innocent might stop the
flying lead. I often had to squeeze myself into a doorway
while bullets whizzed uncomfortably near.' Typhus was
raging and he saw queues waiting at the cemetery gates to
bury their dead. 'Coffins were a thing of the past, anything
did for a shroud. There was thirty degrees of frost; the streets

were like extended ice rinks. Moustaches and whiskers were adorned with icicles caused by breath freezing. Business was stagnant, shops were shuttered, and practically all transactions were confined to the market square.

'I made a few cautious inquiries for a doctor who would give me a certificate of ill-health which I needed if I were to get out of the country. I tried a good many without any success, but eventually found one who, when I produced money, gave me the necessary certificate. Two other doctors appended their signatures. The certificate was worded as follows: "This man is an English prisoner escaped from Germany to Moscow. He is in very bad health, and ought not to have been passed for a soldier at all. He is suffering from paralysis of the heart, and must be sent home at once".' Passport and transit to the seaboard, St Petersburg, were completed for him by the Danish Consul. The next stage of the journey was across the border to Finland, thence to Norway and finally England where he landed on 11 April 1919, exactly two years to the day after his capture.

Tommy Taylor had not expected, on his arrival in London, any great fanfare, but neither did he expect to be swept away from the ferry which had brought him across the Channel and taken to Army Intelligence headquarters in London and questioned for three weeks about everything he had observed in the new regime of Bolshevik Russia. 'I didn't think it was fair', Tommy said sixty years later. 'But that's the army for you!' No other Britisher had crossed the new Bolshevik country as far and in the observant way Tommy Taylor had done.

Private Bertie Giles, 53rd Battalion, who was captured at the Battle of Fromelles in 1916, had remained a prisoner in Germany to war's end when a polite notice was posted in the barracks on the night of 10 November 1918: 'Comrades, the old government has ceased to exist. Government, which is represented here by the Council of Workmen and Soldiers, has succeeded in obtaining an armistice with the powers of entente and there is no doubt that definite peace will be concluded before long.' The notice contained a promise to send the prisoners to their homes as soon as possible, but stated they must realise that there were hundreds of thousands of prisoners and if they all started wandering around they would never be able to get things organised, so they were asked to stay. 'Remain where you are and keep the peace and we will get enough ships into the harbour as soon as we can.' The Germans made clear the volatile state of the starving, defeated country.

'It is no good going out on the roads, so don't attempt to leave your camp, it would be dangerous for you, the food you would be able to carry with you would not last more than two or three days and it is impossible for you to obtain more on the road. Marauding and pillaging would be the only means to get food and we trust that with the good sense you have shown up to now you will not fall in with that idea. You are liable to be caught and shot on the spot. On the other hand, prisoners who are arrested in flight will have to stay until all other prisoners are gone. Comrades, don't act hastily. Don't create chaos or anarchy which would follow your trail and would not stop at the War Office in your own country. General disorder would break out under which you would have to suffer as well as everybody else. The terms of the armistice accepted by Germany are very severe, they are willing to carry them through although there are great technical difficulties to overcome.

'We must withdraw our armies, send food to the troops of the entente which are going to occupy the western districts of our country. We have to convey home thousands of prisoners within the relative space of a few weeks. It won't be possible to carry these through if you do not assist us; therefore remain where you are and don't make trouble or cause disaster. Comrades! Where many of you have been in captivity for three or four years we trust you will be able to stand it a few weeks longer. The German government has the ardent desire to send you home without any unnecessary delay. It will only be possible if you lend a helping hand and do your duty until your train comes.

Kommandantur, the Council of Workmen and Soldiers.'

On the following morning, on the 11th hour of the 11th day of the 11th month of 1918, the Armistice was formally signed and Bertie Giles was free to come home.

The Merchant Navy Man

'The *Wolf* has returned from the Atlantic, Indian and Pacific Oceans with 400 Merchant Navy crew members of ships she has sunk.'

German Government Pronouncement, 26 February 1918

NO RECORD WAS KEPT of the number of Australian merchant seamen lost or captured by enemy ships during the war. They were not enlisted men and although they had to go wherever government ordered (including the war zones – as were all the waterways of the world including those of Gallipoli), they were not given any recognition or pensions when the war ended, despite the fact that their cargo ships were prime targets as they carried life-giving supplies to the Allied cause. With token armaments, sometimes none at all, they moved troops from one end of the world to the other.

At the outbreak of war, the SS *Pfalz*, a German merchant ship, was seized in the port of Melbourne and renamed SS *Boorara*. *Pfalz* was the first vessel to be fired on by an Australian gunner and was one of five enemy cargo ships seized at the outbreak of war and sent off as a troop ship. The crews of these ships were not Royal Australian Navy but merchant seamen of the Mercantile Marine, or Merchant Navy as it was commonly called.

The *Boorara* later carried Turkish POWs from Gallipoli, was rammed, beached, patched up, returned to sea, was torpedoed with five crew killed; then on 20 March 1918 a torpedo ripped open a hole 40 feet by 22 feet on the port side. Captain Buchanan, Master Mariner, sent out wireless messages for help, had his ship towed to Southampton and patched up enough to head for Newcastle for docking, but was again torpedoed, this time wrecking the engine room. 'The ship was gutted, her back almost broken.' Buchanan again called for a tow and she was repaired and again sent to sea. The ship was fully in the service of the government until after the war when she took servicemen and wounded back home to Melbourne in 1919.

Being fired upon was not an isolated occurrence for merchantmen. The 'flying convoy' of 15-knot vessels was often fired on. On 1 May 1918 the SS *Indarra* (Captain M.M. Osborne, NSW) was attacked in the English Channel by two submarines and torpedoes 'just after clearing the swept channel at 4.30 p.m.' A fog came down and the ship escaped only to be attacked the following morning at 7 a.m. by guns and depth-charges. And so it went on until 26 June when they reached Alexandria. 'The air was full of dirt and debris', Captain Osborne wrote as submarines and ships were being hit around them. For a time the ship had been without any escort; it was not considered necessary to protect the merchant mariners once the troops they had been carrying were put ashore.

Captain C.C. McKenzie of the SS *Wandilla*, a vessel that had attracted bombs on several occasions (and skirted four vessels 'lying awash, having struck mines in the English Channel'), said of his men, 'They were all Australian Merchant Navy seamen and I had no trouble with them throughout,' the straight-forward, no-frills reply of any sea captain but to the seagoing fraternity it read A1.

These were just some of the many merchant ships requisitioned by the War Office as troop and war materials ships. Other Australian merchant vessels were taken as hospital ships, indeed several had already been used as such at the Boer War and would be used again in World War II. Crews of these merchant ships received no recognition or repatriation benefits from government. Most had to find their own way home to Australia after their ship had been sunk by enemy bombs or torpedoes. But many of these brave seamen were captured and taken through the dangerous mine-strewn channels to Germany and prison camps. Captain Osborne said, 'We were just Merchant Navy men doing our duty'.

Early in March 1917 the Australian Naval Board learned that an enemy raider was in the Indian Ocean. This vessel, the *Wolf*, brought the war into Australian waters after a fashion fortunately unique. Her mines destroyed an Australian mail-steamer in the Indian Ocean and a large Australian cargo-vessel within a few miles of the Australian coast – besides taking Australian merchant seamen and civilians prisoner and inflicting havoc on Australian sea-borne commerce.

The *Wolf*, with a maximum speed of 13 knots, was origi-nally a German cargo-steamer, but now she carried a crew of 350 men, an astounding number for any vessel let alone one so small. The reason for this was to supply crews to sail selected prizes back to Germany. Although in appearance she was a merchantman, she was in fact under the command of the German navy (as were all German raiders in World War I and World War II). When equipped for raiding, she was almost as well-armed as a light cruiser and carried a disman-tled seaplane (*Wolfchen*) and several hundred mines. In November 1916 the *Wolf* left her home port of Kiel and began a most successful voyage.

To leave Kiel was fraught with danger: the British fleet were blockading the entrance to the North Sea. But *Wolf* passed the Kattegat and hugged the coast of Norway, plunged into storm after storm (which saved her from discovery by the British scouts), passed Iceland and into the Atlantic on her way to the Cape of Good Hope.

Captain Karl Nerger's orders were 'to interfere with the enemy's shipping in distant seas, and above all in the Indian Ocean; to wage war on commerce and to carry out other warlike operations' (of which mine-laying was one of the most important). The ship did not seek naval vessels but unarmed merchant ships (including the big wheat clippers) carrying vital supplies of food to England. By the time she was in the vicinity of Colombo, *Wolf* had laid 275 mines in the entrances to four strategic ports and had begun her great run of piracy with the taking of the 7000-ton *Worcestershire*, the *Turritella*, *Jumna*, *Wordsworth*, and west of Leeuwin (off the south-west cape of

Australia) the sailing vessel *Dee* in ballast to Fremantle. The raider swept round south of Tasmania and New Zealand and over to the Kermadec Islands where the little *Wolfchen* was sent aloft to have a look around.

Roy Alexander, the young radio operator on the Union Steamship Company's *Wairuna*, was having afternoon tea when a cabin boy called for him to come and see a large black vessel lying in the shelter of some rocks off the Kermadec group of islands. 'She was rather suspicious and I returned to my interrupted afternoon tea but only after taking the precaution of closing switches and preparing for transmission from the accumulators since the dynamo was not then running. There was no sound of life in the phones.

'At 4.45p.m. there was a rush on deck, an aeroplane motor could be heard; I got on deck in time to see a bomb dropped off the port bow, and a message attached to a sandbag falling on deck from the small two-seater biplane overhead; its German naval ensign was clearly visible flying from one of her stays. She was so low her pilot and observer could be distinctly seen, the latter ready to do some serious bombing. I made to the bridge for orders but before reaching the companionway, instructions came down [from the seaplane] "not to use the wireless!" I ran up to the charthouse as the chief engineer was asking the captain for permission to destroy the wireless station and spent a busy half hour smashing up the work of the last fortnight and putting the codes, the log-book etc. overboard. The receiver was wrenched from the table and followed the papers. By the time I got out of the wireless cabin door I could see the Hun boarding party coming towards us, but by now there was very little of the wireless gear left.

'A party of armed sailors led by an officer swarmed over the side and one went immediately aft and lowered the Red Ensign [the Merchant Navy flag] and hoisted the German flag.' Roy was taken on board the raider with the chief, second and third officers, all the others to remain on board *Wairuna*. 'The German senior officers were waiting on top of the boat ladder and saluted each of us as we came over the side, with the hundreds of German crew ranged around the deck watching us. I noticed the deck was covered with mine rails.

'After a while in the darkness of the hold, through the smoke haze, we saw the grinning half-dressed British prisoners who bombarded us with questions. This was No. 4 hold mine-chamber, with 200 mines resting in long rows of rails. There were nearly 100 prisoners here. (Before I left the ship there were 400.) We slept in brown canvas hammocks and an armed sentry marched to and fro among the prisoners night and day. [The corner in the hold where Roy and his young mates camped was called by the older men the Hotel du Wolfchen – Child of the Wolf.] The *Wairuna* was brought alongside and was plundered. A coaling party transferred all her coal.

'*Wolf* had two 5.9 guns under her foc'sle head, two of same on forward well decks, another two after and one on poop, with broadside again of 5.9s, four torpedo tubes, seven 12 pounders, 500 mines, a large quantity of rifles, machine guns and bombs. The *modus operandi* of the *Wolf* was to capture ships, take the crew off and sink the vessel after transferring all the coal and supplies aboard, because *Wolf* depended on this means to keep herself afloat. When she captured a ship of value she put a prize crew on it and usually some prisoners to relieve the cramping on the raider and sent them back to Germany.'

The survivors of several captured ships were on board *Wolf* when young Roy joined the ship. He soon learned the ship could be so successfully camouflaged that the steamer *Dee*, on sighting the *Wolf*, had hoisted a signal 'Report me all well' which in those days was a usual way for ships that didn't have radio to send a message to their owner. (The *Dee* was promptly bombed and went down with that signal still flying.)

One day Roy awoke to find the *Wolf* was a different ship from the day before: her telescopic masts and funnels had been lowered to give her a low, squat appearance. At 9 p.m. that night mines began to come up from the hold. 'I could hear each mine being brought up in the lift, trundled along the rails and finally pushed out through the mine doors. Over 100 mines were laid.'

The *Wolf* later put down sixty mines off New Zealand. Then, striking across the Tasman Sea, she began on 3 July to lay a large number of mines off Cape Howe (Victoria).

The immediate result of her Cape Howe mine-laying was the destruction of a fine ship, *Cumberland*, off Gabo Island, the *Wimmera* off the Three Kings, and the *Port Kembla* off Cape Farewell; two other vessels disappeared, the *Handa Isle* and the collier *Undola*. (There was a story current in Australia that the *Wolfchen* had been launched and flew over Sydney Harbour but this is most improbable.)

The *Wolf* next captured the Burns Philp ship *Matunda*. This was a great find for the raider: first-class naval coal and 900 tons of general cargo. The *Wolf* now had the *Matunda* tow a wooden target while *Wolf* had some target practice. 'Men on the *Matunda* were giving loud cooees to the Australian captives as they passed and others threw apples at us.' Then the captives came on board. 'One woman was a vision in white with emerald silk stockings and a very purple sunshade. We stared, it was a long time since we saw anything like that.' Among this captured ship's officers was Wireless Operator Rob Taylor, an old acquaintance of Roy Alexander. (When he was brought on board the *Wolf* Rob failed to recognise Roy in his 'rags' – shorts, bath towel, a coat of sunburn and a short haircut.)

The *Matunda* was put down ('the old ship made noises like a crockery warehouse collapsing as she went'), but by this time Roy was in the hospital with violent stomach pains and being treated with doses of 'opium tincture'. The raider had her own well-laid-out hospital and operating room as well as a dispensary and eleven bunks. Roy dined 'sumptuously' on roast horse – one of the horses that had been brought over from the *Matunda* – preceded by meat soup with prunes in it. 'I took one sip of the awful, sweet soup and rushed away to be violently ill; however I came back and did full justice to the horse which tasted delicious to me in my semi-starved state. Horse has a distinctive flavour and odour but is quite edible.'

They met a patrol boat in the middle of the night. 'The *Wolf* cleared for action with over 100 mines in her hold, with the big electric alarms clanging all over the ship, all lights extinguished and the operating theatre cleared for use; the German patients hobbled to their posts to man the guns on deck and the torpedo tubes.

'The patrol boat was coming up on us and *Wolf* intended to bluff that she was an ordinary merchantman, but the compressed air in the torpedo tubes 6 feet away from us was hissing audibly, the torpedo doors outside had been lowered and the crew were now lying flat on deck. In the hospital the two doctors stood under blue lights, medical packs on their shoulders, staring fixedly through the door and waiting, and I and the other patients still in the hospital had to sit on the bunks and look coolly composed, I fanning myself. Hail Marys were rushing through my head at a terrible rate, but I was surprised to find myself in excellent control to all outward appearances. The *Wolf* bluffed through and I knew it when the torpedo doors were lifted and the tension slackened.'

Then it was the Java Sea, north of Australia. After laying 110 more mines *Wolf* was cutting across towards the coast of Borneo, when the prisoners attempted to send a message telling of their incarceration. They organised a singsong on deck and a 'roughhouse' to distract the Germans while a man either side of the ship dropped a float (prepared from a football bladder) with a bottle tied on it with a message inside. 'They were caught and punished by being kept down below for quite some time.'

Ship after ship was captured, ransacked and sunk. The *Hitachi Maru*, a passenger ship from Yokohama, had fired back at *Wolf* and twenty civilians had been killed during the bombing that followed. The corpses lying on No. 2 hatch were put over the side. 'There was chaos', Roy wrote. 'Chocolate, hams, surrounded by pools of blood and ghastly lumps of human flesh. Blood everywhere. On a cane lounge was a draftboard soaked with blood, nearby a wounded man with his leg in pieces was lying in blood underneath a chair. *Hitachi Maru* was patched up and made seaworthy and was left behind in the islands as a base with a prize crew on board.'

The *Wolf* now steamed off on a south-west course at full speed. 'Second Mate Johnson of the captured *Beluga* died of heart failure following an alarm. His body was laid on a hatch, covered with an American flag and at 9 a.m. he was buried from one of the gun doors under the starboard gun. We were all dressed for the occasion, the first time we'd had socks on for months; the show of uniforms was dazzling, most of them creased and covered with mildew. Later that morning the *Hitachi Maru* met up with us in the vicinity of Mauritius, but since no coal ship had been caught, condition of the bunkers did not permit us to keep another vessel any longer and she had to be sunk.' (Alexander, and doubtless the other long-term prisoners also, had by now identified with the *Wolf* and spoke of 'we' and 'us' when referring to the enemy ship.)

Wolf was now crammed with passengers, including women with their husbands and children. Roy notes again, 'That lady by some mysterious means still appears in well-laundered whites resting easily on a foundation of cerise or emerald silk hose, an admiring train usually following bearing cushions etc., not forgetting the purple brolly. In comparison with the other female prisoners she looks quite brilliant, the others primly respectable. The ladies are permitted to visit the after well deck to gossip at certain times. There they cling to the outer semblance of civilisation to the last, and still look with horror at the sunburnt seminudity on the poop.

'Then it was off on our now familiar chase, hatches closed down, excitement on deck, the bulkheads of the prison closed, bulwarks dropped, then the prize surrendering without even a stopping shot being necessary. It was a Spaniard, the *Igotz Mendi*, deeply loaded with coal, waddling along on our port quarter, perhaps the most valuable prize the raider has yet caught, as the coal problem is now solved for a month to come. So now it's back to the anchorage with the prize alongside us.' His youthful jauntiness bubbles constantly.

'We're going on the prowl for a passenger vessel which is required to be sent to Germany as a prison ship now that we have plenty of coal available.'

On his 21st birthday, 18 November, 'Soup from the horse's bones, the same bones have been used over and over again; I was served up a shoulder blade which once belonged to the horse; then came Mrs Crippen's [referring to Crippen the notorious murderer of the period] unnatural and dried potatoes, but there was beer and lemonade and they wished that my birthday may be better next year'. The ship was now down towards the Cape, the first albatrosses they'd seen for months arrived, and Cape pigeons. They had cruised all the Australian and Asiatic trade routes and now swung to the north.

Roy, in hospital, was told that he had appendicitis but as there was not sufficient anaesthetic on board to operate, the only chance was complete starvation. Two days later the white screens were brought out and the men told to prepare for another burial. But Roy refused to die. A captured passenger came to the hospital daily to bathe him and the other patients, the first bath they'd had for a long time. Roy was semi-conscious most of the time, heavily doped with morphine and opium. On Christmas Eve men were saying 'good luck' to young Roy instead of 'Merry Christmas'. The Germans brought a gramophone into the ward and played 'Rule Britannia' and 'God Save the King', and sang carols.

'By 30 December there was a rumour that our ship [the German *Wolf*] was off to rush the blockade up through the English Channel and into the North Sea.' Conditions were very hard for the boy patient even though the Germans did what they could for his comfort. They carried him on a bamboo chaise longue to the deck under an awning while the band played 'Uber Alles' and Wagner as well as the 'Hamburger Homeward Bound' song and all the Germans sang the chorus, which Roy thought was 'incredibly poor music'. From now on he was taken on deck each day and could listen to bands on Sunday afternoon. 'A neutral ship passed by but the Germans decided to sink her since "dead neutrals tell no tales".'

(An interesting entry in his diary on 10 January 1918: 'The captain taken off the Japanese ship prophesised that Australia would soon be "under the Rising Sun", the Japanese flag.')

The *Wolf* by now was leaking heavily, the captured *Igotz Mendi* having crashed into her during the storm and buckled some of her plates. 'The water can be heard swishing about underneath the hospital deck.' Disease was beginning to spread on board, scurvy-stricken prisoners lined up outside the hospital door twice a day. 'We are now literally rotting with scurvy in the filthy holds. There had been no typhoid until the Japanese came aboard. We have all been inoculated three times against it. Several chaps have died of beriberi, also many of the Japs are in the various stages of syphilis and a half rotten wretch was put into hospital today and occupied the next bed to me. The quarantine consists of the Germans washing their hands whenever they touch him. Another patient is my old pal Josh, Cadet E.C. Cuthill. We were thrashed by another storm, with the *Wolf* rolling on to her beam ends.' A new hospital was rigged up aft to accommodate some of the more serious scurvy cases because there was no longer room in the hospital.

'7 February 1918, in the Arctic Circle, the vessel is coated with drift ice floating on the lead-coloured swell. Instead of the shorts and bath towels, we are now wrapped in old sweaters and rainbow-hued alpine caps made of all sorts of old things like bits of blankets, scarlet edging being used for tassels, and someone made a high Cossack snow hat from coal-sacks and blue and white bath mats confiscated from the *Hitachi Maru*. The temperature outside is 19° below (Fahrenheit). We passed huge fields of ice as we pushed up into the Denmark Straits between Iceland and Greenland to avoid the British Naval patrols blockading German ports as we dashed across to the Norwegian coast. But, the *Wolf* is well crippled; leaking badly. The pumps stopped on the Kaiser's birthday in the hurricane when 40 tons of water came pouring in in one hour. Our speed is only 10 knots.'

They had odd entertainment, such as The Lyric Lambs, resplendent in some mildewed gold lace uniforms, orchestra consisting of a violin with two strings, a banjo, a flute and a mandolin. 'The mandolin player was the only one who could really play.' They had lifted a piano from one of the captured ships and 'Webby' was playing 'So Long Letty' when the news came around that Captain Naga from the *Hitachi Maru* had suicided.

The *Wolf* deserved all her prizes, her master was a brilliant, intelligent pirate. He now lowered the ship's top-masts and extended her funnel as disguise and headed home – but not before taking another three ships.

A captured ship was sent off to Germany with some of the 400 prisoners (actually she was recaptured on the way and the prisoners freed in Denmark) but the *Wolf* sailed triumphantly to the Fatherland and on 26 February 1918 anchored once more in German waters. The ship had been fifteen months in enemy seas during a voyage of over 64,000 nautical miles and had captured fourteen vessels.

The German government uttered its cockcrow of triumph: 'The auxiliary cruiser *Wolf*, commanded by Captain Nerger, has returned from the Atlantic, Indian and Pacific Oceans with 400 members of crews of sunken ships, including white and coloured British military men. She has also on board several captured guns and great quantities of valuable raw materials, rubber, copper, brass, zinc, cocoa beans and copra, worth many millions of marks.'

Nine months later, after release from his German prison at war's end, Roy Alexander returned home safely after one of the most remarkable voyages in maritime history and an experience as daunting as few persons on shore were likely to know.

The Aviators

'they shall mount up with wings as eagles ...'

Isaiah 40:31

THE WONDER AND ADMIRATION of earth-bound men for those aviators who sailed high above the blood and slaughter and mud was never-ending throughout that war. This was a new fighting arm and everything about it was novel. It lent itself to hyperbole. 'The heavens are their battlefields', said Mr Lloyd George when giving the vote of thanks to the Flying Service in the House of Commons in November 1919. 'They are the cavalry of the clouds ... their struggles by day and night are like a Miltonian conflict between the winged hosts.'

There was a lustre surrounding the young flying men, a mystique that was part disdain for death, and part jousting with the old man with the sickle, as though it were the jolliest jest. To a man, on both sides, the German and Allied airmen were delightful, sparkling, the golden young men of an age. Today they seem to us to be crazy with the ecstasy of the contest; they crashed, were shot down, got tangled in balloon-wires, their flimsy machines buckled, but throughout they saw it all as a game.

The French christened these star airmen 'aces' and their daring skill encouraged designers to improve their machines. Numbers of men began to transfer from the AIF to the new service. In the early part of the war the number of airmen from all Britain's overseas Dominions amounted to over 50 per cent in both the Royal Naval Air Service and the Royal Flying Corps. Amongst the large number of Australian airmen who had transferred from the AIF were men from the Light Horse regiments. But an aviator could be killed or taken prisoner as quickly and as cruelly as any man down in the mud and slaughter of the trenches.

The genesis of the Australian Fying Corps was at Point Cook (Vic.) two weeks after war was declared, when four pupils, seconded from the AIF, began a course of flying instruction. Among those early Australian airmen was Captain Thomas White (later H.E. Sir Thomas White, Australian High Commissioner in London). He had transferred from the 60th Battalion to the new fighting arm and had been one of the first four officers to do the training course beginning on 17 August 1914. He was to become one of the best known of the pilot prisoners of that war.

Both sides in World War I found that the best raw material for the making of an air pilot was the accomplished horseman. 'The demand for good heart, good hands and a quick eye is the same in each case', Thomas White believed. 'A pilot must qualify by study and examination but beyond that he needs to be a bit of a dare-devil, to be able to judge to a nicety a risk, when both flying and fighting.' And, as well, the desire for flight was irresistible for men sweating in the dust and flies of the Middle East (as it was for the men in the mud of Flanders when Australians were sent there in 1916).

Above all, this was the only fighting service that had opportunities for individual men to use their initiative; it had the scope, almost the necessity for young men to exercise all the daring that youth commands. That is not to say a pilot had to be reckless, but that his finely tuned nerves, courage and determination, coupled with the confidence of knowing what both the machine and himself were capable of, brought him to the apex of perfection. Among the aircraft they were to learn on was a Bleriot monoplane similar to that which crossed the English Channel in 1909, and two Deperdussin monoplanes that 'fiercely resisted any attempts to get them off the ground', according to Thomas White. For the duration of the war the Australian Flying Corps served as part of the AIF, its men wearing the same uniforms as the army. (Australia was the only Dominion of the British Empire to form her own air arm.)

In April 1915 the British Government asked whether Australia could supply flying personnel for service in India and this request was met the following month by the despatch of three officers and forty-five other ranks comprising a unit known as the First Half-Flight. The men left Australia to sail to Mesopotamia (Iraq) taking with them horses and mules for transport as well as farriers and drivers.

These pioneers of the Australian First Half-Flight were first sent north of the Persian Gulf where the rivers Euphrates and Tigris flow through the desert, past the ruins of Babylon and beyond Baghdad and Kurna, the traditionally accredited site of the Garden of Eden. Here in Mesopotamia was the Anglo-Persian Oil Company pipeline to be protected and here, too, were unaligned desert Arabs and three armies of Turkish soldiers plus German airmen.

The heat of the Persian Gulf remained true to its reputation. The men watched the barren coastal hills of Persia slide by their ship as it slowly approached Basra, their first 'home' in Mesopotamia. Then it was off to Kut-el-Amarah, recently evacuated by the Turks. Here White witnessed a public execution of two Arabs caught robbing and killing wounded prisoners, never thinking that he would one day be a prisoner in this place.

At first the pilots were almost entirely occupied with reconnaissance, flying as far as their fuel tanks would allow over Turkish lines and bringing back information and film (from hand-held cameras). Sometimes they could get far enough to sight enemy groupings and strategic posts that the artillery could bombard.

Captain Williams (later Air Vice-Marshal Sir Richard Williams) said of his days as a young airman, 'At that time we had no guns firing through the propeller, so could not fire straight ahead. We really had very little chance with him [the opposing German pilot]. Our observers were in front of the pilot whereas the German observer was in rear of the pilot who could fire straight ahead. When bombing we had to go without observers (because of weight) and although we carried a machine gun, it was quite impossible to fly the machine and use the gun too. We depended mainly on luck.' They carried

2-pound bombs to drop by hand over the side on to a target, in some cases a hole was cut in the floor of the cockpit and the bombs pushed through this aperture. Later they had heavier bombs but it was still a crude and clumsy exercise even when an 'interrupter-gear' was invented and fitted to enable a machine gun to be used by the pilot without shooting his own propeller off. They always carried a rifle, mainly for use if forced down in enemy territory.

At first the German planes were superior in almost all ways to the British, whose aircraft 'in a strong wind literally moved backwards', according to Captain White. Some mechanics had never seen an aircraft close up but once in Mesopotamia they found they were no more ignorant of the machines than the similarly inexperienced English mechanics. The Rajah of Gwalior had donated two Shorthorn Farman aircraft – they trundled along at 40 miles an hour, the pilot and his observer armed with revolvers, but no guns.

The Australians were soon in action and on 30 July 1915 had their first casualty when Lieutenant G.P. Merz (a medical practitioner and one of the original four trainees at Point Cook) was forced down among well-armed and hostile Arabs and taken prisoner. He, and his New Zealand observer, Lieutenant W. Burn, were never seen again. Evidence of their game stand was given by 'friendly' Arabs, who said that 'after a running fight of about 5 miles during which the two airmen killed one and wounded five of their adversaries one of the men was wounded and his comrade died fighting beside him'. The machine was found a few days later, 'hacked to matchwood'.

New aircraft arrived but much of it 'was reluctant to depart from the ground' as Captain Richard Williams said when he had to drive his Shorthorn aircraft along the ground like a motor car for 20 miles 'after it refused to stay in the air'.

Captain Thomas White had several memorable escapes before he was eventually captured. In November 1915 he had set off in a Maurice Farman 2 aircraft to search for a sea-plane that had been grounded by engine failure between Kut and

Aziziyeh. The importance of this mission was that the sea-plane was carrying no less a personage than Major-General A.V. Kemball, Chief of General Staff, Mesopotamia. It was imperative that he be rescued. White found the sea-plane beside a river, beside which was a large Arab camp; the Arabs opened fire on him, bullets went through his propeller and an aileron rib was broken. White landed half a mile away, and, as he later said, 'put on an act' to suggest he was not alone, grabbed a spare rifle for the General, ran to the river and assisted the eminent gentleman back to the MF2 and set off safely for home ground.

Shortly after this foray, White set off with another airman, Captain F.C.C. Yeats-Brown DFC, an Indian Regular army officer in the 17th Cavalry who had taken to the air as an observer. This sortie seems in retrospect to belong in the realms of adventure fiction. In order to isolate Baghdad from enemy bases before a battle, the two men were to fly out, land behind the town and cut the telephone wires running north and west to the Euphrates, Constantinople and Kifri. What a sight they must have presented as they set off at dawn on 13 November, with necklaces of gun powder and extra tins of petrol and oil strapped on. They had to fly 68 miles to the target and 68 back; however, both knew they had not enough fuel to get back if they met adverse winds.

They reached the Baghdad area safely but once there realised the wires ran westwards from Baghdad along the main road, not out into the desert as the maps showed. Turkish troops were constantly moving along the road, and the ground was rough, so choice of a landing place was limited. Finally White chose an area bounded by canals, with the telegraph lines about 300 yards from the road. It was 8 miles from Baghdad, and the airmen considered that the few individuals in the vicinity could be kept at a distance. But the narrowness of the ground and the unexpected arrival of a mounted policeman led to their colliding with a telegraph pole which badly smashed a wing 'and brought the aeroplane to a stop'. Arabs, soon joined by a party of Turks, attacked the airmen but

Yeats-Brown managed to blow up the wires under fire, while White filled the petrol tanks and with the rifle kept off the enemy. The two then started the engine, buoyed up with the hope of escaping by ground-running as they had done on other occasions when beset by the enemy and unable to get their aeroplane airborne. But this time when Yeats-Brown tried to taxi the motor totally refused to turn over. 'In a moment we were surrounded', wrote White (in his popular book *Guests of the Unspeakable*, published in 1928). 'The first man to approach me was a hideous black Arab with shaggy hair who was stark naked but for two broad bandoliers of cartridges across his chest. He covered me from about 10 yards with a large bore rifle that would have slain an elephant. His ferocious looking companions, yelling "Ingrazzi" [English] and showing their teeth in the most repulsive manner, rushed at me with clubbed rifles.' White attempted to ward off the blow with his arms, but, dodging and ducking, a blow struck the top of his head, another and another followed, cutting his scalp. Blood poured over his face and clothes.

Yeats-Brown was being beaten by another group brandishing rifle butts and bitumen-knobbed clubs. White, glancing across between blows, saw his companion struck between the shoulders with a hammer whilst another assailant stabbed at him with a dagger. The Arabs were all for murdering the airmen, the Turks although happy to beat them unmercifully dragged the two to the dubious safety of the local police headquarters. As the door slammed shut on the howling mob White had no doubt that he and Yeats-Brown had fulfilled their mission but both men knew they would not be able to rejoin their colleagues for the duration of the war.

The men were taken to Baghdad, spat upon, humiliated, then moved on to Mosul, the ancient site of Nineveh. Here, in a dingy cell, the airmen saw two feeble, wasted figures stretched out on ramshackle cots, and suddenly they recognised them as Captain B.S. Atkins and Lieutenant W.H. Treloar who had been captured two months earlier. Now, with fever and dysentery, they were hardly recognisable to the newcomers.

They had been in Mosul scarcely another week when two more aviators joined them, Major R. Reilly and Lieutenant E.J. Fulton whom they had last seen in the mess back at the aerodrome. These two men had had to ride donkeys from Baghdad to Mosul whereas White and Yeats-Brown had experienced the dubious comfort of a cart.

Here at Mosul White bought a small pocket-book, ink and pen and began the diary he was to continue until his final escape. This, of course, was a forbidden exercise and the devious places of concealment included his puttees, hat, and boots. In this little book he recorded the treatment meted out by what he termed 'the Unspeakables', the beatings, killings, starvation and neglect that was the lot of all who fell into Turkish hands. He recorded the forced march from Mosul north to Nisibin, with Fulton too weak from fever to walk, jolting across on the back of a donkey, and from there to Ras-el-Ain, the rail-head for the journey to Constantinople. It was on this rail line that Australian seamen, sailors and soldiers were toiling and dying. At the time of White's passage the mountains had not yet been pierced and with the rest of the passengers, including the ailing Atkins, he must proceed by road vehicle over the Taurus Mountains until they reached where the rail line began again on the other side.

Here they learned of the Australian prisoners working in the Taurus Mountains. 'Prisoners from Gallipoli and naval prisoners from submarines sunk in the Marmora.' And here White learned another side of the novelty of this war: airmen and crews of submarines related stories that were unique in the annals of battle. Unlike the soldier or sailor they had no traditions of regiment or ship to uphold, and had their own history to make. 'In the light of some of the exploits of the submarine men at Afion Kara Hissar, it is certain future generations will claim they commenced well.'

Until now White had heard nothing of the result of the battle in which he and Yeats-Brown had played a part before being captured. The battle had been a failure, the Allied army retreated and the airmen were ordered to leave Kut by air;

because of lack of transport nine Australian NCOs and mechanics were among those left behind to become prisoners of the Turks. Captain White later met Air-Mechanic L. Hudson in captivity in Asia Minor. 'During the siege the mechanics had worked incessantly, and after the capitulation of Kut the 13,000 prisoners, including these Australians, were marched over 700 miles of mountain and desert to Anatolia. Hundreds died on the way through exposure, fatigue and starvation', Hudson told White. The men 'had been driven like barbarian captives of the ancients' and they arrived at Afion 'gaunt skeletons ... staggering along like drunken men stumbling and falling, rising, tottering, falling again'. Corporal J. Sloss, whilst on this forced march to Afion, had tied his wrist to the back of a cart so that he wouldn't drop out during the march.

The survivors of the march were set to work on railway construction on the Taurus Mountains, where many died of typhus, malaria or dysentery, brought on by malnutrition or exposure (as happened to Australian mariners and soldiers captive in this region). Of the nine Australians taken in Kut – one of whom, Air-Mechanic Rayment, was badly wounded during the siege – only two, Sloss and Air-Mechanic Hudson, survived their captivity. Corporal Soley and Air-Mechanic Curran died at Nisibin, and Air-Mechanics Williams, Rayment, Adams, Lord and Munro in the Taurus Mountains.

White, feigning illness, was sent to Constantinople in July 1918 and escaped while travelling on the railway train. Disguised as a Turk, he stowed away on a Ukranian steamer in company with a British airman. The ship remained thirty-three days at anchor in the harbour at Constantinople and the two men spent an uncomfortable time below, sometimes hidden in the ship's ballast tanks by the engineers whom they had bribed.

Eventually they reached Odessa, false passports describing them as Russians enabled them to remain there for one month; they had made arrangements to join the anti-Bolshevik army when they heard of the impending Armistice with Bulgaria. With the help of an interned Englishman and a Russian Merchant

Navy captain, they stowed away in a Ukranian hospital ship, sailed to Varna in Bulgaria, there met up with the Allied forces and eventually arrived at Salonika a week before the Armistice with Germany in 1918.

With so many ex-Light Horse men in the air, it was to be expected that they would turn on their best efforts to assist their erstwhile comrades – to the death if necessary. Near Amman, Jordan, one of the finest examples of this brotherhood occurred early in May 1918 when the horsemen were almost captured by the Turkish army. All day before this the airmen had been reconnoitering the battle and recording its progress. When they saw that the Light Horse line of retreat was about to be cut off, the pilots took to the air in force, even though a strong south wind was blowing over the whole of the Amman area, making for most unfavourable flying weather.

Two machines were caught in heavy fire and one, piloted by Captain D.W. Rutherford with his observer, Lieutenant J. McElligott, had its petrol tanks punctured by bullets. Rutherford managed to land the plane and the two men then set it on fire to prevent the enemy using it.

The other aircraft, with Lieutenants J.D. Haig and R.T. Challenor, landed nearby to pick up the first crew. Haig attempted to take off with the three men on board but the weight was too great and one wheel collapsed as they were taxiing along the ground and the aeroplane toppled on to its nose, snapping the propeller. This plane was also fired by the crew who, by this time, were being pursued by the enemy. They were taken captive and later a German aircraft flew over the Australian lines and dropped letters from the four men telling of their mishap. What the opposing aviators had in common was their skill, and both sides recognised this and openly admired and respected one another while not deviating one jot from the task at hand: to kill one another, man to man.

An incredible chivalry burst forth and those of us who grew up between the wars listened to their stories, read their letters, diaries and the books they wrote with astonished awe. The story of Lieutenant C.H. Vautin, an ex-Light Horseman from Perth (WA), is an example. On 8 July 1917 Vautin of No. 1 Squadron with Captain C.A. Brookes was escorting two reconnaissance planes in the Middle East. Near Gaza, two German scouting planes attacked the escorts and with their slower machines the Australians spun away to avoid the attack, but Brookes's wings buckled upwards, his tail fell off and, to quote the official report 'he went down like a stone', and was, of course, killed. Vautin was driven to the ground by the superior manoeuvring power of the Germans and was taken prisoner. His capture sparked a series of events that demonstrate the camaraderie of pioneer aviators.

Two days after the fight which took Brookes's life and made a prisoner of Vautin, a Lieutenant Felmy, one of two brothers serving in the German squadrons as pilots, wrote a letter. In this he told that Brookes had been buried with military honours and that Vautin was well and hoped the Australians would send him some kit. This letter was dropped from a German plane over the Australian aerodrome of No. 1 Squadron, AFC, in Egypt. In the dropped bag were two photographs of Vautin with Felmy and two letters from Vautin himself, one to his father and one to Captain R. Williams to say he was safe and well and had been 'shown around Jerusalem by Felmy'.

On receipt of these letters, Captain Murray Jones (another of the pioneer aviators) flew over the enemy lines to deliver a parcel of Vautin's clothes and letters to him from home. Felmy and other airmen waved to him as he flew down to 16 yards before dropping the bundle and flying back safely to the Australian lines. A few days later Felmy appeared over the Australian aerodrome, looped the loop to show he came in peace, and dropped a message bag and then flew back to the German lines. The messages told of the deaths and burial of two pilots shot down on a photography patrol over Beersheba.

Pilots were not only in danger from fire from enemy planes, but because of their low flying could be hit from ground forces.

Lieutenant G.V. Oxenham was killed on 3 May 1918 by a bullet fired from ground forces, his plane crashed and his observer, Lieutenant L.H. Smith, another ex-Light Horseman, was wounded and taken prisoner. He later wrote to his squadron describing the final battle that took Oxenham's life.

By now the airmen were flying planes far superior to the early pioneer machines. They could fire through the propeller and carry a greater amount of bombs. Another change in fortune also assisted the airmen: the Bedouin who had previously ill-treated airmen who were forced down on the desert now admired them greatly and treated them hospitably until they could hand them over to the Australian Camel Corps – at a reward of fifty sovereigns each.

Many Australian airmen flew in support of T.E. Lawrence ('Lawrence of Arabia') and his Arab followers. In September 1915, while Lawrence's men were blowing up the railway in Jordan, Captain Ross Smith (later knighted after his prize-winning flight home to Australia in 1920) flew Lawrence to the Plains of El Kutrani. A special detachment called 'X Flight RAF' had been formed to work alongside Lawrence in the desert. A number of Australian mechanics were landed at Akaba (Jordan) and from there they trekked overland to the headquarters of Prince Feisal at Ma'an, and thence over the desert to Azrak. The railway was blown up, assisted by Australian airmen in their 'large, new' DH9 machines. They dropped one and a quarter ton of explosives, including six bombs of a hundredweight each (quite a feat in those times) on the railway station at Der'a. One DH9 (with engine trouble) was forced to land and was captured by the enemy. (The following day four Australian airmen searched for the plane, found it covered with branches from trees and set it alight.)

On 19 September 1918 began the final victorious sweep across the desert, the brain child of Field-Marshal Lord Allenby. The airmen had great and exciting successes in this battle across the ancient Plain of Armageddon. Lieutenant D.A. Mulford DCM, who had earlier transferred from the

Light Horse to No. 1 Squadron, was in the hurly-burly of a dogfight in this battle when he and Lieutenant D.R. Dowling were wounded and 'obliged' to land. They were promptly taken prisoner only to be recaptured a few hours later by their old friends, the Light Horse.

For two months prior to the attack all enemy machines destroyed on the whole British front – fifteen totally destroyed and twenty-seven driven down – had fallen to the airmen of No. 1 Australian Squadron.

In the beginning, Allied aircraft (which, of course, included the aircraft flown by Australians) had been no match for the superior German machines but by the end of the war in the Middle East – from July to 31 October 1918 when the Turkish Armistice was signed – all this had changed. With the coming of some of the most famous aeronautical machines, stable, fast, manoeuvrable and better-armed, the record of No. 1 Squadron was unparalleled. In those four months the Squadron flew 2,862 hours, did 157 strategic and 77 photography reconnaissances, photographed 604 square miles of enemy territory, flew 150 bomb raids dropping 21 tons of bombs and fired 241,000 rounds of machine-gun ammunition in air combat or against troops on the ground. Seventeen German machines were destroyed in combat and 33 others driven down. And it wasn't only the coming of aircraft of greater speed and superior manoeuvrability that won the battle in the air: the German airmen received the new Pfalz Scout, a splendid aircraft, and still they were beaten.

Major-General Salmond, commanding RAF in the Middle East, inspected No. 1 Squadron at Ramleh in July 1918 and declared that, 'The results that have been achieved by the Royal Air Force have been to a very marked degree due to the fine work of No. 1 Squadron, Australian Flying Corps. It is a matter of pride to me to have had this Squadron under my command since its formation.' He was to see three more months of the work of this much decorated squadron.

In all, nineteen of the pioneer pilots fighting in the Middle East were killed, twenty-three were wounded and twelve captured. And now, the man-to-man battles over the desert were coming to an end, a whole era of aerial pioneering had already moved into another phase, another realm.

The Australian airmen were late arrivals in France and Belgium, their work having up until now centred on Mesopotamia and Egypt. On arrival in France these desert-experienced airmen and new pilots from Australia found that war in the skies over Europe was not the individual combats they had excelled in so much as fighting in strong formations. Three squadrons, No.2, No.3 and No.4 of the Australian Flying Corps, were to play a part in the final campaigns of the European war.

The arena and the style of fighting may have changed but the basic strengths and origins of the Australian Flying Corps remained. An instance of this was No.2 Squadron which, apart from ten of its ground personnel, was composed entirely of men who had been on service in Egypt with the Light Horse or No.1 Squadron or both.

The squadrons arrived at the period of some of the fiercest battles on the Western Front and remained fighting until the final day, flying back to base only when the signal that the Armistice had been signed was given.

The first battle casualty in the Australian squadrons to be taken prisoner in Europe was Lieutenant I. Agnew who was forced down in enemy territory over France and taken prisoner of war on 2 October 1917. Others followed.

One of the liveliest of these very lively men, Lieutenant H. Taylor MC, MM, No.1 Squadron, was shot down behind enemy lines in France, 20 November 1917, during the battle for Cambrai. The official report read that he then 'attacked parties of the enemy with a German rifle, joined an advanced British infantry patrol, led it forward and brought in a wounded man'. He found the crashed aircraft of Lieutenant J. Bell who had been shot down (and subsequently died of wounds), tried to get it airborne but it was too greatly damaged. Another pilot, Lieutenant G.C. Wilson, reported watching from his plane above, while Taylor fought on the ground to evade capture.

'We were in thick fog, machine-gunning enemy troops on the ground, when I saw a red pilot-rocket show up beside me. I guessed by this that Taylor was in distress. Another red light followed and then I saw him down on the ground wrecked, among the enemy. His plane was a heap of wreckage, one wing lay 20 yards away from the heap where Taylor was firing rockets to attract my attention. The enemy were raising their rifles – 50 yards away – I dived at them immediately and scattered them, thus letting Taylor know I had seen his signals. He crouched behind a small mound firing his automatic at Germans who were rushing at him. I dived again, the Germans scattered, Taylor dashed back a few yards then dropped to the ground to fire again; I dived again and the process was repeated until Taylor was about 60 yards from the wreck and nearer our own men, and when he reached them, he grabbed a gun from a fallen man and with the soldiers lay firing at the creeping enemy. I dived and zoomed repeatedly to try and scatter the Germans, then there was a crashing sound against my head and I was blinded.'

Two bullets had pierced his windscreen in front of his face and the glass-dust had been flung into his eyes. Momentarily blinded, he pulled back the 'joy-stick' and climbed back up into the fog to get away from hostile fire and 'flew about anywhere until the glass-dust washed out of my eyes and I could see again'. He descended through the fog to search for Taylor but there was no sign of him or of the Germans. 'Then rips showed up in the canvas of my wings and I realised others, unseen, were firing at me. I assumed Taylor was dead, or captured, and the Germans held the ground.' He returned to base and reported what he had seen.

But that was not the end of Taylor, indeed why Wilson hadn't been able to see him was because Taylor had set off in command of the leaderless men he had found and, fighting all the way, led them back to the main body of troops. Here he left them to try to get back to a landing ground and 'get hold of another aircraft'. He again found Bell's crashed plane but couldn't start it and just walked on until he reached the aerodrome in time for dinner.

Battle in France was very different from that of the desert. Here it was, in the main, offensive patrolling. During the five days, 21–25 March 1918, the Germans claimed to have shot down ninety-three Allied flying machines (and six balloons). British pilots destroyed or captured 137 planes and 'drove eighty-three more out of control' (and burnt three balloons). Many of the machines on either side were shot down from the ground while flying low. It was stated that there was not an aeroplane in the Australian scouting squadron which was not riddled with bullets, yet during all this flurried period of flying low near the ground against infantry, they lost only two pilots, Lieutenant T. Hosking who was killed and Lieutenant O.P. Flight, shot down and taken prisoner.

Captain F.R. Smith, the leader of No.2 Squadron AFC, was shot down by gunfire on 9 November – two days before the Armistice. He walked back through the enemy lines three days after the Armistice.

The squadron was fighting up to the eve of the Armistice on 11 November 1918, and thereafter there was the logistical problem of getting all the great armies back to their own homes. Forty-one Australian airmen had died in action in France, fourteen died of wounds.

The majority of airmen taken prisoner were officers and this difference in rank made all the difference between life and death (as of course it did for men of the other services). Officers were badly off as prisoners if we compare their surroundings, treatment and harassment with pre-prison days, but to compare the life of an officer with that of a man from the rank and file is to learn that the mores, class divisions and traditions of civilian life carry over into military stance with scarcely a ripple. Officers are said to be gentlemen and are, in the main, treated as such by an enemy in wartime. Officers and NCOs are not required to work – even in Turkish camps they were exempt. Their quarters were better. Perhaps one example is sufficient to demonstrate how fine the line is between life and death in a prison camp: officer class could write 'chits', notes to say IOU and would repay a loan when the war is ended. They could *borrow* money against their return home. This brought food, medicine, clothing and some feeling of independence and manhood.

Men from the ranks had no such bolster against the chill winds of imprisonment. In the main they had no funding back home, their service pay was poor and all, including their gaolers, knew it. There have been in all wars and all services the odd men who could run a racket, work a swindle, 'make a quid', but the average man has little talent in this regard, and bearing heavily on prisoners is the ruling, agreed to by International Red Cross, that prisoners of war can be put to work by the captors. Red Cross did state hours, type of work and minimum pay but there was little opportunity to police this.

At the close of the war Lieutenant Colonel L.A. Strange DSO, MC, DFC, British Commander of the 80th Wing RAF, 1918, wrote: 'The two Australian Squadrons, No.2 and No.4, were the finest material as an attacking force in the air, just as Australian infantry divisions were the best that the war produced on either side.'

Après La Guerre

'When they saw us hobbling back down I never heard anyone say,
"Would to God I'd *been* with you boys!"'

Private T.E. Taylor, 14th Battalion

THE PRISONERS FROM WORLD War I received little attention
on their return at war's end. Tommy Taylor, who had
escaped to Russia, said: 'They didn't see any difference
between us and the other returned men. Of course we all
swapped stories with fellows who hadn't been captured, and
each brought the other up to date, but all of us captured
men had had at least one good fight under our belt before
they got us so we were seen to be little different from a man
who hadn't been caught.'

There was no help from the government or sympathy for
their particular suffering or hardship. 'No, no one took any
notice of us. They just brought us home when World War I
ended and most were left to fend for ourselves. It was funny
to think of the politicians as they were when we left in 1914,
"Would to God I could go with you boys!" they said as we
marched up the gangway. When they saw us hobbling back
down it I never heard anyone say, "Would to God I'd *been*
with you boys!" No politician even gave us the time of day.'

Tommy Taylor had written a little booklet, relating his experiences when crossing Russia during 1917, and sold it for
threepence. 'In the Depression I cut it down to a penny a copy
but found it hard to get interest from people, they were not
only that poor, but were dispirited and certainly didn't want
to hear an old digger's story once the war was over.'

For Australians, the difference between prisoners of World
War I and World War II lay in the change in numbers. In
World War I relatively few men (3647) were captured, though

almost 60,000 men were killed and 68.5 per cent were wounded. In World War II a far greater proportion of men (and women) were captured as opposed to the number killed and wounded.

World War II
1939–1945

PRISONERS OF THE GERMANS

Twenty Years On

'They took our two brothers in 1914 and didn't bring them home, "Missing, believed killed at Lone Pine, Gallipoli" the Army said. They waited twenty years after that for our sons to grow old enough to face the guns and then they took them too.'

Mrs Margaret Whelan,
'Calrossie', Yarram Yarram, Victoria 1939

WHEN WORLD WAR II 'broke out' Australia had a population of a little over seven million people (the last census taken in 1933 showed the number as 6,629,839, the following, taken in 1947, recorded 7,579,358). From the 1933 figure, which included the aged, the halt, the lame and the children, 922,000 Australian men and women enlisted to go to World War II (the vast majority being volunteers).

For Australians, World War II was a totally different war to that earlier bath of blood, having in common only the spectre of mothers searching the battlegrounds of their minds for their sons who were reported 'missing', 'believed killed' or 'prisoner of war'.

One of the great differences in this latter war was the casualty lists showing more Australian men and women taken prisoner (28,565) than there were servicemen and women killed. The other difference from World War I was that in that war men were being captured from all divisions from the time Australians went into battle in 1915 until the end of the war, and in almost all spheres of that conflict, whereas the majority of Australians taken prisoner in World War II were captured during one short period in the early months of 1942 in the south-west Pacific, 'at our front door' as people said. And most of these men were from one division, the 8th. Quite understandably this affected the people back home, and later, the evidence of the men's high death rate and suffering shocked the nation: but in doing so the travails and triumphs and the day-to-day life of those men of the Second AIF who were taken prisoner in the Middle East, Greece and Crete were to some extent overlooked.

Of the 7116 Australians who were captured by Italians or Germans, 242 died as prisoners of war; many made escape attempts and some made successful attempts, while others, although they failed, should be recorded for their immense élan, courage and daring. 'I never knew a day when I didn't have escape on my mind', Peter Oates says, while Skip Welsh didn't like being pushed around. 'I couldn't stand barbed wire.' For the young merchant seamen, time dragged unbearably, as it did for the airmen who had known the thrilling tension of battle: 'pilot against pilot, nothing could ever replace that high pitch of excitement', as Ken Watts knows. However they were captured, the men in German camps behaved impeccably as prisoners: that is, they made themselves as great a nuisance as possible in an attempt to cost the enemy the use of manpower in guarding them.

For men who had known the heart-thump of battle (as most of those taken prisoners by the Germans had done), the years dragged interminably, but their spirit and humour was superb. The German guards knew them as Kriegsgefangeners, prisoners of war. To themselves they were Kriegies.

When the Australian divisions were sent overseas, Italy was not in the war and neither was Greece, but soon the Second AIF was to fight one and to go into battle alongside the other.

Ah well, we all know the lunatic convolutions of a world at war. The Greeks were fighting in Albania; Italy was fighting Greece who feared attack by Germany and promptly reminded England she had promised to help and ... Once a major war erupts it keeps rolling along. Italy marched into Tripoli and

North Africa, intent on taking all before her across to Egypt, which Britain, to all intents and purposes, controlled. And Australia was bound to Britain.

At home the pathway to and from the battlefields was followed like a litany: Cairo, Alexandria, Mersa Matruh, Sidi Barrani, Bardia, El Adem, Tobruk, Derna, Benghazi – places where men fought and sometimes lost (and their courage often betrayed by the foolishness of High Command as is the lot of all soldiers), places where they died and in the dying literally made a name for themselves. From Tobruk and the preliminary battles 941 were captured, from El Alamein 130 (and later, in Greece 2030 and Crete 3102 were taken).

To Australians, war in the Middle East was almost kin to the holy wars of medieval times, but with a larrikin élan. The distant echo of artillery (some of it captured from the enemy), the set battle pieces, the signals for attack and retreat, the slightly scallywag yet death-dealing-and-receiving sorties through barbed-wire perimeters at night to raid the enemy, were proudly shown as 'news reels' at home in Australia.

Private George King had sailed with the 2/11th Battalion from Perth (WA) to Palestine. 'Met the Italians at the aerodrome at North Bardia. Well, that was a piece of cake wasn't it! We went across the aerodrome and what'd we take? Thirteen thousand prisoners. Never even dreaming that one day I might be one myself.'

'Bluey McMahon was wandering along with a whole battalion of Ities, yacking away as usual, and he gave his rifle to one of these blokes to hold while he rolled a fag and this Itie took the rifle apart and cleaned it for him while they plodded through the sand to the barbed-wire paddock we called the cooler, the boob,' wrote Private John Hall, 2/11th Battalion.

German forces were rushed down to North Africa to assist the Italians, entering Tripoli via the Mediterranean. Field Marshal Erwin Rommel's desire to capture Tobruk had been an obsession from the beginning of the desert campaign. The rout of the British (including Australian) forces at Benghazi beguiled the great Field Marshal into believing he could

retrieve the Tobruk area with its port, which would be very
handy indeed. But the defenders were as superb as any
Rommel had under his command.

Benghazi was an unhappy memory according to Major R.
Serle, 2/24th Battalion. It had begun gently enough, the Italian
army had been routed and it was believed in senior intelligence
quarters that the Germans, who had landed recently at Tripoli,
wouldn't be ready to go into action for some time – but no
one had taken into account the recent arrival of Field Marshal
Erwin Rommel, the man who became known as The Desert
Fox.

The Australian 6th Division, which had been most successful
in the North African battles, had by now been sent to Greece
and was replaced by the newly arrived 9th Division: to retreat
was unthinkable, but it happened. As in many wars, those in
high command were unequal to the task and some men died
and all suffered the indignity of retreat 'before we could use
our own weapons against the enemy'. But it left the survivors
toughened, determined. 'We had no wish to be known as the
Division which had revealed its ability to retreat further and
faster than any formation on our side ... we certainly didn't
want to meet any of the 6th Division until we had another
record to show', Major Serle wrote.

They had learned one thing: the Germans under Rommel
had initiative, courage and daring and were a foe to be
respected if there was not to be another Benghazi Handicap,
as the men named the retreat from that place. The running in
the Benghazi Handicap had been made even more difficult by
the necessity to clear away the enemy prisoners to Egypt – if
they were going to take and hold Tobruk they couldn't handle
any excess, but eventually some 5000 German and Italian prisoners were inside the perimeter of the garrison when the siege
began. The enemy had followed the retreating Australians,
shelling and gunning them and giving them a taste of the artillery that would be their constant accompaniment to life in that
place.

Tobruk defences had originally been built by the Italians

using the terrain of 100-feet-deep wadis at each end of their area, steep rock defiles with concrete observation posts over-looking the whole area made anti-tank obstacles and these the defenders would need because the German army would attack with tanks. On the first morning of their siege an armoured column rumbled straight down the road towards them and the defenders showed their mettle by immediately knocking out so many vehicles that what were left had to withdraw. It was by way of an announcement to Rommel that they were there to stay, the retreat had ended. They would stand and fight behind anti-tank obstacles, mines and wires – their actual firepower gave a false impression of strength though they had two Italian artillery pieces they had captured.

There were now approximately 35,000 troops as well as the 5000 prisoners inside the perimeter of fortress Tobruk, and a 'howling' blinding dust and sand storm swept down upon them as a foretaste of what their nine months here would be; they used the cloud-like dust as a camouflage to move up and take the posts on the perimeter. The besieged garrison was in a mood not so much euphoric as confidently, cheerfully deter-mined. The front line was too long for the number of troops – some posts were out of sight of the next – there were never enough men or ammunition or telephone communication and they were up against the well-equipped and trained force of the German Afrika Korps and their Italian satellites. But the defenders had their backs to the wall (actually the sea in this case), and the unspoken vow was, Here We Stand.

For nine months during 1941 Tobruk was held as a fortress behind enemy lines. Its fame rivalled that of Malta, the island which itself was awarded a George Cross in salute to all its people for bravery under constant attack from the air.

Once inside the dusty, rocky perimeter of Tobruk, encircled by barbed wire, their backs to the sea, the men settled in to the longest siege in British military history. But that doesn't mean they were settled: any night, any day they were bombed. In daylight, encircled as they were, they stayed low, many in caves dug in the ground, but when darkness fell they were ready. Night after night small groups went out through the wire and laid mines, observed and infiltrated the enemy in the daring way Australians had raided German lines in World War I.

There may be time hereafter to recall
These things, and laugh at how we talked and cried;
It may be pleasant to retell our hopes and fears
And scoff at them – if none has died.
                    Lieutenant A.G. Austin, Tobruk 1941

'Lord Haw-Haw', as the men knew his 'plummy' voice on German radio, broadcasting on a frequency heard in Tobruk, tried to sap their morale. 'You are living like rats in the ground.' How surprised Lord Haw-Haw would have been to learn that his words delighted the men – after all, they *were* living in underground dugouts, where else would they live when they had little air support and their enemy had much? They quickly took 'the Rats of Tobruk' as their motto. On their return to Australia in 1942 their banner proudly flaunted a rat, along with the figure 8 on their Africa Star ribbon to show they fought with 'Monty's' Eighth Army in the desert. Their colour patch on hat and sleeve was henceforth to be changed by army decree to the shape of a T in remembrance of their stand at Tobruk.

In my cave lives a solitary rat
(A celibate rat I can vouch for that);
He hasn't a mate for miles around
And he lives on what he finds on the ground,
Though the country's such
That that's not much.
I don't like he
And he can't stand me
But we need the roof, so there we be.

In my cave lives a type of flea
(A scurrilous flea believe you me);

And though he's such a tiny thing
His bite is worse than a scorpion's sting.
He lives on rat,
But worse than that
He lives on me,
This scurrilous flea
With all his numerous progeny.

Near my cave lives the octave bird
(The queerest bird you've ever heard);
He sings eight notes as he climbs the scale
Though the topmost note is known to fail.
He's very small
Just like us all.
So in we fit though we're cramped a bit –
Old rat,
And flea,
And bird
And me.

Lieutenant A.G. Austin

Once again, as in World War I, Australia was a long way from the battle lines. No amount of letters or newspaper articles could give those at home the heightened atmosphere, the nerve-sharpened tenor of the soldiers' days, their changed perceptions of life. They were singing a German song while fighting the Germans, sometimes *in* German, and always with a tinge of yearning as if for something that will never come again.

Underneath the lamplight, by the barrack gate
... My own Lili Marlene.

We'd forgotten the bonding that on occasions men have with the enemy they are sent to kill. We should have remembered how our fathers, home from World War I, spoke of such strange, almost ethereal matters 'that surpasseth all

understanding', an emotion that all fighting men respond to.
The song drifted across the desert from the German lines into
the oasis, garrison or fort of the Australians, a delicately
unifying refrain, 'Darling, I remember the way you used to
wait'. And we remember that soldiers are young men.

Along with the unsung heroes of the Merchant Navy, the
Royal Navy and the Royal Australian Navy made dashes on
moonless nights to the beleagured men at Tobruk. One merchant ship, the *Destro* (a liner in peacetime), endured sixty-
eight bombing raids on one voyage. Reinforcements coming
up that unlit coast at night were crammed down on C Deck,
14 feet below the waves, trapped if the ship were hit by
bomb or torpedo. A silence born of hovering death filled the
packed mess of men. Private Jim Burns, Australian Army
Service Corps, was on one such trip. 'The men were sweating
in the blacked-out hold, the air stifling, when a roar of guns
told us our ship was shelling the diving conning tower of a
submarine: the torpedo was on its way. Frail threads held
the men there, pride, discipline, whatever it was, but skin
crawled. Thirty seconds to go, all were silently counting. But
the threads were parting, one groan would lead to terror.
Then a hoarse, bull-frog voice carried to the farthest corner
in the darkness, 'Does anybody want to buy a good
watch?"'

Some elderly people back home could remember their
parents telling them of the Siege of Mafeking last century.
'Starving, cut off from aid for their wounded, burying their
comrades.' Things hadn't changed much. At Tobruk, they had
sinus problems, scabby sores from lack of vitamins, amoebic
dysentery, running eyes encrusted with fine sand that constantly swept their domain; there was a lack of water – in that
place where they would dearly have loved a shower; there were
infantry raids by both sides and German air raids on the
defenders who had few anti-aircraft weapons. (But they did
scrounge abandoned Italian guns and put them to work 'sort
of effectively'.) The men at Tobruk mirrored the image of what
Australians saw as the 'real Australian'.

On a desolate Libyan foreshore
In a land that God forsook
Lie the bodies of our comrades
Killed in action in Tobruk.
                                        Anon.

Ruin Ridge

Ruin Ridge was one of the many (mostly unnamed) ridges that tower above the deep and ragged wadis or gulches that through the ages have torn and ripped their way through sand and rock from the Mediterranean down to Africa. The odd ruin of no merit at all scarcely stood out.

This ruin the army was looking for squatted on the Qattara Track crossing the Miteiriya Ridge, 8 miles south-west of El Alamein and the coastline. But there being more than one ruin, and their wireless having broken down and the minefields not being where they had been reported to be but in the path of their tanks – of which twenty were destroyed – the men of the 2/28th Battalion soon were literally on their own, surrounded by two of the world's greatest armies, the British and the German.

Word was brought in that an aircraft had spotted 500 enemy vehicles stretched along 1000 yards of Miteiriya Ridge, with infantry digging in and twenty gun positions located. There was no time for reconnaissance, no time for detail. Men who were to ride on the tanks were unsure if they were to go on the first or the second wave of tanks and those who got on tanks had no sappers on board with them when they set off.

The 2/28th Battalion found they were 2500 to 3000 yards short of Ruin Ridge: other ruins had deceived their officers into thinking this was the ruin spoken of. Men were sent to tell the tanks they were too far ahead and to come back. Promptly at midnight, 26–27 July in bright moonlight, they began their advance at a rate of 100 yards in two minutes.

Because of enemy fire on the flank they must reply by firing from the hip without changing direction or halting. Within 800 yards of the start line the battalion came under fire from field guns, mortars and machine guns. Among the casualties were three company commanders, a foretaste of what this battle would be. The vehicles bearing the supporting arms were fired on by anti-tank guns. Five vehicles were on fire – and the men were halted by a minefield until they could clear a track through. But by 1.10 a.m. the leading companies were on Ruin Ridge, clearing their way with a bayonet charge. But they couldn't get through the enemy fire to lay the telephone cable past the minefield and their wireless was still broken down. The whole area was under fire and the ground too rocky to dig a shelter. Only five carriers out of the original ten remained and they began carrying the fifty wounded men and escorting back 115 Germans and 12 Italian prisoners.

The battalion was short of ammunition, the supporting arms unable to reach it. Major B. Simpson tried to get the trucks through the minefields and burning vehicles across the track with guns on the flanks bombarding his convoy. Seven trucks reached their objective, many more were hit by anti-tank guns and the blazing vehicles 'lit up the area like day', as the men were aware, their silhouettes startlingly etched on the skyline.

Captain Fielding, 2/7th Field Regiment, set off to Brigade Headquarters to try and bring forward the ammunition trucks and telephone cable. On the way back he was killed, firing his Tommy gun to the end. Another attempt to get ammunition in failed. The carrier was then disabled by a mine but the driver, Gunner Manning MM, made his way through the minefield under fire and got through with the message he had heard Fielding receive before he was killed. The 2/43rd Battalion made a dash with ammunition for the 2/28th while the artillery bombarded the German gun covering the minefield, but the attempt failed as had all the others. The astonishing news was that the battalion was consolidating but under fire from machine guns on the left, an anti-tank gun and machine guns on the right and a light gun in front of Ruin Ridge with a further eighteen trucks unloading German soldiers on the right flank – and dawn with its inevitable counter-attack was coming up fast. The various English armoured regiments in the area had been held up for one reason and another for most of the time this fire-bombing battle raged. All night anti-tank and machine guns had lashed the gap through the minefield and little help could come through.

The beleaguered battalion fought off the dawn raid. Then the 2/28th Battalion wireless came on air. They heard it at Headquarters. 'We are in trouble', was the first message from these embattled men and one of the last. At 10.30 hours they got another message past the tanks that now encircled them. 'We have got to give in.' Some of the men, exhausted, bitterly disappointed that their stand had ended in this way, wept as they were formed up in a column and marched off to captivity.

The poet and war correspondent Kenneth Slessor reported (as much as army censorship would allow) the capture of one Australian battalion, although he was not permitted to name it. (It was the 2/28th Infantry Battalion.) 'Cairo, Sat. The news is not good. Grave fears are expressed for the fate of a Western Australian Battalion that recently stormed Ruin Ridge and hung on to it heroically for eight hours, without sufficient protection from the enemy's tanks to save the situation. The men fought to the last, they could not have done more; not men against tanks. Of the Western Australians, 320 men and seventeen officers have been captured or are casualties. An intercepted German report says two Australian machine-gun posts were still holding out. They admitted they themselves had suffered heavily. It was known that among the Germans at Ruin Ridge were units of "K Force", Rommel's own bodyguard.

'The following day, at dawn, Bren-gun fire was heard on the ridge and the occasional thud of an enemy mortar. But there was no hope. Patrols had gone out in dark of the night searching for wounded men but found none. Their ammunition exhausted, they are surrounded by enemy infantry and tanks. In spite of the success of two counter-attacks, there is no doubt that the Jerries won at the cost of a heavy beating. Their

wounded limped back, and our men taken prisoner remained
to be transported to Germany.'

From 17 to 27 July the battalion had, in fact, lost thirty
officers and 700 other ranks killed, wounded, captured,
missing or sick. And for over a month after this battle neither
of those opposing armies launched another major attack:
neither was strong enough. And not until the war was over
did Australia know of the stand of the 2/28th Battalion, a story
that makes the flighty, censored despatches from far distant,
safe, comfortable Cairo as false as most reporting of war must
be. Ruin Ridge was an unknown fly-speck in the midst of
nowhere before and after these young men were trapped there,
but it would be a sad commentary on a nation if their courage
and endurance were not remembered.

Captain R.J. Rudge, an observation officer who had been
directing artillery fire against the enemy attacking the ridge
when it was surrounded, wrote: 'About 100 men of the lost
battalion rose from their position and charged downhill with
fixed bayonets into the strongly held wadi. They disappeared
from view. What happened can only be known when prisoners
are released, but the epic story of the West Australians' last
stand will be worth hearing however long.'

Among these captive men of that night were many of the
old families that had settled Western Australia including John
Hall, who had been 'pulling' sandalwood in the bush for the
China trade when he learned of the war. 'I already had my
load on so I hooshed the camels and walked beside them back
to Kalgoorlie (the streets there had been built wide so camel
teams could be turned round), got my dad to look after the
load and went in to Perth and enlisted. There were two other
sandalwood pullers who had beat me in and we met up in the
Middle East and later as prisoners in Italy and Germany.'

Although it was Germans who had captured those left alive
on Ruin Ridge, this was Italian territory and so the erstwhile
camel driver was sent off to imprisonment in Italy. 'It wasn't
that it was too bad in Italy: just awful being cooped up and
ordered round.' When the Italians withdrew from the war in

1943, the camel driver 'decided to hot-foot it to Switzerland'. He did well for a short while. 'It was spring time, warm, pleasant in all ways tramping northwards, skirting villages, trying to live off the land. Crowds of farm workers were in the fields working. I got a little help from them but they were all very frightened of the repercussions if they were caught helping an escaped prisoner.' Then, one day, crossing a bare patch in the hills, he saw a group staring up at him, waving. He returned the wave and a girl climbed to him and said to wait and her family would come and give him help. What came was the carabinieri who took him to the military. 'I spoke Italian by this time and I told the Ities what I thought of them, adding a few Australian terms for good measure.'

He finished the war in Germany and his tiny diary lists his occupation when locked in for the long nights: he read two or three books every week, from Molière to Shakespeare, Steinbeck, Victor Hugo, Thomas Mann, Voltaire and biographies by the score. He read everything the Red Cross sent to his camp. 'It helped to keep a man sane as did the letters from my mother; she wrote homely news, never anything that may upset a man, nothing to disturb him in any way.'

In peacetime the story of even one young man in imminent danger of his life and with little hope of rescue would be followed up day by day in the newspapers of his own land. And if that one young man were multiplied by 800 young men it would grasp the front page of the reputable papers of the world until the last man – or death – could be accounted for. Following this, there would be the public enquiry into the reason for these young men having been placed in this death-dealing position. However, the lunacy of war admits no such civilised refinements.

The story of one battalion of young men, isolated, cut off, alone and lost and being hunted amid the might of two great armies cannot be conveyed in the haste and topicality needed by the newspapers of the day and written safely far away from the thunder and blood and screams of battle. For this reason has Australia officially documented the history of her men at war.

'We were ill-prepared and ill-outfitted for going into a war,' Dr Alan King of the 2/7th Australian Field Ambulance declares. 'We started off with horse-drawn (artillery) vehicles in WA. Our drug panniers were stamped 1926 and contained drugs most of us had never heard of and had been thrown out of the Pharmacopoeia years ago. When we went to the Middle East there was one truck for each company and we later equipped ours with captured Italian equipment on the first desert campaign. Thousands of prisoners were being taken; we had a mobile unit and there was myself and a dozen men, a ute and a 1300-weight truck and we went up behind the 8th Battalion, we saw the ambush where the men were shot up there.

'One company usually had an Advanced Dressing Station as well as a Field Ambulance, both looking for similar sites to set up and get in one another's hair. Here we were too busy to worry much about what each was doing. The 6th Division were a superb fighting unit, physically tough, very proud, as were all of us, to be part of the new Division. They had fought well at Benghazi and Tobruk. Our units felt confident with them at all times.'

Private Colin Horman, 2/24th Battalion, a prisoner first of the Italians and then of the Germans, was working in the Federal Woollen Mills in the dye house in Geelong when war broke out. 'I was 24 and I still didn't have any brains. I had an old uncle, an Anzac, who got shot up in the boat, he didn't actually land. Then they discharged him, unfit for war. He said to me as a boy, "They couldn't get me aboard a troop ship again at the point of a bayonet". And after that I went and voluntarily enlisted. Well, there's just nothing between your eyebrows when you are young.

'I used to work in this dye house, we were making stuff for the Services, navy, army, air force, work from 6 a.m. to 6 p.m. plus Saturday morning. I was earning seven pounds ten shillings a week. At that time a lot of people were only earning four pounds. And I gave that away to get five bob a day and every chance of my head being blown off by some German.

Well, you are definitely *non compos mentis* when you do a thing like that. It was just the Germans and British fighting another commerce war like the last one as far as I was concerned, until the British got bundled out of France at Dunkirk in 1940, and then a lot of people who had jobs like myself thought, by jingo we've just got to go now.

'And I ran into Tobruk like all the rest. The Jerry beat the bejesus out of us at Benghazi and we called our retreat the Benghazi Handicap. But by God we made up for it in Tobruk. We were up in the lines except when we used to get a "rest" and even that meant going all night carrying supplies to the blokes that were relieving us in the lines. It was only from Easter to May when I realised it was too dangerous. I was posted at R5 [the perimeter]. We were with Gordon Porter, wonderful fellow old Pud, and I think that applied to all our officers, NCOs and even Brigadier Toffel, our Brigade Commander, a 1914–18 veteran, a champion fellow.

'The night before I set off on the road to Berlin, old Pud sent me up with a party to bring up some arms, ammunition and stuff, and that was when we brought our water up too, a water bottle a day per man. (Except on one occasion they let their heads go and gave us a mug full of soapy water and they said we could have a bath in that. Of course, not being altogether silly, we let it stand still and the soap sank to the bottom and we drank it.)

'So we are back there at company headquarters with Captain Bird, our OC, to get this stuff and he said, What are they doing firing away there on the flanks? Don't they know how short we are of ammunition? We were forbidden to fire at Jerry aircraft because we were so short of ammo all the time. You could only fire when you could more or less see the whites of his eyes. So up I go to the lines. We used to have to get through this minefield. And then it was really on, all that night, first the Stukas came over and flattened all the wire and detonated your minefield in front of you. So when their Panzers came up all the mines in the minefield had been detonated. And their infantry, not being altogether stupid, came up behind these tanks which meant that you couldn't get at their infantry and all our blokes could do was keep firing at the slits in the Panzers; that's how we were losing men, because our posts had pretty wide slits in them and the German fire came through, their Spandau machine guns were killing our blokes, poor old Corporal Gazard, that's how they got him, and Laurie Baker, all the blokes mounted on the machine guns. You couldn't stay on the top, you had to be under cover because of the Jerry shells coming in. And so finally, at about 11 a.m. in the morning when they started throwing hand grenades down on us, well, we decided that this was enough ... Berlin for me!' Colin Horman jokes. The stand these men made during that night and morning is written in official histories.

'The Germans said we'd have to help with our wounded, so myself and another bloke carried a mate (Windsor) out on two bits of sticks. He'd got a machine-gun burst through the legs and we were taking him to the dressing station back behind Jerry's lines. And this is where these two Yanks were. Big strong bastards and I reckon if I'd had a bomb or something then there would have been two Yanks less. "Tough luck Aussie", they said when us prisoners went by with old Windsor on the stretcher. As though it was a game. At that stage they probably thought Jerry would win the war. The Yanks weren't even in the bloody war then in 1941 and they wouldn't have been in yet if they hadn't been bombed into it. And when the war was over and I got back to Australia they said, "The Yanks saved Australia while you were away!" I'll never forget those words.

'But you've got to give it to old Jerry, he looked after wounded enemy as meticulously as he did his own people', Colin bounces back.

The captured Australians were held behind German lines until they could be handed over to the Italians because North Africa was their war. 'We weren't officially registered with Geneva as prisoners out on the desert, and when one of our blokes complained the German guard said it would get us killed, because not being registered means in army terms that you don't exist. They could just put in the records that you were shot while attempting to escape. That would save them a lot of trouble. They said, "We hope you boys appreciate that".

'We were ten days in Derna, quartered in the camel station. The Jerries had told us right from the start, "We have come here to help the Italians, so although we took you people, you are actually Italian prisoners. We're doing you a good turn by feeding you, so don't expect us to do more than that, because you don't belong to us. Any medicines, hospital, medical attention, food or anything, that's really their pigeon. We're only interested in you as units of labour."

'I was very fortunate, because at Derna those who were kept in the camel stations all the time contracted dysentery in a very bad way, but I was sent to the field workshop with twenty others. My job was the blacksmith's striker. I hadn't had anything to eat for two days. First time I raised a hammer for the blacksmith I fell on my face ..."Frau!" the striker called. "Hausfrau!" The next thing a private came along and he marched me to the lieutenant in charge of that field workshop. He was an Austrian and had about as much interest in the war as I've got in Iceland. In this building he had this lovely piano and he said to me, "If you don't upset me, I won't be worrying you". He had an endless supply of wine, and he'd be playing the piano, and his warrant officer was running the workshop. We were there for ten days; I had to get him lunch, and it was always boiled broad beans and mashed potatoes. But he was that pickled he couldn't eat anything so I used to go up to the cook and say he had a guest. I'd get two lunches and I'd knock them both off.

'When I had to move on he said, "Here's 10 lira. Money always helps anybody." I'll never forget old Streicker playing his piano and drinking the grog and me eating his midday meal.

'At Benghazi, the RAF were bombing the harbour where us prisoners were unloading ships. They'd already sunk so many that they had platforms from one wreck to another. We were unloading ships actually in the middle of the harbour and could roll these 44-gallon drums of petrol from wreck to wreck right to the shore, guarded by a Jerry with a fixed bayonet to prod you along.

'The RAF would come and bomb the ships, then there'd be a great stampede to the shelter which the Arabs always won, the Australians were second, and the Germans third. One day we heard the siren and the next thing the first bomb came and we were all sprinting and Private Cocky Walpole of our battalion just got in ahead of the German, and the German behind him almost got a bomb right up his bum. That's how close it was.

'Then another day we were down the harbour, away went the siren, along came the dust and the RAF came in bombing again. And the Ities (they, as well as the Jerries, had machine guns on buildings), they always opened fire and ran for their life. But this day they opened fire and the Jerry was suddenly applauding the Ities: they'd shot down an English aircraft! Five minutes later they found that what the Ities had actually shot down was one of the Messerschmitts chasing our bombers. Gee, they were savage. We laughed like anything. Oh, they used to get speechless with rage at us.

'Then I cracked up. Jesus, I got crook. The black bread, it just about killed us, that was the only thing we were getting, and two-thirds of a tin of sardines at lunch time, and at night when you'd get back they'd open sauerkraut, straight out of the pickle, for your main meal. That diet and heavy work took toll on a man. If the RAF didn't happen to bomb it, they'd keep you going until dark at the harbour. We used to hope that the RAF would come over because everybody used to down tools and take off.

'Each day the Jerries would march us off from the Itie camp to work. They had captured a lot of big naval guns in France and brought them and the shells here. So this morning, Poidervin, our sergeant, got wind that we were to unload artillery shells and he objected, said prisoners wouldn't do it. So we came back to camp with a full platoon of soldiers with rifles and bayonets around us. And the Jerry lieutenant said, "Now sergeant, is that strike still on or is it off?" Old Poidervin looks at the bayonets, then at us and says, "I yield". "Well," said the German, "I'll teach you blokes for holding us up", and he doubled us all the way from that Itie camp to the wharf and made us start work straight away.

'Benghazi was the worst part of our whole imprisonment with long hours of heavy work, the heat and deprivation. At one stage my boots fell off with the sweat, everything fell to bits. Most of the men just had a pair of slacks or shorts and boots.

'Sergeant Gordon Porter was one man in a million. He used to get on to the Germans during the day when we were gasping for water as we worked. Look, he'd say to the guard, "the fellows have got to have some water, they're going to collapse and you'll get no more of their labour". He never thought of himself. He was the most unselfish man you could ever get. Officers and NCOs didn't have to go out on work parties but Porter did: "I'm here to look after my men", he'd say, and the guard, being a pretty decent bloke, he appreciated that position.

'We did a bit of sabotage if the Jerries weren't watching. It's about as much as a man can do to lift a French naval shell but we used to drop the ammo into the water between the ship and the wharf. A hell of a lot of naval shells are probably still there. It made the Jerries bloody mad, they used to kick our faces right, left and centre. But I was like a ballet dancer in those times, they rarely connected with me.

'Although German soldiers weren't all bad I tell you. One day Cocky Walpole was caught talking through a boarded-up window to an English RASC bloke who had been caught escaping. The old Kraut in charge, elderly like most of them, told Cocky to repeat the conversation. Cocky just stood to attention and said, "You can shoot me, but I'm not going to tell you". And the old Kraut put his revolver back and said, "I couldn't shoot a brave man. You'd better get back into the camp and don't let me catch you again." That says a lot for old Jerry, doesn't it?

'We worked here from the end of May until 13 December, when the push was begun on the outskirts of Benghazi; they then put us in a leaky cruiser and sent us across to Italy. We had no decent clothes to protect us in the snow. A lot only had shirts and shorts. But I had my old army uniform, and had managed to pick up a light Itie summer jacket in Benghazi, so I gave it to poor little Muir, a shell-shocked bloke. He only had shorts.

'First we had sixteen months in Italy, up at Camp 57. The mob already in this camp had that much food that instead of eating the big Itie biscuits, they'd etched pictures on them and hung them all round the walls. But when the drought set in and they got no Red Cross parcels, they all came down. We were very hungry. Two or three of the New Zealanders died and two Australian doctors of the 2/8th Field Ambulance that the Jerries had captured said there was no disease, no nothing, the men simply didn't have anything to eat. We had a chap there, an Alpine captain. Oh, he was a champion bloke. We found in Italy that any officer or member of an Alpine unit was a good bloke, others were mongrels to beat all mongrels. And we had one fellow there, Father Cotter, he'd been a missionary in British West Africa. He was about five feet nothing. Oh, he was a lovely old bloke. And he would do anything. This is what he was like: [Private] Titch Messenger hadn't got a letter from home (I got a letter after a year, and others waited fourteen months), and the time was going on. Titch was very worried about his two little daughters, so he saw Father Cotter and the priest got a message through the Vatican radio to a radio in Sydney; they got on to the Australian army authorities and found that Titch's wife had shoved off to New Zealand. They then straight away started enquiring about the girls, to look after them. Father Cotter couldn't do enough for us.

'Early in 1943 we were sent to rice farms where they grew fourteen varieties on the River Po. There were forty of us in this camp. We had to go to work but didn't draw a pay. So we were flogging our clothes for vino. Bang would go your shirt, or if you had a spare pair of socks or something they would go. Brown even flogged his boots. And then Dino, the Itie cook would bring a big demijohn on Saturday night, oh, terrible bloody claret; sometimes we tried better wines, and then the Ities would come in with us and the blokes would get full and do the guards over. They got frightened to come in in the finish. We had a red-haired sergeant, Charlie Fraser, who could speak Italian like nobody's business and when he got full he would grab an Itie and would call him anything but a Christian.

'And then one day up comes the greengrocer and says that Mussolini was in prison and Bedolio was Prime Minister. The Italians had chucked it in. The Ities thought the whole war was finished. Well, I thought, I bet the Germans won't give up so I swapped all my clothes, my jacket for an Itie's coat (and it went nearly two laps around me), and an Itie had trousers too short and wouldn't meet, so I swapped them for mine, and I still had a straw hat with a lovely blue and gold band to swap for a khaki shirt. (The farmer had given us all one hat each to keep the sun off. Can you imagine an Australian in a get-up like that? I would have been a sight for sore eyes.)

'An Italian woman gave me a big loaf of bread made from rice flour and a big piece of cheese and I headed off for Switzerland. Just kept going north. There was just one place in the hills where you could get through. I was near Torino, I was tired, I'd been sleeping all day and most nights on the road where the Po runs in a gorge. In the finish I got that bloody tired I thought I've had enough of this, so I just walked through in daylight. And this seemed to be one place in the hills where you could cross over. I went round the corner and thought, oh well, it's only another farm house.

'It was the Guardia and they were changing the guard, and the corporal says to me, "Documento?" I said, "Niente documento, Australiano." So he bunged me in the cell there and he said he'd have to tell the Germans because if one of them puts a prisoner up, the Germans will shoot Ities. Next day the German major got me. "I know you're an RAF flyer that has been shot down. I'm going to fix you for this. I'm going to shoot you in the morning." By Christ that was a bad night for me.

'I had nine days in solitary confinement and then they took me to France in a German troop convoy. Finally I got up to Grenoble and I came off the convoy, and there were two Germans, one with a rifle and bayonet and one with a big Mauser pistol, and they marched me up the main street, like Bourke Street, to the gendarmerie quarters to the old lieutenant there. In the vernacular English he said, "Geez, this is a pickle. You're going to be a pain in the neck for me. You'll have to stop with me in the headquarters." He took me out to lunch and all he was getting was a sort of pumpkin soup and a bit of bread and the French waitress gave me two helpings and only gave him one and he never budged.

'Once a month here they got a Red Cross parcel from Morocco and I was only in that joint four days and I was tinny enough on the second day to get a parcel. But things were not rosy. The French prisoners here were going to make a break. The day beforehand they told me I was to lead it. And I thought Christ, I'm going to get shot to pieces with the Jerry out there. What the hell was I supposed to be doing? Smashing the glass window while he'd be putting burst after burst in? Come the morning, this is how tinny I am, in comes the Jerry. He said, "Where's the Englander? You're on your way to Poland." Franz Klodowski was to escort me. Franz had been a prisoner in England in the first war and the English had treated him well, so he said, "I'll treat you well". So I got on well with him and also with the little Prussian corporal who took me right through Leipzig and finally to Poland.

'I still had part of this Red Cross parcel in a little haversack, and when I got there that night, a big fat German confiscated it. I'm called up the next day to the office to be tried for escaping. The German said, "What's your defence?" "Well," I said, "I escaped from the Italians in Italy. I haven't escaped from the Germans." He said. "That's right, you're acquitted." He could have easily said, "Right, down the coal mine." I told him the guard took some bread and the remnants of my Red Cross parcel. "Oh, did he", the German said. He came back with the bread: "But all the choice little bits you had left, he's eaten them all."

'So, it's yet another camp for me. An Australian was in charge of the working parties. He said, "The Escape Committee have got an RAAF chap here, Charles Price Watson, from Elwood, Victoria, who wants to escape. Are you game to swap over with him? He's got two food parcels coming up. The Jerries will rumble you eventually, but think of it, two food parcels!" Christ, you would have murdered your own mother for two food parcels.

'The RAAF had a little camp within the camp up there. So I went up and Stan Moss looked after me, telling me what to do. (He was the Canon at St Paul's Cathedral, Melbourne, later.) All I had to know was that my wife's name was Peggy and that I had a little daughter, 4 years old, and my army number. He said, "That's all you've got to know and all you can tell them when they put the screws on you. You can't tell them any more, because you don't know." Later a German came in and said, "Mr Watson?" and I said, "Yes". You see, I thought of myself as Watson. He said, "Your commission has come through, you're being transferred." I told Stan Moss and he said, "You could be in some trouble now. You don't even look like Watson (he was a big fellow)." Moss said, "There are three dinkum Australians going to another camp. We've got to make you look like an air force bloke." So he got hold of an air force hat somewhere and Moss took the wings off his own jacket. He was a bomber pilot when he was shot down over Germany. And he had all my buttons polished up. Christ, I was looking like a real fair dinkum RAAF coot and, unbeknown to me, they were all making bets on what the chances were of my getting through.

'When I became Watson I thought I was Watson. When anyone said to me, "Hello Col", I stared at him. I'd forgotten I was Colin Horman. Soon everybody said to me, "Hello Price", "G'day Price", and I became Price. We lived in Grey

Street, Elwood. I was a flying officer. I became this person. In the meantime, somewhere else, Price became me, Colin Horman.

'So out we march. You've got to check in the office and I got rumbled straight away. "Oh", the Jerry said, "another swap over. Look, you're obviously not Charles Price Watson, I'll check these prints at Lamsdorf and I'll soon find out who you are."

'And then of course I crashed. It looked as though nothing could save me from getting a month in the coal mines. Straight into solitary confinement. But they gave me a Red Cross parcel. A Jerry came in and said that if I gave him the chocolate I could eat the rest, he wouldn't confiscate it.

But Horman was 'tinny' again. There was an acute shortage of orderlies and, with a little suggestion from friends attempting to save him, Horman was kept at the camp as an orderly. He had hardly settled into this work when the escape committee again approached him. They knew he had worked in a woollen mill and could strip cloth and do dyeing. Thus began a period of working on the odd garments and clothes the committee managed to get by nefarious means and turn into outfits for escapees. 'I don't know how they got these things into the prison. You are not told, you do not ask, then you cannot tell if the screws are put on you. But I had to have various agents to strip material back to the natural wool, dye stuff, chemicals. They got them in. They could have bribed the Germans, I don't know. Lots of things went on.

'I was in my room, number fourteen, in barracks fifty-three and Gunner Sam Weaver, an artillery man, came in and said to me, "Now look here, Colin. Very soon something is going to happen, so just shut up." Then, knock! Up came part of the floor and out came a hand with some matches in it. And Sam had a sandwich and he put it in the hand, after taking the matches, and the hand withdrew and Sam replaced the floor. Sam told me he'd had that "ferret" organised for a long time. These "ferrets" were to intercept our blokes' tunnels under all the huts. Sam was the only man in the camp to have matches.

The RAAF officer in charge knew this and the story went that he said, "Sam, I've told you time and again not to trade with the Germans," but it didn't stop Sam.

'Before I got there the wooden horse escape had taken place from our centre camp. It's common knowledge how the men were bobbing over the thing while underneath they had the tunnel, concealed by bits of hessian coming down from the horse, and while there were many men around, one bloke would go down. The Germans couldn't see them with so many men all around. But that happened before I got there. While I was there they had another escape attempt going. They were playing rugby and when they'd get in the scrum, one bloke would come out of the hole in the ground and another bloke in the scrum would go down. I watched that time and again and I could never pick who was the bloke who came up and who went down and the Germans would be up in the guard tower looking over them and they never found out. Finally the men had to abandon that tunnel as it got nearer the wire because the Germans had put down metal detectors and you had to be a tremendous distance down otherwise they could detect you.

'Life in the bag was what you made it. What our wonderful old Colonel Spowers said was, "What you lot have got to get into your heads right from the word go is that the German is a tough man, he's well trained. Every German has had an education and they're efficient, and the only way we'll ever beat them is to be physically fitter and we've got to be better trained, otherwise they'll walk all over us. It's only by better training and dedication that we're ever going to win," he said.'

War spins a fine net, it ensnares the splendid, the seedy, the poor, rich, coarse and the gentle. Lionel Jones, 2/24th Battalion, was one of the gentle; he was a nurseryman, getting up at 4 a.m. to pick violets 'fingers blue from the spring frost on the plants' to send on the 4.30 a.m. train to the Melbourne market.

He kept a meticulous diary while abroad and flowers burst

through the lines. 'At Sea' he writes home and tells of gardens he saw when the troop ship touched in at Perth (WA), 'Noel's garden not very startling, his main trouble is the watering, the soil is like Black Rock, very hungry and dry.' He uses three pages to tell more about the garden, 'ideal for Stroblanthus, Coleus, Crotons, all the other foliage plants of the tropics. Very disappointed not to see orchids as leave was up.'

Colombo had delighted him. 'A blaze of colour in all gardens.' When he reached Tel Aviv he was looking through a florist's window when the owner, Mr Aron Halevy, came out and said, 'Not like the flowers in Melbourne, eh?'. Mr Halevy had once lived in Berwick (Vic). At Palestine, 'the roses are lovely, unbeatable'. He names a dozen varieties and, 'Today saw a wild cyclamen, white with a pink eye, no bigger than a violet'.

His diary chronicles his days from embarkation to North Africa where he fought in the desert battles that made the Australians famous for their valour, dash and daring. He saw friends die, others wounded or captured, and wrote to their home folks telling them all he knew of the men they waited to hear from.

In Tobruk all able-bodied men were front-line soldiers, fighters carrying a gun. Being a batman in an infantry battalion may cover a multitude of tasks, but is no 'bum-brusher's job' as some may disdainfully name it. Apart from caring for his officer's clothing etc. and waiting on table behind the lines, Lionel had to attend semaphore school, map reading, study Italian and German mines and booby traps, as well as constantly digging-in while camped in the desert and, 'when the chips were down', fighting in the front line.

'1 April [1941], digging in all day.

8 April, nothing but dig and run.

9 April, camp dive-bombed and machine gunned.

10 April, camped 3 miles from Tobruk, 4.15 p.m. under fire – artillery and machine guns, tracer bullets, searchlights.

11 April, Good Friday, in front line.

14 April, in action. Heavy dust storm.
15 April, Stand by at 5.30 a.m. as usual. At Observation
          Post all day. [The OP gives warning of approach-
          ing enemy and is always in advance of the front
          line.] Started picket at midnight.'

It was the last picket he would do. '16.4.41 We are now
in the front line over the wire entanglements from Fritz and
Ities. They get lively at times. We kept our end up all day
yesterday. Could hear Fritz and Itie officers giving orders all
night around us. Dawn, and fog lifting to see the worst row
of enemy tanks all round us open fire. Alan Hempel
wounded. Fred Barlow killed. Captain Bird and three other
mates wounded. Kept at them until taken prisoner at 1930
hours. Fritz courteous. Met most of battalion taken prisoner
during last night and day.'

He had fought through Benghazi, Derna and Tobruk. And
when his post was overrun and the dead and dying out of the
battle, he and the other survivors were taken POW by the
Germans and handed over to the Italians 'whose bailiwick this
is, here in North Africa'. He was put to work sorting, folding
and packing inner tubes for tyres on military vehicles, worked
patiently – all the while sticking a safety pin through the four-
folded rubber tube; the holes would not be seen and the
damage would occur far away on the desert patrols. By 3 May
he had sent a letter home through International Red Cross and
writes in his diary, 'Derna, a pretty town with plenty of green
about, geraniums, bougainvillea, roses, oleander, lilly-pilly,
Moreton Bay figs, date palms a plenty.'

He may be a prisoner but he had kept his humour. He
writes, 'Heard on parade: SM [Sergeant Major] to Aussie:
Where are you going? Aussie: Latrine. SM: There's only five
seats and six have gone already. Aussie: I'll sit on someone's
knee.'

As if working out a blank jigsaw puzzle the families back home
struggled to make a picture or pattern of their man's life in a

world alien to them. Letters from the battle-front areas came in no order at all (one can imagine the difficulty for the Army Postal Service in transport as well as the time taken for detailed censorship of all letters coming from areas such as Tobruk). And many letters arrived after the death of the man. A network grew up in a haphazard yet totally warming fashion between the families whose men were 'missing', 'POW' or 'killed'. Letters crisscrossed the whole of Australia. These far-distant families craved news but were afraid of what it might bring. When families heard mention of some other mother's son, they would write and pass word on in case the family had had no news. Lionel Jones's family received and sent many such letters.

A letter from 'Mr Barlow' to 'Mr Jones': 'We had a letter from your brother Lionel telling us how our son Frank was killed. We were very grateful for his kind thought and when the war is over and peace once again reigns and your son returns to you, we should very much like to meet him. We received a few odds and ends of Frank's belongings.'

Another letter: 'When I was up at Wodonga, I met a girl that Alan Hempel went with, she remembered all the boys, Frank Barlow, Lionel Jones and Alan Hempel.' These three had been 'cobbers' and had 'been in the thick of it'. Frank Barlow was now dead, Lionel Jones was a prisoner and Alan Hempel an escaped prisoner.

Alan Hempel was captured outside the wire perimeter of Tobruk and was first reported 'DOW' [died of wounds], but shortly afterwards a letter from him arrived via the Italian Red Cross, stating he was a prisoner and the family breathed again. But next news was that he and another Australian, Dick McLeish, had escaped from a prison camp in Italian-held North Africa and had walked 110 miles through enemy-occupied territory to rejoin their battalion in Tobruk. Corporal Frank Petzke, who was sent to HQ to bring them back to their unit, took a snapshot of the pair and sent it home. Alan promptly wrote to his sisters.

Rat of the Western Desert   Corporal A.L. Hempel
Date: 23/6/41   VX23993 D Company
                                             2/24 Battalion
                                Australian Imperial Force Abroad.

My Dearest Darling Sister Pearl and All at Home,
I bet by this time you have been wondering what on earth has
happened seeing you did not hear from me, but I am still in the
land of the living and feeling fine. Well Pearl, I guess that you
were let know that I was missing. I had been up to the front for
over three months. We were all 'standing to' behind our guns
one morning, just at dawn, and hoping for a bit of action.
Well, we got it. Aeroplanes diving down, bombing and
machine-gunning us all day long and being shelled by the
Germans' long range guns, tanks running over the top of our
trenches, and using flame throwers on us. The noise was deafening, I thought my ear drums were going to burst wide out.
After two days and nights of this we had to give up as there
were too many for us. It is not a nice sight seeing men shot and
getting blown to pieces, but when it means either you get him
or he gets you, it is a different matter. So on May the 1st I was
captured by the Germans, along with a lot of my own cobbers
and sent back behind their lines to work on a big aerodrome.
    On June the 2nd after being a prisoner for thirty-one days, Dick
McLeish and I broke out of prison camp, got past the guards and
set off to walk 110 miles to our own lines where the Australians
were. We travelled at night and rested during the day. We had to
go very careful, because we knew if we were caught we would
have been shot dead on the spot, because anyone who escapes
from a German prison camp here is classed as a spy. Water is very
scarce as it is nearly all desert country. So we waited till they were
all in bed and sneaked up and drained the water out of their truck
radiators and find what tucker, if any at all. I will not bother to
tell you how many times we were nearly caught, but after nine
days and nine nights of sneaking through their camps and missing
being caught by inches, we clambered through their barbed wire
entanglements out into no man's land and headed across the

desert towards our own lines. At last we reached them and there was the sight we thought we would never ever see again, the Australians there in their trenches just having breakfast and we had not had anything to eat for two days, but even then we did not eat too much, as we were too excited to know we were safe again. All the boys gathered around my cobber Dick McLeish and I and congratulated us on our great effort as we are the only two that had escaped from the hands of the Germans up to date. Anyway you can be proud of your old brother, I have done something that no one has done and brought back a lot of valuable information about Germans. The Brigadier and the General gave us great praise and told us it was something to be proud of. But a few days spell and I am back with my battalion again in the front line. It is very quiet here today, except for a few Jerry planes flying overhead, and a few shells landing around. [Next sentence censored.] Up to the front are little white crosses with tin hats on them, it kind of gets you down when you pass by one of them and know that it is one of your own mates lying there.

Well Pearl my dear, I suppose you are still lairing up with the boys around the place. If I'm not home save me a bit of your wedding cake. Remember me to everyone at home. I have not had a letter for over three months and it is now three months since I have had any leave. So think of your dear old brother sometimes and I hope to be home soon.

I am your ever loving brother Alan.

He had written a letter to his grandmother, Mrs Vincent of Albury NSW. 'Nearly all my mates have been killed or taken prisoner.' Then, 'I would love a big feed of those lettuce salads you used to make'.

Alan wrote to another of his sisters, 'My dearest darling sister Alice . . . I bet you were worried when I was missing over a month but don't worry any longer'. He tells of the run for freedom he and McLeish made, 'getting so close at nights we could hear them snoring in their beds while they were asleep'. And picking their way through the German minefields 'and at last arriving at our own minefields, getting through that, the barbed wire and the tank ditch. Just as we arrived the German bombers came over and bombed the trench but it was like being in a new world after being prisoners for 31 days. Now I am back in the front line again with the boys, having another smack at them. Jerry bombs us hard in the day and we have to lie low and come out in the night like rabbits. The AIF have done a wonderful job over here and will keep on doing it. It is very hot here today and a few bottles of cold beer would be wonderful. But some day we will get leave.

'There's as many fleas as flies here. I haven't had a shave for two months, neither have I had a pay. But darling I am the happiest soldier in the whole AIF today to be able to write to my darling big sister again. I hope the romance is still going well. Dear sister, I must go and see that my men get their tea. Wish me luck that I may stop a few more tanks. I am your ever loving and dearest brother and also ex-German prisoner, Alan XXX'

This was the last letter Alice had from her brother. He was already dead before any of the above letters were received. On 3 July, less than a month after his escape from the Germans, Alan Hempel had been wounded and died shortly after.

A letter was sent from the McLeish family to the Jones family passing on news (and, incidentally letting us know how hard life was for the women waiting at home).

Bridge Inn Hotel,
Maindample.

Dear Mr Jones,
Received your letter to Mrs McLeish, and as she is away I opened it; I am her auntie and she has lived with me since her husband was missing. I do all her writing for her now. I went to town last week and got one of the two little children as Mrs McLeish is going into hospital. It was good of you to write. We get a lot of letters from people and they all help us to find out something new. We didn't know where Dick was for a time. But now we've got good news to say he's got away . . . and is back at Tobruk. I hear from Dick nearly every week. Also get a lot of parcels from him. Hope you have news from Lionel. Wish him

all the best of luck. Anything you would like to know we will be happy to tell you.

Yours sincerely, Betty Gleeson.

Then she writes, 'I also hear from Alan Hempel's auntie. Dick told me about Alan getting shot before it came out he had died. He is buried at Tobruk.'

And so we learn Alan Hempel is dead. The three cobbers had fared badly, two dead, one a prisoner. The shock to Alan's family was numbing; at first was the news he was missing, then he was a POW, then he'd escaped and reached the Australian lines. Now he was gone.

The wife of Captain Arthur C. Bird, Commander of D Company 2/24th Battalion, kept in touch with relatives of her husband's men missing or reported captured. 'I took the telegram I had from Arthur into the Army Friday and they couldn't understand how it came from London (seeing that he was a prisoner in Italy). But I don't care how it came. All I am glad to know is he is well again.' She had typed several copies of Corporal Alan Hempel's last letter as she thought people such as Lionel Jones's father may wish to read it. 'I do hope they will be better treated in Italy and am glad they are out of Tobruk. What a terrible ordeal they have been through.'

Lionel Jones's brother Keith, a sergeant in the RAAF, was a part of the loving chain of relatives and friends trying to help one another in the void of silence and the terror of an official letter. Captain Bird, in an Italian prison, was grateful for the interest and care of these people.

> Ospedale Militare
> Caserta Napoli. Italy.
> Captain A.C. Bird
> Prisoner of War
> 23 November 1941

Dear Keith,

I have just received a letter from my wife, telling of your kindnesses. It means a lot to one to hear things like that and I thank

you very much. Have you heard from Lionel? I have not seen
him since the 1st of May, when we were taken. I cannot
express my admiration for his services, wherever I was Lionel
was close behind me and I was the one that gave up our post
when those lads wanted to go on to fight to the finish. I had a
grand company and we suffered for it by getting the worst jobs,
but we were proud of it. I think that we suffered most in casualties that day, but have been unable to get any real news, as I
was always behind the rest of the wounded as they passed from
hospital to hospital. This is the last one, after this the Pen. I've
had six months next Wednesday here, and when you write to
Lionel, tell him Corporal Leach [5th AGH] is still here, but is
to be repatriated to Aussie. As letters are limited, I would be
pleased if you could drop the enclosed card into the post. Once
again Keith, thank you very much.

Yours sincerely, A.C. Bird.

Lionel's family had at first been informed by the Minister of
the Army that Lionel was 'missing'. International Red Cross
sent word that he was 'officially missing', then the Red Cross
Bureau of Wounded, Missing and Prisoners of War sent word
he was 'Missing, believed prisoner' and the Apostolic Delegate
in Sydney reported to His Eminence, the Papal Secretary of
State in Rome, with a request that he do everything possible
to trace Lionel. They later sent word that he was 'a Prizionieri
de Guerra'. His address, 'Campo T Benghasi, XII Centramento
Postale'. Australian Red Cross wrote on 27 November 1941,
'Our records now show that VX32717, L.A. Jones is a prisoner of war', and added, 'As you know how eagerly letters are
looked for by prisoners of war, we urge you to write at once.'
Australian troops were pouring in from the desert as prisoners. Lionel Jones lists scores of names. He is sent to Italy
with his mate Shonta (Private John Hynes). Rations in Italy
were 'tight' but when Shonta went past girls they'd say, 'Look
under the potatoes', and there he'd find food.
Then in September 1943, Lionel's diary reads: 'Good griff'
(gossip, news). 'Armistice signed. No sleep.' Italy was out of

the war. Next day, 'Vino laid on, very drunk. Standing by ready to escape capture by Germans.' Lionel and Shonta are wearing 'crutch bags' secreting food for the break-out.

Lionel says in a letter, 'I'm missing a good old feed of meat and veg and mum's cakes and Fowlers bottles of fruit. At least we are given a Red Cross parcel per man per week.' Then, in his diary, 'Team with Shonta, get civvy clothes. Hid out. Spend afternoon fishing with kids. Started work picking beans. Ransom of 1800 lira per prisoner offered by Jerries.' Up the mountains, sleeping on oak leaves at Prato, down the auto-strada, eating chestnuts, across hills covered with 'azaleas, daphne, cyclamen, many with first buds bursting'. Sleeping at villages, eating pani.

When Italy deposed Mussolini and retired from the war in 1943, an estimated 40,000 Allied ex-prisoners of war are said to have escaped and tried to reach Allied lines before the German army could arrive to recapture them. (One man, John Peck, is said to have been recaptured and escaped four times.) With the help of Italian alpine guides, Lionel Jones set off to cross the Alps from Italy into Switzerland, climbing over glacier country east of the Matterhorn. His guides knew the area well, they had not only been illicit traders on this route for generations but were actually following the age-old smuggling route through the mountain passes. It is an indication of the strength and stamina of the flower-gardener that he climbed these mountains that men to this day try their mettle on.

When they neared the Swiss border, the guides whispered and Lionel looked up above him on the mountain and saw two grey-clad soldiers, rifles at the ready. Germans! He knew by the uniform. He spun around but his guides were gone, disappeared down into the Italian mountains they'd been bred in. Lionel tried to hide but the stunted growth at that height would not shelter him. He began to run, but one of the soldiers called on him to stop. He heard a snap, the click of a rifle bolt, then for one moment the fleeing man heard what he thought must be wishful thinking. 'You are all right. Safe.' He hesi-tated. 'You've crossed the border, we've been watching you climb all morning.' They were the grey-uniformed Swiss border guards. He was in luck. Many hundreds of men had been turned back when attempting to cross the border into Switzerland. The guards had orders to shoot if necessary.

Once in the country, Jones was able to live in Switzerland under the protection of an Emergency Certificate (No. 661) issued by the British Consulate General, Zurich, on 20 November 1943. He would no longer be known as an escaped POW but as an évade (as in evading an enemy). The Swiss immediately had his status referred to International Red Cross and he began to receive the standard food parcels. His Emergency Certificate stated that he was a British subject by birth 'having been born at Tunstall Potteries [now Nunawading] Australia. This certificate is valid for residence in Switzerland. The validity of this certificate expires two years from this date and must be surrendered to the Immigration Officer at the place of arrival.'

Lionel's notebook of flowers is redolent of turned earth, the scent of the blossom of broad beans and new roses, baby birds falling out of their nests, bees drunk with nectar and the rhythm of the seasons. He wrote of times and depth of planting, how to mix the necessary soils, the rate per rod of fertilising each species of plant and the growing seasons. He remarks on the different needs of soil and plants in the mountains of Switzerland to those in sunny, yet well-watered Melbourne. He is amused at having to 'prick out' blackberries in a market garden instead of 'digging them out as pests back home'. He purchased a camera and took many snapshots including the particular type of lettuce frame used in Switzerland, and of the high bedding of spring bulbs.

'Found first postage stamp with flower design!' For a while he is working some miles from any Australians. He becomes very lonely. 'No one to talk to.' He asks to be sent back to Dägerstein, his first stopping place in Switzerland. 'Talked and walked with Shonta.' Like all soldiers he needed his mate. He worked in a restaurant at Wil and at a nursery planting trees, and carted hay on farms.

He had come from a very ordered life, a quiet, respectable family. His father had taken over the running of the flower farm when two sons of the family had been killed in World War I. The family had helped pioneer the country; his grandfather was a wheelwright whose wagons were known in the district up until this second world war. These settled memories helped him in this new unsettled gypsy life wherein men knew frustration, boredom, discomforts, anxieties and moments of awful fear along with occasional pleasures.

The great thing was to fill in time. 'When there is nothing to do I wash my socks and take one sock to the clothes line, then the other.' But gardens are never far from his mind. 'There is always compost to be got for potting.'

The flower man, who had lost some of his best friends in Tobruk, made friends easily, and with them he worked at the restaurant Ochsen Metzgerei, at Wil. There is a photo of many of the Australian évades outside this establishment and yes, there are girls well in evidence and yes, Lionel had a friend, Antoinette. A snapshot of her on skis shows her to be pretty, and relaxed, skiing at Gilbach with Lionel. He also spent much time with Christian Hari, the brother of Mata Hari, the most talked-about female spy of all time. Christian was as intelligent and kind as was Lionel and they spent nights in discussion. He was also a close friend of Emil Guttinger of Wil and his wife Martz. Emil was a craftsman jeweller and made a gift in the form of a beautifully wrought silver brooch for Lionel to take home to Australia when the war should end. Again, these friends and Lionel talked late into the night. When Emil died in August 1944, Lionel and his friend Shonta sent flowers and a card to Martz and she replied with a card of deep affection and memories of the good hours they had spent together.

In one way all men's experience was the same – The Bag. Yet all were different. Bert Lockie and his companions had been captured and taken to Italy where they worked on a farm. He tells of some recaptured Australian prisoners. 'They were lucky in one thing, the camp kitchen was run by the 2/15th Battalion assisted by our transport drivers. They made sure special meals were cooked for the recaptured escapees and delivered by a man so popular even the Italians liked him. This fellow had a terrible singing voice but always sang when the guards were escorting him to the cooler with the meals for the escapees. Such a voice made the guards laugh and Butch sang on – his words in English, telling all the latest war and camp news to ease the isolation of the prisoners.'

A news bulletin was 'issued' with war news from a variety of sources (one source being bribery), and each night out of hearing of the Italians this was read in each hut to the men. Later, when they were sent to Camp 106 at Pronzana in the north, the men worked on farms and the farmers would daily relate the BBC news to them.

Bert Lockie's farmer-employer 'spoke Oxford English' and would talk for hours with Corporal Fraser, the camp leader, who was a farmer in civilian life. Listening to the BBC news bulletins was a punishable offence, but the owner of Casa Foglietta ignored that and relayed the news to Corporal Fraser.

'So we always had an idea of what was happening outside.' It was here, in Camp 106 on 8 September 1943, while they were playing cricket in the long twilight, that they heard the guards quarters erupt in cheering, along with the civilians of the area: Mussolini had been deposed and the Allies had landed in Sicily. Once the prisoners got over their jubilation, they remarked that the Allied forces were 650 miles away to the south, the border of Switzerland 100 miles away – and Germans holding the key passes over the Swiss Alps. Some men grouped together to try to get across the Alps, others to head south before the Germans could recapture them.

Bert Lockie, along with his friends Jack Fullarton, 2/23rd Battalion, and Fred Vardy, 2/28th, were joined by Matt Knight from the 2/24th Battalion and headed south. Matt left the party to join the Italian Partisan movement and later was to figure prominently in the fighting against German troops. The other three met with happy, friendly farmers who fed and housed them in return for their help with the grape harvest.

'Two snow-white oxen hauled the wooden cartload of grapes to the farmer's home and we three, stripped to shorts, stamped the grapes, and juice flowed, and the grapes sank lower until only the skin was left.

'The stamping was hard on the legs at first but we got used to it.' The good food and physical work strengthened them and after three weeks they left, 'while we were fit and healthy', hoping to meet up with the Allies. They climbed mountains, trudged for days through snow, slipped on ice – by which stage Fred Vardy had only one boot, one shoe, both in a sorry state, almost falling off his feet. Italians guided them up hills, rowed them across rivers, gave them food and bed in their poor farm houses; a 'rich' woman, who assisted POWs as a sort of one-woman endeavour, cared for them in her home for three days; boy shepherds of 13 and 14 up in the higher mountains were delighted to have company. 'Sometimes they went without a meal so we could eat.'

As the trio came nearer to Rome and closer settlement, farmers would take them in at night, giving them a meal and allowing them to sleep on hay in the barn, but asking them to leave before daylight as Germans were installed in most villages. Soon they began seeing and nervously avoiding them; at one time they dived for the undergrowth as a German artillery unit went by. 'One went by me so close I could have grabbed his boot.'

'We were told that some POWs including two Australians were living in a cave in the mountains. We were taken to them and stayed for some days. Italians brought food regularly to these men. This was courageous in the extreme as the Germans had burnt houses and taken families away when found to be sheltering escaped POWs.' It was here that the men realised how weak they had become in the hard, constantly moving life they led. 'Two peasant women we met on a mountain path indicated to us to give them a lift on to their heads with bundles of wood they had gathered, but we could not lift them. The women were disgusted, helped one another to load and off they went.

'Villagers were providing money and food for quite a number of POWs here as well as those in the cave. Couriers brought food to farmers who were hiding men, and gave warning of any German movements in the area.' Again they headed south, towards Cassino. 'All roads were thick with German vehicles so we must move on mountain tracks. Italians were worried now when we approached, and although friendly were obviously apprehensive and very frightened.

'One day in the hills we met a well-dressed Italian who said to meet him in three days time when he would "return from the Vatican!" We were wary of betrayal, but met him at the arranged spot, a barn. We then learnt that he was a courier for the Irish priest in the Vatican, Monsignor Hugh O'Flaherty, who had organised an underground to help escaping POWs, Jews and others, right under the German noses. They did a marvellous job for POWs, and the priest was a brave, wonderful man; we hoped he survived to prosper after the war ended.

'And then, panic: the Germans had raided and burnt down a house and taken the family away. Italian fascists had betrayed them. At that time we were sleeping a few hundred yards away in a stable.

'We decided to keep moving on. Overhead, wave upon wave of Allied bombers were now constantly passing on their way north to bomb Turin, Milan and the Rumanian oil wells. We heard of the landing at Anzio, in February 1944, but we were cut off from them by the German army. Italians in the Sora Valley told us we were not welcome, they were angry and frightened. This was the first time this attitude had been displayed to us and we hurriedly back-tracked in case they betrayed us.'

And so the nerve-clutching odyssey continued, with them crossing the railway, highway and river by dark of night. 'We met two old-timers who told us to go to a cave where an American parachutist had been dropped in the wooded hills nearby. It seemed that this American and his assistant were looking for escaping POWs and were distributing clothes, food and boots. How we three needed them! We took a calculated risk, and it paid off. We stayed overnight in the cave and ate well. Two English POWs arrived the following day, their sergeant had been back and forth three times through the lines near Cassino and had mapped a route for escaping POWs.' Afraid of a German trap, the small party set off in a different direction, but intending to eventually attempt to cross the Allied lines at the point given by the American sergeant.

There was no shortage of surprises for them for now they were joined by two escaping Gurkha soldiers, dressed as Italian farmers. The American had told them that once they got near to Allied lines, an Allied patrol passed a certain spot once an hour during the night, retiring at dawn. They were determined to make a bid to end their long journey but, stumbling on to a camp of Germans, they were split up, Bert, one Gurkha and Fred remaining together. An Italian fleeing from the approaching enemy with his few possessions in a mule cart told them the town they were heading towards was being evacuated. 'Prima linea', the man called as he continued his flight. They were in the front line. 'Buona fortuna!' They would need luck.

They cut up their remaining blanket and wrapped the pieces around their feet to maintain complete silence – and as they did so two Germans with mules passed by. 'In the ghostly light of a late-rising moon, we could see the bombed out monastery of Monte Cassino.' They were on course. Now down into the wadi of a dry river and then a deep ravine, a straight drop of 50 feet. The American had told them that here he had tied a parachute cord on to a rocky outcrop to enable a fugitive to lower himself and here it was, as was another cord, securely anchored to the next cliff edge. Down they went, then down the ravine. It was now two hours to dawn so they must hasten if they were to contact the Allied patrol. A German work party was laying land mines so the three men lay low, then crept along out of the gorge, Bert leading. Fred, partially deaf since the bombardment at Tobruk, could not hear so well so must watch for hand signals. 'Nerves by now were pretty tight.'

At daylight they moved off. 'This was our final fling for

freedom.' They waded along the river, 'flitting from boulder to boulder', until they came to signals and communication wires. 'We didn't know if they were theirs or ours!' They waded forward for four hours and in the half light saw the welcome sight of the familiar British battle helmet. It was on the driver of a jeep creeping over the bridge. 'With one accord the three of us bounded out of the river and jumped on the back of the trailer.

'The sudden appearance of three half-drowned hoboes on the back of his vehicle was a severe shock to the driver, there was a look of alarm and fear on his face. When Fred crawled over to tell him who we were, the driver made "gutteral sounds" and Fred turned to me and said, "We're in the bag again, this fellow's a German!" We crossed the bridge and two fellows came out of foxholes beside the road, indicating with machine guns for us to put up our hands.' The impasse continued until Bert slowly withdrew his paybook from his pocket and proffered it to the nearest gun holder, who suddenly, excitedly, in broken English said, 'Me Tobruk!' It was a Polish Military Police traffic point. Their journey was over. The Poles had fought beside the Australians in Tobruk.

As if on order, the Gurkha divested himself of his old peasant's clothes and, 'Lo and behold!' he was fully dressed underneath as a Gurkha soldier.

'Where do you want to go?' they were asked. 'The further back the better', they answered.

Jack Fullarton and the second Gurkha also reached Allied lines. After war's end, Monsignor Hugh O'Flaherty was honoured by many nations, including Australia, for his fine work for POWs.

The White Ensign

They that go down to the sea in ships, that do business in great waters;
These see the works of the Lord, and his wonders in the deep.

Psalm 107.23–4

'I NAME THIS VESSEL *Perth* and may God bless all who sail in her. A safe voyage and the best of luck.' With these words the young, elegant Princess Marina, Duchess of Kent, christened HMAS *Perth*, 10 July 1939.

The young sailors – or the older officers for that matter – never thought that war was only weeks away and that they would not see Australia again for almost a year. The ship set off for what was to have been her triumphal home-coming. At her first port, New York, she celebrated a special Australia Day on 11 August at the World's Fair; the officers and men of HMAS *Perth* were paraded in a special ceremony and a motor-cycle police escort with sirens blaring escorted the buses taking the men to and from the fair. Film stars including 'Tarzan' (Johnny Weissmuller) were at the reception along with the Australian Arctic explorer Sir Hubert Wilkins, and the famous Esther Williams Aquacade was performed. Hospitality was superb, clubs opened for the men and tickets to the theatres were free. It was more exciting than any young sailor could have imagined.

The next port was Kingston in the West Indies, but the fun of this port had not begun before hands were mustered on deck to be told, 'We have just received a signal from Admiralty which reads, "Total. Germany Total". We are now at war with Germany. Three cheers for His Majesty the King!'

Convoy duty and the surveillance of German ships in neutral ports followed before they were sent to Libya, Colombo, Aden, Tobruk, Alexandria and east of Crete, travelling 10,515 nautical miles in twenty-nine days at sea over a period of thirty-four days. Then to Malta, where on 16 January 1941 HMAS *Perth* was strained by a near-miss off the starboard quarter, and HMS *Essex* lying astern was hit and set on fire. *Illustrious* was damaged and later a bomb lifted the deck of *Perth* almost 4 feet and she 'jumped' sideways. After repair from the Malta bombing *Perth* was in the Dodecanese Islands, Derna, Alexandria, the Aegean Sea and Greece, often under fire. She carried 658 fighting men (almost as many as the ship's entire complement) to Piraeus, port of Athens, on 7 March and 466 a week later. She then sailed into the Battle of Matapan, a fleet action with the Italian navy, the bombardment of Tripoli and constant patrolling around the Mediterranean.

On 6 April the ship was in Piraeus when Germany invaded Greece and the port was attacked from the air. A ship berthed near *Perth* was hit and sunk in seven minutes and after helping to rescue survivors *Perth* shifted anchorage, leaving 200 of her men stranded ashore.

Some were bedded down in HMS *Calcutta* and this ship was bombed at 3.30 a.m. shortly after the *Clan Fraser*, which was loaded with ammunition, blew up. The *Perth* men spent the rest of the night 'on the footpath' and were picked up next morning.

From that date the ships were constantly bombed. If it was not Malta it was Suda Bay, Crete, Alexandria or Greece. Then, as spring moved in to summer there was yet another of the disasters that had befallen the British in this war: first Greece and then Crete were evacuated. Twenty-three ships were sunk in Greek waters in twenty-four hours as a flotilla attempted to rescue the troops who had retreated down to various beaches. *Perth* was sent to Porto Rafti, east of Athens. Because the Luftwaffe had command of the skies, evacuation could only take place round the midnight hours thus giving the ships time to get in and out within the hours of darkness in the hopes of getting far enough away before daylight to escape the vigilant bombers. The Australian destroyer *Stuart* along with *Perth* took 1620 troops off on the 27th and were about to sail when told of another 600 Australians ashore. A message was sent to these men to move down the coast where they would be picked up at daybreak the following morning. These rescues were difficult, with unreliable charts, on unknown coasts, with no navigation lights ashore or on ship, and in darkness and in the presence of enemy mines.

Perth's aircraft, the Walrus, was shot down on 28 April but the crew was rescued. This night of 28–29 April was to be the last attempt to evacuate the troops from Greece. With other ships, *Perth* was to go after darkness fell to Kalamata where 7000 servicemen as well as hundreds of Yugoslav fighters and refugees were said to be waiting. This exercise developed into a tragic foul-up.

Force B, of which *Perth* was a part, comprised two cruisers and nine destroyers. At dusk they formed up and made their run up the coast. A scout from HMS *Hero* was sent to contact the troops: he reported that the harbour was already occupied by the Germans. The rescuing fleet were immediately ordered to retire seaward at full speed. Tragically, the wireless on board *Hero* was defective. The scout's message was not complete. It had told that the troops were to the south-east of the town and that evacuation was considered possible from the beach. This message was not received until forty minutes after the rescuing fleet had scattered and was 20 miles away from Kalamata. It was a disaster for the party on the beach who were taken into captivity for four years. Although some other ships picked up a few hundred men over the next two nights *Perth* was not available, having been sent on orders to North African waters.

Crete was a repetition of Greece. Here *Perth* survived eight attacks in one day. HMS *Juno*, sailing with her, 'was sent to her grave', as Alan Watson, Australian Provost Corps, says. HMS *Carlisle* was hit but *Perth* was 'flung all over the place by our captain and we survived', say that crew. She set off after German troop carriers bringing their army in to invade

Crete and sunk a caique carrying troops before dodging from 'a near miss' after an attack that lasted three hours. The *Perth*'s war diary for these days is peppered with names of vessels sinking beneath the waves around her. Admiral Cunningham sent a signal to the ships: 'Stick it out. The navy must not let the army down.'

Perth took on two landing craft and set sail for Sphakia Bay and rescued 1188 troops including twenty stretcher cases and over a hundred walking wounded.

Captain R.P. Longstaff, DSC, of the *City of London*, a merchant ship, described his arrival in Kalamata Bay at 10.25 p.m. to assist in the evacuation. The night was black; neither he nor two accompanying ships had the necessary charts, but they anchored close to land. 'Half an hour after midnight a destroyer came alongside packed with troops who got aboard us by gangplanks, boatside ladders and so forth. This was done in complete darkness and almost dead silence. It was difficult to keep the troops moving, for they had had a hard time and many collapsed in sleep on the deck; by 4 a.m., 3000 to 4000 troops were aboard, mainly Australians.'

Petty Officer Vic Duncan, RAN, was on the *Perth* when she eased in to shallow water to rescue men abandoned on Crete. 'You could never describe the feeling between army and navy after Greece and Crete. "How are you Jack!" the diggers call to us. "Have a drink?" The soldiers knew nothing about the navy and what it did until a hand reached down and helped haul them up the landing nets we'd put over the side of HMAS *Perth* to rescue them. Bombs dropping, terrifying, but the crew didn't turn a hair.' Petty Officer Duncan was keeping the deck clear, calling to the exhausted soldiers, 'Get below and have a mug of cocoa sport.' The hours he'd spent up on that deck with the bullets flying and German planes overhead making his ship constantly zig-zag seemed not to affect him. 'Mountbatten's ship HMS *Kelly* went down, many others with it. We were out of ammo but our captain ordered, '"Take aim! Fire!" and we let fly with tracer bullets fired from .303 rifles.'

Many men were left behind on the beaches as *Perth* sailed

out into the aerial attacks that followed her to sea. One of the five long attacks scored a hit and thirteen crew were killed, several near-misses 'shook' the ship severely. Men in the boiler room tried to rescue a trapped stoker but he was badly scalded and was dead when they reached him.

It is said that the naval casualties of over 2000 at this period for the first time in history exceeded those of the army they accompanied. But the number of prisoners eventually taken on both Crete and Greece filled many a column of the casualty lists in newspapers back home.

Behind the cold, formal release of names, loved ones down south in Australia could sense the tragic and huge disasters that had swept over their sons. Some names were singled out for attention. On the day that Mrs D. Elder of Balwyn was advised that her husband 'WO David Elder, previously reported missing, is now a prisoner of war', Mrs H. Treloar of Surrey Hills read in the *Argus* that her younger son 'Lieutenant Rupert Treloar, aged 21, has been reported missing, believed drowned'. In a boxed-in area we learn that 'an elder brother, Lieutenant Ian Treloar is missing with HMAS *Sydney*'.

Many a minnow, undetected because of its size, darted with immense daring through the waters where the big ships sailed with majesty and with the adulation of the newspapers and radio. Australia's 'Scrap Iron Flotilla', as Lord Haw-Haw dubbed the five naval ships *Vendetta*, *Waterhen*, *Stuart*, *Vampire* and *Voyager*, were known for many actions, and because of their supply runs by moonless nights to Tobruk. *Waterhen* was sunk in Tobruk Harbour. Her crew swear 'she went down more like a water-logged duck than a hen. Squatted there with her head above water as though she was nesting.' The Royal Navy called the run to Tobruk 'Dangerous Corner'; the defenders called the harbour 'the forest', referring to the masts and upper structures of sunken ships sticking up out of the water. Australian ships made 139 runs to Tobruk during the siege. But the little corvettes (officially known as minesweepers because of their size) received less acclaim, even though they saved many men from drowning or becoming prisoners of war. But they were awarded a fine laurel by the author–war-correspondent, George Johnston.

'Somewhere at sea: These little ships built in Australian seaports of Australian materials by Australian men have steamed in the aggregate hundreds of thousands of miles. When the war came to Singapore they survived up to eleven air raids a day. They were the last Australian ships out of Singapore, and later from Java, they fought their way through the Japanese naval blockade of Sunda Strait.

'One had rescued seventy-eight men and seventeen officers from the sunken British ships *Repulse, Prince of Wales* and *Jupiter*. Later, when one large convoy was caught by Japanese planes and the big liner *Empress of Asia* was destroyed, listing over, in flames from stem to stern, the Australian sloop HMAS *Yarra* (later to be destroyed off Java), brought off almost 900 survivors whilst two corvettes raced out at full speed to rescue 200 men from the gutted liner, most of them burnt, wounded or injured.

'When the Japanese invasion of Sumatra began they left only one jump ahead of the swiftly advancing enemy. One corvette picked up survivors from a sunken ship and found more than 200 in the water, most of them floating on makeshift rafts. Then, with three tankers and fourteen other merchantmen, it fled down the Sunda Strait to escape the Japanese warships and bombers. Two ships following were trapped by the enemy and sunk.

'There were ticklish days and nights for the corvette flotilla immediately afterwards, when they were detailed for "anti-infiltration patrol" off Tanjong Priok, and in Sunda Strait, which by this time had earned its name of "Suicide Lane". "We hid in troughs and dodged behind wave crests," the men said. Most of the time they patrolled by night and sheltered off shore "disguised as coconut palms" in daylight hours. They had orders to tackle any ship attempting infiltration, no matter what its size.

'The waters of Java, lacking in air support, had already

become too hot for Allied shipping. These ships had been the saviour of many Australian men who, but for them, would have become prisoners of war, but it was time to get out. A strange motley collection steamed southward – tankers, liners, tugs, tramps, minesweepers, warships. But the Japanese fleet had also come round to the south coast of Java, smashing every Allied ship encountered. And the corvettes were still to northward of the enemy fleet. They were given only one chance in ten of breaking through the blockage. They accepted that chance with a fatalistic cheerfulness, they were eager to take the chance simply because the course would be southward – in the line of the Japanese fleet, but towards Australia.'

The Road to Suda Bay

Then we heard the wireless news when portly Winston gave his views,
The RAF are now in Greece, fighting hard to give us peace.
Then we scratched our heads and thought: This thing smells just like a
   rort!
For if in Greece the air force be, Then where the bloomin' hell are we?

Private Laurie Ryan, 'The Poet', 2/6th Battalion

SOMETIMES IN WAR THERE is absurdly exaggerated secrecy on matters of little value to the enemy, and sometimes matters that should be treated with extreme delicacy are broadcast for all to hear. On 8 March 1941 Private Howard Vinning, Australian Army Service Corps, was on leave in Alexandria, a city of many races and political loyalties, and while having a meal the restaurant he was in was disturbed by military police. 'They came in, shouted for all to hear, "All troops back to camp! Orders are we're moving out tomorrow morning!"'

'You'd never believe it could happen. And to make sure everyone knew, they stuck posters up on street walls, "All troops back to camp!" You should have seen the cavalcade, old-fashioned horse carriages, every taxi in town and some blokes heading off on shanks' pony. When the 2/2nd Battalion got on the boat they were only two men short. We'd raced back so quickly you'd think we were going on a holiday.' They were off to Greece.

It was the first time Australians were to experience large-scale mountain warfare; they were spread inland with little air support (they believe they had none, hence the lines of doggerel, 'For if in Greece the air force be, Then where the bloomin' hell are we?').

I'm tired of living in Greece Sir!
Snooping around in the hills;

Sleeping on rocks in the open
It sorter gets under your gills.
Each day seems like a month Sir!
And blanketless nights give one chills;
I want to get back to the Mob Sir!
Among the slit trenches and pills. [Concrete pill-boxes]

I'm tired of living in Greece Sir!
Where there's not a square foot without rocks;
My boots have worn down to a frazzle
And it's weeks since I've worn any socks.
This war will have to end soon Sir!
Or I'll peter right out at the hocks.
I want to get back to the Mob Sir!
I don't want to live like a fox.

I'm tired of living in Greece Sir!
And slowly I'm fading away;
I'm no use to myself or my country
Growing older with each donkey's neigh.

                                        Anon.

Their only joy was that the Australians immediately struck
a great and lasting rapport with the people of Greece who
prized their independence and were brave fighters, courageous,
skilled, resourceful. But they stood little chance against the
German army and air force and they died on the narrow
passes, high mountains and rocky cliffs. Greek troops hauled
mountain guns up precipices only to have bombs rain down
on them from the air.

On 19 March Australians began to come ashore at Piraeus.
One month later, 20 April, Greek resistance had ceased and
the Australian retreat and evacuation began. It had all been in
vain. Another bungle by the 'Big Wigs', as the men called the
top brass – when they were being polite, that is. But this bungle
was followed by, or rather flowed on to, a bigger bungle. On
Anzac Day the first of the Australian troops came ashore on

Crete, tired, bewildered and disillusioned by the Greece experience. They received no joy in Crete where upwards of 25,000
men (including almost 9000 Australians) were bundled off
ships in the next four days, regardless of what battalion or
company they belonged to and some with no officer known to
them to care for them or advise.

Greece and Crete represented all that was bad in warfare:
without control of the Mediterranean it was too great a distance from North African bases for shipping, and for air
support. It was not possible to bring up reinforcements, petrol,
equipment and supplies and there were no workshops, repair
facilities or depots. The troops were thoroughly 'browned-off',
a saying they had picked up in Egypt (and later brought back
to Australia).

Australian nurses at the 2/5th Australian General Hospital
in Athens saw the first AIF patients arrive, haggard and worn
out. They had been fighting in the snow and the Germans had
seemed to come in never-ending droves. Athens was being
bombed heavily and the nursing staff were wearing their steel
helmets night and day. Much of the equipment for their hospital was at the bottom of the harbour where many ships had
already been sunk. When the nurses were evacuated their
Commanding Officer, Colonel Kay, began walking wounded
out through the sea water to a ship but planes flew low and
he was killed. Most of the other men from this hospital were
taken prisoner.

The confusion from the top brass to the youngest private
during the short, frantic period the British services fought in
Greece is well summed up by 'Blue' Butterworth. Private
Milton 'Blue' Butterworth came to Australia from England 'for
adventure' in 1938, aged 18 years. The following year, on 20
October 1939, he enlisted from Sydney in the 2/1st Battalion.
Blue 'went touristing' – Egypt, Palestine, the Western Desert,
Tobruk, Greece, Crete, Java, 'the whole bloody itinerary'. As
well as being a 'Desert Rat', he is one of the 'Java Rabble'.

The 2/1st Battalion sailed on the first convoy to leave
Australia on 10 January 1940. 'We disembarked in Egypt,

went up to Palestine and down to Egypt again and then to the Western Desert. I was in the first push up the desert and then I was back as a Rat of Tobruk and believe you me there aren't too many of us around. Then we were shipped over to Greece, and the Germans overran us. I didn't have my boots or socks off my feet for seventy-two hours and they were saturated. A Greek soldier riding by on his donkey took pity on me and gave me a dry pair of socks made of unscoured goatswool, harsh as steel wool. Soon my feet were wet through as we were on a 17 kilometres forced march over Mount Olympus and down to the river; we spelled and had a cup of tea produced by the engineers before anyone could cross on a punt, and then they said, "Right! On your feet!" and when we went to get on the punt I just fell over because my feet refused to carry me any more and they had gone cold, no circulation; so I was carried across and put into a makeshift ambulance and taken into an underground station and a doctor had to chop the boots off my feet and the socks were impregnated with blood. Both feet were a dreadful mess – it was like trench foot.

'All forward troop movement had been cancelled because the Germans were ploughing down through everything. So the next thing I'm on is a makeshift hospital train, shipped down to Athens into a British hospital. The wounded then started to come into this hospital and as I wasn't really wounded I asked the English doctor to let me out. They had posted on my bed, "Unfit as further infantry", so when I came out I was supposed to report to ex-personnel at Daphni, just out of Athens.'

On arrival Blue was 'tossed' a bunch of keys. 'A fellow said, "How is the car, alright? Petrol, oil and water?" And I said, "As far as I know". I knew bugger all about cars. I'd never driven a car in my life – I had no licence. This bloke said, "Right! Stay by your vehicle and we will let you know when we need you". It was about one o'clock in the morning so I settled down on the ground sheet and out came the bed roll. At two o'clock in the morning, Peewee, a 2/1st man, called, "Hey, Blue! Blue! Come on mate!" He said, "Every bugger's pissed off, they have just walked out and left everything". I said, "You're joking". He said, "Come and have a look for yourself". And sure enough there's all the tents, the gear, everything, they had just got out of their bunks and stretchers and pissed off. At first light we saw them all coming back, sheepish. They had done a false evacuation alarm. Of course there was a lot of those sorts of things going on. Later I thought, Well! those buggers! I was being put there to drive for those lousy buggers. You'd have thought before they pissed off they would have had the common decency to come out and tell me to go back to where I came from.

'Then I was told that I had to pick up rations and report to a Major Dunlop at the Acropolis Hotel which was Force headquarters in Athens. So I'm there, waiting, getting a little bit nervy about actually having to drive and be responsible for some poor bugger. Eventually I saw him. I thought, "Shit! He'll never get in this car". It was a small Chev. He was 6 feet 4.

'Major Dunlop wanted to go to the King George Hotel. Well, you can imagine the schmozzle. By this time it's quarter to five and people are coming down the street, out the tube and pouring everywhere and there's tooting, and a Greek Air Force Attache car stopped and I threw the wheel and my front bumper clashed with his back one, just went cling-cling and we were interlocked and the Major – who I learned was called Weary – said, "Shit!" and "Christ!" and I said, "It's no problem". I got out and everybody else too and we all walked around. No problem. They had to push my car that way and I had the others down on the other side and they had to push this way and in two seconds we were freed.

'It's getting dark and I'm starting to get panicky and I am tired because I'd had a bugger of a night previously. As we're going north the cunning buggers were all coming back south, with all the big heavy stuff: it was the convoys retreating. It's dark and you can't put your lights on in a blackout area, so Major Dunlop said, "I'll relieve you, I'll give you a spell". So he took over. Away we go and these big trucks are hogging most of the road and we're going up in the mountain area and everyone else is coming down. "Get down you so and so's", yell some of the Poms, with choice Pom lingo added.'

In the dark they ran off the narrow unsealed road and had to wait until morning light to recover the vehicle. Doctor Dunlop's duty was to try and keep the wounded moving. 'We picked up two Kiwis, one a captain and one a private, both wounded, so we've got to bring them back.

'Things were happening and I was starting to get the old proverbial shits. Weary said, "Right, back we go". Away we go, drop the two Kiwis at the hospital then did another trip and the next thing they bombed Piraeus, the port of Athens, and we're headed there.

'We stayed overnight. Weary went down on the ships helping people who had lost everything; he'd gone back to Force headquarters and what he saw surprised him: some of those officers, the top brass, used to have bloody travelling trunks, the big ones. Oh, Jesus yes, thought they were on holiday, going over to the south of France or to the Riviera. They had more bloody gear than King Farouk took up the Nile and someone went and busted all their cases. That night there were privates going around with brigadiers' clothes on.

'And that was that. The next thing he said, "Right! I want you to take me to the 2/5th AGH". Off we went and the writing was on the wall, and all hospital personnel there knew it. A Scots bloke came out and said, "Are you staying or are you leaving?" That's how things were, as bad as they could be, but at this stage I'm leaving, because I wasn't attached to Weary or anything, I was sort of on loan. Weary said, "Well, it looks like you'll have to return again to where you came from". I felt a bit upset about that you know, I said, "Oh well, it's been nice knowing you". But a British brigadier passing by said, "Dunlop old boy, you know you're entitled to a batman if you haven't got one", and Weary said, "Would you like to do this, Butterworth?" I said, "I don't mind". He said, "Right". I've got a new job. I thought, ah, beaut.

'The Germans were in Athens now. We shot back to Force headquarters, straight across the lawns like you'd see in some comedy movie. He said, "Right, wait here". He was straight back out. "The stupid bastards, they've burnt everything". They'd burnt gear that he really wanted. He said, "Right, let's get to Daphni and see if we can catch up". We took off, going along once again flat out and a bloke came out of an alley and began to cross the road with a cart full of boxes. They just went arse over turkey. I'm going to hit the brakes and Weary swung around and he said, "He's alright, keep going". There was no damage to the bloke himself. We got to Daphni and we saw the nine million drachmas of the Australian Corp payroll being burnt, all the villagers crying, "Why? Why they burn? Why not make rich Daphni?" Of course it was to prevent the Jerries getting their hands on the money.

'We caught up with the convoy and came to a dead stop. On each side of the road was Greek cavalry horses, dead; when they capitulated the Greeks had been ordered to shoot them and leave them there. In the dark the trucks were belting into them. This Colonel calls, "That you Dunlop? The brigadier wants to see you." So right round the convoy we went, and the next thing, down we go, I'd run into the crater, and we're on a forty-five degree angle this time: a bomb had been dropped and half the road had gone in the crater. I'm holding on to the wheel, and saying, "You right Sir?" "Yes, are you alright?" I said yes, he said, "Right, let's get out of this thing". Gingerly I started the motor up again and he gingerly got out of the car and stood in the crater and he's holding the car, "Give it another go". He's holding it up. Oh, you could smell the burning tyres and what have you, and I said, "Look Sir, I'm sorry, I'm not going to do it", because if the car had slipped it would roll straight on him; and we could see two army trucks down in there already. So he came around and he's on the back of the car. Just then a nice little English voice came along and said, "You'll have to abandon your vehicle and get in the truck, join the convoy". Weary very nicely said, "I don't know who you are or what you are but will you please fuck off". "No", I thought, "there'll be no doubt about this bloke: he's tops".

'So away the convoy went and I thought, shit, we might have

done the wrong thing because as the trucks disappeared all became silent. But the next thing we heard was singing. In Greek. The Greek leaders had capitulated a week prior and they'd told their soldiers to get back to their homes spread all over Greece. These strong, courageous Greeks looked at our vehicle and in two minutes flat we were back on the road. I had the glove box full of cigarettes, Woodbines and Players, so I just threw them to the boys and away we went to catch up with the rest of the convoy.

'The big thing was, all the trucks had to be got together and the evacuation worked out. We were to get off Greece. Piraeus was bombed, the troop ship *Stirling Castle*, which was coming in to take troops off, ran aground and five minutes later wave after wave of German planes came in dive-bombing.

'We were abandoning the car and I said to Weary, "What say I pour petrol over the engine?" "No", he said, "leave the car there", and he also left a map just in case anything went wrong and we had to come back this way. And I'm always upset about the fact I left two bottles of beer in that old jalopy.

'It was getting dark and the men were all queuing up waiting to come off; we came off first on a wooden boat, it was dangerously loaded, there's blokes all over the rigging hanging on to it. You were just standing up like sardines and everyone was told to abandon their gear, all bar their rifle if you were a combatant, and as I was still combatant, I still had my rifle and full pack. I also was carrying Weary's valise. "You can't take that bloody thing", some voice said but I still held on to it. The voice grabbed it and tossed the valise away; there's the red glow of the *Stirling Castle* going up, it looked like the Inferno, and you knew how hot the plates were, you could feel the heat of it. She's afire. We veered off and into the darkness and the next thing we're up alongside of this anti-aircraft cruiser, scrambled up the side and just fell in, some had to jump, some blokes slipped down between the ship and our wooden boat. I realised I wouldn't have got the valise up on board anyway. Everyone is pulling everyone up, officers and NCOs to the right, other ranks to the left and you went

through the blackout curtains down below. When daylight
came many were still asleep on their backs when Woof! Woof!
Woof! the Germans were bombing the convoy. We are all
below deck, right next door to the magazine.

'So there we are, whipping up the shells, three point nines
coming up from the magazine. When it's all over and the mist
has blown away, the poor old navy boys, dead-beat and sweating, came down smacking their ship on the side and they said,
"They'll never get this bloody tub, never will". (But she did
go. She went off Crete later.) Every kind of confusion was here.

'So I was coming off with Weary when a bloke covered in
red tape said, "He can't go with you!" Weary slipped me a
thousand drachma note – this is a big one and said, "If and
when we get back to the mainland I'll make contact". Away
he sailed and I was on shore for about another week or so. I
came off on a little merchant Greek, a 6000-ton boat, one of
Onassis' fleet, and arrived in Egypt, then back to Palestine. But
it took time to find Weary.' Dunlop was at the Casualty Clearing Station on the Tobruk waterfront when Blue Butterworth
arrived on one of the little vessels that ran the gauntlet in the
dark of night.

'When Weary sees me he says, "How the bloody hell did
you get here?" Of course, he had difficulties himself getting
there until he happened to meet the right bloke at the right
time – otherwise he might not have got to Tobruk. He had
wanted to get there so as to get off the administration work
and get on to the tools (surgical instruments) again.

'We used to take the casualties out and meet HMAS *Vendetta*, or the other little ships of the Scrap Iron Flotilla in the
harbour; we'd work all the night, taking the wounded out in
the lighter, board them up, crowd them in. They'd only be in
there a short time, but the ship had to clear before the moon
came up and be a certain distance out and down the coast for
safety from bombing and the rest of it.

'Anyway, I'd only been up there about a month when Weary
said, "Right! We're off!" We came out on the destroyer HMS
Hero. These ships had to go like stinking hell to escape being

bombed. Anyway, the next thing we know we were being sent back to Australia on the *Orcades*.

'We didn't get there. The ship was diverted to the Dutch-held islands that are now Indonesia, and after escaping all that crap in the desert and Greece, we were taken prisoners by the Japanese within a few days of landing.'

Staff Sergeant Bill Gamble was serving in the 2/5th Australian General Hospital on the outskirts of Athens when the Germans broke through the northern border.

'We knew we couldn't get away. The last hospital ship to go was bombed, and our Commanding Officer killed. We had a hospital full of patients. The staff not essential to the running of the hospital had been evacuated first. The nurses, specialist doctors and other sections of the hospital then went, and the third part were told they had to stay, and I was one of them. I was in charge of the male nursing staff, and also I knew how to do x-rays. The nurses went away on 26 April 1941 and we were caught on the 27th and taken over by an Austrian alpine regiment.

'Three weeks later we were all moved – patients, staff, the lot – just north of Piraeus. It was a big, brand new building – three and four-storey sections of concrete, and we had to establish the hospital there. We couldn't make out why, because by now we only had a small number of patients. We learnt the reason a week later when the Germans invaded Crete: they were bringing the British wounded back to us (they took their German wounded to their own hospitals in Athens). Gradually, as Crete fell, they evacuated all the wounded from that island.

'They were flying them over to us. Many of the wounded had been lying on the beaches for some days. Explosive bullets when they hit make a hell of a mess and it was summer and maggots were in these open wounds. They were bringing these men to our hospital and putting them on my x-ray table and the maggots were crawling off them. It turned out to be most effective as the maggots cleaned up the wounds and loss through gangrene or such was minimal, and we got those patients on their feet fairly quickly.'

Six months later, all but the blind, the amputees and those whose wounds hadn't healed properly were moved up to Salonika on a German hospital ship coming back with the German wounded from North Africa.

'We stayed in Salonika for three months until all that were left were on their feet and able to look after themselves. We now heard we were to be moved into Germany by a hospital train, so Staff Sergeant Ted Bryant of the 2/5th and I decided we would get out. There was no escape committee, we were too small a unit. I was the acting RSM and there were three doctors, so we got permission from them to attempt escape.

'We hid a few tins of food and things we'd need on our break in a coal cellar with windows level with the footpath, and waited for darkness. A guard was sent to search for us and we heard this German tramping down the stairs to the cellar. My friend got out the window and I was close behind him, I heard the door crash open and was expecting a bullet in the rear at any moment, but I got out clear.

'I got malaria pretty badly on the run so when we got to the village of Katerini we went up the hills to the shepherds looking after their sheep, hoping fresh, cold air would help with the malaria. It didn't, but the shepherds were able to supply us with food for two months. Then we met Lance-Corporal Sidney (Slim) Wrigley, also of the 2/5th AGH. The three of us decided to get guns and go down towards Bolas and steal a fishing boat. I had a small Luger with only one bullet in it so I left the Luger behind and decided we could get another later. My friend had a .45 with a holster belt so he hung on to it. Slim had gone to another village to get hold of a gun for himself and we had decided that the three of us would meet at one of the villages.

'As the two of us walked towards this rendezvous we passed a country policeman who had been friendly previously and he suggested we wait in a copse of trees while he went into the village to get food, but what he got was the Gestapo. After about a quarter of an hour, we suddenly heard cars pulling up around us and we peered through the trees and there they were, coming at us with automatic rifles.

'Knowing the result of being caught with civilian clothes and arms was death, I walked out towards them and put my hands up to give Ted time to undo the buckle of his belt, drop it, and put the revolver under the trees and join me, and they never bothered to search the place.

'They got us down to Katerini and bunged us into a civilian prison, and we were in this small, 9 by 9 feet cell with ten or eleven Greek prisoners who were in for murder, stealing, everything – they were a pretty rough old bunch. It was summer, scorching hot, and the toilet was a tin in the corner. I had the fever bad. On the third morning we were handcuffed together and put on a train under guard of half a dozen Greek police and taken up to Gestapo HQ in Salonika. They made blooming sure we couldn't get away. My mate had dysentery and when we got to Salonika he had to go to the lavatory which was in the centre of the square, opposite the railway. So they phoned up – and in a few minutes the square was surrounded by Greek police as we went into the toilet. Ted was sitting on the toilet and I was getting as far away as the handcuffs would allow me and a woman came in to sweep the toilet and she was looking at poor old Ted there and weeping, "What a pity, what a pity". The Gestapo at headquarters in Salonika were most unpleasant, but they could afford it: at that time the Germans were at Alamein and looked as though they were going straight on to Cairo, they were also at Stalingrad and it looked like that was over too.

'But they weren't as bad as they could have been. They bashed us around because they knew there were some partisan troops in the hills up above where we had been and they thought they had artillery and all sorts of things up there and that we had been with them. If we'd only known where the blooming people were we *would* have been with them.

'Slim had gone to the rendezvous the three of us had arranged and learnt what had happened. So he went down and dealt with the policeman, and after that met up with the partisans. Eventually Slim got pneumonia and these partisans organised to have him evacuated out by submarine to the Middle East.

'In the meantime, the Gestapo had questioned Ted and me for a couple of days and eventually believed that we didn't know where these partisans were. We went back into the prison camp that we'd escaped from, but now there were other people there that had been down at another hiding place where we'd stayed for a while over near Turkey. They'd been rounded up too. We met up with them and the ten of us were moved up to Austria to Stalag VIIIA, Wolfsberg. We eventually had an escape committee and they wanted maps, so somebody drew up a map and it was photographed and a negative taken. I had to print these escape maps and the escape committee was handing them out to any successful-looking escapee. Eventually the Germans found one of these maps and knew there was only one place where they could have been printed, so they removed my x-ray machine. I then had to organise the patients who needed x-rays and get them down to the civilian hospital in town.' There he became friendly with the radiologist, a young woman who lived in the Ruhr Valley. 'She was teaching German, I taught her English. We were getting along fine. We were never alone because the guard was right behind me and there was no fear of anything else because if you were caught getting too friendly with a German lady you were in a concentration camp very quickly. If she'd been caught I suppose she would probably have been sent somewhere unpleasant. But it didn't happen. One night her home was bombed and her whole family were wiped out, and from that moment on we just didn't talk, because she blamed me. I was the only person she could blame.

'I was there until September of 1943 when there was an exchange of prisoners and I, with my malaria and being medical staff, was put on an exchange list. My pal, Ted Bryant, was to be exchanged but he had hopped it, escaped before he heard the news. (Ted had lived near me and we were friends and worked together pre-war, and after the war we met up in

Ballarat – he'd got home before I had as it turned out. And Slim was home in Ballarat before either of us.)

'The exchange of prisoners was to be in Marseilles. We all assembled in Mulhouse, a little town in central Germany, then crossed to the north of Switzerland and down the Rhone Valley to Marseilles in a long train. We only needed one guard; there were no escapes because we knew we were going home. When we got to Marseilles, two hospital ships were tied up, one on each side of the wharf with the Germans on board one and us on the other. Every couple of hours one side got down on to the jetty and walked anti-clockwise around, and later the other ship's complement went for their exercise so that we didn't meet each other. We would have liked to wish the Germans good luck because they would have needed it.

'We sailed off to Alexandria and were put in a convalescent camp there, and looked after by a unit organised by the Australian army just for the purpose. Then we boarded the hospital ship *Wanganella* and sailed for home.'

Many of the men speak about the terrible waste of all their splendid training that they'd put so much enthusiasm and energy into. 'We'd put everything we had into training, we were going to show the world. It was all waste', Private Raphael Wirth, 2/1st Battalion says.

'I didn't go much on the desert in Libya, no man could like it; but then I wasn't ready for snow in Greece, up near the Yugoslav border, miles away from where everyone else was running back. I didn't go on that at all. Well, I hadn't seen desert or snow or the inside of a prison camp before and now I saw all three.'

Raphael had left home, aged 20, his father, of German descent, not wanting him to go, his mother crying and he saying he'd run away and change his name if they didn't 'sign the paper' for him. He fought up the line at Bardia in the desert, saw the huge columns of prisoners coming in. 'The Libyans with their long gowns flapping about them as they ran in all directions, like chooks in a hen house. And then these

unending columns, thousands upon thousands of Italians surrendering. A young man could have been forgiven if he had
believed it was all because of his superb training. Then we
found ourselves in Crete.

'On Crete when we saw the parachutists floating down it
was very surprising. We'd been bombed almost every morning
at the same time but there was something about this that gave
us a warning, immediately, that all the horrible things that had
happened to the campaign in Greece were to be repeated right
here on Crete. Some men counted nine flights of transport aircraft. We could see the German crosses clearly as they turned
because, of course, planes in those days didn't fly near as high
as they do now.

'I stood bewildered, looking up, the sky had filled as I
watched, there were fighters, gliders, troop carriers, great
things like big ducks in the air, and each one of these flights
were flying in close formation, the sky was blotted out with
them, and when the Huns began to jump out of the planes we
could see the planes still lined up behind, still coming over. All
colours, red, green, yellow and white, coming out of the sky
like deflated balloons. It was cold standing there watching
because we'd left our overcoats and blankets back in Greece.

'We could hear machine guns rattling, could hear parachutists screaming in the air and a lot of our firing was coming
from among the olive trees, we were fairly well camouflaged
there. We had only a few Bofors and their staccato beats were
coming out, with the odd mortar trying to lob a bomb high
up, but above all, above everything was just the roar of the
engines of the planes and the bombs streaming down and the
fighter planes diving. I saw a whole olive orchard coloured
with parachutes hanging over the trees.

'We didn't then know that one of the crack battalions, a
whole parachute battalion, had landed in the morning. You
had to admire them because the parachutist is unable to do
much for himself until he lands and gets out of all the gear
strapped to him. On our side everything was confusion. Any
time an order was given it was countermanded, or whoever

brought it had cleared out to take messages elsewhere, you'd never know whether it was a command or not.'

All men say that they were never told of any of the skills of the enemy so they could learn to counter them, they were never taught about such a position they were in, a parachute battalion coming in on them, or indeed what to do if they appeared to be losing the battle. How do you best retire to fight again?

Where shall I hide my head and my face?
The rocks are about me: between them
I have wormed and lie prone,
While over me, sheering through shot-riddled space,
Engined vultures of doom – I have seen them
Swoop avidly, peer, and depart.
My heart is as cold as the stone
Which shelters my dread and my heart.
How long since I scrambled and lay –
A year – or a day?
I am fighting the terror that laps
My bones and my body in ice.
A tremor of prayer, perhaps . . .
A whisper to Him – would a whisper suffice?
(For the ghost of a sound would betray me.)
'I have lifted up mine eyes.
'Father, God, I shall arise – '
'Now I lay me – now I lay me . . .'

Hunted and breaking, alone with the dead –
Where shall I hide my face and my head?
                    Private J.A. Allan, 2/1st Battalion

Signaller Howard Vinning, 6th Division Signals, was there: 'You kept expecting orders before the Jerry built up, but he built up quickly and we weren't ordered in. It was certainly the greatest aerial supremacy that had yet been seen in the war. Men were coming back claiming all sorts of things, some said many thousands had landed, and others said we've got them on the run. Looking back you realise that for the first twenty-four hours, if we'd been led with initiative, things may have been different. The numbers against us, of course, were out of all proportion so perhaps leadership would have made no difference. But it would have been nice to have seen it.

'The Germans had put men in the airport right from the beginning and they just kept reinforcing these men, transport planes were rolling in with big crates full of their weapons, while some of the weapons came down attached to parachutes. We were battling all this time but by the third night of the battle, just after midnight, it was decided that all British forces would be withdrawn from the Maleme area.'

'Most of my fighting was done on the back foot', Private Vic Hillas says. 'I joined the boys of the 2/7th after Bardia. I had a fortnight in Greece, then we were taken off by the *Costa Rica* and it was sunk and we were then on British destroyers and they put us on Crete, and in a month we were gone from there. My war career was short-lived.' Vic had gone into the army aged 18 years 'looking for adventure'.

'Does a young man think he might be killed? I think it was worth the risk, really. In my case anyhow. I was out in a little backwater in western Victoria. Never been out of Macarthur. It grew on me that there was nothing in Macarthur. I had an inkling to do better than just be a butcher boy for the rest of my life. I thought that this was an opportunity for me to get out and probably get into something after the war.

'Not that I knew much about what happened after World War I, except that the soldier-settlement people generally went broke on the poor land they were allocated. But it was the only opportunity I'd ever get of seeing overseas. And the war didn't look like lasting more than one year anyway. For all that it was an adventure and it was worth the risk. A lot of people came back alive from that last war. And I have no regrets. If I hadn't gone ... well, I went back to Macarthur the other day and it's still a backwater, so as far as I'm concerned the war was an experience that was well worthwhile. And it *was* just adventure as far as I was concerned; God, King and Country really wasn't part of my impulse to join up. It wasn't until I was a POW that I began to see through propaganda and that sort of thing, and see what actually was going on.

'By the way the war was run it seemed to me that English officers never had much regard for their troops, they just never seemed to be fighting a war. With our chaps, when we had a job to do you knew what you were doing, until we got to Crete that is. We wouldn't think about backing off until we *had* to back off, but we'd reckoned without Crete. However I can't class myself as one of those fighting Australians because I was never really in the rough and tough. I only know that if it had been winnable those Australians I was with would have won it.'

Howard Vinning was moving from one side of the island to the other. 'By the fourth day the bodies lying around from both sides were swollen and the stench was beginning to come up and the enemy's heavy weapons were really coming to bear on us. Occasionally we saw a really good target, a whole concentration of enemy, but we didn't have any planes. And we didn't have guns to get at the German planes. Eventually we were told to surrender. Some of us found our way to the few ships that managed to get in and escaped that way. The rest went into the bag.'

Private Ryan, 'poet' (Laurie Ryan of the 2/6th Battalion), was at his best in Greece and Crete. Of the hurried, muddled evacuation by ship from Greece he wrote:

At length they came, and on we got,
And hurried from that cursed spot
And then they landed us at Crete
And marched us off our blasted feet.

When the last of the departing ships sailed over the horizon, those men left stranded on the water-fronts or fighting from inland caves with the local resistance knew they had been abandoned. And what about Private Ryan, poet?

Here I sit on the Isle of Crete,
Bludging on my frost-bitten feet

The next we hear from the poet is that he is 'in boob' on
the Isle of Crete.

So now it looks like even betting,
A man will finish up a Cretan,
And end his days in darkest gloom,
On Adolph Hitler's 'Isle of Doom'!

With the 1071 men captured in North Africa and the 2029
in Greece, Private Ryan and his cobbers went 'into the bag' to
Poland, Czechoslovakia, Germany, Italy and Yugoslavia.

Private George King, 2/1st Battalion, was taken prisoner on
Crete. 'There were several young Greek girls, oh very young
girls, scarcely in their teens, and one put a big overcoat on one
of our wounded lying near a house. I don't know how long
she'd had that on him, because all over it was blood. Another,
right in the middle of the road, looked as though she'd pulled
a carpet off the floor or something, she came and wrapped it
around a fellow. And they brought out some bread and water,
but these fellows were pretty far gone. Some of them had been
lying out for days and you could smell them as you came near
them, their wounds and excrement. We were under orders, we
couldn't do anything. We were prisoners now and were being
moved on.'

Like most other soldiers he resented the way the island fell.
'Oh the confusion! With us it wasn't a case of putting up your
hands because you wouldn't fight, it was a case of the whole
island capitulating. When we were told that we had to capit-
ulate, I already had two bullet wounds in the leg and I was in
the RAP when the Germans first came through. A couple of
days before it was over the Germans had came up with a white
flag and said, "Why are you carrying on fighting? The war is
finished, the whole island has capitulated. General Blamey's
gone!" They knew more about it than we did.

'The colonel of the 2/1st was with us at the time and he said to them, "I'll give you fifteen minutes to get back to where you came from and then I'll open up with everything I've got". Machine guns, that's all we'd got off with from Greece. We finished up using the Germans' rifles when the parachutists came down. Oh God, they were a piece of cake, we knocked them off, shot the parachute and that split and the man just came down; motor bikes and side cars on two parachutes didn't last very long: when you split one parachute that was the end of it. So we had their ammunition and that's what we were fighting with.

'The Greek women, they were real fighters. They'd see a parachutist hanging by his 'chute up in the trees, they'd climb up and kill him right where he was. Oh, they were real fierce women! They were fighting for their homes.

'We had the Germans behind barbed wire in just a few days. It wasn't until the main army came across in Italian ships with tanks and what have you that Crete fell. I had no boots, only one sandshoe I'd scrounged, and they made us walk all the way down to Suda Bay. How far? Oh, crikey, right from Retimo, it'd be a good 30 miles. And then I lost my only sandshoe. My wounds weren't even bandaged up, I had to bandage them myself with a piece of shirt.

'Down at Suda Bay they loaded us on to ships and took us across to Greece. We saw the Acropolis and also the German flags flying from the Parthenon. Then we were off to German-held Salonika, the historical old port with stone walls around the medieval city. Twenty years earlier Australians from the First World War had been here in hospital. Lieutenant Colonel LeSouef, who'd been captured with his unit, the 2/7th Australian Field Ambulance when they were overrun at Heraklion in Crete, was with us. He did all he could for us. But all men say Salonika was bad. Bad.

'When they shipped us up country they paraded us all through the streets showing us prisoners off to the Greeks, thinking it would frighten them, but the Greeks were all on side for us and they were throwing lumps of bread, cheese and everything into the trucks and the Germans were shooting at them from the back of the truck as they did it. Of course everybody by that time was hungry and thirsty and stinking because we didn't even have a bath or a shower or a shave or anything.

'In Germany I had a go at escaping. I had a big mate, he was 6 foot 4 and he was all brawn and no brains. I had to work everything out and I used to save up everything from our Red Cross parcels, chocolate, tea, coffee and things like that. When we did make our break, instead of going straight ahead we went right around the back of Berlin and up through that way into Holland and got caught. Another time we went during the day – just headed into the woods and travelled at night time. We saw this car come with very dim lights and we dived into the gutter and the car pulled up and a woman got out and she says, "You can come out boys", in English. So I whispered to my mate, "I'll get out first". The woman said, "And where's your friend?" I said "Who wants to know?" "Oh", she said, "you'll never know who I am". But anyway, she put me under the back seat, my mate in the boot and she took us all the way through the German road blocks.

'We never knew who she was but she got us right through to the River Rhine. "This is as far as I can take you", she said. "From here on you're on your own". We were hiding in the bulrushes and we could hear someone rowing a boat, hear the oars, and we were going to knock him on the head and pinch his boat and go across to France, but we didn't have the chance. The German patrol could smell our cigarettes and picked us up quick smart.'

Private Roy 'Blue' Heron, 2/11th Battalion (naturally he was a redhead), was a typical Western Australian of his period, wiry, tough, outspoken, with an inexhaustible flair for improvisation and adaptability. Before coming to Greece he had been in action at Bardia.

'We had no motor bikes, hardly anything at all, so I nabbed an Alce motor bike (with a high frame), made for the desert.

All the young blokes grabbed the fancy motor bikes, but the old Alce took me right through until I had it shot from underneath me in Greece. So then I pinched a new Pommie VSA bike and finished my journey on that until we got off Greece. I had to leave it behind. We threw everything over the cliffs, guns and all the artillery and trucks. The whole game was lost in that part of the world, that was for sure. We carried our rifles and anything else we could on to the boat, but most of the troops from the front line had no chance to get their haversacks or anything like that, and they got on with only their rifles. We nearly all had a rifle and we got out on the destroyer HMS *Hastie* and landed at Suda Bay, Crete, and marched to Retimo where we settled in.

'The only communication we had with Suda or anywhere else was to walk, and it used to take a couple of days there and back. That was before the German parachutists came down, shooting as they came. And we were shooting back, and most of them got wiped out. They had big Yonkers, those three-engine planes they used to use in New Guinea before the war. You could always hear them coming with the noisy, uneven beat of the motors, and there was one heading towards us and one of my mates picked up an anti-tank rifle and went bang and it knocked him over and knocked the plane over too. It came down and crashed right in our lines. The pilot got out with a gun in his hand and he was going to shoot the first man he saw. He didn't last long enough, someone got in first. Then the plane started blowing up, full of ammunition, so we all laid low until it was more or less over and for the next couple of days we were picking up bits of body from everywhere because they never had a chance to get out of the plane, except for the pilot.

'Because we had no communication with other groups we were still fighting three days after Suda Bay threw in the towel. The Germans came up with a couple of small tanks and armoured vehicles and an officer lifted the lid of the tank up and said, "The island has surrendered. Throw down your arms". He was greeted with a machine gun, so the next half hour, boy was it hot! They opened up with everything they had and a lot of men got killed for nothing in that last few minutes. So then we had some German prisoners, we hurriedly made a compound and when we put them in they said, "Oh, we won't be here long. You'll be taking our place". Which turned out to be true.'

'Blue' Heron was taken from Crete back to Salonika. 'Everyone knows about the lice and bugs and dysentery there, no medical supplies, no food, clothing, nothing to wash yourself with and everybody dressed in rags more or less, and some of our boys were shot. Many others too. Then in the cattle-trucks to Germany, nine days from Salonika to Munich. The Red Cross made them let us out at Belgrade and they gave us a couple of biscuits and a cup of mint tea, which we reckoned was beautiful. And when we got on the train again Red Cross gave us a loaf of bread and a tin of meat between six of us. The first tin we emptied had to be the toilet and we only had the little window up top in the cattle-truck and after we went to the toilet we had to throw it out the window. Somewhere along the line, one bloke threw his out of the window all over a guard who was standing on the platform. So next time the train stopped, the guard came in and wanted to know who threw it out. We thought he was gone, but no, they took him into the guard's carriage and he stayed in there the rest of the journey cleaning the guard up.

'We landed in Munich, all sick. Marched out to Stalag VIIA and the commandant of the camp spoke perfect English and he said he was disgusted by our treatment. "I've never seen any prisoners come from a German prison camp in your condition". So he ordered the German cooks to give us a feed which was sauerkraut and kartoffels (potatoes) and milk, which made us all sicker. And everybody went out to the toilet and brought it all up again. We couldn't take it, no, not that sort of food. And he thought he was doing us a good turn by feeding us.

'I was a carpenter so I went into Munich and Pensburg building barracks for Russian prisoners. Then we pulled all the bells out of the churches because Hitler wanted the metal. The smallest was about 2 inches high and the biggest weighed twenty tons. We stayed in a hotel at Pensburg as there were no barracks. Doors and windows were not locked if we gave our promise not to escape, which we did, because it was useless trying to escape up there. It was a beautiful town and we were well treated.

'The Allies now started bombing Munich and we were shifted up to Stalag VIIIB in Lamsdorf. Bad treatment and mad people. I got sent to a carbide works. (Kalgoorlie miners' lamps came from the same factory before the war.) Then I was shifted to a steel factory. I wasn't there very long because in January I made my escape.

'Me and some others were planning to escape but the *actual* escape was not planned, it happened on impulse. Some of us were standing at the gate one night, just looking. The guard was walking up and down and a German came in, leaving the gate open. It was dark, so I said, "I'm going out the gate. Is anybody coming with me?" And two chaps said, "Yeah". So that made three of us. And I said, "Righto. Once we're out, don't look around, just keep walking. If we get shot in the back, bad luck."

'Anyway, we got away without the guard seeing us. We went back into the factory where we knew of an old disused sewer and we went down there to hide out for a while, but we met some other blokes that had been there for some weeks and they were all mad. All off their head. No lights, it was pitch-black dark. They had a bit of a candle and they lit it for a while and they'd put it out again. That's all they had. Two of us made up our minds we weren't going to stay. We went out and walked through town at midnight back to another village to a Pole who had been willing to help me with an earlier planned escape. He told us the Germans did their rounds every couple of hours, because the Russians were on their way down. "They go into every house and flat and every-thing, checking." They didn't have much food but they gave us what they had. And his wife and family brought hot water to wash our feet in because it was bitterly cold outside, about twenty-five below zero.

'The Pole hid us down in the rabbit hutch. It was full of straw but it was freezing cold and we stayed there until about four o'clock in the morning and he came down and said, "You can come out now. The Germans are finished their rounds." We had a bit of breakfast, what there was of it, and didn't want to put him in jeopardy so decided we'd take our chance and nick off.

'We walked quite a few miles and found ourselves in the middle of a tank battle. We jumped into a big hole until the battle was over and then we saw the Russian tanks with the Red Star coming towards us so we hopped out of the hole. And one pulled up alongside of us and the door of the tank opened and a girl hopped out and I knew a few words of Russian from the prisoners and I said, "Tovarish" which means comrade. "Australian comrade." And oh, they threw their arms around us and they all got out of the tank then. The tank crew were all girls. This was January 1945. The Germans were going back, they weren't caring about anything. They just wanted to get back. Horse and carts and walking, and of course they were just getting mowed down with aeroplanes shooting at them, tanks blowing up the earth around them, you name it!'

Blue Heron and his mate went back and reported to their commandant and were given travel passes to go through the lines and make their own way back to Odessa. The railway lines and bridges were still being repaired. 'Farmers with horse and cart, and the odd vehicle coming through gave us a ride part of the way to near Cracow.

'The chap I was with married a Ukranian girl there. He'd met her earlier as a prisoner of war in the factory at Cracow and we met the Polish commandant and he interrogated us. We had to tell him of any Germans we knew that had done bad things. We just answered what we could. They put on a bit of a banquet for us and said we had to stay in Cracow until they repaired the railway lines and bridges to Odessa.

There weren't very many people in Cracow then because the Germans had gone. So this Polish bloke said, "You can have a hotel, a block of flats, any building you like". We selected a flat, furniture in it and everything. The Pole told us there was an English chap had the YMCA nearby and we went up there and met him, and there were hundreds of girls there, nice girls, all trying to get to Australia and England. "You marry me, and when we get to Australia or England, we forget about it. We want to get out." I didn't fall for it but I know some did.

'Finally we got on the train to Odessa, a long crossing to the Ukraine as they hurriedly relaid the lines and built temporary bridges ahead of the train. There had been some pretty big bridges destroyed. It was very cold, the beginning of March, and we scrounged every bit of coal along the railway line to build the fire up at the end of the carriage. No blankets, hard boards to sleep on.

'When we got to Odessa they put us in showers and deloused us and gave us a bite to eat and we got on the boat. They wouldn't let my mate's wife on the boat, and he wouldn't get on the boat without her. Eventually he cut all her hair off and dressed her in British army uniform and got her on that way.' (This girl later worked in Anzac House, London.)

'I landed home for my birthday, 18 April 1945. Everything was hush-hush when I arrived home because the war hadn't finished. So there was no big reception. The Red Cross just got my sister and my father and they were the only ones who met me and the Red Cross took us up to their place and had a talk and something to eat.'

Private Arthur Robinson, 2/11th Battalion (WA), was another soldier who married a girl who had been a prisoner. 'We used to feel such anger when we saw these beautiful girls being worked like cart-horses: they laboured on farms, in forests, factories, you name it. They had it as hard as we did.'

Bombardier Alan King, 1st Anti Tank Regiment 6th Division (with the unusual Army number of NGXT), was a government man in the Treasury in New Britain. 'Ten of us there enlisted in January 1940 and were sent overseas early and got caught early; when the Germans attacked on the Yugoslavian front on 9 April with tanks, they broke through the Greeks and encircled us on the border. A New Zealander and I escaped. We had a map and compass. We'd been out nineteen days, living on the land when we were picked up. We were so far from the Swiss border that although we'd travelled nearly 150 miles, we had no hope of getting there. That was my one and only escape attempt.

'In the early stages there was no organised escape committee. It was only later in the bigger camps that they organised and in Mahlberg POW camp there were people from all walks of life who could assist would-be escapers: three were able to manufacture compasses, precision work, perfectly accurate. They cut the needle from a razor blade and somehow magnetised it. A group of us helped dig the first tunnel at Hohenfeldts but I didn't participate in the escape. We had brought the soil up in Red Cross boxes. We had to distribute it round the place. I can't understand why they didn't find it because the underground soil was a different colour to the top soil. Another problem was that you had to be able to circulate air down in the tunnel. We made hand bellows (they could make anything in those camps) and worked underground in pairs: one cove would dig and the other cove fill it into the little boxes while a cove at the top with bellows circulated the air.

'The first job I had for the Germans was digging a canal at Weinberg. We jacked up, we reckoned we weren't getting enough food and as a result, they sent us to a Straffelager (punishment camp) where I worked quarrying stone for a cement factory. Two men working as a pair had to load twenty-two railway trucks a day. Then I went into an NCOs camp because my rank was bombardier (equivalent to any army corporal).

'Here I, and others, were handcuffed. We were told it was because apparently in the Dieppe raid the Canadians had captured some German prisoners and in trying to get them back to England to interrogate them, they tied their hands behind their backs, and the Germans, as a reprisal, decided they'd handcuff us. As we NCOs were a non-working camp, we were chosen as the example. They wouldn't have handcuffed us if they could have got work out of us! We were handcuffed for exactly a year. They used to come in at eight o'clock in the morning and put them on and at eight at night take the handcuffs off. There were fourteen men to a hut and they'd handcuff thirteen and leave one free for the day and he'd do the collecting of the food, helping with our clothing and all that sort of thing. So we used to rotate it in our hut so that every fourteenth day you were without cuffs.'

Captain John Berkely Fitzhardinge, 2/3rd Field Regiment (army number WX9), served in the desert campaigns and was then sent to Greece. 'April Fools Day 1941. We went up to the Yugoslav border. We did almost every rearguard action for the next month. Like all others there, I believed we had no air support and we said unrepeatable things about that. The German air force were with us in force. We held fire when they came over the top and became very good at camouflage. We had twenty-five pounders and .303 rifles. We ate well because Australians are very enterprising, we had chickens and goats. It was very sad to see the Greeks moving south in their carts. The Greek army had put up a brave resistance and now in retreat they couldn't hide. The German planes came down and killed their horses. Very sad.'

Captain Fitzhardinge came off Greece on the destroyer *Ajax*. 'Before we left we damaged the guns so they couldn't be of value to the enemy, took the breech blocks and firing pins out of the artillery and dropped them into the water. Not having slept properly for a month, we got on the destroyer and died. The ship was being bombed but we didn't care, it was no longer our responsibility. We reached Suda Bay on Crete the next day, and came ashore in barges. We were given Italian field guns which had been captured in the desert. They didn't have range finders. We went to Retimo and at the airport there were four old Gladiator planes. And so it went on. Nothing was right.

'The 2/11th Battalion and some Greeks were there, so we occupied the high ground above the aerodrome in olive groves. We saw the parachutes, we saw the gliders, we saw the planes coming, it was awesome to see the men and the guns and the supplies fill the sky, hanging on the parachutes, each colour-coded red, white and blue, the men camouflaged, it was great organisation on the enemy's part. It was all so different from the way we had been treated. The Germans hardly knew we were there. They were going to occupy the airstrip and prepare it for their planes. The Australians killed many and took prisoners, even captured one of their guns, which they then used. But we were running out of ammunition and food and everything else. Then we heard on radio BBC that Crete had been successfully evacuated. We looked at one another. I don't remember what we felt, whether it was surprise, disgust, it was just this most awful shock.

'A few days later the Germans put a motor-cycle patrol around the whole area, we were prisoners.' With fifteen men Fitzhardinge 'made a break', they picked their way through the patrols and crossed to Retimo and thence to Mt Ida on the south coast.

'We milked goats into our tin hats. Locals were very helpful. One attached himself to us as a guide. So we moved on, freezing. We slept in a line, near to one another to keep warm. We arrived at Timbaki. There were two Scots regiments there and a landing barge on the beach, it had been shot up by the Germans; a mechanic said, "It's beyond repair, we can't do anything".'

The party with Fitzhardinge got fuel from shot-down-aircraft, 'got hold of' a battery, and three men and Fitzhardinge got a fishing boat going and decided to try to cross the Mediterranean. Fitzhardinge had a revolver, the only arms on the boat. With another good swimmer Fitzhardinge towed the boat out. There was some rifle fire; Fitzhardinge 'only got a splinter in the face'. Another man was wounded in the chin, hand and foot. 'There was blood mixed with water in the boat, it looked like a slaughter yard.' But Fitzhardinge had sailed all his life and now decided to sail back to Timbaki. (By then the other party had got the barge off, with seventy people on board, and plotted a course for Mersa Matruh, North Africa.)

'We left at midnight and at 8 a.m. one of the sailors woke me to say that "One of our subs" had surfaced across our bows.' Fitzhardinge ordered the men to lie down in the boat, he knew it wouldn't be 'one of ours'. He dived in and swam over to the sub and in schoolboy French said, 'I have sick and wounded on board'. The Italians searched him and then said his sick men and officers could come on the submarine and those left on the tender must return to Crete.

Throughout his prison days Fitzhardinge was one of the most popular officers in any of the several camps he was sent to in Germany. He was enterprising, could adapt himself to any circumstances – he believes that all Australians can do this. He was a talented man who could make the most of what was available. He sketched as well as painted water colours. He was helpful with designs for play backdrops, he had great spirit, an outgoing man. He brought home with him on his return photographs of the prisoners performing *The Mikado*, another of a 'dinner dance' (very difficult to tell that the 'women' are just other POWs dressed up for the occasion).

In between all this he made several attempts at escape. One was via a tunnel that began beneath his bed (the soil was hidden in the ceiling above his bed). To bring the soil out the men had joined Players cigarette tins to make a pipeline and filled boxes that were attached to string and pulled out of this long tunnel to be put up in the ceiling. 'The tunnel was only wide enough for the widest man, it was quite a squeeze.' Hair oil (bought from the Italians) with a piece of pyjama cord was used for light, but this was using up air in the tunnel so eventually they rigged up electricity. (The camp had been used in World War I when Italy was on the British side, and in 1941 while they were working in the tunnel the Australian prisoners

found the skeleton of a German POW of that earlier war.)
They had planned to come out on the other side of a tree, but
when they got to the tree, there was a huge rock in front of
them so they had to tunnel around it. There was great excitement when they poked a rod up and daylight came down on
them.

'The men wiggled their way backwards and gathered the
civilian clothes they had been making for months. These had
been dyed khaki – with coffee.' Fitzhardinge was a good forger
and one of his passports had already got one man to Switzerland. Now he went back to the senior British officer in charge
of escape. 'We must go tonight. The tunnel is too close to the
surface and if it begins raining, it might fall in.' 'No, the dye
will run in the uniforms', said the officer. Fitzhardinge wanted
to head off to the mountains where they could perhaps change
clothes. He thought that later he'd go to the coast with a mate
and get a boat and escape that way.

He spent most of the night 'propping the tunnel up'.
Morning broke into a beautiful day. He looked out where he
knew the tunnel to be. While he was watching, a woman came
down the mountain riding a donkey and the donkey's back
legs went down, into the tunnel. The lady screamed and this
sent the Italian soldiers running to see where the tunnel had
come out and, of course, to find the other end – under Fitzhardinge's bed. He said, 'Oh!' in feigned surprise. He knew
nothing. Later he wrote a report that he believed the British
had done it and said that the soil had been put in another
tunnel built specifically for the purpose. Fortunately for him,
the weight of the soil in the ceiling over his bed didn't give
way until he had escaped on another bid for freedom.

'I found the Germans much less human and humane than
the Italians. On the train coming up to Germany after the
Italian capitulation, there were SS fellows on board and men
were shot for getting off the train. Some cut holes in the floors
of trucks and dropped down between the rails to escape. If
you didn't move quick enough a German rifle butt belted you
in the back of the neck; the food was poor, if it was not for

the Red Cross, we would have been as badly off perhaps as those who later were prisoners of the Japanese. Some of us had gone from 14 stone to 9 stone.'

Fitzhardinge, like other prisoners, spoke of the Russians. 'There were 85,000 Russian prisoners treated like animals in one camp. Dogs were sent in to get them out. They only had standing room, at least we could sit and stand and had some area to exercise in. They sent Russians into the town to sweep the snow, without boots. They were hovering on the stumps of their feet with frostbite, pathetic.'

Corporal Charles Parrott, 2/8th Infantry Battalion, had his 21st birthday at Benghazi. 'A mate told me my brother Lawrence was wounded in a bad way in a gully so I went back and got him. Then to think we went off to Greece, got bombed off the *Costa Rica*, got on to the *Defender* and got caught in Crete. You should have seen us trying to get under tiny stones when the big bombing started. Lawrence had been pinching chickens and had them over his back in a white pillowslip. What a target!'

Like other captives he and Lawrence were sent to bury the dead or, as Charlie says, 'Trying to make whole bodies out of odd legs, no arms, one head, three trunks'.

Then it was off to Germany – where Charlie Parrott had the most bitter-sweet love affair in Munich. It began when he winked at a 16-year-old girl cycling past. 'Hello darling', he said. Charlie spoke German and worked as an interpreter at a workshop; this girl, Lili Schneider, had a neighbour who worked on a lathe in this factory. Through him the two young people exchanged 'little' notes. 'Once she sent her month's meat ration ticket so Lawrence and I could have a steak each, another time a small roast beef came.' Prior to Christmas 1942 Lili wrote that she would smuggle meat and a bottle of wine in for the brothers.

Tragedy now swept in as unexpectedly as tragedy always does. The lathe worker who exchanged notes for the pair had a son in the German navy. This sailor, home on leave, heard the story from his father and set off to report it to the military police. In his absence, the now disgraced father hanged himself in the bathroom of his home, his wife ran next door to tell Lili and before the police arrived they searched for any note that would incriminate Charles and Lawrence and destroyed it.

When he learned of this Charlie Parrott was 'alarmed for Lili. Everyday I watched for her to pass by our camp but I never saw her again.'

Corporal Syd Sinclair from Perth (WA), 2/7th Field Ambulance, was taken prisoner on Crete. 'We went down some wadis and carted some wounded fellows out on blankets and loaded them onto an English ambulance. One of our mechanics got it going and a chap named Johnny Greaney (Private, 2/7th Field Ambulance) and I brought it back to a hospital down on the coast. From there we went down into a prisoner of war compound for about two months. Then we went back to Salonika (it seemed like years since we'd left Greece), from there we were in the train for a fortnight on the way to a camp in Poland, 58 miles from Danzig, in a series of forts on the Vistula River. We were in Fort 15 for NCOs and men who couldn't work, plus a lot of the 5th AGH boys from New South Wales. And that's where I was till we were repatriated, in Poland all the time.

'Sergeant Brian Wright, a New Zealand Expeditionary Force man, and I tried to escape. There were high iron struts up around the prisons and then about 6 feet of barbed wire above that. We took our boots off and were climbing this wire, just got to the top and we heard the guard slam one up the spout so we both jumped, the rifle went off and the Kiwi landed on his tummy and busted his knee up properly and I landed on my right knee. I reckoned we'd been up the best part of 30 feet when we jumped. Had we got to the top we would have dinky-died because it was high tension wire on top of the fence. We were pretty fit at the time because we had Red Cross parcels coming in. Well, the Kiwi went to hospital because he'd busted his knee up properly but they threw me in the bunker for a week, nothing was done for my knee.

'The next time I went was in '43, Private Bill Fenwick, Private Alex Sutherland (both 5th AGH) and an Englishman, Joe someone and I decided to go in the daytime. A friend of mine, Corporal Peter Leach, 5th AGH, was in the workshop and so we built a ladder and put it down in the dry moat that was 15 feet deep. Spikes and things like that came up from the moat and they also had barbed wire on top of that. We had this ladder to take us out of the moat and no one had said who was going to go first and who was to go last, so we drew lots and I drew number four, only one man was to be on the ladder at a time, only one chap going up the wire at a time, but at the actual scene one bloke was behind the other on the ladder and on the wire, on each other's tails going over. A fantastic short time it was from when we left till we got over. But then Alex Sutherland said, "I've dropped my glove", which was on the outside where the guard walked around, so he went back and got the glove. By the time he got it the guard came around; however, Alex got out and he was coming back through the trip wires, not on his hands and knees but standing up like a dog. At one stage the guard saw him and said, "What are you doing?" Luckily Alex could speak pretty good German so he said we were Poles going up country, and the guard said didn't we know this was a prisoner of war camp? Alex said no, so the guard said, "You'd better get on your way". But I still think that bloke must have known who we were.

'We were out for three days. We'd walked about 25 miles in the night and were going to try to get over to Sweden. Fenwick and I were together. We'd taken stuff from our Red Cross parcels with us. I was wearing a Pommie battle-dress sewn together like overalls and dyed blue, and Fenwick had got some civilian clothes, a coat, trousers and shoes off a Pole that used to come in to clean out the latrines. We were of military age and looked fit so we stood out in a land where all fit young men were at war. Fenwick was picked up on a railway station, I was nabbed on a street. The four of us got picked up and I got a fortnight in the bunker because that was my second attempt.'

Corporal Reg King, 2/11th Battalion, at Crete, May 1941: 'After the island surrendered rations were meagre and we foraged out into the countryside. On one occasion the boys brought in a live donkey and someone slaughtered it by cutting its throat. Everybody was that hungry that the man who cut its throat hardly got any of the flesh, everybody was tearing at it as it was still quivering.

'The Germans put us on small fishing boats and sent us to Piraeus, then by train to Salonika. We were hungry. And everybody grew weaker by the day. Everybody in this camp was infested with lice. They were that bad that when an English soldier died, the coat he had been using as a pillow had that many lice in it that it actually moved on the floor.

'After weeks in this camp the Germans shifted 1000 prisoners, mainly Australians, to Germany. We were loaded on to cattle-trucks the same as World War I men had travelled on, with "forty men or eight horses" painted on the side. The Serbian Red Cross contacted us at different points as we went along and gave us enough food to keep us alive. The worst part of this trip was that we were locked up for a week and only allowed out for five minutes a day for toilet needs. They would surround one truck at a time, open the doors and allow us out, and almost as soon as we pulled our pants down to relieve ourselves, a Sudeten soldier came along, jabbing us in the rear with his bayonet to hurry us up.

'At Hammelburg we had a very good regimental sergeant major, Bill Brown, in charge of us. He was a regular soldier and gradually brought us into line with our uniforms and behaviour, and made sure that everywhere we went we marched instead of straggled. And this impressed the Germans and I'm sure we were given better treatment because of it for the German commandant in charge of the camp was an old regular soldier. Quite often we heard him drilling his men and telling them to be "upright like the Australian prisoners of war".

'One hundred and fifty of us were sent out to construct a road; we had an open ditch for a toilet with a rail alongside, which you would sit on, and you had to relieve yourself here, irrespective of whether the local people were passing by or not.

'We were sent to Wolferhausen where farmers came to select what prisoners they wanted. Us prisoners lined up. One chap looked at our hands to see if they were blistered or calloused, to see if we'd been working hard. He wasn't very impressed by most of us until he came to an old Scotsman and accepted him. It was funny, for this farmer used to make the schnapps for the district and Jock was quite a boozer. Jock now had to make the schnapps and test it every now and again, and for the rest of the time that I was at this village, I never saw Jock sober at any time. The next farmer to come up was a lady named Hedwig, and she had a look at us all and was apparently impressed by my youth, for at that time I was only 21, and after quite a few signs, including one asking whether I could milk a cow, she eventually selected me. She asked my name "namen". I said it was Reg but she found difficulty in pronouncing an "R", so eventually I said, "Oh, call me Digger".

'In this particular part of the country, the farmers all lived in a little village and went out to work their farm by day. We prisoners were housed at night in one particular house in the village under a guard, with barbed wire and bars on the windows. Each morning we would go round to our particular house and be under the supervision of the farmer during the day.

'The guard would say to us, "I understand that it is your duty to escape, but if you must, escape during the daytime when it is the farmer's responsibility". And the farmers would say, "If you want to escape, escape during the night-time, because then it is the guard's responsibility".

'We settled down in the village into a way of life which was not too bad. Although the Red Cross had not at this stage contacted us, we had enough clothes to carry on. In fact on quite a few occasions I wore the clothes of Stefan, the husband of Hedwig. He was an occupation soldier on Crete, where we had come from. War is like this.

'Each of us lived as one of the family and ate with them, therefore we were reasonably well fed. Of an evening, if we had a good guard, we could go to the gasthaus, the local hotel and drink beer, provided we went home at a reasonable time. The hotel keeper had a couple of daughters, which kept some of our chaps interested, and the young girls also used to come out during the clearing of the snow, and there was quite a bit of frolicking then, as there was in the loft of the barn at harvesting time.

'The main occupation in winter was sitting in the lounge where the ladies would spin wool and we prisoners would shell dry peas and beans. During the first winter I sat in the lounge with a German-English encyclopaedia and with Hedwig's help could soon converse freely.' The guards were none too diligent in this bucolic settlement and went home to their wives at weekends and the prisoners often got out and spent Sunday at the hotel. Once, they rollicked back through the middle of the village singing 'Waltzing Matilda' and 'God Save the King'. 'The villagers came out and cheered, because they didn't like the guard.'

The Red Cross sent them warm underclothing, socks, boots and English battle-dress uniforms, plus one English-issue overcoat as well as one eleven-pound food parcel per week. 'From then on we did well because we were fed by the farmers plus the food parcels, and on most Sundays we would not go round to the farmers for food at all. Normally the arrangement on Sundays would be that we would go around and look at the cows either in the morning or in the afternoon, and the farmers would do it on the other occasion.

'We POWs lost the mock modesty Australians have. We worked in the middle of the fields with a woman alongside us all day and not even a bush for a quarter of a mile. When it first came time for me to relieve myself or pass water, I wondered what I was going to do. Eventually I knelt down on the ground with my back to Hedwig and pretended to be weeding while I relieved myself. She thought this was great fun, she leant back and laughed her head off. And I thought at the time, well, I wonder what you're going to do when it's your turn? But this didn't worry her because these women wore a fairly full, long frock and they don't wear any pants. Therefore when they went to relieve themselves, they just simply leant forward, pulled the frock away from the back and relieved themselves standing up. And nobody took any notice. So of course from then on, even though we were working together, whenever I wanted to relieve myself, I would just simply turn my back and go ahead.

'As Louie, my friend, was a sergeant and I was a corporal and therefore not obliged to work, his frau, Wilhelmina, and mine, Hedwig, were not confident as to how long they could keep us. They competed with one another to see who could treat their prisoner the better.

'By spring, we decided we were doing the wrong thing volunteering to work, because helping to keep Germany's economy running was helping their war effort. Poor old Hedwig was quite upset. We went back to the main camp in Hammelburg and we were not particularly happy about it. The barracks were crowded and everybody had nothing to do and, as we had thought, were at each other's throats as usual.

'At this camp they organised a big event, a cabaret with a floorshow of the type of "My Fair Lady" including a "female" revue and chorus, with dancing. The tables were made out of tea chests and we each brought whatever we used for chairs. There were some prisoners came in that morning from Sicily, the first from that battle-front, and they must have wondered what they were coming to because when they arrived in the camp they were given a complete kit of two sets of clothing including boots and uniforms and a greatcoat, and went to a cabaret that night!

'Shortly after this it was announced that there was to be a repatriation of prisoners, mainly wounded men or medical orderlies. In our camp and in the hospital attached, there were several married orderlies, so I volunteered to stay on while the married men returned home. I was transferred as a medic in the hospital that served all the Australians attached to Hammelburg.'

Reg became an instrument assistant in the operating theatre. 'We had two operating afternoons a week, with two tables going at once, doing up to fourteen operations in an afternoon. We never knew when a trainload of any number of new wounded was coming in and we'd have to have a clean-out of patients.

'It was fun one day when we went down to the siding at Langwasser to meet the repatriation train and put our people on board; there were a crowd of English women from one of the Channel Islands that were being repatriated. They hadn't seen any British men for about three years, and they were quite excited. In fact they were trying to get some of us to hide under the seats and go through with them.'

Their days were leavened by a few laughs. 'As we approached Christmas 1944 the Red Cross sent us some special Christmas parcels, and one parcel we got contained crackers and when they exploded they sent out hundreds of little half-inch flags: Union Jacks and Stars and Stripes, each attached to a pin. We mixed them up with the food parcels which had arrived and managed to get them past the censor, and stored them away for Christmas Day. We had a grand old Christmas party for the patients alone. Then, after they were put back to bed for the night we had a party for the twenty staff, orderlies and offsiders, bootmakers and cooks etc., including myself, the South African doctor and the American doctor that was now with us, and festivities went on for quite a while. Eventually guards came in to see what was going on as it was after lights out.

'We plied them with alcohol (from a still in the surgery) and chocolates from our parcels until they got a little under the weather, and as they were walking around drinking and eating we were sticking hundreds of these little flags of Stars and Stripes and Union Jacks on the back of their uniforms. They would certainly have copped it when they went back to their own barracks.

'As for the stories of "Hogan's Heroes" of Hamelberg, I was doing practically the same without even having to dig a tunnel! Fritz, our friendly anti-Nazi guard, asked me if I'd like to go home with him during the weekend. He made out passes for Saturday to Monday morning, borrowed a couple of bikes and away we went, cycling through the countryside to his village. Of a night he and his wife slept in a double bed and I slept on a sofa at the foot of the bed.'

For Sergeant Keith Hooper, 2/6th Infantry Battalion, one picture develops in his mind's eye to reprint his war. 'The cemetery, 5 miles north of Salonika in Greece. It faced the camp where we were dying at a rate of four and five a day, it attracted our gaze time and again, and those daily funerals distressed us.

'This camp was one of the worst known to British POWs in World War II. There were about 12,000 of us confined there. Some had five months of it. The lucky minority knew only two. Irrespective of the duration of our stay, it was hell. We were, of course, all misfortunates captured in the battles of Greece and Crete. This made our lot harder. The Germans, still irate over their gross losses in those campaigns, resolved on revenge. One day they had the whole camp standing on parade from dawn to dusk in a temperature of 100 degrees; another the curtailing for two days of our meagre ration of a bowl of thin lentil soup. When the first autumn winds blew we, who had been captured in shorts, felt them keenly. The cookhouse contained four shallow coppers to cook the entire camp's ration – the serving of the one meal began at 10 a.m. and finished usually after 4 in the afternoon. The only lavatory contained four cubicles, no wonder there was an appalling muster of sick each day at the camp hospital. The hospital was staffed by several British medicos, but they were severely handicapped for lack of materials, nor would the Germans provide any, nor permit purchases from the Greeks.

'Encompassing these conditions were the doubled, high,

barbed wire fence with its concertina network between each fence, and beyond the fence forty alert, trigger-happy guards. Despite these preventive measures, there were constant and numerous attempts to escape.'

Ever since capture Keith had resolved to get away. But it was extremely difficult. He made two attempts en route from Athens, but on both occasions had to scramble back into the column. Once was when marching down the Thermopylae Pass. 'I jumped into a culvert, but a guard had seen me and encouraged me back with Maschinen-pistol.' The other occasion was when they changed trains after crossing the destroyed railway bridge over the Salamvria River at Ambelikia. 'I made a dash for a lane and ran into a German guard.'

'In Salonika I cobbered up with a Kiwi, Terry McCoy, and Mansel Thomas, a Welshman in the Royal Marines, and we made a joint effort. After probing the camp perimeter thoroughly, we began patiently to cut a diagonal escape route through the barbed wire near the corner of the barracks where we slept.' Night after night they worked on the wire, undeterred by the gusts of gunfire which periodically swept the compound, until one night a guard stumbled upon them. 'The result might have been worse had the corner of the barracks not been an easy leap away.'

Their efforts to escape became desperate when the Germans began to shift the prisoners to Austria and Bavaria. On 9 August 1941, the night before the last batch of Australians were to be removed, one of the most daring mass escape attempts of the war was attempted. In the centre of the gap between the junction of the two barracks was a manhole and they discovered that this led down to the sewer, which was just wide and high enough for a man to crawl through to a creek flowing half-a-mile south of the camp. In the beginning, the idea was a secret, but shortly it got about and there was a score of people wanting to participate in the attempt.

'Just prior to dusk that night, a swy game was started around the manhole. Every evening the game operated and the Germans were accustomed to it and therefore were not suspicious. What they did not know was that this night, one after the other, the players were disappearing down the manhole.' Mansel, Terry and Keith were those next to go when, suddenly, there was a volley of shots and prisoners scattered in all directions. 'We three tried to walk calmly back to our barracks. A German lunged at us with his bayonet. I turned it aside with my hand and abused him. The German shouted and pushed the bolt home. Mansel and Terry dragged me through a doorway. By now there was pandemonium outside. Germans were everywhere, grenades exploding, men moaning and crying out.' The attempt at escape had failed badly, all the men already in the sewer had been slain or recaptured.

'Young Ponto? He was a kid you know. He was under age.
Outside Damour, he died – shot through the belly with
a Very light. We bayoneted the dog who did it.
We kicked his head off ... Young Ponto took two hours
to die.
Hell, that's a shocking way to die ... I wonder where
we're bound?' 'Christ knows;
Destination unknown ...'

A hard voice calls, 'Fair go, spinner ... They're in
the air ...
And heads are right!'

John Quinn

Private Sam Stratton, 2/11th Battalion, a guard – before and after the war – on Western Australian Railways, saw Crete and the evacuation of Greece as the highlights of his war. 'That campaign was war, of a sort. What happened after was something else. When we were coming out of Greece, the boat that we were taken on for Crete was heavily bombed from the air. We had everything pointed towards the sky or we would have sunk. We kept them off, but the bombs had sprung the plates on her, and after they took us into Crete they let her sink.

'On that ship we had our own Australian army nursing service, and those girls were up on the deck looking after our chaps that had been hit, blood and gore everywhere, machine-gun bullets thudding around. You could hardly walk on the deck for empty shell-cases, you'd slip on them.

'When we lobbed on Crete we were very poorly equipped, we never had much to eat even. When we were halfway along the road marching from Khania to Retimo, General Freyberg came up and addressed us. "You'll have everything here, you'll have Bofors guns, you'll have machine guns, you'll have air cover, you'll have artillery", he says. "We'll fight to the last man!" Guess who was first off?

'At Retimo on the middle of the island, you could say that we had a complete victory, we kept pegging away at them, but we lost a lot of men trying to get that last pocket of Germans. Which was useless because the island had been surrendered anyway. We didn't know that till later. We didn't know our side was losing. As far as we were concerned, it was going to be a win. You can imagine the surprise we got when they came up and told us that any further resistance was useless. We'd heard that they'd been successful at Iraklion and we'd thought they'd been successful down at Khania, and at Retimo we had a walk-over. So as far as we were concerned there was no reason to think that we were going to lose, until the last day when the whole German army broke through on us, and an officer rushed down to us and said the island's capitulated and any further resistance from us would be useless. He said, "You can either give yourselves up or try your luck in the hills". He was going to try his luck in the hills. So I thought, that's good enough for me and I threw my gear away, broke my rifle up and took to the land, went right across to the other side of the island, with a few other chaps. We camped down there as long as we could, and the Greeks were trying to help us with a little bit of food, but you can imagine there was quite a mob and they couldn't do much for us, they were pretty hard up themselves.

'Our officers made no effort to keep us together or come

with us or encourage us in any way, so it was every man for himself. Perhaps it's fair enough, but I think it was up to the officers to try and do something for us. Anyhow, we were picked up. Alpine troops. That was the beginning of the end.

'Nothing had ever been said to us about laying down arms. They told us nothing. That's the hard part. If they'd told us a couple of days earlier, we could have got a head start and tried to organise something. As it was, some of these chaps that I was with did get off on a submarine. Some got help from the Cretans to enable them to escape.

'The Germans took us on a boat to Iraklion to build an airstrip, and one of our chaps got off the boat and swam over to a sea-plane. His only flying experience had been to pilot a Gypsy Moth before the war. But when he got there a German was waiting for him with a spanner! When we were on this boat, a British submarine, the *Norberg* with a Greek crew, tried to torpedo us. We had an Italian destroyer with us and a German sub-chaser, and these were chucking depth charges everywhere on this thing, but we never saw any more of it. When we got to Iraklion they took us into the harbour, and unknown to us the submarine had been underneath us and we later learned that she got through the sub nets and followed us into the harbour.

'We were fed on rice and raisins and you're hungry and hunger can just about destroy you. It's a terrible thing to be really hungry. It's a vicious thing. But when we went up to build this airport the Cretans really came good for us. Our main task was grubbing out olive trees to clear the patch and we'd find food there under the roots. They would dry bread and make it into rusks, and they'd make little things out of pumpkin flowers and stuff them with rice, and all this sort of thing. And they kept us going with the food they gave us from this little village of Timakion and that was one of the highlights of the war for us.

'For these first twelve months it was very hard. I don't think I would have survived if it hadn't been for the Cretans. They made the difference between living and dying. Any of the chaps of the time would tell you that. You never forget people for this. Out of the worst of times some things stay with you forever.

'If the Germans found Cretans helping you, they shot them. Without any hesitation. They dropped leaflets warning us of the consequences if we were caught ... that the Greeks would be shot, not us. And they did shoot them. When I was picked up the Germans wanted to know how I'd lived, what I'd been doing, where I'd been. I told them I had some bully beef and stuff on me when I got away and was able to pick grapes and steal fruit, and they said, "What about the local population?" "I never saw them, wouldn't have gone near them", I lied.

'I was on Crete until 1942. They eventually took us by ship to Greece and on to a Bulgarian boat to Salonika. You could see land on both sides all the way, and we were always looking for a chance to go over the side there, but there was none. Salonika camp had been a hell camp for most of our chaps who'd gone through there much earlier. One of my friends saw the Germans throwing stale bread to the horses, and he had a fight with the horse; he said, "I got a bit of it, anyway!"

'They took us by train from Salonika and we were on it for three weeks, right in the middle of winter. It was a hell trip. Some of the chaps that'd joined up when they were about 35 couldn't stand the rigors of it, four died on the trip. I could see that train going on forever. It was just the usual cattle-trucks, with "eight horses or forty men" written on the sides of them; there *was* a window up high, but wired up with barbed wire. A lot of the chaps had dysentery and you could see all of this muck hanging out of the bloody window where they emptied the tin.

'We were lousy, and we never got rid of those lice till we got to Lamsdorf and were put through a delousing process. They got into the seams of your pants, they're little grey things and they just suck your blood. And it doesn't matter what you do: you can get a lighted piece of paper and run it along, but you just couldn't get rid of them. They can cause typhus too.

'We were always after food. I was down by the German

barracks one day and I saw this bloody old tom cat sitting there, so I grabbed him and put him under my coat and took him back to the barracks. I was in with a mob of pretty rough blokes and one of them grabbed the cat and battered it on the head, and we skinned it and were going to eat it because things were very grim at this time. Anyway, we had a lot of Canadians come from Dieppe and they were very flush with cigarettes, so we got a brainwave and one of the blokes decided we'd sell the cat to the Canadians for cigarettes. So the cat became a hare! Anyway, we got 500 cigarettes. And the bloody cat stunk to high heaven ... Stunk! It was old. This bloke that took it over to them was back there the next day and they were cooking the old cat and they offered him a bit and he said, "Oh Christ no, you've paid enough for it, I don't want to eat it". I've always regretted I picked up that cat in some ways, I like cats.

'Cigarettes were the most valuable thing in Germany at that time, you could buy anything with cigarettes. We got fifty cigarettes a week from Red Cross. We used to barter with the Germans, if we had cigarettes we'd get bread, soap, coffee, cocoa, tea, anything.

'The first job I went on was a railway job in Czechoslovakia. We'd just come from Crete and we were in a bad way, starving, and they sent us to do fettling, and the ground was half-frozen, as hard as hell. You had to keep your hands and your ears covered, otherwise you'd get frostbitten. I got my toe frostbitten. They took the darn skin off, it was like a raw sore for a while. We used to wear wooden clogs, no socks, wrap pieces of rag around our feet.

'Anyhow, we stuck it as long as we could, and then we just refused point-blank to work. Which was a pretty risky thing to do but we were lucky and we got away with it, and they sent us back to Lamsdorf. But some stayed. I don't blame them; why put your life on the line? Which we did. Back at the main camp things weren't too good; in the boob for a couple of weeks for refusing to work.

'When we got out things picked up a bit, the Red Cross

parcels were starting to come through. In the Canadian parcels you'd have a tin of Spam, a nice big tin of milk, some dried fruit, a packet of tea, meat loaf, sugar, a tin of butter and a nice big packet of very thick biscuits, which you could soak and mix up with that milk and make a sort of porridge. If you balanced it out you'd get a nice week's ration out of it. The English parcels were not quite so good, but they were good enough, but you can imagine England wasn't in the same position as Canada. Sometimes we got what they'd call bulk from the Argentine, big tins of meat and you'd cut them up and share them.

'Eventually we got supplied with a British battle-dress uniform, British army boots and a cap, singlets and underpants. We were eventually very well equipped in that way. After I did the straff [punishment], I went out on a working party, cleaning out a river bed, then they sent us to a factory in Silesia where they made sugar from sugarbeet. Most sugar they had was used in munitions, not for food.

'But I wasn't feeling too good in the stomach and they sent me back to Lamsdorf, the main camp, for treatment. When I eventually had to get regraded for work, our blokes (Australians are live wires you know), they knew the Jewish bloke that takes you down to the German doctor who graded me 1-A; so the Jewish bloke marked it 4-A. That meant I was damn near dead, just about due for repatriation. Consequently I never went out to work any more.

'I stayed in that camp till you could hear the Russian guns roaring and the planes were strafing the camp. They shifted us up to Hammelburg by train to a prisoner of war camp that was completely Australian; there were the Russians in a different part and you could intermingle. The chap that was in charge of that camp was our regimental sergeant major, Bill Brown. Of course when I got up there, I sort of fell on my feet because he was in charge.

'I went out to work on a farm for a week, at a little place called Untfinden in Bavaria. This old frau had a daughter about 18, and I used to go out with her spreading this muck out on the paddocks, scheit and stuff, and sawing up wood, doing odd jobs in the vineyard and that. I was out with the girl one day in a German wagon, with a cow and a horse harnessed up together, and a bloody American plane strafed us. I ducked, but the girl like a fool hung on to the horse's head. I was yelling out to her but she wouldn't take any notice of me, but fortunately the bullets scattered everywhere all around her feet and missed. The Americans at that time seemed to be hell-bent on shooting up everything. But I never thought they'd shoot a German cow-horse-wagon with a couple of peasants on it!

'Then they put us out on the road again and we walked from there to Munich. That was a starvation trip, we had nothing at all. They turned us into beggars, we used to go and beg at the houses to try and get a bit of food. Some of the people gave us a bit of bread, they very seldom took whatever we tried to barter with ... you'd pull off your balaclava or your scarf or whatever you had and try and sell that, you felt you had to have something to offer. And we'd get a bit of bread and stuff here and there. Our guards were old blokes, the poor old buggers could hardly carry their rifles any more, and they'd been on the road for weeks and weeks, zig-zagging all over the place.'

Sam Stratton was among those being marched away from the advancing Americans. 'We eventually staggered our way up just outside Munich, and the Americans overtook us there. They told us to stay where we were and we'd be taken out, but I didn't trust the situation. I thought there might be a counter-attack or something, so I got to buggery out. Me and a South African chap got hold of a couple of push bikes, and when we found on the autobahn it was too dangerous to ride a bike because no one'd give a bugger whether they ran over you or not, we dumped the bikes and got a lift with some Americans. We went through Regensburg and were going across the Danube where they'd built one of these Bailey bridges, and there was an American officer at the side and he said, "Any prisoners of war? Get 'em out. They're a bloody nuisance." So they took us over to Nuremburg to an airstrip where they were flying petrol in and flying POWs out. The Americans there gave us K-rations. I was at that time about 9 stone but by the time I hit England I'd put on about 2 stone weight from the K-rations, I couldn't stop eating them.'

Yarning over a beer on the Poland–German border, forty-five years later, was a group of ex-prisoners of war:

Corporal Les Latty, 2/1st Field Company Engineers: 'I wasn't that unhappy getting on the marches because as least we knew all the clues on farmhouses and they'd bunk us in that little yard near the barn and we'd be watching for the chooks coming through'.

Sam Stratton: 'First thing you'd do you'd light a fire. You'd get some wood and you'd sit there; four of us we were hanging together. There's three of them dead now. One bloke, Trevor Munro, he could speak a little bit of French, he'd go round and see if he could get some bread or something or put us on to where the kartoffels (potatoes) were. And there was some-times a chook. By God they were good boys!

'We had a lot of Yanks with us later and they all marched on the road. At night each Yank would throw his blanket down in the barn and he'd reckon no one could share it. They'd each want the full blanket and they'd start pushing and shoving and finally a poor old Yank's lying up in one corner and he says, "Goddam, that's my place. Someone's got my place!" You'd just have to hope the Yanks didn't get in the loft over the top of you. They went to the toilet anywhere. They'd just let her go down in the barn. You'd be laying underneath.'

Alan King: 'You'd lie down at night and you'd hear someone say something about buying and selling. Then about three minutes later – "Whaddya got?" "I got this." They'd be arguing till someone'd say, "Shutup".'

Peter Oates: 'I think the thing that rocked me most about the Yanks was when I got to Italy and had no gear. You'd get a klim tin (milk tin) for a mug and a klim tin to make your billy tea with. So I said to a Yank, "You got any spare klim tins?" And he said, "I'll sell you one". Sell you one! They got 'em from the Red Cross free and they want to sell me one!'

Les Latty: 'I used to feel sorry for the poor fellows, the Yanks. They couldn't scrounge, you know. They'd trip over something to eat, they weren't good at foraging. They'd even trip over potatoes. You'd say to them, "Look, there's potatoes". And they'd say, "Hey, them ain't cooked!"'

Peter Oates: 'There might be a hundred of you all sitting down and somebody finds something. It might be a few spuds or whatever. Before you know where you are, phew! The mob have got them.'

Les Latty: 'Talk about grasshoppers! We weren't bad. I tell you what, we could eat better than a team of those cardiganed old ladies on one of those tourist buses.'

Sam Stratton: 'If everyone could put it down in a film as it was, not the "Hogan's Heroes" rubbish, the real thing as it was, it would be the funniest film in history.'

At Oflag VIIB, Einstatt, Bavaria, some of the Germans asked the returning ex-POWs, 'Do you still hate us?' In the town square another German watched the men for a while, then approached and told them he had been a POW and had been taken over to North Dakota by the Americans. The men talked in broken English, broken German.

In the village Blue Heron found the hut he'd worked in. While Blue was walking around the old haunts, a German leaning over the fence called him: he too had been a prisoner – of the British.

Blue Heron: 'The Germans were really hard up by 1944. The bread had sawdust in it. We use to say we got splinters in our hands loading it on the carts.'

Sam Stratton: 'The Yanks bombed the zoo by mistake and we knew it. Got lots of meat and we couldn't recognise any of it. Me and my mate were carrying the big soup cans into the prison and my big wooden clogs tripped me up, and the soup went everywhere. Men have been killed for less. I think the sight of a horse's eye in the mess on the floor took the men's attention off us.'

At Wolfsberg: 'Nothing left of the old camp, nothing.' Another man says, 'But flowers ought to grow here. The ground is laced with Russian bodies. You'd think flowers would grow.'

Another ex-prisoner: 'We weren't permitted to sing "God Save the King" so we played "There'll always be an England" on our gramophone. For lights out we always played "Good Night Sweetheart".'

Driver Ray Norman (the troops called him Punchy) was an ambulance driver in North Africa. Word got around, 'If you get a hit try and get Punchy to take you in'. When several ambulances were lined up, the wounded would say, 'Which is Punchy's bus?' But Punchy was taken prisoner at Bardia. 'When they got us to Germany I didn't do too bad.'

After an escape attempt, Private Ray Fairhall, Signals 1st Australian Corps, was imprisoned at Markt Pongau in Austria when recaptured. He says now that there is one German guard buried here that he wishes he could dig up and kick. 'He was very hard on prisoners. Escapees would be taken out every morning for exercise (as opposed to just being POWs) and if you looked sideways, if you did anything, he'd give you a great jab with the butt of his rifle.

'One day a Russian was beside me and the German just ran his bayonet through him, killed this Russian and the man dropped to the ground and we went on marching on our exercise, through the almost fairy-tale setting in the Austrian Alps, beautiful firs like Christmas trees all around, Austrian houses clinging to mountain-sides with their little balconies, pretty cows in green fields ... and the Russian dead behind us.'

Doctor Alan King, 2/7th Australian Field Ambulance, who had been 'on the other side of Benghazi' before his unit was shipped to Greece, said: 'We were bombed before we got there, nine men were killed; we had to get equipment off one of the destroyers, theirs. Ours was shot up. There was no air cover at all. We went up the line twice there, that made heavy work for the ambulancemen.

'Then, we had to leave Greece, we were ordered to destroy

everything, to take only a haversack on board the boat. It was terrible to destroy equipment, to slash tyres of a vehicle that had served us so well. We were shot up, most who served on Greece were shot up. I had a complete medical case that the boys had got for me from the Italian army and I wasn't able to take this to Crete.

'Crete was a shambles. We had about forty wounded in a schoolhouse, New Zealanders, Australians, Greeks. The chief New Zealand medical officer arrived there and was captured, with the rest of us. We were captured by very pleasant Austrian troops. They tried to help us in any way they could, then the machine took over. We had nothing to treat the men with, no drugs and few bandages.'

It was 28 May 1941. The doctor could have escaped, but there were many wounded men from two battalions left on the island, much diarrhoea and sickness and he decided that he would stay on Crete and do what he could for them.

Later he and his men were taken back to Greece. 'When we arrived at Salonika it was awful, trying to get transport for the sick blokes, trying to speak German, no food, a lot of shooting going on, sickness, Christ knows what. Awful. Some of our blokes were shot on the wire there. Then the men were piled into cattle-trucks and the Red Cross gave us bread and jam and we were on our way to Stalag VIIIB Lamsdorf, in Silesia, looking like scarecrows. Once there morale was helped by getting Red Cross parcels of clothes and food.'

Konigswartha gaol was for tuberculosis patients, Merchant Marine and British (including Australian) POWs. Alan King was the only British doctor there. He nursed his men in two-tier beds. 'Many died from haemorrhage. At least the Germans gave them a small military funeral, I couldn't complain about them in this way, they showed great respect to our men. The doctor in charge was a reasonably kindly TB specialist but there were no drugs in those days for TB. There were men with collapsed lungs, adhesions, lesions, there was very little meat or protein, everything was bad news for the TB patients. They were given two needles a week, there wasn't much else to be done, except constant care. Those of us who cared for the tubercular men were as hungry as they were. Once being escorted by an interpreter into Dresden, I saw German sausages in a butcher's window. I felt faint. But they were not for me.

'Tens of thousands of Russians were here, it was forty degrees below zero and they were exhausted, shut out in the snow and cold outside the buildings. One day I saw one dying of typhus. Two of my doctors volunteered to treat him and both died of typhus. From our hospital we could see these young men walking round and round locked outside their huts, all terribly ill. No help was available to them. I asked permission to go in to see what I could do. But it was no use. They were all to die.'

These memories are indelibly tattooed on Alan King's memory and on his doctor's heart. A quietly spoken man, he becomes embarrassed when tears pour down his face on to his shirt as he tries to tell of the agony of this huge number of young men, 'left to die or to contract most painful diseases before they eventually succumbed'.

Some of Alan's people had been together since they left Australia for the Middle East, others joined him later. Dr Maurice Blondeau, a TB specialist, had taught the doctors much about surgery on TB patients. (This doctor escaped the year before the end of the war and joined the Resistance and was later decorated. He and his wife, the Mayor of Clichy, have since visited Alan King in Perth on several occasions.) 'Doctors saw an average of ninety-two patients per day here.' (Alan, who was 12 stone at enlistment, weighed 8 stone when released.)

By early 1944 when the war was being brought home to Germany, there were air raids day and night, up to 1000 bombers at a time. 'The Russians were getting close from the other direction and the Germans used us as hostages. They put us staff and our patients on trains and left us at the railway siding overnight in an attempt to stop the planes bombing the big marshalling yards that were necessary to send their troops and supplies forward.

'We were six days on the train to Hohenstein-Ernstahl. We got 1000 or so patients in, frost-bitten airmen who had marched for ten days, Russians with TB, as well as all the ailments of soldiers. We took over chalets and filled them up with patients. It was all higgledy-piggledy. General Patton's Third Army pushed forward fast enough to liberate this camp and he took us in, thank God. We saw the first jeep coming down the road and the officer, from Chicago, said, "How long have you been here?" "Four years." "Perhaps you need this." He pulled out a bottle of brandy. Did I what?'

Alan King was always the working doctor, always one of the men. 'Before evacuation, Americans took us out for the night. It was good.' Then came the organising of the evacuation which was done 'in orderly fashion' until the Australian pilot of an RAAF crew said, 'Where do you want to go?' 'Out!'

'We got twenty men on board, stowed them along the fuselage. Most had got hold of some booty. The men had thought we were capturing a motor bike and sidecar of medical gear before we left Germany, but there were no medical supplies in it, only Italian notes, worthless, but I got a very nice Italian medical case. The men liked that, cheered when they saw me with it.'

It had been a long road back from Suda Bay.

Why does she weep, why should she cry?
Her boy's asleep so far away.
He played his part, that terrible day,
Now he lies asleep in Suda Bay.

An early copy of this song stated: 'Written for the Anzacs, 26 May 1941, as they made a last-ditch stand, a holding action, near Suda Bay, Crete, to assist others to escape. These men were among the last to withdraw.'

Many, perhaps most men criticise their officers' lack of leadership and care. Peter Oates: 'At Greece I was put out by the fact that we surrendered when we weren't beaten. If you take the idea of being beaten – like a boxer – you've got to be physically beaten, knocked out, incapable of fighting on. We weren't like that, we were some 3–4000 fit, well-trained, competent soldiers and we had to surrender to someone we didn't even see. The same on Crete, we were beating them there but were told to surrender. That is inexplicable to ordinary soldiers.

'I don't have much time for the Australian officer corps, they were fairly easy to get along with but they didn't know what they were doing. You ask any ex-POW from Germany or Italy, most wouldn't own them, the moment we were captured they forgot us, abandoned us, every man for himself; we were looked after by our warrant officers and sergeants.

'When we were at Kalamata at the end of the Greek campaign we were told that we had been ordered by the brigadier to surrender. I looked around for him to find out what to do and he'd gone, got away. It was every man for himself. Legally there may be a point, but morally their first consideration is surely to the welfare of their soldiers. In my experience I didn't see that occur, with the exception of Major Brookmore. He was the finest Australian officer I ever met. Most people thought highly of him at Stalag III. He's known as Brookie to all and sundry, a very fine man.

'But as for the others, you began to wonder as a young soldier, has this guy sitting back in an office lost touch with what we were trying to do? The generals would say it was a strategic decision etc., but I don't believe that, not in World War II. There is an angry feeling among a lot of us that we might have done more if we'd been allowed to fight on and that no soldier, certainly no Australian soldier, wanted to be told to put his rifle down.

'On the whole the quality of our NCOs was better than that of our officers. The Australian doesn't need officers so much as other armies do, he's a more caring soldier. Australians cared for their mates much more than the English did. Any fault in the Australian military man is almost entirely the responsibility of leadership.'

Skip

'After fighting in Greece for a couple of days the Germans outflanked us into the mountains', Private Skip Welsh tells. 'We were under constant aerial attack all the way back in retreat as far as Kalamata.' He was one of the men embarked on the *Costa Rica* which was bombed and abandoned after the soldiers were picked off the deck by the destroyer HMS *Defender* and taken to Suda Bay, on Crete. A high-level bomb attack was under way, the harbour was littered with merchant and war ships. 'I can remember the calmness of the British naval commanders, each standing on the bridge of his ship smoking a cigarette, lackadaisical as you like. I was marvellously impressed with their control, their orderliness, the way they carried themselves, their courage.

'We disembarked and were taken to an area between Canea and Retimo and there some effort was made by the commanders to organise a force which would deny the enemy the island. But after some two weeks our 2/6th Battalion was so depleted by men they'd lost in Greece, in particular around the Corinth Canal, that we only had odd riflemen; I was in mortars, we had a base plate and a bipod but no barrel, so we had to find a barrel and then we couldn't find enough ammunition. The result was that when the airborne invasion came we were formed into a composite battalion, the 2/5th and 2/6th and some of the 2/8th.

'We had to do a withdrawal across the island under heavy attack from both the airborne troops and a division of Austrian alpine (mountain) troops and we went right across, over the mountain range 12–13,000 feet high, completely exhausted, until we came to the western village of Spakia and it was there we put up our last withdrawal because we had run out of ammunition, water, food, *sans* everything. The navy was doing its best, it was coming in every morning early and taking men off, but it was under heavy attack itself and lost an enormous number of ships as a result. Finally, Admiral Cunningham decided enough was enough, no more ships would come, so we raised the white flag.

'It was then a process of travel in reverse. We had to march back the way we had come across the mountains of Crete and that took us two days. We were starving by this time and weren't getting any food from the Germans, we were just picking up a few eggs or whatever we could get on our way back through these devastated villages. At that time some of the men decided they would go for the hills; some were successful in getting away, others failed and were picked up by the Germans, a few were killed. The Germans were very brutal with the villagers, anyone found harbouring an Australian or any British troops was instantly machine-gunned and the village burnt to the ground. There were many heroes, particularly among the Cretan villagers, they had marvellous courage.

'We were taken to Skeles prison camp just outside Canea, and were occupied for the next couple of weeks burying our own as well as the German dead. It was easy to find them in the olive trees and grape vines, you became familiar with the smell of the dead. It was then that I decided I was going to have a crack at getting away. The camp was loosely guarded by paratroopers, it was only a makeshift prison, it had barbed wire around but being an experienced infantry man it wasn't hard for me to get away.

'I slipped out one night and made for a beach to the west of Canea. I came upon a little sandy bay and saw a small rowing boat with the oars in it so decided I'd row to Alexandria. I was getting the boat into the water when another Australian turned up. I said "I'm Dudley Welsh" and he said "I'm Titch". He said, "We'd better get out otherwise the tide would stop us getting away", so we got in the boat, got out 4–500 yards and suddenly we realised there were a couple of Messerschmitts coming towards us just over the top of the waves so discretion was the better part of valour and we went over the side. That was the end of that little episode. I didn't see this man Titch again. When I got back to the camp no one had even noticed I'd gone.

'The camp was full of dysentery, there were open latrines, men were very ill; we were on very light rations, whatever we could forage; we were given some German bread and we found some rice but the Germans had taken over all the British and Australian provisions. They were walking around taking bites out of whole pounds of butter, just eating it like that. They thought it was wonderful.

'I had this idea that I'd get away but I'd wait until they got me closer to the Turkish border. They eventually loaded us on to a ship and took us up to Salonika. There we were disembarked and moved to Strathmore prison, the notorious First World War camp for British prisoners. The guard towers were situated to sweep the camp in both directions day and night with searchlights. I found myself with 4400 other prisoners spending most of the day delousing ourselves and turning our trousers inside out. In the evening the bugs came out of the walls and if you struck a light to try to find them a machine gun opened up and the bullets would come flying through the wooden walls so naturally no one used a light unless they absolutely had to. If you wanted a cigarette you'd light one and pass it round. We had to bunk straight down on the floor with whatever we possessed, which was very little.

'I joined up with a group of men who had organised escape parties, and we decided to send out fifteen men at a time in the latrine drains. These drains serviced the two latrine blocks between the block houses. There was a huge manhole between them and by lifting the manhole cover and dropping down, you came on the outlet pipe, approximately 2 feet 6 inches in diameter. It went down under the cookhouse and out into a distant creek outside the limits of the camp. We organised this party and I led the first group of fifteen men into the latrine drain. We progressed hundreds of yards down the drain when I came upon the body of a Cypriot who had been working on aerodrome construction for the British Air Force when he was captured. He wasn't a part of the official escape. Unfortunately he had his army greatcoat on and as a result the refuse and water going down the drain saturated the coat and he got himself stuck. It was impossible to straighten him out as rigor mortis had set in and he'd stiffened up and his body was jammed in the tunnel in such a way that you couldn't shift him. I broke my fingernails trying to pull him away, it was all slimey. I couldn't do any good; then, the chap coming behind me was pressing on, of course he wanted to get out, everyone wanted to get out, nobody believed it was blocked up. I told the chap at the back of me, "Move back". He said, "What's going on, why can't we move forward?" I said, "This fellow's dead and I'm running out of air", and he said he was too. I said, "I'll tell you what I'm going to do if you don't move, I'm going to kick you right in the face, I'm going to smash your nose, I'm going to go beserk". The others were still coming into the drain and as a result what oxygen there was was being depleted and I could feel myself coming out in a cold sweat and my heart was starting to pound and I thought, "Oh my God, I don't want to drown in this". So he passed the message back. We couldn't turn around in the drain, we could only go backwards, crabwise.

'Searchlights were sweeping the area. As each man reached the manhole, he'd raise it only enough to see where the beam of the searchlight was. When one beam passed over there was a period when the whole area was in blackness before they reversed, so he'd climb out, let the flange go down as quietly as he could and run for the barracks building. This was successful until one of the last to get out panicked, and in his haste let the cover fall with a bang which the guard on the tower heard and, sweeping his searchlight down, picked us out. Within minutes they had dogs and guards surrounding the manhole and of course they started firing in all directions; they hit a Cypriot who was out snooping around and he was writhing on the ground screaming. The chap who came out before me, the man I'd been yelling at in the drain was hit in the thigh with a bullet and he slipped on the slime around the sewer entrance and collapsed. I got a bit annoyed and let fly at this German, I said, "You rotten bastard, if I had a gun I'd shoot you". And he called me all sorts of things and as I climbed out got into me with the boots and I got a good hiding and was knocked unconscious.

'The next thing I remember was lying on the floor in the guard house with the rest of the fellows standing against the wall with their hands high, with bayonets stuck in their stomachs. A German officer in a little white jacket (he had evidently been to an officers' mess dinner) was abusing the guards because they had let us out of the drain. He tried to interrogate us but we were too sick to take any notice. I collapsed again on the floor and don't remember anything until I came to in the camp hospital on a stretcher, covered in blood. I had blood coming out of my ears and nose, I must have been pretty close to passing out because of the lack of air in my lungs. There was a red-haired Australian doctor attending to me and he said, "Just lay where you are son". He told me the Germans had taken those who were still conscious down to the cells and left them in the clothes they'd come out of the latrine drain in. He said, "We're going to keep you here as long as possible, there are a few things to fix up and we've got to go over you". Which he did.'

But the red-headed doctor, though he argued the dangerous condition of his patient, couldn't keep him safe. Within a week Skip was taken out of the hospital 'forcibly' and put into the cell occupied by the men who went with him into the latrine drain. 'They were still in the same clothes, so it was pretty rich!' They were then interrogated, one by one, by the SS. 'I was tied to a chair and they tied my thumbs behind my back. They asked me questions and one moment they'd be putting a cigarette in my mouth and the next minute knocking it out again because they got the wrong answers. During that time they broke my jaw, kicked me in the ankles [he still has the scars] and generally made themselves a nuisance. They didn't get any useful information out of me; sometimes I wouldn't tell them anything if I did know, but I didn't know a lot of the things they were asking. I didn't know who organised the thing for instance, but I did know, as did the SS, that there were people out there in the Greek community who were in the underground and would take us in if we escaped and would have put us in a "safe house" situation, but I didn't know names, addresses, etc.

'Anyway, that was the end of that and I was returned into the prison camp yard and after a couple of weeks I decided I was going to do it again. After many days of sitting down and watching everything that was going on in the camp, the movement of guards and of civilians such as Greeks who came in and sold food etc. to the guards, I got on to a scheme. I saw that the men had access to different places and could move around a bit when working parties were sent outside to clean stables out. I noted everything and decided I'd make the third attempt on my own. This way I felt it was my responsibility and I had a better chance of getting away. Here we had no organised escape committees such as were formed later in Germany, so it was entirely up to the person concerned whether he wanted to make an escape or not. Quite a lot had tried it over the wire and it didn't work; others tried it on the trains to Germany, some got away and some didn't. However, with this scheme I had it was necessary to obtain Greek clothes and the only way you could obtain them was from Greek prisoners who were with us, and the price was food; so I saved my precious bread ration and starved myself for three or four days and swapped it for a Greek shirt, and I managed to get hold of a Greek pair of pants because one prisoner was wearing two pairs. I swapped my good Australian army boots for a pair of Greek sandals and put those clothes on underneath my uniform.

'What I worked out was this: each day a group of men assembled at the gate nearest the German horse lines and the Germans methodically counted out thirty men, then another thirty and another and so on until they had sufficient people to do the work they wanted. As a reward for doing this, they gave people in those working parties extra food – a loaf of bread, another mug of lentils or whatever – but if anyone escaped they'd punish the whole thirty by giving them no food when they came back in. So I devised a method by which they were going to count thirty out and thirty would come back. No punishment, no alarm for an escaped prisoner. I would just hang around the edges of the thirty; after they had counted the men out, the Germans were always in a general scramble to get back into the cookhouse or whatever was their normal business for that day, and in that general scramble I got a couple of my mates to make a bit more of a diversion. While they were doing this, thirty men and me went out through the gates. When they brought them back they still counted thirty men, so there was no punishment and they didn't raise the alarm.'

Once out the gate Skip had to rid himself of the prison uniform without being seen by the two guards in the guard tower. He went inside the nearby horse stalls and got a German horse. 'I can still remember its name to this day, it was a huge old mare called Matilde – and I led her out to the big cement water trough about 4 feet high. I pushed Matilde sideways so nobody could see my feet or legs on the other side of her and since she was pretty big she would have blocked out the view from the guard post. The horse had a halter which I tied to one end of the trough and I'd found a piece of rope and tied it to the other end so she couldn't move back the other way. I had to make split-second decisions, get out of the prison clothes, put them under a heap of old straw rubbish and then walk out of the camp, past the guards, singing a little song which was very familiar to the Greeks in those days. I can still feel the barrel of that German machine gun on my back as I went past the guard; he thought I was a Greek who'd come in selling food and he ordered me off, which I was only too pleased to do. I walked down the road and as soon as I got round the corner in among the suburbs I went off like a hare.'

He knew he had to be careful in selecting accommodation as many men who had escaped were recaptured simply because they were obviously Australian or English: most were in uniform and were thereby protected under military law, but Skip was not in military uniform, he was in civilian dress, so could be shot as a spy – the Geneva Convention didn't cover such a man. He had to get into a safe house as quickly as he could, he could not safely roam the streets. 'I reckoned that if I went to a rich area there would be a chance of me being given up; I've found that the more possessions people have the more they want to protect them. On the other hand, in poor areas the people are friendlier and happier, so I chose an area near the Salonika railway station. After walking around for a good two hours, I went up to a big fat Greek lady who was sitting down with two little children in front of a row of cottages and said, "I am an Australian prisoner", and without any further ado, she grabbed me by the arm, heaved me inside the house and slammed me in a room. Of course I got a bit nervy but within a quarter of an hour I was being overwhelmed by Greeks, food and drink were being pressed on me and I was being called a hero – by a Greek who could speak English because he'd been to America; they then decided to move me out of that area into a safe house.

'In this safe house there were four other escaped prisoners, among them Private Wally Strickland of the 21st Battalion, and we stuck together. We were joined by a Scotsman, I won't mention the name or regiment because he was responsible for having that family destroyed, not deliberately, but because he didn't obey the rules we had for survival, not only of ourselves but of these people. The rules were simple enough: we were to carry nothing of the past with us. Enesta Costa and his sister Despinis and his mother and father and little Helen, his younger sister, were the people looking after us in that safe house; they provided us with the food necessary to keep us alive and took us out of that house every day to walk the streets so that if there was a surprise raid we wouldn't be discovered; we came back each evening just before the German night patrols came on. Being Australian, we couldn't tell the difference between a Rumanian, a Bulgarian and a Greek, and, as well, there were Fifth Columnists in Salonika moving around feeding information to the German secret police. They were capturing POWs one after the other by this method, so if you went into a restaurant or cafe and sat down you needed to be with a Greek, someone who could get up if the Germans came at you and offer him a cigarette or whatever to distract him. I had my face stained with juniper berries and I grew a moustache like a Greek and acted like a Greek and I felt like one, but not good enough to fool a Bulgarian or other neighbours, because sooner or later you'd give yourself away.

'Therefore, this strict rule we had was absolutely essential. But, each day, unknown to us, on these excursions this Scotsman took with him a little bible in his pocket. On this particular day he left it in the safe house, in a drawer, and in it was his regimental name and number and the village in Scotland that had given the bible to him. Whilst we were away that day the Germans did that area over and they found nothing in the whole street until they opened that drawer and got the bible. They then simply sat down and waited for us: they knew they had found a safe house. Therefore, we were going to walk right into it. But little Helen pretended to be sick, went into the lavatory and got out the small window, climbed over the stone wall in among the grape vines and got away, the Germans surrounding the street not taking any notice of this child. She knew the way we would come home and her one idea was to warn us. And she did. So we didn't see the Enesta Costa family again. We found out later they were killed. I don't know how that Scotsman felt afterwards; just a tiny bible, that's how life is, it hinges on small things. He had a sentimental attachment to that bible.

'The Greeks were extremely kind to us. It amazed me that people who have everything to lose and nothing to gain could open their arms to us.'

They were now taken to other safe houses and spent most of the day moving around, going to German movie newsreels, sitting behind Germans and 'laughing like hell when they laughed'. They watched the invasion of Russia and the rest of the war news, 'a real treat after the long time of hearing little, or nothing'. They went to the waterfront and took notes of the shipping that was coming in and aircraft activity and the railway station. 'Many times I almost yelled, "Hey Jim!" or something like that, as I'd see friends come down from the prison camp and go into the railway station on their way to Germany.' They raided German army dumps 'to return some of the favours the Greeks had done us', but finally the time came when 'it got a bit too hot for us'. They took off for the hills, into the peninsula running down from the top of Macedonia. They went from village to village; before one guide would hand them to the next and return to his own village, he would go alone to the next village to 'case' it for Germans or suspicious strangers. And so they progressed along the Ayion Oros peninsula with its ancient holy mountain of Athos and dozens of monasteries, painted in pastel colours, some six or seven storeys high, containing hundreds of cells for their hundreds of monks. Rumanians, Greeks, Bulgarians and Russians were there and the escapees had to be wary.

Skip hid in the monastery of Panthakratha. 'The monks were all in the underground (and so were the Greek policemen as were the villagers with the exception of the few that the Germans had in their pay, particularly the Bulgarians and Turks who had always hated the Greeks). In the monasteries there was an ancient rule applied to travellers. No female was allowed in these monasteries – no female donkey, dog or whatever – just males, so we were okay! They also have an ancient custom that if a traveller hammered on those huge doors they opened the slot and your guide would say, "This is the one", and they'd open the door and you'd go in, alone, for the guide would return to his home. They'd take you through the large hall, up to a small whitewashed cell facing out across the Aegean, maybe four to five storeys up, a marvellous view. Then a priest would come and wash your feet because that's what Jesus did for the wayfarer. You were invited to join them in the main hall in the evening for the main meal, during which they'd chant their prayers – got a little bit tedious as anyone who's ever been to a Greek religious ceremony could tell you – you had a plain meal of whatever they'd grown themselves, olives, walnuts, fish, sardines, etc.

You were made very welcome. Nothing was said about you, you were just there.

'The next morning when you got up you were given a loaf of bread and were invited to come again the next night, but they would prefer that you kept moving. Sometimes we marched 13 miles a day over this very stony peninsula, sometimes a thousand feet or so up to a monastery. Soon my feet were busted out; you couldn't even get a donkey over some of these places. The early Persian armies even cut a staircase up there where they crossed to invade Thessaly and Athens, through Macedonia. And I marched over every one of those 1000 steps.

'After doing this for a week we found a hermit, Father Savvas who lived in a cave and prayed all day. He had previously been a famous brigand until he "saw the light" and became a monk, but he had been such a bad character that he decided he would rather spend his time alone. He'd go to the monastery every so often and get enough supplies to keep him alive. He had a fairly good boat and agreed to row us to Imros Island, 90 miles away.

'Our supplies were a couple of loaves of bread and a kerosene tin of fresh water and some olives.' The Germans had announced a curfew in Greece, Greek fishermen were permitted to go to sea to fish but must return before darkness when the curfew began each night. This meant that if the escapees could not reach safety in daylight the German aircraft in the area would 'shoot us to pieces'.

'The first day we took off from Panthakratha we kept rowing but when the tide turned we had no option but to row back to where we set off from, with hands covered in blisters. There was a New Zealander, a Yugoslav (never saw them again afterwards), myself, Father and another Australian. The Father was about 6 feet 6 inches and he didn't row at all, he just told his rosary beads and said his prayers all day, with his feet on the tiller, and I can tell you they smelt! On our second attempt the same thing happened as before, the tide turned; we were seasick, feeling unreal as we rowed back but we were determined and so was Father Savvas. On our next attempt a submarine periscope came up, went right around us in a 360-degree circle and evidently decided we weren't worth wasting a torpedo on and the periscope went down and disappeared. It made us work all the harder on the oars. After rowing for thirty-six hours, having the tide and wind with us, we finished up on Imros Island, just off the Dardanelles.

'We got out of the boat and the Father ignored us and hoisted a little sail! He was sailing back to his cave! Maybe he had wanted us rowers to do it the hard way.

'As we landed on the beach at Imros we heard popping noises, I thought they sounded familiar, then realised, "My God, they're bloody bullets!" The Greeks and Turks don't like each other much, even to this day, and they thought we were Greek civilians coming on their island, so they were having a go at us. We didn't waste any time doing a dash up into the rocks. One of the guys had a piece of white stuff, he put it up, they came down and took us prisoners. When they found we were Australians etc., they couldn't have treated us better. We were taken to a Turkish village, put into a schoolhouse and the next thing a Turk arrived to ask us what we would like. Food! So the villagers all got together and made things. Then we all got sick, we were half starved and this food was too rich for us. We finished up inside the Dardanelles in a hospital in Canakkale.

'During the time we were in the hospital recovering we were most kindly treated by the Turks, they even brought us a box of Turkish Delight one day – and we made complete pigs of ourselves. Then they took us to see Gallipoli. We went across and stood on the beaches where the Anzacs had gone up the cliffs; I walked up to Lone Pine where my father had been wounded in 1915. [He had been killed the following year in France and was buried there.] When we got better we were moved from Canakkale to Konya in central Turkey. By this time we had British emergency passports and were wearing civilian clothes because the Turks were neutral in this war.'

In early November they crossed the Turkish/Syrian border. 'We saw a familiar old slouch hat on the border post, the diggers were brewing up a cuppa. It was the 18th Brigade. Someone said, "Oh my God, it's him!" And someone else said, "Well, wouldn't you know it, the bugger was always on the move!"'

Kriegsgefangener

'The only difference between what I was doing and what a juvenile delinquent does these days is that the King gave you medals for it.'

Peter Oates, Multiple Escaper

THE YEARS OF CAPTIVITY of Australians taken prisoner by the Germans in World War II have been overshadowed by the fate of those who later were victims of the Japanese. Yet the lives of these kriegsgefangeners, cut off from the world as they knew it, were scarcely less traumatic. Some had been prisoners from early in the war: all had fought hard battles in the Middle East, Greece and Crete, some at sea and others in the air, before they were captured. The escapes and escape attempts by some of these prisoners were made with all the daring and danger of any made before or after this war.

Signalman Peter Oates, a dedicated escaper, had been working in the purser's office on the Merchant Navy ship *Oranje* before he joined 1st Australian Corps Signals in 1940. He was then aged 17 and by 1941 was a prisoner of war. 'Most men in the German prison camps were fortunate in the sense that they were with an army that related their treatment of prisoners to that which was being accorded to their own men. (That is, of course, as opposed to what is "good" treatment. We were, after all, prisoners and treated as such.)

'If you capture a thousand prisoners of war in a far-distant place (and we were caught in Crete, many days travel from Germany), there are several things that have to be done. You've got to get the prisoners under control; the best way to do it is to shoot them, and that is an option frequently exercised by some captors, or you can lower their resistance and morale, and a sure way to do this is to cut their food. By the time you get people in a situation where they are fairly debilitated, all they're interested in is survival and as a consequence become docile, don't resist or attempt escape.

'Then there is the situation where you have to cart these people long distances and by the most convenient practical means; but there is a limit available to transport in any country, particularly in time of war.

'So they pack prisoners as tight as they can into cattle-trucks and get them to their destinations as quickly as the congested traffic will allow. When they arrive there are probably no facilities to govern them – who could possibly have anticipated the number of prisoners Germany was going to take between 1940 and 1942?

'In those two years the German army claimed to have captured almost 10 million prisoners-of-war, giving the country immense problems, particularly when thrust on to an economy which was strictly geared for all-out war for which everybody was rationed to the maximum point. Of course there are government policy issues involved. In the eyes of that government Russian prisoners were totally expendable; so the treatment varied between those two extremes.

'The better end of the scale of treatment started five upwards for us "British" and the treatment of Russians remained always at zero. So, when men came back home after the war and said they were not too badly treated it was a purely relative term.

'If we say we were well-treated, it is because we cast our mind back to the Russians. It is not possible to adequately describe the bestial treatment the Russians got. There are literally thousands of mass graves all over Germany (and the countries Germany overran) in which Russian corpses rotted with quick-lime after surviving for a couple of years as breathing and pain-filled corpses.

'Probably the single biggest thing the Germans did for men of the British Empire was to allow us to keep our identity. We dressed correctly in army uniform. (The French had to run about the place with a great big rubber stamp on their back, "KGF": Kriegsgefangener.)

'And that did an enormous amount for identity, dignity and morale. We were soldiers, not criminals, or any kind of lower orders and in fact the very strictures that the Germans sometimes imposed upon us was, in a way, like a modicum of respect. They said of us, "If you turn your eye away from them for two minutes, half of them are gone".'

Peter Oates wasn't with his unit for long.

'When I got to the Middle East, as an indication of my age I promptly got measles and was sent to hospital. When I recovered I chased the unit around Africa and finally caught them in Greece. Then we promptly evacuated the place even though there were still troops coming in. I did my best to be a good soldier and got down to Kalamata ... from then on it was unbelievable. They left. I understand a despatch rider was sent round to find several hundred men and tell them of the evacuation, but they missed many. What an inefficient way to evacuate an army. There wasn't even a rearguard. There was nobody there to pick up the bits. The British simply surrendered. The Germans had threatened that if we didn't surrender they would bomb the place to pieces. Kalamata should have been evacuated earlier and I couldn't understand why we didn't put up a fight for it, so that if the navy did try to come in at least we were holding the line while being evacuated. But nothing like that happened. When the navy did come in, for the last time, they had to buzz off smartly because the place was already in German hands. We should have stood fast. That's what fighting troops are about. If we'd held the perimeter maybe we would have got a lot of people off there and maybe we'd have gone out of the place with a degree of honour, because there's no honour in running away.

'I was in the height of the fight when we got a prisoner of war and I was told to take him off. But he and I got to the beach just as the last boats went out. I got his handcuffs off, and we camped the night together. Next day the Germans arrived, I became a prisoner of war and the ex-prisoner produced a couple of loaves of bread, margarine and a few other bits and pieces, and shook me by the hand and went back to his unit. Next day we Australian prisoners were to set off to the Peloponnesian peninsula, to Corinth.

'I was at the very end of the column, going through the town of Kalamata. Greek women were running forward handing the boys food, the men kept away but Greek females are absolutely magnificent. I saw an open door. There's a long corridor, a couple of rooms off the corridor, and a kitchen at the bottom. I was on the flank of this march, and there was no guard. I went straight for the door, thundered down the hall (you can imagine in army boots) and straight across the back of the day-bed, a sort of couch. There was an old lady, grey hair in a bun, black frock, and she sees one digger go past her, swish! boing! About four seconds later another bloke goes swish! bang! And then another. And the old girl didn't change expression. She turned very carefully on her old legs, walked slowly up the corridor and locked the door that led to the street. Then she went back to the kitchen. She didn't say a single word.

'We all sat there for a minute, waiting for a bloody bunch of Krauts to come belting down, but there was nothing. About half an hour went by and there were Greeks peering around the curtains and congregating in the kitchen. The old lady provided coffee, that dreadful grainy stuff, and a thick slice of brown bread and the three of us gave her a kiss and over the back fence we went. Swish! And up the hill.

'We had no direction. We kept going until we were clear of the town, out into the scrub; we were all rather surprised that there appeared to be no pursuit. Quite obviously the Germans hadn't seen us go, and they hadn't done any counting, their few troops were too busy getting all of us out of the place and up to the railway station.

'So we walked what we hoped was south. You don't know where you're going and you've got no plan. And you don't know where *they* are either. We bumped into a bunch of people in the mountains under the command of an officer, a few Kiwis and Aussies among them. They invited us to join them. "You! Over there!" That sort of invitation. They informed us that they were heading for the coast.

'We three huddled together and decided that a very large group like this was worth the Germans sending a navy patrol after us so we went off without them. We subsisted by begging. It's not a very dignified way of going about. We went from house to house. One of us would take the left flank of the house and one the right in case anyone tried to shoot off and tell the Germans we were around. The third guy would go up and beg. Once, when a fellow dashed out as soon as we arrived, my friend grabbed him and threw him back in the room.

'Then we found a convent. I knew from history books that if you said, "I'm a fugitive can I please be given sanctuary?" they'd give you a feed, and a place to bed and wash. One thing I couldn't understand was why everybody in the place shunned us like the bloody plague and why we were locked away on one side. The mother superior saw us when we arrived and saw us when we left. We only saw one other old duck we thought was detailed off to see that we didn't run amok. I was very naive and patriotic at the time. I thanked the mother superior and told her that she could take great satisfaction for helping three British soldiers. Then she told me she was a German. I have always had a great deal of respect for the Catholic church since that time.

'We three were arguing all the time about which way to go. We never had a consensus of more than one at any given time. It was all very unmilitary. We were astonished when we were contacted by a Greek who said he represented the Royal Navy in the south of Greece, a sort of shipping agent for the King of England.

'He gave us a letter, a single piece of Admiralty notepaper with his photograph stuck to it with glue, and a general statement that the bearer was an agent of the Royal Navy and that His Majesty's Forces should assist him. Bassett, my mate (Trooper George Bassett, Queen's Own 4th Hussars), muttered that it was a strange type of bloody letter. He wanted to kill him, to make sure that we at least got one of the King's enemies before we left the scene. And we'd say things like, "Well, you know, there's no real evidence that he *is* one of the King's enemies. He *has* got a letter".

'We were given what looked like a couple of kid's rockets and told to go to a certain piece of coast not far away at a set time and send up the first one. We did, then: Foosh! It was guaranteed to bring the whole Royal Navy to our aid. Bassett nearly had a breakdown, because every bloody German this side of the border had seen that rocket. To our surprise a light came on out on the breakers. We had a light you'd use on a push-bike and we diligently put this on, and the boat came towards us. A distinct English voice said, "Stay where you are". So we stood there in this rather ridiculous position by the boat, which was manned by a couple of matelots and a couple of rather bloodthirsty-looking Royal Marines who were armed to the teeth. We were dragged aboard and instead of the warm, fraternal greetings we were expecting, somebody said, "Sit down, shut up and don't say a bloody word". After an interminable period, we were picked up by HMAS *Stuart*.

'We landed in Crete on the evening of 19 May 1941 and the Germans came next morning. I don't think the British wanted to keep Crete; they thought it was too much of a problem. I was now attached to the 2/1st Battalion, we were actually winning, and the other battalions won theirs. We only got beaten by a technical knockout: our leader told us to surrender.

'Then it was back to Greece. Conditions were as bad there ... Marilyn Monroe could have walked through Salonika naked and no one would have noticed. We were interested only in survival.

'Then we were shipped to Germany on trains, packed seventy odd to a cattle-truck, you can imagine sightseeing through scenic Yugoslavia with the floor of your carriage totally awash with excrement and blood. For five days a bloke was sawing away at the cattle-truck window with a pocket knife. It was a small opening and he was enlarging this and worked bloody hard carving through the thick timber to allow his under-nourished body through it. "No, you can't help", he answered when I offered. So I went to my 3-square inches of wagon and sort of contemplated: "Nobody really owns that hole. Therefore I have a right to go out the hole if I wish to". So when he went I went after him. The train was moving much quicker than I'd anticipated and I clung to the outside of one of this string of cattle-trucks as it moved along. I jumped, rolled a bit and came to a stop on a patch of gravel. There was a stream and I washed myself and my uniform, got all the muck off, and laid it out on the rocks in the middle of enemy Croatia, then, naked as a newborn bloody babe, I waited for my clothes to dry.

'I went from village to village and in about nine weeks covered an incredible amount of territory and was down near Macedonia, heading for Turkey. All of that was absolutely no credit to me whatsoever: peasant to peasant they sent me. I finally had to make a piece of ground under my own steam without any accompanying loyal peasants. I felt quite confident: I was dressed in all sorts of hand-me-downs, the weirdest-looking cloth cap and a suit that looked as though it had been bought in Myers about 3000 years ago and had deteriorated steadily ever since. I came to a bridge that was guarded by three soldiers. I looked at them very carefully: they were something I'd never seen before, but around the cap was a red band. "Russians!" They were on our side! So I greeted them like long-lost cousins. It turned out they were bloody Bulgarians. They weren't a bit friendly and I finished up in a village boob which had apparently been used to store pigs before I arrived, it was filthy and full of vermin. God I stank! It was made of rough stone and had iron bars on the windows, and a big wooden door.

'The second night I peered through the bars and an officer was walking past. "Hoy! You!" So he stopped and peered at me and said, "Vas?" And I said, "I'm one of your prisoners. Would you mind getting me out of here, please?" He came and peered in this place, had me taken to the village pump and allowed to wash and clean up a bit, then had food brought to me and put me on a train for Wolfsberg [a POW camp].

'One very hot day I was sick of standing about . . . far away there were more pleasant places . . . and there was not a soul in sight.' So off he went. 'There I was, out in the middle of Austria, not a clue how to get home or even back to camp. I was wandering through paddocks, totally lost, and I came across a young Luftwaffe airman and he didn't seem terribly surprised to find an Australian soldier wandering around in a paddock. I said to him, "I'm a prisoner of war. I think you'd better turn me in". "No", he said, "I'm on leave". We talked in pidgin-Deutsch. He had a date with a girl and as far as he was concerned I could wander around Germany for the rest of my life, but he wasn't going to be involved. I insisted. I pointed out to him that it was his duty as a German soldier to get me to my dinner. Well, the two of us marched up to the camp, this bit of a kid from the Luftwaffe and me – we were probably the same age.

'I was charged with escaping, which I suppose was techni-cally correct and was put into the boob. The guard did lots of shouting – Germans are completely incapable of conducting a normal conversation without shouting. A couple of days later I was sent back to Stalag for punishment – 21 days, the usual . . . but I only got fourteen days because the bloke in charge of punishment said, "Well, this one hardly counts as an escape". But I was put in what was called the disciplinaires' hut, which was where the incorrigibles were kept.

'I got quite good at getting out of camps but I wasn't sure what I was going to do when I got out. The scale of this started to add up a bit. Shortly after this there was an occasion when two other blokes, Wood and Squires, one an Australian and the other English, came to me because of my tremendous expertise in the area of escapologising! They decided to appoint me leader of an expedition that was to leave Austria and head for the Vatican City. The nearest neutral territory was Switzerland but the border was very closely watched and the Swiss guards' task was to physically prevent you getting into Switzerland.

'I planned a route carefully from the camp to the Vatican. I hadn't taken the Alps into consideration. So we stumbled on these mountains, 16,000 feet high, walked for hours and the slope got steeper and steeper and we got to a place where we were literally wading through the snow waist deep when we saw a notice which in effect said, "Artillery range". We got out of that and found a barn so went in and got a fire going and brought out the Oxo cubes. We tried to get our feet warm. We were very sore, I had frostbite. A farmhand saw us and the next thing we knew the fuzz are all over the place so we got out of the barn and were avoiding the police when I saw a church. Sanctuary! Ridiculous. The police car pulled up outside and here's three thoroughly disorganised, disoriented, tired, hungry and cold prisoners of war. We looked outside and the bloody place was ringed by soldiers. "Come out with your hands up", so out we came.

'We were being frogmarched to town by the local police sergeant when we saw this bloke standing on the footpath with a great smile, giving us the thumbs up. We were locked in an old police cell, the bars were very rusty and this bloke came along and had us out of there in about five seconds flat. So we thanked him and went on our way. The following night we were going through a small town and were spotted by the police and chased into a back alley and were promptly taken prisoner again.

'Once I was in solitary on bread and water with one hour a day out in the small yard. The gaol was guarded by German paratroopers who had served on Crete. And I had been on Crete. So when my 20th birthday came round, they got some booze and came down to the cells and we all had a party. The Jerries are pure professionals, if you escape you take your chance of being punished and that's what it amounts to. And you knew that. No hard feelings. So we had a party. I remember the officer came round next morning and I was still talking shorthand, and he said, "He's drunk". They tried to work out where we got the booze from but no one was saying.'

Peter had no contact with the German people during his

escape attempts. 'No, kept away from them as much as possible. If your German wasn't good enough you'd be picked up immediately. The Germans weren't in any way pro-enemy. I often hear since the war about an "underground" Germany. I never saw any signs of it. They were all pretty solid with the Führer as far as I could see.

'Almost every camp had an escape committee. You should have permission from them to go. But it depended on what kind of camp. If it was a working camp, or in an area where there was less formal discipline on the British side, you'd have a situation where you'd please yourself a bit. But if you were in a camp like 383, you'd front the escape committee. Occasionally, by error, a few lance-corporals would be sent up to Stalag 383. (NCOs didn't have to work.) Once I swapped jackets with a bloke who was being sent back to a work camp; I got away with it for two days before they tumbled to me and threw me into the boob.'

Waldenstein

The Australian, New Zealand and United Kingdom troops who had become prisoners of the Germans after the battles of North Africa, Greece and Crete arrived in the Reich during the period June/July 1941. About a third were sent on to Germany proper, whilst the other two-thirds were divided between stalags at Wolfsberg in Carinthia, and in Marburg in Croatia. Both stalags already had some hundreds of thousands of prisoners from all the occupied countries of Europe on strength, a figure soon to be swelled by tens of thousands of Russians. Consequently, Australians were a comparatively small group.

In August 1941 British Red Cross parcels began to flow through Switzerland and with the nourishing food the starving men recovered in an amazingly short time. To cap it all off, new (British) uniforms, great coats, socks, underwear, soap and toothbrushes arrived, and through the magic of the Red

Cross, starving scarecrows were turned into well-dressed, healthy soldiers.

Peter Oates, the dedicated escaper, saw it happen. 'Once the men were able to lift their collective minds above the needs of their stomachs, and once the pride was back, they were able to consider the world around them, and it soon became obvious that the Germans, the local civilians, the foreign prisoners, and even the Americans who were not yet in the war, all thought that the British Empire countries were finished. It was only a matter of months, weeks even, before we would be "compelled to accept terms from Hitler". To combat this opinion, and to help maintain morale, Allied prisoners began to adopt practices that were calculated to irritate and annoy the Germans: pinpricks like non-cooperation, deliberate insolence, a little sabotage. In a limited number this general behaviour led to escaping, not necessarily escaping to reach a neutral country, at that stage of the game that was too much to expect, but rather escaping as a tactic to make the Germans work at keeping them prisoner, to cost them money and resources, to make them deploy additional troops.

'At this time the Germans had not taken the idea of prisoners escaping very seriously, they took the view that there was nowhere for a prisoner to escape to. If a Russian escaped, they shot him. If a European prisoner escaped and got home to his German-occupied country, his local police simply sent him back. When the British peoples started to escape, the Germans were rather amused. Only these people, they thought, would turn escaping into some kind of sport, and they were rather tolerant with the first few escapers. But when the few turned into dozens, and the dozens turned into hundreds, the German army realised they had a first-class problem on their hands.'

By the end of 1941, only four months after the first Red Cross parcels arrived, British escaping had reached epidemic proportions; whereas five cells in the local lock-up had been adequate to cope with the disciplinary needs of the several hundred thousand foreign prisoners, there were now around

250 British prisoners waiting to serve the statutory twenty-one days in solitary confinement with bread and water, which was the punishment for escaping laid down by the Geneva Convention. To cope with this the Germans built a modern fifty-cell prison block, and allocated a special barracks holding 200 prisoners awaiting punishment. But prisoners for punishment still arrived faster than the Germans could accommodate them, and the answer to that problem was seen to be a grim, 800-year-old castle named Waldenstein, situated high on the old pass called the Packsattel, 16 miles north of Wolfsberg.

Waldenstein Castle had been selected for several reasons; with only one entrance it was easily guarded. The walls were between 6 and 12 feet thick, the prisoner accommodation could be patrolled by sentries on three sides, the fourth side was a sheer drop of about 200 feet, all the prisoner accommodation windows were caged by 1-inch steel bars. Nearby there was a stone quarry where it was intended that the men would be worked to the point of punishment. The plan behind this was to keep the men in these conditions until they were prepared to sign an undertaking never to escape again.

In the first group to be sent to Waldenstein were forty-six men: five New Zealanders, ten Australians and thirty-one assorted English, Irish, Scots and Welshmen.

Peter Oates remembers arriving at Waldenstein. 'It looked like a scene from a bad movie. The huge gates leading into the courtyard were wide open, on each side was a sentry box, painted in the German colours. Standing in front of each box was a German soldier in full battle order. We crossed the courtyard, which was covered in lichen and moss, past a small baroque chapel, stables, and storage rooms and newly installed prison cages on the ground floor, past two more guards, up a flight of circular stone steps to the guard room. At the guard room our name was checked against our photographs, then we were subjected to a thorough search of our person and baggage before being marched in file to the gatehouse where we were ordered to remove our trousers and boots, and hang them on pegs which had our name on them. Our gear was again searched to see if we were secreting spare trousers or footwear, after which we were dismissed to our quarters.

'There were six metal wash basins, the total facilities provided for forty-six men with which to bathe, shave, do our laundry and wash our mess gear. Leading from this room was the lavatory, which consisted of one seat over a chute on the outside of the castle wall, which had been in use for at least 800 years (and smelled like it too).

'The night we arrived the castle held its first camp meeting and elected the first camp leader, who in turn appointed the castle cook, a Private Charlie Westwood, and cook's off-sider (me).' The discussion then turned to the future, and the Germans' intentions towards using the castle as a deterrent to escaping. It was agreed that the castle appeared escape-proof and therefore the only course of action would be passive resistance in the form of a general strike from start of work the following day. The argument the camp would put forward to the Germans was that detention in Waldenstein was illegal, in that the men had already been punished for any escaping they may have done and that to continue punishment by confinement under the conditions there was contrary to the Geneva Convention. 'The only other matter before the meeting was the castle's official name "Sonder Kommando Waldenstein", which the men refused to use. Someone suggested "104 Mobile Laundry and Bath Company" in honour of the speed with which one had to grapple with the castle's bathing and laundry facilities. This suggestion was agreed to with great hilarity and Waldenstein's inmates always referred to themselves by that name whilst I was there.

'The next morning the cook, Charlie Westwood, and I reported to the cook house, and the men departed for work in a fairly orderly fashion escorted by seven or eight guards. About 11.30 a.m. we heard a tremendous commotion and looking out we saw the men coming into the courtyard surrounded and out-numbered by German alpine troops who were armed to the teeth. There was much shouting and screaming going on before the men were marched to their quarters and locked in. At first Charlie and I were not allowed out of the cook house, so we watched the Germans rushing about shouting at each other. Apparently, when the men arrived at the work site they had sat down and informed the civilian supervisor that they considered their presence at Waldenstein as a contravention of the Geneva Convention and as a consequence they could not do any work. The supervisor screamed at the guards to use force to get the men to work and the guards got a little too free with their rifles and bayonets, with the result that a general free-for-all ensued and the guards were disarmed. Unfortunately, Jerry had rather thought our chaps may prove to be a little troublesome and had taken the precaution of having troops handy, and these fellows quickly rounded up our lot and marched them back to the castle.

'A phone call brought two German officers who told the men they could not possibly win a confrontation with the German army, but if they would return to work the following day the officers, on their part, would overlook the events of the morning. The camp leader thanked the officers but declined to accept on the grounds that to do so would contravene the Geneva Convention. They were warned that if they failed to return to work they would be court-martialled and sentenced under German military law, which included the death penalty for mutiny in wartime. The men refused to be swayed by threats and the senior German officer formally charged the whole group with mutiny.

'We were marched out of the castle and back to Wolfsberg under heavy escort. Six weeks later, the court martial was convened, the court comprising a colonel, two lieutenant colonels and two majors. Two German captains acted as prosecuting and defending officers and the Senior British Officer was also present in court. The boys thought they were being railroaded, and as a consequence played up in court which did nothing to please the old colonel and this showed up when the verdict was handed down. Forty-three were found guilty, with sentences ranging from life imprisonment to ten years at the military prison in

Graudenz. Three were found not guilty and were discharged: a Kiwi medical orderly named Bruce Grainger, who had continued to work as a medical orderly, Charlie Westwood and myself, who had been working in the kitchen.

'I never again saw any of the men found guilty. I was told that two of them, both Australians, managed to escape from the German military prison and by pretending to be Canadians from the Dieppe raid managed to submerge into normal prison camp life. But of the others, from what I have been told not a lot made it to the end of the war.

'After the trial, poor little Charlie Westwood became very depressed, he felt somehow that by being found not guilty, and escaping punishment, he had let down his mates; he kept saying that he should be with them. He was ordered to report to the gate with his gear to return to Waldenstein. When he got to the gate he refused to go in and he refused to work. The Jerry in charge of the gate tried to reason with him, but to no avail, and Charlie was charged, found guilty and sentenced to three years. In nine months he was dead.

'I arrived back at Waldenstein a few days after Charlie's one-man mutiny, there was a new group there, thirty-six men in all: eight Australians, two Kiwis and twenty-six assorted Brits. The work place had changed, the quarry was no longer used, the men were supposedly employed on repairing a country road, but most of the time they just stood and talked whilst leaning on a shovel. They were not going to get caught on this mutiny bit, but they came as close to doing nothing as was physically possible.

'Shortly after I arrived back, the camp leader took me aside and told me that on the following Saturday an escape was on. The camp had been divided into two teams, a staff team which would run the escape, and the escape team which comprised the rest of the camp. If I wanted to go I would have to be the last man out, number 24, as the other twenty-three positions had already been decided by lot. I told him that I didn't have much in the way of escape gear, and probably wouldn't last more than two or three days, but "yes, please".

'On the Saturday afternoon, the Kiwi padre Captain John Ledgerwood came up to the castle from stalag [the general prison camp]. He came for two reasons, to bring the Senior British Officer's permission for the escape to proceed, and to give Holy Communion to those in need of it. We had all been a bit worried, the SBO had not been very keen on the escape, he was a believer in the escape-proof theory, and had been worried that he would have a blood-bath on his hands if he allowed a mass escape to go out. It had taken the camp leader two trips to stalag to convince him that it was a goer. During the afternoon Captain Ledgerwood took several photographs including one of the twenty-four man escape team. Later, every man in the camp turned up for Holy Communion, and although some joked about doing anything for a free drink it was a pretty fair indicator how people felt that day.

'The key to the success of the escape that night depended on our camp leader's reading of the German garrison. He believed that the Germans were convinced that once we were locked away for the week-end we could not get out. He was right. The camp commandant, a sergeant major, shot off into the local village on Saturday nights, and the two sergeants took advantage of this and usually spent Saturday nights at the local pub, and were seldom home before midnight. This left two guard details, each consisting of a corporal, and nine men. One corporal was a right little bastard, and his blokes were generally on the ball. The other fellow was a bit on the lazy side, and could be relied upon never to leave the fire in the guard house after 8 p.m. Our camp leader had acquired a copy of the guard roster, and he picked the night for the escape when corporal Lazy's detail was on duty, and when a particular soldier, who was noted for his fondness for the odd pot and the odd chat, was rostered for the cat-walk beat. Hopefully, the cat-walk sentry would spend most of his time chatting with his off-duty mates, and the two sentries out front, being unsupervised, would spend most of theirs chatting to each other.'

Just after 10 p.m., the staff team commenced operations,

they posted sentries on the windows overlooking the cat-walk to monitor the guard, and true to form he spent most of his time talking to his mates; then the team started on door no. 1, an ordinary wooden door with panels at the top and bottom held in place by 1-inch beading. This door had an ordinary old-fashioned lock. On the outside of the door there were two 2-inch by 1/2-inch steel bars running horizontally to prevent anyone getting through the door, as well, there was a 3-inch steel slide bolted to the door, and running into a 3-inch by 2-inch mortice slot in the door-frame. 'With the flat end of a pickhead made red hot in our small stove, the staff team removed the beading from the bottom door panel, then removed the panel. One of them slipped his arm through the two steel bars and pulled the steel slide just clear of its slot. The bottom panel was then replaced and held in position by wooden matchsticks. One of the staff team, who was something of a locksmith, then unlocked the ordinary lock, and the door was open.

'The locksmith doubled across the gatehouse door to door no. 2, which was only secured by an ordinary lock, and picked it. Then six men from the staff team doubled across the gate-house, and through door no. 2, two men moving to the front windows of rooms 1 and 2, to monitor the guards at the front of the castle. One moved to the back window of room no. 2 with a green cellophane covered torch, to act as escape control, another to door no. 4 to act as a listening sentry. Two men, together with the locksmith, moved to the window in room no. 4, and, on the green light, lowered one man down the castle wall, using 60 feet of plaited string made into a rope. This man pulled back the steel slide on the outside of door no. 3, the locksmith went down the stairs to the inside of door no. 3, and let the man in. The rope was hauled up and now every door between the prison accommodation and the outside was open.

'The staff team, acting as marshals, moved the escape team by lot number. Wearing rope-soled espadrilles they went through door no. 1 where they picked up their trousers and boots, covering the empty space with their greatcoats, then through door no. 2, and into room no. 3 where they completed dressing, but leaving their espadrilles on and carrying their boots tied around their necks. Down the staircase to door no. 3, then on the green signal down the outside steps and away.

'As soon as the last man was gone, one of the staff team stepped outside door no. 3 and pushed home the steel slide, and was pulled up the castle wall. The staff team then returned to the prison accommodation, the locksmith locking doors nos 3, 2, and 1 as he went. The bottom panel was replaced, and previously prepared beading glued into position. All incriminating evidence was gathered and dumped down the lavatory chute. The biggest mass escape from a German high security camp had just taken place in slightly less than two hours.'

The following morning the staff team who remained in the castle 'watched Jerry going berserk' when the Germans finally had to accept that twenty-four men of the camp strength had vanished. Army officers arrived, then the civilian police; finally the Gestapo who questioned everyone. Eventually, the German commandant and all his guards were marched off under arrest, and were replaced.

Peter Oates says, 'Of the twenty-three other escapees, I only ever saw five again. I don't know what happened to the other eighteen, but they certainly did not come back to Waldenstein in my time. Of the others, I saw three in the stalag cell block at Wolfsberg, but they did not arrive at Waldenstein over the next couple of months that I was there. Driver Jock Dreever, Royal Army Service Corps, and Leo "Jesse" James, New Zealand Expeditionary Force, turned up at Waldenstein a couple of weeks after I did, but as to the rest, well, God knows Jerry can be a vindictive bastard.

'In my little effort I was right that I would last only two or three days, I was picked up near the Hungarian border whilst attempting to steal a bicycle.' After ten days solitary Peter was taken to Vienna where he was put in a cellar. For three days no one came near him. 'I was visited then by two German generals who at first didn't say anything, they just looked at

me, then one said "How old are you?" I told him and he
nodded, then gave me some cigarettes and they both left. Next
day I was returned to stalag, and after the mandatory cells,
back to Waldenstein.

'Most of the original staff team were still at the castle, and of
course there were some twenty-odd newcomers. They were different to the old lot, they were quieter, not as much bounce,
maybe not so arrogant. All they wanted to do was get out of
Waldenstein.

'Down the road, just outside the village, Jerry had established a new working camp and it sure was different. There
were nice lawns around the barracks, curtains on the windows,
no bars, proper beds (not bunks) and sheets, pillowslips and
real blankets. There were rugs on the floor. In the mess there
were tables and chairs, cutlery, china plates and decent food,
a bar which sold real beer, even women available, Russian
female prisoners who would sell their soul, and pretty much
anything else for a bar of real soap. The work was said to be
not half bad, all one had to do was supervise Russian captive
labour and sign a bit of paper promising not to escape from
the nice Germans again.

'One day, a new Jerry came into Waldenstein asking for
volunteers for this paradise down the road. Quite obviously
he was not aware of my criminal past because when I accepted
his offer he accepted me. Of course I wasn't going to make
any promises, or sign anything, but a few days in paradise until
they caught up with me wasn't to be sniffed at. Off I went and
the camp was just like they said. Everyone was very nice, I was
shown my nice bed, my place in the mess room, I was taken
out and shown the work place, and the labour force, then the
nice German took me into the bar and bought me a beer. I
had just put the glass to my lips when the German camp commandant from Waldenstein arrived. He smiled happily around
the assembled suckers and then saw me, and bloody near blew
a gasket. Shouting "Gangster", "Terrorist", and "Schwindler",
or something like that, he had me out of the place in about
five seconds flat, and back to the castle. It was the only time

I ever got the sack without even starting the job.

'For the next couple of months I behaved myself. Mostly because I wasn't given the chance to do anything else. Then Jock Dreever and Jesse James got together with me to plan another run. We knew that when the morning work party left for work they were counted and their identities were checked at the gatehouse; after this they passed through doors nos 2 and 3, and down the outside steps. Here they formed up, and marched away, but they were not counted again. This meant that with the guards at the front and rear of the party, men in the middle of the work party would be out of the sight of the guards when they passed the door into room no. 4. We checked this theory, and it worked. So, on the day planned, we put our home-made civilian clothes on under our uniforms, packed our escape rations, (mostly chocolate bars and Oxo cubes from Red Cross parcels) into the rucksacks we normally took to work each day, and wrapped 20 feet of string-rope around our waists inside the fall of the battle-dress blouse, and joined the work party. Everything was okay, we got to the top of the staircase, ducked into room no. 4, and left the door ajar. The rest of the work party marched past, followed by the guards who didn't even look at room no. 4. From the window, we watched as the men formed up, and, escorted by the guards, marched away. We looked at each other and grinned. Broad daylight escape from Waldenstein! Jerry would go off like a fire cracker! We thought it was the coup to end all coups.

'Quickly, we each brought the rope out of our battle dress and knotted it to make one rope. I tied the end around my waist, as the others prepared to take the strain, then climbed on to the sill of the window, preparatory to climbing down the castle wall to pull back the steel slide. Being left-handed, I automatically looked to my left before commencing the descent. Standing in the fold of the castle wall between rooms 2 and 3 was a German soldier, and as he saw me emerge he raised his rifle and aimed as I yelled "Pull me up, quick!"

'The speed with which Jock and Jesse responded probably saved my life because the German's bullet hit the edge of the window as I flew through it. Simultaneously, the door to room no. 4 burst open and in poured German soldiers in full battle-rig. As I landed, some German belted me behind the left shoulder with his rifle butt and I promptly lost interest in the proceedings. When I came to, we were in the room with the cages on the ground floor of the castle. When I asked Jesse and Jock what the score was, one of the two Jerries there told me to shut up.

'Popular opinion had it that we had been betrayed. I suppose it stands to reason that Jerry must have had a spy, a stooge, in a place like Waldenstein. There was a suspect, an Englishman who had few credentials to be in a place like the castle, there was a lot of evidence against him and I suppose it is enough to say that the fellow finally came to a sticky end.

'Shortly after we had completed our term in cells I was ordered to report to the gate with my gear, where, to my surprise I was sent to Stalag 383, a non-working NCOs' camp in Bavaria, which was considered to be one of the best camps in Germany. I waved goodbye to Jock and Jesse, and have never seen them since.

'I was told to report to the commandant's office. Here an SS officer said to me, "You can stay here and we will leave you alone, but if you escape once more we will send you to a place you will not like".'

Oates made two more of his wild attempts to escape before being sent to Hohenfeldts. On arrival he was sent before an officer in the beautiful silver-grey uniform of the SS. 'He put it to me very coldly. "You've made a bloody nuisance of yourself".' The Senior British Officer told Peter, 'You'd better cool it. If you don't, you'll be in very serious trouble.' They had begun sending people to Theresienstadt in Czechoslovakia, the old fortress that was now a particularly vicious concentration camp.

Young Oates tried to settle. He began to study at the camp, he matriculated and then began tertiary subjects. 'This set me up for life.' But eventually it did not stop him from bolting. By this time he believed the end of the war was in sight.

'Hohenfeldts was the most difficult place I'd seen to get out of, more difficult even than Waldenstein. So I decided to swap places with a fellow who'd been sent from Wisbeck to Hohenfeldts by mistake and had to be returned. The first morning in Wisbeck I was sleeping when "Raus, you people, out you go and work". It's a working camp. I'm half asleep, and somebody jabbed a bayonet in my bottom. I said, "Piss off!" The German started shouting, half asleep I flew out of bed, grabbed my jacket, waved my stripes and started screaming, "Treat me with respect due to my rank, and stand at attention when you speak to me", and all of this garbage. And he started shouting back. The people who were standing round were all newly-captured prisoners, still scared of Germans, whereas we'd been in prison the best part of four years and knew how far to go without going too far; old lags learn. Then the English Regimental Sergeant Major who was commander of the place appeared and ordered me to go to work. I asked him who the hell he was giving orders to and he said, "To a British soldier" – I'd forgotten I was supposed to be a British soldier on this escape, not an Australian soldier. So I'd given my own pot away. He ordered me to go to work, "Until you've been investigated then we'll find out who you are".' In the meantime the German commandant called Oates to his office.

'I couldn't remember the name and number of this Englishman I'd swapped identity with at Hohenfeldts. I knew his rank, a lance-corporal, so I wrote Lance-Corporal Bloggs. This commandant looked at it, then filled in my correct name, number and rank across the top of it and said, "The game is up, Oh-ah-tess" (Oates).' Oates was marched out and put into a special holding compound, Barrack 20, where court-martial cases were held. The Germans hadn't forgotten that they had promised him he would be severely dealt with if he tried again to escape.

He was kept there for six months 'awaiting the worst', but then he was put to work at the nearby railway station, the hauptbahnhof in Munich, and soon he was off and away again.

He had noticed that some trains coming in had chalk-marks on the carriages in Italian. 'We thought they were going to Italy. As it turned out, they were *from* Italy. Anyway, I jumped aboard the rattler. But, instead of getting the little disguise kit I had organised, my civvy pants, shirt and civvy jacket, as usual I ended up escaping in full uniform. I could have been the worst escaper of his day. I got out an awful lot of times but mostly made a complete hash of it.'

When the train was clear of the marshalling yard, he left it and was again caught. 'I had twenty-one days down there for "something", the charges always were foolish, they never gave the true "crime": that of boredom with POW life and a desire to escape or at least cause a little mayhem.'

Speaking with a number of escapees and would-be escapers, it appears that the instant a dedicated escaper walked through the gates of a prison they assessed the opportunity to escape. (The author was with Peter Oates in 1984 when he visited Colditz for the first time. As his eyes swept the courtyard he muttered, 'Only one exit'.)

But not every man agreed with the escapades of escapers. The day Peter Oates was brought back from his failed break from the Munich hauptbahnhof area was Easter Day, a holiday. 'I was being marched up to my own part of the camp on the way back to the guardhouse, when I was booed by the majority of the prisoners who were watching the various sporting activities. My own people! Basically, because the activities of people like me were causing them to suffer disciplinary actions from the Germans and therefore put them out a little bit. To them us escapers were a nuisance.

'Escaping *per se* didn't become fashionable until well into the war, when it became reasonably obvious that our side was going to win. In the early days of the war when Jerry was winning and going from strength to strength, the vast majority of our blokes would not have liked to rock the boat. Jerry took an opposite view. Whilst they punished you strictly in accordance with the Geneva Convention, they tended to respect you.

'Colditz was an officers' prison, whereas the camps of the vast bulk of ordinary soldiers or NCOs weren't so literate or well-educated. But I think there were much more hair-raising events went on from the men's camps because the men were more dedicated to their King and country than were the officers.

'At the disciplinaires parade every morning, the Germans checked us separately to make sure we were still here, that we hadn't left. They attempted to get some form of discipline into this parade which was a shambles; you'd stand with your hands in your pockets, cigarette hanging from the corner of your mouth. Sergeant Pinder (Popeye to us) would say, "Achtung, achtung", all this sort of stuff, and "Ah, morgen, Herr Oh-ah-tess". "Morgen bitte." And you'd light your cigarette and sort of puff it contentedly, while he wouldn't say anything because you were obviously one of the upper classes, you'd escaped more times than the average, therefore, in the early days particularly, you got even more respect from the Germans as an escapee than you ever got from your own kind.

'To them you were a bloody nuisance that was rocking the boat and causing all sorts of problems to Red Cross parcels and things of this nature. Some people stuck spikes through tins of Red Cross parcels so they wouldn't keep, so they couldn't be hoarded for escape stores. And when the vast majority *aren't* escaping and their food is going bad because of a bunch of people who, as they put it, are "selfishly indulging in escaping" ... well, you see how it was. Society doesn't change whether you are running about free, or imprisoned in a POW camp.

'You get the mutters of political dissent even among those like us who should have had so much in common. Each camp was a tiny mirror of society, vastly selfish, and vastly introverted. Self-preservation was part of it but *self* was paramount. Man does not alter because he is a prisoner. These two-bit heroes like me were a bloody nuisance and there was a fair degree of resistance amongst non-escapers against the activities of the escapers. I am not in any way suggesting that the people who protested or got very angry with the escapers were in any way disloyal, they were just trying to live a quiet life and survive the war and they couldn't see what the escapers were achieving. For our part, escapers were achieving a hell of a lot because, though few in number compared to the millions of others, they tied down enormous numbers of troops to look after them, the whole thing was calculated to deploy German resources searching for them – police, army, etc., plus the trouble, time and publicity making them look foolish. As for the escapees, a lot of it was a fair degree of bravado; I was privately delighted and imagined the Germans thought I was one hell of a Digger: they probably thought I was a flaming little nuisance, "That bloody kid again!", but that's not the point. I never really visualised I was going to get anywhere. *I* thought I was doing what I was supposed to do, and I still think I was.

'I can't speak for others, but I escaped for the fun of it, for a lark, the excitement of getting out, the few free days; the notoriety flattered my ego, I was flattered the Germans considered I was a dangerous character.

'Escaping was as much a diversion as anything else. There's nothing more dismal and depressing than sitting in a bloody prison camp. My escapes were not mirrors of soldierly virtue but I got a great charge out of them. At least I was doing something. It enabled me to swagger a bit; when you are 20 years of age, there is a great need to swagger. In your imagination you walk into a big barracks and it's full of 300 soldiers, and someone says, "That's Peter Oates, he's made six or seven escapes". The only difference between what I was doing and what a juvenile delinquent does these days is that the King gave you medals for it. Basically you were bucking authority, and you could do it with a clear conscience. I thought I was one hell of a fellow, even if nobody else did. They all probably thought I was a bloody nuisance: and I *swaggered*. It probably drove them mad. But the point still remains, that *I* thought I was pretty good.

'I believed the ideal number to escape was two, but the more I went out I preferred to go solo because I found I was much less obvious, the Germans looking for prisoners tended to overlook me, I didn't look old enough.'

In mid-1945, as the war was ending, Peter Oates and a friend had another failed attempt at escape and were being held by German citizens. 'Ah well', he thought, 'Any minute now we're going to be knee-deep in Geheim Staatspolizei' (Gestapo). 'I must have been there for four hours, and then a citizen brought me quite a good feed and some fags and took me off to another bloke and we went for a long walk. We only walked at night. At daytime we were usually sheltered in a barn. Then we got to the east of Paris and my guide said, "Go down there, lots of luck". So off I went. And the next thing I knew I ran into an American patrol, and that was it.

'They stuck me in a cell, wouldn't believe me. "There ain't any Australians around here. All the Australian soldiers are in the Pacific." I said, "I know that, but I've been a prisoner of war for the best part of four years". They said, "I'm gonna check on you, boy". They were pretty paranoid, arresting Russians, Frenchmen, Belgians and all sorts of people. They didn't feed me, they just left me locked in gaol with an American guard outside the door.' Next day a British officer arrived. 'You claim to be an Australian?' Peter was 'a bit cheesed off at the whole business' and did not reply. 'What does the name Donald Bradman mean?' 'What does it mean to bowl a maiden over?' Later the interrogator said, 'I've been to Sydney. I know Australia. I've been talking to you for ten minutes now and you haven't stood up and you haven't addressed me by my rank.' Then he said to the Yanks, 'That's an Aussie. No other soldier in the world would go on like that.'

'The Americans received a signal back from Australia House in London to say that yes, they did own a fellow called Oates, "He's one of ours". They relaxed. Gave me a great time', Oates remembers.

'I was consistent: I had to be the worst escaper. I could sit down and plan getting out of the camp, and I was very good at that. I had it all organised, I'd do it all right. The thing that used to confound me was what you did when you got out of the place. It's just like chasing a cow: what do you do when you catch it?

'My citation, which I received from the King, states "For gallant and distinguished conduct". If that's gallant and distinguished conduct ... hell! I didn't do a thing right, even when I did do it right it was a fluke. All I could have been decorated for was sheer perseverance, nothing else. I enjoyed it thoroughly.'

The Winged Eagles

'Any landing you walk away from is a bloody good landing.'

Squadron Leader Ken Watts, RAAF

FOR MOST AUSTRALIAN COMBATANTS World War II was the war when each knew least about the part the other services played. Because of this, Australian airmen suffered almost as much flak from their own countrymen as the Germans threw at them.

'Where were they when we were bombed night and day in Tobruk? Where were they when we were bombarded in Greece? Where were they when the bloody paratroopers came against us on Crete?' And the men who were captured on Java, Sumatra, Malaya and the necklace of islands above Australia join in: 'Where were they?' Sometimes the answer is, 'They'd been and gone before you even got there'. Often they flew in crude aircraft, endangering their own lives more than did the enemy, as did pilots such as Squadron Leader Ken Watts who was flying out from Tobruk before he left for Europe, where he flew some hundreds of death-defying runs before he was eventually shot down. His story is typical of the men who flew in the northern hemisphere, as is the story of the airmen in the islands north of Australia. 'We saluted those who were about to die', Private Stan Day, 2/22nd Battalion, said of the eight airmen on New Britain who went up in their little 'string and cardboard' Wirraways against a squadron of the lethal aircraft of Japan. The casualty rate of Australian airmen was as high as any British country, none would wish it to be known that in some areas it was even higher.

Australians were in the air from the opening of the war. Many were trained in Canada under the Empire Training

Scheme and went from there into almost every squadron based in England.

These men followed the curvature of the earth, higher than any plane had yet gone – often their planes were so iced up they saw nothing for hours, did not even see their target. It was the days before solid-state electronics. Many travelled in wooden planes on bombing missions, fine for avoiding radar detection but once found they were sitting ducks.

It was said they flew by the seat of their pants, and they did. The war was coming to its end when the best of navigational aids and aircraft were introduced.

'Fighting on the desert of North Africa was the best of all', according to Squadron Leader Ken Watts. 'It was clean, no towns to be razed, no innocent people to be killed: just pilot against pilot. You could see one another you were so close. It was a thrilling thing, you knew the enemy pilot was out to get you if you didn't keep your mind clear and get him first. As for the lovely aircraft, you were bound together, beautiful little things, just touch the stick, edge the rudder and off she'd slide; oh, no pilot forgets the beauty of that.'

It must have seemed to the foot soldiers in their holes in the ground by day and on their sorties into enemy territory at night that they had no air cover because the sky over Tobruk was so heavily speckled with enemy bombers. But, among others, Australian Group Captain Eric Black of the RAF was there during the siege from 8 April to 23 December 1941 and his men went up for as long as their planes could fly. 'Number 73 Squadron went up in their Hurricanes daily against sixty-plus Stukas or ME.109 fighters until they had no aircraft left. Number 6 Squadron pilots did daily reconnaissance flights until they too ran out of aircraft.'

The camouflaged underground hangars from which 451 Squadron RAAF later operated were built on Group Captain Black's suggestion. Black had some great ideas but he liked to tell of the one that didn't work. 'I had wooden decoy Hurricanes made to put across the road west of El Gubbi – until the Germans dropped a wooden bomb on it!'

The siege of Tobruk was such that each side was forever being surprised by the other. One day the airmen woke to find twenty German tanks on their airfield – both doubtless alarmed at the error until each swung into action.

The English Flight Lieutenant Geoffrey Morley Mower (later Professor of English, James Madison University, USA) wrote of Australian pilots, 'They all resembled pentathlon contenders. Ken Watts was tall, fair and had the best physique in the squadron. I have a photograph of him in his briefs, shaving outside his tent, it rivals Melville's besotted description of the sailor, Billy Budd. Nowadays his kind of bodily perfection is rare.'

THE AVIATOR'S LAMENT

A young Aviator lay dying.
Amidst all the wreckage he lay, (he lay;)
To his sad friends gathered around him
These last parting words he did say.

Take the piston rods out of my kidneys
The sparking plugs out of my brain, (my brain;)
From the small of my back take the crankshaft
And assemble your engine again.

Prise the rudder bar loose from my knee caps;
Take the main spar out of my hair, (my hair;)
The petrol tank's lying around here
You'll find all your aeroplane there.

Take the cylinders out of my armpits
The joy stick you'll find in my thigh, (my thigh;)
Put the whole lot together once more,
But I doubt if it ever will fly.

When the court of enquiry assembles,
Tell them the reason I died, (I died;)

T'was a flat spin that closely resembled,
The maximum angle of glide.

Stand by your glasses steady
This world is a world full of lies;
Here's a toast to the dead already!
Hurrah! for the next man to die.

Sung to the tune of
'A Gallant Young Stockman Lay Dying'

Ken Watts was a fighter pilot with the RAAF and RAF. His first entry of flight in his flight log-book is dated 7 February 1941, the final on 6 April 1944 when he bailed out of his Kittyhawk fighter after being hit by anti-aircraft fire near Todi, Italy. By that time his log recorded 877 hours in the 'Hurribus, Spits and Kitties' over Africa and Europe. ('Hurricanes, Spitfires, Kittihawks and every other fighter plane in the British air force.') He stayed in fighter planes by choice: 'I didn't care to have a crew to be responsible for or to suffer if I were to make an error'.

His training began as a *sprog* pilot taking his first flight in a Tiger Moth trainer and then Wirraways at Wagga Wagga under the Empire Air Training Scheme.

The air commodore at his training station at Somers (Vic.) had been Air Commodore 'Tommy' White of World War I fame. Here the sprogs ('young, incapable, untrainable') learnt meteorology, morse code, the theory of flight, lift and drag, and flight plans. 'Flying solo for the first time was thrilling. I sang and laughed, for here was something that seemed so easy, so natural.'

Then he was off on the *Queen Elizabeth* to the Middle East. As the great ship was getting under way the airmen fished into their pockets and pulled out the air force issue of four condoms, blew them up, pushed a note in with name and address, weighted them with two pennies for a stamp and dropped them overboard to the flotilla of little ships on Sydney

Harbour to post for them. (Marjorie, his wife, received her letter from Ken the following day.)

Ken was 'Off to the aerial war in the Western Desert landing in places with names like Gaza, Beersheba, Damascus and Jerusalem where my father had been with the 10th Light-Horse in 1914–18.' Added to these names he'd heard from his father, his log-book shows he landed at (the young pilot's spelling) Dekhaila, El Daba, Fuka, Sidi Azeiz, Sidi-Herrish, Sidi Barrani, Bardia, Tobruk, El Adem, Mersa Matrouth, Gazala, Derna 'to name just some of the beaches and landing grounds we were forced to'.

'We of 451 RAAF were chased up and down the desert by Rommel. Going backwards and forwards along the coast of Libya according to my log-book I landed on fifty-three landing grounds. But you could land anywhere. Often, four petrol drums and a wind sock made up our landing strip.

'There was no drama or grieving if your closest mate was shot down. It was a male club that could not be excelled. "There are old pilots, and bold pilots, but few old, bold pilots", we said. Sometimes men turned up after being reported missing. "Natter" Forstrom, a week after his kite was reported as a write-off, called in from a field phone to say, "Tell all those bastards to put everything back in my tent!" He'd been rescued. There was always bags of humour along with esprit.'

Watts was dedicated. He spent much time with his 2E (fitter), the air frame rigger (2A) and the armourer. 'These were the most important men in the squadron to me. I spent more time with them than in the mess with my peers. I didn't drink alcohol except when the occasion demanded, I wanted to be fit to the maximum degree in order to use that aircraft most effectively. With the fitter and rigger, in between times "on readiness", we would clean the kite down, beeswax the leading edge of the main plane and fin, and polish it to cut down friction; this is assuming all other aspects had received attention.

'Our ground crew could be strafed and captured at any time and many of us treated them as real mates, ranks notwithstanding.

'This extract from the diary of our ground staff helps to illustrate what they went through.

'Friday, 29 November 1941: We move 40 miles west, about 20 miles from Madelina. We hear that ALG party are POWs. When last heard of they were with 2000 Kiwis while a tank battle was on, but Sidi Azeiz saw their capture. We move to Tobruk shortly.

'Friday, 5 December 1941: Of the ALG twenty are still missing. Fred Gowland and Sid Maddison turned up with some of the boys and they look rather done in. They had moved out at night leaving a crew to get the kites away in the morning, the crew are now missing.'

But there was little time for regrets.

'Monday, 8 December 1941: At 1330 we were strafed and bombed by twelve ME110s and fifteen ME109s, killing seven and injuring twelve. It was all over in half a minute. To make matters worse we heard over the radio that Japan has entered the war against us.

'Tuesday, 9 December 1941: Orders last night was a move on Tobruk and are now on the way. Passed through the wire below Sidi Omar. A shoufti [enemy spy] kite let four bombs go on the convoy behind us.'

Watts remembered: 'At the time our troops occupied Tobruk, the only way to get in to the landing ground safely was to approach from the sea at approximately 1000 feet, fire the colours of the day, wheels and flaps down at approximately 100 miles an hour, with IFF on. Forget any of the above and the Aussie gunners would blast you out of the sky, and quite rightly so. Every day the Stukas and JU88s would be over, trying to bomb our troops into submission.

'These were the days before sophisticated pressurised cabins, but the harbingers of these aircraft were appearing. One day a long vapour trail intrigued me, it was a Shoufti [spy plane] JU886P. So, with permission, my fitter and rigger prepared a Spit IX. It climbed to 40,000 feet, balls out, hanging on the prop. Up there it was a new world, the sky was an intense indigo, the darkest deep blue I have seen. The outside temperature was minus 45 degrees. The Spits have no cabin heating and my breath iced the windscreen and perspex canopy. The curvature of the earth was quite apparent. After what seemed an age I saw the vapour trail approaching about 20 miles north-west of Benghazi. It climbed right over the top of my kite and with chagrin and admiration for the technology of this large slotted-wing aircraft, I tried to lift the nose of the Spit to fire the single machine gun, but in the thin air the kite spun off. I felt hazy and dozey because of the oxygen lack, so straightened out and went for the deck. Two blood wagon bods from the ambulance lifted me out and took me to the Ops room, where Air Vice-Marshal Sir Sholto Douglas and Group Captain Bain had witnessed the "do".

'Desert flights were ending but Squadron Leader "Crash" Currey and I had some memorable tail chases: both kites to 35,000 feet. The CO said, "Get on my tail and try to stay there". (What a lovely war!)'

After the outbreak at Alamein, Montgomery had neither the manpower nor equipment to undertake prolonged, large-scale operations. But the soon-to-be Field Marshal Viscount Montgomery of Alamein ('Monty' to the troops) was about to attack Italy. 'Our operations against Italy from North Africa should take the form of the most terrific bombing, a prolonged and sustained effort.'

After his tour of duty in the Middle East, including Tobruk, Watts was sent to No. 3 Squadron, Italy, and by 26 March 1944 he was ready to make a dawn raid on two northern Italian airfields. The squadron's fitters and riggers had fitted detachable long-range fuel tanks to twelve Kittyhawk fighters and the pilots were briefed the night before on tactics. 'The adrenalin begins to flow then, before first-light take-off. It wasn't only the Kittyhawks that were fired up!

'After take off, navigation lights out, a loose echelon was formed in three sections line abreast, height 50 feet, "on the drink at Fanny Adams feet" to get underneath enemy radar over the coast, then RT [radio telephone] silence broken.'

The official history of the war in the Western Desert and the invasion of Italy states, 'A section of No. 3 led by Flight Lieutenant Watts, searching for Wellington crew missing over the Adriatic, found a troop-carrying JU52 which was shot down and crashed into the sea; also a few days later an SM79 was shot down. The highlight for the Australians was an attack led by Watts on 27 March by twelve Kittyhawks from 3 Squadron. The Kittyhawks were fitted with long-range tanks and attacked Rimini and Forli airfields where a mixed bag of Italian and German aircraft were strafed, leading to eleven destroyed and two hangars set on fire. A train and coastal steamer were also damaged on the way out.

'During April 1944 [after Italy had withdrawn from the war], 3 Squadron flew 354 missions and 450 Squadron flew 430, escorting Italian aircraft to drop supplies to partisan forces in Yugoslavia, and repetitive attacks against railway lines causing much damage. The Kittyhawks had to face increased and very determined anti-aircraft fire through April and several pilots were forced to bail out.

'Kittyhawk pilots had been the toast of the Desert Air Forces. They had earned this by their victories against the German and Italian Air Forces, as well as from their prolific support of the Eighth Army in the desert and now the Allied armies during the Italian campaign.' Ken Watts's flight log-book lists 300 take-offs and landings.

'The flying was a great challenge. You took off THAT way, the alternative was 180 degrees. It was wing down to wind-ward always. "Crash" would take six planes strafing and bombing. I would take the other six.' Watts and Currey were now attached to the 244 Wing. Suddenly, briefly, Ken notes in his log, 'Squadron Leader "Crash" Currey was shot down.' "Crash" became a prisoner of war.

Ken was hit several times. The following diary entry is just one of these 'incidents'. 'Machine-gun bullets through port wing. Jock Stephen A/c holed by flak. Ray Hudson ditched over convoy (A/c on fire). Picked up by Aussie corvette. In hospital with burnt bum and arms.'

Then came the one that put Ken out of battle. He was now Squadron Leader Watts.

'About 1845 hours on 6 April 1944, while looking for more strafing targets in the Todi area, heavy flak burst all around my aircraft which was in the centre of the formation (a fluid six). It was the most accurate 88mm I had ever encountered. There were no previous sighting bursts, it was bang on. One burst was immediately ahead at one o'clock, the noise of it was deafening. I looked right into a huge orange red centre and black smoke enveloped the aircraft. The aircraft rocked violently, and I called out on the RT, turning right and diving to lead the formation out of it as quickly as possible.

'My aircraft was streaming glycol smoke from the starboard tank and oil covered the windscreen and perspex. I knew then that the kite had "had" it. Half way around the right turn another burst nearly turned the aircraft upside down, I felt her take some very hard knocks, and the stick became peculiar in my hands as if someone was playing about with the elevators. As I clutched the stick I must have pressed the gun button. I hoped fervently that none of my cobbers' aircraft was hit. I couldn't see through the windscreen at all. I knew the motor would not last long and gave it full bore and fine pitch to gain as much distance as possible from the flak batteries before bailing out. My No. 2, Tex Gray, knowing I could not see through the windscreen, called up and said: "You've no height, Sir". I wondered whether I should try and belly lob instead of bailing out but the heat of the aircraft and fear of it suddenly bursting into flames decided me. The altimeter showed 3400 feet, we were over very hilly country, 2000 to 3000 feet above sea level. The glycol temperature was rapidly rising and finished up right off the clock. I needed more height for safety as I would have to bail out very shortly. I called up Tex: "I'm going to step out. Don't tell my wife. I'll be home in a month." Tex came back: "Okay, good luck".

'I pulled off the oxygen mask and the earphones out of the rubber sockets in the helmet. I'd always vaselined the earphones so they would pull away easily. I remember throwing the oxy mask on the cockpit floor and stepping over the leads. Quickly I wound the elevator trim fully forward, grabbed the stick with the left hand and, again, all six guns blazed away. I pulled back the cockpit hood, the smoke and fumes poured in, so I grabbed the rip cord handle with my right hand, rolled the aircraft upside down and rammed the stick forward. After a slight pause I was catapulted head first out and I immediately yanked the rip cord. As soon as I had done so, I realised I had pulled too soon and thought the 'chute would be tangled up in the tailplane. When a terrific jerk occurred I was convinced of it. Immediately, all sorts of thoughts flooded through my mind: "What a hell of a way to finish up; Marj back home receiving the dreaded news, trying to be brave about it, and resolutely trying to choke back the tears and steeling herself to the fact that I was dead. Scenes from the squadron mess that night rushed my head: Tex and the boys around the bar, "Christ, you ought to have seen the CO going in today, all tangled up in the tailplane". How disgusted they would be after drilling so often about flak evasion and tactics to keep the gunners guessing. Then, why the hell did I fly on every trip? What a terrific silence, it doesn't seem natural. Jesus, what a silence. Everything will be over quickly. Hell, why doesn't it hurry up and happen? Why doesn't the ground rush up quicker? I saw the Kittyhawk just as it dived into the deck, followed by explosions. Ammunition from the .5 calibre guns banged in all directions, tracers whizzing off like a fireworks display. What a tremendous feeling of relief it was that I couldn't be hitched up to the tail plane. But it took me some moments to fully understand that if my aircraft was down there and I was up here I couldn't be mixed up with the bloody tail! A ridiculous sensation came over me: I must be hanging from my 'chute! Hell, yes. There it was above me. What a stupid feeling hitched up around the crutch and legs. Do all parachutists feel this way? It seems such a *silly* feeling!

'My squadron boys were flying around me in tight circles. Gosh! "How pretty those kites look, banking steeply and slightly below. I had never seen kites flying from this angle before – they look beautiful! If I kick and wave, they'll know I haven't been hit and they'll tell Marj I'm okay." So I yelled and kicked like a bastard, then thought, "Jesus! I'll come down right on top of the burning kite". I tried madly to twist the shroud lines; it had some effect. "I'll miss the kite but will land in the trees", I thought. "Let's try and grab a branch". Glad I had my helmet and glasses on. The trees are coming up fast.

'Next thing I was slithering through the branches. I hit the ground fairly solidly, rolling over. "I'm down okay. Hope the boys can see me. I'll rush into the clearing and wave. They'll tell Marj I was quite okay." Though it couldn't have been more than a minute or two since I left the aircraft, it seemed ages. Anxiety to get away from the aircraft filled me. The flak batteries were just over the ridge of hills to the west and I could hear a motor bike some distance away but I could not distinguish which way it was heading.

'I decided quickly to run in an easterly direction and charged off into the undergrowth. The ground was matted with dry leaves which made running hard work. The bushes cut my trousers. Dressed up as I was in a Mae West with its paraphernalia, scarf and gloves, I was soon in a lather of sweat and felt rather shaky, but they had to be carried until such time as I could bury them.

' "Tedeschi!" the Italians whispered from the cover of trees. Police! When he considered it safe, a lad gave me a bottle of wine and showed me the way to go to avoid Tedeschi. Another Italian voice said softly, "Tedeschi!" and pointed for me to run in an easterly direction.' When he couldn't run any more he crawled into thick scrub and lay down in the leaves. 'I considered what articles I'd rather retain, bearing in mind the possibility of future searches of my person and buried my Mae West, a metal mirror, silk map, a letter from Marj, a whistle, phial of iodine, first-aid anti-burn outfit, a rolled length of heavy twine, escape maps, some string and a leather bootlace. It hurt to bury my white silk scarf. I'd always worn it when flying.' He kept only some chocolate, a handkerchief, his watch, emergency rations, benzedrine, money (all pilots before setting off on a sortie are provided with currency of the country they are to fly over in case of just such a need as Ken was now in), and a compass. 'There was no time for sentiment.' An Italian gave him clothes, bagged, patched trousers, 'too short', a work shirt and a coat.

They took him in and sat him near a fire. 'My teeth began to chatter, I was shuddering, but then they gave me wine and that fixed me up.' But he couldn't eat. The young woman of the house showed him pieces of paper on which were the regimental numbers and names of five army privates who stated they had received food and shelter at this house, and that the owner should be remunerated when the Allies took over. Ken followed suit with his name, number and address, and wrote that he too would see they were remunerated.

He asked if he could sleep a while for he was suffering from shock and exhaustion. The father of the family showed him a bed in a room upstairs, 'I rolled in. And the old Italian rolled in too!'

In the morning they sent him on his way complete with a hat for which he had exchanged his watch. Later, as he walked the roads, some young girls brought him wine, and the next family he met took him in and also gave him wine. Then, 'I heard the girl scream, "Tedeschi!".'

'From the window across the room I saw the soldiers running towards the house, rifles at the ready. I took off and ran doubled up, trying to keep the house between us. I made for a creek which ran beside the road. I had only about 200 yards to run and expected to hear rifle shots. It seemed a nightmare run, the legs could not go very fast while bending over. I made the creek, jumped in, and waded along under cover of the bank until I reached a deepish hole, part covered by a bush. I crouched down with only my eyes out and hoped like hell it would get dark very quickly. After a while I cautiously turned my head around to see where the hobnailed bastards were and a Carabiniere levelled his Biretta rifle and yelled. Soon, a squad of Germans was around. A German bawled something at me and I was fished out of the river and searched for weapons.

Some sort of self-loathing and extreme weariness came over me, it all seemed such a rotten anticlimax. I could hardly realise I had been caught and may not see the squadron boys again. I was too exhausted to think of my chances of escape, but dimly felt I'd make it. Others had.'

He was taken to the nearest German camp where, beneath a large picture of Hitler, he was searched and asked, 'Well, what prison camp did you escape from?' Watts did not answer.' Numerous officers entered, clicked heels and Heil Hitler'd. 'The commandant of the camp took off his gloves and cap and stood before me. He was covered with Iron Crosses and medals and looked like a small edition of Goering. He asked me who I was, how I happened to be here. I told him I was an Australian pilot. He asked for identification, of which I had none. He started to talk a lot about the Gestapo, and "spies are shot". He searched me, found the benzedrine tablets, compass, etc., so I told him I was a pilot shot down by flak. This seemed to start the cogs moving as he consulted papers and rang telephones and said, "Todi flak?" I jaja'd and was bundled out into a big lorry with thirteen Germans, all carrying automatics, tommy guns or rifles. As soon as it became daylight, one guy kept aircraft lookout on the back of the truck, and another guy at the front. Soon the lookout shouted "Achtung!" and the truck squealed to a standstill. I was hurried out and the guards disguised the truck with a mesh camouflage net. Fighters were overhead about 7000 feet, Kittyhawks! Civilians were rushing hell-bent for the shelters. The guards had donned their panic bowlers and unslung their rifles, and crouched up against the wall. They could not understand my grin. The Kittys went into echelon and dive bombed about a half to three quarters of a mile away. Hell, they looked good! I wondered if they were the old shark-nosed boys of 112? Many were my emotions. Another raid by fighters caused a similar flap about two hours later. I was rough-handled while getting into the truck after this raid. They had heard me mutter: "Where's the bloody Luftwaffe?"

'Late that afternoon we reached Florence and I was

detrucked in front of the rail station. There is a beautiful fountain there – little stone boys in the fountain peeing all over the place. The guards protected me but the civilians spat and I received a few direct hits. I couldn't blame them. There were hundreds of German troops in all sorts of uniforms, including ski troops. After an hour's wait, during which I seemed to be the cynosure of all eyes, German and Italian alike, I was herded into a train with many German troops. The guards muttered "Swinehundt". It was a helpless, undefended feeling being in a packed compartment full of armed enemies.

'The train passed through Arezzo marshalling yards where terrific bomb damage had caused trains to be overturned, rails torn up and a hospital train overturned and burnt out being recognisable only by the charred Red Cross markings. It now looked like being a one-sided rough house. There was a great deal of excited gutteral comment between the guards and the German troops. At several stations along the line, our bombers had done extensive damage. A lot of civilian houses and non-military targets near the rail track were also hit. The soldiers would point these out to me. The situation would have been much worse had those vociferous German troops known I was a captured "Terror Flieger". I was thankful for my ill-fitting farmer clothes. I was not allowed anything to eat or drink and sat cramped up among their rucksacks and steel helmets. Passing through Bologna, girls came running alongside selling vino. My tongue hung out. At Verona I was bundled into a truck and taken to a large, very old stone building like a fairy-tale castle with semi-circular, cone topped spires and inset windows; hurried through the large mitre-shaped entrance, through stone corridors, down a number of well-worn stone steps, and pushed into a real old-fashioned, story-book dungeon.

'I was not the first Allied fugitive to be thrown in here. The walls were covered with names and service numbers scratched there by earlier inmates. One I remember was a PRU pilot shot down by 88mm flak at 20,000 feet. "Wouldn't it s... you!", I thought. I cannot recall the pilot's name but it was the same

88mm anti-aircraft flak which also claimed my kite.

'I could hear moaning and groaning in the cell next to mine. Talking through the grill, I discovered it was a P38 pilot who had bailed out, aircraft on fire, and was suffering from burns. He was in terrible pain. Later I was allowed to visit him in his cell. He wanted me to remove his bandages and put them on more loosely but they were stuck to him with flesh growing over them. I thought he would pass out. I was able to comfort him a little; even talking to a compatriot helped. His name was Tex Crowe. Flak had knocked out one motor and cannon fire set him ablaze. He jumped and parachuted but his green overall was so badly burnt around his shoulders and legs when he was picked up by Carabinieri he could not lie down to sleep so he sat up. We talked until midnight.

'Next morning I was escorted to a room, seated at a table with a Gestapo-type in sinister black uniform who started questioning me relating to squadron and location. I said, "Sorry, I can't answer", and pointed out that the Geneva Convention required that I need only state number, name and rank. By this time, two jackbooted German soldiers wearing helmets and carrying Mannlicher rifles had moved in, one on either side of me. More questions. My reply, "Sorry, I can't answer". The interrogator nodded. I lost consciousness with blows to the head from rifle butts.

'I wakened in a solitary confinement cell and, next day, was taken back to the interrogator who asked the same questions. Again, I wakened in the same cell. The third time the hated bastard had a folder in his hand and among the German words I saw the figures "239", the number of my Wing. With the Germanic pride of efficiency of his race he said, "The flak battery which shot you down has claimed you as their kill. You replaced Illingworth as CO of 112 Squadron!" I was still alive, now no longer a spy, although I was a POW to be interrogated, transported, guarded and fed in a POW camp until hostilities ceased. Wearing no identity discs, speaking English, claiming only number, name and rank, I was fortunate the aircraft in which I was shot down had the distinctive painting of a shark's mouth on the fuselage, and also that German flak batteries were zealous of their efficiency and record.

'From Verona railway station we set off for POW camp. Tex Crowe was fairly done in from the pain and lack of sleep. He had put up a very gutful show and now was in a sort of delirious state, but eventually dozed off in the corner seat. We had four guards, one of whom had been educated at Oxford University and was apparently quite a big noise in the Nazi Party.' At Frankfurt they left the train for the night to sleep in a small barbed-wire enclosure, where there were approximately 500 air crew, mostly American B17 and B24 crews with five 'fighter boys'.

A few days later the German authorities issued a command that 150 prisoners would be leaving for a German POW camp. 'I was asked as senior officer to sign a statement that on the way to Frankfurt railway station the prisoners would not attempt to escape. I said "Bullshit!" but then Captain Thornton, a USAAF pilot, said, "Watty, you're not taking this on your own, let's put it to the other chaps". The alternative was that we would have to carry all the wounded and the Germans would take away our boots, belts and braces. After a while, with a few dissenters, the men agreed and we arrived at Frankfurt rail yards.

'The transport was grim, a steam engine with side-covered trucks, First World War stock intended to hold the usual eight horses or forty men. Our truck held the majority of the wounded and it was pretty tough travelling for them. There was nothing on the wooden floor, and insufficient room for everyone to sleep lying down. Several of us stood up all night, hanging on to the horse tethering rails.

One of these was the American Lieutenant Greenwood Gay, who had almost recovered from a 20mm shell through the lung. Though he was still very weak, he insisted there were worse cases than he and refused to sleep during the nights. 'It was a very game show. The boys were a great lot and were very unselfish. We had been issued with one Red Cross parcel between five of us and we certainly tucked in. Sanitary arrangements were nil. There being no latrines we leaked out of the truck door and took a rear at a siding on the third day. During the night the guards rigged a wookey fire which helped to keep everybody warm, the nights being very cold with heavy frost. The shunting and jolting in the goods sidings was a nightmare to the wounded. Some of the boys went to pieces with the pain. We had two medical orderlies amongst the prisoners, parachute troop types, but they could do very little, having no bandages, dressings or medical supplies. Tex Crowe would not travel in our truck as he considered his injuries were not as bad as others. I admired the unselfishness of these Americans. During the late afternoon of the third day, while at a goods siding, we were lined up and marched to a two-berth latrine. We were a sorry lot, very dirty, and very smelly, some of the chaps not having had a bath for two or three months. We looked forward to a decontamination shower at the POW camp.

'During the fourth night, eight guards took myself, Captain Firestone, Captain Thornton and Lieutenant Van Epps to Lehr rail station to get water to make coffee. While there, the sirens went and search lights picked up a couple of kites. We were made to shelter in a concrete building and civilians poured in, one white-haired old lady very grim; the civilians made it fairly hostile for us and we were taken outside to keep out of trouble. Railway officials and German soldiers at the entrance to the building gathered together and it seemed by their actions that we would be done over. Our guards took us away before the raid was over, and we made it safely back to the trucks.

'During one of the stops in a railway siding we heard the roar of Merlin engines and the crack of machine guns and cannon and we were strafed by Mosquito aircraft from England. They sounded bloody marvellous! The guards could not understand why we were laughing and cheering. It seemed our boys were over to say "Hello, but mind our bombs and cannon fire!" It felt very homely to hear those Merlin engines!

'The following day was Hitler's birthday, and numerous red background swastika flags flew from buildings. By 1400 hours we were in Barth station, lined up and counted and, with heaps of guards with Alsatian dogs, escorted on a 3-mile march to Stalag Luft I.

'In captivity the instinct for survival reasserts itself with great force. It becomes a serviceman's duty to survive. A live prisoner is a hindrance to the enemy, a dead one saves him trouble. From the first moment of capture there is in the back of every prisoner's mind a firm determination to come through with a whole skin. "Be a survivor. Just keep on breathing."

'During the first few hours or days of capture, if prisoners did but know it, their chances of escape are best; yet, it is just then that their initiative is apt to be at its lowest. A man alone, and on the run for many days, or having spent a long time in the hands of some underground organisation, suffers prolonged nervous strain. Once in enemy hands the temptation to relax becomes almost irresistible. He is no longer hunted. Instead of having to take lightning decisions, any one of which might cost him his freedom, the power of decision passes from him. Events have taken charge. It requires almost superhuman qualities to wish to be hunted again immediately and begin to contrive a means of escape rather than to wait for one to be presented.'

Ken Watts 'palled up' with Squadron Leader A.I. McRichie, RAF, known as Mac. (McRichie's plane had been with Leigh Mallory's famous attack on the gaol at Amien. This raid in France was a low level assault to knock down the prison walls so that the inmates, mostly Resistance people, could be released. The raid was successful, but McRichie's plane was shot down, his navigator killed and he was wounded by shrapnel. In Stalag Luft I he and Watts met and have been close mates ever since.) At first they were housed in Block 5 but then asked permission to move to Block 9. 'The main reason was the rank-conscious British officers. We believed that as we were all POWs, we should not be compelled to address Wing-Commander Hilton as "Sir". And also be torn off a strip for wearing American strides and a zippered blouse.

'Mac and I had a much closer affinity with the Americans.

In Barrack Block No.9, we roomed up with George Hill, a Canadian Squadron Leader, and a British Flight Lieutenant; the latter was replaced by an Aussie because our Flight Lieutenant felt he was culturally superior to us. He probably was, but he caused some bad blood in our little sanctum. Over the passage were housed three most agreeable Canadians, one a Wing-Commander. The rest of the block had four large rooms housing approximately 200 bods of varying rank.

'There was little to feel superior about in a Stalag Luft. The communal toilet block for approximately 1200 bods was a sight to behold. The seating arrangements were a long piece of 3-inch by 2-inch over a deep trench; viewing quite a few bods balancing like chooks on a perch meant it was no place for a chat. It was easy to realise the possibility of the saying, "In the deep Schizen".

'Boiled barley was the basic meal; there were turnips and potatoes; horse meat once a month in 1944 but not in 1945 – they must have run out of poor old horses. Depending on Geneva Red Cross inspections of the Vorlager stores, we had a Red Cross parcel every two and a half months. The contents were absolute luxury – small containers of marmalade, cocoa, sugar, biscuits, tea, two packets of cigarettes (American) and the most prized of all, a solid chocolate bar called a D-Bar. Men were known to exchange their motor car (back home) for two D-Bars. (This transaction actually took place because Mac became the owner of an SS Swallow, the forerunner of the Jaguar, in 1945.) The poor old German guards, semi-starved as they were, would commit all sorts of non-Germanic acts, even treason, for a D-Bar, such was their desperate need for nourishment.'

Home was a long way away and most men admit that it was only on odd occasions that a wave of homesickness struck them. Ken had always loved dogs. 'The guard locking and unlocking our barred window had a German Shepherd which, on command, would put his front paws on the window ledge and that great big beautiful head with its erect ears could be stroked, usually preceded by a quick glance at its keeper.

Having had a dog of my own it reminded me of a very far away home and of different circumstances.'

As the year 1944 rolled on the guards kept disappearing and their replacements were very much older: the Russian front needed all the able-bodied men. 'As prisoners, we were not privy to outside news except the rantings of Lord Haw-Haw, which was compulsory listening. He was hated by all of us. The strongest indication to us of the changing fortunes of war was Allied bombers by the hundred. We later learned that it was 1000 bombers at a time on their way to Berlin or other targets. Above the bombers were the vapour trails of Allied and German fighters. It was an awesome sight. We could imagine the death and destruction to both sides, but being prisoners we were also survivors, and many were the emotions among us in the camp.

'Shortly after the bomber raids, we would congregate at the entrance gate to welcome in the new contingent. "What got you, flak or fighters? Tell us your tough luck story." It was not long before our new sprogs were secure and reasonably contented. An airman is very fortunate to be a POW.'

Geoff Breaden had one obsession. 'When war came I joined the RAAF. That's all I wanted.' He did part of his training in Australia, and was then sent to England and became a navigator in Bomber Command and Pathfinders. 'Our training was kept up to fever pitch. We were given a period of familiarisation then upgraded to bigger aircraft, Wellington bombers. They were huge things for those days.'

Their first operational trip over enemy territory was usually a leaflet raid. 'We were so keyed up for this it never struck us that we might get killed; we were caught up with improving our skills because we thought that if we were smart enough we'd get through.

'Nearly all the aircraft on our squadron at Litchfield near Birmingham, UK were Wellingtons, but there were a few fighters there as well and going out to our aircraft one morning I was going past these fighters and it suddenly hit me: that's lethal! That's what I am in the force for! I'd been sort of apart from it and I'd developed this to a very fine degree, shutting myself off from something I didn't like, pulled the shutters down. If we hadn't been like that I don't think we could have done it. Histrionics and all that sort of thing aside, when you look back on it I've often thought that the Charge of the Light Brigade that we learnt all about as kids was a bloody Sunday-school picnic compared to what we did because we used to do that night after night.

'The charge of 600–800 aircraft with seven or eight blokes in each one, shot at all the way over to Europe and all the way back; these are the facts and they outdo the Light Brigade by a mile. We used to say the only badge we wanted was the RSL badge. We didn't want any gongs, we just wanted to get home in one piece. So a man learnt not to dwell on it.

'At that stage my total flying hours were 174 in daylight and 102 hours at night. When you think of it, it's not a hell of a lot of flying to be getting ready to give your life away. Ken Hutton, the pilot, and I applied to be posted to the Pathfinder course and were accepted. We had the most advanced equipment and training, and had to be prepared to do two tours of operation consecutively, without a break, over Berlin. (One tour was nominally thirty trips – if you made it.)

'Once we were in the briefing room where the target was exhibited our nerves and senses were tightly strung but there was plenty of occasions when we got prepared and briefed, and for some reason or other the flight was cancelled. You've got no idea the let-down of tension. We'd never know why, maybe someone leaked the target or something happened that shouldn't have happened. It was a terrific let-down; we were keyed up, ready to go, at that stage we would have far sooner been on the job. Just imagine standing on the hangman's platform with a noose around your neck and a voice says, "Oh no, we'll leave it till tomorrow". Unbearable.

'The briefings were quite extensive, not at all like Hollywood shows it with air crews sitting around and smoking and lounging. It was not at all like that. You were keyed up, listening, you had to know the rationale of the raid, what it was for, whether it was a factory we were trying to bomb or just blanket bomb or drop certain markers to show the target to the main force bombers or where the defences were most heavily berthed. We listened attentively to the tactics we were to use. Then the crews were divided up, the gunners were given special briefing on what to expect by way of night fighters, the wireless operators would be briefed separately on any special messages to give, and not to give, and bomb aimers would be specially briefed again. The captain was briefed separately, and the navigators copped the longest of the lot because we had to be briefed on the weather and any other factor that could affect our calculations. This would take at least an hour or sometimes longer.

'The preparations for a flight could take up to three hours irrespective of the length of time of the flight itself, and after a flight of six hours (if you were lucky enough to make it back), there was a debriefing when you had to give an account of yourself and explain that you did what you were supposed to do, or couldn't carry out your duty and why. And finally, in a state near emotional exhaustion you got to bed and couldn't sleep no matter how hard you tried.

'Timing, for a navigator, was critical and we were specifi-cally trained for this at the Pathfinder Navigation Training Unit in England. The timing of our navigation had to be spot-on because the main force of bombers were relying on our accuracy: we had to be right. The officer commanding us was an Australian, Air Vice-Marshal Donald Bennett and he was the sort of fellow I would have followed to hell, a real leader, he could do anything; he wouldn't ask us to do something he couldn't do; he was inspiring, but boy you knew who was boss – you had to. He'd written books on navigation and was keen on debriefing the navigators. One night at debriefing (I was young and maybe showing off), I said, "Oh, I was only half a minute late tonight sir", and you would have thought I'd made some improper suggestion to him. He jumped up and said, "It's not bloody well good enough, remember you've got

to realise that the main force of bombers are relying on you!"
I wondered, "My God, what did I say that for!"

'We had to fly hundreds of miles through flak and crap and
snow and ice and rain, get there on time and then be able to
drop the target indicator markers at acutely precise timings,
on half-minute intervals. It was a tall order. On 18 November
1944 we did our first trip on the milk run to Berlin with 8000
pounds of bombs. That trip took seven hours forty minutes
flying time; and with briefing and debriefing it took the best
part of twelve hours altogether from go to whoa.

'We got that way we thought if we could survive six trips to
Berlin nothing could shift us out of the sky because it was the
farthest target there and back. There was always opposition
crossing the European coast and the fortifications on the way;
Berlin itself was fortified for miles and miles around. You could
see it from the air, a 50-mile diameter circle with Berlin in the
middle, the whole thing lit up with searchlights, heavy flak guns
and we had to go in to the middle of that. You had to see it to
believe it. I, as navigator, was mostly too busy, flat out, head
down and tail up but I knew what was going on and I used to
have an occasional look. It was a fantastic sight from 20,000
feet up, just imagine looking on Sydney, but then looking right
down as far as Bulli and right up the coast as if that was all one
concentrated mass of light and you know that they are out to
get you. We used to say, "shits were trumps". It was never a
coincidence that on every dispersal point there was a lavatory –
there was never any trouble with constipation.

'Anyone who wasn't frightened wasn't there. Tall tales were
sometimes told to the civilian population, after all, much of
the truth was too preposterous and sounded like tall tales and
stranger than fiction.

'We navigators, pilots, gunners, radio operators, all took
pride in our skills; we had to be good. We would have been
thrown out if we weren't.'

On Geoff's final trip he was concerned. 'Zero hour as far as
the target was concerned was 2300 hours, eleven o'clock at
night, but our plane had to be there at 0-5, five minutes before

the main force arrived. It was suicidal, because we'd be there on our own. But, as it turned out, we were there first because there was more of a head wind component than the Met forecast, consequently the main force of bombers were later than expected. We, who had all the expertise in navigation could compensate for that and we were there on time, but we were still too bloody early for our safety. We were alone. We were sitting ducks. The night fighter activity was waiting for us. As we lined up the target, everything was perfect, we were cruising down our last time-and-distance leg and all of a sudden the rear gunner screamed, I'll never forget that, and right on top of that there was an echoing clatter like unloading a ton of rocks on to a tin roof, which was the fighter's cannon blasting into our fuselage. From then on the fighter, a radial engine Fokker Wolfe 190 was on us and armed with 20mm explosive cannon shells, while all we had arming our own plane was .303s – about as thick as a pencil, therefore the fighters could stay a little bit further back than we could reach them, but their higher-powered projectiles could knock the hell out of us. That's quite a tactical advantage. He made another attack, put out our two port motors and then he came in again and raked the fuselage. By this time we were on fire and if anyone reckons that aluminium and magnesium (the material our plane was made of) can't burn they ought to try it.

'But it all seemed so unreal, time was compressed, time virtually stood still. My bomb aimer was sitting on the bench next to me with his radarscope, I was sitting at my desk beside him with my charts and instruments. He was wounded under his left arm with a splinter of cannon shell. The wireless operator, an Irishman, standing up in the astrodome was giving us a vivid ball-by-ball description; I tried to attend to Mac's wound, the fighter was coming in again to deliver the *coup de grâce*, and by this time our two gunners – the tail and the mid upper gunner – didn't exist any more, they'd had it, were the first to go as they were more visible. Then Ken, our pilot gave the order to abandon aircraft.

'We'd always discussed this, which we *knew* would never

happen, but each had always said, "Now look, if the rest of the crew have to bail out, I won't, I'll stay and get the aircraft back to England somehow"; I suppose it's bravado and wishful thinking. But now when I made that comment Ken said, "Go!" and the last I saw of him he was holding the aircraft steady while we jumped. We had developed an expertise after all these months of training in what to do in an emergency, "ditching drill" (landing in the sea), parachute drill, dinghy drill. We'd moan, "Oh no, not again!" and you'd have to go through all these drills. But when the time comes things are happening so quickly you've only got that drill to help you know instinctively what to do.

'My immediate thoughts were, okay, I've got to get out now, we're about 20,000 feet, and starting to go down a bit because we'd been manoeuvring, jinking wildly to get away from the fighter, and I didn't want to pass out through lack of oxygen because, of course, we were always on oxygen supplies at that height. So, my immediate reaction was to grab a portable oxygen bottle to hook on to. I looked at the gauge and it was empty so I threw that down and thought well, I've got to get down quickly to get to the more dense air so I can breathe, and without even thinking I jumped with my hand on the D-ring and I free-fell (that's without pulling the parachute cord), until I went through the low cloud which that night was around 4000 feet; so I'd free-fell 14,000 feet from round about 18,000 to 4000 feet, and then pulled the ripcord of the chute. My second thought was to get down quickly so I wouldn't be picked up by searchlights for the fighter might get me again and pick me off.

'So with all this bang, bang, bang in the old computer that governed my actions, I landed a long way away relatively from the target which we were bombing, whereas the rest of them who bailed out landed in it as they had pulled their ripcords straight away. They were picked up that night, badly bashed up, badly treated and Ken, our pilot, was shot on the ground after being picked up. And the other two, the Irish wireless operator, and my friend Mac who was wounded, they were

bashed up and the Germans were going to lynch them (they
had the rope round their necks but the police arrived and
stopped it). But up to that time they'd been knocked down and
kicked and Mac had his ribs broken as well as suffering from
his wound. When I saw my wireless operator a week or so
later, his face was blue right across where they'd kicked him.
I was lucky because the Germans didn't catch me till the following day, otherwise I probably would have got shot as well,
because at that time Hitler had decreed that the real criminals
were the pilots and navigators and they were to be shot on
capture, because we were responsible for getting the aircraft
to its destination. But I wasn't caught until the following afternoon so you can call it luck if you like, I prefer to think that
the Almighty had his hand on me.

'I was in a state of shock, I just didn't know what to do.
What *do* you do when you're in the heart of Germany in the
middle of winter and the temperature on the ground is zero?
Well, I finally wrapped myself in my parachute, rolled under
a hedge and tried to go to sleep. But I didn't sleep very well,
I kept dreaming that I was back on the squadron, and when
we got back from an operational trip over enemy territory we
always had steak and eggs, special rations because of the job
we were doing, and I remember dreaming, "thank heavens I
made it after all, I must have been dreaming". And of course
I was. Dreaming that I was just dreaming.

'I was finally apprehended in the early afternoon by a
German soldier, an Alsatian dog and a couple of civilians and
taken to a quarry where there was a crowd of German youth.
They'd obviously been organising a search party because on
the way to this place there was an aircraft crashed in a forest
and it might have been ours, I couldn't tell, they're a bit hard
to identify when they crash. I'd hardly say I was given the red
carpet treatment at the quarry, but I tried to be nonchalant;
once again, what do you do in a case like that? You haven't
got many options left, but my very nonchalance seemed to
infuriate these Krauts and I made a big mistake, I said
"cigarette, cigarette?" And this bloke just about exploded, he

picked up his rifle and slapped the bolt, rammed one up the pipe and pointed it at me as if to say this is the only bloody cigarette you'll get you bastard. So, well, what do you do? Nothing. They argued, and some of them wanted to shoot me; although I didn't understand the language then I knew what they were on about!

'Finally I was taken to the village about 11 miles away from our target. I was stripped and searched and while being marched up to the local lock-up a great big fat Kraut walked up beside me and abused me and started to belt me over the neck with his walking stick. The soldier that was ushering me shook him off.

'Being by myself was desolating, that was one of the worst aspects of it, being suddenly deprived of the fellowship of the other blokes, being on my own so far from anybody, any friends, that really was awful.

'That night I was in a little lock-up, like an animal's cage with a big iron grille open to the main concourse and every so often a local policeman brought a crowd of young kids along to shout abuse at me. Looking back, I must have been in a sort of protective psychological shell somehow, it was like when you knock your elbow and it goes semi-numb. It was all so unreal, it wasn't happening to me, it was an out-of-the-body experience. I was sitting there watching it happen.

'We had been given certain escape materials and we always carried them. I managed to save some of those, not that they were any good to me. One was a pencil that you broke at a certain spot to find a little compass in it, and I had some maps printed on silk in my flying boots, they didn't find those. Back at base we had had photographs taken in civilian clothes so one could use them for passport photographs if we were caught. But the trauma that you experienced when you were captured, and the knowledge that you hadn't got a great deal of time to be smart and hide things, was numbing. My mind had been so intent on navigating I'd had no time to prepare – but who has in war? The overwhelming feeling was one of loneliness or desolation and just wishing I'd wake up.'

From the little lock-up he was taken, along with an English airman, by rail to Magdeburg 'where we had been bombing' and there met a few other airmen he knew. They were all then transported down to Frankfurt-am-Main in southern Germany, to the big interrogation centre for airmen who had been shot down. 'The first shock on being herded in there with lots of other dishevelled-looking airmen was that all the German soldier-guards spoke English with an American accent (they had been to the United States pre-war on the German Bund Scheme). That was really a shock to see these German Yanks.

'We were searched and processed and then shoved into little cells. There the German Hauptmann started to shout and rave and ask questions. Well, you know the drill, you're only allowed to give your name, rank and number and, of course, when he saw that was all I was going to give him he started to get a bit persuasive, but the line that he took was "Well, look, we understand you're only allowed to give your name, rank and number but if you don't give us other corroborative evidence such as your crew members ..." But you hold out, and you are still in a shell, it isn't happening to you, you are there watching it happen.

'There is no training that can adequately prepare a man for the time when he becomes a prisoner.'

PRISONERS OF THE JAPANESE

Singapore

'Fight to the end, even to the ruins of Singapore City.'

Winston Churchill, 1942

AS PEARL HARBOUR IN the far-away Hawaiian islands rocked to the shock of the 'despicable', unannounced air raid on that lazy Sunday morning, 7 December 1941, so too had the Japanese bombed the British-held Kota Bharu on the Malay peninsula and Singora (Songkhla) and Patani in Thailand one hour earlier on the same day (8 December on the Australian side of the international date line).

Perhaps Australians today may find the date of this attack to the north of Australia surprising. Pearl Harbour has been preserved for all time in folklore and legend, but who remembers – or scarcely knew at the time – that bombing attacks were made that would so affect Australia that same morning of 8 December?

With brilliant strategy by their generals and the tenacity of their troops, the Japanese swept down the Malay peninsula in a three-pronged attack, and within one month had fought their way down to Kuala Lumpur. Many of these invaders rode bicycles that could be folded and carried when necessary, carried enough rice to feed themselves for two days, and all wore clothing suitable for jungle warfare. It was warfare so different, never before contemplated, that the British command (and Australians were then under British command) was taken by surprise. High fallutin' orders rang out, including one from Churchill that he 'expected a fight to the end, even to the ruins of Singapore City'.

Resistance to the Japanese was fourth in a list of priorities drawn up by the British Government and came after defence of the United Kingdom, the Middle East, and aid to Russia. Yet Churchill insisted that Singapore would be held, 'no matter what happens'. These admonitions belonged more to Crimea and the 19th century than to the way Japan would conduct warfare in the 20th century.

The war-lords spoke of Impregnable Singapore and in that time before widespread travel became possible, most Australians thought of Singapore as an almost make-believe land of Somerset Maugham, languid nights, gin slings and exotica, as well as relying on it as an unyielding shield behind which Australia was as snug as a bug in a rug.

In retrospect, it would appear that the excited, naive boys who were shipped in to defend the island may have known as much as did the august leaders in London and Australia. The great guns that made Singapore 'Impregnable' pointed aggressively out to sea awaiting the coming of a great armada which they would sink or scatter, as surely as had Francis Drake defeated the Spanish Armada. But the enemy came swiftly, victoriously, by land.

Much has been made of Churchill's seeming disbelief and anger when told that the guns faced only seawards, but why would he or any other soldier be surprised: wasn't it the habitual placement of guns since medieval times? Mankind simply had not yet rid itself of the old method of doing things. (And, as the empire diehards in Singapore said, 'the damned things would have blown up the Club if they were swung in-shore!')

Battle

Those who have seen battle only in Hollywood movies or on television can have no idea how battles in the mid-20th century have been fought. Men who fought the Japanese in World War II came across a type of warfare they had not been trained for, leaders had not expected – and indeed at times they faced they knew not where, because they knew not from whence the enemy would come. The men who fought and were taken prisoner in Malaya knew this.

Captain Bernie O'Sullivan, 2/4th Machine Gun Battalion, found it difficult to understand the reasoning behind many of the orders and movements. 'It seemed to me that we were running around in circles, moved east, west, north, south. Units moved from our flank and we were not told of it. We were overlooked, abandoned. The movements of this battalion were the same as most of the Australian battalions who fought in the Pacific. To quote the men, "We were buggered from start to finish. First our side buggered us around, then the Japs buggered us around and finally buggered us up!"'

On 24 January Bernie O'Sullivan's machine gunners set off to battle posts in Malaya and the Japanese attacked on 8 February. 'Many of the men were only partially trained, not having been in the army very long (some men had no bayonets for their rifles), yet they were the best trained men of any of the battalions to which they were sent. Major Saggers took his position with his troops and of the seven officers he took into the line from the 2/4th Machine Gun Battalion, six were lost when caught in an ambush. They were my best and oldest friends, Wadhurst, Dunoolin, Hodgers, Mercer, Green, Till. Vic Mentiplay was the only survivor. Our Colonel Ankatell was hit and died. Our company commander was killed, our quartermaster was killed. (So I then took over as quartermaster.)

'The units were contracted to a smaller line of defence. I was given men I'd known from the battalion, formed a platoon and took them to an area to support the line. The men frantically dug tank traps. Young Indian troops, untrained, confused, afraid, without officers, came wandering back through us. They had no leadership, they were abandoned.'

O'Sullivan and his men were heavily bombed from the air. By this time the few British aircraft in the area had either been shot down or withdrawn. 'Our position was hopeless. Now we were almost completely surrounded. The artillery came to our aid and enabled us to get out by their fire blanketing us on both sides of the track. There was much enemy movement around us on this march and even with the artillery help I still don't know how we made it.

'Major Green, by now a Colonel, was in charge of the battalion, he had ordered me to the right flank and here I contacted the officer in charge of the battalion next to me in the line so that they would immediately inform us if they were moving. But we heard nothing from them. It was no fault of any of the commanders I suppose, just overall confusion caused by the swift advance of the enemy and their knowledge and cunning in fighting in jungle conditions, many of them having already fought for some years in their invasion of China. We had no stores to feed our battalion so we had to try to pinch food. I then sent back to the brigade major to ensure we were informed of any movement because we realised that withdrawal was imminent, but we heard nothing and the men had to fight their way out.'

Few awards are given to the losers and while most men deserving of such were ignored, a few were selected. Captain Victor Brand MC was one such. He was Regimental Medical Officer with the 2/29th Battalion and had won his Military Cross in Malaya in January 1942. The official citation read, 'Captain Brand was with the battalion near Vakri [sic]. The Regimental Aid Post was in the centre of the perimeter which was constantly under heavy shell and mortar fire. With total disregard for his own safety, he left the slit trenches in which all personnel were forced to shelter, and remained in the open during the heavy and continuous bombardment, attending to the wounded, both Australian and Indian. Shortly afterwards the battalion withdrew and left only a small covering group of carriers. Captain Brand, however, remained behind and refused to leave until he had attended to all the wounded and placed them on vehicles. He was wounded while out on the road, but owing to a road block was unable to be moved. He then went through the vehicles collecting the walking wounded whom he personally escorted to the battalion.'

No quarter was given; men wearing Red Cross brassards on their arms were as vulnerable as a man with a rifle. Private Harold Ball of the 2/9th Field Ambulance was killed on 2 February. Ball, the Australian Rules premiership footballer (Melbourne premiership team 1939, '40, '41), had orders to withdraw but decided to stay to relieve Captain John Catchlove who had been wounded. With him was another fine athlete, John Park. Their bodies were later found.

The 2/10th Field Ambulance had moved up into forward positions along with the 2/30th, 2/29th and 2/26th Battalions who were to make first contact with the enemy. The 2/10th was advised to establish its main dressing station further back but Colonel E.M. Sheppard, the commanding officer, said that was 'much too far to the rear' and moved his station up amongst the infantry. Casualties arrived the following day. The battalions were therefore among the first of the fighting and offered the fiercest resistance the Japanese met in the Malayan campaign. They carried in the wounded, buried the dead, transported some men to casualty clearing stations, others further back to a base hospital. After three days of strenuous fighting, word came to the Field Ambulance that the Australians, outnumbered, could no longer hold the Japanese; the medical group was to make a strategic withdrawal at night. The doctors, Captain Roy Mills and Captain Peter Hendry, each had a full haversack and pack ready to move at a minute's notice 'when things got sticky', as Captain Mills said.

All men, including clerks and cooks of this body of men, were trained as stretcher bearers and medical orderlies. They had sailed from home in August 1941, their commanding officer, Lieutenant Colonel Doctor E.M. Sheppard, already proving his mettle. 'No battalion had a more egalitarian leader', the survivors claim. 'We called him Mac.'

The 2/10th Field Ambulance came down the peninsula setting up casualty clearing stations as the retreating troops fought a losing battle. The battle was moving so fast that at times the wounded were scarcely attended to when the station had to pack up and move; patients were carried to ambulances and 'we got to hell out of it with the enemy hard on our heels', as Driver H. Barnes said. 'You had to pick a way for your ambulance to get through the packs of refugee civilians trying to escape the Japanese and there were also our own units retreating.'

Captain Roy Mills had all the qualities of a great medical man in the field. He had his men commandeer big brass trays from deserted bungalows and each medical officer had two teams of two orderlies attached to him. One, called 'the dirty pair', had scissors, jack-knife, soapy water, washers and towels, so that a wound could be quickly exposed, boots and clothes cut off and a quick cleansing made. The 'clean tray' was like an ordinary hospital ward dressing tray, with sterile forceps, dressings, antiseptic in bowls etc., artery forceps and ties to arrest major bleeding and needle holders and suture material for special cases, although he expected to transport most patients quickly back to the main dressing station south of Segamat, thence to the casualty clearing station further south.

'One of the first casualties was Lieutenant Des Makepeace from 2/15th Field Regiment who came with a mouth wound, a missing tooth and holding in his hand the bullet that caused it. We learnt at that time that Sergeant Stark, who had transferred from our unit to the 2/30th Battalion, had been killed in a bayonet charge, from a head wound. That night we were withdrawn to our main dressing station south of Segamat and the next night Major Rayson called me up and told me that the Japanese tanks had broken through and the 2/26th Battalion was in danger and heavy casualties expected – I was to go north of Segamat on a road I had reconnoitred the previous week, to wait at a certain point to meet (hopefully) the 2/26th Battalion coming through.

'It was eerie. Shells could be heard above us going back and forth. I had four ambulances facing south, ready to move at a moment's notice. Lloyd Noakes was the corporal in charge, my driver was Keith Offord. We had a kerosene tin with a cross cut out of the side and red cloth pasted over it, with a hole in the back to flash a torch on the red cross. We heard vehicles coming, were they bren-gun carriers or were they Japanese tanks?

'They were about 70 yards away, I was lying on the ground with arms outstretched and flashed the torch in the kerosene tin. Great was my relief to be challenged by an Australian voice! It was a company of the 2/26th Battalion. We got back to our main dressing station just after dawn and then the Segamat bridge was blown by our engineers.

'Days and dates just seemed to go by with withdrawal after withdrawal – being shelled, bombed and machine-gunned without respite.' During this period, and at all times following, the bearers, drivers and doctors worked tirelessly to attend to the sick and wounded, offering any comfort available. 'Our aerial defence was next to nil and the Japanese were able to dictate each phase of the unfortunate mess we were in.'

'Large numbers of casualties came through, including survivors from the Muar area battle and they were in bad shape. There were Australian infantry and support units, Gurkhas and Indians, all were treated promptly and despatched to our Advanced Dressing Station.'

Ray Connelly, 2/10th Field Ambulance, wrote: 'When the Japs attacked the Muar area, Headquarters in Singapore received the information that a Japanese force of 500 was involved. The 2/29th Battalion was detached "temporarily" to assist the 45th Indian Brigade and "to return when they had mopped up". The force involved however, was a division of Japanese guards, efficient, highly trained and well-equipped troops, with tanks and planes. The Indian resistance crumbled and the 2/19th Battalion was sent in across from the east coast to assist the 2/29th. With a few remnants of the 45th Indian Brigade, these two battalions stood off the Jap division for a week, suffering massive casualties. They destroyed thirty-eight tanks and killed probably a thousand Japs. Finally, almost surrounded, and in an impossible position, they fought their way back in groups to safety. They were carrying their wounded, short of food and medicine. Ammunition was running out. Those who could walk were ordered to attempt to reach the Australian lines through swamps and jungle to the eastward. The wounded were left propped against the trees or lying on the ground. They would, we believed, be taken prisoners of war. "We lit cigarettes for them and left them smoking and laughing. They were calm", a survivor wrote, "not afraid". But the approaching Japanese shot and bayoneted them. It was the first hint to the Australians of the barbarism they might expect if they fell prisoner to these people. The 2/19th had only 271 men left and the 2/29th had 130 and these survivors marched off ready for yet another battle.

' "A" Company, 2/10th Field Ambulance, was forward at the 118-3/4 mile peg on the main road, assisted by Captain Mills and a section of B Company under Major Murphy, and sending back casualties in ambulances three and four at a time to the 110 mile peg on the main road. Mobile sections were established with one medical officer and ten to twelve other ranks and two to four ambulances attached. Captain Hendry, Captain Mills and Captain Crabbe of A Company were now mobile. The official history of World War II states: "the Ambulance Mobile Sections were truly mobile and retired only when the front line troops moved out and were often the last to leave".

'Headquarters moved back to Mengapol Estate, where Doctor Tom Hamilton's CCS was operating. Sergeant Tom Purdon was sent forward to find and aid wounded and try to contact the 2/19th and 2/29th Battalions. He returned with a bullet-riddled ambulance and reported no luck. Sergeant Mick Lumby described the numbers being evacuated as five stretcher cases and ten walking wounded per ambulance, and numbers were so great that they called in the Australian Motor Transport Unit with big trucks to help. Some confusion was caused by men looking for mates, and for wounded, and so crowding the area.'

The Indian Field Ambulance moved forward to assist the Indian Brigade and, with the 2/19th and 2/29th Australian

Battalions, suffered massive casualties. 'There were a large number of the Indian Field Ambulance men killed in this action, they had done a great job while they could.' When the 2/19th and 2/29th had originally tried to evacuate their wounded with the Indian Field Ambulances manned by 2/19th and 2/29th personnel, they were refused thoroughfare by the Japanese, who demanded total surrender. This was refused by the battalions. But the badly wounded men had to be abandoned when the troops withdrew.

At Yong Peng, some of Ray Connelly's men scrounged 'a couple of pigs, which were quickly killed and dressed and most of the company had pork chops that evening.' The mobile section was now at Socfin to aid stragglers, and there they waited until a Provost sergeant rode up on a motor cycle and enquired 'What the hell are you blokes doing here?' Captain Mills explained he and his men were there to treat stragglers until ordered out. The sergeant then said, 'Hear that rattling noise just down the road? Well that isn't the garbo truck, they're Jap tanks! Now get out! That's an order!' 'We went cheerfully', Ray Connelly recalls.

They set up at Ayer Hitam crossroads. Ray arrived there with a car and two ambulances and on his first trip up was halted by a sergeant waving him down saying, 'Hold it you silly bastard, this is the forward platoon – the Japs are just across that paddock there. And get that bloody ambulance out of sight, you'll draw the crabs.' 'We loaded the wounded aboard after about ten minutes of heavy mortar fire. The feature of our stay at Ayer Hitam was regular bombings and machine-gun fire from Jap planes. During breaks from casualties and bombings, we would usually have a game of contract bridge in progress as Captain Hendry was a keen player, and we'd play until the planes appeared or casualties arrived.'

Ray Connelly had asked to be sent to help with the forward platoon from the 2/26th Battalion where fifteen men were left out of thirty of the platoon. Most of the trip was on hands and knees, the whole area was under shell fire. On arrival at the platoon post he was asked where was his rifle?

'I'm a medical bloke', Connelly replied. 'We want riflemen not zambuck', he was told. 'What will you do when they come over? Hit them with your Red Cross haversack?' He was thrown a rifle and a hundred rounds in a bandolier. 'Can you fire this?' Connelly said, yes. 'Well, take that red cross off your arm and bury it and get out in that firing pit. They'll be over tonight.' After dark, the order came, 'Check your gear, here they come'.

'All hell broke loose, firing from right and left and yelling and screaming from the Japs. We were under fire from left and rear when we were ordered back. There was a machine gun firing along the railway line.' Then the order came, 'Between bursts, three at a time, nick across and we'll take up positions on the other side.' Connelly got across and was sent off with eight walking wounded. He flagged down the Red Cross utility and loaded the men and headed back to his unit which now set up camp in beleaguered Singapore.

'Sister Salmon, who I knew from Bathurst Camp Hospital back in Australia, gave me a good tumbler of brandy. As we took up our positions the nurses were being loaded into ambulances, all protesting loudly, some in tears. "We want to stay with the boys", they called. But they were sent away to the waterfront. (Their ship, the *Vyner Brooke*, was sunk off Bànka Island and many of these women were murdered by the Japs.)'

Ray, by now wearing his Red Cross brassards again, got on with the bloody business of the day.

Another of these men, Private Bob Wilson, also 2/10th Field Ambulance, was working in the Cathay Building where ambulances were bringing wounded men and stretcher bearers were trying to get them into the building. 'Civilians and high ranking officers milled round in the foyer, doing nothing but obstructing and being bloody pests.'

The shelling of Singapore was intense, shrapnel, black smoke and fallen debris everywhere. 'When my partner and I were trying to unload a patient from an ambulance the scene in the foyer was utter hysteria. When a high ranking officer got in our way, Fred Kelly kicked him in the arse and shouted,

"Have a go or get out of the way and let a man do his job!" The Cathay Building received seventeen direct hits, the streets were littered with rubble, lives were in danger every time the men raced out to the ambulances to bring patients in.' Every medical man was a hero, they all earnt praise and admiration even though they may not be mentioned in despatches.

The 'front line' was retreating by order, and all the army with it including the medical parties which had fought their own fight under fire the whole way down the peninsula. During the final stages of the Malayan campaign, when the weary troops were retreating across the Causeway into Singapore and the last of the 2/10th ambulances were retreating with them, a soldier trudging along the road patted the side of the vehicle and said, 'Good old 2/10th!' Sitting beside the driver, Keith Offord, was Captain Roy Mills, the young doctor, scarcely out of medical school, already a legend for his valour under fire.

Sapper Bob Berry, RAE, had arrived in Singapore on 24 January 1942. On 5 February he wrote home. 'Dear Mum and Dad, Things are not going too good over here, they are always bombing the island. We expect an attack any day now. I hope we can hold them off for a while. Hard to write, we are moving about a lot. Has George gone back to the front yet? Did his arm get alright? [His brother George had been wounded in North Africa.] Well mum it is getting dark so I will close hoping to hear from you soon. Love Bob.' (At the end of the war Bob's parents received a 'deep regret' telegram from the Minister for the Army stating that Bob had died as a prisoner.)

On Sunday 8 February 1942 the Japanese landed on Singapore Island and continued the bombing that caused more casualties on three separate days than London had experienced at the height of the blitz. In twenty-four days there had been eighty air-raids on this small island which held over one million people.

Captain Alan Rogers in Singapore, pharmacist, Medical Supply Unit, 8th Division, was caught up with the confusion but he performed miracles.

'From the Sunday night the "landing" was made [across the causeway to Singapore], the roar of guns was terrific; we had a battery of 4.5 Howitzers just behind us and also a couple of Bofors anti-aircraft guns, and these were truly nerve-shattering.' From that Sunday there was a continuous barrage going on from both sides, and air raids were becoming more frequent. 'As I had all the medical stores for the AIF you can imagine that I was a bit worried, not only for these precious stores which could save so many lives and which would all be lost if a single bomb hit them, but also for myself. However, there were no safe places left on the island and we had to take pot luck.'

Activity was so intense during the night that Rogers decided to find Administration. 'We found them at 0830 and I was again reassured that I would not be forgotten if there had to be another move. All day things were decidedly unpleasant. At lunchtime we all got into the truck and went to the barracks for something to eat and when we got there we found the whole place completely deserted. So, grabbing a few tins of meat and a loaf of bread from the Q store, we went out to get into the truck just as the Japs started to shell the place. I yelled to the boys to drop and we dropped pronto and stayed dropped for fifteen minutes flat out on the top of this exposed and unprotected hill, while the shells were cracking and bursting all around us.

'When we got up, all around us there were smoking buildings, smashed to the ground, roofs blown in, dust and smoke everywhere and the air almost unbreathable for the reek of powder and cordite. We cautiously made our way out, and found a 3-ton lorry lying across our track. In it were two Indians badly smashed about and beside it was Lieutenant Lewis who had been out at Serangoon with us. He was very badly hit and all his staff of Indians who had survived the barrage had fled and left their wounded comrades there. Of course we jumped to it but just at that moment the shelling started again. But this time we could not hug the ground because we had to give these poor fellows what assistance we could and get them to some place where they could be attended to. Lewis was the worst so we put him in the truck we had further down the road and Reg drove him to Tanglin Hospital. In the meantime we had got stretchers and carried the two Indians down to the road where we eventually managed to get a passing ambulance. I went back to the 3-ton truck but couldn't get it to go so I let off the brake and ran it into the gutter so we could get our truck past.

'The shelling had now stopped so we went back to the store and got a few clothes together and I collected all the morphia I could as well as all the thermometers and forceps and decided to go to headquarters and see what was happening. There was a great deal of fighting going on in the Botanical Gardens opposite us, Jap snipers having been there for several days. The building next to ours had been damaged by shell fire and the battery behind us was again in operation. We found head-quarters desolated, it had recently been shelled and bombed and damaged vehicles littered the area; there was no one in sight. Nippon bombers were still flying overhead.'

He decided to go back and see if he could rescue some more supplies. 'I borrowed the ARCS truck and drove it while Reg drove mine and we made the pilgrimage back again through the city, which by this time was a bit of a shambles. As well as the Air Force leaving us, the Navy had evacuated about ten days before so we were left on our own – there could be no withdrawal for us earthbound troops, we could only retreat on land, and as there was no land left we would have to fight, or die – or what?

'All this time I was anxious to know where [Doctor] Glyn White was and wondering how to get in touch with him. So I was up very early next morning, Thursday 12th, but I could get no information as to the whereabouts of Administration Headquarters. However, I did the best I could and made two more trips to Tanglin. We brought back all the ether and local anaesthetics, antiseptics, dressings and what I thought would be the most useful things. There were still a large number of planes flying around the Botanical Gardens and a lot of sniping

on all sides. I spent another night at the hospital and word
came through that we were outside the perimeter laid down
by Command – in other words we were beyond the front line.
There cannot be many instances in history when a *base* hospital has been in such a position.

'We were told that the hospital would be taken prisoner that
day. I thought this over for a few minutes and decided I would
probably be more use if I were not a prisoner. I routed out the
boys and told them to get dressed while I went to St Andrews
Cathedral where I'd learned Glyn had established himself. He
agreed with me that I might be able to do a job there, so we
took what gear we had and went to the cathedral. There was
an Advanced Dressing Station being run there by the 2/9th and
2/10th Field Ambulances and there was also present the 2/2nd
and 2/3rd Motor Ambulance Convoys. Things were fairly
quiet that morning, only one air raid, but just before lunch we
were fairly heavily shelled. Down on our bellies while shells
were dropping all around us, a couple of vehicles were hit,
several men were killed and others wounded. I was particularly
lucky as I was going over to yarn with Peter Chitty when the
show started and he was in the middle of the ructions and was
himself wounded.

'That was Friday the 13th, a black day indeed. We made a
couple more trips to the store, taking a couple of ambulances
as extra vehicles. It was as hot as ever out there now, as the
front line was coming back down Holland Road and was
getting very close to our doorstep. All the afternoon casualties
were pouring in, not only AIF but English and Indian troops
and civilians. There was intermittent shelling all that day and
a couple more air raids.

'During the whole of Friday we had been told that relief
would reach us by the 15th and we were all keyed up expecting
help if we could hold out till then. So there was a day to go
and attacks were getting fiercer every minute.

'Saturday morning dawned with the air filled with smoke
and dust, planes constantly overhead, a continuous roar of
artillery, both ours and Nippon's, and the sound of small arms

ammunition fire getting closer every minute. Early in the morning I took my truck, an ambulance and a 30-hundred-weight vehicle up to Tanglin and again we put on as much stuff as we could manage and again we got away safely. It was an unpleasant trip and the city was much more damaged than the previous day. We were up in the front line no doubt about it. There were four of our boys dug in with their automatic weapons in our garden, next door was a Bren carrier hidden in the hedge waiting to pounce when need arose. The artillery was still pounding away on Tanglin Hill.' This remarkable man continued to salvage all medical supplies he could get his hands on. He bade farewell to friends.

Acting Corporal, Joe Barnett, 2/20th Battalion, 'had established his depot at Fort Canning and from him I collected some more morphia. Gus Thorpe [Private, 2/19th Battalion] was there and I said goodbye to him. From what I hear he sailed that night and from all reports there seems little doubt that poor Gus is at the bottom of the sea.'

Children had earlier been evacuated followed by civilians and women (Europeans, that is). There was no chance of escape for the Chinese people: they stood fast, stalwart and brave. Thousands were killed by bomb and shell every day and the planes came over without respite, and without British planes to contest right of way. Much of the city was on fire, the smoke and flames rising in great fiery clouds into the sky accompanied by the booming and rattle of big guns, bombs, mortar shells and machine guns. By Wednesday the last real chance of evacuation went on amid chaos ashore, with escapees climbing over and around hundreds of cars abandoned near the waterfront by people who had fled earlier, skirting the fires and diving to the ground when bombs fell, and eventually scrabbling on to sampans and small boats that acted as tenders to the larger ships anchored out in the bay. These fleeing ships were bound for Java. In retrospect we may well ask, given the speed, skill and bravura with which the Japanese had sped southwards, would nearby Java be any safer than Singapore?

Older even than Britain's holdings in this part of the southern hemisphere, was the empire of the Netherlands East Indies, the empire of the Spice Islands that had yielded vast wealth to Holland.

In what is now known as Indonesia, the Dutch had built fine roads, splendid public buildings, cities, towns, schools and hospitals and were renowned for their business enterprise and unremitting labour. A large colony of Dutch descendants of the early NEI colonisers had been there for 400 years, and Holland, like England, had never envisaged the day when it would lose its wealth-producing colonies. The Dutch had treated the natives with even more scorn, harshness and lack of understanding than had British colonists. It was a rich empire and could afford arrogance.

It was to this 'sanctuary', where the Japanese missionaries of the anti-white, Greater Asia Co-Prosperity Sphere movement had been most successful, that the Singapore evacuees were fleeing through daylight bombing, mine fields and in disastrously overcrowded ships of any condition. Many were killed on the way, many ships were sunk even before they left Singapore harbour or indeed the wharf. Some men bobbed around on the water on bits of flotsam of wrecks, until Japanese planes spotted them and blasted them to death; a few got ashore on islands and lived miserably for a few days, even weeks before they were found and killed, others died of exposure, disease and hunger. Few had mosquito nets or quinine, at that time the only remedy for malaria.

All who escaped remember one thing in particular, the blue-black fog-like clouds that reached hundreds of feet into the air as far as the eye could see, the result of the firing of oil dumps and high octane fuel tanks (used by aeroplanes), set alight on Singapore Island to deny them to the enemy.

Ray Connelly didn't leave. He continued to collect every thing he could by way of medical stores.

'I put in some more anaesthetics, dressings, morphia and x-ray film and decided to risk a trip out to Katong. At this time we did not know if the hospital was prisoner, surrounded, wiped out or what, so we'd be serving a twofold purpose by making the trip. Taking courage in both hands, Reg and I set out. There was little activity out this way at the time but as we passed the drome a row of houses were on fire as were several oil dumps, doing their share to maintain the pall over the dying city. Twenty planes were on the ground, one of them still burning and others twisted and smoke-blackened skeletons. A Hurricane was standing on its nose, a huge ammunition dump was going off and bullets were flying everywhere.

'We reached the hospital and found everything very quiet there and going on much as usual. Then back to the cathedral after sheltering under a tree while twenty-six Nip planes went overhead on their way to bomb the wharves and docks.

'Wounded were still pouring in and the surgeons and dressers were toiling, Doctor Frank Cahill in particular doing job after job in the little improvised theatre in the back of the cathedral, and coming out for a breath of air, and Bert Campbell lighting a cigarette and putting it in Frank's mouth so he wouldn't have to waste time scrubbing up again. The orderlies of the ambulances and MACs were going flat out, doing dressings, administering morphia and getting other poor devils ready for the theatre.

'The whole thing was a never-to-be-forgotten sight – the stately old cathedral, blinded by having its stained glass removed and replaced by boards, was standing in its grounds, which were not lined by the cars of worshippers but serried ranks of ambulances and other Red Cross vehicles. A small Red Cross flag was flying out front, another had been rigged up out of sheets and red blankets and we all hoped it would be seen and recognised. Inside this lovely old place were row upon row of stretchers and blankets and mattresses, each one bearing its poor shattered man. The orderlies were rushing hither and thither and as cases were treated they were shipped out into the waiting ambulances and taken to their various destinations. The AIF were taken to the Cathay Building where the 2/10th AGH was operating at this time, the Pommies were taken to Raffles Hotel which had also been turned into a hospital, and the Indians were taken around the corner to the Raffles Institution were Indian Field ambulances were running another hospital. It was a pitiful sight to see some of the poor little kids carried in all knocked around and damaged and probably maimed for life. The ambulance drivers were doing a fine job, carrying on through air raids and artillery barrages, driving right up to the front line and bringing back casualties with speed and despatch. They were responsible for saving the lives of many poor wretches.

'At every explosion some of the shell-shocked would cower into their blankets, others would endeavour to leap up in spite of their wounds, while others would scream and hang on to their mates, and the whole of them would be a shivering, quaking mass terrible to behold. It was no use trying to comfort them by telling them that the guns were ours – they just did not believe us.'

It is necessary when referring to the 8th Division to correct a widely held impression that these men were easily defeated. Doubtless their own government at the time was happy enough for this rumour to spread and so cloud the truth that they were damnably betrayed by a government which had neglected the country's defence and so sent young men to fight without the years necessary for training of both officers and men, and without modern equipment to maintain a stand and save lives. They had poor, sometimes defective arms, some of the rein- forcements had little training or none, some of their leaders from the top down left much to be desired, and at all times they faced a foe experienced in warfare and using new and surprising methods of locomotion as well as strategy. Not only had the 8th Division been tenacious and brave as the men battled a long, fighting retreat, sometimes driving the enemy back in hand-to-hand fighting and with bayonets, but they had withstood the courageous, tough, well-trained, battle-experi- enced Japanese for ten weeks.

When the end came it was not the decision of the men in the field to lay down their arms, indeed they believed they were able to fight on, and were willing to go on. The British General Percival commanding all the Allied Forces in this region made and relayed the decision that his troops were to lay down their arms in surrender to the Japanese.

Capitulation followed. Bernie O'Sullivan, like other soldiers, had never seen this as a possibility. 'At no time in my experience in the army was there any thought of the action of surrender. We were physically over-tired, mentally exhausted. We had only fought for a week but of the 961 men on battalion strength we had lost 133 killed in action (and 239 of this battalion later died as POWS). All had fought splendidly, bravely and without any more thought of their safety than the average well-trained soldier. But now we were completely at the mercy of events.'

There was no evacuation from Singapore as there had been in other campaigns such as Dunkirk. No flotilla of little ships could come to their aid. The time bought by the troops in Malaya and the surrounding islands is claimed to have allowed the Australian troops then in the Middle East to be brought home to defend Australia; and this country should never forget the cost they paid.

Private Alan Davies, 2/29th Battalion, was only 20 years old. 'We didn't know anything about the jungle. Nothing at all. And our rifles, .303s, were useless, great long cumbersome bloody things and they'd catch on vines and you'd finish up on the broad of your back. You'd see a Jap and you'd have one shot at him and he was gone. Automatic weapons were the only thing that would have been any good. Word came through that there had been a landing of 500 Japs at Vila, and they sent two companies of the 2/29th Battalion up, a few odds and sods which I was amongst, workshop people and a company of Hyderabads, Punjabis and Sikhs. We were supported by Pommie artillery. When we got to Muar, there wasn't 500 Japs, a division of the Japanese Imperial Guard had landed. Anyway, we formed a line across.

'We were fighting them, and holding them there in front of the Muar River, but like the others they went round us. They

put a big road-block across the Muar bridge. We didn't have
any tanks or anything like that to clear a way through. They
were fighting us from the back and the front. By this time there
was about fourteen truckloads of wounded fellows in a pretty
bad way. Our Don R [Despatch Rider] under a white flag on
the back of a motor bike, went down to the Muar bridge and
asked could the wounded be allowed out, under a Red Cross.
And the Japs said yes, they'd allow them through if all the
others would surrender.

'It was put to the fellows who were wounded and they all
said, "No, we'll take a chance". We got the order to disband
and it was every man for himself to make our way through
the jungle and try to get back to our own lines. Eighteen of us
walked for five days, straight up along the banks of the Muar
River, about 25 miles, and then we got old trees and logs and
began to paddle across the Muar but the river was in a raging
flood with the monsoonal rains. By the time we got across we
must have floated 10 miles down stream, and there were many
who hadn't got up as far as us who tried to get across and
they just floated down and into the bloody Japs, because the
river was a mile and a half wide. And the Japs shelled them
as they floated down river. Not many survived out of that. We
were formed up again at Krangi.

'There was no barbed wire to put between us and the Japs
across the Causeway. It was just open country. We tried three
times to fight past them but they went round us and broke
through the Indian lines. And came in on us. That was the fight
for the island of Singapore. We had to retreat back to Bukit
Timah where we fought again. And from there we retreated to
Tanglin Bay, and that's where we finished at 6.30 p.m. on Sunday
15 February and that was the end of the war for us.'

15 February 1942

On that fateful day, Sunday 15 February 1942, the notice
board at the Adelphi Hotel read: 'Singapore must not, shall

not, fall!' All the night and all that day English, Australian, Indian and civilian ambulances poured in their cargoes of bleeding humanity to the cathedral, some able to walk, some so badly wounded that their stretchers were soaked with blood. Stretcher squads were always ready to unload (and load patched-up soldiers being poured out again); spare drivers and wagon orderlies were ready to go out again as soon as required.

The men who were there tell the story. Private Charles Stuart, 2/9th Field Ambulance: 'Inside the cathedral, to the left of the font, a regular supply of hot sweet tea was always ready day and night for the patients and medical workers. And when the stretcher bearers and ambulance men came in and unloaded their wounded they went straight to the tea pot before they set off for their next dangerous run to God knew where. Nearby was the "Admission and Discharge" clerk keeping a record of the wounded and dead. On the right of the font and handy to the entrance to the cathedral, the smell of ether was always present from the small room used as the operating theatre. The cries of men going under or recovering from the effects of ether were joined by the pitiful cry of wounded children. Sometimes buckets, covered over, were carried out which indicated that limbs had been hastily amputated under surgically primitive conditions.

'By the font was a table of bandages, bottles, hypodermic syringes and the rest of the equipment of a field medical unit. Under the nave wounded men were lying on dozens of mattresses, all ranks and colours together.

'The padres and the burial party carried a wooden cross knocked up from a bully-beef box. Some men were dead when brought in to us and some died after a few hours. One was a mate of ours – an ambulance driver who was with us in the early days of our unit at Nagambie Road, Seymour. A shell burst near his ambulance and a femoral artery was severed. He was rushed to the cathedral, given a hurried transfusion, but it was too late. The dead were temporarily buried in the cathedral grounds.

'Singapore at this time had abandoned sounding air-raid sirens for the simple reason they would have had to work non-stop. A few fellows had given away under the strain of the never-ending racket and sobbed unrestrainedly at the loss of pals. So far the enemy had respected the Red Cross flag. This Red Cross flag flying at the cathedral had been with the original 10th Field Ambulance in France in 1916, 1917 and 1918 and had been given to the 2/9th by the old survivors.

'As well as the military casualties, civilians poured in with their wounds and their wounded. Another of our ambulance drivers was mortally wounded. He "flattened" when danger came, but the "daisy-cutter" effect of the bomb fragments tore through his stomach and he died later in the day. The whole area was ablaze. Many of the walking wounded Australians rushed to help us haul the blazing Red Cross trucks and ambulances clear, attaching tow-chains to haul petrol tanks away. Officer F.L. Wright of the Red Cross put out the fire on his truck with water from the radiator.

'At about 1600 hours the Bishop of Singapore conducted a short service and passed among the wounded – a blessing here, a few words of comfort there. The bomb attack had destroyed many of the windows and put the electric organ out of use. There was confusion in the heart of the city, troops forced back from the front lines had nowhere to go, and hundreds of them gathered themselves into groups and outside buildings where units of the medical corps were in evidence. There was no other symbol or standard for them to rally to.

'About four o'clock an air raid was launched at us – we could hear the roar of the planes and then the whoosh! as the bombs came down. I was in the vestry of the cathedral where Des Brennan was running an RAP and as I heard the noises of the descending bombs I flung myself flat. There was a terrific explosion and the air was full of dust and smoke, I was covered with broken glass and dirt but unhurt. But the noise of the poor shell-shocked wretches was awful to hear. All the cars parked outside were in flames, some of them total wrecks.

'At this time we were told that we had capitulated unconditionally and that the cease-fire would sound at 2000 hours
that night. But the war still went on and many more of our
boys were brought in wounded and some were killed after we
had really surrendered. After 1600 hours a strange silence
seemed to come over Singapore – the gunfire had stopped.
"What's wrong?" It was uncanny. Then the sad rumours
started. "An Armistice has been arranged." "We have given in
to the Japs." "The fighting is over." It was a terrible thought.
All the bloodshed and loss of lives – all for what! It was a
relief mixed with bitterness – we had been let down, and with
cold, calculating deliberateness. First and chiefly, as a result of
England's criminal unpreparedness for war and, secondly, by
the muddle-headedness of the manner in which the Malayan
campaign had been conducted. Some of us have modified our
views since that date, but I venture to say that a large proportion have not.

'I have heard since that the capitulation should have taken
place on Saturday night but owing to some misunderstanding,
a junior staff officer was sent out to interview the Japanese
general, when, according to the Japanese, our GOC, General
Percival, should have gone out in person. And so we had to put
up with another day's useless slaughter owing to another blunder
by our leaders. Still, this appeared to be the last one they would
make for some time.

'The ground floor of the Adelphi Hotel was also covered
with stretchers with wounded and it was hard to find a place
to park the body. We had set up a sort of dressing station in
the middle of what had been the dining room and I stayed on
duty here until midnight. About all we could do was to dish
out water and morphia.

'At approximately 2030 there was a wild moan – it was an
air-raid siren giving the signal that all was over. As it went on
one wounded fellow called to his comrade, "It's all over mate".
All the senseless, useless throwing away of young lives had
stopped.' It was defeat, but these men had fought the enemy
longer than any country in Europe had yet fought the German

army. (France, for instance, had surrendered in six weeks.)

Much of Singapore water came from across the narrow causeway from the Malay peninsula and now, with the Causeway blown up, the water supply was failing. All supplies were dwindling and the Japanese were now on the island and within the city itself. A siege was not possible with the enemy holding land, sea and air superiority (even though overall they were not superior in numbers, the Japanese fielding between 33,000 to 36,000 combat troops to the Allies with almost 70,000 fighting men – Indian, English and Australian. Each had several thousand more non-combatants).

On 15 February, at midday, seven days after the battle for Singapore had begun, General Percival admitted the end had come and later in the day 'terms' were signed. There is a newsreel showing Percival on the following day at the head of his troops marching in, the white rag of surrender being carried beside the Union Jack. English, Indian, local and Australian troops followed, each having dutifully laid down his arms as agreed in the terms.

For the medical services the work would go on as long as they were held prisoners and had the wounded to care for, and the sick who up to now had been too busy to come in. Charles Stuart was there: 'Our Unit Quartermaster praised sincerely and feelingly our ministrations in those days in the bloodied cathedral, and that to my (very surprised) ears was praise indeed, because only God and an army private know how unimaginative and stony-hearted a quartermaster can be! Over the three days (13, 14, 15 February) we had handled 960 military battle and 500 civilian casualties and the RAP dealt with countless minor casualties in the cathedral.

'When I reached the Adelphi Hotel that night there was no space left on the ballroom floor to sleep, so I spent the night in an upstairs passageway. There was shooting in nearby streets during the night and shouts and screams punctuated the eerie quiet of the darkness. So ended 15 February 1942.'

Following the White Flag

'I'll never forget the surrender as long as my life lasts. I felt, absolutely, as though the world was going to end.'

Private Alan Davies, 2/29th Battalion

THE 'IMPREGNABLE BASTION', AS Singapore had been known, was gone, and in the most humiliating way: the historic surrender of a white race to what had been called a 'yellow Asian horde'. The effect was devastating in a way we can scarcely conjure in our minds today. The British Empire was the largest and farthest flung of any in history. 'The Empire on which the sun never sets.' It had a fabled navy on which Australia, isolated at the furthest end of the earth, relied for protection. Two months earlier no one could have doubted it when HMS *Repulse* and the British aircraft carrier *Prince of Wales* arrived at Singapore to show the flag. But now these ships were at the bottom of the sea and the white flag of surrender was being trailed as witness of defeat.

Back home in Australia bewilderment, fear and rage built up as bit by bit the government let out snippets of news. But, of course, nothing surpassed the news that Singapore had fallen. The great old patriot, Mary Gilmore, expressed the frustration, anger and fear of the people.

SINGAPORE

They grouped together about their chief
And each man looked at his mate
Ashamed to think that Australian men
Should meet such a bitter fate.
And black was the wrath in each hot heart
And savage the oaths they swore

As they thought of how they had all been ditched
By 'Impregnable Singapore'.
Whose was the fault she betrayed our troops
Whose was the fault she failed?
Ask it of those who lowered the flag
That once to the mast was nailed.
Tell them we'll raise it on Anzac soil
With hearts that are steeled to the core
We swear by our dead and captive sons
Revenge for Singapore!

The poem so mirrored the mood of the nation that it spread like wildfire. The huge windows of David Jones emporium in Sydney were covered with a massive blown-up copy of the poem.

Back in Singapore the finale to battle had been played and the men left wandering on the brink of the no-man's-land they were about to enter. At 6 p.m. on Sunday 15 February 1942, firing ceased on the island of Singapore. The campaign of sixty-nine days was over. Earlier in the afternoon the British General A.E. Percival had crossed the enemy lines and in the office of the Ford Motor Company had interviewed General Yamashita, his conqueror. There, according to a Japanese report, he had answered the thundering question 'Do you surrender unconditionally?' with a quietly spoken 'Yes'.

And what of the feelings of the 70,000 British, Australian and Indian troops upon whom the door to freedom had so swiftly and yet so finally closed? Warrant Officer II, David Elder, AAMC: 'It was difficult to generalise on so sweeping a panorama as the secret thoughts of an army facing the unknown for the first time. There was, of course, dismay, astonishment and an uncomfortable impression of guilt. There were mixed feelings too of having let Britain down and of being let down; of having fought well, of having fought badly, and over all a feeling of relief. The din, the shrieks of Singapore's death agonies, were replaced by the blissful silence of evening.' Too weary for self-analysis and reproach, the defenders of Singapore sank that night into sleep – beaten, but too tired to think. Only occasional firing broke the stillness, only the red patches of old fires pricked the darkness of night. For the 8th Australian Division the war was over, but a different battle had begun.

Elder says: 'When dawn broke on the first morning of captivity the confusion of thoughts had begun to take more definite shape. The initial humiliation occurred early. It was the order that each soldier, save for a small band appointed to act as local police, must divest himself of his arms. Even those to whom a service rifle had been nothing more than a penance, a useless article that must be occasionally cleaned, felt keenly this act of parting with his arms. It is the final signal of defeat. There were few who did not experience deep emotion as they threw their rifle and ammunition on to the ever-growing pile which littered the padang [open area] at Tanglin Barracks.'

Private Alan Davies, 2/29th Battalion: 'I'll never forget the surrender as long as my life lasts. I felt absolutely as though the world was going to end, because we all knew how bad and hard these buggers were, and we thought tomorrow would be the end of the world for us. We all thought we'd just be taken out and shot out of hand. Too much had happened in a short time. It was only three days before, on 13 February, that in pursuit of some Indian troops, Japanese soldiers massacred patients and staff in the Alexandra Military Hospital, Singapore. They killed men lying on mattresses on the floor and in beds, shot, stabbed and bayoneted staff and patients including a patient on the operating table. There was total confusion. We'd heard from people who had been in their hands. And I'd read the book *The Rape of Nanking* and about the Japanese occupation of China and knew of the deep-seated hatred they had for us white people. A lot of fellows said, "Bugger this, I'm going to have a go at getting away". They did and were never heard of again. There was nowhere to go.'

In Crete, when the end came, the men had headed for the coast, risking the strafing and bombing in an attempt to escape to the ships lying off-shore. In Singapore, the surrender

forbade this before the men could run. But some did run, and
some ran gamely.

Rohan Rivett was one who made a good run for it. He had
been a leading radio broadcaster and journalist in Australia
and had been transferred to Singapore shortly before the city
fell. His material was 'top-hole' for the period although it may
seem 'over the top' for us today. It was he who broadcast to
the world the news that the Japanese had landed on Singapore
Island, a broadcast that caused the BBC to interrupt its news
to replay his message, a hitherto unheard of action in that
august body. Rivett and a friend sailed southwards in a boat,
ran the gauntlet of Japanese ships 'moving in to Singapore for
the kill', as he said. He was 'hounded' by islanders when he
came ashore and was eventually handed over to the Japanese.

Alan Davies: 'We were ordered to lay down our arms. The
.303 has a bolt which only fits that one rifle, so we threw the
bolts away. We had to throw all weapons in heaps. There were
great heaps, bloody hundreds of them. We stayed where we
were that Sunday night and they pulled the Japs back from us.
Some of us went out scrounging, we hadn't had a drink of
water for about four days, or anything to eat. Things were in
a pretty bad way for us because the water supplies to Singapore came from Johore. The Japs had taken Johore nearly ten
days ago and the water supply in Singapore had about finished
and this made black news. And they were bombing and shelling. Thousands of the civilian population were killed in Singapore itself because they'd all just fallen back from the
mainland. They'd never thought they'd be taken or would have
to leave with one suitcase. They walked out of banks, business
houses, jewellery shops, just left everything.

'After a few days there was nothing to eat. Then all of a
sudden all these Japs came in their trucks with stout barbed
wire, miles and miles of it, and they surrounded the whole
area. There was enough to go right around the camp, four
strands at the bottom, three, two and one. *And this was the
wire that we were told our army never had when we wanted
to put it in front of us.* It may have saved a few of our own

men. Then the Japanese came in one morning and said men were to go out to the Bukit Timah area. I was amongst a couple of hundred chosen. This was five weeks after our war had finished and was one of the rottenest jobs I've ever had. We had to clean up all the dead and we found our own dead that were there and we had to bury them and the dogs and the bloody pigs had been at them. It was a pretty bad job that.'

Sergeant Arch Flanagan, 2/3rd Machine Gun Battalion, 'never thought of rescue'. Neither has he talked of his war as a prisoner. 'Those experiences can't be told, it's not possible. A man underplays or overplays if he tries. We didn't think we'd be in Japanese camps for long. "Out by Christmas!" the troops said at first. Then it was, "Out by Queen Wilhelmina's birthday!" After a while getting out was not mentioned.'

Bill Hood (born in 1900) had been in the British army in World War I, he later migrated to Australia and in World War II was 'an Aussie in Changi'. 'No need to tell you which was the worst war for me. We were 100 per cent fit when we left Australia. The Japs soon changed all that.

'As for surrender, I know the boys in my section wanted to go on with the fight but we were told to lay down our arms and that was it. Our padre came and told my section, "It will all be over at eight o'clock, surrender, capitulation, complete". He said, "Eight o'clock's the deadline or else all men finished, the Japs say". Our first guards were renegade Sikhs who had gone over to the Japs, and they treated us as badly as the Japs did later. The food was poor and scarce. We'd go out on various work parties and drop off to reconnoitre places for food. We found pigs and chooks. We went out one night, cut a hole underneath the barbed wire and streamed through. A chap had a big knife; this fellow jumped into the pen and killed the pig and turned it over with his hand on the slit in its throat, and in the dark he grabbed a hand near him and said, "Just hold it there for a moment, mate" and ... there was a scream – it was a Chinese and the pig was his. Anyway, we brushed him aside and grabbed the pig and away we went before they could raise the alarm to the Japanese or the Sikhs, it was cleaned up and chopped up and made into nice pies.'

Sapper Horrie Brown, RAE, has always spoken highly of the assistance the Chinese gave the men. 'They took a great number of risks, they were often in danger in their attempts to help us. I was in a Singapore working party, and a Chinese kid ran alongside and pushed a bundle of notes into my hand and ran on his way so the Japanese could not see him. He would have been killed if they got him. Many of us wouldn't have got home if it hadn't been for the Chinese. There was a woman called Mary Seah, we knew her as "the angel of Changi". (She came down to a reunion in Perth in 1965 and the Governor received her.)

'Before the war ended the Japanese were watching Mary's house, she was arrested and placed under sentence of death. Mary noticed a senior Japanese officer in charge had a skin complaint and told him she could cure it, and she did. He then spared her life. She had lost her husband and had to protect her children. It made her all the more brave in our eyes.

'The Japanese occupation was very hard on women. Mary supplied food and drugs for the camp, these things were life savers for us. She took her life in her hands. Her kids had nothing, she was battling to survive herself.'

Bombardier Pat Blythe had come down the peninsula with the 2/15th Artillery (Mobile) in a fighting retreat. They crossed the Causeway hauling their guns with them behind tractors. Pat was weary but fit until the sudden end of vitamins in his diet almost immediately took his strength. He lost most of his sight. But still he must work; he laboured on the waterfront at Singapore. 'A Chinese drove the crane unloading slings full of goods for the Japanese. He was a skilful operator but when there were boxes of tinned food and the guard wasn't looking, this Chinese would lower the sling until a metre off the dock and then drop it: a splintering crash and in we'd rush for tins of food to hide.

'We slept anywhere round the wharf. At nights, if we were lucky we'd get a brazier going and what with the tins the Chinese dropped to us, we did better than we ever did back at the camp. Then our doctor got some Marmite for those of us almost blind and in my case my sight recovered sufficiently for me to see in a few days. The Marmite did it!'

Pat used to wander up a small hill in the evening and stand, 'not thinking, not admiring the view, just being there'. A few other prisoners did this, 'probably thirty. Not talking, just standing. I learnt that other men called it "No-hopers hill". Be that as it may, I can't say what it was, I never analysed why I went. And not one of the handful who went up there spoke about it to one another either. I'm not religious but I think it was to do with our spirit, the soul.'

Back in Australia, when the news of Singapore broke there was a cold and terrible rage. Mary Gilmore roused the nation with her verse.

NO FOE SHALL GATHER OUR HARVEST

We are the sons of Australia,
Of the men who fashioned the land,
We are the sons of the women
Who walked with them, hand in hand;
And we swear by the dead who bore us,
By the heroes who blazed the trail,
No foe shall gather our harvest,
Or sit on our stockyard rail.

Changi

'If Jesus Christ were to walk in the gate, none of us would recognise him.'

Captain Leslie Greener, Australian Military Intelligence Unit,
Writing at Changi, 1944

CHANGI SPRAWLED OVER ALMOST 10 square miles of undulat-
ing land and in this area, in the pre-war days of British supremacy, were the Selerang barracks that housed up to three British
battalions with family accommodation, a gaol, hospital and
parade grounds. In 1942, after their capture, up to 50,000
Allied prisoners of war lived in this large compound but it was
not until 1944 that they were moved into the actual gaol
(which had originally been built to hold 600 Asian and fifty
European criminals). By this time the large number of men
originally captured in February 1942 had been sent off to
labour camps inland, leaving Changi with a smaller floating
population of roughly 5000 men.

When Singapore fell, the Melbourne doctor Colonel Glyn
White was ordered to have the sick and wounded Australian,
British and Indian troops marched from Singapore into
Changi, a distance of 16 miles. Colonel Sekiguchi, the Chief
Medical Officer of the Japanese forces, ordered that this must
be completed in seven days, no field equipment was to be taken
and no more than five ambulances could be used to bring in
the hundreds of sick and wounded.

As the buildings at Changi could not accommodate such a
large force of men as were now to be marched in, they must
bring everything with them including their atap huts – concrete
bases, wood-framed walls and roof of palm fronds. It is said
that the last thing expected of an atap hut is that it should be
moved, but moved these huts must be.

An article written by Sergeant David Griffin, MAC, in

Stand-To, March 1952, tells of this extraordinary movement: 'To appreciate the magnitude of the task of moving the Singapore camp, one could imagine the movement of an Australian country town of the size of Goulburn to a new location, and not only its population and furniture, wire, kitchens, hospitals, forges, power stations, workshops, diet centres and theatres – all to be accomplished by hand. The time allowed for this tremendous task was one month.'

An impressive fleet of 'trailers' was drawn up in the barrack square. There was nothing more intimately associated with life in Changi than the trailer. Save for the bedridden there cannot have been one man, from colonel to private, who has not pulled one of these cumbersome vehicles. They were constructed by stripping the bodies from abandoned motor cars and trucks and substituting a wooden platform in place of the body. A stout rope or wire hawser was tied to the front axle and wooden poles were attached at regular intervals, each pole giving pulling space for four men; the trailer teams varied between sixteen and forty men (the last drew the massive steel bones of a Marmon-Herrington lorry). 'Up hill they were immovable and down hill they buffeted the hapless men in the shafts with the malignancy of a Japanese sentry.

'The spectacle of a heavy trailer fully loaded, preceded by a phalanx of brown and sweat-streaked backs, the rhythmic crunch of eighty feet, and the bored nonchalance of the helmeted guard riding like a potentate on top of the load, is perhaps the most striking memory of Changi. Wherever there was movement, there were trailers. Rations were collected on them as was water and the sick, the dead went to the cemetery on them. "Fall in trailer party" was the call heard a hundred times a day. "More men in the traces." "Swing wide on the bend!" "All together, stick your toes in!" – exhortations that will never be forgotten. Trailers took their toll of lives. Skids at high speeds doing downhill runs, capsizes and collisions killed men who had escaped the hundred-and-one other menaces of death. Some trips were 6 miles each way, returning with 3 tons of wood. By the end of the day, legs ached, heads were dizzy with exhaustion and eyes were smarting with sweat. "All together, wop it into her!" came the cry again and again.'

So, on the great exodus to Changi the trailers took to the road, preceded by men with axes who felled trees to make a path for the ungainly loads. Beneath the blazing sun the long column wound like a pioneering trek to the goldfields, but with men in the traces instead of oxen, and by the roadside stood the native children watching the antics of the white men and perhaps marvelling at their change of fortune.

While Dr Hedley Summons, 2/9th Field Ambulance, with great courage set off with his own vehicles marked with a red cross, Glyn White set off with his five ambulances to the 13th AGH. That was on 17 February, only one day after the encounter with the Japanese medical commander, and Glyn, stripped to the waist, labouring to get hospital equipment stacked in as safely as possible, looked up and saw Sekiguchi, alone, watching him. Glyn promptly said once more that it was an impossible task he had been given but Sekiguchi was adamant he would give no transport other than five ambulances. Glyn tried a desperate gamble. 'If I can get more transport can I use it?' Sekiguchi, knowing Glyn could get nothing from the Japanese, said yes.

The following morning Colonel Sekiguchi appeared at 8 a.m. to see twenty 3-ton trucks, fifty-five motor ambulances and a staff car for Glyn White lined up. Many of the trucks were driven by World War I veterans who were living up to their reputation, willing to take any risks to make sure nothing of value fell into enemy hands.

Sekiguchi looked at the convoy stretching along the road and said to Glyn White, 'Wait here'. He drove away and on return, in less than an hour presented White with seventy-six passes, one for each vehicle. Glyn White later wrote, 'I wondered if he was remembering that he was a medico and perhaps, on the previous day in front of junior officers, he had not wanted to appear "soft" '. Again Glyn White absorbed a lesson in how to manage in this alien new world he had been thrown into. 'If you wanted to ask for something it was always better to wait for the opportunity to speak alone to the officer concerned.'

The day following the collection of the grand convoy, a Lieutenant Nakamura arrived, an infantry officer who spoke English. He asked White for his plans and Glyn White, thinking on his feet, said, 'I have a week to shift the Australians, a week to shift the British and a week to shift the Indians'. When he got away with this three weeks instead of one week, Glyn tried again. 'Is Colonel Sekiguchi coming back?' 'No,' said the infantry officer. And Glyn, realising the officer knew nothing of the edict handed down by Sekiguchi, there and then decided to get away with as much equipment as possible. 'I suppose', he later said, 'it's not surprising that after three weeks with seventy-six vehicles manned by the best scroungers I have ever met much useful contraband arrived including 4500 hospital beds instead of the 250 expected, along with 7000 mattresses, much needed medical supplies, reading material and a couple of pianos.' And none of the 12,000 sick, wounded or dying men had to march the 16 miles into captivity. They were all transported in the seventy-six vehicles. It was surely one of the greatest scrounging feats in medical history.

Changi was not only a hospital centre, it was the Japanese camp for their prisoners of war and up to 50,000 men were in the camp at one time. When Glyn White first went to Changi there was no water, sewerage or lighting system, the whole area was dirty 'and flies were breeding everywhere'. Modern barrack buildings housed the first intake but within two months crowds of prisoners were herded into the compound and 8000 were without shelter.

In the rough bivouacs bacillary dysentery appeared. 'This boded ill for the maintenance of health under crowded conditions', White knew. 'A couple of hundred deaths took place before we could make the troops realise that we were not talking a lot of rubbish about hygiene.' But this most humane of men had correctly assessed the men whose lives were truly in the hands of the doctors. 'You couldn't blame them, exhausted, fighting a losing battle and finally a long march to the area. They were dirty, unshaven, hungry, their fondest dreams shattered. There was only the unknown to look forward to. These were the men we had to call on to dig latrines, clean up the area, clean themselves, remember the principles of hygiene and all on half a gallon of water a day.'

Two buildings were allotted to the hospital at Selerang for the 2/10th AGH, and for the 2/13th, a three-storeyed block facing the barrack square. They now had to provide accommodation for over 2000 patients. There was no water supply, sewerage system or lighting, no kitchens, showers or means of transport. The only labour available was men exhausted by warfare, stunned by defeat and appalled by the prospect of captivity. For every man in camp, aching for rest and longing only for sleep, those opening days were a succession of shocks. There was no time to ponder on the even greater problem: the personal adjustment to the violent changes of this new and terrible life.

For AIF (HQ) which, even behind the wire had retained its title, the problem was twofold: for survival, discipline had to be preserved and a huge programme of public works launched. Scraps of galvanised iron were collected to build field kitchens in which the few available stores were installed. Water points were established at several wells, or 'tongs' as they were invariably called, after the Malay word for water dipper. 'At first it seemed strange to be one of a thousand naked men moving forward in a slow queue towards a few pints of water. But this strangeness was all too soon eclipsed by others', Leslie Greener said.

'Owing to the absence of a regular water supply and the dense concentration of men, the camp hygiene officer, Major C.E.M. Gunther, was faced with the work of constructing latrines. In Changi he found small numbers of augers used in peacetime by Chinese labourers for digging post-holes, clumsy affairs operated within a straddled tripod of steel poles, and Gunther utilised these. To rotate the auger, a team of men trudged in a narrow circle about the central pole. A few shifts on the auger and the prisoners were fully alive to their already weakened condition. There was acute shortage of augers, as with everything else in Changi, so squads were forced to work in relays all day and all night. Thus arose the first "boreholes", a word which rapidly became the most common in all the prisoners' vocabulary.' It originally meant 'latrines', but soon 'boreholes' also stood for all rumours or news.

In addition to the arduous camp fatigues, the Japanese called for working parties for clearing war debris in Singapore. The officers in charge of these parties were in a delicate situation, obliged to make unwilling men work for the enemy. By the end of the incarceration, however, both officers and men had evolved a perfect working-party technique, the sole object of which was to accomplish nothing. Working parties, like rice and starvation, were simply things which had to be accepted as part of a prisoner's lot; even such tasks as the burial of scores of Chinese who had been machine-gunned on the beach where subsequently the camp drew its salt water and staged swimming races, parties for the recovery of identity discs and burial of men who had been killed in the campaign, parties to clean the Singapore sewer, parties to work waist-deep in decaying offal seething with putrification, parties to do work too nauseating to mention, while Japanese guards beat the sick or weary about the head. 'Slaves they were by occupation, but by temperament they were still and always were free men. The Japanese shrieked, screamed, kicked and bullied in an effort to secure complete submission and hang-dog obedience. But they failed, and to the last, with very few exceptions, the spirit of proud defiance remained unbroken.'

To all prisoners of war, food and everything connected with it rapidly becomes an obsession. 'To gaze on a sack of rotting shrimps moving slowly under the impulse of a million maggots was a poor prelude to the meals which followed. Constipation of astonishing duration was the immediate result of this unnatural diet, only to be replaced as the years wore on by an almost universally chronic diarrhoea.'

The sudden change of diet, environment and overcrowding, and the lack of water closets, made the outbreak of an epidemic a certainty. The dreaded scourge of armies down through the centuries swept through the camp. 'You won't catch me collecting this dysentery', said hulking men, 'my gut is a damned sight too tough'. By the following day the speaker could be an abject bundle of fever, twisted with agonising pain, and a few days later may be lowered, coffinless, into the hastily dug grave in the little cemetery off Changi Road.

The hospital, despite valiant efforts, was swamped with patients for whom, owing to lack of drugs, the doctors could do little. 'Scenes in the dysentery ward at the height of the attack beggar description, and the entry of Florence Nightingale complete with lamp would have surprised no one' wrote Glyn White. The dysentery epidemic passed, leaving the camp exhausted, but the experience emphasised more potently than a hundred routine orders how precarious is a prisoner's life. (It was not until later that M&B693, the saviour of Changi, was used to combat the disease.)

At Changi, Glyn White depended on Major Burgess, RAMC, a nutrition expert, for advice on vitamin deficiencies. Among officers and ORs were trained engineers and leaders in every type of manufacturing endeavour, including Captain Michael Woodruff who had degrees in medicine and engineering (later Sir Michael, Professor of Experimental Surgery at the University of Edinburgh). Together, the officers and men 'performed down-to-earth miracles' as Glyn White said. It was known that a source of riboflavin was found in grass and green leaves, but first the cell walls of the plants must be broken down and this must be done mechanically before extraction with cold water. The troops at Changi made scythes and reaping hooks and harvested up to half a ton of grass a day. This was chopped into half-inch lengths, washed in diluted potassium permangamate by an electrically driven, stationary lawn mower, then crushed between rollers and packed into large percolators made out of the steel lockers which were in the barracks office when the men first arrived, and wire from the boundary fence wired it together. The pulp from 200 pounds of grass was fed into a hopper with 16 gallons of slightly acidified water, and six hours later the cock was opened and the thick brown fluid trickled out overnight into collecting vessels. From May 1943 onwards, 30,000 gallons were produced annually. 'The troops called it what we might expect them to, but they swigged it down knowing it would help prevent blindness. Each pint contained 5 milligrams of riboflavin.'

Without doubt the mortality rate in Changi was comparatively low, largely due to the constant work done by the medical staff to prevent or cure most of the serious nutritional disorders. They even had a hospital poultry farm producing over 40,000 eggs in the last two and a half years of captivity and men were encouraged to breed ducks and chickens for their own private consumption.

Despite being just a prison Changi had, by the end of the war, become something else. The officers, NCOs and men of the Australian Army Medical Corps had turned what might have been a far more terrible catastrophe into something noble and grand.

The Chinese community of Singapore and Malaya were consistently supportive of the captives and the help did not flag for the three and a half years of the occupation. This succour ranged from single acts, such as the man who heard the prisoners would like some musical instruments and threw a violin over the wall at Changi to a waiting Australian, to men such as Boon Pong who smuggled medicine and health-giving supplies up the river to the men on the Burma Railway.

In any army there are adventurous spirits prepared to risk death for reasonable reward and the 8th Division were second to none. Chinese and Malays living in kampongs near the camp let it be known they had large supplies of tinned goods for sale. In return the Japanese announced that any prisoner found outside the wire would be shot. Accordingly, those who slipped through the wire to found the 'black market', one of the most famous of all the Changi institutions, took their lives in their hands. In one of the valleys of the compound there was a weak spot in the fence adjacent to a storm-water pipe passing beneath the Changi Road. It was here that the forbidden but precious food that saved so many lives was brought into camp. Prices were high and profits enormous, but the risks were great.

Initiative and resource became part of most men's natural equipment. Before long the gaol area was restored, and soon gardens and grass plots gave to this collection of huts an air of neat suburbia. 'The men refused to live permanently in squalor, and there were always men prepared to devote their scanty leisure to "making the place look a bit like home".' Life in Changi Gaol settled down to a routine of monotony, work and hunger. It was not the worst of prisons or the cruelest of treatment meted out in that war, but men were in a warp of time wherein no thing was real, either past or present. As Leslie Greener wrote, 'If Jesus Christ were to walk in the gate, none of us would recognise him.'

The Selerang Incident

On 30 August 1942, after the senior Allied officers above the rank of full colonel had been shipped away to Formosa, Major General Fukuye of the Imperial Japanese Army produced a document which every prisoner was ordered to sign. It was a promise not to attempt to escape. This order gave the prisoners clear witness of what their time as prisoners was to be like.

No serviceman is exempt from attempting to escape the enemy to rejoin his regiment, and the then commandant of the camp, the British officer Lieutenant Colonel E.B. Holmes MC, Manchester Regiment, refused to sign, stating it was against military law to make such a promise. The Japanese promptly ordered all prisoners scattered outside Changi (except those in hospitals) to move on to Selerang Square, a small area lacking facilities. Into this small area thousands of men (including Australians) were packed and with them they brought their cooking gear, bedding, odds and ends of personal gear and facilities for a temporary hospital. There were only two water taps and rations were cut to one-third. They were issued with picks and shovels to dig holes as latrines in the square, men taking turns during the night as there were already dysentery cases walking into the compound.

Sergeant David Griffin, MAC: 'Before the sun was up the amazing pilgrimage had begun and by nightfall the last man had squeezed himself into the area. Thus 17,000 people found themselves living on a flat asphalt surface some 260 yards long by 155 yards broad, bounded on three sides by high concrete buildings. The only water came from one miserable well, the only food that which they had carried in with them. The response of the men to the demands of the Japanese and the inspiring leadership of their commanders was magnificent. All ranks were welded into a single body with one resolve – to stick it out to the end. By day they worked until they dropped and by night they sang. The Japanese mounted machine guns and smashed faces with rifle butts, fearful lest the singing would cause a riot. "God Save the King" has had many settings but none stranger than in the Selerang barrack square on those sweltering, dangerous nights.'

Three days after the 'no escape' document was tendered and the prisoners were still refusing to sign, the Japanese executed four soldiers, two of them Australians, Privates R.E. Breavington and V.L. Gale. These two had been recaptured after escape from another camp in May. They had rowed a small boat almost 200 miles to Colombo Island where, starving, they were recaptured. Now they were awaiting death. The senior army commanders were forced to watch the executions.

Breavington, a 38-year-old police constable of Fairfield (Vic.), was cool and dignified. He risked the Japanese rage by appealing for the life of Gale, stating that he, Breavington, had ordered the younger man to escape. His appeal went unanswered.

The official version of the 'incident' states: 'As the Sikh firing party knelt before the doomed men, the British officers present saluted and the four men returned the salute. Breavington walked to the others and shook hands with each of them. A Japanese lieutenant came forward with a handkerchief and offered it to Breavington who waved it aside with a smile and the offer was refused by the other men. Breavington then called for one of the padres present and asked for a New Testament whence he read a short passage. Thereupon the order was given by the Japanese to fire.'

The men on the square were again ordered to sign the no-escape document and their senior officers agreed that as they would be signing under duress, such a promise would not be binding. And so the incident ended.

David Griffin: 'When release came seventy-two hours later, the force had won an *esprit de corps* which remained with it until the long imprisonment was over. The Japanese had their bits of paper but the prisoners had their pride.'

B.J.

In uniform all servicemen are astonishingly circumspect in their use of terminology: a corporal may be called Jack or Bob in relaxed situations by any private, although the same private would need to know his Ps and Qs to address a staff sergeant or warrant officer by the name his mother gave him. As for officers, it was always Sir! Of course, in the privacy of their barracks men called officers everything except nice and ser-geants were fair bastards 'because they had to pass on the bad news handed down from officers', Private Donald Stuart believed. But there were some officers who had nicknames that stuck and usually for the good reason that the men admired the man. 'Soldiers need not necessarily *like* their leaders but if they admire them the battle is half won', Stuart rightly repeated this truism.

Brigadier (later Sir) Frederick Galleghan DSO, OBE, ISO, ED, who was a private in World War I and commanded the 2/30th Battalion in World War II, was such a man; he was known as Black Jack. He was superb in military matters and had studied textbooks on the subject since he was a lad. In 1937 he was given command of the North Sydney regiment (17th Battalion), 1000 men to be shaped into the image he saw

as ideal for the cohesion and standard of fitness and knowledge of not only their weapons but their whole army life. This
meant discipline harsh and unyielding and no man was better
fitted to hand this out than Black Jack Galleghan, or B.J. (as
he was known 'privately' to other ranks and to his face by a
select few high ranking officers). The 'nickname' was a soldier's accolade to a firm leader. Black Jack didn't give a damn
what his detractors thought of him. While many officers were
relatively unknown, Galleghan was a legend.

In 1942 his gallant battalion (the 2/30th) had been driven
down the Malayan peninsula and eventually to Changi Gaol,
and in August 1942 when all senior officers above the rank of
colonel had been removed, he was placed in command of all
Australian prisoners in that area. David Griffin writes: 'This
legendary figure had, prior to the imprisonment, been surrounded with such a reputation for ruthless discipline that
knowledge of his return was greeted with mixed feelings, much
as those on the *Bounty* would have felt had they observed
Captain Bligh unexpectedly approaching in a pinnace to
resume command. Thus "Black Jack" came to Changi as
leader of the Australians; and so remained until the end, a
powerful influence on the life of every man there. Few there
must be who do not regard him with admiration and
affection.'

'He had one little annoying habit', Doctor Glyn White who
shared quarters with him recalled. 'Each morning when he
awoke he would call out from behind his screen, "Glyn, are
you there?" "Yes." "Have I ever told you what I think of
Hitler?" Then he would mumble a few words to himself.'
White put up with this for three months and then told him
that he should wake up happy and bright. The following
morning, "Glynn, are you there?" "Yes." "Well, listen to
this." And Black Jack sang "Jesus wants me for a sunbeam".

'He was a psychologist', according to Glyn White. 'When
the officers first received pay before the working troops I
believed that the great majority of the pay should be pooled.
On mentioning this to B.J. he demurred. He called a conference

316 PRISONERS OF WAR

of the eight senior officers in camp, but he still argued against my recommendation so I went into the conference full of fight. He asked each officer their views but passed me over and I thought he was not going to give me a chance to speak; it seemed that my idea that only 10 per cent of the pay should be retained and 90 per cent pooled was to fail. I was really fuming. Then, quite casually he said, "What have you got to say, Billy?" (He had given me this nickname as he said I reminded him of another Welshman – Billy Hughes.) So I stood up and in the most forceful Australian language that I could muster I told them just what an officer's responsibility to his troops was. And when I finished, Galleghan simply said, "Well gentlemen, you have heard what he has to say – and I so order it".'

His second in command, Lieutenant Colonel N.McG. Johnston ED, has written of B.J.'s impact on others: 'It was not always an impact of admiration, often it was quite hostile, but *the man's very personality left no room for half measures*'. He did not look for admiration or adulation 'not even the goodwill of others'. He could never have accepted a title of 'the Christ of Changi' or any of the similar titles some men in postwar years have used thinking to elevate their leaders; indeed, with his splendid upright soldier's physique he may well have become physical had any man been fool enough to try it on him.

He was a contradiction in terms, some formed a lasting friendship with him. Johnston says, in his orientation to Stan Arneil's book on B.J. '... contradictory and full of surprises even to the opposite range of sentimentality and humility'.

Colonel Glyn White said of B.J.: 'He was in every way a truly remarkable man and an outstanding character, hard as nails but basically so kind. When the senior officers were removed from us in August 1942, "Black Jack", as he was then affectionately known, was appointed to command the AIF component of the prison camps. At the time morale was at its lowest, as was the standard of discipline. He was a strict disciplinarian, he considered discipline to be a state of the mind and though he could be justly harsh, he preferred to gain respect by his own personal example. He was a stickler for military etiquette.'

White knew that if combatant officers and men are ill-disciplined, no medical service, no matter how excellent, can function efficiently. 'He was the right man in the right place at the right time. It was not long before discipline had improved and by the end of our incarceration it was at a high standard. I can still hear B.J. telling the troops, "You are not going home as prisoners of war: you will march down Australian streets as soldiers!"'

On one occasion he complained to the local Japanese camp officer that his troops were going on leave improperly dressed, and instructed him to have the Japanese parade before him. 'They duly arrived and he inspected every man and made each one correct anything which was out of order in his dress. When he finished, he dismissed them and they did not salute him so he ordered them back and they *did* salute him!'

It was the most difficult command. He not only had to contend with the Japanese and the welfare of all the Australian prisoners, but with other commanders who were battling to get supplies for their own troops. Mostly this was resolved with the tactful and often forceful help of Doctor Glyn White, himself a lieutenant colonel. One unfortunate impasse took place between B.J. and Lieutenant Colonel Edward Dunlop, a doctor known to some as 'Weary' (a name given, it is said, not because of his stooped figure but from a convoluted joke on Dunlop tyres) who had been brought to Changi with the men who had been imprisoned in Sumatra and Java.

Six months after arriving in the NEI the group of Australians, who had been on their way home to Australia from the Middle East until the *Orcades* deposited them in Java, were transferred from Batavia to Singapore in the hold of a Japanese cargo boat. Captain John Kennedy: 'It was pretty grim down there. When we landed in Singapore we were dirty and scruffy. We'd lived cheek by jowl with the Japs, we'd lived in prison with pigs, whereas, particularly in Changi, half of them hadn't seen a Jap as far as I could make out. We were referred to as the "Java Rabble". Our clothes had rotted off us. That put us on the wrong foot immediately, and remained a constant irritant. I suppose it got up my nose a bit and that's why I took a bit of a dim view of Changi, silly little things really.

'At first some believed that we were those who had got away, deserted Singapore, gone to Java. They didn't know we'd come from the Middle East and landed in Java and had been trapped there. We were truly outcasts, our clothes were rotting off us. We were grubby and they were all immaculate, new boots, good uniforms, they looked like lifeguards marching around the place. We had virtually no clothes. We had had it hard. We did look like Java Rabble. Those who had been stationed at Singapore had things fairly well organised.

'Perhaps the pertinent thing was that we had fought in the Middle East. They believed we thought they had given in too easily. Sure there was a bit of resentment and I don't suppose we were very reticent about letting them know about those things.'

It was unlikely Lieutenant Colonel Galleghan would approve of the style of the men accompanying and under command of Lieutenant Colonel Dunlop, and the inmates of Changi did indeed refer to them as the 'Java Rabble'. Dunlop himself wrote in his published diary of 'our ragged mob' as well as recording that his parades 'are a great worry to me, as the troops fidget continuously and move about with a constant buzz of conversation'. Galleghan was unlikely to forgive Dunlop for the state of the men in his charge, but of course he should have done: Dunlop was a doctor, not a soldier or combatant.

On 9 January 1943 Galleghan, from his command at HQ, AIF, sent a memo to Dunlop asking for the name of the Senior Combatant Officer with the Java party. He suggested that this soldier should be officer-in-charge of the party replacing the present non-combatant officer-in-charge, that is Doctor Dunlop. Dunlop replied that Major W. Wearne was the senior combatant officer and the reason for he, Dunlop, having assumed the post of OC was 'the result of Nip policy in Java not recognising non-combat personnel'. As senior officer travelling with the group, Dunlop had been instructed by the Japanese to command the party in transit to Singapore.

That evening Brigadier Blackburn, who had known Dunlop on Java, learnt from Dunlop of the exchange and wrote for him the following memo: 'I desire Lieutenant Colonel Dunlop to retain command for administrative and disciplinary purposes so long as the troops brought over by him remain together as one body. Arthur S. Blackburn Brigadier.'

This letter had not been delivered when, at dinner the following night, Galleghan said that Dunlop's position was quite incorrect and that as a non-combatant he had no authority whatever to give commands to or punish combatant soldiers. In his diary Dunlop later wrote, 'This is nonsense I know, as I have already had plenty of combatant soldiers under my command in units and, anyway, note the case of a large Convalescence Depot (these are commanded by medical officers) and that sort of thing. However I could not be bothered arguing; I simply agreed with everything and said coldly, "You are the Commander of Australian troops here, so take appropriate action."

'However, after a while I produced Brigadier Blackburn's note very casually and he [Galleghan] read that. He then asked what he could do for us. He said he was now satisfied, but that in order to regularise things he would now give me a formal authority to command the troops. I remained bland and friendly and assured him I bore him no resentment (for meddling in my affairs) and that it was nice of him to go to all these pains on my behalf!'

The two men were intractable. Dunlop wrote: 'I am frightfully annoyed to learn from Glyn White that Black Jack turned down his offer re rice polishings because we had 2000 gulden and he said we must buy it (approx. 90 gulden), as "he had his own 10,000 men to look after". I wrote a rather dirty letter pointing out the difference in the lot of my transit party and his command and their correspondingly lighter rate of sickness.' Dunlop's men believe to this day that this 'dirty letter' read 'My men marched into this place without clothing or boots and despite my request for these items they march out tomorrow without clothing or boots.' In retrospect, it may be said that B.J., having treated Colonel Dunlop as he treated all men under his command, could have done no more than he did. At the same time one sees that Galleghan did not originally approve of a non-combatant being in charge of soldiers, particularly when even Dunlop himself wrote that they were ill-disciplined. B.J. had pulled his own troops up to scratch and expected no less from any other man who aspired to leadership of fighting men.

But the antipathy between the two men, according to Dunlop's diary, resulted in the men of Dunlop's party departing to work for eight months on the Burma Railway with '178 men without boots, 204 with unserviceable boots and 304 with boots urgently needing repair'. In reply it could be pointed out that neither Galleghan nor Dunlop knew the troops were off to the Burma Railway: information from the Japanese was that they were being sent to a health camp.

In the meantime, B.J. had Changi to care for, a difficult administration in the field of prisoners of war. Later, the leaders of the various parties that had been working on the railway were, on return, to liken Changi to 'a five-star hotel'. And those men who were obliged to spend the rest of the war there agreed that their war was not as tough as some others had had it: but it still was not a 'five-star hotel' nor was it home.

A Bookman in Changi

Warrant Officer II David Elder, AAMC, was a bookman in a prisoner of war camp. (He was later to be part of the great publishing firms including Oxford University Press.) 'Life in Changi was not so dismal or restrictive as most people seem to believe, prisoners were resourceful and imaginative in their efforts to keep themselves sane. I had expected that I should be deprived of good books and literary matters during that terrifyingly vague sentence "the period of captivity", but at Changi camp there were books; not a super-abundance to be sure, but a wonderful assortment of surprising quality.

'When the camp settled down and the initial lethargy and depression disappeared, there was a great demand for entertainment. Educational classes quickly commenced – in the case of the AIF, just fifteen days after the capitulation – aided by a small number of textbooks found in the ruins of the regimental schoolroom. A feature which developed surprisingly was the willingness of the troops to listen to lectures. It was sometimes difficult to decide which one of several lectures to attend on a particular night. The majority of the men had not spoken in public before but many of them quickly acquired confidence. Modern Art, International Polo, Sadlers Wells, History of the Violin, Law, Philosophy, Civics, Architecture, Music, were a few of the subjects about which we heard. From civil servants we learned of various (and frequently remote) parts of the British Empire; Dutchmen told us of their own country and of the East Indies. Captain (the Hon.) Richard de Grey, an itinerant lecturer in the subject at Cambridge, gave lectures in English History. Signalman Lavender related his experiences as an ice-cream inspector in Canada, whilst Major (the Lord) de Ramsay outlined holidays in Europe.

'A theatre was built by prisoners at the gaol and this lacked only a revolving stage. Lighting and stage effects were marvellous and the standard of acting high. Variety and light musical shows proved the most popular, but straight plays drew good crowds: *Arms and the Man, Dover Road, I Killed the Count, Outward Bound, Love on the Dole, Hay Fever.* Scripts were written out entirely from memory and others were adapted from novels. Shakespearean readings were also given, and rehearsals for *Macbeth* had reached an advanced stage (several actors growing imposing beards) when movements of personnel prevented its appearance.

'Some wonderful talent was available for these shows, professionals with Shakespearean experience at the Open Air

Theatre, Regents Park, repertory, stage and screen. Many of the female impersonators were excellent and put their acts across splendidly. On Christmas Day 1943, a burlesque soccer match was played, with the kick-off by the "Princess" of the current pantomime *Aladdin*. As the Princess and her consort were being pushed round the camp hospital on a car chassis, the entourage was passed by a Nip staff car. The goggle-eyed look on the two Nip officers is something I shall never forget. Impersonators were so realistic that Jap guards would force their way into dressing rooms and demand proof that the stars were men!

'If prisoners couldn't continue their hobbies, at least they could talk about them. In March 1944 the following clubs were in existence: Travellers, Yacht, Ski, Farmers, Horticulture, Music, Mountaineering, Rostrum, Model Railway, Hiking and Cycling, Town Planning and the German Circle. In addition there was a Rover Troop, and the Freemasons, the Buffaloes and others held their meetings. National sporting contests were held: cricket, baseball, soccer and basketball were played by English, Dutch, American and Australian teams. Some of these matches attracted thousands of spectators. Racing enthusiasts were confined mainly to a discussion of the past, but many found an outlet in the Frog Derby. Frogs were numbered and placed under an inverted bucket which was surrounded by a large circle marked in the earth. The first frog to jump out of the ring after the bucket had been removed was declared the winner. A tote was run and bookies were in attendance on the course and there were instances of "batteries" being used. (In this case a piece of sharpened wire was attached to the frog so that it would prod him as he landed from a hop and thus induce him to make another.)

'Few prisoners who were in Changi in 1943 will forget Smokey Joe's. Housed in a pre-war canteen equipped with a bar at one end and an attractive stage at the other, Smokey Joe's became Changi's popular rendezvous. Here one could purchase coffee and "doovers" (rice cakes) and consume them to the accompaniment of Smokey Joe's orchestra, or the tap-dancing of a "female" star from one of the concert parties. Unfortunately, Smokey Joe's had one serious drawback – its popularity, and the crush, the noise and the heat, added to an already sticky Singapore night, are likewise not easily forgotten.

'Reading became increasingly popular and individual exchange soon gave way to libraries which obtained books by amazingly devious means. Transport units moving equipment to the area brought in a good selection; one hospital managed to do the same; many books were found in the ransacked Changi barracks – for example, the library of the Gordon Highlanders yielded nearly 1000 novels. In April 1942 the AIF were permitted to collect their base kits and these furnished a wonderful selection; troops returning from work in Singapore brought back books from residences in the city.' The camp libraries were kept busy. One library at its peak contained more than 5000 volumes, had 4000 subscribers and employed a staff of ten. Permission was granted to collect 700 books from Raffles College, the local 'university', and these formed the nucleus of an excellent reference library, staffed by teachers from that institution. It contained one of the camp's most treasured possessions – a set of *Encyclopaedia Britannica*.

Eventually a central library and three branches catered for the camp, offering more than 6000 books to 5000 subscribers. The subscription to Changi libraries was the provision of a book in readable condition. With the constant handling, the books rapidly deteriorated and ingenious binding work was carried out with poor materials. 'Changi Bindery' used tails of shirts, black-out paper, twine from unravelled fire-hose and rice-flour paste to keep books in circulation. Some books were rebound five or six times at the gaol and twenty men found it difficult to keep abreast of the work. 'There was the paucity of camp resources, but ingenious devices were constructed and a satisfactory paper was produced from lalang grass. Smokers had to "roll their own" in Changi and they were sorely tried by the paper shortage. This proved hard on books, particularly thin-paper editions – a *Concise Oxford Dictionary* brought $50. Half of the twenty-eight volumes of Halsbury's *Laws of*

England made their way into a camp library; the remainder went up in smoke!'

David, who had been in book publishing all his life, found other members of the book trade in the camp and exchanged views and gossip with them. 'I made the acquaintance of a member of the staff of Kelly and Walsh, the large far-Eastern booksellers, an acting manager of one of W.H. Smith's branches, a Dutch bookseller from Java, and several librarians from England and Australia. In all, the period during which we were cut off from the latest trends and publications of the trade enabled us to consolidate our past experiences and to catch up with many books we had "always meant to read", publications which we had heard about in rare letters from home, and to look forward to the time when we should be able to restore our connections with the trade.'

Leslie Greener, the Egyptologist who spent his summers in Tasmania and his winters in Egypt, 'began the war in Intelligence and finished it in jail'. He later wrote a rare novel, titled *No Time to Look Back*. This is a delicate book, quite out of pace with the times when it came out in the early 1950s. After the war he said, 'It wasn't so much that we felt we were without hope, helpless in a situation we could never have anticipated, but that subconsciously our survival instinct warned us not to dwell on our uniquely awful situation. Hence the grim and sometimes macabre humour generated in all camps.

' "If we don't knit ourselves into a cohesive group we are done for", was the almost immediate revelation we had. Men learned the art of living together in a way we never had before. No man had individual space, privacy or purpose, everything was out in the open for the first and perhaps only time in our lives: and all because we were deprived of everything in life except the desire to survive, to hang on until the end.' It has been written that most, if not all of the men 'knew the war would end in us winning'. Leslie Greener believed that no deep thought was given to the ultimate end of their time, 'We had hope, and no doubt faith in the future was buried in us but you can't go on for three and a half years expressing these things to others or even to oneself, all our energy was taken up with staying alive. We didn't intellectualise about how we would best survive but the inner strength we automatically, unwittingly drew forth was such that it came out in its purest form. Had it been less pure we may well have survived physically but the independent spirit of mankind in us would have been debased. As it turned out, there are few ex-prisoners who cannot "look another in the eye". Some bent a little at times as if a too rigid stance would cause a fracture, while at the other end of the spectrum there were men whose refusal to bend at all gained them much punishment albeit much admiration from other inmates.

'Who will ever forget the Western Australian author Donald Stuart? Intelligent, sharp, a delight to discuss the ways of the world with, literature, art, politics or history, yet the greatest larrikin of them all. His clothes had dwindled to half a hat and a G string but he'd snap to attention when he came on any of our medical officers and salute in an exemplary fashion, yet made such an arrogant, studied point of not saluting any Japanese officer, under any circumstances, that he was bashed often, and badly. I once asked him why he persisted, and he said, "It's my way of expressing my feelings".'

Leslie, in an older-age bracket than most of the men, became involved in education in Changi. (He had been a schoolmaster 'in civilian days' in Egypt.) 'The only total pleasure I knew in that waste-land of my life was the comfort of being a total part of mankind; and the look on a man's face when for the first time in his life he mastered some abstract thought or recognised the beauty in something he had hitherto ignored; those things kept me going.'

At the outbreak of war, four YMCA officers were sent to the Malayan peninsula to provide recreation and canteen facilities at Mersing, Segamat, Malacca and Johore Bahru. One of the officers was invalided home and, shortly after the fall of Singapore to the Japanese, another was transferred from Changi to Borneo. That left Ivor Hanger as senior welfare officer and George McNeily to carry out the association's work. Before the fall of Singapore, 'YM blokes', as the troops knew them, helped to organise games and sports meetings, ran libraries and concerts and drove mobile canteens distributing tea, confectionery and cigarettes to the men at the front. After the capitulation, given the choice of being allowed to leave Singapore or being imprisoned with the soldiers, the YMCA officers chose to stay with the men.

The 'YM blokes' found themselves in Changi and Hanger wrote a book as a record of the YMCA's work with the men. This battered tome, with pages made of scrap paper and illustrations drawn with clay and iodine, is now in the Australian War Memorial in Canberra. The contents include drawings by British cartoonist Ronald Searle (also a POW) and show contrasting pictures of POW life. Gaunt, naked Australians are shown harnessed like horses to trucks hauling firewood; others are pictured sitting quietly listening to a YMCA recital of classical music played on the camp's most treasured possession, a gramophone, with needles fashioned from bicycle spokes.

Hanger estimates that more than 3000 lectures on various topics were delivered by prisoners to prisoners. The two YMCA men conducted music appreciation, art, public speaking and debating classes and in several cases taught men how to read and write. To cope with the demands for education and entertainment a special YMCA hut was built in Changi in May 1943 and it became the centre for plays, lectures, church services and band recitals. A painting of the hut done at the time shows it surrounded by hundreds of prisoners listening to an orchestra playing its camp-made or donated instruments.

'Music, whether orchestral, classical, jazz or in the form of simple sing-songs, was the life-saver of the prisoners', Hanger says. When the survivors of the Burma Railway returned to Changi, one of the first requests was for the YMCA officers to play their gramophone. They played records for hours. Music cheered up the patients in the gaol's hospital and in the camp music programmes were given six days a week.

'It was during personal talks you had from time to time with the great number of men you came to know that the most vital work was done. The subjects discussed were endless, ranging through every aspect of life – and often death.'

Midnight in Sunda Strait

'You miss your lost ship. In the prison camps the crews of USS *Houston* and us from HMAS *Perth* were like brothers we had so much in common.'

Petty Officer Thomas Mooney, HMAS *Perth*

BACK HOME IN AUSTRALIA all news was censored, but there were columns of good news about German U-boats being sunk in the Atlantic, air attacks on 'Japs' at Moulmein and Germans in peril somewhere in Russia, as if these distant, doctored snippets of information would divert us from the disasters a few hundred miles from our coast and make us believe that the war actually was going our way. HMAS *Perth* had come home when Australia was in danger. But her time was running out. The Melbourne *Argus* of Saturday 14 March 1942 announced, 'Two RAN ships missing after Java. Presumed loss of the Australian warships HMAS *Perth*, cruiser, and HMAS *Yarra*, sloop, in waters around Java, with 833 men on board, was officially announced by Mr Curtin, Prime Minister last night.'

HMAS *Perth* had 'covered herself with glory' in the Mediterranean, as the sailors said: 'Malta, Matapan and Crete!' Many an army veteran remembered the *Perth*'s attempts to rescue them when the Germans had control of the skies and were 'throwing everything they had at her!' 'Took every risk trying to rescue us from Crete, that Island of Death!' It takes exclamatory encomiums to describe that time. But when speaking of their ship's final battle, the voice of the sailors is different from other fighting men.

Petty Officer Thomas Mooney: 'We left Fremantle on the 14th of February 1942 at 0030 hours, our Captain Hector Waller waiting until after midnight of the 13th before sailing'. But even that conciliatory gesture towards fate and tradition couldn't save them or their ship. Mooney, born in 1901, was

328

a *Tingira* boy, having been on that earliest RAN training ship during World War I. He was, therefore, an 'old hand'. The story of his final days at sea in World War II are part of the evidence of the extent of confusion of that time when he and his shipmates were ushered into captivity.

When *Perth* sailed on the 14th the battle for Malaya, Singapore and the rest of the South West Pacific region was in its final awful, dying throes: there were only two days left to capitulation of the Allies. And *Perth* was being sent to the Java-Sumatra area that had far less defence to offer than Singapore had had. There was a worse dilemma: communications were becoming chaotic, and when we learn that this was the third time in four days the cruiser had been sent off – and twice recalled from the port of Fremantle – we, at this distance from events, are bewildered, amazed and finally angered at the tomfoolery of war games far from the smoke, the roar and the pain of battle.

The Australian cruiser *Perth* was steaming to join a force of ships not under orders from the Australian Naval Board, the Admiralty or any British authority; she was to be under the command of the shore-based Dutch Rear-Admiral Helfrich. The flagship of the motley fleet of American, English, Dutch and Australian ships was the Dutch *De Ruyter*, commanded by Admiral Doorman who spoke English, which was just as well because it was one of the few things this polyglot, politically motivated fleet had in common. It was named the ABDA fleet, an odd jumble of ideas put together a few days previously with American, British, Dutch and Australian contrivance to defend the Dutch island of Java.

Perth had scarcely arrived in Fremantle on 9 February when she left port for the Netherlands East Indies. On the 10th she was recalled and left again that evening to join a convoy of five empty Dutch tankers and a Dutch freighter she was going to escort to Java for oil from the supplies at Palembang. Again she received a signal ordering her return to Fremantle. When 600 miles off Fremantle, she left the convoy to the care of HMAS *Adelaide*, and putting on all speed headed back alone to Fremantle to refuel and head off once again, but now alone, to the battle zone, Sunda Strait and her death. Fully fuelled and unhampered by a slow convoy, she put on her 28 knots to swiftly close the beleaguered islands of the Dutch. But General Wavell, in the Netherlands East Indies, had already told Churchill that naval resources were too weak a force to divide and so protect either of the threatened ends of the 600-mile-long island of Java; and if kept concentrated the ships could not reach vital points in time of attack. 'Moreover', Wavell concluded, 'wherever this fleet is it is liable to heavy air attack'.

On the 21st, six days after the fall of Singapore, Wavell informed Churchill, 'the defence of ABDA has broken down and the defence of Java cannot last long'. On the 25th Wavell ceased to be Supreme Commander of ABDA and flew to India to take command of the defence of that country and of Burma. The end was not nigh, it had already come. Because brave, occupied Holland was on the Allied side, Australia must defend these doomed islands where the Netherlands East Indies Dutch in the South West Pacific had, for centuries, harvested their wealth from spices, rubber and oil.

Little news reached Australia and little of that was accurate, some of it just silly. Chaos reigned not only on the battle-grounds, in the air (what little air power we had) and on the sea, but in the south where strategists and their ilk were attempting to assess and plan, as well as keep faith with Australia's allies. Thomas Mooney's observations tell us a little of the vast armadas of small ships and boats putting to sea from Singapore and nearby islands in an attempt to escape the catastrophe. 'We entered Sunda Straits before moonlight and were kept busy challenging (identifying) ships getting away from the Java area.' Perth entered the port of Tanjong Priok, Java, on the 24th and was taking on oil fuel when suddenly HMS Exeter hailed on her intercom, 'Bandits approaching!' It was a formation of nine Japanese bombers and Perth let fly with her ack-ack guns and almost to their own surprise the planes, to quote Perth navigator Lieutenant Harper 'were inspired to let go everything, scattered their bombs and turned tail'.

HMAS *Perth*, along with Royal Navy ships, sailed through bomb and submarine alerts to join the Rear Admiral's chaste fleet in Surabaya. They arrived in the midst of an air-raid alarm with one ship burning in the harbour. After a conference with Doorman, the captains returned to their own ships and put to sea. 'We were in company with USS *Houston* and the few Dutch, British and Australian ships of war. We had never exercised as a fleet in action or even trained together in fleet movements', Mooney says.

They steamed all night long looking for a large Japanese convoy heading for the invasion of Java, and made contact the following day. The opposing fleets were evenly matched except that the Japanese had observer and spotter aircraft and the Allied ships had none, the Japanese had more and better torpedoes (Japan was far more advanced than the Allies in their development and use), and these two advantages proved to be the decisive factor of the battle. Making smoke, and sending their spotter planes aloft, the enemy cruisers could fire at will at the sightless Dutch, American, English and Australian vessels as they zig-zagged and dodged in an attempt to confuse the enemy they could not see. Within fourteen minutes the Japanese had fired sixty-eight torpedoes. The Dutch *Kortenaer* 'blew fair in half and sunk in five minutes'.

Admiral Doorman suffered from lack of reconnaissance to the degree that he could be said to be blindfolded. But he was courageous. Instead of a concerted attack and defence, it was almost independent firing. The battle raged over two hours. *Perth*'s commander, Captain Waller, believed his ship had hit two Japanese vessels as there was a large explosion aft in one ship and Mooney saw 'volumes of bright lava-like emissions and pink smoke'. Another ship was immobilised for forty minutes and then rejoined the action. *Perth* continued firing through gaps in the smoke while being peppered from any Japanese ship within range.

The dusk of night was stealing visibility when Doorman signalled his fleet to make smoke and, with some confusion, to cover his retirement and follow him. Then the moon rose and in the bright light the striking force steamed and searched for the ABDA ships while the Japanese Second Destroyer Flotilla was 2 miles from them, their Fourth Flotilla 5 miles, their Fifth Cruiser Squadron 9 miles and the Japanese invasion convoy 20 miles north-west of them. Soon the enemy reconnaissance planes watched Doorman's fleet by moonlight and dropped bright calcium flares across their line of advance. They again crossed the area of their afternoon battle, passing through a large number of survivors of the torpedoed *Kortenaer*. USS *Houston* dropped a raft and flare and HMS *Encounter* stopped and rescued the survivors. Later HMS *Jupiter* blew up, thought to have hit a mine: unknown to the fleet the Dutch had that day laid mines in Tuban Bay inside the 10-fathom line. *Jupiter* sank with the loss of a third of her complement. The Japanese now launched their fifth torpedo attack and 'blew up and sunk' the Dutch ships *Java* and *De Ruyter*, the flagship of this fleet; Admiral Doorman went down with his ship. His instruction from shore had been that any ships disabled must be 'left to the mercy of the enemy'. The shore-based Admiral Helfrich had signalled 'you must continue attack until the enemy is destroyed'.

Captain Waller of *Perth* ignored this suicidal instruction and took USS *Houston* under his orders, made a feint to the southeast then turned direct for Batavia at high speed. 'I had', he wrote, 'under my orders one undamaged 6-inch cruiser and one 8-inch cruiser with very little ammunition and no guns aft. I had no destroyers.' His next words were the most telling. 'The force was subject throughout the night and day operations to the most superbly organised air reconnaissance, enabling the enemy to play cat and mouse with our forces. I had therefore no hesitation in withdrawing what remained of the striking force and ordering them to the pre-arranged rendezvous after night action – Tanjong Priok.'

They arrived the following morning to a deserted wharf with a bombed fuel tank burning on shore. On the wharf where the ship docked, the NAAFI stores (Navy, Army, Air Force Institution) stood with doors blown out by gunfire.

Captain Waller gave permission for the men to take anything they wished with the proviso that any liquor must be handed to the master-at-arms for storage until later release. Young William 'Buzzer' Bee was 'in like Flynn'. 'There were cigarettes, chocolates, everything. There were even sewing machines coming on board. You should have seen the men sweating up the gangplank with gifts to take home to their wives and girl friends! We also took on wooden rafts (merchant marine issue).'

Able Seaman Bee was not to know how soon these rafts would be needed. 'We left harbour that evening at 8 p.m. in company with USS *Houston*. We were in second degree action stations.' Thomas Mooney was sitting on the starboard torpedo tubes, 'talking to torpedo-gunner mate Petty Officer Bill Davies and Able Seaman Butch Stayt'. The sea was calm, the air still, sky clear and a full moon gave visibility up to 7 miles. Captain Waller was unaware that the enemy lay in strength across his path. He had received no recent radio intelligence report on the area. General Imamura's invasion convoy steamed toward him escorted by two light cruisers, eight destroyers and a mine-layer with, to seaward, four more cruisers, one destroyer and the aircraft carrier *Ryujo Maru* with a number of destroyers farther north. 'At 11.6 p.m. we challenged a ship we thought may be one of our Australian corvettes of the Sunda Strait patrol but she replied unintelligibly with a greenish-coloured lamp and turned away, making smoke. She was then seen to be a Japanese destroyer. Captain Waller sounded the alarm, made an enemy report to warn other ships and all hell broke loose as he ordered the forward turrets to open fire.'

The encounter must have been as great a surprise to the Japanese as to the Allies. Leaping up with his mates from their perch on the after torpedoes, Thomas Mooney learnt that immediately after the first sighting, many destroyers and cruisers had been sighted. The ship's armament was split to engage different targets simultaneously. Captain Waller himself handled the ship throughout the action, altering course 'violently and repeatedly', with *Houston* conforming while engaging the enemy so as to keep the guns bearing as necessary with the mean course describing a circle of approximately 5 miles diameter.

'There were so many targets that enemy destroyers attacked from all directions and at close range while fire from cruisers from further attack dropped around us.' HMAS *Perth* suffered her first hit at 11.26 p.m. and a third near the waterline in the ordinary seamen's mess at 11.50. 'We continued to fight and with *Houston* used every effective gun we had as well as our eight torpedoes. Lieutenant Commander Harper told us we scored hits on the destroyers.'

A Japanese report later gave Japanese losses as 'one mine-sweeper and one transport of convoy sunk and several vessels seriously damaged and three more sunk, though apparently later salvaged. *Sakura Maru* sank as the result of shell and torpedo hits, and in the *Ryujo Maru*, "the facial expressions of the soldiers changed to anxiety".' This ship was hit soon afterwards and Imamura, his aide and adjutant Tanaka jumped into the sea where the commander-in-chief floated around on a piece of wood until a boat picked him up. There were some 300 or 400 persons in the water when suddenly *Ryujo Maru* listed and tanks and automobiles fell into the water. 'Freight which was loaded on deck fell into the water beside us with a dreadful sound.'

Around midnight, *Perth*'s gunnery officer, Lieutenant Commander Hancox, told his captain that very little 6-inch ammunition remained and Waller, deciding to try to force a passage through Sunda Straits, ordered full speed and set course direct for Topper Island at the entrance. 'But shortly after midnight a torpedo struck on the starboard side, the report came forward, "Engine room out, speed reduced"; and our captain acknowledged, saying, "Very good". Then Lieutenant Commander Hancox told Captain Waller that our ammunition was almost gone, the turrets were firing practice shell and the 4-inch guns were reduced to star shell. Again our captain said, "Very good". But when a second torpedo hit beneath the bridge, on the same side, he said, "That's torn it. Abandon ship". Lieutenant Commander Hancox asked, "Prepare to abandon ship?" "No. Abandon ship." Word went out and many got out of the ship.'

William 'Buzzer' Bee went to the aid of a mate, AB Don Briney. 'I knew if they fired again, given the position we were in, we could get blown. When these guns go off, everything goes forward and you've got to keep clear of them. Instinctively I said to myself, "Well, you'd better get going, get out of here". And I got Don by the legs, because I couldn't stand. I was crawling, my foot seemed to have gone, and I felt sick because I realised then that he had his arm blown off, because I was pulling him away and his arm was staying on the deck. And he was groaning, "Ooooh, Jesus, don't, don't, leave me alone". I said, "Alright. Don, I can see what your trouble is mate. You've lost your arm. I'll go and see if I can get a stretcher for you." When I pulled him back over the main part of the flag deck all I could see of the officer who was in charge of the flag deck was half his body, he'd been decapitated, and I crawled a bit further and I saw his head. Other bods were laying around, blown too. Because that's where we copped the full blast there. Then I went round and got myself into the Signal and Distributing Office, what we call the SDO, and there's about half a dozen blokes in there. My mate, (AB) Tom Lesley was there, and I said to Tom, "Don't worry about me, but you get the stretcher that's up against the bulkhead and grab someone and take Don Briney down to the sick bay". I said, "He's alive, the others are dead". And he grabbed another bloke and they went out there and put old Don on this thing and they were taking him down below, and the sick bay unfortunately was right above where we stopped the next torpedo. The torpedo came in and of course they got blown to bits down there, the whole lot of them. So they never made it. And I was the only one on the flag deck, or any part of the deck that's still around today. A third torpedo struck a few minutes later, again aft, on the starboard side, followed by a fourth torpedo which hit on the port side. All who could do so got out then. *Perth* listed to starboard then came upright, heeled over to port and sank twenty-five minutes after midnight. We were roughly 4 miles NNE of St Nicholas Point.'

The American ship *Houston* was on fire but still afloat and fighting. 'Shells were ripping into her and torpedo explosions tore her open (the Japanese fired eighty-five torpedoes in this action) and she sank about twenty minutes after us in *Perth*. Of a total complement of *Houston*'s 1000, some 368 men survived as prisoners of war.'

Perth had been repeatedly smashed by shells while abandoning ship after the second torpedo hit and many of her crew were killed or wounded in the water by the exploding shells and the last two torpedoes that hit her. Of her complement of forty-five officers, 631 ratings and four canteen staff, twenty-three officers and 329 ratings were killed in this, her last action. Of the survivors who were taken prisoner of war, some 105 ratings died. (There was also one officer and five RAAF ranks on board.)

Captain A.H. Rooks of USS *Houston* and Captain H. Waller of HMAS *Perth* went down with their ships, only a mile apart from one another. 'Captain Waller had much to do and when the boys in the water saw him up there, still on board, they cheered him and he looked down and saluted them and then he was gone.'

Buzzer Bee was 'squirting blood like it was coming out of a tap. The blokes had got a piece of halyard and tied it around my leg as a tourniquet. And I had this around my leg when the ship started going down. I crawled out to the side of the ship and the water was just a couple of feet below the flag deck by this time because we'd heeled over. And all I did – I just rolled into the water, with this thing on my leg.' By this time the leg had doubled up behind his back owing to damage to the tendon.

'There was about a dozen or more of our fellows in a boat. I was swimming around and they just pulled me inboard. I'm not a strong swimmer, but I was pretty strong that particular morning – it's surprising how strong you are when you've got to do something! When I got out of the water into the boat, I took the tourniquet off. The oil on the water was that thick that you could hardly recognise anybody because your hair, eyes, nose, every part of you was covered in this oil. I had had on my action station gear, a pair of blue overalls, anti-flash gear, a helmet and gas mask nearby but I'd discarded all this rubbish when I abandoned ship. I fell into the water with no shoes, just the pair of blue overalls, my watch on my wrist and my wallet and a handkerchief in the pocket of my overall pants. That's all I had when I went over the side.

'A Jap destroyer loomed up the following day and pulled up alongside our boat. We were done in. They told us all to climb up the iron-runged ladder at the side of the destroyer and come on board. I clambered up with one leg. I got on board somehow or other. And this oil film was right over the whole body. All I had was a big hole in my leg. And the hole was filled up with oil fuel. When we were all on board they brought out a 4-gallon can of kerosene and everyone had to wash off this oil with it. It left a smear on you of course, it didn't completely clean you, and you couldn't put kerosene into your eyes and your ears. And of course it stung my leg. But we cleaned ourselves up as best we could. We were completely nude at this stage. As soon as we came on board the Jap destroyer, the first thing they made us do was take all our clothes off and throw them in a heap. But in those overalls were my handkerchief and wallet which I never saw again, nor my wrist watch, which came unclipped as I was clambering up the side of this destroyer, and it fell down into the sea, so I lost that too.

'The Japanese ship had a submarine alarm while they were transferring our fellows from the water and one boat was left with fellows still in it. They just pushed it off and didn't take them on board because they had to get their destroyer underway, being stopped as it was in the water, it was a sitting shot for any torpedo. Left in the boat with the others was a very badly wounded bloke, Lieutenant McWilliams, one of the RAAF crew of the Pussers Duck, the amphibious aircraft we had on board. Some of the others were picked up, some of them weren't. Some of them made the beach. They all had different experiences. Everybody has an individual story.'

Arthur Bancroft, an AB, had been detailed to report on effects of shellfire amidships on *Perth*. 'It was just a shambles so I reported back just when the abandon ship was sounded. It was passed by word of mouth to many of us. I climbed up on the starboard side and jumped from there. I swam clear as she rolled over. Shells were landing as blokes got over the side of the ship; one of the propellers scalped Frankie Nash. He slipped, and we pulled him on a raft with us.

'My abandon ship station on board *Perth* had been No. 5 Carley raft. All that training went for nothing when the *Perth* went down, we couldn't use our experience of launching the rafts and lifeboats when a thing like that happened. We saw an officer sitting on a raft and he called out, "Not very healthy, is it?" And he floated off, not able to do more than the rest of us.

'Being adrift at sea is like nothing anyone can be trained for. The current and wave patterns on the waters of the world differ, not only from region to region but sometimes within one small region: it is as though you are in a place which has never before been sailed by man.'

When abandon ship was ordered, Petty Officer Mooney was on the gun deck manning fire hoses. 'Petty Officer Heddrick came past me and said, "Let's get out of this, abandon ship has been given". After we hit the water I tried to blow up my Mae West but found it impossible to seal off the tube as oil fuel was very thick on the water and prevented me from screwing the valve tight, so I kept the tube in my mouth and kept blowing air into the belt as required. I had been in the water for about an hour when a black object rose to the surface 50 yards away. I thought it was the conning tower of a submarine but it was one of our oiling fenders 4 feet in diameter and 6 feet long with a spar through the centre. Eight of us grabbed timber that was floating past and as the fender had lengths of rope each end, we managed to make a raft to hold us.

'After we had been in the water for about two hours everything was so quiet after the din of the battle that some of the boys could hear Red Lead our little black kitten crying nearby, most likely sitting on a piece of timber. I hope he made it to shore. Captain Waller was very fond of him.' PO Mooney added more to the story of the observer from the ship's aircraft. 'We were drifting along when we came upon a badly wounded shipmate, Lieutenant McWilliams, and we placed him on the raft and did as much as we were able to give him some comfort.

'In the water the survivors' spirits were pretty high, some were clustered in groups singing "Roll out the Barrel" and "Bless 'em all". There were many individual acts of courage this night, it made one feel proud to have been a member of such a ship's company. We caught a small paddle that was drifting by and proceeded to make for Topper Island and had nearly made it when a riptide swept us out to sea again. We then decided to make for Sangiang Island and were nearly there when the riptide caught us again. By now it was about 8 a.m. Japanese cruisers and destroyers had continued to pass us during the night but they didn't pick any of us up. They were only picking up their own soldiers who were in the water from the sunken ships of their convoy.

'Some of the survivors were able to make the beach at Java Head, but they were so weary after their night's ordeal that the Javanese bastards cut them down when they hit the beach; we had several men killed by them. Some of the survivors who made Sangiang Island stocked up a lifeboat that had been washed ashore with fresh water and coconuts, and set sail down the coast of Java, but the wind and tide were against them and after eight days the Javanese got them too.

'We drifted about all day under a very hot sun, and what with the oil fuel on our bodies it made things very uncomfortable. About 4 p.m. we hailed and came alongside a lifeboat that had come from a Japanese troopship, manned by our RAAF pilot and six other survivors who were picking up our lads as fast as they could. I explained to the pilot officer that we had his observer on the raft and that he was badly wounded. He was lifted aboard the boat but died two hours later.

'A Japanese destroyer came up and told us to come alongside and come inboard. They made us throw our oily clothes overboard and issued us with loin cloths and this became our only article of clothing for six weeks. They wouldn't allow the wounded on board, so some of our uninjured men elected to remain in the lifeboat with them. Those of the lightly wounded who managed to get on board received no treatment for their wounds. Petty Officer Davis, the captain's steward, had a compound fracture below his knee and not even a bandage was given to him, and sitting or lying on those steel decks under a tropic sun is no picnic.

'Next morning we were placed aboard a troopship who had emptied out her troops. There were quite a number of *Perth* survivors aboard this ship and we remained for eight days, with tinned fish and rice for one meal a day. But the old Japanese bosun was a kindly old fellow and he did all he could for us, even to bringing us petrol tins full of tea as often as he could. Then the crew of a Royal Navy minesweeper came on board, their ship had been forced aground and set on fire, but they were able to salvage quite a few stores in the way of smokes and tinned food and in true navy spirit shared them with us.'

AB Joe Hurst had earlier made the interesting observation that as he watched the many ships coming out through Sunda Strait in the dying days of the battle for Malaya, he thought, 'what a lot of old ships, perhaps they're being sacrificed'. Joe reached Java with eleven other members of the crew, and there was helped by a Javanese lightkeeper, until he was captured.

AB Clarrie Glossop and OS Fred Skeels had been two years on *Perth*. 'I was in the Caribbean on her after launching', Clarrie remembered with pleasure. 'You get very attached to a ship, you know. We were surprised when we were attacked', Fred Skeels says. 'We had been in action before, but a sailor never expected us and *Houston* to be sunk.' Clarrie says that when four torpedoes hit the ship it reminded him of the thump and shudder of a horse taking a jump. Both men were on the starboard side of the *Perth* and saw the ship's aeroplane blown off by shells, 'then the catapult itself went'. Their turret had no casualties in a sixteen-man gun crew. Skeels had been sent forward to report that the ammunition electrical line had broken down. 'I had to go past the sick bay. There were bodies lying on deck. The sick bay had been hit too.'

Fred Skeels went off the starboard side off the quarter deck. 'I had a couple of 44-gallon drums lashed with a plank that had been a painting party pontoon, one half of the pontoon was submerged because of the shell holes in it. We were float-ing, not pushing or swimming.' Skeels was later on a Japanese lifeboat that had been abandoned. 'All night we rowed until we hit a reef off Java and that left us with a very large hole in our already fairly useless vessel. By 4 a.m. we got ashore on Java. Two had died in the boat overnight and we put them over the side; one died as we reached the reef and we buried him ashore. The sun was bubbling the oil on our bodies. We began to walk inland having no idea where we were going. After two days we reached a village and they brought the Jap-anese to us. Later we met all the chaps at Serang and for the first time we knew who did and did not make the shore; it was a reunion of survivors.

'I lost my closest friend, OS Bob Johnston, he was in the shell-handling room deep down in the ship; men down there had no chance of getting out. Another cobber of mine from the next street down from our house at home, we'd gone to school together, went to sea on the same day, he got home and so did I. It makes a man think.'

These men later went through the same areas as many other prisoners – Batavia, the Burma Railway – but, Skeels said, 'No matter where we went no matter what happened to us, Aus-tralians stuck together more than any other nationals who were around us. Of course the navy had strong common bonds.'

Photographer's Mate Gene Wilkinson from USS *Houston*, like many other *Houston* men, has kept close contact with men of HMAS *Perth*. They had not only fought two battles together but had been sunk within an hour of one another and then spent three and a half years in prison camps together. 'I was at my battle station forward range finder and I heard the call to abandon ship given two or three times. My liferaft station was No. 13, near the forward funnels. But the liferaft had gone, full of people. I was leaning on the shield of the pompom gun getting my balance on the way to the catwalk when I saw a young sailor standing in a coil of rope that had tangled around his foot. I cut the rope loose and both of us climbed down the rope to the water, and tried to get away from the ship because of the undertow. There was a 3 to 5-knot current running. Along the way as we were swimming, we came on others in the water, Japs had torpedoed boats and machine-gunned the men and tried to run them down. We had got off the *Houston* at midnight and by early next morning we had swum ashore to a small island, then, under protection of a rain squall swam to the mainland.

'I wore only a shirt and this became entangled so I swam back to the island and took it off. "I was dumb, eh?" And then I swam back. Now I was away from the regular party. I swam on up the coast to a banana plantation, where natives were cooking green bananas in coals. With sign language I learnt that a group had gone up a ridge here, I guessed, rightly, they would be my friends. We were up on a ridge looking down at the beach as a boat load of Aussies got ashore. Natives with knives were waiting for them and carved them up, every one. We could do nothing.'

Gene was 'on the run' for nine days before being captured. 'The Japanese took a small piece of string and tied it around our thumbs in a peculiar knot, tying us 3 feet from one another and like this we remained for three days.

'They then used us as labourers to carry supplies forward. Several days later we reached Serang, the camp where pris-oners were locked in a theatre and there we eventually met the men from HMAS *Perth*. Although we'd fought beside them and lost our ship with them, we had not met individually before. There I met Buzzer Bee and Ron Sparkes. We all stayed together through Batavia, Singapore, Malaya, Burma, Thailand and Saigon, and we are still like family.

'The Japanese had the men penned off like sheep and bashed us if we spoke to each other, but we were so pleased to see one another we put up with the bashing. We were hungry, and sweating bodies herded together didn't help much. We were in a filthy condition, still covered with oil fuel, and after a few weeks this stench became unbearable.'

Buzzer says of Gene Wilkinson, 'He was my mate, just the same as I had a mate back home in Australia, Gene was my mate in prison. A real nice bloke. Still my mate.'

Young Buzzer Bee still had the crippling leg wound he'd received in the last fight of HMAS *Perth* in Sunda Strait.

'For my first operation there was, of course, no anaesthetic, no injection, not a thing. All they had was boiling water. The only stuff they could lay their hands on was mercurichrome and that often did more damage because it hardened the skin. I was absolutely emaciated. I lay on my stomach and these four Yanks from the *Houston* sat on me. My leg had doubled up backwards because the tendon was broken. Sitting on my back, they all put weight on me so that I couldn't move, and others grabbed my foot and bent it back to straighten the leg out. And when they straightened it out the doctor went in with this hacksaw blade that they'd been sharpening up for a couple of days on the concrete. And when they started cutting my leg I could feel everything. I went out like a light. That's the time when they reckoned I was dead and they told the Yanks to take me off to the morgue.' He awoke in the morgue. Two men were going out the door. 'I'm not dead!' he called.

'As soon as I came back to this gaol, a mate came over to me, "You were supposed to be dead", he said. I bloody felt dead too, I was really feeling crook. But a mate used to make these little rice cakes and things, special little titbits, and he'd come and push it down me bleedin' mouth, "Now eat! Eat it!"

I was on an angle with my feet up and my head down and it's pretty hard to eat like that, but I'd swallow the stuff. The leg healed up; I know some people would think it is ugly and deep and ragged. They had put rice string over the wound and sewed it up and it eventually healed, but my leg was always jumping and I couldn't sleep at night. It gave me hell.'

Wildebeestes and Wirraways

'These were the sickest Wirraways we'd ever flown, no parachutes, no ammunition, couldn't get the undercart up so I flew mine at 100 feet.'

Flight Sergeant Geoffrey Dewey, RAF

THE AUSTRALIAN AIRMEN WHO flew in south-east Asia suffered from a greater lack of recognition from the other services than had the pilots who flew out of Tobruk, Greece and Crete. There were even fewer planes here and many that were here were so obsolete they could not compete successfully against the superior Japanese machines. Geoffrey Dewey was one of the handful of airmen who flew – in vain – in the defence of Singapore. He and his companions' war has scarcely been recorded. Like many RAAF men on enlistment he had been sent to the Empire Air Training Scheme in Canada and then transferred on loan to the RAF in Britain.

'In July 1941 we set off on the armed merchant cruiser *Aurania* en route from Canada to England. On the way we hit an iceberg which tore the bow off the ship. In an attempt to save the vessel and the men we had to sail stern first, backwards, to Nova Scotia. It was a relief to be transferred to the *Strathnaver* in a fast convoy to the UK.'

Then followed posting to Bicester Blenheim day bombers and long-range aircraft on Atlantic convoy escort. Following that he flew via Gibraltar to Malta and then to the Middle East with aircraft spares, then to Egypt to set up a series of fuel dumps to aid the sending of reinforcements to the Far East, and then to Singapore. 'I was in Singapore when it was being bombed from Christmas 1941 until 25 January 1942, and by this time the Nips were in range with artillery fire down the Malaysian peninsula, as well as on our aerodrome, so we were sent to Sumatra. On 15 February, Singapore had gone.

'We fought on at Sumatra until the Armistice on 16 February. The first and only time I heard of Japanese parachutists was when they dropped them on us in Palembang. We were then evacuated; one aircraft took the last four bombs out and we had no more left, and we had no more bullets and were trying to use Dutch ammunition in our weapons and it split our guns. When we got to Java we used Dutch bombs but they didn't fit which meant our bomb bays were half-way open all the time; we had baling steel around them to hold the bombs in. The bomb aimer flew as a passenger, nothing he could do. The guns on these planes used American ammunition and we had .303 ammunition. That is what it was like then, nothing had any commonality.

'We flew quite a few trips in Java and Sumatra, just knocking Japanese aircraft off on the ground, and we bombed all night until the Japanese landed on Java and were on our aerodromes by ten o'clock in the morning, with tanks. So I baled out on the back of a water tanker and my observer pedalled in two days later on a bike with a buckled wheel. I was then sent with five other pilots, an engineer officer and a mechanic to the north of Java behind where the Japs had landed, to pick up six Wirraways that were hidden in the jungle at Andir. In those days the strips were just carved out of the jungle as a refuelling dump and that's all we needed to fly back to Bandung. These were the sickest Wirraways we'd ever flown, no parachutes, no ammunition, couldn't charge the guns anyway, couldn't get the undercart up so I flew at a hundred feet', Geoffrey Dewey recalls. 'To this day I've still got tinnitus from flying without any protection from the noise of the engines because I couldn't shut the enclosure. It was four or five days before I heard anything at all, and ever since I can barely hear anyone through background noise. (It's a standard thing with service people, from guns or bombs or things like that, almost an occupational hazard.)

'We went to Tjilijap and four Japanese aircraft carriers bombed us with 300 aircraft, they made a hell of a mess. It was finish for us.

'We got two lifeboats and a launch, that's all we could find. I was on the requisitioning party, which meant I was looting tucker. We loaded the boats and set out for Australia with sixty-three people on board – five in the launch and the rest were on the two boats which were loaded up with tucker and we were sitting on top, the launch towing the two lifeboats. We got out of the harbour of Tjilijap as the Dutch blew it up and the Japanese were coming in. We sailed all night. By morning the launch was done for. "What the hell are we going to do now?" So we sunk the launch, mounted sails on the two lifeboats and then the lifeboat I was on ran over rocks and ripped the bottom out, and the other lifeboat stood off. So we dived all day in 12 feet of water and recovered all the rations which were of any use, rigged a sail on our now-only-lifeboat and twelve men set sail for Australia. The rest were to hang on and wait for them to send a flying boat or submarine back. They made it to Australia forty-four days later. But we never saw any flying boats. (Thirty years later I went to Broome and found out that the Japanese from Timor had strafed the flying boats that were at Broome and sunk them. You can still see them on the sea floor at low tide.)

'We stayed on the island on starvation rations for six weeks until 21 April; we were down to 2 ounces of bully beef and four ration biscuits a day, except for what we could scrounge.

'We ate hermit crabs, anything we could lay our fingers on. On one end of the beach there was plenty of fresh water but the other end of the beach was malaria-ridden and we didn't know that at first. All the Brits and the few Canadians that were with us were down there and they all got crook. We had no drugs so we reconnoitred the island and found there was a native prison at the far end of it and what we could read of Dutch or Indonesian on the gate was that it was for murderers. So we lay in the bush most of one day watching it and all we could see were Javanese warders, there were no Nips around. So we started carrying our sick blokes in at night, took about four hours to carry a man in through the jungle, drop him off at the gate and clear off back into the jungle. We used to come back exhausted. We did this for two or three weeks and my tally is that we carried twenty men in over the period, until the Japs got very agitated about it.

'By now there were only twenty-five of us left because three days after we landed on the beach an empty lifeboat had drifted in and eight men went off on that; they never made it, we heard they were captured in a storm after getting about 200 miles further down Java. We lost three more men shot by the Japs, so we went back to the mainland looking for boats, but no luck.

'Now the Japanese turned the Javanese warders loose over the island to find the source of the malarial patients. There were no tracks down to where we were and they took a few days to find us, but they burst in one night. I'd never seen rifles with bores like a forty-five gauge until I looked down the end of one.

'They took us across to the mainland and as we came off the boat at Tjilijap they got stuck into us. They lined us up with three machine guns and five Japs with fixed bayonets and they turned the garrison loose on us. I don't know how many of them, they were probably young, as they usually were when they did these sorts of things. They belted us for about two hours with anything they could lay their hands on – boots, lumps of wood, bayonets, scabbards, rifles and then they took us up to the Japanese command post which was a Dutch residence, lined us up and separated us. From recollection there were seven Australians and eighteen British. Here, a Japanese officer came out with an interpreter, and I looked at him and I knew him. He was what we called 'works and bricks' in the air force, a sort of maintenance chief at the aerodrome I was on in Singapore; he now acted as interpreter.

'They stretched one flying officer out and said, "We're going to take your head off". But he talked and talked, and never whimpered or whinged once and he finished up talking them out of it. I've never seen or heard of anything like it being done since. They charged us with being guerilla fighters. They said, "You all go in the cells and in the morning you'll have the choice of beheading or shooting". (Beheading is the honourable way with them, shooting is just for the scum.)

'Needless to say we weren't very happy; they crammed us into two cells, each made for three people, there were now twelve of us in one and thirteen in the other, and a little bucket in the corner. Our cell was running deep in pee and crap and one thing and another. Down the passageway we could hear yells and screams going on all night; we didn't know the Japs at this stage, didn't know they were past masters at psyching people; we thought it was the cell next to us, and it was terrifying. The next morning, through a grille in our cell, we could see out to the road and down came this squad of twenty Japs and we thought, "Oh hell, this is it". Down the end of the passage, screaming and yelling was going on, changing the guard etc. and then the noise comes up the passageway and the doors were flung open and in comes this big Dutchman with a wheelbarrow full of fried rice. He said, "Good morning boys, how about breakfast".

'I never knew what had happened, it wasn't logical what they did (remembering what the Japs did later in the war). I was the only one that was convinced they weren't going to kill us in the morning and my only reasoning was that that was not Jap logic: when they had us stretched out, why didn't they do it then? So 21 April is the day we were sentenced to be beheaded and weren't! Three days later they took us to a tiny little wired-in enclosure with a couple of huts and we went in and there were twelve survivors of the cruiser HMAS *Perth*. They'd set up trestle tables with white paper on them and they'd pinched everything they could off the wharves and had a meal of Uncle Toby's oats and tinned milk for us. We thought it was wonderful!'

Geoff was shipped off to the north-eastern corner of Kyushu, Japan. 'Companies employed us, clothed, housed and fed us; and this was the best prison camp I was ever in. The clothing was good, the warders were good. When the town got a mandarin, we got a mandarin. For the Emperor's birthday everyone at the factory got a biscuit and we got a biscuit, so

they did us very well there. But Bill Belford, a Spitfire pilot
and I drove a decrepit old train up and down carting material
to dump down the shutes for the furnaces. We had both gone
to sabotage school in the air force, so we blew up the electric
motor. We were never allowed to forget it! On our train were
eight men and us two, and the Japs made us push the train for
six weeks. The other blokes said, "If you bastards blow up
that bloody loco again, we'll send *you* down the chute". It was
a long hard winter pushing that train through the snow – eight
trucks at a time.'

Ivor Jones, RAAF, joined the Empire Air Training Scheme
and after initial training at Somers, went on to No.1 WAGS
(Wireless Air Gunner School) at Ballarat (Vic.) for six months,
then No.1 BAGS (Bombing and Gunnery School). Then he
waited.

'Firstly we were posted to England and that was scrubbed,
then posted to the Middle East, that was scrubbed; we finally
got posted to Singapore and were the first Australians to go
into No.36 RAF, a torpedo bomber squadron equipped with
the obsolete biplanes called Wildebeestes. The idea was to fly
the Wildebeestes to the Indian north-west frontier, leave them
there, come back to Australia, pick up Beauforts and do a
conversion course. But we didn't finish our advanced training,
instead, the Japs came into the war and we had to fly on operations in the old Wildebeestes. We just went in raw, straight
into action.

'We were one of the few squadrons that saw action from 7
December 1941 to 8 March 1942. Some of our planes had
been at Kota Bharu when the Japanese attacked there and a
flight of three of our planes attacked a Japanese cruiser but it
was in shallow water and the attack was not successful. [For
a torpedo to run a depth of water is necessary.] We got annihilated one day; our top speed was 90 miles per hour and they
sent us out on a daylight raid and our squadron lost eight out
of the twelve planes in half an hour. It was a blunder by some
idiot sending us out in daylight. We'd been night bombing,
doing a terrific job; the Japs couldn't work us out, us being so

slow I suppose; one night we destroyed twenty-one planes on the ground. We'd sneak up and bomb barges, we dropped supplies to the battalions when they were trapped up the Malayan peninsula. Then we came back and got torpedoes on and we'd stand by every morning at dawn with the torpedo (we could only carry one torpedo each of 1500 pounds). If we weren't carrying the torpedo we carried extra petrol tanks and took six 250-pound bombs. The bombs were on racks outside the aircraft, not like modern planes where the bomb bay opens.

'This day we went out with two 500-pounders in our racks. The pilot was wounded, the left wing was hit, the observer had a wound across his arm, I was the gunner, on the deck, standing up, the gear was only an old thing like a bicycle brake and a 1917 Lewis gun; ridiculous! I could have done as well with a pea shooter. I leant forward at the right time, the bullets went across me, otherwise I'd have lost my lolly! Anyway, the pilot struggled back. There was petrol coming out of the tank, the structure of one wing was gone and it was flopping about, one of the 500-pounders was jammed in the rack underneath us. We should have gone at least a half dozen times, apparently we just weren't meant to go that day. I tried to bale out and forgot to unhook my monkey strap and I went over the side with the parachute, next thing I've flipped back. Buck, our pilot yelled, "Stay where you are, I think I'll get her out of it". I would have landed right in the middle of a Japanese guards division. That was a remarkable day. Buck got us and the aircraft back and never even got a mention in despatches; in a losing campaign you don't get many medals.' Fifty years later men may say to their leaders, 'You led us to slaughter', but Ivor merely says, 'You didn't say those things back in those days. That doesn't mean you didn't think it.

'We operated from 7 December until 26 January, Australia Day, when we got annihilated, the two squadrons. We got knocked around and then they joined what was left of the two squadrons together. About 28 January we flew out of Singapore, over Sumatra, then on to Java. Then we started a lot of chasing around Java on secret dromes; we didn't have any ground crew and the tyres on a couple of our planes were stuffed with grass. We eventually got our ground crew then flew down to join up with B17 bombers. I wasn't in that raid but it destroyed several ships. We lost two more planes and that left us with a total of three, and on the night before capitulation in Java two of our planes went off bombing and we lost one of them. We were the last squadron to operate in the campaign. And, together with one squadron of the RAAF, we had been the first.

'In Singapore and Malaya we only had 145 planes to start with and none of them were modern. As well as the old Wildebeestes, we had Bristols and they were old, the Hudsons were the most modern and they were converted passenger planes. There were seven Buffalo fighters which were no match for the Japanese Zeros, they did a magnificent job just the same, and half a dozen Wirraways. From day one we had known the score. The day we bombed the Japanese landing at Endau I looked up and saw all these fighters just circling around waiting, they dived down on us, some of us got to the target. Of four planes that got back two were badly damaged, ours was one of them, it was one we borrowed from the navy – or the navy gave it away. Alex Kelly was in the midst of that fight. He bailed out, we thought he was dead. I packed his bag and sent it home.

'Two of our boys bailed out from the plane we lost on the final night; the pilot made sure they jumped, but he went down with the plane and was killed. Then next morning came capitulation. We tried to escape, we got down to the coast, I was driving a truck full of provisions; it was pretty hopeless, the natives were hostile then, they knew which side was winning. You could trust a few, not many. We found some other Australians on the beach from No.1 Squadron, they had a wireless set and were in contact with Australia. Word was that Catalinas were to land at night and take off as many as they could, but those Catalinas were machine-gunned by the Japs at Broome. So we went back to the squadron and they said, "Here's the bloody Australians coming back with their tails between their legs". We didn't like that very much. We'd been in camps run by Poms and we'd had a bellyful of that so when we heard about the Middle East troops that had been off-loaded and caught in Java, we asked to be transferred to the Australians.'

Sergeant Air Gunner Alex Kelly, RAAF, arrived in Singapore in September 1941 with a contingent of observers and air gunners for posting to RAAF Squadrons 36 and 100. They were flying Wildebeestes, the old biplanes of the 1920s, single engine and torpedo bombers, lumbering old things with a Vickers gun firing through the propeller and one Lewis gun in the back. That was the whole armament. The Wildebeestes were covered with fabric, a fixed undercart, no retractable carriage. But they were dependable. 'They'd get you over and get you back', Alex claims. 'The cockpits were in line, the pilot was up front with the observer-navigator right behind him and then the wireless operator air gunner was further back. There was a tunnel between the observer and the wireless operator air gunner, each could crawl into the other's position if need be but there was no communication to the pilot apart from the intercom.

'Singapore was a very nice place before the Japs had the temerity to come; it was a tropical station, we only worked in the morning, knocked off at twelve-thirty every day and had our lunch, maybe a rest, played snooker, went into town, oh we were having a whale of a time. All that suddenly ended.'

Alex was posted to RAAF 36 Squadron; their battle position was Kota Bharu where the Japanese first landed. The RAAF Hudson squadrons were up there, and when the Japanese came in before bombing Pearl Harbour No.1 Squadron was the first of the Allied forces to contact the Japanese. 'Saliti was bombed that night, so we knew immediately that it was "on" though we didn't know they'd landed at Kota Bharu. We sent up nine aircraft the day after war was declared.

'For the first part of the war we were bombing up at Kuala Lumpur, an eight-hour trip, about the limit of our range, and we had to do it with long-range tanks and we could carry only four bombs. We strafed the Japs coming down by boat, and nearly always flew at night.

'There was a bomb release mechanism that the observer used (he sat behind the pilot facing backwards), the bomb aimer's position was in the nose of the plane, face down, looking through the bottom of the aircraft, with a switch to release the bombs. The pilot could also let loose the bombs from his position. We did quite a bit of bombing on transports coming down the main road, we dropped supplies, didn't know who we were dropping them to, we were just given a position. The stuff was in canisters, medical supplies, food and ammunition. While doing this there was always someone firing at us. There was a Japanese landing at Muar on the east coast up near Malacca. We had to strafe the barges and that had to be done in daytime. Quite a few of the aircraft were shot up.

'The Wildebeeste was manouvrable, it could turn on a three-penny bit, but it was so slow. We only tangled with the Japanese gliders once, they made mince meat of us. And that was the last trip we did, at Endau, about 100 miles up on the west coast. The Japs were landing a force there. We went off in two waves, 36 Squadron went first with a dozen planes, we got off about 12.30 and by the time we got to Endau the cloud had rolled back, fighter protection (what there was of it) hadn't arrived and the Japs had fighters up (their planes were about ten times better than ours). They got amongst us and we got four planes back out of the twelve. When 100 Squadron went up in the next lot they were a bit lucky; clouds had rolled over and they could get in; even so they lost four planes. So, out of twenty-four planes we lost twelve in one day. On that day I baled out at Endau. We had managed to pick up three Eldicores – similar to the Wildebeeste except of metal construction; a monoplane, enclosed cabin, quite a deluxe job, slightly faster but not much. I was flying in one of these in the squadron leader's flight, our plane was attacked, the pilot took evasive action and I was thrown to the floor and got knocked out. When I came to, the cabin was awash with petrol. The observer got out and I followed.

'I don't remember a thing about parachuting out of the air-craft, my recollection is standing on the ground with branches all around me and the parachute ripping. I don't know whether I hit something going out or whether I flaked out from what happened before I jumped, but I've no recollection of pulling the cord, nothing. I had gone through all the tall timber. It took me two or three days to get out of the jungle, I was alone, lost, and in the dark of night blundered straight into a Japanese camp. I was the only person who came down that day to be taken prisoner and survive. The others were picked up by front-line troops as they went through and were given the slash. I was lucky to miss the front-line troops. (In a battle, front-line troops have copped your flak and are there-fore not so reasonable as troops behind the line.) I was taken back to Endau and put in the Japanese guardhouse. I didn't know what was going to happen then, we'd heard all these tales.

'One night they came and got me and I thought that was the finish; I was walked up the main street and taken into an officers' mess; they sat me down, gave me a bit of grog, smoked for a while, then sent me back again. I was quite relieved!

'After I'd been there a few days they brought in Spud Spur-geon, the pilot, so we were together again. We spent a week sitting in the guard-house, then they put us on a truck for a journey through Mersing and that was horrific because it was where the Australians had fought the Japanese and their corpses were lining the side of the road and by the time we got there they were pretty high and swollen up after a fortnight in the hot sun. Eventually we got to Kluang in the centre of Malaya and were put in to a gaol, which was chock-a-block with Australians and Indian troops. I was upped in rank because I was still wearing flying boots and that impressed the Japs. They later took us up to Kuala Lumpur. When they were giving instructions about the movement they deferred to me despite the fact that we had a brigadier there and me a sergeant air gunner with long boots! We went by bus and truck to

Kuala Lumpur and ended up in Pudu prison.

'I was surprised by the English camps, they were shocking, you could smell them miles away. I spent twelve months at Kuala Lumpur in the gaol, a sort of clearing house where they'd bring the Chinese in and hold them for a while then take them out and knock them off. We'd go on working parties around Kuala Lumpur and come across a big plank above an intersection with a row of heads on it.

'I had a peculiar experience there, a priest came in from somewhere and said mass. There I was at mass and I suddenly realised I was talking to mother, I could see her there and I just had time to say "I'm right mum" and I think that message got through to her. (I never saw her again because she died before I got home but my sister Margery told me mum used to go out on the verandah every night and say the rosary, and she came in one night and just said that I was alright.)

'We got back to Changi in December (I had baled out on 26 January 1942 and was taken prisoner a few days later). There was myself, Spud Spurgeon and Derek Charters, a New Zealand fighter pilot, who had also been shot down, plus a couple of Dutchmen (a pilot and an observer). Just five air force amongst 1000 army personnel. One of the Dutchmen tried to escape, he got caught and they beheaded him, so then there were only the four air force blokes left.

'When we got to Changi, the Dutchman went off with the Dutch forces, and Spud Spurgeon, Derek Charters and I were put in an army camp where we met up with three other New Zealand airmen who had tried to pull out of Singapore but got bombed just as they were leaving, were blown up and landed in hospital. We were marked people among the army fellows there because most air force men had got out of Singapore to Java, and army men were bitter.

'When the two squadrons escaped to Java they combined all the remaining aircraft and personnel into 36 Squadron and 100 Squadron ceased to operate. We did operations there until the final capitulation. At the end of hostilities there were just two planes left. Eight of the crew decided they'd fly out with these two planes, their idea was to head north along the east coast of Sumatra and pick up a junk somewhere along the way and sail over to Ceylon. It didn't work out and the two planes eventually ditched in the drink. One got fairly close to land and all the crew got ashore and the other came down further away where the currents were going out fast and only one man got ashore. That was the finish of our squadron.'

Flight Sergeant Paul Thomas (Bluey) McKay says, 'Things were chaotic; we were supposed to be picked up by Catalina coming from Port Hedland to the beach on the south side of Java, and we were waiting for that. But the aircraft were bombed in Port Hedland or Broome and of course there was no way we could learn about this. We had come down from Kota Bharu in Malaya where the Japanese landed initially, and we had backtracked all the way to Singapore, then over to Sumatra and Java.'

As a POW he went to Burma on one of the notoriously over-crowded decrepit ships. He then worked on the northern section of the railway. 'We started off in Burma and worked in various staging camps up to the Laotian border. After the line was finished we were transported down to Tamarkan in Thailand. We were only there a few days and, still being able to walk, were considered fit enough to go on what they called the Japan party. We were sent to Phnom Penh in cattle-trucks and then along the Mekong River in a boat which was quite pleasant considering the other circumstances we'd been in.

'We reached Saigon and were there a couple of months because the Japanese couldn't get us out as the Americans had the port blockaded with their submarines. So it was decided to take us back by land to Singapore which was a five-day trip again in the trucks. Eventually, on 4 September 1944 we set sail for Japan on the *Rakuya Maru*. It was a hazardous trip. The captain had said he wouldn't move the ship until we were all down below but there were so many of us – almost a thousand – and we couldn't even stand up in the hold; so he had to have the sick and some of the others on deck.

'I was sound asleep on 12 September at about five o'clock

in the morning when there were a couple of loud bangs, one in the bow and one in the engine room. An American sub-marine had got us. I was in No. 2 hold and we missed direct hits. When daylight came I asked Vic Duncan (he was the Chief Petty Officer of HMAS *Perth* so I thought he knew a bit about sinking ships having once been on one) and he said, "If I were you I'd get off", so I climbed down the side into the water.

'In the morning there was the ship, it had settled down to the deck but it was afloat because of its cargo of rubber; there were about twenty of us hanging on one of the oregon hatch covers and I suggested why not paddle back to the ship and see if we could get something to eat. But this wasn't well received at all, so I kicked off and swam. It took me till late afternoon to get anywhere near the ship and I've often thought, had the ship sunk I'd have lost the landmark and been in a watery grave. I met up with a raft of men not far from the ship and we managed to get back on her and got a couple of tins of beef but in the meantime the sea was getting rough and the raft we had tied up to the ship was going up and down about 20 feet. We tried to drop the bully beef over to a chap on the raft and we lost that. And the ship looked like going under any minute, so we get off. And we did see the ship sink.

'The Japs were in the lifeboats but they wouldn't take any of us at all and they were then picked up by their own escort vessels. We managed to get into the lifeboats when the Japs left them, I think it was seven lifeboats all together, it was just on dusk and we rowed around trying to see if we could pick up a few more men. The sea was rough so we couldn't stay together, but individually floated around. In the morning there were three boats in the area, all the others had disappeared. We heard machine-gunning and we were sure that was what happened to the other boats.

'We had a sail so we said we'd try to make China. In the meantime a Japanese corvette picked the leading boat up and the men told them there were more back further, so we were also picked up. There were eighty of us all together (and I think

American submarines picked up 127 out of 1000 men). Eventually those of us on the Japanese ship went to Hainan Island and were put on board a tanker. There was no shelter, they wouldn't give us anything to eat or drink; your tongue starts to swell. It is bad. The deck plates of the ship were red hot, and to walk anywhere you had to get a bucket of seawater and throw it in front of you to make any distance at all. The Japanese had picked up a number of Englishmen off a ship they had sunk near Hainan Island so these men were on the tanker as well. The only shelter was under the superstructure. Men were covered in oil, had great pieces of skin and flesh coming off their legs; one chap had both arms and a leg broken and the Japs wouldn't give him a splint. Life became very miserable.

'Eventually we were transferred on to a mother whaling ship, but although there was enough room to hold a ball the Nips had us crowded up into one little part, fenced off. When we got nearer Japan a typhoon blew up and it was pretty rough. Previous to this there were depth charges going off as the Japs were after the US submarines.

'We arrived at Moji on Kyushu Island, the port most POWs went to in Japan. Because of the quarantine we got our first hot bath for a few years. That was October. It was starting to get a bit chilly then, coming on to their winter. I had a pair of shorts and a shirt, some chaps didn't have any clothing at all. I was in a group taken to Kawasaki, midway between Tokyo and Yokohama, a wholly industrial area. Even the Japs gave us a rest, saw we were done in, we didn't work for the first week. All we wanted to do was sleep; we couldn't eat. I gave a bowl of rice away rather than bartering it which I should have done we were that poor, but we were that weak I didn't have the energy to barter.

'We were sent to work at a factory and it was a war of nerves all the time. They had civilian guards. There were plenty of bashings. In our barracks there was no heating, no washing facilities, it was down to 5° below zero. We had little clothes, what they gave us to go to work in was like hessian; and rubber shoes. It was just plain misery. Obviously the Red Cross sent all our names home but we never saw any goods.

'Then we had to contend with the B29s; the Americans were getting on top, coming over bombing every day and night, they burnt us out of one camp and we got shifted to another camp for the last two months of the war. A B29 dropped a bomb right where I used to sleep and killed twenty of the boys there. We were bombed out twice. For sheer misery, oppression and threat, Japan was the worst I suffered in the war. One year there was equivalent to two years on the Burma Railway.'

The Islands

Mt Vulcan to his breast, holds them in their last rest.
Oh, could a thousand hearts recall them to us?
No. The years must mellow with our tears the memory
that shall live to be – Rabaul.

Five little Wirraways soared up, their guns ablaze –
Our boys knew well that death would be their due
Behold them die, ye Gods.
Eighty to five the odds. Still to the name of Australia
they were true.

Louis H. Clark, New Britain

NEITHER CHANGI NOR THE Burma Railway were the worst things that happened to Australian troops by way of percentage of deaths or degree of brutality or outlandish means of the final killings. Few Australian newspapers reported the findings of the separate and various War Crimes Tribunals that investigated the deaths of these Australian troops.

But, like Simpson and his donkey of World War I fame, these two, Changi and the Burma Railway, were clearly definable experiences and, like the legend of Simpson, they remain. That is not to say they were not notable, nor that the crimes committed against these men as prisoners up the Burma Railway were not dreadful and in some cases barbaric: they were all these things. But it must be stated that it is almost flippant of a community to so grasp at an easily assimilated story rather than search for the whole; in this case, to take hold of what was offered them by way of selective communiques by government rather than search the battlefields for the sons of their land and learn how they died.

On the islands of Ambon, Borneo, Timor, New Britain and

New Ireland, Australians 'died game' as Bill Cook a rare survivor said, but nevertheless died a cruel death.

New Britain

Not one survivor of the tiny garrison on New Britain (isolated,
furthest east of all Australian army cadres at the time) forgot
the sight, or fails to tell the listener of these young gladiators
going aloft 'eighty to five the odds'.

The little AIF garrison itself was about to face similar odds
and many to die a worse death.

Australian troops had been at Rabaul on the island of New
Britain since March 1941. L (for Lark) Force comprised 1420
men, the majority of whom were the officers and men of the
2/22nd Battalion; completing the force were twenty Australian
Army Service Corps, twenty-two medical personnel (2/10th
Field Ambulance [Detached] including six nurses), an anti-tank
battery plus small units of artillery, anti-aircraft and engineers.
There were ten Wirraway pilots, two anti-aircraft guns and
four trench mortars' crews.

Private Bill Harry, 2/22nd Battalion: 'Truk was only 650
miles north of Rabaul, and the first indication we had that the
Japs were on their way was a patrolling Catalina that picked
up the invasion force of forty-eight vessels moving in our direction. The Catalina radioed Port Moresby and was told, "Drop
your bombs and come home". So they tried to drop their cargo
of bombs but the Catalina was shot down, three of the crew
got out of it and were brought into Rabaul by the Japanese
invasion fleet.'

A 'few' Japanese planes had been over but early on 4
January twenty-two Japanese bombers and eleven flying boats
bombed Rabaul airstrip and the compound area. From then
on there were daily raids. On 22 and 23 January 1942 Lark
Force met the enemy. The encounter was almost instantane-
ously disastrous and was to rapidly deteriorate to become the
most gruesome memory for the Australian survivors.

Strangely, it was a crime that few back home in Australia heard about, yet it was not as though we had too many military disasters as yet to deaden the communal mind.

This was the earliest. Government, of course, knew and promptly embargoed the news, for what reason we can only guess: did they think citizens back home would panic, become afeared that should the Japanese now hop over into Australia, they too, after surrendering, would be massacred so hideously? A few doctors and nurses in a few army hospitals in Australia knew of it but it was not their place to broadcast such things about their patients.

Not until forty-seven years later was the official report on this matter released, and then it was scarcely mentioned in the news; some of the media believed it was too 'sensational' (not in the sense of disbelieving the facts but of 'titillating the senses of those no better than the perpetrators themselves'). Others believed that, as it had happened almost fifty years ago, we should not 'open up old wounds'. Those few victims still living, say, 'Whose wounds?'

Private Bill Cook (2/10th Field Ambulance) said, 'From the time the first bomb fell on Rabaul we knew we were done for'. Billy was in charge of a ward set up in a private house, the rest of the hospital was in nearby Government House. 'We who are about to die salute you!' said Billy, speaking for the pilots of the little Wirraways as he watched them go up against the Japanese Zeros, one of the best planes to take to the air in that war.

'Six pilots were killed, four wounded. While the little Wirraways were still airborne, trying to win an advantageous position to outwit the fast, manoeuvrable Zeros, eighty Japanese bombers and fighters roared in, taking one strategic post after another.'

Sub Lieutenant C.L. Page (RANVR), a planter in civilian days, was now a coastwatcher on Tabar Island, east of New Ireland. On 20 January he had sent word to Rabaul that twenty enemy aircraft were on their way. Another thirty-three planes were coming from the west and Page, of course, could not detect these – neither could the garrison at Rabaul until they struck just after midday. Eventually 120 aircraft were bombing the town, port and troops at will. Kavieng (New Ireland) had been heavily bombed and four enemy cruisers were heading for Rabaul. On the morning of the 22nd, forty-five fighters and dive bombers came over, and as twenty ships approached – destroyers, cruisers, troop transports and an aircraft carrier – the radio transmitter was put out of action, leaving the garrison out of touch with the outside world just as the enemy arrived. The end had come. The Japanese poured ashore and overran the Australians.

Privates Stan (Bluey) Day and his mate, Bill Gault (both red-heads), of the 2/22nd Battalion were waiting at their camou-flaged machine-gun post on the beach. 'We were proud of that camouflage', 22-year-old Bluey said later. 'We'd spent months working out just what we were going to do – until they landed and then we might as well have picked the gun up and thrown it at them for all the use our few men and arms were. They came in their thousands across the beach and over the rough jungle mountains like a tidal wave and rolled over us as we ran.' Men were picking up and firing rifles from the dead but it was 'snowflakes in hell' as Private Claude Lunn said. Bluey Day recalls, 'It was still dark when the first of them landed, they were all around us. Nothing we could have done could stop them. And then those of us who could, ran. We called ourselves the Rabaul Harriers.'

Those not dead, wounded and captured, or encircled, took to the bush. Already Major Palmer (2/10th Field Ambulance) had moved his hospital and patients inland to Vanapopi Mission (where there were civilian nursing sisters and a doctor) and as there were trained staff there he then left to go to help the 2/22nd who had no doctors with them. 'The field ambulance party carried a medical companion (the 'bible' of all doctors), a surgical haversack and a shell dressing haversack.' Dr Palmer himself carried a heavy pack of dressings and drugs and treated the men en route on the nine-day trek over the 3500-feet mountains and down to the sea where fleeing civilians had earlier been rescued by a flying boat. They were constantly harried by Japanese, some died of their wounds, most others suffered from the host of diseases peculiar to all islands in the tropics, several varieties of malaria, dengue fever, beriberi, ulcers, tinea, hookworm and urticaria.

The Japanese had by now landed large bodies of men at odd spots around the coast line, others were moving along the steep mountain terrain, pushing through the thick jungle-like growth.

Bill Cook of the 2/10th Field Ambulance fled with one party. 'Rabaul was in a sorry plight. Stretcher bearers and ambulances were bring casualties in – Air Force, Army and Merchant Seamen whose ship had been sunk in the harbour – none complaining while waiting for treatment. The doctors, nurses and orderlies worked until the early hours of the morning, probing, injecting and bandaging. The operating theatre was like a slaughter-house, bloodied swabs and dressings were thrown into a corner, none of them being cleaned up until the last of the patients were treated.

'The total loss of life was between thirty and forty, most of these through being buried when the bombs blew our fortress guns over. The natives were hit with anti-personnel bombs, legs and arms were missing, while detonation killed a few. Our position was very insecure, a few mortars and anti-tank guns to combat a huge task force.

'At Kokopo we took over the mission to use as a hospital. Our nursing staff consisted of six army and six civilian sisters, a few Public Health Department personnel and twenty from the Medical Unit. When the Japs surrounded Rabaul, Major Palmer called for two volunteers to stay with the wounded. Privates Laurie Hudson and Max Langdon were selected and these men, together with the army and civilian nurses and the Public Health men (who were able to operate in an emergency) stayed with eighty patients. After blessings by Padre May who also was staying behind, we set off by road, an ambulance leading the way and an assortment of cars and trucks following.

'Just before midday a party of Aussies caught up with us and handed over their casualty, Private Tom Connop. The MO splinted his fractured leg and, after an injection of morphia, he was placed in the wagon. We were in a hurry to pass Toma drome before the Japs occupied it. Connop's ride was not to be envied. The jolting of the ambulance could not be offset by morphia and it was a godsend when Tom eventually fainted.

'At the deserted Malabunga Mission we stopped and again Major Palmer called for men to stay, this time with Connop as we were near the end of the road and would have to walk over 50 miles of mountains.' Billy and four other men were detailed to stay while the rest moved on. 'On several occasions a Japanese float plane came over and we could see the pilot looking over the side at us. A few soldiers called in for food and then moved on. Tom begged us to leave him with food and water, and morphia tablets, and so give us a chance to escape. Albert Fernandez and Alf Hawkins of the dental unit said that they would stay with the patient to allow the rest of us to move on again.

'We crossed the first of what proved to be scores, hundreds of rivers. At first we removed our shorts, puttees, boots and stockings, walked across the river, carefully dried our feet, put on our boots and stockings, wound our puttees around our legs and began walking. A few hundred yards further on we found another river to cross. This time we walked across, then lay down with our legs sticking up in the air to allow the water to run out of our boots. During the afternoon we met another soldier and two civilians. We reached the mission, Lamingi, and after a short rest moved on as one big party, Captain Robertson leading and Major Palmer at the rear. We were in the centre of very mountainous country and the journey was slowed down as we climbed mountains, slipped down mountains or crossed rivers. A very long stretch of down-hill gave us a feeling that our troubles were over until we reached the bottom and saw the Worongoi River, the swiftest flowing and widest we had yet encountered. It was only after a few natives had forced their way across with a thick monkey vine and secured this on both sides that we could make our way across. Some few hours later the track ran along the bank of a slow-moving river which meant that we were near sea level. Anchored near the mouth was a schooner which, as we found out later, had been provisioned by some civilians for an effort to reach New Guinea. As we neared the boat, we saw standing out to sea a Jap destroyer which had evidently sighted the schooner and now opened fire to sink it. In all, fourteen shells came over before a hit was scored. You can imagine us about 30 yards off the schooner and the Jap shells exploding around it. My personal opinion was that they were shooting at me.

'A mile or so further on we met the civilians who had prepared the schooner. They were very disappointed and told us that it was the third time the Japs had tried to destroy the vessel. They had planned that the boat would sail that night. Further on there was a sawmill and this seemed to be a rendezvous for the troops. When we arrived we were given some Granose biscuits by the civilians who were going back to Rabaul by canoe to surrender.

'There were eight of us, all 2/10th Field Ambulance, until now – the party would be bigger, then smaller, some dropping out and some joining. The eight of us spent the night at this spot, most of the time spent swatting sandflies which were very troublesome. After a breakfast of rice and chocolate, we were preparing to leave when we saw five barge loads of Japanese moving down the coast. We left a note on a tree informing anybody following of the possibility of being cut off by the Japs.

'Towards midday on 4 February, Staff Sergeant Michael Bowers of the 2/22nd met us and said that the Japs had landed ahead but had moved on again. He told us to wait where we were while he went ahead to find out where the Nips were. We moved a short distance off the track into a clearing and, while half of us played cards, the rest started to cook rice. Our game of bridge was interrupted by Mick Bowers running to us crying out "The bastards are here" and, looking towards the track, I saw a Jap with fixed bayonet looking at us. A party of Japs signed to us to sit down. More Japs came along, bring-ing more prisoners until our numbers had grown to twenty-three. A Nip officer made us sign our names and numbers in a book which held many other names. Later, another wounded Australian staggered into our midst and we treated him, using the supplies we had.

'At last we were made to carry the rifles and ammunition the Japs had captured and two of us were detailed to look after the patient who was suffering from fatigue. The travelling was slow so we were made to leave this patient behind with a Jap soldier while we moved on. A short while later the Jap caught up with us, alone, so we could only surmise what hap-pened. When we arrived at the Jap outpost, Sergeant "Mick" Bowers joined us, also a civilian. We were then taken to the Tol Plantation where the Japs had established their headquar-ters. We were made to put all the gear we had carried, both our own personal gear and that which the Japs had captured, in a heap and then sit down some distance away.

'We were given a piece of very stale bread and one canteen of water between the party. This seemed to be a signal for the Nips to ransack our packs. Everything was strewn about the ground in their search and they seemed to be after photographs (particularly female) and tobacco. Medical supplies were trodden on and spoilt, thousands of quinine tablets were ruined and, in the case of our (medical) gear, drugs and hypo-dermic sets which would have benefited anybody, were left lying around. While the searching was going on, I noticed two Japs grinning and one gave the impression of shooting the other. They looked at us and laughed and I realised that we were to be killed.

'When all our belongings were taken, even to our handker-chiefs and our pay books – in fact, as I realised later, every-thing which could be used to identify us, they started to tie our thumbs together behind our backs with new cord fishing line. They were not gentle and our thumbs soon were swollen and started to pain. The Japs had overlooked the fob pocket in our shorts and so had left me with a "cat's eye" (a New

Guinea penny) and a packet of razor blades. They next tied us together by passing cords, belts or native lap-laps between our arms, thus grouping us into twos or threes and, after signing us to shake off our tin hats, we were led off into the jungle. The medical personnel had been kept together and it looked like our last minutes had come or, to use an expression of one of our mates, "Well fellows, this looks like it". Ron Cantwell was trying to work his thumbs free but one of the guards saw him and jerked at his bonds, nearly pulling Ron down. At a small clearing, looking down at the water some 150 yards away, we were halted and signed to sit down with our backs to the sea and not to look around.

'The first of the party was signalled to stand up and walk down the hill with a guard. Another of the party looked around and was bashed on the jaw with a rifle butt which, incidentally, was an Australian rifle which is heavier than the Japs had. This Jap had a rifle and bayonet which he was going to use against us in preference to the Japanese type that has a thinner and narrower bayonet.

'When the first man was taken away, one of the Victorians pointed to our Red Cross armbands and protested at the treatment but the Jap officer just grinned and ripped our armbands off. By twos and threes the rest were taken away – no noise, just the English word "Next" spoken by the Japs, and the next group would stand up, say, "Cheerio, fellows" and walk away to their death – head erect and without a falter, truly a grim indication of those boys' guts. This was something which helped the remainder keep their chin up, they died like men, without a sound.

'Seven men were left and the next two were Field Ambulance men. I tried to be taken with them but this was not allowed. When they were gone, the Jap officer pointed to his revolver and then to the bayonet, seemingly to ask us what method we preferred to be killed – shot or stabbed. Needless to say, we wanted to be shot. At last my turn came and, with two Victorians, we stood up and one of them said, "Well, Cookie, now we will know what the next world is like". We walked

down a slight slope and could see to our left three Japs converging on us until we were about 50 yards from the water
when they swiftly lunged at us from behind with their bayonets. During the walk down I could see the Nips plainly and
could recognise the one who stabbed me even now – a big
fellow, easily 6 feet tall, built in proportion and at least four
gold teeth in the front of his upper jaw.'

The first stab knocked them down. 'In my case the wound
was in the back about level with the lower ribs. The Japs stood
over us stabbing, each stab being accompanied by a snarling
grunt. In all I received six wounds in the back – two just
missing the spine, two more breaking ribs and the last two,
one under the shoulder blade and the other sliding across the
shoulder blade. My two companions had not uttered a sound.
I think one of them must have died very quickly and the other
lingered a short time because, when the Japs started to leave
us, he groaned a little and one of the Japs returned and stabbed
him again. I had been holding my breath and feigning death
but could not hold it any longer. When I breathed again, I
either made a noise or moved, and the Jap started on me again,
stabbed me another four times in the neck and another
through the ear which entered my face at the temple, severing
the temporal artery, and the point of the blade finished in my
mouth. Each of the wounds which I received had not hurt a
great deal except the last which grated across the cheek bone
and, when he withdrew the bayonet, it lifted my head. Blood
spurted from my mouth. He then covered the three of us with
palm leaves and bushes, and left us. I just lay there waiting to
die and I heard two distinct shots followed by a scattered
volley of rifle shots which meant that the last two had been
shot.

'For a space of time I lay there – I don't know how long.
Flies attracted by the pools of blood started to worry me and
I heard a voice call to me. Although it was a voice in my
imagination, this saved my life and I decided that I would die
trying to get away rather than stay as I was. The native loin
cloth which tied me to my dead companions was my first

obstacle but, after a little manoeuvring, I got the knot between my hands and managed to get it undone. This freed me from the others but my thumbs were still tied. I spoke to see if either of my mates had survived although I do not think I could have helped them much if they had. My legs were rubbery and could just support me and my head seemed a long way from my body. In the first few yards I had to step past the body of the first of the party to be killed. There was no bleeding evident and he was lying on his side. Several times I fell down and realised that I would have to free my hands to save myself from further injury. I collapsed and lost consciousness – for how long I do not know. When I came to, I tried to saw the cord binding my thumbs on the iron "horseshoe" of my boot. I had often read about this method but it failed in my case as my swollen thumbs got in the way.

'Finally, after a lot of bending, I managed to work my hands down over one leg and so get them within reach of my teeth. I then chewed the cord until I was free. All this had started my wounds bleeding again and, when I started walking again, I suffered another "black-out".

'After another unknown period, I walked to the water and waded out waist deep and let the salt water wash my wounds. This caused a lot of pain but it just had to be done. I realised my position – the Japs were between me and freedom and the only direction I could take was towards Rabaul, hoping for the best. Walking in water to avoid leaving footprints and blood stains in the sand, I staggered along until I reached a patch of rocks where I could move without leaving marks and I crawled under a tree trunk and went to sleep. A short nap and on again, trying to reach a river to quench my thirst. The beach I was on was about 3 miles around and, as darkness came, I saw smoke from what seemed to be a camp fire at the end of the beach. It was after dark when I reached the river and I just lay there drinking. I wanted to rest but decided that I must put more distance between myself and the enemy.

'The walk along the beach was nerve-racking. Tree stumps looked like Jap sentries and several times I nearly panicked.

My only chance was to keep going until I could find somebody who could give me dressings, not that I gave myself much chance of surviving, but with this in mind I walked until I reached where I thought I saw camp fires. The possibility of the smoke coming from enemy fires did not enter my head. There was a path leading into the jungle. Following it, I walked into a few Aussies asleep. Lieutenant Colonel Scanlan was in charge of the party and they were going in to surrender. There were about seven or eight other officers, the colonel's batman and a native in the party.

'I woke them up and related what had happened and asked if they had any dressings or antiseptics. Colonel Scanlan took my shirt which was caked with blood and gave me one of his. His batman gave me some rice gruel and tobacco but neither of these had appeal as I felt I only wanted to sleep. They let me sleep for a couple of hours, then woke me, dressed my wounds with what material they had and told me that they would send me back with a native to contact one of our Field Ambulance boys, Bob Kennedy. (The idea was good but it happened that Bob was dead and the medical pack which the Jap sergeant was carrying when we were captured had belonged to Bob.)

'Capture with me meant almost certain death for both of us so, after about a mile of travel, the native shook hands and said "Goodbye, master" and left me. Again I felt helpless. I had to wade across a river exposed, but, on the other side I saw three Aussies walking along. I called out to them and they asked me to stay with them and we would try to climb the mountain ridge and get around the Japs.

'The hard climbing aggravated the wounds and my broken ribs. One friend gave me a piece of mosquito net which I bound around my chest and helped support the broken bones. The only food these three had was about half a pound of barley and a piece of young palm trunk, which we chewed, and some tea leaves. All these they shared with me, the barley being counted in grains to ensure an equal share. This was the spirit one found on the whole of that long jungle journey.

'We would climb a ridge and then find our progress barred by a huge drop so we would have to retrace our steps. At times we would pass one ridge and again find our progress stopped. Our barley was eaten and near a stream of water we found a specie of water snail, rather small, but we boiled them and ate them.

'Each day one or other of the men would tell me my wounds were healing and this gave me heart, but the side of my face was swollen and discharging and the smell was hard to bear.

'Six days of mountaineering and we discovered a path and marks of those two-toed boots which the Japs wore. We didn't tarry too long at that spot.' They twice met natives and one volunteered to guide them to a mission station. 'We then realised that we were in the same place where we had started our mountaineering a week ago.

'We had to pass the spot where the massacre had been committed and it took all my willpower to keep going. I carried a razor blade in my hand with the intention of committing suicide rather than be captured again. My mates could see my panic and they kept me in the middle of the party. Passing by the Tol Plantation I could see boots and tin hats lying around.

'We had barely passed the plantation when we saw the tops of rifles and a red cap over the top of the kunai grass, coming towards us. I, for one, did not waste any time running into the long grass to hide but my mates called to me as it was only Colonel Scanlan's party. They had passed the Japs but, with comparative safety in sight, had retraced their steps and were going back to surrender. Scanlan had a loaf of bread in one hand and a white flag in the other and was in full colonel's dress. To my way of thinking, his surrender would have been in vain as the Japs had left Tol and the atrocities had been committed – practically all the troops had either passed Tol or had been captured. However, they wished us the best and we went our respective ways. We purchased some bananas off a native and had a meal, keeping some for later. Our native guide made the pace a cracker and it was not long before I started to lag, frequent rests being necessary. I saw a patch of congealed blood and an eyeball but whether it was human or not, I don't know.'

They crossed fast-flowing rivers and climbed more heights. Once they saw a Japanese warship steaming into the Tol Plantation wharf. 'We lost no time moving out of the danger zone. Later I met a few Aussies who said that some mission boys were getting a boat to take us across another river. Where they got this boat astounds me. It was an ordinary pulling boat, the first which I had seen in New Britain. Some of us were sent on ahead to contact a Lutheran priest who would certainly have some medical supplies and possibly some food, but the missionary, a German, treated us coldly, giving me only four bandages, a little rice and showed us the way out of the plantation. We found a Nazi flag here and some of the soldiers wanted to shoot him but his religious position saved him.'

On 15 February the party struggled on, knowing nothing of events outside the island, therefore not knowing that 'Impregnable Singapore' was that day surrendering. They caught a pig, cooked it and shared it with natives – 'whose pig it was'.

'From then on everything went well for us. At each village we were given food of some sort – bananas, oranges, taro and one native gave us a tapioca pudding. But one man was sick and I was not much better and our thought was to catch up with Major Palmer to get treatment.' Once some natives gave them 'honest to goodness' tobacco, another time some vaseline for Bill's wounds, as well as oranges and pumpkins.

'Each time we met natives, we asked if the lic-lic (little) doctor was far ahead and we found that we were gradually catching up with him. He had two other survivors of the massacre with him and was moving slowly.' And then they met.

'Major Palmer asked me my trouble and I showed him the eleven stab wounds on my back. His only remark was, "Cook, you're a tough old bastard". These words certainly meant a lot to me knowing the major and I realised that he was paying me a great compliment. He then tried to strap my wounds together with sticking plaster but, with the exception of my face, these had begun to heal.

'Four survivors from the massacre (Webster, Hazelgrove, Cliff Marshall and I) were together while another of my unit (Des Collins) had gone with another party. At each village Majors Palmer and Owens bought food and distributed it evenly. Each day seemed alike, except some days we would see some of the boys carrying a bag-enshrouded figure and we knew that one or more of our comrades had "passed beyond".

'At night, sleep would not come. I went through the Tol experience in my dreams and on other occasions I was back in Australia, suffering the same treatment, always from the Japs. Both the officers and the men cheered Hazelgrove and myself, helping us to carry on, joking to us and keeping our spirits up when things were not so good.' When they arrived at their destination their numbers were too great for the small mission of Father Harris, and some, including Bill Cook, had to walk 15 miles to another plantation.

In their new camp they set up a mini-hospital.

'Our medical supplies were primitive, consisting of one lance, very blunt, one round lucky stone to be used for sharpening the lance if necessary, sundry pieces of native lap-lap, washed and clean for bandages and one tin of Dhobies ointment. Major Palmer, who had stayed at Father Harris's mission, used to walk the 15 miles each way to us twice a week. Lieutenant Selby (later Mr Justice Selby) kept what scraps of news we received, wrote it out and handed it around. One of his jobs was to carve the crosses with the name and army number of those boys who passed away there. The medical treatment was administered by Max Pearsall, Jim Peterson, a NGVR man and me; and our hospital had six makeshift beds, full nearly all the time.'

Recurring malaria kept Bill Cook in and out of bed. Many of the men died and the grave-digging party was hard put digging through the solid coral-like earth. 'Some gave up hope, some had every hope and a number said that they would stick with me as they considered that if anybody had luck it was me.

'We had hoped that two parties would get through to Port

Moresby, Captain Cameron on the other side of the island and Lieutenant Best on our side. Each of these had a boat and had made a break but our hopes were dashed when news was received that Lieutenant Best was captured at Gasmata, some 80 miles away from our camp.' In the first week in April, the men moved back 15 miles to Palmalmal Plantation where rescue was said to be imminent. A flutter was caused when Major Owen compiled a list of names, if married, number of children and weight. 'This was to be the order of evacuation. There was no rank in the order of priority but sickness got preference and my name and Cliff Marshall's were first and second on the list.

'When we arrived at the plantation house, I heard one of my unit speak: it was Les Fawcett. He told me that he had a surprise for me and was it a surprise: a plate of hot scones with butter and a cup of Ovaltine to which I did justice. While I was eating, he gave me a cigarette, good old Fine Cut, and I felt like a king. I had to go to another room and sign a nominal roll. As I entered, somebody said "Here he is" and I was given another smoke (I had not finished the one which Les had given me – greediness) and asked a few questions as to my health. Major Palmer came around to each and every one, issuing a dose of liquid quinine. All next day men were arriving and I met Max Hazelgrove again, Jack Holah and others from our mob. Jack told me that they did not give me much chance of ever leaving the island and I had been given two weeks at the most to live.

'The boat was to be here on Thursday. We learned that our rescue was made possible by three men with tommy-guns who had volunteered to come to New Britain in a 16-foot launch to look for us. Three native police boys helped them. They had planned to work along the coast until they found us and they would not have been shown much mercy if captured as they had a radio transmitter.

'The ship was due at daybreak on Thursday and nobody had slept very much on Wednesday night. We were all looking for the ship's approach. It was not until 8 a.m. that it was sighted. Were we surprised! Instead of a destroyer, it was a small schooner, the *Laura Bada*, some 150 tons. Realising that it meant our freedom, it looked like the *Queen Mary*.

'There were roughly 140 of us. We all went to bed together down below and stayed there until everybody could get up, as one could not move about without treading on those on the floor. Captain Rose, a medical officer, had come over on the boat to take charge of us, he handed out Atebrin [for malaria]. There were some sick men on board. One soldier died the first night out and was buried at sea.'

They travelled in the dark of night, hugging close to islands. When a wireless message had to be sent, the ship was stopped. 'After three days, we entered the China Straits which meant that we were close to Port Moresby. Two planes flew over us – a Kittyhawk and a Catalina – a marvellous sight to see our own planes above us. At last Port Moresby was sighted and a naval launch came out to inspect us, calling to all hands that we were to sail for Sydney that night (Sunday) on the *Macdhui*. Long streams of ambulances were waiting at Moresby and a crowd of soldiers came as close as rules allowed. Cigarettes were thrown to us and it made us glad to think that here were men eager to face the enemy.

'We were then lined up on the wharf and, in single file, it was then that we realised the state of our clothes. Most had no pants (their only adornment being a native lap-lap or loin cloth), very few had a hat and those who possessed shirts were lucky. What few private belongings we had were in an assortment of corn sacks or army packs. When we were assigned to our cabins, there was a rush to the bathrooms, hot water and soap, something we had not seen for months. We had no modesty, three having a bath together, taking it in turns to wash our neighbour's back. My turn in the bathroom brought a group of curious officers who, having been told of my wounds, came to have a look. Each and every one, from the highest to the lieutenants, wished me luck and promised to get square for me.

'After dinner, roast turkey! George Smith (2/10th Field

Ambulance) came with three dozen pairs of shorts, shirts, tobacco, razor blades – in fact, everything we needed. One of the NCOs had called his men together and said, "Fellows, there are a lot of poor bastards on board the ship who have no clothes and I want you to give what you can. If any of you hold back, Christ help you as I will do you over." A few other lads took up a collection to buy tobacco for the 2/10th boys on board and we received 20 ounces of tobacco and fifteen packets of cigarettes each. When I was handing out the clothes, one of my cabin mates asked if there was a piece of string which he could use for a belt. Immediately one of the soldiers took off his belt and handed it to him, another asked me if there was a bigger shirt and, again, one of the visitors took off his shirt and handed it over. Well, the giver and the receiver looked at each other and tears started to flow. And I nearly followed suit. These fellows again demonstrated what friendship means.'

Then Sydney. 'Down the harbour we moved, under the bridge, a mere handful of what had left some thirteen months ago. At the wharf a large number of people were waiting, some gladly and others hoping against hope, then walking away crying.

'My wife had been working in town so I went to where she was employed, not knowing if she was still there. When I knocked, a young woman asked what I wanted and when I told her she said, "You must be her husband". She brought my wife to me and, as she told me afterwards, watched through a crack in the door to see us embrace.

'Later I was ordered to attend an official inquiry into the Tol massacre and learned for the first time Private Max "Smacker" Hazelgrove's story. He and seven others had been taken prisoner after us and one of his party had a pamphlet the Japanese had dropped stating that, if the Australians surrendered, they would be treated as prisoners of war. When this soldier was searched and the pamphlet found, the finder grinned and waved the paper across the Aussie's face.' They were tied and marched in single file to a clump of grass where

Embarkation for any war is cluttered and messy. Above all, however, it is exciting. There's no thought here of dreary, dangerous years in prison camps.

Arthur and Harry Simpson 'before they left home and did not come back again', as their mother wrote on this photograph, which was taken in their backyard at Officer, Victoria.

No man who saw the war out as a prisoner in Turkey could forget the bitter cold.

When Leslie Richardson was taken prisoner he set off on a six-day walk, 'the thermometer registering 120°F in the shade'.

Captured men were marched through the town in the hope of lending fear to the French citizens. (Australian War Memorial, A02239)

Men of both sides sheltered in shell holes. Here German prisoners carry Australian wounded; the next day things could be reversed.

Near every camp was a graveyard.

Above: The men complained constantly about the food in German camps but, as this 1917 photograph taken at Schneidemull camp shows, the feeding of vast numbers of POWs cost Germany dearly in human resources as well as supplies.

Three of the most famous Australian aviators were (left to right) Lieutenant C.H. Vautin, who was captured in July 1915 on the Palestine front, Captain T.W. White, captured November 1915 on the Mesopotamian front, and Lieutenant W.H. Treloar, captured in September 1915. (Australian War Memorial, A02265)

Opposite: Small, close-knit communities such as those in Tasmania suffered grievously when large numbers of troops disappeared. Corporal K. Jensen, Staff Sergeant A. Bull, Privates C. Tabart and N. Skinner were captured in 1941 along with many other servicemen from their island home.

'Going up to battle or down in retreat, donkeys were a man's best friend in Greece or Crete', wrote Howard Vinning. (Australian War Memorial, 7851)

Escaping POWs fought with the partisans of several countries bordering Italy. Sergeants Ross Sayers, Ernest Brough, Allan Berry and Staff Sergeant Harry Lesar fought with the Yugoslavs until evacuated by the RAAF at the end of the European war.

On 8 May 1941 this group of Australian officers and men of the 2/2nd Infantry Battalion escaped from Greece to Euboea Island in the Aegean Sea. They eventually rejoined the Australian forces by escaping across Turkey. (Australian War Memorial. 134872)

The mountain tracks in Servia were rough. (Australian War Memorial, 007797)

Some wounded and protected personnel (such as medical staff) were exchanged by
Germany and Allied nations. This group has just arrived safely in Alexandria, 22 November
1943. The ships sailed under special arrangements for their safety, agreed to by the warring
parties.

To all Prisoners of War!

The escape from prison camps is no longer a sport!

Germany has always kept to the Hague Convention and only punished recaptured prisoners of war with minor disciplinary punishment.

Germany will still maintain these principles of international law.

But England has besides fighting at the front in an honest manner instituted an illegal warfare in non combat zones in the form of gangster commandos, terror bandits and sabotage troops even up to the frontiers of Germany.

They say in a captured secret and confidential English military pamphlet,

THE HANDBOOK
OF MODERN IRREGULAR
WARFARE:

". . . the days when we could practise the rules of sportsmanship are over. For the time being, every soldier must be a potential gangster ~~and~~ ~~~~

~~own country~~ ~~~~
~~stances, such neutral countries~~ ~~~~
supply."

England has with these instructions opened up a non military form of gangster war!

Germany is determined to safeguard her homeland, and especially her war industry and provisional centres for the fighting fronts. Therefore it has become necessary to create strictly forbidden zones, called death zones, in which all unauthorised trespassers will be immediately shot on sight.

Escaping prisoners of war, entering such death zones, will certainly lose their lives. They are therefore in constant danger of being mistaken for enemy agents or sabotage groups.

Urgent warning is given against making future escapes!

In plain English: Stay in the camp where you will be safe! Breaking out of it is now a damned dangerous act.

The chances of preserving your life are almost nil!

All police and military guards have been given the most strict orders to shoot on sight all suspected persons.

Escaping from prison camps has ceased to be a sport!

Posters were distributed widely to discourage escapers.

Sergeant E. Butterfield (centre), who was captured in Greece, kept the battalion flag, and 'stuck to it all the way through. We used it to cover the coffins of pals when they died'.

RAAF ex-prisoners arrive home in Australia.

September 1944: POWs from the Japanese *Rakuya Maru*, covered in oil from the sinking ship, are near to rescue.

Bill Jinkins was well trained for the trials he would undertake. 'We had a stern taskmaster at Bonegilla, he pushed us to the limit.' One trial was to swim the Murray River at a point 800 yards wide 'carrying as much weight as would drown unfit men'.

Captain Sam Dealey, US navy, who twice took Jinkins to Japanese-held islands in the Australian's attempts to rescue prisoners.

Captain L.C. Matthews GC MC arranged a radio link with the outside world, brought medicines into the camp and organised escape parties while directing an underground intelligence organisation. He was executed by the Japanese on 2 March 1944. (Australian War Memorial, 59358)

Australian nurses (civilian and army) after being held POW for almost three-and-a-half years by the Japanese. Seventeen women had been captured at Rabaul and one at Kavieng early in 1942. They were taken to Yokohama and kept there until 1943, when they were transferred to a camp at Totsuki.

'Two of the greatest heroes of the war', as the captions read when Major K.J. Fagan and Lieutenant Colonel W.A. Bye returned in 1945. 'They carried out medical and surgical work under great difficulties despite their own poor condition.' As with the majority of the great doctors they slipped back into civilian practice and looked for no plaudits from their patients or the nation. (Australian War Memorial, 116634)

Wives search for husbands, children for fathers on this most terrible Golgotha. Beverley Lynn (née Connor) was 2 years of age in 1945 when her father 'went missing'. In 1986 she went to Borneo to search for him.

The crowd waiting at YMCA hut, Sydney Showgrounds, to greet men returning from German prison camps, April 1945. Many of the men had sailed away five years previously.

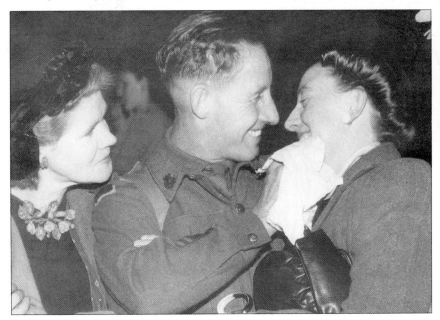

Private L.R. Oates, over five years away (four of which were spent in Stalag XIII C, Germany), dries the tears of his girlfriend, Winifred Corringe.

And yet – five years later, 'Mo' Gwyther (arrowed), whose father had been to World War II, rushed to enlist for Korea.

the firing began. Max told me that when he was hit in the shoulder he feigned death, and afraid the enemy might burn the grass and bodies he later freed himself from his mates and crawled away. On return home the surgeons removed his shoulder blade where an explosive bullet had lodged back at Tol.' Ironically, Hazelgrove's escape route was along the track while Bill Cook's was along the beach and they must have been very close to each other for several days after escaping the Tol massacre.

In all, six Australians survived the massacre by pretending they were dead, but two of these died of their wounds in the following week. Driver Wilkie Desmond Collins, 2/10th Field Ambulance, gave his account of the massacre and two other soldiers told of the aftermath.

Driver Collins: 'About 10 a.m. they split us into parties which all went in different directions and I could see only our own party of twelve. An officer pulled out a sword and cut one joker loose and walked him into the bush. A soldier followed with a fixed bayonet. I heard a scream and the Japanese soldier came back wiping his bayonet. Another two or three went like that. One Aussie broke loose and jumped up and tried to run for it and the officer shot him with an automatic revolver. I was the last one left and the officer was there by himself. He put away his sword and took a rifle and motioned me to get up and walk. I took a few paces and he shot me through the shoulder. I fell to the ground and kept still. He fired again and hit me through both wrists and in the back. He decided he had finished me and went away.'

Collins was able to make his way into the bush where he hid for several days before returning to the plantation after the Japanese had gone. There he found two other surviving victims of the massacre. Collins left them in a plantation hut with some bananas for food and went with a party of civilians who came by looking for help. Soon after leaving they saw a Japanese destroyer come in and later saw that the hut where the two men had been left was on fire.

He was later evacuated to New Guinea by boat. The fate of

the two wounded men in the hut was reported to another soldier who escaped the massacre – Private Alfred Robinson of the NGVR. He said natives told him the Japanese put grease on the men and poured kerosene or benzine over the house and set fire to it. A few days later Lieutenant Hugh Mackenzie, RAN, walked through the ruins of the hut. 'We lifted out several sheets of iron and found a corpse which had been burnt', he said. 'The corpse was within a few feet of the back entrance of the house and was on its hands and knees with one arm flung around a watering can. The attitude was that of a man attempting to crawl out of the house. There was a smell as if there was another corpse in the house but I did not see it.'

Mackenzie also saw the body of a man, who natives said was an officer, half-buried on the lawn outside the house. The natives told him the officer was questioned, forced to dig his own grave, bashed on the head with a piece of wood, bayoneted and shot and then half covered by loose turf in the grave.

Lance-Corporal Clifford Marshall of 2/22nd Battalion told this story of the massacre: 'As soon as the first one had been motioned off into the bush we knew what was going to happen to us. Each Australian was taken off separately with a Japanese soldier, we would hear those who went before us cry out. There was no shot fired. We took it for granted they were bayoneted. When my turn came I was motioned to move off into the bush. There was a Japanese soldier walking behind me. I sort of turned, my hands being tied behind my back, to see what he was doing. He was making a rush at me with the bayonet.

'I received three wounds, one in the back just under the shoulder blades, not very deep, another through the arm and into the side and another into the side lower down. I shammed dead. I could hear cries from the other men for a while and then a lot of shooting. I lay there for a while and then wriggled into the underbrush. Later another Australian party picked me up and took me to Major Palmer.'

A senior officer of the 2/22nd, Major W.T. Owen, said of

the medical officer, Major Palmer: 'Four soldiers who had been victims of Jap brutality at Tol were never allowed away from his care. All realised that to be caught by the enemy in the presence of these men, thereby disclosing a knowledge of these happenings, would lead to almost certain death. Major Palmer, however, saw that his duty was with these men and their lives can be credited to his work.' Some believe the luckiest man at Tol the day of the massacre was a Private Robinson, who was one of the last to be tied up, and although his hands were tied behind his back he was not tied to the rest of the group. He told the inquiry: 'All the Japanese had fixed bayonets and some were carrying spades and I decided we were going to be done in. An agonised scream was heard and the whole line halted to listen. We then continued and at one stage I noticed the men in front, when rounding a bend, were temporarily out of sight for a few seconds. When I arrived at this point I noticed a small bush just off the path and I nipped out of the line and hid behind it. One man in the line said, "Lower sport". I crouched further into the bush. My departure was not noticed. After the line had gone by, I made off. I heard six or seven shots coming from the direction in which the men had gone.'

Robinson wandered through the jungle with his hands tied behind him for two and a half days until he ran into a party of civilians who freed him.

Reports by natives and by Private Robinson indicated that in addition to the Australians captured on 3 February and murdered the following morning, other small parties who surrendered or who were captured on 4 February were also immediately killed, and at least one party of eleven was shot at Waitavale Plantation adjoining Tol.

Many soldiers who passed through the plantations in the days and weeks following reported seeing half-burnt piles of Australian equipment and commented on a strong smell which came from certain areas of the plantation. One officer reported that when the Japanese destroyer returned after the Tol massacre the Japs poured fuel on to 'something' piled on the beach under heaps of leaves and set fire to it. He said he went close enough to see the half-burnt limbs of one human body.

The escape from the island of some of the men was due to the dedication of a handful of daring men. Bill Harry: 'We were in Jacquinot Bay, and sent a message across to Keith McCarthy who was organising the north coast evacuation. Keith was Assistant District Officer in New Britain. He sent Frank Holland over the island to contact the troops on the south coast and any troops in the vicinity and made contact with our party; there were seventeen of us and some civilian police further back along the island, also a couple of survivors of the Tol massacre. While the rest of the men went back with Frank Holland on to the north coast and teamed up with Keith McCarthy who had the only tele-radio in New Britain, six of us, Hughie McKenzie, a naval officer, Peter Pickus, intelligence officer, two naval telegraphists, an AWA radio operator and myself continued on down the south coast and sent a message back with the party that crossed to the north that we would concentrate the troops at Palmalmal Plantation, hold them there for a period of six weeks and keep a lookout between dawn and dusk on Wednesdays and Sundays.

'By the time we got down to Palmalmal, the troops we thought would number about 200 had been reduced to 120 or 128 because they were dying at a rate of about four a day, with malaria, hookworm, dysentery, malnutrition, typhus, etc. By the time the radio message got through to Port Moresby, they said, "Look, we'd better not take a punt on this, we'd better find out more of what's happening at Palmalmal". They sent Alan Timperley, an old New Guinea hand, on a little boat with a tele-radio to contact us and radio back reporting the situation. Alan had to come into New Britain under cover of night because the Japanese had a base at Gasmata about 90 miles down the coast. As soon as he came in we grouped all the troops and radioed Moresby, and they sent Ivan Champion out on the *Laura Bada*.

'It was a bit chancy whether it got through or not so when Ivan set off he headed for the Trobriand Islands and came into New Britain under cover of night. We camouflaged the *Laura*

Bada and held it there all day (pulled it up close to a little island off-shore and hoped that nothing would fly over and see it). About five o'clock in the afternoon a heavy squall came in and this was a heaven-sent opportunity so we headed for the open sea flat-out. These heavy conditions continued most of that night and the next day and we came up to the Trobriands, headed down through the China Straits at Samurai around Milne Bay. Once we got there we knew we had a fair chance of getting through. When we got through to Moresby about four days later, we went straight aboard the *Macdhui*, a coastal trader heading down to Cairns.

'However, it should never have worked that way. If we'd had a proper defensive system and a secondary plan, or alternative plan, but that never existed; it was just one of the tragedies of the whole business. Out of the 1339 men of Lark Force, roughly 400 survived, including those who were on the *Laura Bada* and the *Lakatoi*, which McCarthy organised off the north coast.

'Keith McCarthy was an interesting character, he went to New Guinea in 1926/27 as a cadet patrol officer and was an extraordinarily good performer; he served in many areas including the Sepik and had five arrow wounds in him. He was around in the days of Errol Flynn who was knocking around there living by his wits and his charm. Keith had worked on New Ireland, down on Bougainville in the Solomons and was the Assistant District Officer at Talasia on the north coast of New Britain at the time of the outbreak of war. As soon as the show broke, Keith went into action as coast-watcher, with instructions as to what to do when the Japanese came in. But the radio station had been blown up before Rabaul was evacuated and the codes destroyed and that meant that the only tele-radio that was in operation on New Britain was at Talasia with Keith McCarthy. The army got in touch with him and said, "Find out what's happened to the Rabaul garrison". So Keith then went up the coast and found a few of the survivors starting to come through. With two or three old New Guinea hands he then started to shuttle the troops

384 PRISONERS OF WAR

down the coast, intending to take them right down to the bottom end of the island and somehow get them across the Strait to mainland New Guinea.

'In the meantime there was a Burns Philp boat, the *Lakatoi*, loaded up with copra in a lagoon out on Vitu Island, and the skipper was frightened to move; the Japs had apparently called in there and he'd given them an undertaking that he'd stay put so now he wasn't prepared to budge. Keith McCarthy heard that the *Lakatoi* was there, went across in a small pinnace and commandeered the boat, heaved the copra overboard and when all the troops were collected, he got them aboard and headed for Moresby. He came down the island, ran the gauntlet and got away with it.'

Bill Harry: 'We had a few weak officers, every unit had those. Tom Blamey sent them home in droves from the Middle East – first action no good, out! Quite ruthless. But we only had the one action. We were never re-formed, we all went in different directions. We had some delightful fellows in the battalion, but we were left for dead.

'Following the First World War Australia had accepted the conditions of the Mandated Territories to the letter. There were to be no troops, no fortifications, only a native constabulary. Finally, in desperation, in 1940 the Australian government with directions from Britain said, forget all about that, you'd better do something about defending the airfields and the various harbours that exist in the general area. When the 2/22nd were sent to New Britain, the First Independent Company was put on New Ireland minus a detachment which went to Kieta, Bougainville, and another detachment of thirty men on Manus in the Admiralty Islands and that was all we had as the first line of defence against the Imperial Japanese Navy.'

In his report on the massacres on New Britain Commissioner Webb said: 'I am unable to find any justification or excuse for the bayoneting, shooting and cutting down of these Australian soldiers and civilians by the Japanese armed forces. This dreadful massacre was, I think, a fulfilment of the threat contained in Japanese pamphlets that those who resisted would be killed.

'There were at least four separate massacres of prisoners on the morning of 4th February, the first of about 100, the second of six, the third of twenty-four and the fourth of about eleven. None of the survivors could give any explanation of the Japanese onslaught upon them, and none saw anything which might have provoked it. All the men had surrendered or been captured and held in captivity before being slaughtered.'

The Commission accepted as absolutely reliable the evidence of the men. 'Each had a clear recollection of the events he was describing, each of the five bore wounds consistent with his account, and Robinson's hands were tied when he was picked up, and each of the six was subsequently picked up, quite independently, by other parties and gave an account of his experiences agreeing with his present testimony. It is in the highest degree improbable that such an account could, in the circumstances, have been concocted.'

At the end of the war a sad addendum to the travail of New Britain gradually unfolded. In the euphoria of peace this caused little interest, even though it was one of the most disastrous tragedies of the war.

By early January 1942 most of the European civilians had been evacuated from New Britain and New Ireland but there were still some 300 remaining when the Japanese attacked on the 22nd. The reason for these people being trapped can partly be laid at the door of bureaucracy. Acting Administrator Page had sent an urgent radio message to Canberra on 16 January stating that invasion was imminent and asking for the civilians to be evacuated on the merchant ship *Herstein*, then in port. The Prime Minister's Department replied on 21 January, five days later, asking for details. Attempts to contact Rabaul by radio the following day failed: the colony had been attacked that morning and the ship *Herstein* that the Administrator hoped to use to send the civilians to safety was burning in the harbour.

Many men had wanted to stay, their life's work was here in the plantations they had hewn from the jungle, far from the comforts of home and civilisation as we know it. Most had felt a responsibility to protect as well as they could their native workers, and the men in administrative positions would stay at their posts because they saw it as their duty. Whatever the bungling, it cost almost 200 civilians their lives along with 849 prisoner servicemen who sailed on the *Montevideo Maru* en route to Japan in June; an American submarine torpedoed the ship and the sea claimed every soul on the vessel.

Unheralded at the time for 'security reasons' and occasioning little interest later except to their bereaved loved ones back in Australia, the fate of the *Montevideo Maru* was forgotten and, to a degree, remains so today. Among the casualties were 164 civilians, sixteen missionaries, one RAAF, one RAN and three unidentified/unnamed persons, along with 849 army men, including 129 men from the 1st Independent Company who had been captured on New Ireland. The dead were from all States: Queensland 46, NSW 165, Victoria 530, South Australia 29, Western Australia 9, Tasmania 35, New Guinea 36, making a total of 1035.

There were no survivors from this sinking. Eventually, a report was released: 'New Guinea missionaries previously reported missing, now presumed lost at sea'. Among these men were two Catholic priests and a Catholic missionary, two Seventh Day Adventist missionaries and eleven men from the Methodist Missionary Society of Australasia. The other civilians included planters, merchant ships officers, overseers, mine managers, medical officers and government administration and public service officers, the baker from Rabaul and C. Campbell, listed as 'Visitor'. The men comprised a large part of those who pioneered the opening up of New Britain and New Ireland, the Australian Mandated Territories.

It was later officially reported the *Montevideo Maru* was sunk by the US submarine *Sturgeon* off Luzon on 1 July 1942 without survivors.

The *Naruto Maru*, 'a dirty old freighter', departed Rabaul ten days after the *Montevideo Maru* and got through safely to Japan. Aboard this second ship were forty-eight officers and six Australian Army nurses – ex-Lark Force, fifteen officers from the 1st Independent Company who had been taken on New Ireland, six civilian nurses and four Methodist Mission nurses and three RAAF officers. The prisoners were 'all mixed together for nine days sweating and starving before we reached Japan'. In between the sailing of these ships and the preceding landing and swift seizure of the island by the Japanese back in January lay a story that the authorities believed Australia was not prepared to hear.

And so, the pattern was set for all the island garrisons that were to tumble, and even after the war we scarcely heard their tragic tale of abandonment and death.

At the end of the war 101,000 Japanese surrendered in New Britain and New Ireland, and it was then found that there was a POW on the island who had been there since 1942. This man, Captain J. Murphy, had been captured after landing by submarine in the Gazelle peninsula in an attempt to contact the fleeing men and assist them to escape. HMAS *Vendetta* took him 'back to Aussie' in 1945.

The Fate of the 2/21st

They loaded us in cattle-trucks in steamy Katherine,
Where mosquitoes tackle by the score and metho substitutes for wine,
A few miles south of Darwin where there is no railway station,
Our train came slowly to a halt: it was our destination.

Anon.

From the poem *The Fate of the 2/21st* – an AIF Battalion later lost at Ambon –
written by a member of the Battalion, 1941. The poem bewails their 'fate' of not,
at that time, being sent overseas to fight.

WHEN MEN ARE ENLISTED, an urgency infects them, they want
to get going – anywhere in, or near, the firing line; they loathe
hanging around in their own land while the fighting goes on
elsewhere. They give all sorts of reasons – usually patriotic,
such as 'helping our mates over there' – but the truth is that
war engenders its own magnetism. The 8th Division was an
example.

In World War I five divisions were formed; the 6th was
formed at the beginning of World War II and then the 8th.
Naturally enough the men of the 8th thought they would
follow the 6th to the Middle East and France to what had been
the traditional battle grounds Australians had fought in. But,
to the chagrin of the men with the oval colour patch, the 7th
Division was founded in the Middle East from reinforcements.

Brothers Doug and Pompey (Stan) Jackson of Lang Lang
(Vic.) who were Privates in the 2/21st Battalion, 8th Division,
were sent up to Darwin. ('Darwin!' they wrote home to their
mother – known to their many cousins and friends as Aunty
Gert Jackson. 'We'll rot in Darwin while everyone else gets
overseas!')

Len Scott of Darwin, guard on the Northern Territory Line,
remembers, 'The 2/21st Battalion looked like kids off for a

picnic when we got them on board the little train. Some put their faces to the bars of the trucks and mooed at us like cattle as we went along attending to the couplings. In a few months we heard that most of them were dead.'

The Jackson brothers sent the following anonymous lament down south to their cousin, Jean Smith.

A few miles south of Darwin, where there's no railway station,
The train came slowly to a halt, it was our destination!
To conclude our story, our luck is surely 'cursed'
It's not our fault we're not abroad,
It's the fate of the Twenty-First.

Ironically the letter arrived from Darwin two days after the 2/21st Battalion was suddenly ordered on to the ship that took them off to Ambon 'where their souls walk' as their mother, 'Aunty Gert', says of her dead sons.

Three Forces had been put together to defend the northern perimeter of Australia. Sparrow Force was sent to Timor, Robin to New Britain and Gull Force to Ambon. The main component of Gull Force was the 2/21st Battalion. The Dutch had been in possession of the rich spice islands for 200 years before Australia was settled by Europeans. Therefore it was 400 years after Dutch merchants had first settled these fever-ridden outposts where the Japanese arrived on their armed conquest to capture the Pacific and thereby become one of the largest empires the world had known.

By the 20th century the Netherlands East Indies were almost a race apart from their distant motherland, Holland, and, in any case, when war came, they would get no support from her as Holland had already been captured by Germany. The Netherlands East Indies' nearest ally was Australia, and the two had agreed in 1941 that Australia would hold men ready to reinforce them if the need arose. Ambon was the capital of the spice islands, the seat of government for the Molucca Islands and the biggest of the trade centres outside of Java. Strategically, Ambon was part of the battle plan for the South East

Pacific. Japan needed Ambon for the large bay which could have accommodated the whole of the Japanese fleet at anchor and the air strip for a hopping-off point to south and east. (It was from this airfield the forty-four Japanese bombers took off on 19 February to bomb Darwin.)

From the beginning this defence planning was bad, and the men to suffer were those of the 2/21st Battalion and those medical, engineer and anti-tank units who sailed with them to Ambon. Lieutenant Colonel L.N. Roach commanding the 2/21st appealed for arms and more men the day they landed on Ambon, 17 December 1941. 'Health and morale good', he stressed. But, 'surgical equipment inadequate'. He appealed again for arms for his men on 23 and 24 December. Arms on the island were, 'Inadequate to repulse an invasion'. Melbourne refused to reply to his signals, even when he stressed that his present forces were so inadequately armed they could not hold out for more than one day against a determined enemy. The Deputy Chief of the General Staff, Major-General Rowell, signalled, '... Your task in cooperation with local Dutch forces is to put up the best defence possible with resources you have at your disposal'. Which meant in plain language that the 1000 men were expendable, they were there merely to delay a little the Japanese advance. Roach, unwisely, even though understandably, wrote, 'I feel it difficult to overcome a feeling of disgust ...' He was ordered to 'cease sending messages at once'.

On 15 January 1942, learning of Roach's reports, the British General Wavell told the Australian General Sturdee: 'So far as I can judge position at Ambon not critical. I am opposed to handing out important objectives to enemy without making them fight for it. Quite appreciate feelings of lonely garrison but am sure Australians will put up a stout fight whatever happens. No doubt it is wise to change commander'. The new commander, a man from General Staff Melbourne, arrived four days before the Japanese attacked. As Colonel Roach had predicted the force could not hold out for long. (Actually they held out for three days.) They fought with neither air nor sea support, no anti-aircraft guns or field artillery, only twenty-six light automatic weapons among the whole force, and there were no spare parts for these. No satisfactory army liaison was established with NEI forces.

Ten days previous to the Australians landing on Ambon, Japan had shown her might, power and intention with the attack on Pearl Harbour. Australia, with a population of under 7 million people, was spreading its few battalions of the 8th Division around isolated islands in the Pacific to face a nation of many millions, their armies trained and blooded in battle in China and their belief that to die for their Emperor was honour beyond belief. The Japanese Greater South-East Asia Co-Prosperity Sphere was to be the greatest land-grab aim of the century.

In the scented air of this spice island, villages had names as gentle as the trade winds. There was Hitoelama, Mamala, Wakasihoe, Laha, Nona and Hoetoemoeri, where the Japanese came ashore on 3 February 1941. When the war came to this island, another difficulty was added: this was the jewel of the spice islands, the rich empire of the Netherlands East Indies where authority was invested in the Dutch, whose troops were NEI natives with little, some no, training or belief that this war was anything to do with them. Twelve days before Singapore fell the Japanese came to Ambon and, like the guns of that city, the gun emplacements of Ambon also pointed in the wrong direction – or, as some would have it, the Japanese came the wrong way. Ambon and Timor were said to be vital to the defence of Australia but, if so, were 1100 unblooded, poorly equipped young men going to make much, if any, difference?

Lieutenant Colonel W.J.R. Scott, a general staff officer, had been, at his own request, sent to replace Colonel Roach whom the troops had trained with, known and trusted. (Scott, an insurance inspector, at 54 was older than any other battalion commander in the AIF.) Before the new leader of the Australian troops could get to know his men, or they him, the enemy landed 5300 trained men to face 1092 Australians and 2500

natives and their Dutch officers. Worse still, the main body of
their officers over the age of 26, with whom they had trained
and been with in the unit from formation, had been withdrawn
and sent away to Malaya to build newer battalions. On the
day of battle they were bereft of the long-term respect for, and
binding trust in, their new commanding officer. Much of the
weight caused by the loss of the transferred officers fell on
young officers in their early twenties.

By 5 p.m. the day the Japanese landed, Colonel Kapitz, the
senior Dutch officer, had capitulated, along with his officers
and NCOs. Lieutenant Bill Jinkins, 2/21st Battalion, says, 'I
don't think there was much resistance from the Dutch. The
local troops around the coast just took to the jungle, threw
away their gear and put their sarongs back on. There wasn't
much loyalty between the locals and the Dutch. All was confusion. The Dutch had no intercom radio, only telephone, the
enemy cut the line after landing and thus Colonel Kapitz lost
sight of the broad movement of the battle. As the separate
Australian parties fought on, an attempt was made to get the
wounded men to hospital in the town of Ambon but the Japanese when approached said no wounded would be allowed
through their lines until the Australians surrendered.' Time
was telescoped; much happened in a short time.

'Our battalion headquarters, "B Echelon", took the first of
the Japanese attack after the Dutch had capitulated. These
soldiers were not fighting troops; Sergeant Martin, a carpenter in civilian life, got a party of cooks and headquarters men
together and they quite professionally took the brunt of the
battle in the town area and held up the Japanese advance
for a time. As well, Martin and his men relayed orders for
the mortar crew led by Sergeant Smith, who was under fire
from the advancing troops. All the while the scene was being
confused by over 100 Dutch and Ambonese troops drifting
back through the Australian firing lines throughout the
afternoon.'

Up on the plateau on top of Mt Nona, Lieutenant Jinkins
with twenty-five men was reporting that Japanese were around

his position; Sergeant Kay, Jinkins's 'right-hand man', had been killed. 'Attacked by heavy mortars, J.B. Lewis wounded.' Sam Anderson, in charge of the platoon that was coming up from the Amahoesoe line to reinforce Jinkins's position, was wounded. Jinkins, with two volunteers, went out to rescue the wounded man and under covering fire helped carry him in on a stretcher. 'About 1 a.m. we moved to our alternate defensive position on the mount, a pre-planned move, carrying Anderson. The next morning at daybreak we saw the hordes (600) of Japanese on top of the mountain where we had been.

'We had a couple of Lewis guns but the range was too far for effective fire. We then realised there was no way we could get a wounded man down the mountain as we had to go over a 300-foot sheer cliff to rejoin the unit. Art Buchanan and Harry Walseling carried Anderson back through the Japanese lines all the way to the Japanese RAP at Benteng Barracks, where Anderson was given medical attention, and the exhausted bearers, now prisoners of war, were able to rest.'

After the Dutch forces left the fight at the end of the first day, there was little hope for the Australians, far from any help. The battle may, in one sense, be considered yet another example of the futile and cruel use of young men by leaders far from the hurly-burly of battle; yet, these men, for three days, held up a whole Japanese division that had naval and air support, a division and support that some military men say could well have gone straight to Darwin.

Jinkins formed the opinion of 3 February, the day of the capitulation, that had Colonel Roach not been relieved, he would have fought on to the last round and not surrendered. Bill Jinkins: 'When we got down the mountain we found that the Dutch commander had sent a surrender note to our CO, Colonel Scott, and asked him to surrender. But the Dutchman who had been sent with the surrender note didn't deliver it, didn't find the battalion. One of my fellows had been hit by mortar shell in the chest and I'd sent him back to the RAP as a walking wounded to get attention, he met this Dutchman on the way, so he turned round and came back with him to our party and told me about the Dutch surrender. I then decided to go into Benteng to ask for the surrender note because I knew my CO wouldn't have known about it, and would not know that the Dutch had already capitulated. So I went off walking to the Japanese lines, had a talk with the major in charge of the detachment, who allowed me to talk with Anderson and see my two fellows who had carried him down on the stretcher, and then took me in to Ambon town to get another surrender note from Colonel Kapitz.

'In front of the Japanese headquarters (the house of the Governor of Ambon), I had to kneel down with my hands clasped behind my back in the middle of a big circular lawn to be interrogated. That was a bit surprising as I'd only come in to get the surrender note. There was a large group of Japanese round the perimeter. The officer's final question was, "Why don't you answer me?" He was really getting wild, he was boiling – and I thought oh well, here it is, and I said, "I can't understand you because you don't bloody well speak good English!" Someone was just behind me, I'd heard him take his sword out, I couldn't look around, but when I said that, there was a bit of a silence and I thought my head was going to go, then I heard the sword go back in the scabbard and I heard someone march away. After a while I stood up, then after about five minutes I walked towards the verandah of the residency to get this surrender note and they took me in and allowed me to talk to Kapitz, the Dutchman. We sat at a table, I told him I was surprised that he capitulated so quickly, and that though he had sent a signal down to my commanding officer, his men hadn't delivered it and I'd come to get it. So Kapitz wrote another note addressed to Colonel Scott, gave it to me in an envelope, Major Harikawa (educated at Oxford) gave me a captured motor bike which I was able to ride for only about half a mile, because I couldn't get it over the bridge which was already blown up; I ran it over the gorge, let it finish up in the bottom of the ravine, climbed over the blown-up bridge and walked back to my platoon, got them to hold the position at Amahoesoe while I went back down to the end of the peninsula where our troops were to give the note to the CO, only to find that in the meantime he'd sent the doctor in by ambulance to negotiate with the Japanese.

'The commander down on the peninsula couldn't do anything, he was surrounded by water except for an area almost one and a half miles wide facing the enemy, which left him no flexibility. Some little time before I got there, a fighting patrol was deployed to go along the south coast and if they met the enemy they were to engage them; if not, they were to leave the island and endeavour to get back to Australia to tell what had happened. Major McCrae was in charge with another subaltern, Lieutenant Chapman who was my close pal. When I heard that the fighting patrol had been sent away, I asked for permission for my platoon to join them because we hadn't been captured, and we hadn't finished the fight, but permission was refused. I was told that Major McCrae had eaten some berries off a bush and was in a pretty serious fever but Chapman, with his platoon, was able to successfully go the whole length of the south coast without meeting the Japanese (these men left Ambon and went via the islands to Thursday Island, sailing in two different boats to safety).'

On 3 February Jinkins was ordered to march his platoon into the compound for holding prisoners (their old barracks). 'I knew my men did not want to march in, nor did I, I objected to it and requested permission to join the fighting patrol that had been established but was refused; I was again ordered to march in with my men to captivity. I believed we could have evacuated the island some way. During the night we slept in a grove of nutmegs and next day we marched in. The Japanese were making a lot of publicity about the capitulation, and took a lot of films. They mistreated Alec Chew, my right-hand-man, an Australian-born Chinese, and that angered me as much as anything else.'

When Jinkins arrived at Geser, he learnt that Lieutenant McBride and his platoon had been in hand-to-hand fighting in long grass when McBride trod on a Japanese who shot him in the arm. While in the Advanced Dressing Station, schoolmaster

McBride began to organise an escape party. When he set off he had twenty walking wounded in his care. On the way up the island he learnt that ten RAAF personnel with their leader had got away by boat but had been captured and in three days had subsequently 'died while prisoner'. McBride's party went on, island-hopping at first in a prahu, taking turns to row, then collecting Dutchmen, soldiers and officers and a Dutch doctor, women, children and Dutch native troops plus sixteen Australian army men he picked up from Merauke in New Guinea. He had 112 people in two motor boats when he arrived at Karumba (Gulf of Carpentaria), a free man.

Bill Jinkins said, 'When I was ordered to march in to the camp, I did, but five minutes after I moved my platoon to their allotted quarters I went back into the officer's lines and requested a parade to see the commanding officer. I told him that I was now a prisoner of war and my first duty was to escape and I would do so at the first opportunity. He shook me by the hand and said, "Good luck son". He said he would give me every support possible but he wanted nobody else to know I'd got his help or permission to escape. Then he called the 2IC in and said, "I've agreed that Jinkins's is the first official escape plan".'

When Bill Jinkins was planning his escape, two men came to his colonel and said they heard that Bill was going to lead a group out and they wanted to go with him. The colonel said no, there was no such escape planned, and even if there were he wouldn't permit more men to go. He called Bill in and Bill said, 'Well, anyway, I wouldn't take Johnson.' The reason was that Johnson was a very big fellow, much bigger than Bill. Bill said, 'I knew that I couldn't drop him, couldn't knock him out and I had to be able to totally control the men with me. I wouldn't have minded his mate, Redhead.' Redhead and Johnson made an escape two nights before Bill's men were ready to go off, and got safely to Thursday Island, and home. Jinkins was held in the prison camp on Ambon for six weeks. During this time he was the officer-in-charge of the platoon who were to erect a barbed-wire fence around the camp. 'I fixed one place where I could negotiate the fence. I planned an escape; Alec Chew and I left the camp thirteen times and on the thirteenth occasion we didn't come back, we evacuated the island.

'I had to decide how many men I was going to have. The first fellow I spoke to was Alec Chew and Alec immediately said, "Sure I'll go with you". He had been my batman. Then I had another pal, a signals officer, and he said yes, he was quite prepared to escape with me. I said, "All right Gordon [Gordon Jack], you can pick one man that you'd like to take with you and let me know who it is, let me have a look at him before we make any firm decision and before he knows". He picked Arthur Young. I had a good look at Arthur before he knew anything was on and decided he'd be all right. By that time I had four men – Alec, myself, Gordon and Arthur. Then I decided I needed somebody who knew something about diesel engines. I scoured the camp and found a fellow named Harry Coe from Wonthaggi. Harry had a diesel engine to drive his milking machine back home and there was nothing that could go wrong with that diesel engine that he couldn't fix. So I approached Harry and he was a very willing volunteer.'

He still needed a man who had some experience in boats. 'I went to the school of navigation held in the camp and found a young fellow there, Cliff Warn, who used to be in charge of the supply ship for Zane Grey when the author was in Australia fishing for marlin out of Bermagui. He readily agreed to be in an escape team. Another officer told me he had sailed yachts on Sydney Harbour and was quite willing to escape. The CO refused to allow me any more than the seven I had lined up. In hindsight I realise I could have taken another twenty, we had the capacity in boats and I could have got the twenty-seven out alive. What the CO was primarily concerned about was that if we got caught there would be reprisals taken on all those left behind. During a period of six weeks from the time I first went in to prison, to the time I was ready to go, there had been three escapes out of the prison camp – two men at a time – and none of them had been caught. But the CO was worried that accounting for seven people at roll-call would be a hard enough job, without there being any more. The other arrangement made before I left the camp was to select three men who would come up out of the general camp to sleep in the officers' lines in my bed and the beds of the other two officers I took with me to hide our absence.

'During the thirteen different occasions I had left the camp I was able to make contact with the three Gasperz brothers, sons of the Dutch Chief of Police on Ambon. Bill, the eldest of the three, agreed to help me organise the escape from the outside of the prison camp and made available to me one of his servants, Peter. I used to go up to the jungle house of the Gasperz family in the hills at the back of the prison camp to meet Bill and Peter and so made arrangements for the escape. On one trip out of the camp, the CO had asked me to go back to the top of Mt Nona and with binoculars learn whatever I could about the force on the Laha air strip, of whom we had heard nothing since the Japanese landed. But I learnt nothing of those boys. On that occasion I was out of the camp for forty-eight hours. On the mountain I picked up a tommy-gun with ammunition, a .303 rifle, several hand grenades, a 32-calibre pistol and two bayonets and brought them back into camp and hid them, ready for the night of our escape.

'With Peter, I explored the possibility of stealing a sailing boat and also some navigation material and maps from the office of the harbour master. (All we were able to steal from the harbour master's office was a school atlas calibrated to 120,000 and marked with the route of Orient Line passenger ships, plus wind and current.) This contact with Bill Gasperz, his brothers, and with Peter worked to a degree where we had four canoes, each with a native paddler from the village at Narcoe; we planned the escape for the night of 17 March.

'At dusk, we moved through the perimeter fence at intervals and rendezvoused at the house at the top of the hill. The Gasperz family served us sweet biscuits and coffee before we set off. They had six men ready as our escorts through the jungle areas to the south coast of the island. The men carried lengths of hollowed-out bamboo to hold coconut oil with wicks, and these were kept alight for the trip across the mountains until we reached Narcoe and were only extinguished when we had to pass through inhabited villages. We were given a hearty meal and then descended 700 feet down to water level where the canoes were ready and waiting with our three kit bags, two containing food and one with warm clothing for the party, and paddled away at 2.30 in the morning. Soon a wind squall hit us, battered the canoes and drove us ashore only one hour after we set off, at exactly the same place where the Japanese had made their initial landing.

'By 5 o'clock we headed out again, paddling past Japanese positions in broad daylight, each of us wearing an Ambonese pyramid hat of woven grass. The Ranee of Haroekoe had fêted us and negotiated for the hire of an orambai – an Ambonese single-masted sailing boat, 24 feet long. For 240 Dutch guilders the owner of the orambai bargained to take me to a village at Amahai on the south coast of Ceram. I was now able to pay off the paddlers and let them go back to Ambon.'

But it took them fourteen hours in total calm to row the sailing boat to Amahai. The owner of the orambai left to go back to Haroekoe and they again searched for a suitable boat until a Chinese rubber planter permitted them to use his 30-foot diesel-driven work boat 'on the assurance that at the end of the war we would give it back to him!' Alec Chew, the Bendigo-born Chinese, and the diesel engine expert Harry Coe, the dairy farmer, had travelled to see this vessel and negotiate for its use. We lost no time in victualling the boat, got fresh water in jars placed on board, an abundance of fruit – pomelos, papayas, bananas and pineapples, and, after the ship was victualled and we'd said our farewells, set off down to the island of Geser where we found the Dutch controller was still in charge.

'We invited the controller and his very pregnant German wife and two children to accompany us but he said he felt it was his duty to remain at his post until the Japanese came. We said farewell, got on board our boat and then spent two solid days trying to start the engine. We had a horrible suspicion that we were not going to get that boat going because it would have been a valuable means of transport for a very pregnant wife.' There were nine Dutch servicemen on the island and Bill had agreed to take them, and in the meantime he had picked up two more Australians who were escaping on foot as best they could. The party was now nine Australians and nine Dutchmen – with one sabotaged boat.

Never beaten, Bill then chartered two sailing boats, one with a crew and one without. 'The one with the four-man crew I allocated to the nine Dutchmen, making thirteen on board that boat; we had nine Australians and Peter from Ambon and we hired another native to help us sail the other boat, so we were eleven. We set sail after victualling both boats – at our own cost. The Dutch controller, his very pregnant wife and two children remained – with our original motorised vessel, that was now mysteriously "broken down". We headed for Toeal, the capital of the Kai group of islands.

'We didn't know whether the Dutch here had been captured or not but the welcoming party at the end of the pier were well armed; we were prepared to shoot it out and fortunately one of them indicated that he was police, so we came ashore. We were introduced to the Resident of the Kai Islands and the district officer, and housed by the Resident who wined and dined us that evening. The Dutch soldiers were allocated to the hospital.'

In the harbour of Saumlaki there was the *Aleida*, a 250-ton government supply ship with a crew of seven, a skipper and a navigator. 'We persuaded the reluctant Resident of Saumlaki to allow us to take this vessel.' (One wonders what option he had with these determined brigands.) But the crew 'flatly refused' to accompany them. So, for three days Bill Jinkins and his men took lessons in steering, maintaining the engines and sailing this (to them) large vessel. They victualled the ship ready to leave at 5 p.m. on the fourth day. In the excitement of preparing to sail they failed to realise that a heavy southerly storm had sprung up and by dusk, when they were ready to leave, the storm was at its height. Being soldiers, not mariners, they were oblivious to the problems of this and set sail, and finished up high and dry on a coral reef, on a high tide. By morning the ship was on an angle of 45° to starboard with the water lapping against the gunwales. 'Two of the boys rowed across to the jetty to tell the controller that we were in a spot of bother. We were taken off on native canoes back to Saumlaki and I believe that ship remains on the reef to this day.

'We realised as we had wrecked one boat we had to be sharp to get hold of another. In the meantime, a 48-foot motor cruiser with cabins fore and aft, toilet facilities and showers, arrived carrying nine women, seven children and four Dutchmen, including the Resident from the Kai Islands. We were glad to see him and the *Groeffoen* tied up at the end of the jetty. By this time Gordon Jack and Arthur Young had been to the Dutch radio station and spent three days trying to make contact with Australia. They were able to make contact with the Dutch radio at the Aru Islands and ask them to pass a message to Darwin indicating that there was a large party of servicemen and civilians at Saumlaki wanting transport to Australia. The message was received but no reply was given. We were able to hear news of the progress of the war and realised it would not be long before the Japanese spread themselves through the outer islands of the Dutch East Indies. Time was running out for us.'

Bill 'endeavoured to negotiate' the use of the *Groeffoen* to get to Australia on the promise that an Australian warship would immediately set out to pick up the rest of the women, children and other civilians. But the party insisted that he leave one of his officers as a guarantee of a pick-up. This he would not do. The crew of the *Groeffoen* refused to man the ship and sail it to Australia. The Australians decided they could not afford to try to sail the *Groeffoen* on their own because they had already wrecked the very much larger *Aleida*. So Jinkins decided to hijack the crew and command possession of the vessel 'because of my military rank and the fact that we were at war'.

'I called for a conference with the crew and the controller of the island – there were no other refugees present. I had placed Harry Coe, wearing a groundsheet over his shoulders and carrying a .303 rifle underneath it at one entrance, Alec Chew was stationed at another entrance with a .45 tommy-gun under his groundsheet, and Arthur Young was at the third and last entrance to the conference room, similarly dressed and with my .32 calibre pistol. We anticipated trouble. The conference lasted for two hours and no progress was made in persuading the crew to come with us. It was then I disclosed to the Resident that whether they agreed or not, the crew were coming on the *Groeffoen*. He questioned how I would do this and by removing my handkerchief from my right-hand pocket and blowing my nose, the groundsheets were dropped and three armed men were standing at each of the exits. I then asked the controller to line the crew up and they were then marched directly to the ship. There was quite a lot of concern and disturbance about it, but I persisted. They were all pleading that they needed to go home to get their navigation instruments and other tools to maintain the engine and a lot of other things, and to say goodbye to their families. On board, one of my armed guards was placed on the sea side of the vessel to see that nobody dived over, the other two were placed on the jetty to see that we were not attacked.

'We had already victualled the ship, and because it did not have enough diesel fuel to get to Darwin, the controller had arranged for the villagers to make oil by boiling coconut flesh. They carried it to us in hollowed out bamboo sections about 6 feet long and there was enough to make two 44-gallon drums of coconut oil which was then strained through hospital bandages into the reserve tanks on the *Groeffoen*. Once the engine was started on diesel and gained maximum heat, it would have no trouble in travelling on coconut oil. We had water and enough food for the seventy-two hour crossing of the Arafura Sea; there were now nine Dutchmen who were allocated the forward cabin and given no duties on the ship, nine Australians and the crew of Ambonese who were coming to Darwin with us, twenty-six altogether. Peter decided he wanted to go back to Ambon so I gave him the boat we had bought and he got back home, the proud owner of his own boat. When we were ready to leave, I went back and gave the Kai Islands' Resident my assurance that there would be a Royal Australian naval vessel come back immediately to pick up the rest of the party. I then ordered the ship to sail. The Saumlaki Resident was the only one allowed on the wharf and he saw us off; we headed out in a calm sea, and I made my bunk alongside the helm.'

He stayed there for seventy-two hours, not leaving the steering wheel in the hours of darkness to make sure that the skipper did not reverse his course; Harry Coe stood guard in the engine room with the threat that if the engine stopped or faltered the engineer would be thrown overboard. Still using the map on the back of the exercise book they navigated southwards, three times hitting the bottom in shallow water near Bathurst Island, and reached Darwin harbour at 5 p.m. on 11 May to be greeted at the boom by Chief Petty Officer Chick Henderson. They were given a great welcome and 'great hospitality' and were housed at naval headquarters at Winnellie, 'the same barracks we had built during the eight months we cooled our heels in Darwin before we were sent to Ambon'.

'Gordon Jack and I had to write reports for the Northern Territory Force and be subjected to questions and answers, from both Navy and Army HQ, but my first request immediately after being welcomed by the naval officer in charge was to acquaint him with the number of women, children, Dutchmen and the Administrator left behind and request that he endeavour to have them picked up with as little delay as possible. He despatched a signal that evening and the following day one of our destroyers on patrol in the Arafura called into Saumlaki, picked them all up and within seventy-two hours they too arrived in Darwin.'

Jinkins had orders to report to the Director of Military Intelligence in Melbourne and was sent south on a Sunderland flying boat from Darwin down to Rose Bay in Sydney.

'When I got back to Melbourne at nine o'clock in the morning, I was still dressed in tropical summer dress – shirt, no jacket, and especially no head gear.' He reported to Victoria Barracks and was taken in to see General Sturdee, the Chief of the General Staff. 'He shook my hand and said, "Welcome home son, we never expected to see any of you again".' This rather shook the young man. 'It took until the scones and tea were served before I got over that.' He was then asked to tell of the battle of Ambon, of the prison camp and of his escape.

Jinkins told General Sturdee he wanted to go back to rescue the POWs on Ambon, and of how he could make a pick-up from the prison camp. 'They enquired whether I had a winter uniform at home and I said yes, so they said, "You pop home and see your mother and come back in a day or two." I informed them I'd be back at one o'clock that afternoon and that as far as I was concerned, time should not be wasted because these fellows were in the hands of the Japanese. I went home, my mother was out, I left a note on the table "I'll be home around five o'clock", donned my winter uniform, found I didn't have a cap so went to Snows in Flinders Street and bought one, and paraded again at Victoria Barracks at 1.30 p.m., finding it was still lunch time. That afternoon I sat in conference with the planning team as I was to do every day for the next ten days.'

The planning for the pick-up was to use two destroyers, the Dutch *Tromp* and the Australian *Arunta* – to make a sortie into Ambon harbour with Jinkins in charge with two landing parties of twenty-three men. The ships would sail to within 100 yards of the camp, drop landing nets to allow the men who would swim out to climb up on board.

'We believed we would be able to rescue at least 800 of the POWs. The rescue was assessed and assumed to be a worth-while risk, especially the advantage of being able to carry out a rescue against the Japanese which at that difficult time would boost Australian morale. The plan was put into effect and the *Tromp* was withdrawn to Fremantle to revictual and the *Arunta* was brought into Sydney. I was to join the *Arunta* at

Townsville with my twenty-two men. In the meantime the plan was submitted to the American command, and some days later I was informed that the Americans had refused to allow the project to go ahead, and the rescue expedition was cancelled.'

He was then taken on to the strength of the Director of Military Operations and Plans under Brigadier Hopkins, who knew he was keen to get back to Ambon. 'I'd promised the 2IC I would arrange to rescue them from the prison camp and was always hopeful that I'd be able to do it.'

He put forward the proposition that he should form some parties who could go back to the islands with enough equipment to be a nuisance to the enemy, and enough radio equipment to be able to communicate back with Australia. And so, a body called Plover Force was formed which was to occupy Jamdena, the Kai and the Aru Islands with small sections, and to establish themselves and remain behind as intelligence gathering parties with a small sabotage role, to harass the enemy and maintain communication with Australia. Jinkins personally selected the twenty-six Plover Force men, all with some technical expertise. Alec Chew and Harry Coe were with him, as well as six other men who had been with Alex Chapman's escape party from Ambon in the first group that came back to Australia. He therefore had eight men already familiar with Ambon.

They left Darwin in September 1943 and headed for Jamdena, some – including Jinkins – in the MV *Southern Cross*, another party in the lugger *Chinampa* under Chief Petty Officer (Chick) Henderson (who had welcomed Jinkins back to Darwin when he escaped from Ambon). Two-thirds of the way across the Arafura Sea the *Southern Cross* had to hove-to while they re-ran a bearing. Henderson in *Chinampa* went on ahead towards Saumlaki and two days later the *Southern Cross* followed them into the harbour.

'The *Chinampa* was approaching the jetty. We heard the sounds of machine-gun fire and then saw the *Chinampa* steering a very erratic course down the bay. I left the *Southern Cross* and got aboard *Chinampa* – to find Chick Henderson machine-gunned right through and across the waist and both legs. He was slumped across the wheel and the rest of his crew were too apprehensive to climb up to the deck, it being exposed to machine-gun fire. I straightened the wheel up to head out of the harbour and nursed Henderson until he died in my arms. I then took the executive officer off the *Southern Cross* on to *Chinampa* to skipper her and we headed down the bay under mortar fire from Japanese positions.

'We subsequently learnt that Henderson had arrived the night before in the dark, had tied up at the end of the jetty, donned his whites and with two other sailors proceeded down the jetty to the house of the Resident. He was challenged at the gate by what Henderson thought was an Island policeman but in fact was a Japanese guard. He went on to the house and saw three Japanese officers sitting around the table with their feet up enjoying a party. When they saw Henderson they rushed to the door with revolvers but Henderson headed down the footpath and was again challenged by the Japanese guard at the gate. One of his sailors managed to punch the guard on the jaw and knock him out (strangely, Henderson had gone ashore completely unarmed). He made good his trip down the jetty, got on board the lugger and put her out to the middle of the harbour. He remained there waiting for the *Southern Cross* to arrive, and when he saw us coming in the harbour at first light, for some unknown reason he headed back towards the jetty. That's when they opened up on him and that's the picture we saw when we were coming up to join him. We learnt that the previous day a Japanese cruiser had entered Saumlaki and landed Japanese occupation forces. We were their first visitors.

'We buried Chick Henderson with full naval honours as well as we could do.' The Australians then endeavoured to contact Darwin and in reply to radio signals they received a clear message asking them to state position and give course. This raised suspicions because the Force had arranged to receive signals in code only and they felt that a signal asking that sort of information in clear could not possibly have come from

Darwin. (Later, on return to Australia they learnt that no such message had been sent and that Hudson bombers had found a Japanese cruiser lying half way across the Arafura Sea in a direct path from Saumlaki to Darwin. The bombers had driven the cruiser off.)

The men made two attempts to land on the shores of Jamdena. Jinkins was still prepared to put a party ashore in the hope they could establish themselves, but without a suitable craft to make a passage through the surf they had to withdraw and head back to Darwin. The whole of Plover Force operation was then aborted.

From the time the Japanese swept down and engulfed the South West Pacific area in the early months of 1942, they were in such complete control until near the end of the war in 1945 that to Australians those lands to the north of them seemed as if enveloped in a grey blanket of fog through which they saw nothing, heard nothing

To the east, in New Guinea, Australian soldiers were fighting the Japanese but nowhere else. 'Prime Minister Curtin', says Bill Jinkins, 'gave Australia away to the Americans when MacArthur came. MacArthur's one desire was to beat the Japanese because they had beaten him on his home ground, the Philippines. He set himself up in Brisbane with an immediate liaison link with the guerilla forces in the Philippines. Everything that was smuggled in to the guerillas had a picture of MacArthur on it and the words "I will return". Packets of cigarettes, all the food packs, the boxes with ammunition, everything that he sent back said, "I will return".

'He had allocated to himself a fleet of submarines, two of which were the largest in the world at that time, the USS *Narwal* and the *Nautilus*, and they were entirely at his disposal for the supply of his guerilla forces right throughout the Philippines. He kept the guerillas going to keep the Japanese busily engaged and occupied. He didn't do this anywhere else, he could have, but MacArthur was only interested in beating the Japanese in the Philippines and to occupy this small piece of land he was willing to pay a tremendous cost in lives. MacArthur wasn't worried

about any Allied prisoners of war at all, he certainly had no
worry for the Australians. He hated Blamey and gave him some
very poor jobs that Blamey couldn't say no to. Curtin was all
for MacArthur and not all for Blamey and so were the AIB,
whose headquarters were in Brisbane.'

Bill now went to a far different war. Inter Allied Service
Department, later the Services Reconnaissance Department,
and Z Unit (often called Z Force) recruited most useful people,
Australian, British and Canadian. From this unit Bill Jinkins
joined men infiltrating the Borneo-Philippines area. 'It was a
clandestine type of operation with AIB's approval; run by Willoughby, MacArthur's right-hand man. Willoughby had all the
power over these special units that were operating over the
line. Six of our Z Unit chaps went into Borneo after the Japanese occupied the island in December 1943.'

The determined young rescuer was now to enter a field he
had never contemplated – but it was certainly tailor-made for
him. It was arranged that he would meet Colonel Edgerton
Mott who had established Special Operations Australia (on the
same lines as SOE in the UK, a newly formed clandestine
organisation).

'Mott was a man after my own heart and was willing to try
any plan that had a reasonable chance of success with the
element of surprise.' Being keen to get back to Ambon, Jinkins
suggested he should get a small party together and go back by
submarine. Mott himself had, unknown to Jinkins, already
been planning that type of operation for other areas.

'It was decided to set me up with three sections – the Kai
Islands, the Tinambas and the Yarawa Islands – I had twenty-
six men, and out of the twenty-six only one was a private.
They were all specialists – signallers, explosive experts, three
medical sergeants, one for each party. My sergeants, Stan
Dodds and Alec Chew, were both original 2/21st men, we'd
been together from the beginning. I have not heard of any
other attempts to rescue men except from Sandakan.'

From now on Jinkins belonged to a world that the world at
war knew little of. He was taken into SOA, and his life almost

immediately became one of constant movement in and out of occupied territories interspersed with trips back to Australia for planning and pooling of information, as well as training others in his own special expertise, sabotage and underground resistance.

Among his many trips – on seven separate US submarines – Bill had only one chance to go back to rescue the men on Ambon and, eventually, it was denied him. 'I learnt that my plan to go back on to Ambon was to be preceded by a Dutchman going into the area before me. I found difficulty in accepting this. However, a Dutch naval officer was selected and taken in by British submarine. I was to be "inserted" six weeks later. I was most worried about the fact that the Dutchman had prior knowledge of my intentions and plans. He was sent in with one Ambon native and was captured. In the meantime, a party sent into Timor by another group had also been captured.'

Bill was appointed chief instructor of Z Special Unit, a device used for registering Australian troops into a unit which could not be traced through army records.

The tension on the 'insertion' attempts was such that only the most thoroughly trained men could be used. One trip Bill did began on 10 January 1944. Jinkins embarked from the US submarine base in Western Australia and ten days later he and his party landed successfully on the Philippine island of Tawi Tawi. Bill returned to Darwin on the USS *Narwal* and flew down to Melbourne, only to learn on arrival that the party he had left on shore was being 'hounded' by the Japanese and 'two men got jumped and were captured.

'The main party were constantly escaping capture and it was decided we had better get them out.' Jinkins volunteered to go back in a submarine and bring the men home. 'When they gave permission for me to go and pick these fellows up, they said, "Find a skipper you can get on with and if he agrees to take you, you can go with him". I palled up with Sam Dealey, the skipper of USS *Harder*. Sam was a little older than me – I was about 29. He was married, a lovely fellow and the most courageous man I've ever known. Two skippers had already tried to pick up the beleaguered men without any luck. I was impressed with Dealey so asked Sam if he'd take me and he said, "Sure, I'll take you", and he did.

'During that trip Dealey sank five Japanese destroyers and one blew up while we were 480 feet underneath it. We were expecting the hull to cave in. We were down for about eighteen hours before we could come up. Later, American Vice Admiral Lockwood wrote a book called *Harder Beats the Mangrove Bushes*. In this he tells how we went in – the range, the signals etc.'

Dealey took USS *Harder* in as close as he dared and Jinkins and Stan Dodds transferred to a folboat (a rubber canvas shell). 'They were just two-man boats but we would put three in each of the two boats. Mine was the only motor that would work, so I towed them out.

'In the folboat I had a little army walkie-talkie so we did a lot of radio tests and the moment I left the submarine they had me on their frequency and could hear me loud and clear. I put the radio between my legs with the microphone facing up and told them all I was doing. We paddled in and they were able to steer me in to exactly the point the shore party had suggested. I signalled, and waited for a little while. Nothing happened, so I moved thirty degrees right and signalled again, waited, and nothing happened; I came back thirty degrees left and signalled. So I thought, "Oh damn it, I'll come back to the original place", signalled and had barely finished the signal when I got the response. From the shore, my marvellous sergeant, Alec Chew, was signalling back to me. But we still must complete the recognition. I asked for Alec to come to the rendezvous point and the voice came back, "Yes, I'm here". I then said, "You'll know what I'm talking about, you'll either recognise the next voice or you won't", meaning that if he was in Japanese hands he would not give the correct response. Dodds, beside me, then asked Chew, "Is that you Alec?" The immediate response from Chew was, "You old bastard, Doddsy!"'

Jinkins was a stickler for perfection. The reason Chew did not respond with the torch the first time was because the man with him had said, "Oh, they're not going to come tonight, it's too late", and walked away – with the torch. When Alec got my signal he ran back down the track yelling "Give us the bloody torch!" And he'd just got back on the beach when I signalled again and he gave the response.

'When they got to the canoes which I had taken to deeper water, I reported to the submarine that I'd made the pick-up. The men were covered in mud so they stripped to their briefs, and off we went – Doddsy took one canoe, I took the other. Alec was with me, Lloyd Woods, Len Crotty.

'In the meantime a fairly heavy mist had fallen over the cove and as I got towards the submarine I could see two distinct black shapes and nothing in between. It seemed to me that possibly there were two boats there and if so one must be Japanese. We got ready with the weapons and went fully armed towards these black objects. We got within 25 yards before I discovered that the rear black object was the conning tower and the forward object was the assembly of sailors on the foredeck waiting to bring us aboard. We got below as quickly as possible, fed the shore party, bathed them and bedded them down. None wanted to sleep but we provided a few appropriate tablets and they all had a good night's rest. The talking began the next day and went on for something like thirty-six hours.'

Jinkins belonged to that rare body of men all armies have – a high degree of competence and bravery – who seek the most difficult, individual battles, often on their own and sometimes with a small, select, chosen group, all with a mixture of various skills, strengths, individual discipline and an underlying dash of derring-do. Jinkins had all these components with an added passion to help free the captives north of Australia.

While Jinkins and his daring, brave (beyond the understanding of those of us who stay at home) compatriots continued so desperately in their attempts to rescue the men on Ambon, more than half of those cheeky young men who had mooed like cows at the guard when they travelled by cattle-trucks to Darwin were dead.

Ambon could be described as two islands joined by an isthmus 'as wide as a car', as the troops said. When war came the two areas were separately attacked and the two separate groups of Australians did not see one another again.

On the Ambon township side were approximately 800 men, while 300 were on the other side of the isthmus where Laha airport was situated. Major George de Vardon Westley (2/21st Battalion), who was a prisoner on the Ambon side of the island, heard nothing as to the fate of the men on the Laha side of the island and in September 1945 after the surrender of the Japanese he sent a party across to trace survivors. He found none. In time, some details were learnt of the fighting that took place there in 1942.

The Japanese landed on the beach at Hitoelama before dawn on 31 January 1942 and three days later captured the Laha airfield and took 'about' 400 captives made up of 'about' 210 Australians, sixty Dutch and the rest Ambonese. According to evidence later given at the War Crimes Tribunal in Japan, the first ten men taken prisoner were 'bayoneted to death before our force left Sowacoad'. These prisoners were killed, as were another fifty taken the following day it was claimed – and this was almost certainly true – 'because they were likely to become a drag on the movement of the Admiral's Force' (commanding officer Rear-Admiral Hatakeyama).

By 4 February the Admiral, by now on Laha airfield, learnt that the small guard placed on the prisoners at Sowacoad was having difficulty controlling the men. Ensign Sakamoto reported that the POWs either rebelled against him or deserted 'because of the misunderstanding due to difference of language'. The Admiral ordered the men to be killed on the following day because of their 'disquietude'.

On 5 February, in compliance with this order, according to Japanese naval lieutenant Ken-ichi Nakagawa, 'I took about thirty Petty Officers and men to Sowacoad. In a forest of coconut-trees, about 200 metres toward the airfield from Sowacoad, we dug our holes and killed prisoners of war with swords or bayonets. I recall it took about two hours from

10 a.m. The process of the murder was as follows: I divided
thirty Petty Officers and men into three groups, the first group
for leading the prisoners of war out of a dwelling house where
the victims were temporarily confined, the second for prevent-
ing disorder on their way from the house to the forest, the
third for beheading or stabbing the prisoners of war. The prisoners of war were sent to the spot one by one and made to
kneel with bandage on their eyes. Our men of the third group,
one at a time, came out in turn either to behead a prisoner of
war with his sword or to stab him through the breast with his
bayonet.

'These prisoners of war were all Australians, including four
or five officers. All corpses were buried in the holes.' Nakagawa, giving evidence stated, 'The names of our men then
employed for this execution cannot be recalled at all. But it is
certain that there were present on the spot no officer, either
warrant or commissioned, except myself. Interpreter Ikiuchi
was in the dwelling house to send out the prisoners of war
from the house. Most of the time I placed myself in the middle
between the house and the place of the killing to do the overall
command; but I went to the spot when the last victim was to
be executed. I reported that the execution had been accomplished to the adjutant in his room on that day, and I suppose
the adjutant in his turn reported it to Admiral Hatakeyama.'

Nakagawa was then asked by the president of the court to
tell about the killings of the other prisoners of war.

'In the airfield barracks were some 200 Australians and
some sixty Dutchmen. When our forces first entered into the
airfield, they saw that the Japanese strength was very small,
numbering only some 170. Some of the prisoners of war, therefore, expressed their view through Ikiuchi, interpreter, to such
an effect that they would not have surrendered but would
rather have continued fighting bravely if they had known the
Japanese strength was so small, and that if they had fought
more stubbornly the Japanese casualties would have amounted
to a considerable degree. In addition to these they behaved
themselves disobedient in their assigned works, though partly

caused by the difference of language. And about thirty of them were considered to be especially disobedient. The commanding officer heard this fact, and he gave Adjutant Hatakeyama and me an order in his room in the evening of 5 February to murder these thirty prisoners of war. I had about twenty enlisted men kill these some thirty prisoners of war about 3 p.m. on the following day, if I remember right, in a coco-palm forest near Tauli, about 700 metres from the airfield, though I cannot recall what platoons these twenty men belonged to. In this killing also, the prisoners of war were taken in a house nearby, then called out in turn one by one, and killed with sword or with bayonet, as before. Their corpses were buried in the hole dug for the purpose. As in the previous case I stood in the middle between that house and the spot of murder to take general command for the most of the time, and I went to the spot to witness the last one being killed and ascertained this bloody work had been finished. I reported to the adjutant the accomplishment of the execution.' Nakagawa then told of another killing of the prisoners of war.

'On 17 or 18 February, I cannot recall which day, while we were taking lunch at Ambon, Commanding Officer Hayashi disclosed his intention to kill all the remaining prisoners of war. His reason was this: our troops available for service numbered only 340 or 350, from which guards in various districts had to be dispatched; the desertions of the prisoners of war began to be noted; rumours ran among natives that the Allied troops would come soon to attack us; enemy planes in fact came for reconnaissance; if the deserting prisoners of war would divulge the situation of Japanese side, we would be faced very unfavourable situation; and all these factors were forming a menace to the position of the Japanese forces. I asked the commanding officer then what is his opinion concerning the provisions of the International Law which I understood to be stipulating that 'Furyo' should not be treated as enemy. He answered me that I was right so far as 'Furyo' was concerned, but that the captives interned there were to be classified and called 'Horyo' and therefore we would not violate the International Law if we would kill them. A few days later, in the evening, while taking supper with the commanding officer and his adjutant at the garden in front of the commanding officer's room, I was told by the commanding officer to kill all the prisoners of war at Laha.

'On the following day, probably 20 February, I gathered up some sixty enlisted men from various platoons and about thirty enlisted men from the crew of the Minesweeper No.9 who were boarding at the barracks because their ship had sunk. I took both these groups of men to Laha from Ambon at about 1 p.m. on the 20th. We dug holes in a place in a coconut forest at Tauli; this new place is a different position from that of the previous murder, being 140 or 150 metres away from it, and was about 200 metres off the headquarters of the Laha detachment. I divided ninety men into nine groups: two groups for bloody killing, three groups for watching the prisoners of war on their way to the killing place, two groups for sending prisoners of war out of the barracks: one group for guard on the spot of the killings, the last one for emergency. The prisoners of war were on foot from the Detachment building to the spot of the killing. The same way of the killing was adopted as in the previous case; to have them kneel down with bandage over their eyes and to kill them with sword or bayonet.

'The poor victims numbered about 220 in all including a few Australian officers. Interpreter Ikiuchi was, as in the previous case, in charge of duty of sending prisoners of war out of the barracks; I was giving overall directions and ascertained the final accomplishment of the affair on the spot. It took from about 6 p.m. to 9.30 p.m. Most of the corpses were buried in one hole, but because the hole was not big enough to receive all of the corpses, a dugout nearby was also used for the burial. On that day upon my arrival at our headquarters, I reported it to the commanding officer directly and also to his adjutant.'

The president of the court asked the witness if the order to kill prisoners of war issued by the Commanding Officer Hayashi was at his own discretion and he replied that in the first three cases of the murder, the orders were, with no doubt, issued by Rear-Admiral Hatakeyama. 'But as for the last case, I am not sure whether the order was issued by the Commanding Officer Hayashi himself, or it was given in compliance with the order of Rear-Admiral Hatakeyama.'

And so, Aunty Gert Jackson's sons died, Doug, aged 23, and 'Pompey' (Stan) aged 22 when they disappeared. Before the fighting began, Pompey Jackson had sent the following poem to his cousin Jean back in Australia.

A SOLDIER'S PRAYER

Stay with me, God. The night is dark,
The night is cold: My little spark
Of courage dies. The night is long:
Be with me, God, and make me strong.

Help me, oh God, when death is near,
To mock the haggard face of fear,
That when I fall – if fall I must –
My soul may triumph in the dust.

Jean, as a child, had written a letter to her mother on Anzac Day 1934. She was then holidaying with 'Aunty Gert Jackson' at Lang Lang. 'Pompey and Doug tease me too much. They sat behind me at the Anzac Service and they tied my hair to the back of my chair and I did not know and when I stood up for the hymn the chair was bumping me because I could not undo my hair and everyone laughed.' During the war years the girl had said, 'If they get back they can tease me all they like'.

On the other side of the island Gull Force had no news of the men on Laha. Lieutenant John Charles Van Nooten of the 2/21st Australian Infantry Battalion had been captured on 3 February 1942. 'On the Ambon town side of that island 809 Australians and approximately 300 Dutch prisoners were captured (a quite separate group from those captured at the airport of Laha). We were confined in Tan Toey Barracks, about 2 miles from the town of Ambon, the Dutch were confined in a separate compound within the main prison compound with only a barbed-wire fence between us.

'On 26 October 1942, 267 Australians and 233 Dutch were transferred from the island of Ambon. I subsequently heard that they had been taken as laborers to Hainan Island. There were then 528 Australians left at Ambon and we had been increased with fourteen Americans and six Dutch prisoners, making a total of 548. There had been fourteen more Australian prisoners who surrendered but during the period between 3 February and 26 October 1942, one Australian prisoner had died and thirteen Australians had escaped.'

The men left on the island began to die of starvation-caused illnesses even though Van Nooten was informed by the Japanese quartermaster that there was one and a half year's ration, sufficient for a floating population from 3000 to 10,000 Japanese. 'In the last three months of the war men died in shocking proportions. In May 1945, forty-two men died; in June seventy-two; in July ninety-four. The health of the Japanese was pretty good. They showed no signs of malnutrition.' Of 528 Australians who had been held on Ambon when their companions had been taken off to work camps on Hainan Island, only 123 were living when the war ended.

Fifty years after the event, the story of World War II has not been told in its reality in Japan. This, more than almost anything else, fans distrust of Japan among the people of South-East Asia and China.

The enquiry into the deaths on Ambon was held in Japan. General Douglas MacArthur, in an attempt not to further destabilise Japan, had already decided the finding. Senior Japanese naval officers (up to the rank of admiral) who had given the orders for the killings were not charged; the NCOs and privates bore the brunt because of their code of loyalty to officers up through the ranks to their Emperor.

Timor

'There was no Dunkirk for us. No ships would come to take us off.'

Sergeant Harry Holder, 2/40th Machine Gun Battalion

TASMANIANS ARE A TIGHT-KNIT island people and know their soldiers and their battalions well. When the original 40th Battalion colours were laid up in St David's Cathedral, Hobart, in 1967, the wonderful old cathedral was packed, and the overflow spread out on to Macquarie Street. These people had already been out to Brighton military camp to see the trooping of the colours of the World War I battalion through the ranks for the last time, the old men of the colour party with tears rolling down their cheeks as they slowly marched down the lines of new young soldiers to the slow drum beat demanded by tradition. It was not the Australian or the British flag they carried but the battalion colours, to which men could rally on the battlefield as men had done for centuries.

Two generations of men had fought beneath that flag, and died under it. In World War II the 2/40th Battalion of the 8th Division went to Timor beneath these colours. 'They sailed to Melbourne first on the old *Zeelandia*', any old Tasmanian will tell you. 'It was January 1941 and the Japanese weren't in the war.'

The men trained in Bonegilla (Vic.), near the Murray River, along with the rest of the battalion from other States including Western Australia and South Australia. There are snapshots of them marching down the dusty, country roads led by their own bands. Some wrote about what followed. Reg Holloway from Tasmania: 'We were sent to Darwin and the trip took twenty-three days, what with "the wet" season washing away the rail track to Alice Springs, and everything.'

Sergeant Harry Holder, 2/40th Machine Gun Battalion, was

418

a weightlifter, wrestler, boxer, PT instructor, a well-known athlete in Western Australia. 'We went up via Sydney, Broken Hill and Quorn (SA). The ladies were very good at the odd places where we pulled up on the way. They always had tea for us and something to eat, but Quorn was well-known for having great meals. The railway men working on the line used to help their wives, they'd keep fires going all day out on the sand of the desert and big coppers boiling out in the open with plum puddings in them. We had a big blowout always in Quorn. We remembered that later on. From Alice Springs we went by truck to Katherine where we got on Leaping Lena (the little Northern Territory train), and then off to Darwin.'

Reg Holloway: 'We had been told for some months that we were soon to receive final tropical leave home to Hobart after being in Northern Australia since 22 April. On Friday, 5 December 1941, at a battalion parade the CO (Colonel Leggatt) read a telegram from the Prime Minister (Mr Curtin) regretting that our leave would be "temporarily suspended owing to the Pacific situation". The colonel told us that we were not to be disheartened as we would see action much sooner than we expected. We returned to our tents with the band playing "There's a boy coming home on leave", which brought an ironic smile from us all. "There'll be a great celebration when he comes home on leave!" The next day passed quietly, until after "Lights out" at 10 p.m. when an order came through to pack the entire camp. At first we thought this was only another practice move and one joker said it might even be a surprise move towards Tasmania!'

On 8 December at 5 a.m. EST (7 December Pearl Harbour, Hawaii, time), they went so quickly they left 100 men still on leave, including their chaplain, their 2IC and their Intelligence Officer behind. 'At Darwin the populace was waving to us. This was supposed to be a secret move but the civilians knew we were off. After hours in stifling heat on the Darwin wharf we were huddled aboard the ship in a haphazard, disorganised fashion. We were told we were off to Timor as the Japs had struck at many places. But we knew nothing of Pearl Harbour.'

Harry Holder: 'Refugees were coming down in boats, boats everywhere, we stopped a few but none were enemy, just people frantic to escape.'

Once on Timor they had only two official leaves to Koepang, 5 miles from their camp, and after a few hours sight-seeing there was nothing else to do but eat and drink. Timorese established restaurants sporting such names as Sydney, Hobart, Australia and Casimatti's Cafe (a well-known fish and chip shop in the main street of Hobart). But there was little time for such capers. Towards the end of January most of the residents of Koepang and other coastal villages had moved further inland by army orders to clear the coast. Everything was prepared for the impossible task to come and no time was available for amusements or leave.

Reg Holloway: 'We had natives acting as batmen for us, all against HQ orders, but apart from the mail, this was our only interest except for mixing with the Koepangers in their oil-lamp lit huts at night, eating bananas and coconuts and learn-ing their language.'

Enemy bomber and fighter raids were increasing and their own few reconnaissance planes were failing to return from daylight operations. Morale among the men was low – chiefly because of the expectation of at least one year's stay in this disease-ridden, forgotten colony of the Dutch. 'Word that the Japs had been sighted took us partly by surprise', Holloway wrote. 'We had long since realised that we were in a hopeless position if invasion occurred, but due to the lack of exact news of their progress, and the fact that reinforcements were on their way from Darwin, we did not seriously consider the possibility of attack. But the Japs had shot up planes on Penfoei drome and other so-called "secret" dromes.

'Many planes were shot down and large flights of our fight-ers and bombers were passing through – when we wished they would stay with us and engage the regular Jap raiders. We stood by to help disembark English ack-ack units, plus our own troops from Darwin. The English landed during a Jap bombing raid and set up their mobile guns that were originally intended for fixed defences. But Australian reinforcements on their way to us received orders to turn back when only six hours off Timor (they received a hearty bombardment back in Darwin harbour when the Japs made their first raid on that outpost on 19 February. We didn't know if Australia had been invaded as this was the last message we were to receive from our homeland.).

'We were notified after dusk on 19 February that fourteen Jap ships with escorts were heading our way and were estimated to land in the early hours of the following morning.' Reg was in charge of transport. 'We packed our belongings for transport to the hills, keeping only equipment necessary for fighting and the bare essentials of clothing. We had drinks with old cobbers, expecting them to be the last, and endeavoured to get a little rest before the landing. At dawn we were informed that the landing had taken place on the south coast at the end of the only metal road. We moved off with the morale of the boys being the highest for some weeks. As we approached Boen the boys left the transports and moved in formation on the look-out for the enemy. Natives were taunting us that we were against hopeless odds.

'We met survivors who had been attacked by mortars and Jap paratroops, and these men were in a very frightened, confused state, being no use to us whatsoever. Up to this time our other companies were still at their allotted positions on beaches and airfields which were blown up soon after our air force personnel had evacuated to Darwin, wishing us all the best as they flew off. We were told that Baboa had to be cleared of Japs and then to engage them in the Tjamplong area, their estimated number being 600. We had about 100 men. We entered Baboa in the late afternoon under continuous bombing and machine-gunning by Jap seaplanes which were apparently notifying their own troops ahead of us of our whereabouts.

'On the outskirts of our bivouac area a native was pointing and gesticulating towards our area and I realised that a Jap was right among us. He was riddled with bullets before grenades finished him off. He had apparently ridden a bicycle into our midst and was as surprised as we were.'

Holloway, with an armored car he had commandeered, and carriers, set off half a mile in advance of two companies in open formation on either side of the road until they entered Baboa area.

The fire from Japanese in palm trees overhead was fierce. 'One dead Japanese officer had in his pocket plans of our whereabouts on the island, ending all doubts about fifth column activities. Due to the disorganised state of affairs at this stage (evening of the 21st), heavy bombing concentration and the knowledge that Japs were encircling us with the main forces in front whilst their troops disembarking at Koepang were gathering in our rear, some men deserted to the jungle at this stage. Some of them escaped to Australia months later, whilst others returned, or died in the bush.'

When word was received after dark that Baboa was clear, the armored car had to report back to where it had been 'borrowed'. Bob Anderson, the cool despatch rider, accompanied them on the rough tracks on his motor bike as they did three trips back and forth in the dark to escort the convoys.

'After the final trip I had only two of my original crew of thirteen left, Ernie Wescombe (who later died of blood poisoning from a wound) and Terry Burgess (who later died of malaria, general debility and dysentery in Thailand).

'At 4 a.m. on the 22nd we had completed the convoy work with the whole fighting force gathered from their scattered positions and assembled at Baboa for the next onward push towards Tjamplong at daybreak. The force was now organised and together for what was to be our last engagement. The various companies went first on general reconnaissance, transport assembled along the road ready to advance, but opposition was soon met with and casualties streamed back for attention. Many tries were made to move forward but the Japs had blocked our only crossing bridge over the deep river, whilst their mortar fire became more accurate on our congested force. They were close behind us and "dug in" in front and scattering to our sides: an offensive against the bridge was the only way out. In the late afternoon we concentrated our complete mortar and machine guns, all our firepower for fifteen minutes to the front, with men clearing the barriers with bayonet charges until our total force moved forward. After clearing the hill it was necessary to set fire to the village of Oesoe, to clear out the Japs (the natives had fled to the hills), and the camouflage of flames and smoke enabled the transports to move forward to safety over the river while foot troops mopped up the remaining Japs in the area and checked to make certain that all live personnel of ours were clear of the area. We gathered everybody into crowded vehicles and moved forward over the now flat, swampy country for about 5 miles and halted near the foothills of the Tjamplong area.'

In three days the 2/40th had lost eighty-four officers and men dead, and 132 wounded artillery men were fighting as infantry; cooks, clerks and mortar men were using rifles and the Lewis gun. And along with these men were the young reinforcements who had arrived the day before the fight began with little, if any, training. The Japanese intelligence service knew who was on the island: they called 'Surrender Australian!'

It was now about 11 p.m. and apart from guard duties the completely exhausted, hungry and thirsty men tried to snatch a few hours rest. 'At this stage we had many wounded and dying personnel, our water supply carts were empty as were our bottles, a few men, not all, had iron rations. The whole force was exhausted and had the job of attacking Japanese-held Tjamplong in the next few hours. Soon after daylight a huge force of mobilised Japs headed by light tanks advanced suddenly around the bend in the road to our rear, taking everyone by surprise to such an extent that the boys first thought they were relief forces for us. When it was realised that they were Japs we opened fire but they now advanced with hands up, shouting, "Peace", "No fight", "Surrender". We could not continue to machine-gun men who were making no attempt to defend themselves, so firing ceased and parlying began in a smattering of Dutch, Malay, English and Japanese. Armaments of both sides were deflected and various compromises were attempted but with the Japs fresh ashore with 23,000 men against our few hundred (and, they informed us, a bombing attack due on our restricted area in twenty minutes), a quick conference was called to gather officers and men's opinions. Apart from suggestions that we be allowed one hour to move our wounded away and then fight it out (the Japs turned this suggestion down immediately), the feeling was unanimous for surrender.

'We did not realise the seriousness of surrender. We had the impression that it would only be a short time before our own Australian-based forces would attack and we would once more put our knowledge to harmful purpose to the Japs. With 23,000 fresh Japanese at our rear and 600 in the hills and in front, swamps on either side of the road and no food or water, no relief for the wounded men and the whole force exhausted and disillusioned at receiving no support from our navy and air force, and no word from Australia, there was simply no option but surrender. After the laying down of arms was completed, the promised Jap bombers came over and dropped their eggs on us: the victors had forgotten to call off their raid and so sixty of their men suffered with forty casualties to our men. We had a rest, with us and Japs who, a few minutes before, were fighting to kill one another, now sitting casually on the roadside eating and smoking. We commenced the two-day hike, without food and with only filthy water holes to drink out of, back to our future barbed-wire enclosed prison camp under a coconut grove at Oie Sapa Besar. It was ironical: we had spent months preparing the wiring of this beach and foreshore to trap the Japs.'

Harry Holder: 'It was all so hopeless. There was no Dunkirk or anything like that for us, no ships would come to take us off. We set fire to the ammunition and there were fuel fires everywhere. The Dutch ladies on Timor weren't rounded up until later in the war and they kept their radios secret and were able to give us news. It was all bad.'

And thus began their prisoner of war life. 'The wounded personnel were transported back by our own motor vehicles. Some of our men in advanced positions and furthest away from the Jap forces continued on towards the mountains, some hoping eventually to join with the commandos in Portugese Timor, others returning to us later, broken in health; some were betrayed to the Japs by natives, whilst many died – twenty-eight men listed as missing were most certainly dead in 1945.'

The prisoners were 'angry about a lot of things', such as the lack of air support. 'Our RAAF forces attached to Dutch Timor wished us luck and took off for Darwin before the Japs landed, and never returned, even though they could have dealt crippling blows to the invasion force of 23,000 Japs. Our engineers blew the drome and ammo dumps at daylight on 20 February to deny it to the Japs but with their paratroops and landing forces occupying our time, the enemy convoy disembarked and prepared to advance unmolested. We had completely annihilated the paratroops, which according to the Jap figures were 500-odd strong and only seventy-eight survived. It was all for nothing.'

The sickness in the camp of 1100 men increased as time went on to 70 per cent of the inhabitants, with the RAP and hospital sections working full time with very little medical supplies. Reg Holloway: 'There were Major Stevens, Captains Brown and Gillies plus two Dutch doctors, Heking and Bloomsmar (who were an asset on tropical diseases and saved numerous limbs infected with ulcers). Seriously ill amounted to 311 in hospital, with complaints including general wounds, malaria, yaws, black-water fever and heart failure. The dead were wrapped in blankets and buried nearby and eventually cement crosses were erected. Numerous men repeatedly attempted to reach the Australian Inpendents in the Portugese end of Timor but returned broken in health or sold to the Japs by Timorese natives. Officers who entered camp with money belonging to the pay office, canteens, etc. handed it over to a battalion fund for use in the hospital section. The engineer unit with us constructed latrines, showers (operated from a sunken well), bakehouse and general camp improvements. Main cooking for the camp was done at the central kitchen, some done by platoons and small groups of friends continuously concocting dishes from coconuts, bananas, pawpaw, wild tomatoes, goela, etc. mixed with our issue of rations. Everything from roots to leaves were cooked as were cactus buds for jam and sea water for salt. Coconuts were our "life blood".

'Early in August the first senior officers and specialists left us for Singapore and were followed by other officers and sick men. These were key men in the units and the Japs knew it, they had full records of all of us, given by us in the hope of information being sent home to Australia as to our well-being. Up to this time we had been more or less organised to play a part should an attempt be made to relieve us. Reconnaissance parties were continually out about the island for days on end gathering information which might prove valuable.

'During the following months large numbers of our men who "went bush" before or during action, plus many Dutch personnel, gave themselves up, broken in health, and drifted in in small parties or singly, and gave information as did the only survivor of a Lockheed which was shot down, Flight Lieutenant McCallister (who later made an unsuccessful attempt to steal a Jap Douglas plane from Penfoei drome). Many of us continually went out of camp under cover of darkness on general scouting parties. Japanese troops were concentrating all over the island, their supply ships at Koepang were unloaded by us and Timorese, and large concentrations of fighter and bomber aircrafts regularly landed on their way to raid Darwin and after refuelling on the return journey would return westward, presumably to Java or the Celebes. Many planes were concentrated on Timor.'

Sabotage kept the Japanese guessing and resulted in many camp searches. 'On one such search Corporal J.H. (Dummy) Armstrong was found missing and as I slept near him and had various papers, the Jap commandant hauled me to his house for questioning. After many threats he told me that I could return to camp temporarily but would be shot as blameworthy should Dummy not return or be brought back to camp. Nothing came of it as that Jap was transferred a few days later and although I knew of Armstrong's whereabouts at the time, he is still missing to this day and must be presumed dead by Jap hands, or by starvation.'

The first Japanese CO, Lieutenant (later Captain) Bugara, was 'a cruel, arrogant monster who always rode a horse about the camp, brandishing a sword'. The second, Lieutenant Horato, treated the men reasonably while the last, with them only a few weeks before the prisoners were moved to Java, was 'very considerate' but took over too late to help obtain better conditions. All natives of the Dutch army were given their freedom and those with wives and families were transported back to Java. A white Roman Catholic bishop was left free in the north of Dutch Timor, a Protestant Minadones missionary, Reverend Roti, who was married to a Dutch girl, was left at Soe in the island centre where the Dutch women were interned under trying conditions. 'When all Allied personnel were rounded up and shifted to Java, these poor women, about forty of them, were left there alone at the mercy of the Japanese and we heard no more of them.'

'About 10 p.m. on 24 September, all Allied personnel were gathered together and told to pack ready to evacuate the camp. In the early hours of the morning the fit men walked to Koepang, 6 miles away, whilst sick personnel were transported by trucks. The natives secretly or openly defied the Japanese by passing us food etc. and were willing to give us anything, and refused payment. Disregarding Jap guards, many acquaintances crawled through enclosures to shake hands in farewell, and left crying bitterly. The Aussies had made a great impression on the natives of Timor (and friendliness was returned to our fellows who landed some three years later).'

The Australians were taken by lighters to cargo ships in the bay, herded down in the holds, crowded together in 'a disorganised rabble among the filth', no washing facilities were provided. The heat was stifling in the darkness of the hold as there was no ventilation. They were told by the Japanese that they were traversing dangerous waters and could expect enemy attacks at any moment, 'not that we in the locked-down hatch would have hoped for any means of escape should we be torpedoed or bombed. We had no life jackets.

'Captain Bugara, who had been our camp boss early in the year, was CO of the move and of course had no sympathy towards our conditions in the hold. There were about 1100 Dutch, English and Australians plus civilians and administrators. The Resident (Governor) and his wife, about 60 years of age, had to share our conditions, the Japs making no special allowances for the lady, who had to live with us in the same crude circumstances.'

In this way the Australians left Timor. Reaching Surabaya harbour, Java, they found it full of sunken, scuttled and bombed ships, remnants of the initial Japanese attack. 'A Japanese Red Cross liner was in port along with a battleship and many naval warships; the air was full of aircraft. The harbour buildings and docks were badly battle-scarred and the native coolies were unloading ships amidst the wreckage. After a long rail journey, Dutch internees were put off in Batavia, destined for the local gaol. I last saw the Resident's wife struggling with her baggage with Japs standing over her.

'We were taken on a railway branch line to the port for Batavia, Tanjong Priok. At this huge, imposing station we received our first brutal treatment and realised that the iron discipline often threatened by the Japanese was about to commence. Our more or less casual prison days were over.'

And so, the men from Timor joined the other Australian captives in the long trail along the Burma Railway, the voyage on the ship *Byoki Maru*, and the coal mines of Japan.

Reg Holloway: 'Out of the 377 men who had left Tasmania to defend Timor, only thirty-one went through the war without dying or being evacuated as seriously ill.'

Formosa

Changi was like a big clearing station with men in transit coming in, while other groups were being transferred elsewhere. Such groups rarely knew their destination. 'We set off into limbo, suddenly Changi seemed like our home we were leaving behind' Colonel Wilfrid Kent Hughes wrote.

'A bit of a band got going in the early days, when we set off to cross the China Sea this band farewelled us with "Waltzing Matilda". For an instant we smelt gum trees and saw wattle, but only for an instant. As we marched to the docks it was interesting to see new sights after being shut up for six months.'

Every group that sailed away was crammed into holds 'until there wasn't room for a gutted sardine'. Kent Hughes once told the author of his being crammed into a ship in Keppel Bay and then, at the last moment, he and some of his group being off-loaded without any explanation. 'We waved as the ship moved off, but we didn't call out to our mates nothing like that, it wasn't a cruise ship. We watched them go, they didn't know where, and neither did we. There would be no one to greet them "over there" wherever that might be, I thought irrationally. And like a ghost flitted through my mind the cheering and chiakking as we climbed all over the ship's rigging when we left Australia such a short time ago. Watching our friends transported away from us made us strangely ill-at-ease.'

But soon he too was at sea, 'herded like a herring catch', with tiers of slats around the sides of the ship and men crowded 'flesh to flesh'. Soon the heat stripped them of all thought and energy. 'The hold became like a stove where human shapes lay broiling in the heat.' When it rained the moist hot air condensed below deck and dripped on the naked men sprawling below. Some sat in slimy puddles until the sun dried the rain. This group of men were mostly senior officers: Kent Hughes saw a general, stripped to his skin, collecting water in a jam tin. 'Our skin dripped sweat from every pore.' Dysentery rampaged through this sty and by the time they reached Tarkao, the southern port of Formosa, the rate of illness was too high to calculate. 'We climbed ashore like ship-wrecked seamen.'

They marched 4 miles to their camp, 'dirty, damp, unhealthy Heito', timber platforms beneath thatched roofs. Kent Hughes wrote, 'A more depressing, fever-stricken hole had ne'er been dreamed of by a single soul'. Here the men were soon debilitated with dengue fever, dysentery, diarrhoea and two types of malaria. 'Benjo!' they called at night to gain permission of the sentry to rush to the slatted, hole-in-the ground lavatory.

Then they were separated again, one party going by train to Karenko camp at the northern end of the island now known as Taiwan. And again there was that sadness that schoolboys feel when a long or permanent break comes. All ranks below that of lieutenant colonel were to remain in sweaty, horrid Heito while higher ranks, that is, generals of several races, plus twenty men from the ranks, went to Karenko. Karenko was superior to Heito where their mates still languished. The Japanese General Ando visited them and brought a pig. The Japanese ate the hams and head and feet but enough was left for all the prisoners to taste a little meat. But, as they learned, 'life in a palace is a travesty when one goes back to famine fare'.

They read everything they could get their hands on; they played cards, grew vegetables to supplement their rations and, when in despair, whistled a tune 'any old tune from home', and suddenly other men would wander up and talk about home and movies and 'houses with doors on them'. In a few months they were removed to an even better camp. Bets were taken as to why the generals were moved – the winner had guessed: a Red Cross visitor was to come to the island and 'it would look bad for generals to be cooped up with "convicts"'.

If all this seemed to be the land of Beulah, then it was all to change when they reached Japan, for this was their next destination. It was not the land of cherry blossom of the picture books to which they were travelling but further still, to the arctic north, to Liaoyuanchow, a straggling town of adobe huts in Manchuria.

The benjo pits froze up. Kent Hughes said that a stalagmite of 'evil, involuted coprolite grew through each opening, rising 2 feet high and Manchus, armed with long spears and red-hot coals, came to melt the dung-formed poles'. When the short summer came the benjo overflowed and the pumps broke down. No prisoner here worked as the men in Southern Asia did but the boredom, as the years went by, had to be constantly attacked and beaten back far enough to allow light to enter the spirit of the men. But time began to drag.

Kent Hughes described himself as 'a slave of the Samurai' and wrote many poems while held in bondage. Because of the total ban (under pain of severe punishment) of the holding of any paper, he wrote on small, flimsy sheets that, when folded, could fit into an anti-tinea powder container. He used a borrowed fine-nibbed fountain pen and 'two pairs of spectacles'. He wrote neatly on each side of the paper with 3000 words back and front. Before he was moved to Manchuria, he could hear through the night the sea beating on the shore and the flocks of migratory birds flying low over the camp. He wrote of it on a tiny sheet of paper.

Through the still watches of the night, the sea
Plays martial music for a soldier's soul
Migrating wings whirr softly overhead
Departed spirits of the noble dead return
To claim a comrade from the grave.

Milne Bay

Milne Bay, on the far eastern tip of New Guinea, was as isolated as any island and no story of the fate of Australian prisoners could be as sad as that of this place. Here the Australians were cut off from the rest of their kind and it was here that the Japanese received their first and only defeat in a seaborne invasion in that war. The hill slopes were littered with bodies of Japanese who had attempted to take Milne Bay. The astounding fight put up by the Australians cost them dearly: no Australian taken prisoner lived.

Later, war crimes investigation revealed that Australian bodies were found spread-eagled in trees, one having been 'dressed as one does a bullock in the outback'. The loss of their many fine young fighting men appears to have driven the enemy into a frenzy of retribution. One well-documented incident was that of the death of Sergeant Siffleet. The Japanese officer detailed to execute this man with a sword assigned a private to photograph him in the act, another took notes of his feelings when watching the spectacle, 'his head rolled off cleanly, I could hear the ssh ssh of his blood falling on the ground'.

By the time Milne Bay was reported in Australian newspapers General MacArthur had claimed the privilege of issuing all news releases in the South Pacific. He headed the story 'Allied Victory in Milne Bay', not mentioning Australians although he had been quick to criticise them when they had, at first, been pushed back on the Kokoda Trail.

Java

'The Colonel had sent me to tell Major Daly that the Dutch report there's no Japs within 200 miles of Java. Just as I arrived all hell opened up. Daly said, "What do you think those bastards are?" I said, "I was only relaying a message".'

Private Bill Garvie, 2/2nd Pioneers

AMONG THE MANY BUNGLES – always couched in high military terms reminiscent of the communiques of Field Marshal Sir Douglas Haig in World War I – was Java. Early in 1942 when all was disaster for the Allies and imminent disaster for Australia, the Prime Minister of Great Britain, Winston Churchill, was badgering the Prime Minister of Australia, John Curtin, to send the Australian troops from the Middle East to Burma. John Curtin refused. Darwin had been bombed, Singapore lost, Timor invaded, the whole string of islands encircling the north of Australia were gone or going and one of Australia's four divisions (the 8th) had been lost to the Japanese.

Churchill believed that if Australia was lost it could be regained when Britain and the new partner in the war, the United States, later achieved victory. Curtin said no: the ships were on the high seas returning with the AIF aboard to defend Australia. Churchill replied by diverting the leading ship of the returning convoy to Rangoon. Curtin saw an almost certain likelihood of a repeat of Greece and Crete. It was even unlikely that the troops could be landed given the overwhelming supremacy of Japanese sea and air power, and much more unlikely that they could be brought out later. 'The movement of our forces', Curtin told Churchill, 'to this theatre therefore is not considered a reasonable hazard of war, having regard to what has gone before, and its adverse results would have

433

the gravest consequences on the morale of the Australian people. The government therefore must adhere to its decision. We feel, in view of the services the AIF have rendered in the Middle East, that we have every right to expect them to be returned as soon as possible, with adequate escorts to ensure their safe arrival. We assure you, and desire you to so inform the President, who knows fully what we have done to help the common cause, that if it were possible to divert our troops to Burma and India without imperilling our security in the judgment of our advisers we should be pleased to agree to the diversion.'

On 21 February Curtin learnt that the American government was sending the 41st US Division to Australia. On the 22nd, Churchill sent Curtin the following cable: 'We could not contemplate that you would refuse our request, and that of the President of the United States, for the diversion of the leading Australian division to save the situation in Burma.'

Curtin learnt that the leading convoy had remained on course up until 9 p.m. on the 20th, when, on Churchill's orders, the Admiralty directed it to turn north to Rangoon. Curtin sent a cable to Churchill on the 23rd complaining that Churchill had treated the Australian government's approval of the diversion of the convoy as a matter of form, and that by doing so he had added to the dangers of the convoy. Rangoon was burning. Refugees fled into the jungle. Their exodus from the Burmese capital gave the city over to fire and looters. The air, sea and land were held by the Japanese. Wavell had already revealed that Java faced imminent invasion. Australia's outer defences were now quickly vanishing and her vulnerability completely exposed. With AIF troops she had sought to save Malaya and Singapore, falling back on the Netherlands East Indies. 'All these northern defences are gone or going. Now you contemplate using the AIF to save Burma. All this has been done, as in Greece, without adequate air support. We feel a primary obligation to save Australia not only for itself, but to preserve it as a base for the development of the war against Japan. In the circumstances it is quite impossible to reverse a decision which we made with the utmost care, and which we have affirmed and reaffirmed' Curtin cabled. Churchill, 'not a little disgruntled', informed Curtin that the convoy had been turned about once again and would refuel at Colombo, and proceed to Australia. It is still, in the 1990s, being argued as to whether the Australian Division could have saved Burma, but few argue in the affirmative; the many shudder at the thought of the final result of doubling the numbers of our men already taken prisoner, doubling the cruel, painful deaths, the life-long toll on survivors.

While this armada of 'battle-hardened' men of Tobruk, of the Middle East, Crete and Greece sped homewards to defend Australia, one ship of their convoy was cut out and sent off to the Netherlands East Indies as a gesture to the Dutch.

The convoy steamed back to Australia – except for the P&O liner *Orcades* (which had earlier been converted to a troop carrier). She was sent to Sumatra. A quite wondrous – to the troops, and also to us at this distance – black pantomime followed the arrival in the roads of this ship.

The *Orcades* carried 3400 men including the 2/3rd Machine Gun Battalion led by Lieutenant Colonel A.S. Blackburn and the 2/2nd Pioneers led by Lieutenant Colonel J.M. Williams. The swiftness of events was confusing for the officers, and much more so for the troops. The island was to be evacuated, orders were issued for the withdrawal from Sumatra of all British troops; naval and air support was sought for protection during the embarkation of 6000 men, Japanese troop ships were arriving, and at the same time, the embarkation of Australian troops was being carried out, including all equipment they could carry. In two days they embarked 2500 RAF, 1890 British troops, 700 Dutch troops and roughly 1000 civilians, in twelve ships, with the rearguard sailing at 7.30 a.m. on 17 February. A steamer was left to pick up late arrivals and a small group of officers remained on shore.

Blue Butterworth: 'On the *Orcades* we had started to think, Christ, what are we going into, what's happening? Some of the 2/3 and 2/2 boys were all ready to be taken off at Sumatra and then, "get back on board, the Nips are coming". Everybody got back on board and we turned around and headed down the coast in daylight and you could see seven smokestacks coming towards us. Oh Jesus, naturally shits were trumps. We all thought it was the Nips but it turned out to be American destroyers and Dutch naval craft trying to get in and evacuate the Europeans.

'We shouldn't have been there, we shouldn't have stayed when we did get there. We were told we must keep the faith with the Dutch. I never knew the Dutch were anything to do with us. We were put off on shore, our medical gear was on another ship. We only kicked off with a little thing like an RAP kit and we had to build it all up again. Naturally we had to liaise with the Dutch and there was a very efficient Dutch matron, her father had been Governor-General at Java. She had got this team of VADs (hospital aides) and they were good and the whole place started to swing. But then, on March the 8th we knew things weren't going too hot. Those of us in medical units were told we could go if we wanted, but a skeleton force to look after the wounded would have to volunteer to stay behind. Well, no one left. And that was it. That was the end. From then on we were prisoners.'

Private Claude Roediger and his brother Eric of the 2/3rd Machine Gun Battalion were also on the *Orcades*. 'They had tried to land us on Sumatra. We got on a lighter and they pulled into shore prepared to disembark – a few had already got ashore when an English officer came along and wanted to know where we were going, and we said to guard the airstrip, and he said, the Japs have taken it already. He told us to get back on the lighter and move away. It was not so easy to regain the *Orcades*. The night was as dark as the inside of a dog. The pilot who was to take us through the minefields to the ship had gone home. They had to call the *Orcades* on the radio and ask them to put the port lights on "so we could see where we were going". A fellow who volunteered to pilot us back turned out to be uncertain about the minefields.'

Then they headed for Java. 'First they told us we were to

get ashore, then no, we weren't. Then, "Greatcoats will be worn". We were all lined up on deck. Shortly after, "Greatcoats will not be worn". Off they came. Then, "Greatcoats etc. etc." One fellow pulled his off and chucked it over the side. "Bugger the bloody overcoat", he said. Next day, "Overcoats will be worn". So it went on. Imagine fussing as to whether greatcoats were or weren't going to be worn!'

Indeed yes. It would have been better had they fussed about whether the men would carry weapons or travel in their regimental trucks. But it was too late to do this: their guns, ammunition and trucks had gone on to Australia in another ship. The *Orcades* could issue the few ship's rifles they had – 'World War One models, some dating back to the Boer War', but the 2/3rd Machine Gun Battalion would go ashore without their own weapons. 'There were orders, counter-orders, disorder. First we were to get ashore, then we weren't, then we were. And so on, day after day; ultimately we went.'

The men were not given any details of their task – did anyone *know* what the task would be? The official records are diffuse and one might well be excused for accepting the findings of the men in preference to the excuses of those responsible for this useless, senseless, blunder. Claude Roediger: 'There was a vast convoy of enemy troops on its way, and the idea as I understand it, was that our role was to engage the enemy, exchange a few shots, pull out, take up a new position, dance all around the place to keep them guessing as to how many troops were there, hoping they would think there were three divisions of Australians on shore when actually there was only part of three battalions.

'We were there to have the Japs think that the Netherlands East Indies was well garrisoned. If they'd known what little strength was on Sumatra they would have felt free to by-pass us and move straight on to Australia maybe. So it was a strategic role, a delaying tactic. It gave them time back home to organise some sort of resistance ... so we were told. We were expendable.

'We knew the *Orcades* was gone. There were nurses, airmen

and naval personnel going back on it to Australia. We were on our own now.'

Eric Roediger: 'We didn't have our own weapons. The old ship's rifles they gave us were pre-World War I. They had been stored away, gummed up with grease and clag to keep them from rusting and when you went to fire them the magazine was pushing against this gum and stuff and the first two or three rounds would come out all right, but as the spring got extended and weaker the last two may or may not come out. I remember our corporal saying, "You guys will have to be careful with these guns. Give it plenty of exercise, bolt action, before you take it for granted there's nothing in it." He went on like that for quite a while, then he pulled the trigger, Bang! We all looked round to see who was going to fall, it tore a hole in the concrete floor.'

Claude: 'Because I had originally been in the Infantry, I was trained with a Bren gun and so it was given to me to man the Bren, but it was a brand new one and terribly rough. It wasn't finished at all. So we were in our positions down there, getting back to the Java bridge, and I said to the corporal, "We're fools. There's never been a round put through this thing, we don't know whether it's going to work", and I convinced him that we at least should see if it was going to work. "What say I run just a short burst through it?" So I ran off about three rounds into the river bed and of course everybody had heard, the whole line jumped for their guns immediately. Captain Jack Hands came rushing up wanting to know "What's all the noise about?" I said, "You've got to prove you're well-armed before you go into battle". It caused a bit of excitement, anyway.

'We were holding that line there when, one morning, we were told the Dutch had negotiated a peace contract with the Japanese. We were most upset about it because our group hadn't been informed about it promptly. So we decided that we weren't going to surrender, we were going to take to the hills. We turned all our convoys around, set off for the south coast of Java, hoping that there would be a bit of flotsam or something that we might be able to float across to Fremantle on. But there was nothing there and every morning the Zeros used to fly around the island and shoot up anything afloat. We had high hopes that there would be some attempt to rescue us by submarine. Talked about it. But all these things were not on, of course. But it was good to think about it. We settled down in the Tea Factory up there for about ten days and more.'

Captain John Kennedy, 2/3rd Machine Gun Battalion, was one of the men of the Machine Gun companies who were put ashore in Java without their guns. He had 'a bit of a torrid time' right from the moment he was caught. 'We hadn't seen Japanese until we landed in Sumatra and Java. We'd been on our way from Suez; thought we were going to Burma, but were held in Colombo, and then told we were going home to Australia. We got as far as NEI and us very reluctant soldiers were put ashore to go and defend Sumatra. We only got inland about a mile, it rained like the clappers and someone said, "Come back home" and we came back "home" as quickly as we could, and got on the boat again. We went from Ouisthaven in Sumatra to Batavia in Java and we got on the boat, off the boat, on the boat, off the boat and they constantly changed our orders and we got off once too often and stayed there. A sore point with us was that we got off the ship and the Dutch got on it and we were left there, on an island of the Netherlands East Indies – with the Japs. We were put ashore there to support the Dutch and they ran and left us. Their navy and their air force fought to extinction, no argument about that whatever. They fought admirably. But most of their soldiers were Indonesians and they had been treated very badly by the colonial Dutch.

'We didn't know anything, it was utter confusion, we were just told we were to go ashore. We knew we were in Batavia because when we arrived there the deserters from Singapore pelted our ships with tins and things. And they were Australians! My commander, Arthur S. Blackburn VC, was a hotheaded old so-and-so, and if he'd had his way he'd have gone ashore and shot them. No doubt about it he would have. Some of them were terrible scum. And, of course, they ultimately joined us as POWs, and we didn't like that very much. The officer that led them was a terrible bugger. Singapore was about to fall, and the *Empire Star* had a lot of women on board and he had forced his way on the ship with a group of men. He should have been court-martialled.

'When we arrived on Java, the 131st Field Artillery from Texas was there. They had been bound for the Philippines but were unloaded here instead. They were National Guardsmen and their great story was that they had been to two wars and fired three shots. We heard the whole bloody three of them go off! When we first saw them we thought, where have all these big fat men come from? We'd been in the Middle East and were lean. But when you got to know them, they were the salt of the earth; I've got the utmost admiration for Yanks.'

Anxious to learn the whereabouts of the Australian 7th Division, the Japanese had subjected Captain John Kennedy, Lieutenants John Haynes and John Redward to constant questioning with extremely rough treatment in an unsuccessful attempt to secure information. Engaged on reconnaissance in Java, they were caught by the Japanese and taken to their forward headquarters on 3 March 1942, before the fall of Java. The Japanese tied Haynes and Redward and handcuffed Kennedy, and they remained trussed up for three days while being put through brutal bashings by the Japanese.

The three at no time gave in but led the Japanese into believing that they still had a big force to meet. 'They hopped into us and knocked us about with their fists. We were kicked to pieces in the face, then they took us out and stood us up against a verandah while a Nip from behind booted us from head to toe. Then a couple of Nips dressed as natives tried to interrogate us.

'They kept on questioning us about the disposition of troops and we replied that we didn't know, and then they started in again with rifle butts.'

During the afternoon of the first day the three were thrown into ankle-deep mud and were kicked, then stood up and taken into a room and flogged with a cat o'nine tails. They all collapsed but were revived again when the Japanese threw water over them. While Haynes and Kennedy were being flogged, Redward was threatened with a big knife placed against his lower stomach and drawn over the surface of his skin towards his neck. The Japanese then intimated that the Australians would be killed. A party of soldiers came up with rifles and went through loading preparations. The three were lined up against a wall and waited several minutes for death which did not come. Instead, they were taken to the Japanese aid post and their wounds patched up. The Japanese gave them cigarettes and they smoked with their hands tied behind their backs and lashed together. Then the end of the rope was tied to a tree and the three were left for the rest of the night. They remained trussed to the tree all next day and at 6 p.m. they were put into a truck and travelled all night. During the truck trip, a Japanese war correspondent took their photograph for propaganda purposes.

Later that afternoon a Japanese guard kicked Haynes 'but was unsuccessful in kicking his lower body'. That evening the men were separately questioned by two Japanese asking for the location of the 7th Division. An interpreter informed the three that if they did not tell they would be shot. But by now the three men knew that they were valuable and would not be shot while they still refused to talk.

After further questioning, the Japanese guard threaded a piece of wood a little larger than a pencil through Kennedy's fingers and tried to break them (his hands were still tied behind his back). Then the stick was worked back and forth quickly, rubbing the skin off. The three still refused to speak and the Japanese gave up for the night.

Next morning they were put in prison where for six weeks they were subjected constantly to further questionings and bashings. On Easter Sunday 1942 they were taken before a Japanese camp commander who talked to them and showed them his sword. He then told them of the Japanese method of committing hara-kiri and offered the sword to them. The men refused the offer. He then treated them to lunch, with beer, fitted them out with clothing and sent them back to gaol. 'You would never understand them in a million years', Kennedy says.

'At this camp where my cobbers and myself were tied to a tree for a couple of days, we saw how strictly disciplined the Japanese were. They did exactly what they were told. A platoon of their bicycle troops went by us blokes on our trees and the officer leading on his bicycle slipped and fell on the ground, the bloke behind him fell over him and the next bloke fell on the second bloke. The first bloke got up, the fourth bloke fell over the third bloke, the whole bloody lot of them! We were so scared stiff we wouldn't have dared laugh, but it was the funniest thing I've ever seen. No one got off their bikes without an order, so they just rode into the mob and fell over. I wasn't in a laughing mood anyway, but it sticks in my mind; it was raining like the devil.

'We were tied to that tree for a bloody day and a half. My personal thing was that I wouldn't sign allegiance to the Emperor of Japan and nearly got myself killed for it. That was on 4 July, a very carefully picked day with all the Yanks there. They got all the men to sign, then the officers. I had Bronte Edwards with me, a funny little fellow with all the courage in the bloody world. We were lined up in a shed, all sitting at attention and we were to sign this allegiance to the Emperor of Japan. And Bronte, he got a piece of rag and kept tying a knot in it, to encourage officers *not* to sign. He conned me into it, and two other blokes, and we got this hell of a doing over because of that. In fact we didn't sign until we got instructions from Arthur Blackburn [their commanding officer] and then we did so. We had a hell of a night on that bloody tree.'

Eric Roediger: 'We got a message from the Dutch to say that under the terms of the surrender, they were responsible for all the troops on the island and unless we came and gave ourselves up under the terms of the surrender they were forced to take up arms against us. That's when several little parties decided they weren't going to submit and they took off in various directions. The rest of us said well, there's strength in numbers, so we thought we should stick together.

'Of those little breakaway parties, not one of them lived, they were all dealt with by the natives because most natives had been caught up in this Japanese Greater South East Asian Co-Prosperity Sphere Scheme – the Japs pre-war had been poisoning everybody's minds down there with the racist, anti-white concept and so natives had turned very sour on Europeans.

'We had a conference and decided as there was no hope of getting away and the area was mosquito-ridden and our medical supplies and food were limited, we believed the only thing we could do was to stack our guns, they weren't worth much anyway, then we reported at a little village called Leles where the Japanese soldiers were billeted. There was a beautiful stream running about 100 yards away and we were able to go down there and bathe and the Japs didn't even bother to say goodday to us. They were walking around town and we were walking around the town. Apparently the officers had some understanding about it but as far as we were concerned we could trade with whoever we wanted to and go for a swim and sleep on the grass. We had a couple of weeks there and then we had a message to say that we were to report to the next town, Garoet, 7 miles away. We marched up there with all our belongings, and were put behind barbed wire for the first time.

'And that's where our rations started to run out. The Japs didn't have anything organised because they hadn't expected us, they were embarrassed by the prisoner of war situation. But they allowed us access to the sweepings off the floor of the barns nearby. It was rancid, had been there for years, it had rat manure and weevils and cockroaches and we'd bring this stuff home and try to pick out all the foreign matter and prepare it for a meal; we had no salt, sugar or vegetables. We started quite suddenly into the bad stuff. Our chaps who were at Garoet before us were skeletons, they'd gone down so quickly.'

Claude: 'I had different values at that stage. We'd been brought up as a Christian family and our parents always taught us to believe in God and we always said Grace before our meals and we used to observe that, but when this food came along I said to Eric one day, "I just can't thank God for this stuff". Then one day I was thumbing through my New Testament and came across the verse, I think it was in *Timothy*, which said, "All food is good to eat. It is sanctified by prayer." And I took that as a guide and I immediately decided I'd better start to pray because this food certainly needed to be sanctified. And from that point I never ceased to ask God to bless that food for the nourishment of our bodies. The whole time of my captivity I always thanked Him for the food. My faith never wavered, even during the worst days. The Japanese were not a Christian people. And they didn't have the standards we have.'

Eric: 'I always thought I'd get home. Always did. Some of our friends, when we pulled out of Fremantle said, "Oh, I'll never see that sight again", and they didn't. But I always thought I'd get back. You might have ups and downs, but right through it we always kept faith and with that you've got peace of mind. It was something that you can take along with you – and there wasn't much we could take with us.'

Claude: 'There was nothing much else to hold on to. I was the same as Eric, I was an optimist and I never thought for one minute I wouldn't get home, even later on when I had cholera. I knew that the church people at home were constantly in prayer for us. We knew, although we received no letters, that the congregation prayed for all those who were serving, every Sunday without fail, and with that backing we never thought of not getting back.'

Eric: 'It was a horrible place but we got the occasional laugh. One of the lads brought some eggs through the barbed wire. A Jap saw him come in so he put the eggs on the ground and threw his hat over them. The Jap was sure that there were eggs underneath the hat so he's yelling and bellowing at him, exercising his rifle and threatening to blow everybody up. We just shrugged our shoulders and walked away from him. There was a basketball match going on and we couldn't hear what he was saying because we were all barracking. When the Jap knew that he couldn't get anybody to lift that hat off, he started to call out to the guardhouse about 100 yards away, and we started to call out louder, "Come on WA! Come on WA!" The others shouted, "Come on Victoria! Come on Victoria!" And as he couldn't get the guards' attention, he had to walk towards this guardhouse and one of our boys swooped back, got the eggs and left the hat. When the Jap got the guardhouse's attention, he quickly marched back and got one of the guards to lift up the hat: and there was nothing there. And we were all shouting, "Come on WA! Come on Victoria!" and pretending not to notice him. There was always something humorous going on. You had a few laughs. One day, to break the monotony, I was giving a talk on the cuts of meat. I drew a side of beef on a blackboard, showing where the fillet steak comes from, the rump steak and the other cuts and joints. The Jap came over and thought we were planning an escape route and he confiscated the drawing.'

Claude: 'Apart from further on, on the railroad, the morale was at its lowest at Garoet for the whole war. Even though we tried to keep our spirits up.'

Eric: 'One guard, the "Singing Fool", made us sing as he rode a bike in front of us and beat time with a stock whip as we marched up the street on the way to work. So we'd sing, "There'll always be an England" and all the patriotic airs we could think of. The Dutch ladies would all come out to see if their missing husbands were there and they'd give us sweets and tobacco. Sometimes we got a piece of garlic sausage, different little things they'd try and press on to you as you passed by.'

The men from the *Orcades* were told, and believed, that they were placed on Java as a sop to the Dutch. The soldiers found the natives on Java and Sumatra were at all times pro-Japanese, anti-white, not just anti-Dutch. Private Bill Garvie, 2/2nd

Pioneers, is outspoken: 'There had been Japanese among them before the war who had whooped up a lot of enthusiasm against the Dutch and against whites generally so that they were no help to the members of the AIF who were landed there. The Dutch were no help to them either, they capitulated without a struggle in an attempt to save their businesses.'

Bill Garvie had the stamp of the legendary Australian larrikin on him. He was one of the men trapped on Java after returning from the Middle East. He remembered only the good times. 'The other times aren't worth remembering', he said. His story begins immediately before being taken prisoner.

'I'd been into a town to get a load of water at the Dutch barracks. I came back and pulled up at the kitchen to give them supplies and was told I had to go out to where we had a company each side of the road and a bridge blown. Just as I was leaving the colonel came over and said, "Tell Major Daly that the Dutch reconnaissance report there's no Jap within 200 miles of the island". Just as I arrived all hell opened up, I saw Major Daly dive into a clump of eggfruit so I followed him and said, "I've got a message for you, the Dutch report there are no Japs within 200 miles". He said, "What do you think those bastards are?" I said I was only relaying the message.

'We had the Dutch each side of us on our flanks but when the firing started they shot through. Eventually our boys had to retreat. When I got back to the tea plantation where we were camped, I said to the transport officer, "I'm short of petrol, I won't be able to do much more travelling". He got the orderly to type up on army paper an order authorising me to buy, and that the army would guarantee to pay for the goods and services rendered. I suggested he give me another half dozen such chits. I went to the service station, got both tanks filled up, as well as a grease and oil change. The Dutch owner was all smiles, came the payola and I produced the form, it's a wonder you didn't hear him back in Australia the act he put on! I said I'd sign it so I put "Thomas Blamey", gave it to him and told him that's all he was getting. I said, "There's a war on and if we win you'll get paid, if we lose they'll take your service station and probably shoot you, so you have nothing to lose".

'Eventually our troops had to retreat so we left the tea plantation, drove all night and sheltered in daylight. Next day the transport officer showed us the map, said he was sending three vehicles into town, one was a staff car with a sergeant with a tommy-gun escort; I'd be on my own in the middle vehicle followed by a blitz wagon. He wanted water and supplies so we set off, passed about ten airforce buses blown up beside the road; had to make a way around them. I got the water, the boys were loading up supplies so I said I'd head back. Remembering the map, I saw a turn-off I could use and so miss the buses. Back at the camp the transport officer said we'd be moving out that night and I'd be the last vehicle and he'd be my passenger. We had to set fire to the place, all the whisky and spirits had to be burnt and then we'd head off after the convoy. He said to go in and see what I could find so I got tobacco, plenty of cigarettes, tins of coffee and milk, dried biscuits and two little portable burners with solidified fuel. Saw a billy so thought I'd better take that too, so loaded them on to the water truck, the best thing I've ever done. Eventually the convoy moved out, we gave them a bit of a start then we set fire to the canteen, got it nicely blazing and headed off. I said I'd go around the other road because there were no buses in the way, we drove for about three hours and I said, "there's the convoy up ahead", all you could see was a little light, no headlights. We followed them, came to a halt a couple of hours later, I looked in my mirror and said it looked like there was a convoy following us and I hoped it wasn't Japs. We moved a bit further and stopped, the convoy caught up and we heard footsteps. I thought, "This is it!" And I was leaning over the steering wheel, the officer was sitting back, and along came our colonel and asked "What convoy is this?" I said, "the 2/2nd Pioneers, I'm the rear vehicle." And he said, "Like hell you are, I'm *leading* them!" I asked what he wanted me to do, pull aside and drop in at the rear? and he said to keep going and he'd follow us.

'On our way into the town looking for rations and water, I saw a hotel three storeys high, so I blew the horn and pulled in. The other two vehicles stopped. I told them I was hungry and wanted a feed. I said I had an order form and it would be right. The poor old sergeant didn't like coming but in we trooped to the dining room, had a Chinese waiter behind each chair in beautiful velvety uniforms.

'I asked for five bottles of Tooths KB nice and cold; got a menu each (it was only in Chinese and Dutch), I said the top one would be soup so that would do me. I saw Peking, thought that looked like duck, we all had soup and duck, didn't worry about sweets. The poor old sergeant kept on about how would we pay for it and I said "She'll be right". When we finished, got to the desk, the Chinese bloke gave me the bill and I produced the typed order from my pocket and said to our two blokes with machine guns to stand each side of me. He was yabbering in Chinese and Dutch and I said for them to stick the barrels up over the desk. I don't know if he understood English, but he did understand guns. "If we win the war, you'll get paid", I told him. "If we don't they'll cut your bloody throat", and I signed it "John Curtin". We trooped out, one bloke said, "You're the cheekiest bastard in the AIF!" I asked if he enjoyed his tucker and when he said yes, I told him not to grizzle about it. That was a decent trip! We finished up in a market place, stranded, and after a couple of days an officer came and said, "I've had word from the Japs, you've got to stack all your rifles and guns, they're going to pick them up, we're POWs now".

'A train took us into Batavia (now Jakarta) to what was called the Bicycle Camp. When we got in some of our mates came and said, "All you get here is boiled rice, you get nothing with it". We had our two-up boys and they produced the pennies, we didn't have much money. They started a game and some Yanks (Texans) came over, they said they'd be in it, so up go the pennies. The guards came and broke it up after about a quarter hour but in that time we got quite a bit of money and the Yanks got quite a bit of experience.

'We settled down into this camp which had been a former Dutch barracks, there was a 10-foot close barbed wire about 5 inches apart all around it and another one 10 yards out. One of my mates borrowed my pliers and files and cut some barbs off the wire, filed one end flat, cut it off and made flints. We didn't think they'd work, but they did. About a week later a Yank came and asked if we had any flints. My mate had half an aspirin bottle full: I don't know what he got for them but he came and gave me 5 guilders for the loan of the pliers and files. The next day the Texan came looking for the guy who sold him the flints but he never found him. The Texans were real hillbillys.

'While we were in the camp I got dysentery and was put into isolation; the only cure they had was a big mug of epsom salts followed by a tablespoon of castor oil and another mug of epsom salts. At least it worked! I was there about two weeks, I remember one big bloke sitting on the bench farted loudly, said "I'm cured", and rolled over dead.

'One evening a guard came in full, lined us all up, goes along on inspection, I had my shirt button undone, he yabbered at me, threw a swing and I ducked; my mates said not to do that as he might kill me, so I copped the next one and the force of it burst my ear drum which discharged for about six months continuously. My head rang all night.

'After a while they got a heap of us together and marched us off. It rained all the way and we were ploughing in about 6 inches of black mud. We moved into bamboo huts which had been a native barracks, with thatched roofs and bamboo slats for beds and full of bed bugs: as soon as you laid down they'd attack you. It was a terrible joint! I'd been there about three weeks, I was going to get my eardrum washed out with metho and they said they were taking nineteen people to a Dutch place where they were going to establish a hospital and would include me as bootmaker, and may be able to do something with my ear. So we marched back to Batavia to this Dutch medical school. The commandant was a Dr Schmidt. He gave a hell of a lecture. Our little doctor was only in his twenties and didn't say a word but we had a medical sergeant who said, "I've listened intently to you Dr Schmidt, now we'll give you our story; there's nineteen Australians here and if you want something done, ask politely and we'll probably do it for you. We're quite prepared to pull our weight, we'll do our share on the understanding that none of us will take orders from a Dutchman. Now tell your fellow officers, NCOs and other ranks if they try to give orders they'll get hit in the mouth." Dr Schmidt started to argue and the medical sergeant told him not to. Two or three Dutch tried, and got hit in the mouth and from then on they left us alone. If they wanted assistance they only had to ask and we'd do it.

'While we were there one of the Javanese was allowed in with a cartful of supplies for sale, and as we were getting 10 cents a day if we were working, that enabled a man to buy an egg, a roll of tobacco which was like a coir mat, or a banana; with a week's pay you'd do well. (By the finish of the war it took you twenty-seven days' pay to buy an egg, but I was still able to buy one.)

'Before we came to that camp we'd been to Bandung, packed sixteen in a small room, sleeping on a tile floor, 6 foot by 2 foot per man which left a 3-inch strip around the wall. I was between two 6-foot blokes, every time you wanted to turn over you'd give them a nudge to turn. It was cold as hell at night and it wasn't bad sleeping between them, just hot in the daytime. We didn't have toilet paper, only freezing cold water to clean ourselves; one bloke claimed he'd had piles for months and after the first dash of this water they'd gone – probably up near his heart.

'We weren't there very long but though discipline was tough, we were alert to opportunity. They'd bring a ration truck in and when the Australians had to unload it we'd form a line alongside it. Once they were bringing white bread into the cookhouse and the next thing there was a loaf of bread gone from one end of the line to the other like lightning, a couple of onions, a couple of carrots. We never unloaded a truck without getting our share; they used to bring in half pigs and the bloke working in there said he'd pinch a chop, so I said take two, one off each half as some smart person might put the two halves together and notice one chop was missing. There were four of us – the two Withers brothers, one a warrant officer, the other a sergeant, Sergeant Kelly and myself, a private – we shared everything, we'd count up what we got for the day and share it out.

'Reg Withers was a jeweller and watchmaker from Rockhampton, there were a few watches about, some rusted, we'd buy or scrounge them, give them to Reg, then he'd set about making a watch from the parts. Sergeant Kelly was the best Malay speaker so he was the salesman, he'd walk past a guard, look at the time and the guard would immediately want to buy the watch.

'They'd haggle about the price and when the guard was about due to knock off (they'd do one hour on and two hours off), he explained he wanted to have it valued. We knew he wouldn't pinch it because stealing carried the death penalty in their army, so he took it to Reg to have it valued, came back and bought it. Reg Withers said, "If any of you buggers are religious you'd better start praying now that the watch keeps going, otherwise we're in trouble".

'At Bicycle Camp at one stage the Japs made a wire netting compound between a couple of huts and they brought 300–400 ducks in. They used to hold a count, morning and night and they had a few blokes in charge and the count kept getting smaller and smaller. The guards put on a bit of an act, one of our blokes said, "Come round here". They'd cut a couple of holes in the wire netting, putting feathers and blood around it and said "the weasels" had been there. But the count kept getting smaller and smaller so the Japs decided to kill the lot and give them to the cookhouse to cook for the prisoners, little knowing that most of the Australian prisoners had been eating duck for a week.'

Leuwiliang

Many old warriors, perhaps all, go back in their minds to the battlefield where, perhaps for the only time in their lives, they walked knowingly towards death. Some go further than the mind, they set off physically on an odyssey to the field where they stood fast in their youth, even when they knew that all their efforts and bravery and fear were probably in vain.

Des Jackson from Tasmania was a young corporal with C Company 2/3rd Machine Gun Battalion put ashore on Java from the *Orcades*. Forty years later, on Saturday 13 April 1985, he returned with Privates Charles Chapple and Alan Whelan. They had been together on 4 March 1942 when their company had joined battle with the Japanese at an isolated spot named Leuwiliang.

The three men, now in their sixties, walked along the road they had then travelled. 'The track was flanked by substantial fruit and coconut plantations in 1942, whereas now in 1985 they are all gone and the road is flanked by houses and shops, very different to what my memory of it has been for all these years.'

But the depth of memory goes deeper than that. They remembered the old bridge that had been blown up in 1942 and a small, pot-holed road branching off in a southerly direction. 'I knew that if we were going to find the area where the battle had been fought it must be down that road. There was always the possibility, of course, that the road that we'd known which was just a dirt track had been extinguished altogether and didn't exist any more.'

An elderly woman told them that only a short distance away, 'Where the cows are', there was a Japanese grave. An old man said 'very positively' that during the war a battle had been fought further down the road between Australians and Japanese and that six Australians who had been killed were buried under a house that had been built since that war where the battle had been fought.

'We could clearly see the two little hillocks and the coconut plantation where the 10th Platoon had been. It was open country and when we were there in 1942 it was a very dangerous stretch of land because the Japanese were able to enfilade it and shoot at anybody who tried to walk along it. The hillocks were greatly overgrown and also a lot of houses had been built. The smaller hillock where headquarter's platoon had been was almost completely covered with very high trees and the paddyfield which had surrounded the two hillocks had disappeared.

'When we were there in 1942 there'd been only the one house. With great pride the people took us to this one house and showed us the bullet holes which were put in from the Japanese side during the fight, about thirty or forty holes all told. They indicated the house under which the six Australians who were killed were buried and their bodies still remain. They took us up on to the hillock where 12 Platoon had been and showed us where the Japanese dead were buried. They didn't tell us how many, they simply said "the Japanese grave", an almost circular piece of concrete from where 12th Platoon fought.'

Des walked over the whole of that hill. 'We saw the spot where Jack Hill was killed, and where Shorty Moys was killed. That fight went on from just before dawn until dusk. We started pulling out at about four o'clock and most of the reserve platoon came forward to the hillocks and started firing to help us pull out. The Japs seemed to be a bit confused. They'd left a holding force in their original position, and were trying to work their way around us in an easterly direction. When we came down that 600-yard stretch of open road we had no casualties at all and we got all our wounded out: we couldn't bring our dead out because it was just too dangerous to do so. We were extremely fortunate to get out at all, let alone get out with our casualties. We withdrew to 10 Platoon and gradually withdrew to the main road and the trucks came up and they removed us from the area.'

The US 131st Field Artillery on Java had been given orders that one man only was to be on each tank and one on each truck, and every vehicle was to keep moving all day long in the hope that they would create an illusion of much strength. Whereas they, like the Australians and the Dutch, were no strength at all.

In earlier days captives were put to death as a sporting spectacle for the victors; in the 20th century, one nation denied
their captives the necessities of life. Food was what they could
scrape up, literally that is, and medication in the historically
virulent tropics was nil.

In the diary he kept during his time with the Japanese, Dr
Edward Dunlop recorded several acerbic comments on his
fellow officers. While still in Java, on 13 October 1942, he
claims that he attempted to collect money from officers to buy
nutritious food for the men who were already falling ill from
malnutrition. But most of the officers resisted. It was the first
but not the last time in the long incarceration that he was to
become disgruntled with the comfortable few for their indifference to the undeserved pain and misery of the many. He
wrote, tongue in cheek, 'Where is that principle: "my horse,
my man, myself"?'

Berhala Island, Borneo, 1943

'It was all bad in Borneo.'

The much-loved doctor, Lieutenant Colonel Sheppard

BERHALA ISLAND, AT THE entrance to Sandakan (Borneo), had been an old leper settlement and gaol until early in 1943, when it became a holding camp for British and Australian prisoners of war who were to build an aerodrome for the Japanese. Whereas Australians on other islands had become prisoners after being overrun by invading Japanese, here the Japanese had seized the island of Borneo and had shipped in men already made captive elsewhere to labour for them. Some POWs were taken from Singapore to Berhala Island and were joined there by some captive white settlers of Borneo; some professional 'old hands' such as doctors and personnel (European, Chinese and native) from vital services were left unfettered in Sandakan while some Australian POWs were shipped in from Singapore and billeted at Mile 8, a camp 8 miles out from Sandakan. The stage was set for a three-way intelligence network to flourish between the prisoners on Berhala Island, the free settlers at Sandakan and the POWs at Mile 8 camp.

The scenario was the stuff of Hollywood movies of the Errol Flynn era, except that this was real life, and real death for the daring men involved. Among the early escapees who fled the holding camp at Berhala Island was Warrant Officer II Walter Wallace, 2/15th Field Regiment, who escaped on 30 April 1943 together with Signallers Harvey and McKenzie-Mackay, both of 8th Division Signals Unit.

Wallace's party escaped to the mainland of Borneo but Harvey and McKenzie-Mackay left Wallace after an argument and the two men were later betrayed by natives to the Japanese, who shot Harvey and clubbed McKenzie-Mackay to

455

death; their bodies were taken to the aerodrome in Sandakan but the officer in charge, Captain Hoshijima, would not permit them to be buried there beside other deceased POWs because he classified escapees as criminals. In the meantime, Wally Wallace had moved to the Sandakan area and on 11 May 1943 he arrived at the house of Heng Joo Ming, one of the patriots who wanted the Japanese off their island.

Another prisoner with escape in mind at this early stage was Captain R.K. MacLaren MC, who had served with a Scottish Regiment in World War I, migrated to Queensland after that war where he again enlisted, this time in the AIF in the 2/10th Field Workshops. He was then aged 42. McLaren met His Excellency, Governor C.R. Smith of North Borneo, who had also been imprisoned and learned of Corporal Koram, 'a Mata Mata (policeman), number 142'. Koram, 'a man who could be trusted', the Governor assured MacLaren, had to work for the Japanese by day as a guard, but he assisted the British at night. He lived in Sandakan and was daily taken by boat across to Berhala Island.

MacLaren said, when he saw number 142 Corporal Koram come on duty, 'Governor Smith said you can help me'. The guard replied that at midnight he would be on his beat up and down the lines and on that night, Corporal Koram drew a map showing where escapees should go – 140 miles east of Sandakan to the island of Tawi Tawi (towards the Philippines) where guerillas were fighting the Japanese.

When MacLaren had first arrived at Berhala Island at the entrance to Sandakan Harbour, he had met an old friend, Sergeant R.J. Kennedy, who had served in the navy in World War I, and was now in the 2/10th Ordnance Workshop. The two men joined members of a wood-carrying party and this enabled them to move all over the small island. At the leper colony on the northern part of the island they found a small boat which they noted for the future. Another prisoner, Major Rex Blow, 2/10th Field Workshops, now joined the party as did his mate, Lieutenant Charles Wagner, 2/18th Battalion, and Sergeant Rex Butler, 8th Division Signals. Butler, 'a tall thin grazier from South Australia', had once been a buffalo shooter in the Northern Territory 'and was capable of shooting out a buffalo's eye at 50 metres', according to Wally Wallace. He was tough and was ideal for the task of paddling a canoe from Borneo to the Philippines.

In the meantime, on the mainland of Borneo, Wallace the escapee had been hiding in the house of Heng Joo Ming in Sandakan and on the evening of 13 May, Heng led him along a trail to meet Police Inspector Ernesto Lagan. With Lagan was Mu Sing, a Filipino-Chinese who owned powered boats used for carting sandalwood in peace time, but now he was using them to help Allied servicemen. These two men were both loyal sympathisers. The three men went to a rendezvous where a boat was to meet them to take Wallace to the Sulu group of islands, but the boat was not there and Wallace had to be brought back to his hideout. Shortly after this the Japanese raided Heng Joo Ming's house but Wallace was not discovered, and after another failed rendezvous he was secretly taken by boat back to Berhala Island on 10 May 1943.

Mata Mata (Corporal) Koram had arranged that when he was coming on duty and expecting to meet the escapees, he would mew like a cat, and this night, after Heng Joo Ming heard the signal, Wallace was handed over to Mata Mata Koram who took him to a prepared hideout on the island. Shortly afterwards Wallace made his way up to the perimeter wire of the POW compound and contacted three prisoners who were sitting inside the fence. He warned them not to look his way but he asked that Charlie Wagner be brought to the fence. Wagner wandered over, pointed out the guard positions to Wallace and arranged a meeting place outside the wire when Wagner would be on a wood-gathering party. The two men met, along with Captain Ray Steele, 2/15th Field Regiment, and Lieutenant Blow and Major L.M. Gillon of 2/10th Field Regiment, all of whom had been planning escape since Changi days. The men learnt of the conditions at the Mile 8 Camp at Sandakan and realised the transfer of the prisoners from Berhala Island to Sandakan was imminent and that it would be far more difficult to escape from the mainland than it would be from Berhala Island.

The actual prison camp on Berhala Island was enclosed by a barbed-wire fence, 160 yards back from the sea. The Japanese guard room was outside the enclosure between the camp and the beach; it was necessary to pass this guard room to get to the latrines which were the native variety erected on stilts above the sea water. These latrines must be used before the gates were locked each evening and their use during the night was forbidden.

The men planned to wander past the sentry at dusk to the latrines as was usual before the curfew at night, except that this night they would squat down at the latrines, hoping they would not be missed at roll-call; if their absence was noted they would excuse themselves as suffering from dysentery. MacLaren was to be in charge of one party and Rex Blow the other, each party was to make their separate ways out of the camp, up through the jungle of a mountain slope and meet at a small reservoir which was the lepers' water supply and there they would compare notes before separating. MacLaren's group was to be the first away.

On 4 June 1943 the Japanese brought a barge across to Berhala and ordered the prisoners to be ready for transfer to the main camp at Sandakan the following day. MacLaren, Butler and Kennedy knew they had to escape that night or their plans would fail. At dusk, each went separately through the main gate, past the sentry at the guardhouse and down to the latrines. When darkness fell, they hurried off, dug up their hidden equipment and gathered near the leper colony with Blow's party. All now went to the beach where Blow and Wagner were waiting to help them with the lepers' dugout canoe. A bundle of bits of old iron had served the lepers for an anchor and now, as the men hauled this up, the noise awoke the leper colony and the lepers hurried down to the water.

Seeing their boat being stolen they cried 'we need our boat to catch fish' but the three escapees had paddled off while

Blow and Wagner stole back into the jungle and joined Steele and Gillon. At 2 a.m. that morning Koram, the guard, brought Wallace from his hiding place to join the other members of the party still on the island.

The men in the lepers' canoe followed the route of the Moro pirates of old as they paddled for eight days, over 200 miles until they reached the island of Tawi Tawi. Filipinos there told them that Japanese had recently landed and burnt down Batu Batu, the main town of Tawi Tawi.

At Batu Batu they were met by the legendary Lieutenant Colonel Allessandro Suarez, late of the Filipino constabulary but now commander of the guerilla force working with the American infiltrating forces. That night, the Filipino guerillas tapped out a message to Australia stating that three men claiming to be escaped POWs of the 8th Division AIF, and who had escaped from the Japanese, had arrived on Tawi Tawi.

In the meantime, their five comrades left behind at Berhala Island were preparing to make their move, thanks to Alberto Quadra (disguised as an inter-island trader but actually an NCO in the Filipino guerilla army). His brother, Bernard Quadra, lived in Sandakan and was in contact with the members of the Sandakan underground under the control of the two Australians, Captain L.C. Matthews, AIF, and the civilian doctor, J.P. Taylor, an 'old hand' in the area.

Corporal Koram was an active member of this group as was the police man, Inspector Ernesto Lagan, the Quadra brothers and many others. On the night of 24 June 1943 the five escapees heard the cry of a cat outside their hideout. It was Mata Mata Koram and Alberto Quadra who had come from Sandakan in a compit (a 24-foot boat) on a 'trading mission' and would be returning to Tawi Tawi in a few days' time. Two nights later the five men set off through the jungle, along the top of the mountain and were met by Mohamet Salleh, a night-watchman and friend of Koram, who led them down to the beach. At 9 p.m. they boarded the compit, hoisted sail and left Berhala Island and Sandakan behind. On 29 June they saw the lush green jungle of Tawi Tawi and there the five gaunt soldiers received a spontaneous welcome with food and fruit 'showered' upon them. With the crowd milling around them they were led for several miles along a narrow road to Colonel Suarez's headquarters where they met their other three comrades MacLaren, Butler and Kennedy.

On 1 July 1943 the eight Australians were taken on strength into the 125th Infantry Regiment of the US Forces in the Philippines. Captain R.E. Steele was appointed assistant executive and training officer, Lieutenant C.A. Wagner regimental intelligence officer, Lieutenant R. Blow CO 1st Battalion, Lieutenant L.M. Gillon 2IC 1st Battalion, Sergeant W. Wallace chief instructor to the regiment, Sapper R.J. Kennedy and Privates R.M. Butler and R.K. MacLaren assistant instructors. (A signal was received shortly after this from Australia appointing Wallace to warrant officer and Kennedy, Butler and MacLaren to the rank of sergeants.) The eight men were a small commando group at large, and almost immediately went into action.

Knowing that there was a strong pro-Japanese element on Tawi Tawi, particularly amongst the Moros whose history had been one of piracy, smuggling, pillage and opposition to the Spanish and American colonisation of the Philippines, it was decided that a patrol should be sent to an old Spanish fort which a particular tribe of Moros were occupying 'in an effort to disrupt their activities'. Blow, Gillon, MacLaren and Butler, with three Filipino guerillas, set off on their long march across to a high hill. Women and children hurried into their houses 'with hate and fear clearly showing on their faces' as the patrol went by, and the Australians were uneasy, eyes and ears alert for any unexpected movement. But there was no sound. Rex Blow was in charge of the patrol and gave the order 'Let's go', and with that they waded through the creek, climbed the bank and walked towards the hill when suddenly 'the air about them exploded,' as MacLaren later reported. Gillon was hit in the left arm, hand and leg, with blood gushing from the wounds caused by the fragments of nails fired from the double-barreled shotgun. Rex Blow rushed forward, tommy-gun at the hip, taking cover, as did Butler. MacLaren lay in the open 'firing at anything that moved', while the three Filipino guerillas found a hollow for protection. Firing from both sides was intense and Rex Butler suddenly clasped his hands to his chest and fell forward, MacLaren crawled to his side and Butler said, 'They've got me Jock', and died. With Gillon seriously wounded and Butler dead, the position of the patrol was perilous. One of the three Filipino guerillas with the Australians now ran forward to join the men of the ambush and MacLaren shot him down, while Rex Blow and the ambush leader 'blasted each other' and the Moros retreated up the hill while Blow and MacLaren withdrew and tore their shirts into strips to dress Gillon's wounds. They recovered the personal belongings of Sergeant Rex Butler, the South Australian, but they could not recover his body as now, down to four able men, they began the return to their base carrying Gillon with them through the mangrove and jungle-clad hills to the safety of Batu Batu. When the patrol was withdrawn, Butler's body was recovered by the Moros from the area, they cut off his head which they sold to the Japanese garrison for, it is said, 2000 pesos, and the Japanese displayed this head on a pole as a warning of the fate of those who sided with the guerillas.

In October 1943, orders were received for the Australians to proceed to General Headquarters at Angusan on north-east Mindanao Island to be repatriated to Australia by submarine. On 31 October 1943 the Australians began their trek to Tarawakan where their craft was waiting for them and, as they had done on their arrival, the local people 'showed their affection and loyalty'. Colonel Suarez thanked them for their contribution towards organising the 125th Infantry Regiment from which they were now struck off strength, and two days later they began the second stage of the voyage home.

These men fought more battles to reach their rescue vessel than most men fought in the six years of war, and in doing so, by the law of averages, some must fall. Wallace later reported: 'As daylight broke MacLaren and Wagner decided to reconnoitre the area they were to cross; each one took a line of palms to follow for protection and, as they stealthily moved from tree to tree, a shot suddenly rang out. MacLaren looked across and saw his companion lying on the ground, face downwards. Diving across to him he found blood oozing from Wagner's head. "This is it Mac", Charlie Wagner whispered and died a a few minutes later.' Shortly after Wagner's death, two senior American officers informed the Australians that the rescue submarine was nearby and Australian HQ wanted two men to return for intelligence purposes. No one volunteered to go but it was decided that Kennedy and Wallace should return on the USS *Narwhal* on 29 February 1944 as both were ill, and, as well, Captain Steele was ordered south to fully report on the POW camps in Borneo and Japanese atrocities.

Steele left on the understanding that after making his report to Australian Army Headquarters he would return as soon as possible with supplies of arms and ammunition. As it happened, the changed fortunes of the Pacific War made his return unnecessary. Gillon returned home a short while later, but Blow and MacLaren remained until 22 April 1945.

Both carried a price of 70,000 pesos on their heads and the Japanese regularly published their photos in news bulletins offering rewards for their capture. They played a vital role in the growing strength of guerilla operations on Mindanao which, it was said, greatly aided the American forces when they came ashore in 1945.

Of this gallant band, Steele was promoted to major and mentioned in despatches, Blow received the DSO and Bar and a mention in despatches, Gillon, the DSO and mentioned in despatches. MacLaren was promoted to captain and awarded the MC and Bar and mentioned in despatches, and Wallace received the American Bronze Star medal. Kennedy received a mention in despatches as did Rex Butler and Charlie Wagner posthumously.

Sandakan

Perhaps it is best that we think in mathematical terms, rather than of human forms, if we are to walk back into Borneo. In

1943 when the rations of the sick were reduced, the prisoners of war working at the aerodrome divided their rations so the sick got an equal share. Captain Hoshijima stopped this by compelling the prisoners to cook and eat their midday and evening meal at the drome (as it was always called). The Japanese on Borneo did not provide the sick with any medical supplies other than a small quantity of quinine.

Cruelty was in some ways similar to that the other Australian prisoners were subjected to. 'Almost every guard on the aerodrome carried a wooden stick about 4 feet 6 inches long and 1 to 1½ inches in diameter for beating the prisoners', Lieutenant Roderick Wells later testified. 'Beatings were a daily occurrence. Sergeant Major Asacod was with me on a wood party when he was struck across the ear with a stick and his eardrum was broken. Private Darlington was so badly beaten that his arms were broken; he was bleeding from head, face, arms and legs and was unconscious. He was then tied up and put in a cage 5 feet by 4 feet and 2½ feet from the ground.

'I made complaints to Captain Hoshijima about the use of the cage, the work required from the men, the low rations they were receiving, the lack of footwear and clothes and referred him to the International Conventions. He said he was not interested in International Conventions.'

While the men were on Berhala Island, or Mile 8 Camp on the mainland and in close contact with friendly native police and the free English settlers at Sandakan, they were able to fight on as best they could and they saw their duty as soldiers. But many paid heavily for this, some with their lives, and not until the War Crimes trials were held in Tokyo in 1946 was the truth known. Lieutenant Alexander Weynton, 8th Division Signals, was a witness at these trials and gave evidence of the remarkable resilience of the men who fought a terrible war.

'As a result of a conference between our Intelligence Officer Captain Matthews and other officers I secured materials from natives and from the camp and constructed a wireless set. From November 1942 onwards, I listened to BBC news and disseminated it through camp. When not in use the set was hidden. Corporals Small, Mills and Richards assisted in the working of the set.

'Captain Matthews and Lieutenant Wells were engaged in getting medical supplies into the camp surreptitiously. On 2 May 1943 I had sent a letter to a camp containing 500 British prisoners of war stating that we were going to send them some medical supplies. This letter was intercepted by the Japanese and I was arrested on the following evening of 3 May 1943. I was assaulted by Captain Hoshijima and then made to stand at attention outside the guardhouse from 7.30 p.m. until 10 a.m. the next morning and was then sentenced to fourteen days imprisonment in the cage along with five others. It was not possible for all of us to lie down together, we had to take it in turns. During this period we were not allowed to wash or shave or to leave the cage except to go to latrines. We had no bedclothes. It rained very heavily and for two of the fourteen days I was in the cage I was wet through. At the conclusion of my confinement I was sent to hospital by the medical officer and remained there until I was arrested by the camp commandant on 29 July 1943 and confined in the cage until the morning of 12 August 1943. I was then called before the camp commandant who said that I had a wireless set and that I must tell him where it was. I denied all knowledge of it. I was then sent back to the cage where I remained without food or water and was not allowed to go to the latrines. On 14 August I was bound hand and foot and thrown into a lorry and taken to the Kempei Tai headquarters at Sandakan where I was put into a room and made to sit cross-legged at attention. There were about twenty-five others in the room sitting in the same way, Australian soldiers, English internees and natives. We were compelled to sit in this position from 7 a.m. until 9.30 p.m. and were not allowed to speak to each other. We were allowed to lie down and sleep in this same room from 9.30 p.m. to 7 a.m. but the lights were kept on all the time. For five minutes every morning and afternoon we were made to do physical jerks. If these physical jerks were not carried out to the satisfaction of the guards, the person offending was beaten or was forced to remain in one of the physical jerk positions throughout five or ten minutes. From 14 August until 26 October 1943 I received this treatment except on those occasions when I was taken out for interrogation, or to the toilet.

'I was first taken out for interrogation at 9 a.m. on 16 August 1943, and had to sit cross-legged at attention on the floor. An interpreter and six or seven members of the Kempei Tai were in this room. I was asked what I knew of a radio set in the camp and of the activities of Captain Matthews and Lieutenant Wells. I denied all knowledge of these matters. I was immediately beaten about the head and shoulders with a riding whip. I was again asked the same questions and again denied all knowledge. The Kempei Tai then held me down, tore my shirt off and burnt me under the arms with lighted cigarettes. I was then sent back to the main room to sit at attention again. Three days later I was again taken out for interrogation. I was asked the same questions but still denied all knowledge of the radio set or the activities of the other officers. I was again beaten and burnt as previously. In addition they applied jujitsu holds on me, throwing me around the room and causing me great pain by twisting my arms, head, legs and feet. I was again taken back to the main room. On 28 August 1943 I was taken by the Kempei Tai to another building and was again treated as I had been previously.

'They then placed before me statements which they had obtained from natives stating that I had been outside the camp compound at night securing radio parts. They showed me a diary which had been kept by an officer at our camp. This contained information about the activities of myself and my two assistants, Corporals Mills and Small, in connection with the radio set. They then brought Mills and Small into the room and we all then admitted that we had the radio set in the camp but denied all knowledge of the activities of the other officers. The Japanese continued to interrogate us until 3 a.m. next day. Later the same day Mills and Small were interrogated separately and when their evidence differed in any detail from the evidence that I had given the previous day, we were all beaten up together and made to agree. This went on for four and a half days.'

He was again questioned about Matthews and Wells and denied knowing anything and was then tortured with burning cigarette butts, tacks were put down his fingernails and hammered so that they went into the quick of the nail and he was tied by the wrists to a beam and forced to kneel on the ground with his legs out behind him. A beam was placed over his ankles and two Kempei Tai officers see-sawed on it until he became unconscious. He awoke after a bucket of water had been thrown over him but like Captain Matthews, Doctor Taylor, Lieutenant Wells and Mr Mavor (a civilian) he could not walk for four days after this treatment.

Weynton was taken to Kuching, tried, convicted and sentenced to ten years imprisonment at Outram Road Gaol (Singapore) even though he had never been told of the charge against him.

Lieutenant Wells was arrested on 24 July 1943 and taken to Sandakan Military Police Headquarters where he was confined for three months, the first three weeks in solitary confinement in a cell and the remainder of the time with other prisoners in a room under observation with lights on all night. All clothing was taken from him except for a pair of shorts and he was frequently interrogated and tortured by the Kempei Tai hoping to extract information. He was flogged with a whip and beaten with a wooden sword on three occasions and racked on an improvised rack. 'I was handcuffed and tied to a verandah rafter by a rope passing through the handcuff chain and around the rafter at such a height that on kneeling I was suspended with my knees about 6 inches above the ground. A beam of wood about 4 inches square and 6 feet long was placed behind my knees, and by means of two interrogating officers standing on either end of the rafter enabled my body from the knees upwards to be stretched. Another beam of wood was laid across my ankles and similar pressure applied. The effect was to stretch my arms and legs and almost break the ankle bones by making me kneel with the fore part of my foot on the ground, with the rafter across my ankle on each edge. It pulled all the flesh away from the ankle. After two minutes of this treatment I became unconscious. I was revived by water being thrown over my head. The interrogation was resumed to the accompaniment of a different type of torture which consisted of my head being repeatedly struck in the same place with a small hammer. I was also beaten across the head with a rafter of wood and as a result my middle ear was broken and I have permanently lost my hearing in the one ear.

'On the 16th of August 1943 I was made to consume a quantity of raw rice. They then introduced a hose into my throat and filled me up with water. After about four hours the rice, as it absorbed the water, swelled and stretched the stomach muscles to an extraordinary degree. The rice pulled a large portion of my bowel out through the anus. I asked for medical attention. This was refused.' (Weynton saw Lieutenant Wells within three hours of him being administered the rice treatment.)

All prisoners when not being interrogated were compelled to sit with crossed legs from 7.30 a.m. until 10.30 p.m. 'During the three months' period, our only food was 5 ounces of rice and a small piece of rock salt or a dried fish head each per day.'

On 25 October 1943 twenty-two Australian soldiers including Captain Matthews, Lieutenants Weynton and Wells, five local Europeans and upwards of fifty natives, all in some way involved with the 'underground' movement, were shipped to Kuching, the capital of Sarawak, for trial. The men were tied on deck throughout the whole eight-day voyage and had no cover from the sun, rain and waves that washed over the deck.

Lieutenant Wells: 'I remained at Kuching for five months until I was tried on 29 February 1944 by court-martial consisting of Lieutenant General Baba. Captain Matthews and a number of others were tried with me. We were not given a defending officer nor told what charge was laid against us. Captain Matthews asked what the charge was but was not told; he also asked for a defending officer but his request was refused. We had previously been compelled to sign or thumb-print statements in Japanese. These had not been translated before we signed them and we did not know what was in them. No evidence was given, we were merely questioned on these statements and the trial was over within half an hour. Thirteen prisoners of war who had escaped and were recaptured were sentenced to terms of imprisonment up to six years. Eight others were charged with planning to escape and were sentenced to imprisonment for up to four years.

'Matthews, myself and three other ranks were sentenced two days later, me to twelve years' penal servitude with hard labour, Matthews was sentenced to death. A firing squad was waiting for him as I left the court and about ten minutes later I heard the sound of firing coming from the direction of the Roman Catholic cathedral about 100 yards away from the court. Eight natives were also executed that morning but the Japanese said they were killed with the sword. On 8 March 1944 I left Kuching for Outram Road Gaol.'

The March

'There's little you can say to a mother.'

Private Nelson Short, 2/18th Battalion

IN THE LAST YEAR of the war the islands of Japan were besieged; American navy and air force had practically isolated the warring nation and left its several captured outposts unprotected and unable to procure food or ammunition. In 1945 when the Japanese on Borneo saw that the war was going against them they began to send their prisoners on death marches; the men staggered rather than marched from the camp at Sandakan to Ranau across the mountains, a distance of about 125 miles. Private Nelson Short, 2/18th Battalion, was one of the six survivors of almost 2400 men who began the worst march any Australian has known, one of the most damnable marches in military history.

'The fittest went on the first march. Parties of fifty carrying a bucket of rice. Half an hour for every man to be out of the camp and they carried them on bits of stretchers and whatever they had to get the sick out and all sat in this big padang in front of the Japanese headquarters. [Warrant Officer] Sticpewich was ordered to cook up for them what was left, if you could call it a meal. Just a bit of stuff. A plane came over, a monstrous Catalina flying boat, at the time the interpreter Osiwa was saying, "All men who can stand on their feet be prepared to march". You could see the airmen looking down at us. No shot was fired. I often wondered about that.

'By evening they had the men all ready to march. There were a terrible lot of First World War diggers with us and this old bloke said to me, "Don't go with them. Stop here. The war is over. Don't go to die." Both my legs were swelled up with beriberi and ulcers on both feet as well as the sinews hanging

469

out of toes of both feet and the old man said, "Stop here. All these men are too sick to walk." But I had to go. They burnt the camp to the ground, set it alight as the men left. Someone said the Japs are going down to the boats. "They'll send a truck to pick up these blokes who can't walk." We all believed if they turned us to the left as we got down the bitumen road, that the war was over and we were going down to the boat. But it was to the right we went, straight in to the jungle. That's as far as the bitumen road ran. It was no distance before the blokes started to drop out, never to be seen again, the Japs called faster! faster! going through swamps, mud, and blokes were dying, two dropped out and they were put together and the bloke with the machine gun coming on behind us shot them. And that happened all the way through, we were bombed all the way on the march.

'Jack Sue, an Australian Chinese who secretly went in to Sandakan for information for the authorities, says that at times he was so close to us on the second march he could have touched us; he described what we looked like. "Like skeletons, horses which had been starved to death." That was true. But nothing could be done it was said. But he would have a radio. Couldn't word have been got out about what was happening to us? But this would have aborted his whole mission I suppose.'

Nelson's legs and feet were rotting. 'They gave us odd rests, but often up to twenty and more blokes couldn't get to their feet when we were ordered to move on and they were shot where they lay. You had to keep going to live.'

'Men dropped out from the march, too weak to carry on. They were immediately shot', Private Keith Botterill, 2/19th Battalion, remembers. Keith had arrived at Sandakan Camp in July 1942. At the beginning of 1944 rations had been reduced to 5 ounces of weevily rice and a small quantity of tapioca daily. Tropical ulcers, beriberi and dysentery became prevalent, and, from the end of 1944 until Botterill left Sandakan in February 1945, men were dying at the rate of seven per day. A total of 400 had died when he left to begin the march.

In February of that last year of the war, 350 Australians and 120 English prisoners were sent from Sandakan to march to Ranau. 'They left daily in parties of forty or fifty.' Keith was in the third party. 'We were accompanied by an officer, three NCOs and fifteen privates as a guard. We had to carry their ammunition and food as well as our own food. Men dropped out from the march as they became too weak to carry on. They were immediately shot. I saw four men shot by the Japanese sergeant major when they fell out from the march. At one time the only food that forty of us had between us for three days was six cucumbers.' Keith gave evidence at the War Crimes Tribunal in Tokyo, 1946.

'When we were about a week out of Ranau we crossed a large mountain, and while we were making the crossing two Australians, Private Humphries and a corporal whose name I cannot remember, were suffering from beriberi, malaria and dysentery and became too sick to travel. A Japanese private shot the corporal and a Japanese sergeant shot Humphries. Altogether we lost five men on that hill.

'As we were going along men would fall out as they became too weak to carry on. We would go on and then shortly after hear shots and men squealing out; when this occurred there were always Japanese behind us, and it was they who did the shooting. Although I did not see the bodies of any men who had been shot in the parties that had gone before us, often I could smell them. Of the fifty who started out from Sandakan in my party, thirty-seven reached Ranau. The trip took us seventeen days, we went straight through, marching every day. The Japanese who came with us were in very good physical condition, they had more rations than we did on the march; a couple of them had malaria, but they were left behind at the outposts and I saw these men come along six weeks later when they felt fit enough.

'After we had reached Ranau I was one of a party of Australians sent back 26 miles towards Sandakan to carry rice for the Japanese and troops coming on the next parties. The journey took us five days – three days out and two days back.

'Each of us had to carry one 45-pound bag of rice on his back over hills and swampy ground. As a result of the hard conditions, several men died carrying this rice. We carried many men who were too weak to walk back to camp. Private Shear was shot 9 miles from Ranau and Private Alberts and a corporal were bayoneted by the Japanese 20 miles from Ranau. They were too weak to carry rice and fell out. I saw the killing myself; the men were on the ground at the time calling out, "Don't shoot me", and putting their hands up, but nevertheless they were shot and left lying on the ground.' Botterill was one of the fittest men in camp and believes this was because he used to go into the gardens for tapioca 'which we would cook up and make a decent meal of it'.

'In March 1945 two Australians, Crease and Cleary, attempted to escape from Ranau but were recaptured and tortured. They were screaming with pain. They were tied up in the open in full view of the natives for two weeks. Cleary had no clothes and was tied up by a chain around his neck. He died within ten minutes of being released.

'Bashings were an everyday occurrence at Ranau. For taking some food from a food dump, Private Murray was tied up outside the guard-house and on the same afternoon taken by a medical orderly and another guard to the cemetery and bayoneted to death. Deaths were occurring from starvation, dysentery, malaria and beriberi but we were given no medical supplies. In recording deaths the Japanese only allowed us to write malaria or dysentery.

'Of the 470 prisoners that had left Sandakan in February when I set off, six only were alive in June, the remainder had died or been killed. On the other hand, the Japs were all in good condition except for a few who had malaria. They had plenty of food and none were suffering from malnutrition.

'In June 1945 a further party of 140 arrived at Ranau from Sandakan. Nelson Short, 2/18th Battalion, was one of those in this party. When they had left Sandakan there were 600 of them, but the remainder had perished on the march.'

At the War Crimes Tribunal held in Tokyo in 1946 a

statement from one Ishii Fujio was tendered in which the ex-soldier tells of the murder of the prisoners left behind at Sandakan Camp after all men who could walk had been sent off on the track to Ranau.

'I was present when the eight prisoners of war that were left behind in the No.1 camp were killed. This is what happened. Second Lieutenant Suzuki and Sergeant Iwabe ordered us [here he named six other Japanese soldiers] to take the prisoners of war to the hospital. This proved to be a lie. We had carried two prisoners of war out and gone about 100 yards from the hut when Second Lieutenant Suzuki said to let those two men walk and go back with the stretchers and get two more. We only had two stretchers so had to bring them up two at a time. As we went back for the other prisoners of war I heard shots and thought that the prisoners must have attempted to escape. I found out later that they had been killed in cold blood.'

The young soldier was then ordered to fire on the next two prisoners. 'Everyone fired at least one shot and most of us two. I personally did, as my first shot entered below the breastbone and did not kill the man. At the time the prisoners of war were killed they were lying on the ground too sick to move and so did not have their hands tied behind their backs. They had no chance to escape and did not make any effort to do so. The same procedure was followed as the rest of them were brought up, and all the bodies were buried in the one hole. I did not have a rifle at the time, but when Suzuki had fired he gave me his to use.'

In December 1945 Sergeant Major Morizuma made a statement to the War Crimes Tribunal regarding the fate of those prisoners who remained at Sandakan when the last party left to go to Ranau.

Morizuma said that after the prisoners marched out on 29 May 1945 there were 291 POWs left under his charge. He made no provisions for their shelter or comfort. They were left out in the open and on 9 June seventy-five POWs were sent away out of that camp with the pretence of sending them to Ranau. He knew that they would be disposed of en route. On

13 July he, in company with Lieutenant Noritake, took twenty-three prisoners of war out to the airdrome and killed them. On this date there were approximately thirty prisoners left in the camp area. He said he 'didn't bother killing them, they would die in time'. They were given no food or water – just left to die. Out of the 291, all were accounted for except 163. He stated that the Javanese coolies had buried approximately 150 prisoners of war in that time and that the rest had all died.

'In November 1945 I was present with the investigation team that investigated into the Ranau area. I indicated the camp areas and graves of the POWs to this team. About 280 bodies were recovered.'

'Did you see these bodies or parts of them?' he was asked. 'Yes, I saw their remains and the greater percentage of them, over 80 per cent of the remains had their skulls bashed in, jaw bones broken and the facial part broken in. They had been brutally murdered.' 'Have you heard anything about a massacre of prisoners at Ranau on the 10th of June 1945?' 'Yes, I was present at the investigation when a statement was made by a sergeant and guards who massacred eight prisoners of war on that afternoon.' 'Of the seventy-five prisoners of war who were alleged to have left Sandakan on the 9th of June, did any ever reach Ranau while you were there?' 'No, a guard by the name of Itchikoawa, sole survivor of the prisoner of war guards, had made a statement at Jesselton to the effect that these prisoners of war were all disposed of before they got to the 30 Mile.'

At Ranau the survivors of the march died quickly and those that were left were killed. John Hore, one man who escaped, was recaptured, killed and his body was placed on the POW camp sign. Hoshijima and Watanabe viewed the body there. 'I think Hore was shot in the chest by Hinata Genzo', Watanabe volunteered during the tribunal.

'Prior to that escape, prisoners were going under the wire at the end of the camp through a drain pipe to get food. These men were taken back to HQ and placed in the guardhouse and were later put in the cage, as we viewed this as a serious offence. I saw the men in the cage but had nothing to do with their treatment. I know that one who was very sick died in the cage. Hoshijima was in charge and gave orders to Noritake as to the treatment of these prisoners.'

William Sticpewich escaped and although efforts were made to recapture him he avoided the searchers.

'Three days after Sergeant Major Sticpewich escaped at Ranau, seventeen sick prisoners were taken on stretchers up the hill to the cemetery and killed. I was in charge and Sergeant Okada and approximately ten Formosan guards were also present at the killing. After these seventeen men were killed there were about sixteen left in the camp and these were also shot on 1 August 1945. Eleven of these were taken about 100 metres along the road and shot. Sergeant Major Tsuji with a fresh lot of about fifteen Formosan guards shot the second batch. These two killings were both at 1000 hours on 1 August 1945.

'I do not know the names of the prisoners killed. Picone, Cook [Captain G.R. Cook, Australian General Base Depot, Singapore], Chopping, Oatshot, Daniels [an English doctor], Maskey and Evans may have been among them. At the same time, Sergeant Beppu with ten Formosan guards took five officers about 100 metres towards Ranau where the party shot the five officers behind the rice store. Sergeant Iwabe was out searching for Sticpewich and had nothing to do with the killings. I did not know that it was a general order from Army HQ to kill POWs. My orders came from my commander, Takakura.'

When the main body of officers was removed from Sandakan to Kuching in 1943 several officers remained with the men, one being the humane and brave leader Captain G.R. Cook, a schoolteacher from Mittagong (NSW) in civilian life. He died on 12 August 1945; the two doctors, Captains D. Picone (2/10th Field Regiment) and R. Jeffrey (2/10th AGH) and the padres Thompson and Wardale-Greenwood had died earlier.

On 15 August the war ended.

Colonel Harry Jackson remembered, 'At the end, the Japanese burnt all the compounds at Sandakan. They took the people who were too sick to march and laid them on open ground to die. They had been left behind from the second march because it was thought they would not live long and would be a hindrance. Fifty-three men were still alive, twenty-three of them could walk. Lieutenant Noritake was very ill at this stage. He was always afraid the POWs would see the Japanese out and decided the walking cases should now die, so on 13 July 1945 the twenty-three very sick walking cases were taken to the aerodrome where they were lined up against the air-raid shelter and killed by a firing party. The bodies were thrown into slit trenches and Javanese coolies completed the burial.' Later, when Colonel Jackson was investigating the deaths, he asked a young native to speak of this. 'When the firing party returned to the camp, I asked one of the guards what caused the shots I had heard. When he told me they [the Japanese] had been shooting ducks, I asked how many and was told twenty-three.'

After this murder, thirty men remained alive and this figure was reduced to twenty-eight by nightfall on 13 July. They were not given any food and those who could crawl attempted to help their comrades. They were too sick to appreciate the fact that the hated Noritake died on 18 July. There were five POWs alive when the waterboy took some tapioca to the men on that day. He said they told him they'd had no food for a week and asked when he would bring them more. 'He could see they were just skin and bone and badly affected by malaria and dysentery, beriberi and tropical ulcers. That was the last occasion he visited the men. At 7 a.m. on 7 August he saw the guards moving into the compound and he climbed a tree to get a better view. He could see there was only one POW alive. He recognised him as a "tall, thin, dark man" to whom he had once given salt and received a tattered pair of shorts in return. He was much thinner now and only wore a loin cloth. He was being coaxed along to a trench drain, Morizuma was the prime figure and some guards had shovels. The POW was made to kneel and a black cloth tied around his eyes, his hands not tied. Morizuma decapitated him and pushed the body with his foot into the trench where the head already lay. The guards then shovelled earth into the trench and covered the remains.'

The Mile 8 camp was left for the jungle to reclaim when, on 20 August 1945, the day Japan surrendered, Sergeant Major Morizuma and the guards left the camp and headed towards Ranau. In the topsy-turvy absurdity of war they too were stumbling towards the unknown. They died unsung by their own people, as losers.

Ishii Fujio (who had been part of the group who killed that last of the men left on stretchers at No.1 Camp, Sandakan) avoided another killing later on. 'The day that the rest of the prisoners of war were killed in the 110 Mile Camp [the point where the march from Sandakan to Ranau ended] I was out looking for the Australian Sergeant Major Sticpewich who had escaped. Our orders were to shoot Sergeant Major Sticpewich on sight. When I returned to camp about 2 August all the prisoners of war were dead. Although I have heard nothing, I should say that from my knowledge of the Japanese the probability is that the balance of the prisoners of war were shot at Sandakan the same as they were elsewhere.'

Evidence of the manner of death of many Australian soldiers was given by eye-witnesses. Some mentioned the Kempei Tai, the Japanese military police. Three Chinese, Chen Kay, Chin Kin and Lo Tong, who lived 15 miles from Sandakan gave evidence at the War Crimes Tribunal that in June 1945 a large number of Australian and other Allied servicemen were being marched along the road from the prisoner of war camp, Sandakan. 'They arrived at the 15-1/2 Mile Post at approximately eleven o'clock in the morning and cooked a meal. As many were very sick all the party rested until about 5.30 p.m. when the Japanese guards ordered the men to march. All the men got up with the exception of seven who were too ill to walk and had been using sticks. Two Japanese guards and one Malay soldier remained behind with the seven Allied servicemen and started to urge the seven men along, kicking them and hitting them with the sticks the servicemen had carried [to help them walk].

'Although the men were very weak the Japanese guards managed to urge the soldiers about 30 yards along the road. The two Japanese guards then took the rifle from the Malay soldier and urging the men off the road, commenced to shoot them in the back. The men were then in the rear of Chin Kin's house. Four of the men were killed instantly and two were wounded. One man escaped and hid himself a little further along the road. After the shooting, which took place about 6 p.m., the two Japanese guards and the Malay soldier continued their march without examining the soldiers, possibly believing them all to have been killed. The soldier who managed to hide himself and who we believe was an Australian was found by a Kempei Tai soldier the next day at about 2 p.m. He shot the two men who were still alive through the head. The shooting of the two men took place as the three of us were digging a grave for the four men who had been shot the previous evening and we all saw the shooting take place.

'The Kempei Tai soldier then left the spot where we buried the six soldiers and started looking around. We then heard a shot fired. After we completed the burial of the six soldiers we then went to look for the other soldier in the direction where the last shot had been heard. We found the soldier who had been shot through the stomach and was lying dead. We buried him immediately.'

Sergeant Hosotani Naoji of the Japanese Imperial Army admitted to having shot two soldiers at the rear of the house of Chin Kin at the 15-1/2 Mile Post. 'The men were wearing Australian hats but their clothes were torn and I could not recognise them either as English or Australian soldiers.'

Corporal Katayama of Okimura Unit was in charge of the last group of marchers from Sandakan which was composed of sick prisoners. 'At the time of the march I was living at 15-1/2 Mile Post because I was sick with malaria. About the middle of June, as Corporal Katayama came past the 15-1/2 Mile Post he said to me [Hosotani] that if there were any stragglers I was to shoot them. I was sleeping at the time the Japanese soldiers came by with the Allied soldiers. I heard shots but did not get up because I was sick from malaria. Chen Ten Choi and another man came to my house the next day and reported that some Allied soldiers had been shot. I came out of the house and saw Corporal Katayama who told me that if there were any Allied soldiers remaining behind that I was to kill them, as he was going on. I found seven war prisoners dead, apparently killed by Katayama's men. I ordered the natives to bury the bodies. On the way back to my hut I saw two prisoners sitting down. They had beriberi. I shot the two soldiers in the head because Corporal Katayama told me to. I was too sick to bury the bodies so I asked Chen Kay to bury them.

'Nakao, an interpreter of the Kempei Tai unit, told me he had shot a prisoner at the 17 Mile Post the same day as I shot the two prisoners. I did not shoot any other prisoners but I was told Allied soldiers were pushed off a truck at the 15 Mile Post and shot as they lay on the ground by guards from the Okimura Unit. They eliminated them because they could not walk to Ranau.'

Hosotani had also killed five Chinese. 'Captain Nakata, OC Sandakan Kempei Tai, ordered me to shoot five Chinese because he said they had been collaborating with a guerilla group. They had given the guerillas money to buy food and supplies and Chinese were getting information from them concerning Japanese dispositions. I shot Sui Chong and Tan Pak An on 27 May 1945. The other three were handed over to me and I shot them about the middle of June 1945. I shot the first two Chinese near the 1-1/2 Mile Post in the rubber plantation.'

Lieutenant Watanabe remembered the total destruction of Sandakan Camp on 29 May 1945. 'They were burnt by us. A POW was only allowed to take what he could actually carry, the rest was left behind and destroyed. This was all done on Takakura's orders, and I was present while the destruction was carried out. I do not think that the destruction of the medical supplies was humane or lawful.'

That night the prisoners heard what was required by the

Japanese: every man who could walk had to be ready, assembled by six o'clock. 'We were then in the open with no protection whatever in the area of No. 2 camp', Sticpewich recalled. 'Parties were formed in groups of fifty, Jap guards in position in front and rear of the parties and no prisoner was to be allowed to lag or to escape. The parties then had to march. The guards were going through the sick and trying to make them stand, belting them to try to get more out the gate. After we moved off I have never seen any of those prisoners who were alive in the camp when we left.'

On 29 May 1945, on orders from Army HQ, Lieutenant Watanabe was ordered to begin the move from Sandakan to Ranau with POWs. 'We were informed that an Australian landing at Sandakan was imminent. Another reason was the severity of air raids. Captain Takakura was IC and I was 2IC for the movement. Lieutenants Suzuki, Fukushima, Sergeant Majors Tsuji, Ichikawa (QM), Tujita (Medical), Kobayashi Ozawa (civilian interpreter) were present (the last named for four days only).

'There were 536 prisoners of war in the party leaving camp, ninety-one English and 439 Australian prisoners.' Sticpewich assumed charge of No.2 group. 'At the end of the asphalt road at the end of the first day I called for nominal rolls of all POWs then present. These were supplied by squad leaders. The first check from nominal rolls revealed a discrepancy in numbers of about six.

'Throughout the march from Sandakan men dropped out along the track, others could not move in the mornings and were left at the previous night's camp,' Watanabe remembered. 'Out of the 536 that had left Sandakan, about 183 POWs arrived at Ranau. Of these 142 were Australians, and also one Australian who died on the last day was carried in dead. Of the 353 unaccounted for, about ninety were ill and put out of their misery by being shot. They asked for death rather than be left behind. I do not know exactly nor do reports show accurately how deaths occurred. Fukushima and Tsuji moved bodies into the jungle. At Takakura's orders soldiers were told to dispose of sick POWs and to see that none were left behind. I was in charge of the disposal of the sick but was not present at the killings. Each morning all those POWs who were unable to travel were placed in groups for Fukushima and Tsuji. The disposal of these POWs was done behind me and I never knew who killed them. I arrived at Ranau on 25 June 1945, and camped at the foot of the mountain. Fifty-four escapees were arrived at as the number unaccounted for on my lists. This was the only way I could account for them. I did not make out any death certificates and I cannot remember any being made out.'

Warrant Officer (later Captain) Sticpewich had remained on the island after the war with the War Graves Commission, assisting to find and recover the dead bodies along the route from Sandakan to Ranau. Shimanouchi, the Japanese Counsel during the International Military Tribunal for the Far East, asked Sticpewich if any prisoners of war deserted or escaped during the march and Sticpewich said, 'I believe so. There were two prisoners of war that evaded recapture and are still alive. There were others who reputedly attempted to escape. At Monyad, where there was a stopping place, a great number of prisoners attempted to escape, fifty-four as stated by Lieutenant Watanabe in his statement; on going back to recover the remains of those prisoners of war I found in a heap forty-seven bodies at this area.'

Sticpewich also acted as guide into the area from Keningau and the Ranau area in November 1945. Shimanouchi asked him, 'What was the condition of the 280 bodies which you discovered?' and Sticpewich replied, 'They were just skeletons, just bones and over 80 per cent of the remains had the skulls bashed in – in fragments'. Shimanouchi: 'Were these bodies buried or were they lying on the ground beside the road?' Sticpewich: 'They had been lying up to 15 or 20 yards off the track. None were buried.' Shimanouchi: 'Were there any indications or evidence that these skulls had been bashed in by those other than Japanese soldiers?' Sticpewich: 'No. And the

Japanese soldiers who have been apprehended have admitted the killing of these prisoners of war throughout the marches, and have been convicted for murdering these prisoners'. Shimanouchi: 'Was there any indication that some vehicle had passed over these bodies, for instance?' Sticpewich: 'The terrain in the country doesn't permit it. There hasn't been a vehicle any further from Sandakan than the 17-mile peg, and from Jesselton to a point 22 miles away these are the nearest motor roads where any vehicle could travel. It is quite impossible, the jungle is too thick, for any vehicle to proceed.'

Sticpewich said that of the men who were left at Sandakan after the first party moved out to Ranau, 90 per cent were unfit. 'If men could walk, they were forced out to work irrespective of their condition. If they could not get the required number, the Japanese would have a full parade of the personnel left in the camp and then an ordinary Japanese soldier would go along and inspect them. If a prisoner had his leg tied up he would probably kick it, the really sick were kicked, and a prisoner who had been crippled had his walking stick taken away; and the guard would go along the line and belt them; and if a doctor objected to a man being sent out, this man's doctor would be subject to a beating from the Japanese soldier for interfering. Approximately 231 deaths occurred in March 1945 at this camp.' By May 1945 there were over 400 stretcher cases. 'Some of them were on sticks or had bones broken, but in such a state they had to be helped along or carried.'

Sticpewich witnessed the end of the camp at Sandakan. 'At about nine o'clock on the morning of 28 May, Captain Takakura, accompanied by Lieutenant Watanabe and Staff Sergeant Ichikawa, who was the QM, inspected the camp. About quarter of an hour after they left, we observed that the old camp was then unoccupied, No.3 and No.2 Camps being burned, destroyed by fire, ammunition dumps being exploded. About half past ten, Captain Takakura called for Captain G.R. Cook and issued the order that he had to clear the camp in ten minutes. We carried the last man out and some gear was left behind. The huts in No.1 Camp were burnt.'

At the International Military Tribunal for the Far East in session in Tokyo Sticpewich was asked how many of the 536 prisoners who left Sandakan on 29 May 1945 reached Ranau, 'One hundred and eighty-three'. As to the distance his party averaged per day on the march, Sticpewich replied, 'Approximately 6½ miles per day, average. The first 30 miles was through marshy country, low land, many creek crossings and heavy going mud and slush. The next 40 miles was in higher country with very short, steep hills and many river crossings. The next 20 miles was over a mountain, and the last 26 miles was mountainous.' 'How many meals per day did you have?' 'There were no camping facilities at our stopping places.'

'On the march did you pass through any other parties?' 'Yes. The parties alternated daily from front to rear, staging right through.' 'Did you observe how the stragglers from parties in front of you were treated?' 'Yes. Stragglers who showed signs of fatigue, who started to drop behind were pushed along with the barrel of a rifle, thumped in the back with the butt of a rifle, and beaten up by the Japanese guards.' 'Would all the men move off after each overnight halt?' 'No. Those who were too sick or ill to move, who were cramped up or suffering from starvation and exposure, were just left behind, and I never saw any of them again. At frequent times during the march I heard Japanese guards referring to whom they had killed that day.' During the 165-mile journey Sticpewich saw stragglers in groups ahead of him beaten. 'A guard would stay with those that were beaten up, knocked down, not fit to travel, and we would not see them again.'

Asked about the camp at Ranau, at the end of their forced march, Sticpewich said no shelter was provided for the men. 'There was a line-up of a morning and afternoon of those who could walk or get on their feet, those too sick to come on parade were checked where they lay.' 'What method was adopted by the guards to see whether a prisoner of war was dead or alive?' 'He would kick him or poke him with a stick.' 'Did you hear anything of the numbers who had taken part in the first Ranau march?' 'Yes. On our arrival at Ranau we were told that our strength would be increased by six, five Australians and one English. These were the survivors of the 470 men of the first march to Ranau which left Sandakan late January and early February 1945. About 240 reached Ranau alive but there were only these six alive when I reached there.'

In reply to the prosecutor's question regarding the work the survivors of the march were forced to do once they reached Ranau, Sticpewich said they covered up to 18 miles in one day carrying rice and vegetables for the Japanese. They died very quickly from the exertion. 'Coming to the 3rd of July of 1945, what happened on that date?' 'I, with nine others, was detailed for a carrying party to accompany the Japanese on a hunting trip to kill cattle.' 'Did the guard in charge of that party say anything about what was going to happen to the balance of the prisoners?' 'He said that all the prisoners were going to die, be killed off. On the return trip back to camp he stated that Takakura had killed off the prisoners of war en route from Sandakan to Ranau, and that he was no good, and that he would die.'

The following night, 4 July, Sticpewich was preparing a meal when the guard came down and said goodbye. 'A few minutes later there were four rifle shots in fairly rapid succession; a short interval, then a fifth shot. I learned what had happened from Captain Cook, who had been called down to the Japanese officers' quarters. Captain Cook was present when this guard came up and shot Captain Takakura, Lieutenant Suzuki, Sergeant Fujita and a batman was dead. After he had shot these four people the guard threw a hand grenade in amongst them but it did not explode, and in the meantime he pushed the muzzle of his rifle in his own mouth and blew the top of his head off.'

'Coming to the night of the 7th of July, what happened then?' 'That night Privates Botterill, Short, Anderson and Bombardier Moxham escaped. Their disappearance was not known until next morning at a check parade by the Japanese. We were mass punished. We were not allowed any more vegetables. By the 20th of July only seventy-six POWs were alive. The main cause of death was starvation and physical exertion and expo-sure. One death was from violence. Staff Sergeant Horder was kicked by two Japanese guards and rendered unconscious. He died a few hours later.'

'What death certificates were given in regard to the deaths of the various prisoners who died at Ranau?' 'The only cause of death permissible by the Japanese on the death certificates was dysentery and malaria, irrespective of the medical officer's opinion.' 'Coming to the 26th of July, what happened then?' 'On the 26th of July a medical orderly who supervised the burial of the dead (checked them when they were being put into the grave) stated that we were all going to die and that he had seen the order from the Japanese High Command in the Japanese officers' quarters. He told me that I wasn't to speak or let anybody know.'

Asked how many prisoners would it require to move the body of one prisoner to his grave, Sticpewich replied, 'It would be as much as four men could do to struggle along with one light body, and it would take about six of us two and a half hours to dig a grave and about four hours to complete the burial. This would only be a hole about 2 feet 6 deep because of our physical condition. At this time the general physical condition of the prisoners still alive was in such a low condi-tion that only about twelve could walk. Of the rest there were eight unconscious when I escaped from the camp with Driver Reither [2/4th Reserve Motor Transport Company] on the night of 28 July 1945. I had been warned by a Japanese guard that if I stayed any longer I would either be too sick to do so or be killed.'

There were thirty-eight alive in the camp at Ranau when Sticpewich and Reither escaped. 'On the 2nd of August I was in an area approximately 5 miles above Ranau in the moun-tains at a kampong. A native informed us that there was still a number alive when he left that camp on the morning of the 1st of August.' Sticpewich met up with an Allied reconnais-sance force on the morning of 10 August 1945 but Driver Reither had died of dysentery two days previously on 8

August. The total number of prisoners at Sandakan had been approximately 2736; approximately 240 were sent to Kuching and 100 to Labuan before the march to Ranau. 'Of the remaining 2296, there were only six of us left alive.'

Botterill had made his escape in July when 'about' 100 of these men were still alive at Ranau. They were then dying at the rate of about seven a day, mainly from starvation. They were given a small cup of rice water a day, with about an inch of rice in the bottom. Plenty of rice was available and the Japanese used to get 600 grams a day themselves; they also used to get tapioca, meat, eggs and sweet potatoes and showed no signs of malnutrition. The Japanese took the clothes of Australians who died and traded them with the natives for food for themselves. Blankets were also taken and traded. 'A Korean guard named Memora told Lieutenant Bombardier Moxham who had made the march from Sandakan with me that we would all be shot by the Japs if the Australian army landed. On 7 July 1945, Moxham, Short, Anderson and I escaped. Anderson died on 28 July 1945. On the first night we were out we broke into a Japanese dump for food. We were in the jungle for six weeks before we were rescued. My weight fell from 132 pounds to 84 pounds while in captivity.'

When did Nelson Short know he was safe? 'When I was picked up by the Z Force reconnaissance. They said to me, You're alright now. You're right! There were still plenty of Japanese around. They were still bringing chaps in who had been shot up while we were in a hut the natives had taken us to. The Japs would have killed the natives if they'd known. They brought us food, took us to shelter, brought us information of the whereabouts of the Japanese, they did this in the sure knowledge that death was all they could expect if found with us. Women as well as men were helping.

'A native came to the hut with a Japanese cap on. I did get a terrible shock, it was bad, they've surrounded the hut, I thought. Even though I knew it was over.' Nelson's first question to the rescuers when he recovered was, 'What are the new songs? What's Bing singing? His latest song? These blokes all sang and they sang the new songs to me. "Don't fence me in". "Down in the meadow in the itty bitty pool, lived three little fishies and their mummy fishie too". And "Coming in on a wing and a prayer", and all those new songs.' Nelson has a splendid voice and today sings as well and as often as he did when he was a young soldier.

Nelson went to many people to tell them of their sons. 'Some said, "How is it that you got out and my son couldn't get out?" There's little you can say to a mother.'

Of the 2400 men who were forced to march from Sandakan to Ranau six only survived, Captain W.H. Sticpewich, 8th Division AASC, Lance-Bombardier W.D. Moxham, 2/15th Field Regiment, Private K. Botterill, 2/19th Battalion, Private N.A.E. Short, 2/18th Battalion, Bombardier R. [Dick] Braithwaite and Gunner O.C. Campbell, 2/10th Field Regiment. Of these survivors only Short, Botterill and Campbell were alive in 1992.

The Footsteps of Dead Men

'We were walking in the footsteps of dead men,' wrote the author Colin Simpson.

'There was no other way. Pushing through the jungle growth we trod on the mud tracks of their bare feet and ragged boots. Sometimes we saw their bones or bits of cloth on the scrubby growth, and often we smelt death.' Simpson had gained permission to join the party of Lieutenant Colonel Henry (Harry) Jackson, who was sent to North Borneo in 1946 to find the natives and other persons of that area who had helped Australian POWs and also to 'discover as much as possible of the story of the death marches', the details of which were relatively unknown.

The local North Borneo authorities helped Harry as did the considerable publicity given the visit in the local newspaper (in Malay and English) and also through the village headman. 'News spread rapidly about the purpose of my visit. Each name led to other names, like a chain letter. We walked for five days to reach Ranau, the terminating point of the death marches. Word had been sent through the local constabulary representative to the surrounding villages and these people then contacted me.

'One handed me a locket which was given to him by a POW when he'd given him food. I handed it to the War Graves Officer; one native had a haversack with a name on it, but because a name was on it, that didn't necessarily mean he was the soldier whom the native met, because when men were falling out on the track, knowing they would be shot, they'd hand things on to others. They'd say, "Who takes size 8 boots?" and hand on things in this way; they'd exchanged belongings so often you couldn't be sure whose it was originally, so I had to be careful.

'I had photographs of nearly all the prisoners who went to Borneo, photos taken when they first joined the AIF – face on and side on – height was noted and colour of hair. I asked the local people to look and see if they recognised anyone; they'd often point to one, I'd ask where they had seen him and write this information on the back of the photo. It was hard, because the faces of the young men when the natives met them would have been sunken, old, no longer did they look like young men; but some natives did recognise the doomed marchers.

'These people, if they thought they could please you by telling you something they'd do so; therefore I was very careful in interrogating them.' Harry spoke fluent Malay, had learnt it with other languages when training for this work. Princess Bureh was helpful as she lived in Pangana in the middle of the town and the death track went right past her front door. 'She used to give eggs to the men as they passed by.'

He heard of attempted escapes. 'In the village of Kamansi they told me they had harboured and fed four POW escapees, but all died. There were other escape attempts but no man survived. The Japanese were establishing supply posts along the death track because the island of Borneo was now isolated from Japan, they had lost their shipping and the only way they could go from one coast to the other was overland. There hadn't been roads, it was virgin jungle before they came and the tracks were put through for the purpose of moving troops and supplies.'

Harry talked with forty-seven people between Ranau and Paginatan then, because of flooding, he had to return to Jesselton and go by sea around to Sandakan, the other end of the track. 'So now we went along the track in the same direction the POWs had travelled.' He interviewed forty people at Sandakan who had been connected with the underground movement which had culminated in the arrest and death of Captain Matthews and Dr Taylor. These people included wealthy Chinese and ex-senior employees of the North Borneo government, people who had helped the escapees from Berhala Island, who helped Sergeant Wally Wallace, others that got the radio parts, money, medicine for the underground movement. Also, Harry met the widows of the Asiatics who were executed along with Captain Matthews.

'I devised a system to reward these people with a "risk bonus" – if someone was in danger of losing his life he was entitled to 100 per cent risk bonus, for something minor I might decide on a 10 per cent risk bonus. I had to use my own judgement, I had nothing to go by. For example, I might say, "He should get three months pay". There were some wealthy people who had money, a lot didn't want anything, but I explained, "It's not to compensate you, it's purely an expression of thanks". When I said I'd be recommending a certificate, that was big news. Everyone who helped our men in some way got a "letter of good name", as the natives termed it.

'Some of these people couldn't write and I had some trouble with the public servants back in Australia who said, "When you give them money we want their signature". So I put their thumb prints on the receipt form which the Department of Treasury gave me.

'After I'd finished the first interview sessions at Sandakan, we proceeded to the 49 Mile Peg of the track. This was the scene of a massacre of seventy-three Australians with rifles and machine-gun fire on 13 January 1945. Gruesome relics of the previous death march became more evident after Maunad was passed, bleached skeletons and decomposed bodies were often seen and many spots on the track exuded the stench of death. Other items thrown away by the POWs were seen, portions of footwear, tins used for cooking rice, pay books and photographs with the image removed by the elements. It was at Maunad that thirty-five survivors of the third death march were executed. The Japanese in charge of the men committed suicide and we knew nothing else about it, we just heard of it from local natives.

'We interviewed eleven people in the area where Braithwaite and Campbell escaped. Campbell was taken to a village, and later evacuated by air. Braithwaite was taken out to sea and rendezvoused with an American PT boat. They both escaped on the same day in different areas and were rescued by different parties from different kampongs.' Further interviews took place at Kuching concerning Captain Matthews and his helpers, who had been tried and executed there.

On return to Australia Colonel Jackson prepared a detailed report and recommendations for the rewarding of the men and women who had helped the trapped Australians; the most treasured and lasting reward, particularly to the Dusan people, was the certificate to be handed to those who had helped in any way whatsoever. He returned in 1950 to Borneo. 'This time I went to Ranau via Kota Bilud, walking around the base of Mt Kinabalu, then over the mountains; it took four days. I then went over the death track through to Sandakan, rewarding people en route. I told the people the documents were coming, "Letters of good name" I said. They weren't asking for money, just to see the looks on their faces when I said those four words was wonderful. They shook their heads in disbelief. Although it's forty years ago, I'll never forget it.'

Harry Jackson has since returned to Borneo to visit the Dusan people who valiantly, knowingly, risked their lives to help the dying and the near-dead. In 1985 he accompanied a pilgrimage which included three living survivors of the march,

Keith Botterill, Nelson Short and Owen Campbell, to Ranau
for the unveiling of a monument to those who died on what
is now known as the Sandakan Death March.

The small mountain people had, with their nimble tread,
walked miles along narrow tracks and were awaiting us in the
ever-present sweltering heat, perhaps 100 of them, faces uncertain, black hair sleeked down as always. Recognising Harry
Jackson, they smiled, that slow, shy smile of tough, timid
people, and as he went to each and spoke their language and
embraced them, the men and the few women certainly had an
expression of pride for being singled out, yet also acceptance.
Their shyness was not directed at Harry, him they knew well,
but at us who Harry explained to them had come 'from far
across the sea' to watch a flag be removed from a pile of
stones. 'A dedication', he said. They were unsure what we
would do. Their eyes were often on the visitors. Harry told
them the cairn was built of stones, one for each young warrior
who died or was killed on the trek along past their holy mountain Kinabalu. They watched as Bruce Ruxton (who, as a very
young soldier had landed and fought on Borneo just a few
weeks too late to help save these men, and who was responsible for having the cairn erected) brought the various digni-
taries forward. Colonel Jackson quietly explained, when Harry
Longey's sister Mary and his three brothers stepped forward,
that their family had nominated them to travel here 'to pay
homage to their young brother who had no grave but the
jungle'. There was Bev Lynn (née Connor) who had come in
search of the father she had last seen when she was 2 years
old – and found only his name on a stone wall; and Dave Cook
who had found a post near where his brother had died, and
brought it home. Then these small, neat people did as Harry
asked them – still shyly, but with strangely undisguised pride,
they each took a small document from a bamboo cylinder and
held it in front of them for all to see. It was the 'letter of good
name' that had been sent to them by the Australian government in thanks for their help in saving some, and easing the
deaths of others, when all of them, the dead boys, the Dusans

and the three still-living survivors were young in one of the few wild, untamed forests, at a time when one of the most hideous acts in the history of warfare, or mankind, was being enacted.

One of the people Harry Jackson had arranged compensation for in 1950 was Mrs Lagan, the widow of Police Inspector Ernesto Lagan who was executed for helping the prisoners. He had also recommended to the Australian government that an annual amount of money be paid to the North Borneo Government for a period of five years for the education of the Lagan children. He told Chris Lagan in 1985, 'I can remember in 1950 seeing your mother and grandmother and you children on several occasions before I was posted to Japan and Korea.' Chris Lagan, the younger son of Police Inspector Lagan replied: 'I knew very little about my father and his gallant deeds. I was only 3 years old. My mother was never the same after my father's death.'

One stands aside and watches all this, questions the survivors, stares at the evidence, listens to natives who were alive at the time, and there is no rhyme, no reason that is acceptable for this most terrible loss. The memorial tells an awful tale of degradation of mankind.

Jesus Wept

Inscribed by his family on the tombstone of a young Australian boy landed and killed in battle at Kuching, Borneo, July 1945, immediately before the bomb that would end the war was dropped on Japan, are the words: Jesus Wept. *John* 11:35.

The decision to drop the atomic bomb had been taken weeks before the sacrifice. The atomic bomb had to end the war, had to stop the Japanese from killing more of our men. There are two sailors buried here. David Newbury, ex-RAN, knew them. 'One bomb killed both of them, both aged 19'. In this graveyard are two VCs. There is a grave of a young boy, the inscription reads 'From Mum, Dad, Mavis, Billy and Jean'. It's a very sad place. There are walls, walls, walls of names of men who were sent too late, who should not have lost their lives because the end of the war was being fought elsewhere, and, perversely, had they been sent earlier to Borneo they may have saved men on the march of death from Sandakan to Ranau, a victory that would have sent the bells all around Australia ringing. But, when the bells did ring out across their homeland it was too late for the poor prisoners.

While the American troops made history, and won honour and glory for themselves and their country by fighting up through the Philippines and direct to Japan, Australians were fighting far away from the decisive battlefields. They were trundled off to backwaters where they fought and died bravely – but for what? Often they were involved in mopping up operations that could have been attended to when the war was won. The pockets of Japanese had little or no naval or air support, they could have been left to rot. Although MacArthur was determined he and his men would take the final glory themselves, at least better use could have been made of our already proven warriors. Couldn't they have been sent in where it was known their comrades were imprisoned, dying?

When the troops went into Borneo in 1945, it was to seize the oil wells and hopefully to stop the Japanese from blowing them up. But there were still Australian soldiers alive at that time and still sympathisers at Sandakan who knew which way the groups had been driven on the death march. Fresh and fit newcomers could have overtaken these sick men and their equally ailing Japanese guards. Perhaps none could have been saved, but at least an attempt should have been made. It would have been seen by Australians as equally as symbolic to us as had been to the Americans the return of MacArthur to the troops he had left behind three years before in Corregidor.

Four Australian Divisions were involved in the mopping up operations of 1944–45. Stalwart men, some war-weary but vastly experienced after six years of battle, many young and fresh. And now, for the first time, we had sufficient and modern arms, ships, planes, 'You couldn't see the sea for the

armada of ships that covered it on the way to the Borneo landings later on', Tom Wratten, RAAF, says. 'The beaches were
bumper to bumper with transport, arms carriers and landing
barges, as were the beaches during the Normandy landings',
says David Newberry, RAN.

Why couldn't we have made greater haste to the rescue?
Bring aid when there were still bodies to receive it. Their flesh
and blood was dear to us, why did we delay? Some lay in a
gloom so deep no light would again filter through, but they
may have sensed that at long last we had come to them.

'It was all bad in Borneo,' said the much-loved doctor, Lieutenant Colonel Sheppard of the 2/10th Field Ambulance AIF.
In November 1943 he was sent to the extreme south-west end
of British Borneo (then of course held by the Japanese) and
transferred from the main hospital at Kuching to a camp hospital which had to serve a population of 2000. 'There were
hardly any medical or surgical supplies. In the dysentery hut
seventy-four patients lay on the ground covered only by pieces
of sacking. Deaths were caused by deficiency diseases. Five
hundred and eighty died in the seven months between 1
January and 31 August 1945. Bashings of prisoners took place
at the rate of ten a day. Japanese Doctor Yamamoto bashed
and kicked me and other medical officers including a woman
medical officer. Propaganda photographs falsifying conditions
were taken. Thus a load of bananas was brought in, photographed, and then removed from the camp.'

When the war ended, Lieutenant Colonel Neville Morgan,
CO, 2/12th Australian Field Ambulance, was in charge of the
medical team that went to Kuching in September 1945 to
attend to the POWs and internees. 'All the Japanese I saw were
well nourished. The camp was still being run as a POW camp,
the commandant, Lieutenant Colonel Suga still exercised his
command over all the POW camps in Borneo. I first visited
the camp on the morning of the 8th. In the Australian camp
all the officers and other ranks were suffering from general
malnutrition. In the British ORs camp, 250 were stretcher cases
of whom 100 were suffering from a degree of malnutrition

which we refer to as famine oedema which was likely to bring about their death within a fortnight. In the male internees' camp a severe degree of malnutrition was also found. The Dutch, Indians, priests and British officers were all suffering from a degree of malnutrition – the women and children were in fairly good condition. Approximately four personnel in the camp were dying each day when I came in. After Major Hudson and I commenced the resuscitation of these people, not more than fourteen further deaths occurred. Of those who did die, several had cancer and several tuberculosis. This is to say, we were able to save all but four cases of famine oedema.

'In the British camp there was only one medical officer, Colonel King, to attend to the 250 patients. Very few of them were on mattresses. A number had new Japanese dressings on their ulcers (before the end of the war there were no dressings given out) and a great number of old rags as they had had for the past three years. Medical stores were in very short supply – surgical instruments almost non-existent. The men's clothing, patients and otherwise, was in a very poor condition but they saved it by wearing loin cloths as much as possible. No member of the POW camp would be classified as fit for any kind of work by ordinary Australian medical standards. We evacuated as sick two-thirds of the camp. Famine oedema is a disease which is caused by conditions of semi-starvation operating over a period of months. Had those conditions continued to operate, nobody would have survived in the whole camp. I expect at least fifty would have died within the next fortnight and about seventy or a hundred within the next six weeks under their present conditions.'

But at least some had lived and were now saved, partly by doctors such as Colonel Sheppard and, after the war, Colonel Morgan and his team: but mostly they lived because they were not in the wrong place at the wrong time as were the men who were sent walking to death from Sandakan to Ranau. Altogether, 1783 Australian prisoners died in Borneo.

The Railway to Burma

In Burma they tell of a Memorial:

When you go home
Tell them of us and say
We gave our tomorrow
For your today.

THE JAPANESE MOVEMENTS OF their slave labourers created statistics almost comparable with their own fighting troop movements in the Pacific. Prisoners were shuttled up and down and across the south, west and north Pacific wherever Japanese needed workers. They moved Australian men to and from Timor, Ambon, Java, Sumatra, Singapore, Thailand, Burma, New Britain, New Ireland and New Guinea, Malaya, Hainan Island, Formosa and Japan and its various islands. The theatre of operation that captured the minds of Australians when they learnt of it at the close of war was the Burma Railway and the prisoners who had been transported there.

The railway had been planned by a British company some years before the war but its survey declared it was not a viable proposition as it would be too costly in lives because of the diseases that were rife in the area the line would cover and the dangerous, difficult terrain. But for the Japanese it was a necessity to supply their troops in Burma and open a route to China and India.

There was already a railway from Bangkok to the Malayan peninsula and now they needed that railway to continue from Bangkok to Burma. When they had done a survey the British had gone around the hills. The Japanese went *through* the hills because they had an unwilling labour force to cleave a railway through 400 kilometres of jungle, mountain and fetid valleys, from Thanbyuzayat in Burma, south to Bampong in Thailand.

Eight months of work on this line were to cost the lives of many Australian prisoners (as well as British and Indians) and a lifetime of illness and distress to the survivors.

There were 4 million cubic metres of earthworks, 3 million tons of rock to be moved and almost 14 kilometres of bridge-work constructed, and all this done by primitive methods and total lack of machinery as used anywhere else in the civilised world. The rough figure of 330,000 workers has been gener-ally accepted to represent the number who worked on the line and this includes 61,000 prisoners of war, while the large remainder were labourers brought from Malaya, Thailand, Burma and India. Of this estimated 270,000 Asian labourers, it is thought that at least one-third (90,000) died. Of these, few have marked graves and many of their compatriots who survived the line would conceivably have died from starvation and disease before reaching the homes from which they had been taken three and a half years before the war ended.

When the Japanese ordered Colonel Holmes, the English-man, and Lieutenant Colonel Galleghan ('B.J.') to prepare a large body of men for a journey northwards by train, Gal-leghan and Holmes were seemingly suspicious. The Japanese added that there would be a better food supply for them 'up there', better facilities and, besides, Changi was too crowded and Singapore unable to provision such a great number of men. The troops were delighted, working on the wharves had palled as had the life at Changi and the skimpy, boring food.

Like troops throughout all wars they soon heard all the news: 'Black Jack has been told to send a complete medical unit including all equipment for the camp hospital. Better still, the train will take us right to the new camp up-country, there-fore no marching!'

Galleghan was said to have been 'suspicious', but the Jap-anese insisted it was a good move and, besides, they had the whip hand. When the time came for the men to depart, Gal-leghan was visibly distressed. He hovered around them, was 'forever visiting the area given over to the group being sent away'. There was a farewell battalion dinner in the open air with whatever scraps of rations men had hoarded. Leslie Greener recalls the leader farewelled his troops 'quite emotionally'.

'He reminded them that they were soldiers, they were of the Anzac mould, but he spoke more gently than was his usual way. It was as though some shadow had come over him. He wasn't Black Jack Galleghan that night in the padang under the moon, he was a leader forced to remain behind to hold the fort while his boys went forth without his leadership or protection.'

Well might the Colonel have felt sad. There was no alighting at a pleasant camp after an easy train ride. The men marched 300 kilometres, night and day. 'Their feet and legs were cut by razor-sharp bamboo and when they reached journey's end they were in a savage wilderness. The eternal heat would ravage them and the monsoonal rains sweep through them as they toiled as hard and with as little labour-saving equipment as did the slaves who built the pyramids. And they fell ill, were beaten with sticks, and died as did the slaves captured in battles of old by Xerxes, Alexander, Caesar, Ghenghis Khan and Attila the Hun. Mankind leapt back centuries to do what was done to these men', Leslie Greener believed.

A later group are said to have left with pianos, books, entertainers, furniture – strange equipment for one of the most protracted agonies of modern times. The men were not to know that their mates were off to the agonies of the jungle march, the deaths in the cholera camps.

Parties followed in quick succession until Changi was reduced to a few thousand men. (As well as shelter for these men, Changi was used as a staging camp for thousands of prisoners being shipped to and from other areas and islands.)

There were two sections of the railway, the Burma section and the Siamese section, and between the two was the Three Pagoda Pass.

Captain John Kennedy: 'This Pass was a sort of watershed that made all the difference between what you died of, although the death rates were much of a muchness either side. In the

Siamese (Thai) section the river runs parallel with the railway, enabling food to be brought up in barges in the wet season. I was on the Burma section, the line ran at right angles from a river, so we died of starvation. The men in the Siamese section died from cholera, it was six of one and half dozen the other.

'So off we sailed to Burma and lodged in the Moulmein Gaol. "By the old Moulmein pagoda, looking eastward to the sea" Rudyard Kipling wrote. But the bloody old gaol looks westward and it looked down over the pagoda. All the romance of my childhood was swept away in one sea voyage!

'The railway life was terrible in the wet weather. At night the rough huts used to leak and we were thoroughly uncomfortable in the day in the wet and heat of the railway line. Men starting at daybreak, getting back after dark, it was hard. And the discipline was grim too, the guards were mainly Koreans, more brutal to us than the Japs. The Japs had ill-treated the Koreans and their nation. They had given their captives the most menial jobs and those men knew their brutality would be approved of. But the Japanese were brutal to everyone. At one stage we were on the railway line and some of the Japanese troops that had been in Burma were making their way back in little groups moving past us and we'd almost feel sorry for them, they were so emaciated and decimated and they were up to their knees in mud like the rest of us were, and if one of them fell down the Japs would just put the boots in and kick him and leave him there. Oh yes, they're a brutal people and they have a brutal code, or they did; I honestly don't think this generation have got that.

'Food was very poor, primarily rice and little things like whitebait that the weevils had got to, all you got were the head and the eyes, terrible muck. We could send a working party out in the jungle to pick things we called violet leaves to get vitamins. We'd boil them, oh, a terrible taste; we got chillies and they were made up into stuff called sambal, but it was terrible muck too, because you'd eat it and it burnt the backside. It was always referred to as ringburner.

'Other than the times spent on the railway, there'd be lulls of inactivity and of violent activity. The thought of escaping was in my mind, and others thought about it too, but it was quite impracticable, because you had to go through Burmese villages, and the Japs would kill the natives if they didn't report you, so consequently the natives would give you away immediately, and not only that, the Burmese were our enemy, no ifs or buts about it. It was their self-preservation they thought of, and I thoroughly understand their attitude. Consequently you didn't escape; I don't know anybody who escaped from the Burma Railway. I believe there are people who claim to have done so and probably did do so.

'When the railway was completed, the officers weren't seen again, whereas during the railway they lived in the same huts as everybody else. We might have slept up one end of the hut, but we all went to the same place and drew our own rations from the same pot, ate the same food and the same quantity of it. My group did anyway. But I'm sure that varied from place to place.

'In the main, my group had no doctors. For a while we had two American doctors, one, Captain Hugh Lumken, a very good doctor, died on the railway line and I often think about how he died. There were a few dogs about, nothing wrong with dog, but all the people who ate dog died, but not from eating the dog, they just died. There was a group of people who used to catch a dog and to the best of my knowledge this group, without exception, all died from extraneous reasons, sometimes months and months afterwards, or maybe even a year, but it just sort of sticks in my mind because there was no reason for it at all. But Lumken was a very good, considerate doctor, and we mourned his death.'

Kennedy resented knowing that the war was going on around him and he was unable to do anything about it. 'We'd hear bits on clandestine camp radios. The blokes that ran these hidden radios were brave men. They'd get the news and then they passed it on to one of the fellows and he'd get a group of people together and repeat the news. We'd memorise it and go around the camp, sit down, and the troops would stroll up and we'd tell them the latest news, making it appear that we were having casual little conversations. If you got it in the morning, it took nearly all day by the time you'd sit down and talk to two or three blokes at a time. Then you'd move on somewhere else.

'At one camp we had a very brutal commander. We had an inkling we would be moving, so the men had to get the wireless out of the camp. One of our soldiers had been forced to be a batman for this officer, so they packed the wireless up in the Jap's luggage and the batman took it out of the camp. When the next commander arrived, he asked, "Where's the wireless?" The original commander said, "I don't know", and the new man said, "Well, it was taken out in your bedding!" Oh, he was a very special fellow, this one, and he got hanged for his pains (not because of the radio of course!).'

Claude and Eric Roediger with the other men from Java went to Changi, on Singapore Island, before leaving for the Burma railway. 'They used to have some tremendous community concerts and theatre at Changi which was good because morale was pretty low then. One night, a fellow climbed up on tall stilts, and he's got these great long trousers right down to the floor and he staggers out on the platform and looks over everybody with a very serious long face and he says in a lugubrious voice, "We'll never get off the island". That was his introduction and of course the response was deafening. I remember nothing else he said except, "We'll never get off the island". That's why there is always a roar of laughter when old prisoners say, in a very flat voice, "We'll never get off the island". That comedian was brilliant. He knew how to lift morale, those few words shooed away the bogeyman.

'Well, we got off the island alright! By train in steel cattle-vans. The one we were in had some bags of rice and we were sitting on top of that. We were tempted a few times to push the Jap out who was sitting in the doorway. At night, he'd be asleep, we could have knocked him off anytime really. We did think about it, but if it wasn't fatal to him then, of course, it would be fatal for us.

'We went into the jungle and they said, "You'll cut all the trees round about you and establish your camp here". That was Konyu River Camp where a lot of hard yacka went on. It was around about July when the monsoons had been going for a while that we got cholera. The rain really came down and the track up through the jungle was just a quagmire. When the pressure was on we'd be out working all day and get home in the dark and you'd have that rice stuff and nowhere to go and eat it. You'd stand out in the rain and the water would run off your head into the food. You couldn't all fit in under the tent. Some of us would be standing behind trees, trying to eat. When you finally did finish your food it was time to go to bed, you'd walk in from out of the slush and mud and you had no way of cleaning your feet before you got into bed. There was no water, there was nothing, only that soggy ground. The thickness of the bamboo was all there was between you and the wet earth and so you'd sit on that and try and get the black dirt off. Then you'd let your feet hang over the end and just pull the blanket around you if you had one; half the time you didn't need one anyhow.

'You'd just get to sleep and the Japs would come around and say they wanted fifteen men to go 3 miles down the road to pull out a truck that was bogged – or something like that. There were about ten or fifteen different tents there and they'd say, "One man from each tent" and so one of them would have to go out to make up the numbers.

'The sergeants in charge of each tent were tremendous. Sergeant Arch Flanagan from Tasmania, when they'd call for one to go, he wouldn't say anything, he would just go himself, and Sergeant Harris from South Australia was in my tent and instead of saying, "One of you blokes will have to go up", he'd go himself.

'But there were times when the whole tent would have to go and you'd be out until all hours of the night and get back in the early hours of the morning and you'd have to be ready for work just the same that morning. It would still be dark and we'd be on parade to be counted. The guards would leave us standing there waiting for the engineers to pick us up and take us out to work. But the engineers worked off Tokyo time and the guards worked on Singapore time and there was an hour difference between the two, so the guards got us out there at six o'clock, guard time, and we'd have to stand there until seven o'clock Japanese time when the engineers would take us out to work. That was an hour every day that was completely wasted, and they were too pig-headed to do anything about it.'

Eric Roediger: 'As soon as we knew we were prisoners of war and the reality of the thing descended on me, I had said well, I'm going to conserve what strength I can. If I'm not out working and I'm not eating, I'll be resting but I'll do my exercises to keep myself in good trim and I'll keep out of the way of the Japanese guards as much as possible, have as little contact as I can with them. I made that resolution early on and I kept it right through.'

But he was bashed. 'Not as bad as a lot of them but the guards would go berserk, go from being a normal, reasonable bloke ... then all of a sudden he'd go berserk. You could never trust him, we knew that early in the piece. Try to keep out of their way.'

Claude Roediger: 'When they got really snarly they'd kick you, hit you with anything they had in their hands. Some shot men. And they were never pulled up by their officers or anyone for doing this. I didn't ever see anyone pulled up.'

Eric: 'No, I think they were encouraged. But what some of us failed to admit was that they were top dog at the time and we had to be realistic about it, that they were the boss now, and as irksome as it was, we had to accept it and realise it was no good trying to push them around because it wasn't us who was holding the rifle. Some people weren't realistic enough to accept that temporarily, at least, we had to submit.'

Claude: 'Oh, by gee. When it comes to preservation ... you learn. But I guess a part of that would have been a feeling of the period, the great superiority that one felt being of the white race as opposed to coloured.'

Eric: 'Yes, that's right, it was hard to take. You had to

restrain yourself. I only ever had hands laid on me once. One night in Java, half a dozen who were Christians had got away on our own and we were having a prayer meeting and a guard came along and we were concentrating on what we were about and because we didn't jump up quickly and salute him next thing we hear a bellow and of course we looked up while we came to our feet and bowed to him but he lined us up three and three and we had to slap each other's faces.

'We tried to explain to him that we'd been praying and I don't know whether he understood or not but anyhow he made us continue to slap each other's faces.

'But the lack of care of the men in their keeping was their most disgusting crime. I came in one night from work and Bill Haskell said, "I'm sorry to hear about Claude". I hadn't heard anything, so Bill told me, "I'm very sorry mate, but he's got cholera". I went to see how he was and it was bad.'

Claude remembers his travail: 'I must have lost 2 or 3 stone in a matter of hours. It just gushed away. I couldn't stand up. I had collapsed by a tree and a couple of fellows had picked me up and took me down to the cholera camp. With cholera, the lymph gland is affected, all your cells are breaking down and allowing the fluid to run out your ears, your eyes, everywhere, just draining out of you. You had to get that fluid back into you somehow if you wanted to survive.'

Eric didn't get cholera: 'I was just lucky. The recovery rate was very poor. It was a most wasting disease.' Eric, working by day on the railway, cared for his brother at night. 'They wouldn't let me near him for a start. Cholera patients were isolated. He was just skin and bones.'

Claude's isolation ward was 'not the best. There was only enough room for two in the old tent, and because of the tropical rains the canvas had perished and the water dripped through all over the place and the floor of the tent was green with mould and we were on the slats of bamboo for a bed. I only had a groundsheet to put over the bamboo and I had nasty bed sores because while I was there in the midst of this, I caught pneumonia.

'The day I went in they put me on the drip and I was there for forty-eight hours and they'd put 19¾ pints of saline into my system. They kept a daily balance of what I was able to take through the drip and orally and everything that I lost was measured and weighed. Unless you could keep ahead you were on the way out. When Doctor Corlette put the drip in my vein he said, "Well Claude, that's all we can do for you, the rest is up to you". I said to myself, "And the Lord". And that's where the battle began.

'At first, in order to get the fluid back into the body, they used a big syringe to puncture the stomach and the water was pushed in and the stomach absorbed the moisture. Then they tried this new idea of cutting a vein and putting it in through there. Kenny Walker (one of the orderlies) was the first to receive it, I was the second and then Paddy Fox and the rest of them got it but even that didn't save a lot of them. Piggy Blockman, an Aborigine had it, they got him over it but he was so weak that pneumonia took him off. In those days pneumonia was a killer anyway without even being in our extreme situation.

'I was just starting to get a little better on 21 July 1943, it was my birthday and ... I got my first message from home. It just acknowledged the fact that they'd been advised that we were prisoners of war and sending their love, that's all they were permitted to say on the formal card. But it was good. The people at home were marvellous, and not only at home but all around the world. We got some messages from American sailors to say that they were listening in to the Bangkok or Singapore or Hong Kong radio and they heard a message that Private Claude Roediger of Western Australia was a prisoner of war, and they said they would write home and pass the message on to mum and dad. Yanks on the battleships, and different people that would be listening in would write. And our people at home, they were listening in one night and they heard the name of somebody in Perth and they went down to Perth and looked up the people and told them they'd heard this message about their son and handed it on. There was a lot of that going on.

'As soon as we were half fit we had to go back to work. I often think of it. Often. The camp had moved down to the river from the road camp and when it was time for me to go down and join the group again, Eric took all my gear on him as well as his own and I'm coming along behind him on two sticks because I'm too weak and it's pretty slippery on the track and every now and then Eric walking ahead with my gear would look back to see how I was coming along and I thought, that's how a sheep and a lamb walk along, the old mother ewe looks around to see if the lamb is coming behind, and that's just how I felt. They closed that cholera camp down and we were the last to leave, they gave us as long an isolation period as they could.'

The two brothers were on the butchering party in the new camp. Claude says it helped him to recover. 'Nobody gave us permission but we used to have a bullock's liver. There were four Australians and four or five English. We'd cut the bullock's liver into slices and fry it. Any other little titbits we'd throw in a bucket and boil for soup.'

Eric had malaria and beriberi. 'Everybody got beriberi; you could press your skin in and the hollow would stay there; I had diarrhoea all the time I was up in Thailand. I'd go five times during the night and five times during the day. Every night when it was dark we'd get our little pile of leaves ready – no toilet paper in those days. You'd cart your pile of leaves off with you. If you worked in the jungle there were always plenty of leaves there. Nighttime you had to have your little heap of leaves ready as they were a bit hard to find in the dark. And men took a heap of leaves in when they visited a mate in hospital.

'We used some choice language there; a man would just have walked a hundred yards to get back from the benjo and oh! I've got to go again. When you had diarrhoea you still had to go to work of course.

'Back in Changi our officers, in spite of what the Japs said, had been of the opinion that it was going to be pretty rough up here, so they decided to cram in all the medical men they could and it was the best decision they ever made and I remember Doctor Coates saying to put in as many bottles of quinine as you can, so if anybody had a spare corner in their kit bag they'd put in a bottle of quinine tablets and when we got there we handed them in to the medics. And just as well. Malaria was a problem. I remember standing out on the river bank one day, it was beautiful in the sun, and all of a sudden I started to shiver and then to sweat and that was the first time I'd ever had malaria. Every beat of my heart felt as though it was going through the whole body. We had plenty of quinine.

'When we were working on the cuttings up on the line, we were on the "hammer and tap", boring holes in the rock for the dynamite to be dropped into. They started us off with 60 centimetres a day per team of two, one holding or picking up the rod and turning it all the time, the other fellow belting it with a hammer. We had to bore 60 centimetres a day and, of course, being Australians, we'd hop into it so we'd get it finished and get back to camp and have the rest of the afternoon off. So the Japs kept jumping the rate up, and in the end we were loaded with that much that we couldn't get it done in time. They wanted 2 metres a day towards the end, so what we used to do, when they gave us a position, we'd start to belt away at it and get it down to about 30 centimetres and say to the Jap, "Deep enough or do you want to go down deeper?" And he'd measure it and say, "Okay, deep enough", and he'd write "30 centimetres" on your little ticket, put a little piece of rock over that hole and take you to a new spot. At the new spot we'd fool around for about ten minutes while the Jap was measuring other people's work. Then we'd go back to the original hole and we'd bang it down another 10 centimetres and we'd call him again and say, "Okay, deep enough?" And he'd say, "Okay, okay, 40 centimetres".

'He'd take us to another place and we'd put one down deep and he'd say, "Okay okay", and give us a credit for it and then we'd go off to another hole, not necessarily the one we'd done before but somebody else's, and we'd put that down another 10 centimetres and get double value for that. It was the only way you could beat them.

'That was on all the time, we were just as cunning as they were. But I learned a lesson there on the railway. I saw it from the employee's point of view and when I got back home I said very firmly that anybody who was asked to work anything over and above their normal hours should be paid for it and I insisted on that. I could see it from the other side and I never took it for granted that the boss should expect anything for nothing. You learn the value of things, what's important and what's not.'

Did they believe they were building a fine railway? 'We didn't think that a train could ever get through on the workmanship', Eric Roediger declares. 'That was one of the ironies because we were amongst the first to go over our own line on the way back from building it. We were like guinea pigs and we suspected that at any time the thing was going to collapse. It was hard for us to accept the fact that we were testing our own work. It had a disastrous effect on the morale I tell you.'

Driver Colin Gooch, AASC 8th Division: 'A year after the surrender I heard there was a crowd being sent away somewhere, nobody knew where, except that it was a camp where there was plenty of food and people would become healthy. "I want to go with them", I said. I didn't know where they were going but I wanted to break the boredom. They put me on the list and it ended up to be the Burma Railway.

'Whatever you had you'd sell to get the money to buy food. Everybody did the same thing, the Japs didn't stop us at first. People just used to come and sell eggs, brown sugar, salt and whatever they had. That's at the beginning. After that we were put on trucks until the track ran out, and we marched from there on.

'Cholera wiped most of our fellows out. Of the 300 patients in my lot there were a bit over 100 came away from there, and cholera was the main killer. A lot of death was just starvation and broken hearts. I saw fellows that seemed able to get around, sit there and talk of a night, and in the morning they'd be dead. It could have been cholera but they could have just given up I think, because that's about all you had to do to die.

'Nobody had any shoes or boots by this time. You're off on the elephant tracks all the time in about six inches of mud. Bamboo and thorns tear your skin and flesh. I eventually got ulcers all over the side of my right foot. Of course that spread pretty quickly. I was out on the working party for quite a while with that foot. They wouldn't let you stop; if you were on your feet at all you had to go to work. I remember the last job I did on the railway. By this time the Japs were taking food including cattle through there up to their troops in Burma. I went up to work this day and I couldn't walk, just lurched along and they said to make the tea. I remember sitting there in the jungle with this tea billy and I thought I'd just about had my time, and a Jap came over and he said, "Kampo!" He had this animal on a bit of rope and told me to take it back to the yard in the camp. I struggled back through the mud with this thing. How I got there with it, I don't know. Anyhow, I put it in the yard. By the next morning I couldn't walk at all. There was one Jap guard that we could have said was a human being. So our sergeant said, "As soon as this fellow comes out of the hut we'll carry you to the fence and we'll show him, see?" And that's what they did. They carried me over to the fence and showed him my feet and he said, "Hospital!" Well, that's how I got off the railway.

'Just after I moved into the hospital the rest of the fellows were moved to another camp and there were thirteen of us left in the hospital plus one medical orderly. The Japs decided to take us back to Chungkai but we had to wait till the medical orderly died, he was on his last legs; I can remember just lying there and waiting till he eventually died and somebody buried him.

'Then we padded up along this elephant track back to the river and they took the thirteen of us down to Chungkai in a barge. One fellow died before we got down to Chungkai and within a fortnight there were two of us left out of that thirteen.

This English doctor came in this day and he said, "Oh, Colin I'm afraid we're going to have to take your foot off". Then he said, "I'll just try something different, iodaform, a powdered form of iodine, and if it doesn't show any sign by tomorrow we'll just have to amputate". He gave me a blood transfusion and that was a sight to see. I had this Scotsman lying beside me giving his blood and they had this bottle of his blood hung up on the tree and we were chatting away, this Scotsman and me, with this great needle into my arm, just watching the blood run from him to the bottles into me. That was the blood transfusion. Luckily, by the next morning when the doctor had a look at the ulcer, there was just that little thin edge of the new skin. Apparently the iodaform had worked on it. It improved from then on but it was a year before I walked.

'They eventually moved us two Australians out of that camp back down to Nakom Paton, which was a hospital camp. Colonel Coates was in charge there and "Weary" Dunlop was one of the doctors who used to scrape my ulcered foot with a spoon. It did eventually sort of heal, but it was like a big dried scar tissue that used to keep shedding all the time. Even after I came home. It eventually broke out again in 1965. The foot's a bad place to get it because you're putting your weight on it. There's no way you can nurse it unless you're in bed, there's nothing much you can do, even today.'

Alan Whelan, who had enlisted in Hobart when war broke out and been sent to the Middle East with the 23 Machine Gun Company, was also on the *Orcades* returning to Australia when his battalion was put ashore in the Netherlands East Indies. He tells about the clothes he was wearing when he was later sent to Singapore. 'Our boots had rotted because that type of climate rots everything, many men were without boots at all. I was luckier than some because I had small feet and could sometimes get hold of a pair of Japanese boots, the one-big-toe type of short rubber boots. I wore a Jap-happy, a sort of lap lap, we made them of anything we could get hold of, rice sacks, anything, and sewed a little turned down seam so you could thread a piece of string in it around the waist.

Sometimes we wore just one straight strip of material and pulled it up between our legs into the front inside the string and let the front bit hang over – a proper sort of native lap lap. I had no hat, few had hats, and of course that was a sad loss.

'Sick men who couldn't get out of bed to sell anything and were desperately in need of food would ask others to sell for them. This go-between would take part of the price himself because he ran the danger. Well, one day I was flogging a blanket for a bloke who was in hospital and needing money to buy eggs. So there was me and an Indian bloke, both trying to flog things over the fence to the Javanese and we hear the Japanese coming. The Javanese grabbed my blanket and ran. So there was me without my bartering garment. Me and the Indian bloke ran off and the next morning we found that two other men had mistakenly been taken for punishment.' Alan and the Indian went to their officers and said, "Well, we don't think it's right, we don't think they should get a flogging for this". The officers said, "Then why not go and tell them and you'll get a lesser punishment surely for owning up to it". So we did, and the other two were let off and me and the Indian were made to stand in the sun for three days.

'You can manage it for three or four hours but then you start to sway and it's very difficult to keep upright, and of course you mustn't lie down. In the middle of the day without a hat it gets extreme then.

'There was one guard who was quite decent, and when he'd see you getting too badly done by in the heat he'd say, "You benjo! you benjo!" Benjo being the latrines. You could go for ten minutes and sit on the latrine and get a little rest.'

Alan Davies, despairing after being nine months in Changi, heard that the Red Cross had taken over 'these big, beautiful camps up in Thailand. A place called Kamburi, on the banks of a big river between Bampong and Bangkok and we'd stay there for the rest of the war! All this time we'd received only one Red Cross parcel, and in it was practically nothing, because the Japs took bloody everything. We hadn't received any letters from home. We were allowed to write one letter (mine was received three years afterwards).

'So everybody was in pretty high spirits when they marched us down to the railway station at Singapore and loaded us into these bloody cattle trucks. There wasn't enough room for everybody to sit down at once, we used to take it in turns. They just left the door open a little and whatever you wanted to do you had to do it out the doors as the train went along. It took two days to get to Kuala Lumpur and there everybody got out of the train and washed under the big water pipe in full view of everybody; you think of it now as awful but you didn't give a bugger then.

We jumped in again and the next stop was on the border of Thailand and Malaya. We hadn't had a feed yet. The trip took six days from Singapore to Bampong.

'We got out there. Oh, what a blasted place. I got a belting there. I was pretty hungry. I had a blanket left and I went to sell it to one of the Thais and he grabbed it and ran for his bloody life down the road and I chased after him and he tripped, I could never have caught him otherwise. But I got hold of him and gave him a bit of a whoofing and grabbed my blanket and this bloody Jap came. He started to scream at me because I'd run out of the camp, anyway he gave me a couple of whacks, grabbed the blanket back from me and gave it to the bloody Thai. I'll never forget that, oh Jesus. I mean a blanket! That was worth quite a lot, you could have got three or four dozen eggs for that.

'Next day they marched us thirty odd kilometres to Kamburi to the railway line. This was supposed to be the Red Cross camp that everybody was talking about, and all we got there was a shelter about four or five feet high, just atap, and all you could do was just lie under it, there was nothing else there. So where's the Red Cross camp? Must be further up the road we thought.

'That night they started to march us. Fifteen kilometres out of Kamburi the road finishes and all it is is a bloody yak track through the jungle. And they marched us every night about thirty kms and she was pretty bad going, it was that black everybody tied a little bit of white cloth or a white bit of paper or something to himself. It was only single file, right through the jungle. It took us fifteen nights marching through the jungle. Nobody can work out why they marched us at night.

'The second night out from Kamburi, they had these big carts with the great big wheels and a yak pulling them. They said they would take the haversacks and whatever you had, and it would only cost you ten cents each, and they would drop them off at the next camp. Everybody was pleased about that. But what these buggers did during the night was, they set off before us and were throwing our gear off the carts to their mates in the jungle. So the next night, when fellows went to pick up what little belongings they had, there was nothing there. So that was the last that we used those bloody things.

'There was a warrant officer of the 2/18th Battalion, a black-belt holder, and the next night he and three other men held on to the carts as they were going along, and when these bloody Thais started to throw off the haversacks and that other stuff, they grabbed them but eight Thais came at them with big machetes, the bloody knives.

'They were going to chop them up. But this unarmed combat bloke got into them and he did them, the other blokes helping him of course. And they pinched their yaks and slaughtered them and ate them.

'At a place 200 kilometres from Bampong we stopped, eleven kilometres from the Three Pagoda Pass. We had a half-caste Malay doctor with us and he knew all about cholera and all the diseases that were in the jungle and he got round and he told our officers that no men were to drink any water that wasn't boiled, not even out of the creeks, not to wash their mouths, do nothing without the water being boiled. This stood us in good stead. In three weeks, the 1200 Pommies who were up from us in another camp had 420 dead. Cholera had struck them. And cholera kills you in forty-eight hours, it's a terrible thing. It's one of the worst things I've ever seen in my life. Every bit of solid in the body turns to water and all the apertures of your body, everything just passes, everything. In forty-eight hours you're dead. The only cure that they knew of was saline, salt and water with sugar added, but you couldn't get it from the Japs.

'We had one bloke, Squeaker Peterson, he contracted cholera and we broke into the Jap cookhouse and pinched twenty pounds of salt and mixed it up and put a bamboo funnel in his mouth, and in about six hours we poured eight gallons of salt water into his body.

And he survived. We lost a terrible lot of our men. There was smallpox in the camp. You would think the blood boiled with it, so frightful a thing it is. That would kill you in a matter of twenty-four hours. Almost everybody finished up with ulcers. I had an ulcer on my ankle and I used to have it scraped with a spoon every bloody morning. But I was just one of them. The ankle bone was sticking out. And they used to scrape that.

'Fellows would be working in the quarries there, breaking up ballast for the railway and you'd get a nick with a rock or something and that would turn into an ulcer. On the other side of the railway there were Malays, Indians, Chinese, Singalese, you name it. I don't know how many of them died, but we used to see them burning up to sixty every three or four days. They'd have a big pit dug and they'd lay a row of logs, then there'd be a row of bodies, then another row of logs. The pit itself would be eight feet deep and the whole thing would be six to seven feet high with bodies, logs, bodies, and they'd cover the whole lot with bamboo and set it on fire and burn all these bodies. They got cholera over there and they had Blackwater Fever and they had beriberi and they had pellagra and they had bloody malaria. It was the rottenest country in the whole wide world. I don't think there's a disease known to man that isn't up in that bloody place.

'We were up there for nine months, we'd build a section of railway line and the next camp would be building a section and then they'd meet. There were railway camps all the way up. Too many men died on that bloody job. It's a frightful place up there, one of the heaviest rainfalls in the world, you could be standing within three feet of somebody and the rain would be coming down that heavy that you couldn't distinguish anything. You could see only a blur in front of you.

'And the work crippled us. If the working elephants refused to pick up a tree they'd get fifteen or twenty men to lift the bloody thing instead. A lot of people tried to escape. We had six fellows tried to escape from our camp and they got into Assam, went right through Burma and then 50 miles to India. And these bloody Indians caught them and gave them back to the Japs, because the Japs had put so many thousand yen on their heads. It was only occupation money, no good, but they could buy something with it I suppose. And the six fellows were brought back and put in little boxes as big as chook crates and they were absolutely skeletons. They'd been starved and tortured and they were rotten with ulcers and they were more dead than alive. They were left there for two days and then they were taken out and the whole camp was lined up and they had their heads chopped off in front of us.

'There was just nothing you could do about it, just nothing, they mounted machine guns everywhere. And they executed those six fellows. Swords. Actually it was a relief that they did do it because they were in such a bad way, they'd been belted and they had broken arms and nothing had been done for them.

'We had nothing in common with our gaolers. For instance, we were working making this road and we used to boil up a 44-gallon drum of water for our tea, cha we called it, made from rice we'd cook until it almost browned, throw it in the boiling water and it came out tasting between a tea and a coffee. It was a quite drinkable substance. Most of the blokes who would be doing this would be getting over malaria or being sick, it was light duties. It took from 6.30 a.m. until 10 or 11 a.m. to get this bloody 44-gallon drum boiling.

'The Japs all used to have their sweat bands around their hats and used to blow their noses on them and wipe under their arms, do every bloody thing. So this bloody Jap came along and the water was just about to boil and he put his bloody sweat band in the bloody water, washing it. And this NSW bloke, a rough nut, did his block and he went wooof! and flattened him, oh he could use himself a bit this bugger, and he really knocked him. Of course the guards saw him and they ran over and grabbed him; they got coils of barbed wire, they laid him on the ground and they laid the barbed wire out and they rolled him in these coils of barbed wire. This is fair dinkum. Anyway they left him there – out on the job. We had a bit of morphine – this was very early in the piece, and the hospital orderlies were going out, with permission to give him a drink but, as well, they were hitting him with morphine. The Japs left him there for about twenty-six hours.

'The punishment was bloody terrible. They'd get you and they'd get a lump of wood and they'd put it behind your knees and then make you kneel down and hold a shovel over your head. A shovel is not heavy, but you hold it there for two or three bloody hours mate, and you've got this lump of wood under your legs; then another time they'd make you jump up and hold on to the bough of a tree for bloody hours, and I mean if you let go and dropped, you'd get a real belting. You'd think your arms were falling out. You'd stand there and hold a rock over your head. It doesn't sound much but you try and do it for bloody hours.

'What they used to do with animals! They were just animals themselves. They'd get monkeys and tape a cork into their backsides, feed them and feed them until they were just about bursting and they'd put them into a refrigerator and then they'd bring them out. Honestly, they were inhuman. I mean, I've seen them lay men down and just put a bit of a pipe or something in their mouth and just keep pouring water in and then jump on their stomach. They did some terrible things.'

'Did anyone ever tell you of the erection in the atap hut?' Jack Chalker asked, in a breezy way. No, no one had. 'We were all too sick and fleshless to do anything but move one bone of a hip carefully and rest on the other for a change, most were dozing in the heat, lying side by side on the bamboo platform when one, as he gently moved a limb to protect it, as he turned said, "Gawd! Look!" We looked, listlessly, and then in amazed excitement. There was this bloke asleep on his back – with an erection.

'We stared, I don't think anyone spoke for a moment, then someone said "Half his luck" and "Never thought I'd live to again see the day!" and things like that. We were fascinated. It was as unlikely a sight as would be plum pudding, turkey and holly. The worst cases had shared a raw duck egg that day and the man still holding the shell carefully forced himself along, till he got to the sleeper, and placed the eggshell over the erection. Whereupon a "Holy Joe", as the Australians called this rather religious prisoner, became most irate and told them they were disgusting and he struggled to his knees and crawled along across sixteen sick men till he reached the man we were all envying – and whipped the eggshell off. Well! In the doing of this the ragged broken shell scratched the tender organ and the sleeper awoke, saw the Holy Joe leaning over him and let fly and punched him. We laughed, even weak men who had little to laugh about roared. And by this time of course, the miracle had dissolved and it took a while to convince the recipient of this largesse that he had indeed been the site of a miracle and that made him mad at having missed it and he said, "Why didn't someone wake me?"'

Another soldier, Private Alan Whelan, had 'all the usual' ailments up in the jungle, and in an attempt to recoup his health he took a turn working in the Japanese mess. Among his tasks was to prepare the officers' baths which they had standing up in the open, 'a thing like a big 44-gallon drum,' under which Alan had to set a fire to heat the water he carried from the river to fill the 'bath'. One day the Japanese officer was furious, he claimed the water was too cool. Alan put more wood on the fire but still the Japanese screamed for more heat. So Alan grabbed an armful of dry leaves and kindling and threw them under the upright tub in which the Japanese was standing. 'Well, the kindling took off, whoosh! and I did too;

I ran for my life because the Jap was screaming blue murder and the flames were blazing up all round him and he couldn't get out and all I thought of was, 'What'll they do to me?"

'Eventually he got out and I heard him running after me, howling with rage and screaming he was going to kill me and that I had tried to kill him. So I kept running and I got in among where the fellows had the elephants (they used to use their trunks to carry water up in big lengths of bamboo to the camp). I ran in among them, the Jap was right on to me and he had a big stick and was belting me and I ran in under an elephant's trunk and sheltered there and the elephant got angry at the Jap who was hitting him while trying to belt me out of it, and the elephant began belting him back with his trunk and getting cranky. The Jap later backed off and went back to camp and I raced off and hid in the jungle for a couple of days, and when I came back, thinking the least he'd do would be to belt me, I found he'd forgotten or something. You could never make them out.'

The men got a laugh out of some things that would be deadly serious back on civvy street. Blue Butterworth tells of an operation he had. 'I was a jack of all trades. First thing I was Weary's batman [Doctor Dunlop], then I was the transport officer, I was a quarter-master, you name it, I was it.

'About four or five months before the war ended Weary came to me and said there was no way he could cook the books any more to keep me in the same hospital camp, and so I said, "Ah gee, that's a bugger". Then I had this brilliant idea. "Couldn't I have an operation on the day of the movement, you know, any old excuse?" He said, "What have you got?" "Oh", I said, "I've got my appendix and I don't need that and I've got my tonsils and I don't need those and I've got my foreskin and I don't need it". "Right!" he said, "the foreskin". So I lost my foreskin.

'The shaving gear was a table knife honed down and the shaving brush had about half a dozen bristles on it and the soap a mixture of any old fat. Weary comes over and he just had this little bit of anaesthetic in a bottle. I was working out what age that was now – three and a half years after we'd been POWs. He said, "I don't want to give you much of this". Then he said, "It'll go black". "What? Me whole cock?" They got two or three other blokes to come up and see this operation, they're standing behind me as onlookers, one of my mates fainted as soon as Weary attacked with the scalpel, down he went, cold. He gave me the needle and waited for about half a minute, then he put the point of the scalpel on me and said, "Can you feel that?" I said no, and he got the old forceps and that's the start of the action you see, and as soon as he did, ooh! I leapt up. He just went bang! and sent me straight back. "You silly bastard", he said, "you told me you couldn't feel that", which I couldn't when he asked, so he had to give me another little shot and there it was. He said, "Do you want to take it back home with you?"'

But mostly life was too hard, too close to death to see any humour in any thing.

Private Len (Paddy) Fox: 'In the early stages of Konyu we were charcoal burners. This Korean who called himself the Mountain Lion was in charge. We had to dig a round hole and stack the wood in up to ground height and on top packed mud hard like the top of a water tank in the bush. To achieve that you had to pat the mud with a piece of wood to get this convex tank top appearance and then they'd stick a flue in to let the smoke out, fire it, and proof of whether the damn stuff had been burnt correctly was, you prod it with a bar or something. But this Mountain Lion bludger, he used to want people to walk on top of it – it was all hot underneath you see, and he wanted me to walk on the coals and I told him barley, I wasn't in it. One day he did the narna and he jumped on to it himself and went into it up to the armpits. He got badly burnt, and a Nip medico came racing over and got a pair of tweezers and was pulling the skin off; it was shocking. Particularly his legs.'

Bill Haskell also did time as a charcoal burner. 'I worked out that if you got a stick that had a hollow in it and you're hitting down it made a hell of a noise and the Mountain Lion would hear it and reckon you were doing a good job. He reckoned the "long bloke" (me) was the "number one charcoal". You wouldn't have got me walking on it, I'd die rather.

'We built the camp there and then went up working on the railway. They were early days and it was good fun. You had no idea of course what was going to happen in the near future. The first intimation we had of our fate was when the Nip engineer officer pointed through the jungle and said, "There's a railway going to go through from here across to Burma". Of course we just laughed because it was an immense area that he was in charge of. Two huge cuttings had to be sunk through capstone, limestone and what have you, and it was all put down hammer and tap by hand. Straight after that there was a three-tier trestle bridge that we had to build and then you ran off the trestle bridge on to an embankment which was about half a mile long and that had to be raised to a height of about 6 feet and it all had to be carried in tiny little baskets. And that led into the other big cutting we called "the compressor cutting" where men were working with jack-hammers. All this work had to be achieved inside a three-month period. They used to call a day off a yasmi day, a holiday. Well, we didn't have a yasmi day for about twelve weeks and this was right through the cholera and monsoon period. They picked the worst time of the year to put the railway through.

'The trestle bridge and the embankment were completed and the Jap officer had a big smile all over his face, and he was fairly well commended. He'd done his job at no cost whatever. When the train came through, it turned out to be an actual motor truck with rail wheels put on it.

'The bridge and railway were rickety. We used to call it "the pack of cards bridge". They had brought all the tractors they'd captured at Singapore, as well as all the explosives they needed. What they used to do was fire the cutting sometimes two or three times a day and there'd be an immense number of explosions and then you'd have to clear it, and you can imagine splintered capstone.

'To understand how the Japanese line of command worked

you must know the command started from the top – "get this railway built", so on right down the line. You have to appreciate this line of command to appreciate the type of discipline that the Nips had – and expected. For instance, there were three classes of privates and the third-class private is the lowest thing in the race. He is everyone's lackey; if he is spoken to by anyone above him, even a second-class private, he stands to attention, he bows. He has to bow correctly and he just jumps to it. This discipline was inherent in them, obey strictly the instructions of anyone above you without question and not once, but a thousand times I've seen someone just say something out of place, not actually *do* something, an off-the-cuff remark and a corporal or a lance-corporal would stand up and unmercifully bash their own blokes, really give them haymakers, and this was just something that they all accepted without question. With the exalted rank of a sergeant you literally had real authority over life and death, and so there was no question of disobeying. If we Australians didn't agree with one of our officers we would tell them, you'd obey them but you'd let them know, because that's the Aussie way. But for the Nips, it was just blind acceptance of the fact, and when it came to constructing the railway, the officer class said this has got to be done, and so, it's got to be done.

'You'd go on to sick parade, real crook when you stumbled in late at night; there was always one of the doctors there, in our camp it would be Weary Dunlop or Euan Corlette or Arthur Moon. Frequently a doctor would say, "The quota is full for tomorrow, the only way I can get you off is for you to collapse on the parade in the morning". The only trouble was that there'd be that many critically ill blokes collapsing it used to be chaos at times. Overnight some would develop dysentery or cholera, causing absolute pandemonium in the morning trying to fill quotas to get blokes out on the line. Often you'd get them out on the line and they'd be not worth a bumper, poor cows, and the Japs would lay into them.'

Ivor Jones: 'We started work clearing the jungle in early 1943. We had showers there because our engineers found a spring and we could drink the water straight out of the spring and Majors Alan Wood and Bill Wearne and a party that were allowed to stay in camp built a water system using bamboo for pipes. After coming in from the railway – had to walk about 5 or 6 kilometres each way – you were absolutely done, you'd pull the wood plug out and feel that water run over your bony frame ... ahhh!

'They did all sorts of things. Our latrines were sealed in with bamboo lids. That's where they were so far ahead of the Dutch and the Poms. The Americans weren't much good either at improvising. Our generation had gone through the Depression, most ordinary people had fathers who would maybe get one week's work out of three. So people grew up able to adapt.

'The three hardest things for us as prisoners were medical, physical and psychological. There was the work. The Speedo period from June to October was indescribable. Before that, the work on the railway and the food we were getting were horrific. But we were probably reasonably fit; but then you could see it happening to us, we became debilitated, collapsed, a dreadful thing for a young, fit man to see happening to him. I stuck it as long as I could, then got into a clearing gang because I couldn't keep up the pace with the hammer and tap. It was a terrible time.

'Dr Arthur Moon said, "You know, it's amazing what the human body can take, how much you can stand if you're determined to live". He was a great man. We had a very good run until cholera hit the camp and that was devastating. But compared with some Brits nearby, we survived in much greater numbers while they died like flies. It was pitiful; they were badly officered, they weren't fed, it was terrible how they suffered, they lost the greater number of their blokes, just died, some only a few hours after onset of cholera.

'You had to be adaptable. The Australians were the most adaptable of all the people up there, they could cope better. The ratio of losses are interesting: the Australians lost about one-third of their men, the British lost 50 per cent. Our cookhouses were cleaner, so were the latrines, men did their best to keep hygiene as good as they could. It wasn't that the Poms had any lack of spirit: the stamina just wasn't there; you get a bloke brought up in the slums of Manchester, Liverpool or London, he wouldn't have the same background, he wouldn't be fed the same in his childhood as we were. And I don't believe anyone had the mateship we had.

'I can remember at one stage the back and soles of my heels were like pulp, I had no boots and I was coming in from the line, walking on sticks, sloshing along in the wet of the monsoon and this bloke, I don't know who he was, he picked me up and carried me the rest of the way into camp.'

Like most ex-prisoners, Ivor is totally honest. 'You didn't really have time to think and meditate, you went out in the morning in the dark and came home in the dark and you were so exhausted you flopped down in whatever you had on. You didn't have much time to ponder over what people were doing at home, you were fighting for survival all the time. You're in a state of shock when taken prisoner, you don't believe it's happening, you expect others to come and get you out. Then gradually it dawns on you. The people who accepted that it was going to be a long-term thing weathered it far better than those who believed they'd be out within a month. If you dropped your bundle you were gone. There's a poem a mate of mine wrote, called "Mates", a lovely poem. It goes, "As we walk through the mud, though you stumble, tell your mate 'now don't drop your bundle, mate'." You watched one another, you cared. "Don't drop your bundle mate" you said, and heard someone say it to you when the burden was too great and you stumbled.

'I remember when rats came, the tent was wet and the rats used to pull at your hair and you'd just brush them off you were so exhausted. That speedo period was the most horrific of my life. When the speedo period finished, we were pretty knocked about; at one stage I didn't know if I had cholera or gastroenteritis. I was sent to look after the graveyard. I had to dig the graves and put the crosses on, the name and number were burned into the wood.'

Ivor Jones had amoebic dysentery, but when there was a call for orderlies he volunteered and was given charge of a ward. 'At the big base hospital at Nakom Paton, where all the "terribly" sick went, was my mate, Scotty Thompson, 4½ stone (on enlistment 13½ stone), we used to carry him around like a baby. We got some condensed milk from somewhere and fed him with a spoon. Anyway, he survived.'

Ivor's party was sent north-west to Nakim Nyak (Thailand). 'I was medical orderly for the whole party of 200; it took us about a fortnight to get to the camp, much of it by foot; we were bombed by our own planes and had six killed, and one bloke lost his leg. The Japs thought I was a doctor so I didn't let on, used to do a sick parade every night. We were building tunnels as stores for Japanese ammunition, right in amongst the front-line troops.

'They talk a lot about mateship; it was there in the prison camp, right to the end: not one man died alone. Everyone seemed to have a special mate, you had to be a pretty crook sort if you didn't. That's where you saw devotion you'll probably never see again.'

Some went by train, some by ship and some walked. Bernie O'Sullivan, who in 1942 had fought down through Malaya, was on H Force on the Burma Railway. (Two machine gun officers went up the line with this group, O'Sullivan volunteered as one of them.) 'H for horror. Six hundred Australians I knew went up there on the line and they lost 43 per cent of them. It was a bad thing. We didn't lose any officers, but we lost a lot of men. Eighty per cent of our men were unfit, lack of food, many kinds of sickness, work conditions had laid them low. We moved north to hell and back. I kept a diary. It was unwise but I did.

'It was a hell of a march up, we tried to help one another as best we could, walking in the night, up to our shins in mud. Many were left behind going up ranges to the mountains, they'd lie on the ground and water covered them. There was a jungle track hacked out. You'd get some kind of meal at times and stagger on. The column was so drawn out that the front of the line was halted for the rear to catch up; then straight on again.

'A cutting had to be dug through solid rock. Parties on twelve-hour shifts, sometimes extended to twenty hours. A little food was taken out to them. This was a bad camp, sickness was rife, beriberi, malaria, dysentery, finally cholera. Drugs we had didn't do much good.

'Dr Fagan was with us, he was absolutely marvellous, every man of us owes much to him. He was a quiet man, a surgeon, gentle with us and strong with the Japs. He defended our men as best he could, Fagan fought like a demon to keep sick men off work parties. If a man could show he was bandaged it was okay with the Japs, but sick men had to go to work because the Japs thought Fagan was sheltering bludgers; what Dr Fagan was doing was trying to help men stay alive. As I said, all of us on H Force owe our lives to this man.

'A British doctor set up a special cholera ward near us, it could almost be called a dying ward. We didn't even have salt to give them. You'd see a huge man go down 7 stone overnight as his body denuded itself of salt. It was hard to recognise your mate if you didn't see him for a few hours. And these were often men who already had tropical ulcers, yet I don't think I ever heard a man complain.' A man is numbed by such illness and the brutal work. He mourns the death of his nearest and dearest.

Bernie O'Sullivan weeps unstoppable tears. All prisoners who had these experiences weep. It is not unmanly, indeed it plumbs the depths of deep and caring humankind, of love, and the sadness of the human condition.

'Men gave strength, one to the other, both moral and physical. I know no experience that could weld men so sincerely as the life of prisoners. They would know that their friend was dying and could do nothing but sit there and hold his hand, and they did that. Blokes knew they were dying and knew their friend was holding their hand. There was strength, the recognition of each man's value. Sometimes a dying man may have lost his own mate, but there was always someone who would take that mate's place and hold him while he died.

'H Force had one of the worst times but the enforced labourers from many nations, certainly many Chinese, had worse times than us. They had no administration, no officers and no surgeons to help or stand between them and the Japanese. They couldn't even speak to one another because of their different languages. They brought the cholera through with them up the line and they died of it in droves without the help of an arm around their shoulders or a hand holding their hand.

'We always had a mate.'

Bill Haskell reminds us how close we were still to pioneering days and ways at the outbreak of World War II. Bill had a friend called 'Middy', Alan Middleton. He says, 'I think that somewhere in the annals of World War II the likes of Middy deserves a bit of a mention. He is not around any more and even if he were he wouldn't speak for himself, so those of us who knew him should do it.

'Middy came into camp the same time as I did in 1940. He was about 19 and I was 20, and he was an immense fellow, strong as an ox. He stood 6 feet 3. He had a likeable disposition, a country lad from down the south-west of WA. When he was a youngster at school, he had a difference with his country schoolteacher who, in those days, used to teach the whole school. The teacher had reprimanded his sister Mary, and Middy didn't stand for any nonsense like that. He just up and clobbered the teacher and said, "Come on Mary, we're going home". So at the ripe old age of 12, Middy found himself out sleeper-cutting with one of his older brothers. There were ten children in the family, several of them axemen of repute. They used to compete at country shows. Anyhow, Middy went out in the camp in thick bush and when his brother was away getting stores one day, Middy cut his instep very badly with an axe and there was no medical attention around anywhere so he just got a needle and cotton and stitched up his foot himself.

'When we were leaving Australia, on the pier before we went

away, he says to me, "I can't swim". Then he says, "I better learn", so he just went in off the pier at Glenelg and somehow by-gosh-or-by-golly he made it to shore. That was the sort of bloke he was, a particularly likeable sort of a character. Overseas we served in Syria and Middy spent his 20th birthday behind his machine gun at the battle of El Alamein, which was the deciding battle in that campaign. He was giving supporting fire to a WA battalion, the 16th, who were engaged with units of the French Foreign Legion. Middy reckoned it was a great brawl because he could see something for all the training he'd done. Subsequently we lobbed in Java and from there we were taken prisoner and finished up on the railway.

'He suffered from dysentery from the word go; he was strong enough and powerful enough to be able to somehow keep working when other blokes just had to stop. He had an infinite capacity to keep going. He endured the absolute full brunt of the hammer and tap on the cuttings up there. In hammer and tap you had one fellow hanging on to the drill or the bit and the other chap, of course, is swinging the hammer. Middy was always on the hammer and tap.

'He would select the weakest of the party to hang on to the bit while he did the hammering. When we kicked off it was a metre a day that had to be sunk in the type of stone up there on the cutting. It gradually increased until it was 3 metres a day which was way above the capacity of a lot of the men. This was where Middy really came into his own. He'd be clobbering holes and giving his tally over to other people and he'd just rouse around like a chook mothering her chickens and work to make sure that the weakest were getting their quota and thus protect them from getting bashed.

'At the end of a day's toil, if there happened to be a barge down the river (which was about 3 miles away), you'd find Middy going down to do business with the Thais, and I should imagine on many occasions to his advantage because he wasn't afraid to use a little bit of force if he had mates who were suffering. He'd get an egg or some salt or a bit of tobacco or something, but always would do that extra 3, sometimes 6 miles to pick up stores so that he'd be able to pass them on to his mates.

'He was a real character; he was a chap who was selfless, big in heart, he personified in my mind the fighting Australian man because he was able to cope. He had a lot of native bush cunning and he was the sort of fellow who could mix in any company. He had a very good sense of humour and at the same time he was there when the whips were cracking. He was always prepared to chip in and do his bit, and where there was someone weak and suffering, Middy was there to help. I well remember when we were going to Japan, the "sick trip" that took seventy days to get there. At one stage, when the American submarines, operating out of Fremantle, gave us a bad time for a while and there weren't enough life vests to go around, Middy gave his away. I was a pretty good swimmer so Middy reckoned that between the two of us we'd be able to work something out.

'Middy did his stint in Japan and we worked in the coal mines. He was a really crack-a-jack joker.'

Ray Parkin (whose trilogy of books on the years he spent as a prisoner of the Japanese is among the finest literature written on any war) mentions Bill Haskell's mate. 'I had fever. Lying alongside me, also with malaria, is Middy, a giant of a man from Western Australia. He has fallen away to a skeleton and shows his big bones clearly.'

Donald Stuart ('Scorp'): 'When a mate died (and any man was your mate then) well, you did your best to be decent. But we were weak and near to death as we buried them and they died in numbers, and we couldn't dig deep and sometimes an RC would see RC on the dead-meat tag on the dead man's neck and make a sign over him as he bundled him into the pits, and once I heard a real young boy say about a World War I bloke going into the cholera fire, "He wasn't a bad poor old bugger". It was as if he didn't want to appear maudlin but he felt a prayer of some sort was called for.'

Donald, who disdained 'the salon's darling Seigfried Sassoon', knew most verses of Wilfred Owen by heart.

Speaking of a dying man on the Burma Railway, Donald said, 'One sprang up and stared, with piteous recognition in fixed eyes, Lifting distressful hands as if to bless.'

Sapper George Scott, of the 26th Field Company Royal Australian Engineers, served in the Middle East, Libya, Syria and Java where he was taken prisoner by the Japanese along with the rest of his unit. He admired the grit of young Sapper Pat Reid. 'It was the practice of all the men to try to get as close to the head of the work party as you could to keep out of the dust that was made by the hundreds of men going out to work on the line. This particular morning, Sappers Reid and Tony Dawson were in the first of two or three lines as they marched to their place to start work, when Sapper Reid went into the jungle to relieve himself without asking the Korean guard if he could go to the "benjo". Pat Reid was squatting down to relieve himself when "Muckin", this Korean guard made a thrust with his rifle at him and Pat pushed the rifle away and made his way back to the rest of the working party. Muckin followed him out, and called Lieutenant Haynes, the officer in charge of the work party, and told him that Sapper Reid was going to "boxing presento" to him. Pat was stood to attention by "Muckin" the guard and proceeded to get a bashing from him with his rifle, he was kicked and then made to stand to attention again. All this time the guard was "roaring and carrying on". Lieutenant Haynes said to Pat Reid that he should apologise to "Muckin" and bow to him and everything would be alright. Men from the same section as Pat said, "If you apologise to that bastard Reidy, don't come back to camp". They needn't have bothered. There was no apology likely to be coming from Pat. Everyone knew that. So another bashing followed. All of this happened in the space of fifteen minutes. The Japanese engineers were carrying on all the time this was happening because there was no work being done.

'Later on that morning two other men on the water party went off, without asking, to the creek to pick up water to boil for the "smoko". They also got an unmerciful bashing. That same night the engineers lined up all the Korean guards in the camp and bashed them one at a time for hours for causing a disturbance in the work of the railway working party. The next day the Korean guards and Muckin came down to the camp lines. Sapper Reid had gone back out that day, but the two men from the water party had stayed in camp and were taken up to the guardhouse and were bashed and kicked repeatedly all that day and night, so badly that they had to go to the hospital camp where one of them died as a result of the treatment he got at 18 kilometre camp from "Muckin" and the other guards.'

Pat Reid received many more bashings from 'Muckin' as the line progressed. From camp to camp he singled him out.

'When Pat went back down the line to 60 kilometre camp with seven other men out of our unit, Jack Ekin, Ern McMahon, Tony Dawson, Jack Parkinson and two of the 22nd Pioneers, Archie Tate and Jim Bell, they were the last Australians to leave the Burma side of the railway after completion.'

In one month, November 1943, there were 200 men in the critical surgical ward at Tarsau hospital with tropical ulcers; seventy-seven died in four months. It wasn't only lack of drugs, liniment, bandages, operating theatres and lack of antiseptic conditions that killed the men up this line. It was lack of food and overwork. Eggs, like all food containing vitamins, were scarce and were doled out as medicine, not food. Avitaminosis and the foul diseases of the jungle were killing the young men.

In spite of a general belief among the men, the officers *did* contribute, sometimes handsomely, to the fund for buying life-saving food from the hawkers who came up the river, and any other source they could find. Some officers did complain heartily but the doctors up that line were fierce when the saving of the lives of their charges was concerned. Captain E.C. Verdy, the medico at Tarsau hospital, wrote, 'Unlike normal times the men are forced to rely more and more on dietetic measures, in fact foodstuffs such as eggs and milk are regarded as drugs, not "eats".

'Dry supplies appear to be practically exhausted and so diets *must* improve. We are trying to raise our standard on the present handsome subscription from the officers but we need extras. The morning ward rounds are becoming more and more difficult as patient after patient sinks into a final total deficiency state which often lasts for weeks before he eventually dies.

'At this hospital alone twenty-seven men have had limbs amputated in five months from ulcers, thirty-one died from cholera, with the two forms of dysentery and chronic diarrhoea accounting for 166 deaths. There are still too many with chronic deficiencies who are already beyond our aid.' He begged for any oddment held by men not in hospital to be given to the hospital workshop. 'Biscuit tins are being made into midget charcoal stoves for sterilising dressings, crutches have been made for one-legged men and hose tops and old socks converted into woollen comforters for covering stumps.'

Summing up the situation in December, he asked for more funds. 'Reduction in expenditure means further loss of life, and the painful necessity to discriminate against men least likely to survive.'

By March and April of 1944 the war had begun to move well away from this area and prisoners were being sent elsewhere. Many were in camps in Thailand at Kanchanaburi, Tamuan, Nakom Paton, Non Pladuk, Chungkai and Tamarkan.

Groups of men were sent off on railway maintenance work such as cutting fuel for the engines and unloading and loading trucks of stores. This work was not as heavy as the original building of the track had been but because there were less men there was less incentive for hawkers to come up the river with food and medicine for sale.

Six of the eight months of construction had been 'speedo', the Japanese term for 'work till you drop and work fast even then', as Donald Stuart said. 'Men were the machines and because they were cheaper and far more easily replaceable, they did not require the maintenance of machinery.'

The report of Lieutenant Colonel (Doctor) E.E. Dunlop,

post-war Medical Liaison Officer, Bangkok, 5 October 1945, includes the following: 'The Imperial Japanese Army showed complete indifference to the fate of the sick and the labourers. This policy was economically so stupid that one can only suppose it was due to sheer sadism. On one occasion one of them killed a patient by putting a pick through his skull, apparently to see how effective a weapon it was. The Nipponese orderlies used to enjoy going about the hospital with a bottle of chloroform and a 10cc syringe, administering the chloroform intravenously to patients chosen at random and watching the subsequent convulsions and death.' And that was in hospital; the men on the line knew all this, and more.

Harry Holder went to Bampong. 'The Japanese soldiers had been there a few days before and there were lolly-lopped heads stuck on posts everywhere. Most were Chinese shopkeepers. Quite a bit of lolly-lopping went on, they hated the Chinese almost as much as they disdained white men. You'd be walking along and suddenly find yourself looking straight into a grinning dead man's face.

'You say all men at war are victims, it was hard for us to see anything but one side being victims when you were looking at heads that had been lopped off and stuck up on posts in front of people's houses.

'We did a five-day march from Bampong to Tarsao in rain, mud, slush; everyone finished with dysentery. We slept in the mud in fields and went down like flies. Australians always buried their dead. That is our way. We were startled to find that other people didn't do this. Like other men I saw the cholera cases burnt. The rain came down and we had to begin to cook them again. There was one place where the top layer was of blokes that died with beriberi. Of course beriberi men blow up, they are very distended when they die and the heat from the pit got to them and they blew apart. Everyone there will tell you the same story.

'This is one story that will never change with anyone, no one could pretend to have been up that line and not talk about it; it was a thing no nightmare could resemble. But everywhere you went you were seeing bad things. You came to accept it. Each of us thought, "My turn may be next". It got a lot of them down.

'I can think of more horrible things in that war than I can think of ordinary things. I think of the burial parties for the Tamils, hundreds of them in one grave. I saw one Tamil getting off a barge on the river. When he moved there was a clicking noise, I looked and saw he didn't have a foot, he was walking on the bones. When you went down to get water on the river, you often had to push two or three bodies away. There were often live men sitting there too, our men, with their legs in the water to let the little fish eat the rotten flesh away from their ulcers. We saw floggings, bayoneting. Even when we were at Changi we got bashings on work parties and there was always the slow attrition of boredom that dulls the senses. We were hungry.'

Bombardier Philip Relf, 4th Anti-Tank Regiment, was an art student when he enlisted in 1939 aged 17. By the time he was 20 he was a prisoner closely observing man *in extremis*. 'The fighting and deaths of the Malayan peninsula receded into nothingness. To a prisoner, self becomes all-important. It is yourself who must survive. That philosophy is above even mateship. Your offsider was important but in retrospect I see that it was self that was paramount. Very few men would give up their life for a mate if the actual pinch came. The "alone-ness" of man was starkly revealed.

'There were a few officers and a few padres I wouldn't want anything to do with but in the main officers were doing their best to survive as best they could, as were we. Officers had privileges but I don't think it really mattered. They managed to liaise with the Japs. Lower ranks could not do this. My battalion, like other battalions, got it in for a bloke and that remains till this day. I don't know what started it with my mob, but nobody really behaved normally. A few officers were bad, but there were as many sergeants and privates just as bad. Officers behaved differently from us but I don't think it mattered because nothing much could have been done for us men given the type of captors we suffered from. We were the serfs of the conquerors and were to be treated as Attila, Xerxes and Alexander treated their captives long ago. Officers and men had one common, vital unifying factor: they wanted to survive.'

Philip Relf had carried a pencil and small sheaf of paper with him. 'It didn't last long. By the time I got to the Burma border it was gone. But, like all prisoners of the Japanese, the scenes were etched into the eye of my mind and could not be ripped away like a cataract. Every man remembers the rage of this enemy, it was as though a seizure came on them.' Before he died in 1988 Philip asked to have the following recorded. 'What happened to the Japanese mentality, morality and lack of civilised mores during the war was no aberration of history.

'I still believe what they were saying at the end of the war: "We'll win the war if it takes a hundred years". A lot of them realised they were going to lose the current war but they knew that in fifty or a hundred years they would have won it. I believe they will. They think differently from us about death, about killing, they believe differently about time. I had a belief in God when I went into war. I tried to maintain it. But I am an agnostic now.

'Time blunts the attacks of horrors. Most of the men who copped the worst of it are dead now, some mad, some from drink.'

Alan Davies, Halls Creek, WA: 'I was brought up in a God-fearing family. As a youngster I used to go to Sunday School and church, the fundamentals were instilled into me as a lad like everybody else. But it got that way at the finish that few of us were believers. A very good friend of mine, Alan Dalton, died. We were in the same company. He was a wool-buyer and good athlete (he ran fourth in the Stawell Gift). He died in such a terrible way, not through sickness, he was in hospital through malnutrition and they gave him maize and the maize had been boiled, but it was so old that it stayed rough and it took all the inside of the throat and the stomach. It just tore it to pieces. That was the cause of Alan Dalton's death. And I think to myself, he was a man who went out of his way to be kind to everybody. In the prison camp he used to do all he could for others. And that did something to me as regards to the bloody Lord and God thing and from then on I've never thought the same about it. Why should somebody as good as him be taken like he was? It makes me very bitter.

'I don't think that I'd be far wrong in saying a big percentage of men lost their faith. I don't think there's very many gone back (to the church) in the sense that they were before. They've formed an idea in their own mind and it's still there. It destroys your whole attitude to everything. And you had believed that the Lord, or God, is the pillar that you try to hang on to, otherwise the whole of your world will change. But in truth there was just nothing at all left to think about or hang on to but one another. We had the padre but nobody took much notice of him. All you thought of was your mate. If you had good mates it enhanced your chance of survival 100 per cent more than if you were alone. You had to have somebody.

'I was laying on these bamboo slats up in Siam. I was skin and bone, 5 stone. Pus was running out of my leg, and I used to dread having to have it scraped. Brian, this mate of mine, used to come and carry me out and hold me while it was scraped. He'd often come in where I'd be lying and he'd have scrounged stuff and give me some and he'd help the fellows alongside me whose mates had gone. He'd come in the night-time and talk. It's companionship and comradeship that pulled a lot of fellows through. There were five of us and two died and three came home. But we all helped each other. And this is what survival is about: having a mate.'

MATES

I've travelled down some lonely roads,
Both crooked tracks and straight,
An' I've learned life's noblest creed
Summed up in one word ... 'Mate'.

I'm thinkin' back across the years,
(A thing I do of late)
An' this word sticks between my ears:
You've got to 'ave a mate.

Someone who'll take you as you are,
Regardless of your state,
An' stand as firm as Ayers Rock
Because 'e is your mate.

Me mind goes back to '43,
To slavery an' 'ate.
When man's one chance to stay alive
Depended on 'is mate.

With bamboo for a billy-can
An' bamboo for a plate,
A bamboo paradise for bugs
Was bed for me and mate.

You'd slip an' slither through the mud
An' curse your rotten fate;
But then you'd 'ear a quiet word:
'Don't drop your bundle, mate.'

An' though it's all so long ago,
This truth I 'ave to state:
A man don't know what 'lonely' means
'Til 'e 'as lost 'is mate.

If there's a life that follers this,
If there's a 'Golden Gate',
The welcome that I want to hear
Is just: 'good on y' mate'.

An' so to all who ask us why
We keep these special dates

Like Anzac Day, I answer: 'Why?
We're thinkin' of our mates'.

An' when I've left the driver's seat
An' handed in me plates,
I'll tell old Peter at the door:
'I've come to join me mates'.

Duncan Butler,
2/12th Field Ambulance

The Artist

Some men carry the history of those times on their bodies:
gunner Jack Chalker of 118th Field Regiment, Royal Artillery,
carries his on his nose and forehead. 'Oh, it was just a beating
up.' 'Did it break?' 'Oh, it fractured my nose and I had a big
hole there [the bridge was gone] and they had to tie the sides
together and they found it wouldn't mend and they were going
to unpack my arm too but eventually got it together. I was
worried because of infection, because you've only got to get it
there and it's through to your brain in two ticks and that did
worry me. But they packed the hole every day for about a
fortnight, and then gradually pulled it together afterwards, so
it was OK. I was lucky.' There is a drawing he did of it at the
time. 'For fun.'

When Singapore fell, Jack had managed to escape. 'War had
been all bombs, batteries, machine guns and shelling, trench
mortars and safe houses and Fifth Columnists, and then we
heard Singapore had finally surrendered and the Japanese
terms were unconditional.

'Tom Albright, me and two others made our way to the
docks which were burning furiously and we hunted for a ship.
The Japs appeared at the top of the road. We and some thirty
others sailed away from the yacht club on the launch *Sylvia*,

a small craft, at 8.50 a.m. on the 16th. We provisioned and fuelled it from the burning warehouses and being daylight we didn't dare run the gauntlet through the channel.

'The Jap planes were over the island. We were running into things so we achored mid-harbour, miles from the shore, in full view of the Japs. We stayed well below deck and over-hauled the engines because they had been sabotaged before we found the boat. In darkness we cast off, and found we had a mooring rope twisted round the propeller. We drifted to the shore. After five hours we cleared it. Anyway, eventually we were caught.'

Chalker, who was later to become a professional artist, was given by a young patient a tin box of Windsor-Newton Artists' Water-colours in tubes, untouched. 'He had no interest in painting and hadn't used them. When you think of those long marches, when we threw most of our stuff away because of the weight, and then Arky, this lad, came up with this huge box of paints. Nothing could have been more fortuitous or more delightful as far as I was concerned. It was with those paints that I did many small paintings up the railway though they had often to be hidden in the ground. It was a find of gold as far as I was concerned, but it was amazingly curious.'

Chalker sketched not only the beauty of the jungle, and the camps, but the medical instruments and conditions of the men. His drawings are true and fearful, full of terrible sound and fury, noise that comes from men who are yet to have their open wounds of ulcers scraped with a teaspoon, or the gan-grene picked out. 'I don't know how they did it, I just don't know. The agony, and this went on for months. They scraped the pus and muck into a dirty pit; and then we used to take all the old bits of mosquito net that we had to scrape the pus off and boil them up in the tin to try and sterilise them because we hadn't got any material in some of the camps; then put them back on the wound again because it was the only thing we had. Bandages were almost unheard of. It got a bit better when we got to Chungkai and better in the compound but even then you had to save them.'

Jack riffles through his miraculously preserved drawings. 'They'd sit there, one with a massive ulcer on his leg and another fellow being scraped and another knowing his turn was yet to come. Some of them used to come in and they were barely human. They were just quiet. They didn't speak. And they didn't want to speak and some of them actually couldn't speak. And they, oh, they just, you know, we always cried. It was terrible. I mean, I can remember weeping and lots of other people ... Just the eyes of those poor men coming in, their mates holding them up. Lots of bad things. Especially when we were unloading at Chungkai. They'd been in the barges for sixteen days some of them. And half of them were dead. I unloaded two friends but I didn't recognise them for about three days. I didn't know who they were at all they were so emaciated. If they sat down they just sat like *things*. It was one of the saddest sights I've ever seen.

'I had a friend, a geneticist made some primitive elementary medicine in camp, and he and others made the rising yeast culture and distilled it and produced 92 per cent alcohol, so you got the physicist, the geneticist, the pharmacist and anybody else that could play the game and this was the magic I think, that people worked together. A water bottle with the top knocked off, they put a seal on it and a bit of rubber around the hole and they could use it as a colostomy bottle. They did all sorts of innovative things.'

His work in physiotherapy realised hundreds of sketches. 'A lot of their legs were all bent up and we had to get them straightened out.' His drawings show how it was done with the camp-made equipment. 'It wasn't very polished, the thing we made was pretty rough. But the principle was fine. We made orthopaedic beds. We got some raw hemp in from time to time to make ropes for the Japs and we'd knock off some for the beds.' He sees a drawing of an old Dutch mess tin. 'They adapted that as a retractor ... you put your femur or your tibula through there in amputations. There was an old bit of a gas mask and with a milk tin it was used for anaesthesia. They made artery hooks, they made a series of artificial legs – and when the beautiful buds of the Kapok trees burst in May we collected the kapok and made pads. All this worked well.'

Doctor Dunlop said of Jack Chalker, 'He has been the living saviour of men in camps of disease and death. From the time when he was sent out sick to a jungle base hospital he helped other patients. He is a generous, open-hearted social philosopher.'

With others, Jack was involved in theatre in the camp. 'We had a lovely natural arena at Chungkai. We slipped across the river, through palm trees, and there nature had left an auditorium at the bottom. For seats, the men had stepped the rising land, cut it out of the ground and you looked right across the river to Chungkai. You could see up to the sky. It was lovely. Some wrote out musical scores for a vast range of music, from memory, and it gave us very great pleasure, particularly with the heavy sickness here. It was absolutely a marvellous thing. At night there was a moon and it was just unbelievable, and they used little coconut oil lamps to light all along the front of the orchestra and the players.'

Costumes took all the ingenuity of the men. 'We made hats of woven bamboo and all sorts of stuff, modern, smart, and we dyed them. We tried to remember what women had been wearing. We had no reference. But we put our heads together and made these damned things out of odds and ends and we made brassieres which we stuffed with prickly, rough kapok. We made our own needles and when we were sewing these damned dresses up we had to drape them on the men and just sew them up. I used to stick the needle into the brassiere they were wearing and it looked terrible and they'd say, "Oh, don't do that!" It was a little joke but I think it must have been agony to watch.

'The wigs were made out of raw hemp. We made lace mittens, elbow-length gloves, all sorts of gloves, day frocks, evening frocks, Grecian gowns, cocktail dresses fully lined, with sweetheart necklines. Once a woman in our play had to undress and when we asked round the camp for underwear, somebody produced a marvellous pair of cami-knickers and a brassiere and he had had it up there in the jungle for nearly two-and-a-half years!

'And other things turned up. There was a handbag. How could anybody ...? We could carry very little because we had long marches and how the hell could anyone take a woman's handbag up there? We could believe the cami-knickers ... OK, yes, but not the handbag. Anyone having a fetish about a handbag must be interesting.

'To write the scripts we had to get paper off everybody. Paper was scarce. Some wrote plays from memory; one man wrote the whole of *The Two Mrs Carrolls* from memory.'

From beneath a cupboard in his studio, like the treasures a young boy hides or the souvenirs a grown man cannot destroy, Jack hauls out a small case. In it are his drawings and he lays them on the floor. A card: 'Wishing you many latrine birthdays'. 'It is a painting of the very refined upper-class lavatories we had in Nakom Paton. There we had wooden floors with bamboo sides and we wrote, "Maggots on stand-by to wave the banners ..." on the card. Another card said, "Immaculate conceptions daily". This was because there was a padre who cut a groundsheet in half. I had some pastels and chalks which I'd hidden and he wanted me to do a religious thing on the Immaculate Conception on these two pieces of groundsheet. He came to me and I remember tying the pieces up and hurling it at him. "Stick your bloody Immaculate Conception up here", I said. "You've cut a groundsheet in half. We've got people dying with pellagra who, if only we could sling them we might save their lives". I've never been so angry. I said, "You've cut this in half!" I tore into him and oh, bugger it, Jesus, I was so angry because there were poor men dying because we had nothing to make a sling with and there was this oaf who had cut a groundsheet in half. I was mad and everybody clapped and then we booed this chap out of the hut. He was a very simpering fellow, an English padre and he was getting higher and higher in church hierarchy to save his bacon, which was really what it was all about, and I couldn't bear that.' And so the 'back stage' crew did this card for Jack, 'Immaculate Conceptions daily . . .'

Jack kept a diary. It is meticulous. 'There was more of it but the rest got white ants and then there were great gaps in it.' He went through the war as a member of the British army. But he had been patched through to an Australian hospital and when he finally had to go back again to the Royal Artillery and return to England, Dr Dunlop wrote, 'This soldier has been a prisoner of war in Indo-China since October 1942, and has seen the most bitter episodes in railway construction camps and the aftermath, and the greater part of a force that drifted with broken debris down to the Menam Quoi Noi, the crude hospital.'

The Return

In the new year, 1944, the main railway work was finished, the surviving prisoner-slaves dispersed. Some survivors of 'the line', including those of Galleghan's 2/30th Battalion, were sent back down to Singapore.

Down south, far from the vast tragedy played out on the Burma Railway, Bridagier Galleghan knew nothing of the travail of his men; there had been no word, it was as if, in a dream, a noisy bunch of boys had surrounded him and then were spirited away, like young men in ancient folk tales who disappeared 'and were never heard of more'. Until mid-December, when Singapore Chinese passed the word that 'some' Australians from Thailand were on their way to Changi; Galleghan was told that the troops were returning but had suffered losses. He warned his men of this. He waited on the road outside Changi for them to arrive, a great throng of Changi prisoners sat waiting along the roadside.

'All stood', Leslie Greener remembered. 'A convoy of trucks was coming. We knew the men would have been brought down by boats and train earlier. Now they were here and the tail-gates of the trucks dropped, and the Japanese ordered the men out. There was none of the old leaping over the tail-gate. They appeared naked, they were wraiths, eerie figures like the Wayung shadow plays we'd seen in Java; they were clumsy, we didn't know what we were looking at; they didn't call out to us, some appeared to be holding one another up, leaning on one another, some leant on sticks. Then the moon seemed suddenly to shine harshly colder, and we saw them as they were, bits of rags on bits of skeleton men.

'They had been almost a week on the journey, crammed into filthy rail trucks, their ulcers suppurating, some bandaged, but with strips from rags of clothes tied round them, sores on bare feet weeping. I was one of the older men in Changi. I'd run classes and taught some of these boys eight months ago. But there was nothing I could have taught them that would have prepared them for this, or me for that matter.

'The emaciated returning men held within them a code of behaviour that had succoured them all the days since they were last in this place. They lined up. They were soldiers. The line may have appeared ragged with some bodies bowed over sticks and others still leaning on the man next to him *but the feet were in line*', Leslie Greener remembered. 'Some couldn't stand at all and their mates laid them down with touching care at the end of the line. (One of their dead had been removed earlier.) They looked at us and we looked at them.'

Some say their sergeant major marched to Galleghan and saluted. 'All present and correct Sir!' Greener says Galleghan said only, 'Where are the rest?' One-third of his battalion were dead and buried. 'Black Jack cried', according to Greener. 'He walked along the ranks on parade and tears ran down on to his collar. He didn't talk to any but put his hand on arms and shoulders and then he motioned to us fitter men to care for them, look after them.

'Few men have been cared for so tenderly. It was beautiful. I remember that night and the days that followed. It was only a few days before Christmas (dear God, it's ludicrous to juxtapose the two scenes!). All our Christmas hoard was delightedly given away to these men we used to know who were now caked with filth and had lice on them. Men had their arms around them, as though it was casual, but we had some need, perhaps more then they had, to place our hands on them. It is not possible to find words.'

The great humanitarian doctor Glyn White, in his capacity as OC Medical Services in Changi, wrote: 'At 3 a.m. on a lovely tropical morning in April 1943, we were there to see them off. I was also there to welcome them back at 2 a.m. some eight months later. What I saw has left a permanent scar on my memory. Many of my mates were missing, and those who returned were so altered physically that I did not recognise some of them. The stories of the heroism and fortitude of the prisoners equalled the highest traditions of the AIF in war.'

The Sick Ship, *Byoki Maru*

'To a man, all who travelled in that ship believe it to be the worst voyage in that war, perhaps one of the worst in modern times.'

Private Alan Whelan, 2/3rd Machine Gun Battalion

THE WORDS TUMBLE OUT when men speak of the 'sick ship'. 'Where they dredged that ship up from in the first place I don't know.' 'They brought her up from the bottom didn't they?' 'Just patched her up enough ...' 'That's all they did, patched her up.' 'Remember bringing the anchor up ...?' 'Oh Christ yes!' 'Bloody layers of rusted metal, that's all the anchor was.'

'On 1 January 1944, after we'd come back from the Burma Railway, we went down to the harbour in Singapore to catch the boat to Japan', Claude Roediger and his brother Eric recall. 'The Japs were terribly nervous. The moment we landed in the middle of the square by the wharf there was kicking and yelling and shouting and blokes were ducking to get out of the way of the rifle butts of these guards. It was really bedlam, you've never seen anything like it. If they'd taken it easy we'd have got in and got out of the way quickly but oh! the performance they put on and I thought gee! It opened my eyes, I thought boy! If this is the start, what's the end going to be like?'

Alan Whelan: 'They were running shit scared about something. We, of course, knew nothing about the terror American ships and submarines were causing on the sea route to Japan.'

Claude Roediger: 'We were speculating which ship we were to go on, and laughing at an old wreck the British had sold to the Japanese for scrap, pre-war. An explosion or something had blown all the plates off, the bridge was completely gone and they were steering this thing from a little dog box up the back. The ship had been gutted and not repaired. Eric saw this wreck and said, "Well, that one will never get there anyway!" But sure enough that was the one we were to go on. And we just shot in as quick as we could to escape the bedlam on shore.

'We each had to carry two lumps of rubber on board, about 10 kilograms, so they got 2000 lumps of rubber loaded. At least we didn't have much gear of our own to carry on, we were still desperate for clothes. The cargo we'd carried on board later came in handy for sitting on, like a little rubber cushion; we used to play bridge and put one lump of rubber on top of the other to make a little table.

'On that boat we didn't have room for anybody to stretch out their full length, you sat with your knees pressed up and the man in front had to put his knees up too, both together, touching one another, all of us in rows like this. We were in the hold but on little shelves that ran round the side of the ship, a big hole in the middle for cargo and us on our sort of platform built around it like the slave trade ships of last century. From the remains of the deck we could look down into the hold and from the hold we could look up at the sky.'

Alan Whelan: 'They packed us into this bloody hold and when there was no moon it was pitch bloody black. Some joker yells out, "Anyone got a book to swap?" To a man, all who travelled on that ship believe it to be the worst voyage in that war, perhaps one of the worst in modern times. We left Singapore and hugged the coast of Borneo, then across to Manila and were left in Manila Bay for two, three weeks; you can imagine the heat, dreadful, because the boat wasn't moving and no air circulated and we were sweating it out underneath there in the sides of the iron hold. The Japs were afraid to go out to sea because there was too much Allied activity out there and Japan had already lost more ships than she could afford – we only learned this later.

'Eventually they pulled up the hook and assembled a group of ships together and we went out through the heads into the open sea. We were only about an hour up the coast, hugging the shore fairly closely when we were attacked by US submarines and several ships went down; our little Jap escort vessels were darting around dropping depth charges and all sorts of things and we were hoping they'd all go down and of course the Japs were very edgy.

'We had to keep down below therefore we couldn't see what was going on. Oh, it was quite a thing that happened there. Then, the ships that were left afloat regrouped, and we carried on towards Taiwan. An incredible journey.'

Claude and Eric Roediger: 'They had ladders for when we wanted to go up to the toilet, a little box laced on to the side of the ship with ropes. It had two slats on the bottom where your feet went, and the rest of you hung over the sea. You had to get permission to go to this thunder box. You sneaked up to the guard and said "Benjo" and mostly they'd let you up. One day I just got my head up on to deck level and the next thing I hear is Bang! There was a Jap oil tanker behind us and the bloody thing blew up, the Yanks had torpedoed it and was there a scare then! They wouldn't let anyone on deck at all, even for the benjo, so that's when we started to panic a bit – we thought well, if the Yanks let one go into this tub we're gone and someone said she wouldn't be worth a bloody torpedo.

'A torpedo could have gone in one side and out the other with no trouble. (We later learned that the Yanks sank a lot of ships in that area around that time. The next convoy behind us had a hell of a lot of ships sunk and we got a pasting ourselves.)

'Once a week they'd let us go up to have a bucket of sea water thrown over us. Oh, the smell down there must have been pretty good you know. Yet, like always, in the worst of times there is something beautiful. One night I was sitting on the bottom of the boat and looked up and saw a blue moon. All the men looked at it. It was absolutely a blue moon. A lovely night. Such moments are rare at any time.

'This voyage was horror. You think of the shape two of our men, Sandy Whitton and Bert Pierce were in when they arrived in Japan. They were blown up like balloons. Bert Pierce was about 20 stone, yet normally he would only be 9 or 10 stone.

But then he blew up with beriberi on the trip. Vitamin problem, holding the fluid. It could be the onset of cholera and other tropical problems. We didn't know what to do for them.

'In the China Sea we hit a typhoon, a lively one. Ray Parkin, HMAS *Perth*, says it was the most hair-raising experience of his life. But we all had to admire the captain, because he kept heading into the wind and at first we were riding it out reasonably well. The guards were all sick, you could've done what you liked while it was on, nobody cared, it was vicious. Down below we were totally drenched. Then, for some unknown reason we got sideways to the wind and the ship rolled over . . . and it was hovering, we could see the water . . . Sitting there in the bottom of the ship we saw the ocean. Oh, it was a terrible situation, and then she rolled the other way and we thought she was going to roll right over this time and one of the lads yelled out, "God save us!" Like a call for help.

'And not long after that the captain got it heading back into the wind again and from that point onwards, gradually there was a lessening of the gale and we came out of it. But boy, I tell you, he must have been some skipper. To save a tub like that in a sea like that was something. And you can imagine what was happening to all the plates, they had been lying on the deck with scrap iron on them to keep them in position and this tub was rolling backwards and forwards, and all this stuff would go across the deck that way and then she'd roll back this way; oh, it was, you can't describe it, it was just bedlam. Later the Jap told us that another twenty minutes and the bloody thing would have broken in halves. She was creaking and cracking like artillery. Was she ever!

'They sailed her into a lagoon, it was like a bottle-neck, just a slight opening and we went in and they beached the bloody thing. The Japs told us there were subs outside the lagoon opening just waiting for us. An isolated place it was, the niggers were over the side with bloody bones through their nose and everything, looking at us. It looked as if she was beached forever, but eventually they got her patched up enough to lurch off.

'We went to Formosa, and after a few days set off for Okinawa at seven o'clock in the morning and we were back in Formosa the same night. Apparently there was so much US naval activity ahead they couldn't proceed. Two days later we set off again but between Formosa and Okinawa they heard something: we knew because they wouldn't allow us to come up for salt water baths or benjo on deck because they expected Allied activity. And then the boat sprang a leak. We could see it from where we were, we looked down and water was shooting up about 6 feet from the base of the ship and we all said, right, this is our opportunity, so three or four at a time went down and had a good old scrub and clean up and then when we were all nice and cool and clean we called the Nip over and said, "You'd better have a look at this". So he had a look at the hole in the hull and his eyes went like organ stops and he went away and got a piece of 4 by 4 and sharpened the ends with a tomahawk and drove it in there and plugged the hole up and we carried on.'

Alan Whelan was one of the men sent to Japan to work in the mines. 'A bugger of a place. We were working in the old mine. The main shaft was under the sea and we were forever shoring it up. It had not been worked since German POWs were put down it in World War I. [Japan was on the Allies side in that war.] There was no vertical shaft but an underlay shaft going down at an angle, we were loading coal trucks as we went down. With the heavy bombing that was going on now the power would often be off and water flooding in and there were earth falls and blokes were trapped. Japanese, Koreans, Australians were all equal then, we were all scrabbling to get out. The thought of burial alive is horrifying to any man. We moved fast and the roof collapsed behind us as we ran. We did our best but we lost several men there. It was hot down there below ground, it was cold snow above, we weren't dressed for either. We did what we could about food but miners did get an extra issue. There were Japanese working down below who had been tram conductors, sailors, the authorities were so desperate they put anyone down in the mine to work.'

Alan was very young. It was difficult for him not to be mischievous. 'The Japanese hung their coats and watches on the side of a pole as we went into the mine and we'd decide some days that we wanted to get off early, so we'd alter the watch, put it ahead. We only put it on a quarter hour. He wouldn't notice if he came back during the day to look at it and then I'd slip in and put on a quarter hour again and we'd get off early. I'd give the game a rest for a few days and then I would have another go and one night I got us off one hour early.'

Alan went out one night looking for 'spinach' greens, 'all dressed up' so he could stuff the greens out of sight. A Japanese came on him and searched him, Alan said, 'For benjo, toilet. Plenty leaf to wipe. Okay?' No, it was not okay. 'The Jap grabbed an axe and swung it, I grabbed his arm and wrenched it away and cut his arm with it. He then flew into his sleeping quarters and I heard two distinct clicks. He had slammed two bullets into his rifle. I rushed off, the Japanese officer was coming in the gate, he said, "Where are you going?" I was really in the soup then and I paid for picking my bits of green, I tell you.

'The Japs treated their own people as badly as they treated anyone else. If a Japanese mine worker was sick and couldn't work, the family were only given half rations.'

When Claude Roediger and his brother Eric disembarked in Japan they were lined up on the wharf. Again the men were reminded of slaves lined up for sale a century ago. 'Civilian employers looking for cheap labour were there and each wanted so many hundreds of us. One half of us went to Nagasaki to the ship-building and the other to the coal mines. Eric and I went to the mines.' Claude, after the fearsome voyage in the 'sick ship', had carbuncles on his thigh. 'They lanced them and I was hospitalised there for a short while.

'In Japan our food was at least as good as the civilian population had, but every month we were weighed and if there was an increase in weight they knocked so many grains of rice off. If there was a big decrease they gave us a little more. Their aim was just to keep us at subsistence level. We were always hungry. There was one good point about the camp: when we'd come in from the work parties they had a great big wash trough the size of a small room full of water heated up by steam pipes. It held about twenty people at a time. We had snow in Japan and this was the only chance we had of warming up, as well as cleaning ourselves, and we'd hop into bed nice and warm and clean.

'The work compared with that we had come from on the railway cutting in Thailand. I got on well with the old Jap in my heading, he was fed up with the war and hoping it would finish. He knew that the cards were stacked against Japan, they couldn't win, and he said so. As soon as we'd get down the mine he'd say "Okay", and he'd get his head down and go to sleep, so we'd fill the skips with all the rubbish we could pick up, broken timbers, and lumps from a seam of yakky that you could break off in great chunks, then we'd put a nice clean layer of coal over the top of it all. When the skips went up top and were emptied into the chute, these great lumps of stuff would keep blocking the chute and they were having plenty of trouble up there. Endless belts ran underneath and Japanese girls used to sit inside that picking out any foreign matter and they were complaining bitterly about this rubbish that was coming up. The Japs were threatening all sorts of action. They issued all men in the mine with tickets, each had a different number for each heading. We'd pick up our twenty tickets every morning and go down the mine and after we finished our skips of coal, we put all our tickets on the trucks the Japanese workers had filled and we took all their tickets and put them on our trucks. That went on for a long time, but we knew we'd have to fall one day, and when we did it was getting towards the end of the war so it wasn't too bad.

'I can remember when the bomb dropped because I'd been working night shift and I came home and had my usual bath and clean up and went to bed; there had been enormous bombing going on for months. This night, Wham! It just about blew me out of bed. The fellows with me said, "Boy! That was close", but we turned over and went off to sleep. We didn't know there was such a thing as an atomic bomb at that time.

'One of the Japs working down the mine was called away next day and when he came back he said, "Oh, Dunny Dunny". Very bad. Very bad. We got the impression that something pretty drastic had happened. Just before that event Yanks used to come over in their planes with their lights on. That's how cocky they were. And towards the end, the work load became less because half the time you'd go down to your work base and the power would go off and all you'd have is your little cap-lamps to see with, and the problem was that as this mine went a mile out under the sea and you'd be going up hills and valleys through the very wet tunnel, and with the power off the pumps stopped and there was always a race to get out before water trapped us.

'It could be days before the power was restored, because the Yanks were bombing power stations, anything, and we'd lie in bed of a night and hear them roaring over in wave upon wave and later they'd all be coming back again. This was the only news of the war we were getting, but we knew it was coming towards the end because this old fellow that I got very friendly with in the mine called me one night. He said, "Understand Englando, Georgie". In other words, "understand, King George the Sixth of England". I said, "Oh yes". He said, "Georgie speak Churchill finish now".

'From our sleeping room upstairs in a double-storey building, I could look down into the guardhouse where there was a monotonous speaking voice going on and on and all the guards were around the wireless listening to this broadcast. When it shut off, these guards all very dolefully walked back to their positions, and you could tell by their appearance that something of a very important nature had taken place. We believe that we actually heard the Emperor's speech of surrender at that point.'

Bill Haskell was working in the mines on 15 August. 'About 3 in the afternoon we were coming up from a couple of miles beneath the inland sea – and we met the afternoon shift going down, and they said, "She's all over!" And of course this is what we had greeted one another with for years. "She's all over!" They said, "No! no! She's right this time". The Nips had been in their own hut all day and there had been a lot of talk going on and no air raids and everyone was very, very solemn. The Nips were quite beside themselves, no screeching, yelling or anything! So we came up to the surface. Always when we came in at the guard room, we had to salute and we'd be searched and be numbered off in Japanese, and do their drills in Japanese. Not this day. The guard was very quiet and obviously there was something afoot. We walked a quarter of a mile back to the camp and it was quiet, things were very still. An announcement was made that we weren't going to work tomorrow – that was the first thing we heard – and they said we could all go into the kitchen and the mess room, which used to be only for Japanese and we were allowed to keep our lights on. And then, of all things, they made a Red Cross distribution. All the time we'd been prisoners we'd seen Red Cross parcels on only two occasions and then it was one parcel to five men, but now they made a distribution of one parcel to two men. We knew that something was really cooking. Then the three o'clock shift came and they said, "She's definitely over. The war's finished and there's no more work down the mine."

'The mine had been our whole universe. Now it was finished we just milled around till about midnight and we weren't told to go to bed; we weren't sure of anything, we thought there could have been a cease fire or Armistice. We didn't have a clue about atom bombs or anything like that of course.

'So then we were in kind of limbo land, betwixt and between, but we weren't prepared to take the punt and say that we were free or that the war was over, because we didn't have it official. It was two or three days before a high-ranking Jap came along in a car and mentioned that the war was over, but he said he would advise all men to stay in the camp "so that they would be protected". Then MacArthur made an edict that all rifles and firearms that the Japs had, had to be surrendered to the local depot. We went down and picked them up and got ourselves armed and went back to the camp.

'A couple of chaps off HMAS *Perth* who knew about making sails made three flags, a Union Jack and an Australian flag and the Stars and Stripes, and we ripped down the fried egg that had been flown over the camp for long enough and hauled up our own flags. The real feeling that we were free was when we were all in the Japs' mess room and we sang "God Save the King". We then knew that we were no longer under the fried egg.

'The Nips indicated that aeroplanes would come over and we had to write POW in white paint on the roof of the buildings along with the number of people in the camp. A Flying Fortress came over and dropped a cylinder with a message that within half an hour relief supplies would be flown in and to indicate on the ground roughly the area where we would like them dropped. We were on the side of a hill which was awkward. Anyhow, we put out a big white mark where they were to drop and sure enough, four of the big planes came over and opened their bomb bays and dropped out 44-gallon drums on parachutes. I can still see those multi-coloured parachutes in the sky.

'About forty canisters came out every time they opened their bomb bays, and there were parachutes and 44-gallon drums everywhere. I saw one drum and one parachute and I made after it. It went about half a mile and when it hit the hard ground the concussion smashed the drum and it was full of chocolate and Campbells pea soup which had broken open and was all mixed up and I'm sitting down there stuffing blasted cold Campbells pea soup and chocolate into myself.

'They dropped everything under the sun, in typical American fashion. We hadn't had any experience with dehydrated food and men were eating the dry food that needed to be soaked in water before you cook it. There were cigarettes by the thousands, Phillip Morris, Camel and Lucky Strike.

'There were about 400 of us in this camp and we had enough to last the village for weeks. We had the complete village collecting stuff. In the finish we had an immense amount of stores and the little Jap kids in the village who had never ever tasted anything like chocolate and the other supplies had a wonderful time.

'I don't bear the boss miners any malice, they were just common ordinary folk; miners the world over are pretty decent people and these people were no different and we gave them a lot of the Yank generosity.'

Then the trek home began. 'We met the Yanks at Wakiama. I'd never seen so many warships in all my flaming life. The American fleet was there, aircraft carriers, battle-wagons and hospital ships, you name it. We pulled into the railway station and were met by great big American marines, the pick of the force, armed to the teeth and expecting all the trouble under the sun. But there was no trouble. Japan had been destroyed, burnt to the ground as was Berlin, not from the two atomic bombs that had been dropped on two towns but the immense waves of bombers that had come over for the past year. Town upon town was flattened, razed, the survivors living in the rubble. It was just incredible the amount of damage that had been done. Tokyo was in ruins.

'On board ship we stripped off on the bottom deck and they deloused our hair and all our body and then we went into an area where there were showers going all over the place, and Lifebuoy soap. We hadn't seen pink Lifebuoy soap in years, it smelt beautiful, a really carbolic smell. We all soaked under the showers and after we dried off were equipped in jeans and white t-shirts and boots and socks and what have you, underwear and all; soon as we did that we were fed ... you could smell bread ...' (Like most of these men, there is something that triggers Bill's emotions. *Bread*. 'I'm sorry, I've done that before', he says. Few of them can connect the word, sight, smell or sound with what makes them suddenly weep hot tears and their body to tremble.)

'When the medical was finished, we went up a deck where

they had the complete record of all service personnel. You were to give them the date and place of anyone you knew who had died, or been killed, anything you knew, or had heard. They showed the service photo to see if you could positively identify a man. Then we went to the war crimes section to indicate crimes that we had witnessed.

'Then you could compose a cable home. It was hard to think what to say. There was an Australian destroyer, the *Nizam*, amongst all these American ships and an Aussie sailor called out, "Is there anyone from Fremantle?" and I said "yes", and his name was Phil Craven and he gave me all the gen about what had happened to local blokes from home and what had happened in the war.

'It was only then that I heard about the atom bomb. We didn't know, we had no means of knowing that ... we were cut off from the world, right in the middle of it, yet isolated. We may as well have been 10,000 miles away. Didn't have a clue about it. We'd been prisoners for three and a half years. We didn't know anything.

'We went on a Liberty ship to Manila where we met the Aussies in the camp. There were troops coming home who'd been in the islands and of course we knew nothing about the island shows and we'd talk to them for hours.

'There were lots of people when we sailed into Sydney harbour. Gordon Bennett came on to the ship and was absolutely tumultuously welcomed by his boys, a heart-felt ovation; we learnt later that there was a bit of mixed feeling in Australia at the time, the big wigs reckoned that Bennett had shot through from Singapore. It was nothing like that at all. He was held in great admiration by all I knew anyhow. And we had quite a few of his crowd on this ship and when he came aboard he was made more than welcome.

'We got on buses and were given a ticker-tape reception through Sydney. But it was quite an anti-climax. After what we'd had, anything is an anti-climax and nothing was real any more. There was a telegram for me to ring a lady and she told me that my brother had been killed three years before.'

The *Moji Maru*

Able Seaman Buzzer Bee, who survived the sinking of HMAS *Perth*, sailed again, and this time was almost sunk by his own side. This was in January 1943. Major Bertram Nairn, in his makeshift hospital, had now 'expertly' operated and removed the piece of shrapnel from Buzzer's right calf thus enabling the young naval signaller to sleep and walk much more easily.

'I was feeling better than I had since my ship went down.' Until he saw the old ship that was to take him to Rangoon, on the way to work on the railway from the Burma end down. 'The *Moji Maru* was waiting for us at Penang, an old rust-bucket with another old ship and an anti-submarine vessel as escort. We were the last ship in line-ahead formation. The prisoners on board were Australian and American soldiers and a few RAAF and sailors from USS *Houston* and HMAS *Perth*. In the ship ahead were Dutch prisoners and Japanese troops, as well as steel rails and equipment for the railway.

'Despite the cramped and humid conditions in the after-hold of the old rust-bucket, good humoured banter, especially between the Aussies and Yanks, was pretty well continuous and amusing. "Chesty Bond" maintained a constant flow of bawdy songs and other dittys while some played 500 with Spud Murphy's home-made pack of cards. Others, legitimately and otherwise, were attending to the requirements of nature on the upper deck. In Japanese/POW parlance, this constant function was called "the Tucsan benjo". Morale generally was at a fairly high level.

'Soon after noon, a day or so sailing from Rangoon, our routine was broken by the drone of approaching aircraft. I was down below at the time explaining to my mate, Bandsman Ron Sparks, how I had, a little earlier, done a good deal with a Jap seaman: I had swapped him a pair of Indian army boots which I had carried with me since Singapore and which were too small for any of us, for a number of essential articles including a new toothbrush and toothpaste and packets of cigarettes, etc. This Jap seaman shared a cabin with another crewman which was directly beneath an old gun mounted on the poop deck above. As it happens this unlucky son of Nippon didn't have much longer to live.

'Two aircraft appeared suddenly coming in from astern of us flying in line ahead at about 4000 feet. We could see them rather fleetingly through the open hatch cover passing right above us, and knew that at any moment we could expect a stick of bombs to fall. Then it all happened, there was a lot of clanging and banging on the deck above as the Nips, realising that we were now under attack, raced to their allocated action stations shouting and firing as they went. Simultaneously, the familiar crump and rumblings of underwater explosions told us that bombs had also found their mark but luckily not on us.

'I decided to get top-side and have a look at what was going on. Halfway up the ladder there was a loud swoosh as a stick of bombs fell down the starboard side giving us a near miss. The next moment a great sheet of salt water came cascading down the hatch, nearly knocking me back to the bottom of the hold. The old tub seemed to lift right out of the water then fall back in again with the explosions. I clambered to the top and looked about me. There were bodies and wreckage strewn all over the after-deck. The old Great War-vintage field piece which had probably been removed from a museum or some such place, had also blown up at the Japs' first attempt to fire it, killing the entire gun crew, the first of the casualties on board.

'The near miss had done more damage than had at first appeared, the ship was developing a list to starboard and was going around in circles as if out of control. We found that considerable damage had been sustained below the water-line amidships. The other transport ahead of us was sinking fast and the escort vessel could not be seen anywhere; and the Liberators were still circling overhead preparatory to another bombing run or perhaps just playing a wait-and-see game.

'A glance up at the ship's bridge platform suggested that it was deserted, and because of the excitement and general confusion existing among guards and crew alike, the thought struck me that this was an opportune moment to obtain a signalling lamp with which to communicate with the aircraft. Having worked our own aircraft with an Aldis lamp in better times, I knew that air crew could receive and transmit morse by light and at least it should be possible to let them know who we were. Even if the ship's bridge was manned I reckoned that I could convince the captain that my purpose in being there was solely to help save his ship (and us of course).

'I made my way up to the bridge via the port ladder and gangway to the bridge, and saw an officer dressed in white shirt and shorts who I presume was the captain standing beside the man at the helm. The captain didn't give me a chance to say much before he wheeled around shouting something unintelligible, at the same time drawing a pistol from its holster. It seemed to be levelled at me for a long time while I made a backward retreat, gesticulating madly as I went. I literally fell down the gangway to the deck below and thinking I was being followed, quickly got to my feet and returned to the after-part of the ship to mingle with the others. It was all over in a few minutes and nobody apart from the two Japs on the bridge and perhaps a couple of my mates were aware of what had happened. I thought it prudent to say nothing and remain inconspicuous for a while, in case the guards came looking for me.

'Back in the vicinity of the hold activity was at a peak, quick thinking by some able-bodied men who had snatched up all available buckets and, using sea water, were dowsing a fire which had broken out on the gun deck, threatening the ammunition lockers. Had we not been able to control the spread of the fire, the carnage, especially among the POWs who were quartered below deck, could have been horrific. The Japs, realising the danger to the ship, were strangely lavish in their praise for the fire-fighters and this behaviour probably contributed most to making life easier for us for the remainder of the voyage. My own indiscretion was possibly overlooked for this reason too.

'Our friends above us, apparently thinking that we were in

a sinking condition, eventually departed the scene, leaving us to clean up and sort ourselves out. I took the opportunity to retrieve the boots which I reasoned were no longer required by their late owner. The unfortunate gun crews' cabins were most accessible and I believe had already been ransacked by some of our more enterprising comrades.

'The attitude of the Japanese was remarkably generous considering the losses so recently and swiftly inflicted by our bombers. At times like this we prisoners were usually the victims of more vicious bashings and less liberties but instead of us being herded down below which was the usual custom, we had the freedom of the after-deck and were allowed to assist with the recovery of survivors from the other ship.

'Johnny Coe, an Australian soldier, dived overboard with a rope to help a Dutchman who wasn't making much progress. Still in his old army greens, he had the biggest haversack strapped to his back that I have ever seen and sitting atop the lot, seemingly oblivious to everything, was a cat. They were all hauled safely aboard much to the mirth of the onlookers. Unfortunately for the poor cat, the Japanese considered it to be an unnecessary burden and immediately tossed it back into the water. The Dutchman didn't appear too happy to be thwarted of his alley-rabbit stew!

'We arrived at the mouth of the Salween River late the following day. We passed a number of dead natives, their bodies puffed up to huge proportions, floating out to the open sea as we limped our way up river, coming to a berth at Moulmein on 17 January 1943. POW casualties amounted to seven dead, including Steward R.W. Smith (HMAS *Perth*) who was badly wounded during the bombing and died later in Moulmein whilst a number of others suffered cuts, bruises and shock of varying degrees of severity.'

An Act of War

'I saw the girls fall one after the other. Then I was hit.'

Sister Vivian Bullwinkel, the sole survivor of the Banka Strait Massacre,
February 1942

WHILE WOMEN'S LITERATURE HAS achieved great momentum
in the years of a relative peace among the major nations, it is
an anomaly that the role of servicewomen in war still attracts
suspicion or, in the case of nurses, gentlemanly protectiveness
that almost negates the matter-of-fact bravery – or is it
common sense? – of the women involved. Brave women have
not been so much coy about their acts as seeing such behaviour
as part of their chosen profession as does a soldier, sailor or
airman. And their acts have been as stoic, their deaths as courageous as the men.

Although they did not bear arms, the nurses served with
bravery. Their quiet remembrances warn us to look beneath
their words.

Military policy was that women were not to be in life-threatening areas, they should be in hospitals well behind the lines,
safe and secure. But Australian nurses have been in danger
areas from the Boer War to Vietnam, and none more so than
the valiant women of World War II.

Nursing reinforcements were despatched to Singapore in
1941 and served in several hospitals until many of these
women later became POWs or were killed by Japanese on
Banka Island or died because of the harshness of their prison
life.

The 2/10th AGH was at Malacca until the swift march
southwards of the Japanese. The hospital evacuated to Johore
Bahru to the 13th AGH but by 30 January troops and hospitals had moved again, this time to Singapore Island. The

Causeway was dynamited, the bombing continued night and day, and soon the oil tanks were burning. The 13th AGH with 240 beds was now handling over 900 wounded and using tents and private houses.

Then came the most chastening move of all: the women were told that half the nursing staff were to be evacuated on the cargo ship MV *Empire Star*; they would be leaving the wounded behind. The women ran the gauntlet of an air raid to reach the wharves and there waiting for them was a vessel that had carried frozen meat, its holds now emptied – and defrosted – ready for the children, nurses and servicemen – 1254 persons altogether, who would attempt to reach the shores of their own homeland. Some nurses had only been a few weeks out from Australia, none more than a few months. They were cooped in the hold as the ship left the dock and anchored overnight in the roads because of the minefield at the entrance to the port. In the morning planes came over and began bombing and machine-gunning the vessel, killing some of the ship's personnel including the men manning the machine guns on deck. When Sisters Anderson and Torney learned that wounded were lying on the deck under fire, they hurried up to attend to them, shielding the wounded with their own bodies. (Vera Torney was awarded the MBE and Margaret Anderson the George Medal for 'conspicuous gallantry under danger'.)

The ship's boats were wrecked but the *Empire Star* sailed on to reach Batavia on 14 February. There the nurses had their first real taste of fear for those nurses who should follow them. They heard the news that Singapore was about to fall and that the seas they themselves had sailed through were littered with wrecks and drifting lifeboats and rafts as well as the dead of many ships.

Two days later they again set sail, sleeping on deck, the ship crammed with women and children fleeing from out of the crammed-with-disaster waters to the safety of Fremantle harbour where they arrived unheralded, unexpected, no word ˙ving reached Australia for many days of the events and disasters of the northern battlefields. It would be three and a half years before they learned why their sisters-in-arms did not join them at Batavia; why they would never see some of them again.

'Where were you shot?' 'Just behind there on my left side, and it came out there. It missed all organs, just went straight through. Luck! Yes, well, you wonder why? I don't know why, I always put it down to the fact that I was in salt water at the time and my wound was clean. Then I took myself up into the jungle and I don't know how long I was up there. All I know is that I woke up at one stage and it was pitch dark and the next time I woke up it was daylight and I was hot and sweaty and uncomfortable and sorry for myself, here I am on my own, and what's happening? I knew what had happened to everybody else. I didn't see any of them although in the fortnight that I was there I used to walk down the beach hoping some food from the sunken ships would be washed up. There were bodies, but never any of the girls, just men's bodies. Well over seventy ships were sunk there, but none of the girls came. I would've probably tried to bury them if there had been any of our girls. But the others, I didn't I'm afraid. I did find a tin of condensed milk but I had no way of opening it.' These are the words of Sister Vivian Bullwinkel.

The brave women are among the most self-effacing. 'I was shot. I didn't do anything about that. I was just shot.' It is a peculiar situation, a woman who has nursed wounded men to herself be shot and wounded by a bullet – not by accident but as an act of war.

Vivian Bullwinkel's saga began when she joined 300 old people, nurses, women and children on the *Vyner Brooke*, a small coastal steamer. That night, Thursday 12 February 1942, the coaster left Singapore hoping to reach Australia. Behind them the city of Singapore was afire, the sky black from burning oil dumps, and the air a cacophany of gun fire. By now the authorities knew that Singapore and Malaya could no longer withstand the onslaught of the Japanese. With the fleeing civilians on board *Vyner Brooke* were sixty-five members of the Australian Army Nursing Service from the 13th and 2/10th AGHs, almost half of whom were soon to die. 'We were told to help the civilians in any emergency before thinking of ourselves.'

On their attempt to run the gauntlet of Japanese fighters, bombers, ships and minefields, they would try to run through Banka Strait. This strip of water between Banka Island and the island of Sumatra is at places 20 miles wide and at others only 10. Within a period of fourteen days, scores of ships would sail through these waters and be sunk in the straits or just outside them or on nearby islands. Every vessel, from row-boats, unseaworthy tubs to liners and the whole of a Japanese invasion fleet, was converging in the area of this narrow water-way in which lay Banka Island, a rich tin-mining area almost 140 miles long and 60 wide, a rocky and swampy strip of land. Apart from the Australian army nursing sisters, there were no other service personnel among the passengers.

Among the nurses on board was Sister Vivian Bullwinkel who had been on the staff of the 13th AGH at Singapore until that city was about to fall to the Japanese. 'On Saturday 14 February, at about two o'clock in the afternoon, we were in the Banka Straits when three Japanese airplanes flew over and bombed the ship and machine-gunned the lifeboats. The ship commenced to sink and the order was given to abandon ship. The civilian women went over when the lifeboats had been lowered, and after they had left the ship we were given the order to follow. All but two of the lifeboats sunk. I, with twelve other nurses, jumped out of the side of the ship and swam to an upturned lifeboat. There were three civilians and a ship's officer also cling-ing to this boat. We drifted for about eight hours.

'Another lifeboat had got away from the ship and it got ashore on Banka Island around 5 that night, they lit a fire so that when it became dark all of those who were still out at sea could see it and this became the central point for everybody to try and get to. Our boat got ashore at ten o'clock that night. It was still upside down of course because it had been machine-gunned. We came ashore and walked a couple of miles along the beach and joined up with the group at the fire. All night, small groups – ones, twos and threes who had got ashore at various other places, kept turning up at the fire, and at one stage a raft with about twelve of our girls got within about 20 yards of the shore and we were talking to them and we were saying to get off and come in, "work harder, get yourselves in", and then a current came and just swept the raft away and that was the last we heard of them.

'That was Saturday the 14th. On Sunday 15 February, Chief Officer Sedgman of the *Vyner Brooke* – with a group of four or five men and another lass and myself, went into the village on the island to try and get help for his wounded amongst us but the natives said the Japanese were on the island and they were just not going to help us. So we came back to the beach. That night we saw a ship in Banka Straits being shelled and later were joined by a lifeboat full of English servicemen whose ship had been sunk out in the straits. There were between thirty and forty with a number of wounded amongst them. On Monday morning, the Merchant Navy Officer Sedgman called everybody together and said, "Right. We're here, we've got plenty of water, we have no food, we have no means of getting away and there are over 100 of us. What do you want to do?" And it was quite unanimous that he and a party should go and contact the Japanese and say that there was a group wanting to be taken prisoner. So they went off.

'Back on the beach we had civilian women and children and the children were pretty testy by this time, having been through a ship-wreck and not having had anything to eat for about fifty-two hours. So Matron Drummond decided to get the women and children together and get them started off towards Muntok and we nurses would stay behind as we were trying to make some kind of stretchers and things to help carry the wounded. So that was done and the women took off.

'Eventually Sedgman and the other men returned plus this party of Japanese. Sedgman said to the Japanese, "This is the group that want to be taken prisoner", and he was brushed aside.

'The Japanese had a little chat together and Sedgman went up again and said, "This is the group that wish to be taken prisoners", and he was once more brushed aside. Then they put all the women on one side. They took half the men off and we heard nothing and the Japanese came back ten or fifteen minutes later wiping their bayonets. They took the rest of the men away and we heard several shots this time. The Japanese again came back cleaning their bayonets as well as rifles.

'At that time there were left on the beach twenty-two army sisters, one civilian woman and about ten or twelve stretcher cases that had been wounded in the bombing of our ship and the shelling of the other one. When they had finished cleaning their rifles and bayonets, the Japanese ordered the twenty-three of us women to march into the sea. We had gone a few yards into the water when they commenced to machine-gun us from behind. I saw the girls fall one after the other. Then I was hit.

'Being young and naive I always thought that if you were shot by a bullet you'd had it. With the force of the bullet I overturned and lay there. As time went by, to my amazement I was still alive but having swallowed so much salt water I became sick and then I was terrified that they would see my heaving shoulders, so I tried to stop being sick and just lay there and the water gradually brought me back into shore.

'I haven't any idea of time but when I found the courage to sit up and look around, there was nothing – none of the girls anywhere, none of the stretcher patients and the Japanese had gone. I became suddenly terribly, terribly cold and all I could think of was to get up in the jungle.'

She dragged herself up into the jungle and there lost consciousness. 'I wouldn't know how long I was there. When I awoke and was lying there contemplating things, I had every intention of getting up and going down and having a drink at the spring and why I didn't get up then I'll never know, because I heard nothing, there was not a sound but I suddenly saw this line of helmets and bayonets going down to the beach again. Well, that was enough to send the heart down to the very bottom of my feet. I don't know how long I laid there but when they came back I swore I looked into every pair of eyes that went past. It took me a little while to pull myself together and when I did I went down to the spring and was just about to have a drink when this voice from behind me said, "Where have you been, nurse?" Well, that was almost as bad as the Japs. I swung around – it was one of the stretcher cases, an English soldier who'd come in the boat and he'd had all the top part of his arm blown off during the sea battle and then he had been bayoneted by the Japs on the beach. He had later crawled into a fishing hut near the beach.

'We exchanged names [his was Kingsley] and the bits of information we had and he said, "What are you going to do?" I said, "It shouldn't take us long to die". He said, "No". I said I was going back to the jungle. He was going back to his hut because he had faith in it and I said no, there's already been a party down here looking around, did you see them? He hadn't. I said, "Well, no way will I stay out here in the open, I'm going into the jungle". So he agreed to come.' She managed to get him and herself up to the jungle and then gathered some life belts that were on the beach. 'They looked comfortable, and still being a nurse I got some water bottles and filled them with fresh water from the spring and found some coconut husk and put that around his wounds. It was probably the following Tuesday, I didn't know, the next day or two I wandered along the beach to see if . . .' But no girls' bodies floated ashore.

She went into the village where she had been on the previous Sunday, 'The native women gave me some food which I took back to the beach. We lived on that food and fresh water until Kingsley was strong enough to walk. We decided to give ourselves up again and I said I hope that they make a better job of it this time. He agreed but said, "Do you mind if we leave it for another twenty-four hours because I'll be 39 tomorrow and I would like to think that I was free on my birthday", so I said, "Well, you know, time is no object".

The morning after his birthday we set off. We got to the village and once the native men knew that we were giving ourselves up they became quite helpful and gave us some tea and biscuits and put us on the track to Muntok. On the way we met an Indonesian who spoke very good English and he told us there were white women wearing Red Cross arm bands at Muntok. After he left us I said to Kingsley, "Well, I really don't think he could be making all that up; maybe they are taking prisoners now and if they are they won't want to know about the story on the beach because that's pretty terrible, so we'd just better forget about it and stick to the story that we'd been shipwrecked and we've been in the jungle and the local people told us to give ourselves up."

'We had just agreed on this story when we heard a car coming up behind us and I didn't think until the car pulled up that there would only be Japanese in it, which was probably a good thing because if we had realised we'd have both most likely tried to break to the jungle and we'd probably both have been shot again. But as it was, we didn't think quick enough and the car was upon us. There was a Japanese naval officer and a soldier interpreter whose English was very poor. They both got out, searched us, then told us to get into the car and we were driven to the island's Japanese naval headquarters. Eight men came out, all dressed in the most beautiful silk kimonos and they looked so clean and fresh to somebody who hadn't washed or changed anything in a fortnight. They questioned us as to where we'd been, how we'd got there and then they started questioning us about Singapore and I said, "I'm a nurse and I was far too busy looking after the men that your army had been killing and wounding and I have no idea". Kingsley said that he had been one of the reinforcements and had only been in Singapore forty-eight hours.

'They asked me if I would work and I said I was prepared to work in a hospital but I wouldn't work anywhere else and they asked Kingsley if he would work and he said yes. Kingsley had said to me, "Don't tell them I'm injured because they have got no time for injured men". One of the Japanese became very interested in my rising sun badge and he asked to have a look at it, so I took it off and gave it to him, and he was about to pocket it and automatically, without thinking I said, "Oh, that's mine", and put my hand out and their leader said something to him and he handed it back to me. They gave us tea and biscuits then they signalled to Kingsley to get into the car. So we shook hands solemnly and wished each other the best and he took off.

'When he had gone one of the Japanese brought out a baby monkey to entertain me and then another one brought out a bandage and offered me his ankle to bandage. When the car came back I was told to get into it so, backing down the steps with my water bottle over this hole in my uniform, I got into the car and we drove off. Soon I saw a line of European servicemen and I thought oh, they *are* taking prisoners. Then there was a white woman with a Red Cross armband on her sleeve. The car pulled up at the entrance to this place and an Englishman came up to me and said, "Welcome sister, it is nice to have you with us, your name, number and unit etc." And I was quite composed because I was just so relieved that I was with *people* again and I started to give him all this information, and while I was talking to him I could see about 20 yards away a sea of faces, women, all peering through the entrance, and from out of that group I heard somebody say, "It's Bullwinkel". Well, that was the end, I just made for this crowd, hadn't any idea who I was going to see, and I said, "Oh, somebody knows me!" The fellow said, "Look, I've only got a few more questions to ask you", and I was saying, "Somebody knows me". It was two of the girls from the 2/10th AGH, I think it was Beryl Woodridge and Jenny Greer who grabbed me.

'I'd made up my mind that I wasn't going to talk about what had happened on the beach. They asked me had I seen this person, had I seen that person and I was saying no, I hadn't. By the time we got to the seventh name I sort of broke down and I said, "Look, yes, I do know what happened", and I told them. Well, of course, they were just so horrified and Nesta James then said, "Oh, I must go and see somebody", and I said, "Well, for goodness sake don't tell too many people because I don't think it's a very pretty story and there might be repercussions". Anyway, James went off and she saw some prisoners who were Army Intelligence and told them what had happened, and they said to her, "Forget about it, don't talk about it, don't mention it, deny everything, don't do anything, don't intimate that you know anything or heard anything at all, because without a doubt if they find out that somebody knows [about the massacre] it won't only be sister who goes out, you will all be taken out", because at that time, every day people were disappearing from the camp. The Japanese would come in and some Malay or English people who had held positions would be taken out and they were never seen again.

'James came back and told us it was to be forgotten, we were not to talk about it. And amongst us we never spoke about it again. I did run into a couple of the civilian women who'd been on the beach with us and they said, "Nice to see you, what happened?" And I just said, "Please forget about it, forget that you were ever on the beach or that you saw us nurses", and fortunately they were two sensible women and what they said to the other women who had been on the beach I don't know, but never at any time did another query come from them. About three years later a group of people were brought into camp and amongst them was a European woman married to a Chinese doctor who was with us on the beach. (He had gone from the beach at Banka with the married women and the children that day as their medical man.) They had each been put into solitary confinement and this doctor was now dead. But after three years his wife recognised me and said, "You were on the beach weren't you?" and I said, "No, no, I haven't been on the beach." "Oh," she said, "yes you were. There were a group of nurses on the beach." So I said, "Yes, we have heard something about that but I certainly wasn't there, and when we are in uniform we all look very much alike". She didn't push it any further.

'The only other time there was any query was after I had to go into hospital because I got a terrible tinea on my feet and couldn't walk. In the hospital was Dr Goldberg, a German, who came and sat on my bed for half an hour and did her level best to find out what had happened to me after the ship had sunk, so I stuck to my story that I'd got ashore and I'd been in the jungle and that the local people told me to give myself up. She asked all sorts of questions in different ways. Whether she had heard or whether it was thought that somebody knew anything about it, I don't know.'

Rohan Rivett, Australian war correspondent, was attempting to escape across Banka Island at the time of the massacre of the nurses but did not then know of the death of the women. His own escape boat had broken down and he and six other escapees headed for the swamp lands of Banka Island, only to be captured later. He said of the massacre, 'It was the hush-hush story of the prison camps because although rumours of the atrocity were common in all prison camps in the southern regions, it was felt that if the Japanese got wind of it they would unquestionably shoot nurse Bullwinkel out of hand'.

Vivian Bullwinkel: 'For the first few months I couldn't lift anything heavy but apart from that the wound just healed. Being in salt water had helped, and I'd had absolute complete rest for I don't know how long after being shot and that must have done me good. We were young and healthy and it healed itself.'

The girls gave her clothes and concealed the tell-tale cotton uniform she'd been wearing with the blood stains and the holes where the bullets ripped through. (In recent years it has been placed in the Australian War Museum.)

'During those first few days when we were in the jungle I wanted to pray but I wouldn't let myself because I'm not a church goer, but I believe and have faith, I'm a Christian, but I thought no, I won't pray, won't appeal to Him just because I'm in trouble. He's got enough anyway, everybody's appealing to Him. It took me about three days and on the third day I just couldn't help it and I sent up a little prayer and from that moment I felt it was going to be all right. It was an amazing experience.

'When Kingsley and I had eventually decided to give ourselves up we both honestly believed that we wouldn't be taken

prisoner, that they would have to kill us. My only fear was
that they would see I was frightened, nothing else worried me,
it was just the fact that I didn't want them to know how frightened I was.

'Kingsley died a week after we gave ourselves up. The padre
from the men's camp was in hospital when I was in there and
he told me. I think it was just sheer determination that got him
to the camp when we walked across the island. I don't even
know what his christian name was. But he had his 39th birthday.

'One thing almost shattered us. This day all the Australian
army nurses were called up to the guardhouse because a high-
ranking Japanese officer wanted to see us. We thought we
might be going to be repatriated or something. But he said that
he had come to tell us how very grateful the Japanese government was to the Australian government for sending the ashes
of the Japanese submariners who had attacked Sydney back to
Japan, and that they wanted us to know that the Japanese
government appreciated this gesture very much indeed. Our
hearts were down in our feet thinking that the Japanese must
have got to Sydney, but we hoped we didn't show it on our
faces. We said well, as they had been so appreciative of that,
what about sending us out – I'm sure the Australian government would be very appreciative of that. We tried to be quite
nonchalant about it, but we couldn't get back to our huts
quick enough to start working it out and try to be logical –
how could they have got to Sydney? No submarines would get
down to Sydney and get into the harbour! And then, after we'd
thrashed it out, we realised that if they'd really got Australia,
the Japs' behaviour towards us would have been very different
to what it was. So we gained faith again that Australia was
still free.

'Mostly we have put it out of our minds but there are some
things which do come back; only when we are together and
talking about things. Mind you, there are things that I haven't
talked about. But when I think of those days I believe that we
were probably all a bit odd by the end. I only have to remember the toilet in the Banka camp to know that. The toilet was

a great big pit but, of course, being cement it couldn't drain or soak away and the time came when it filled and we kept asking if we could do something about it, if we could empty it, but they said no, there is no need. Until one night a Dutch nun fell in and there was such a hue and cry and the Dutch women were so furious and so upset I think the guards rather feared for their lives. The upshot was that they decided they would form a lavatory gang and they called for volunteers. Wilma [Young] said to me that she was going to volunteer and I said "Well, you're mad because you're working in the hospital and doing this, that and the other thing and you'll get ill and I don't think you ought to do it". "Well", she said, "it's the only way that we'll get any money". So off she went and volunteered and she came back and told me, "I've volunteered but I have to have somebody to take my place when I become ill". And I said, "Well don't look at me". She didn't say anything but the upshot was that after a while she got ill of course and all that night I tossed and turned with my pride, all night poor Wilma tossed and turned because she thought she might lose her job when somebody else took her place. She didn't get much money, just enough to get a duck egg when the pedlar came in, or a bit of sugar.

'Anyway, the sun rose and of course I crawled out. Then I got the position of permanent reliever.

'What they gave us as equipment was a long stick that two of you put on your shoulders with a kerosene bucket in the middle to carry à la Chinese, and they gave you a long handle with half a coconut shell on the end of it to empty the big cement pit out into the bucket. Well, you don't get far with half a coconut shell of fluid. It took ages, but it did keep the level down, it didn't overflow any more, and that's about all we could hope for. And then, one of the permanent women retired and they appointed somebody else, and I was so upset to think that here am I being reliever for so long and when a permanent position comes up I get overlooked! I was so upset! So, as I said, we probably were a bit peculiar. The real world was no part of us.'

Betty Jeffrey, whose book *White Coolies* was written after she returned home from three and a half years imprisonment, recalls 'Everything. You forget nothing. Not a thing from years like those.'

Betty was a nursing sister with the 2/10th AGH Malacca for nine months. 'Right in the thick of it when the Japs started the war on 8 December 1941. By the beginning of February we were forced to evacuate and set up our hospital in a Chinese school in Singapore. We were bombed daily. Eventually there were continuous daylight bombing raids. You felt the tenseness in the air all the time as though the air itself was tense, there was nothing to allay the feeling that doom was rolling towards us. Six of our girls had been sent off with some patients on a Chinese hospital ship.

'The *Empire Star* was to sail, there was room for thirty nurses so Matron Paschke calmly sent this number off to the wharf while just as calmly she continued supervising her hospital where the rest of her nurses were flat out receiving the never-ending stream of wounded.

'Wounded and still more wounded', Betty Jeffrey later wrote, 'while the bombing and noise went on and on. On Thursday 11 February, Matron had a call for help and drove Sisters Cuthbertson, Blanch, Davis, Freeman, Halligan and myself to another hospital nearby. We went straight into work. I heard Matron Paschke on the phone saying "Yes sir. Yes sir. Yes sir". She turned to me and said, "Jeff, can you get seventy-eight patients in by midnight?" I said, "Yes sir, yes sir" without thinking. To put the seventy-eight patients in we knocked out the thin walls in this building and by midnight we were pulling their boots and socks off while Matron was in the kitchen making soup for them. By daylight we had been working forty-eight hours straight and I was walking along the ward in the first glow of sunlight and I could hear gentle breathing all around. I thought, "We've done it".'

She, like other nurses and doctors, had not been trained for war, hadn't experienced it, just dropped into it. 'But we were tough, we could do anything.

'Later we were shelled. We had beds out on an old tennis court under a marquee. Because it had been raining heavily, 150 beds began to sink into the soil. Sister Freeman and I were out there and they were actually sinking as you rested your hand on the bed to treat the men. When the bombs began to fall, some of the patients put their tin hats on and for those who didn't have tin hats, we put bed pans on their heads. The planes were firing streams of bullets. I had a tray with a cloth on it marked with a big red cross and I stepped out and lifted it up. The pilot coming in low must have seen it and he stopped the stream of bullets just before getting to us and began again after he passed on. A piece of shrapnel had gone by me, it just missed my face but seared my skin and hair on one side. I don't know how many hours we worked. When we were ordered out I realised I was hungry but there was nothing to eat except jelly, so I ate that. Never had I seen such a sight. There were wounded men everywhere, in bed, stretchers on the floor, verandahs, garages, tent and dugouts. Low flying planes were machine-gunning all round us. Wounded were arriving all the time. Almost 1000 were there, in the 200-bed hospital.

'When we were told we had to leave we said "You're joking" and went on working. "No", they said, "you're going". We said, "we're fit, we're coping with everything. We want to help these men, we don't want to go." But we were sent to the ship. As the ambulance I was in set off, an orderly threw my half-filled kitback in to me. We drove through the air raid in Singapore; once we took cover in St Andrew's church. Later we were joined by the remaining sisters of the 13th AGH and the 2/4th Casualty Clearing Station. There were now sixty-five of us and we were taken to the wharf, straight on to the *Vyner Brooke*.

'Matron was a great and well-known golfer, but she couldn't swim. She said to me, "If this thing sinks you'll have to help me Jeff". When the planes came over the *Vyner Brooke*, she talked to us and told us what our duty was.'

When the ship was bombed, Jeffrey slid down a rope over

the side by hand. They were 10 miles from shore but Betty was confident she would get there. Swimming in the water with her was Iole Harper from 13th AGH, these girls hadn't known one another until now. 'Shinning down the ropes had taken the flesh from my palms and my middle finger as well as from my fingertips, deep enough to remove my finger-prints.' (The scars remain.) She had eventually found a panel of wood from the side of a suitcase and was using it to paddle a raft.

'When I was swimming to this raft, Iole was calling out "Hurry up". But I had a life jacket and the rough canvas rubbed badly under my chin, so I was protecting it with one hand, using the burnt-by-rope hand to breast-stroke. We got so sleepy, even when we were in the water swimming, the sun was on you and the water was cool, it was a strange effect. Some dropped off from the sides of the boats because of this effect.

'I went looking for Matron Paschke in the water and later found her clinging to a crowded raft. She was wonderful.' Later Matron joined Betty and Iole Harper rowing throughout the night while other sisters nursed tiny children. The follow-ing morning they were as far out to sea as ever, the tides and currents assisting them towards shore and then taking them back out to sea. They were passed by numbers of Japanese ships but none stopped.

The load on the boat was too great to make headway and to lighten the load Betty, Iole Harper and two Malays went over the side into the water to swim. Betty found her torn hands were now too swollen to cling to the ropes. 'I was too tired to row too.' So she and Iole swam alongside until the raft was nearly ashore. 'A current suddenly swept the raft about and took it back out to sea. We called to them, but they went too fast for us to catch them and we never saw them again.'

After twenty-four hours in the water, the two nurses reached mangroves that lined the shore. They swam up creeks, along the shore, but always the mangroves drove them out. There was nowhere to rest, the mud below at low tide, the spiky mangroves above at high tide.

Some Malay fishermen found them, took them to a village, gave them food and tea and told them where they were, Banka Island. They also told them it was Tuesday: the girls had been in the water since Saturday. Their women and daughters bathed the nurses' cuts and wounds with clean warm water before taking them to a temple to await capture. 'They had assured us there was nothing we could do but give ourselves up to the Japanese who held the island and we agreed.'

And so the girls met up with the other nurses who had survived the sinking of the *Vyner Brooke*.

In the camps, first on Banka Island then Sumatra, Betty Jeffrey kept a diary on scraps of paper. 'Of course we were not permitted to do this', but she secreted her papers for three and a half years of her imprisonment. 'I was sick, lying on the bali bali one day, the thing where we slept, made like tea-tree fencing, I could see beneath this a broken bottle with spiders and things in it and I crawled out and pulled my papers into it and left the spiders to keep guard.

'Whenever I moved I had to find a way of transporting my diary. I had a little cushion for my head and sometimes I would put it in that. Once I had a bag around my waist and pulled my pants over that but that didn't go too well. They transported us in this boat thing and because I was sick I couldn't climb out so the Japs had to heave me out and I felt the bag go. Next day a Japanese came down asking us who owned the bag and I called out, "Me! me!" It hadn't been opened.

Betty suffered many illnesses. 'Everything was so damn dirty. There was not even clean water to pour over a wound, so things got septic quickly. Once Iole and I were carrying a big container on a coolie pole across our shoulders and the thing slipped and the pole cut my leg, not badly, not enough for me to bother about I thought, but it infected. We had two surgeons in our camp but they had no instruments. We had made lamps using as fuel the cooking oil got from palms and we found that this rubbed on wounds helped us.'

Betty had food poisoning, tropical fever, beriberi, dengue, was unconscious for some time with cerebral malaria. She had rashes, including that which both men and women got in crevices of the body in that humidity where they were unable to wash for days at a time. 'We'd scratch away in front of anybody', Betty said. 'Everyone did. Thought nothing of it.' She had chronic appendicitis and nothing could be done about it except total rest. She vomited constantly. She weighed 4 stone, 10 pounds (height 5 feet 7 inches).

'When looking for entertainment the girls would say, "Come on, let's count Jeff's ribs", and they'd go tinkling along my ribcage. The Japs thought we were mad laughing at this silly game. Unlikely things became commonplace, such as when we would come into shelter from rain, we would bend over double to empty the pools of water in the two hollows at each side of our neck above the shoulder blades. The girls were marvellous, they made me hang on. Living shoulder to shoulder was no great effort, we were used to being in big wards and we nurses were chock-full of discipline without knowing it, and we had a great sense of humour, which you have to have to get through nursing.'

They had arranged their own committees to carry heavy loads of firewood and heavy sacks of rice to the kitchen, to chop wood, stoke fires, cook rice in huge drums, draw water from the well and, if there was enough water, to wash clothes. During the dry season each internee was rationed to a small tin of water each day.

Periodically, squads had to plant potatoes for the guards outside the camp and daily during the dry season go and water these potatoes with clean, fresh tap water while back in the camp the daily ration for nurses was this one can of brackish well water. Twice every day, every woman and child had to be counted, the Japanese called this tenko. The guard blew a whistle, the women ran out of the barracks and the kitchen, lined up, barrack by barrack, and bowed to the guard. Actually they bowed to the Emperor of Japan, or so they had been told. When the lines were crooked, or the women didn't bow at the correct angle or if they had disdain on their faces, the guard prodded them with his bayonet, kicked them or made them stand for hours in the sun long after the others had been dismissed.

'The Japs would occasionally tell us "news". It was always bad. They said their submarines had knocked out the Sydney Harbour Bridge. We were terribly upset. Then they said they had knocked out the centre pylon of Sydney Harbour Bridge and it fell down. We sighed in relief, we knew there was no centre pylon. But there was not much relief to be got, we tried to get something out of refusing to be cowed; during tenko we stood politely with our hands behind our backs looking the Japanese up and down. They hated us.

'We never stopped thinking about the lost girls. The girls on the beach, as we spoke of them, were never out of our minds. But after Viv (Bullwinkel) came into camp we knew we'd all be taken if we spoke of it. It was a most amazing thing to do, to keep a secret so long, for over three years. No one mentioned machine-gunning, always we just said "the beach".'

Betty became one of the singers who performed the 'Song of Survival'. Along with her diary she secreted a copy of this remarkable manuscript of an orchestra without instruments except for the human voice. 'It was a great thing this, to be doing something so like people could have done in civilian days, particularly when we were all so sick.'

But the women still had their voices. The various nationalities had sung separately because not all of them spoke each other's language, but then, 'a wonderful thing happened'. An English woman, Nora Chambers, suggested singing music written for orchestra or piano, another woman, Margot Driver, a 50-year-old Presbyterian missionary, had precise musical recall. She wrote down pages of Beethoven, Chopin, Debussy, and this was rearranged to form a 'vocal orchestra' with thirty Dutch, Australian and British women prisoners as singers. They wanted the concert to be a surprise so rehearsed in a tiny shed behind the kitchen. For their first recital on 27 December 1943 the audience 'dressed'. Sitting on the ground, the women prisoners 'were a sight to see', as Betty Jeffrey says. Some wore dresses they had saved for the day the war ended, but most wore the only clothes they owned, some were in faded, patched dresses, others in the 'camp uniform' of shorts and neck halters. Some shared lipstick they were saving for that great day when the gates would open. The thirty choir members filed in carrying stools to sit on because in their weakened condition it was too tiring for them to sing standing. They had already been prisoners for one and a half years. They were thin, hungry, with tropical sores on their bare legs and feet.

Margot Driver spoke: 'This evening we are asking you to listen to voices trying to reproduce some of the well-known music usually given by an orchestra or pianist in days gone by. So close your eyes and try to imagine you are in a concert hall, hearing Toscanini or Sir Thomas Beecham conduct his world-famous orchestra.'

As Nora Chambers lifted her hands to conduct, the guard came running from the guardhouse, bayonet at the ready, crying 'Hoo! hoo!' Large gatherings were not permitted and the women knew this, but they ignored him and he became so entranced by the music that he stopped shouting and quietly listened to the entire concert.

The impact of the music on the prisoners was intense. 'It renewed a sense of human dignity, of being stronger than the enemy, of staying on top of it all.' The unique vocal orchestra gave concerts all through 1944. By the beginning of 1945, half of the singers including Margot Driver had died, but those living continued. 'Each time it seemed a miracle that among the bedbugs, cockroaches, rats, among the smells of the open latrines, hunger pangs, fevers, and boils, women's voices could produce so much beauty. If they had to hold a note for several measures they got out of breath, but still the beauty remained.' This was now their third year in captivity.

'Wilma [Oram]' said Betty Jeffrey, 'was stronger than many because she was young. As time went on her task was to dig graves. She would do the rounds of us ill in bed to see how many graves she would need to dig each day. Bodies could not be left overnight in that country.'

'Yes, people died in prison camps', Wilma says. 'That's what they were, those camps, places where people died. We buried them, bundled them in by the score. Wild pigs dug down, we covered them up again.'

Mona Wilson had trained with Wilma. 'We were on night duty early 1940, came off at 9 a.m. "France has fallen!" the early paper said. I said, "I'm going". Mona said, "I'm going too". We were together all the time until she was drowned off the *Vyner Brooke*. Mona couldn't swim. I went over the side with her but the ship rolled over.' Wilma came up through the rails and saw the life rafts slide towards her, felt each one bash her head. Blood poured over her face and down her neck. 'Mona didn't come up.' Wilma got on a life raft. A Eurasian girl came up. 'Such was society in those days she asked my permission to climb on the raft. The oars were tied firmly on the raft; I had my duty scissors in my uniform pocket so I cut the cord and we rowed.

'During the night it seemed that shapes materialised around us like great castles. I could clearly see the figures of men way up high above our heads as though they were on battlements and were looking down on us. We banged on the outside wall with our oars but no one answered. We had found ourselves among big Japanese war ships and in the morning they were gone, where, we didn't know.

'Then, we rowed towards shore. We could see the beach but we came and went with the tide, we couldn't make headway. We saw lots of motor boats. We rowed to them. "They're Japanese! Get out of here! Row away!" the girl cried. Well, where could we go? We weren't near anywhere.' But the Japanese merely looked curiously at the women as they floated around. 'Just looked at us, gabbled away a bit to each other, but showed no other interest and then they too went away.' Eventually the two women reached shore.

In the prison camp Wilma was known as 'the girl with short hair' because her hair had been cut off to deal with the wounds in her scalp. 'Viv used to look after me when I was sick.'

'We had an awful trip by ship from Banka Island to Palembang. We buried women at sea as we went. Then a train trip, not allowed to look out. Viv got sick at this place. We got worms, all of us. The treatment killed some, it was too severe for them. Viv was very sick. Her hair fell out. Then she began to mend.

'We had several different orders of nuns with us, many of them died. I remember Sisters Brigitta, Imelda, Pasadea.

'Most of us didn't have handkerchiefs, toothbrushes, none of the things you "can't do without" at home. One of the sailors off the *Perth* came in as a patient. "The thing I miss most is a toothbrush", he said. I said, "Here, have a loan of mine". So we shared my toothbrush. I don't know who he was. Didn't see him again. [Later a woman who died in the camp bequeathed her toothbrush to Wilma.] Yes, food was poor. Soup was made out of a type of local spinach but it was a case of in one end and out the other. You had to ask the Japs' permission to go to the lavatory. If you didn't they just fired a shot after you.

'They put women and children in one room, us nurses in another; lights on all night. We couldn't sleep, mosquitoes were thick on us. They took us on a route march. We looked like pictures I'd seen in newsreel theatres in the early war years of Polish refugees straggling along the road. We reached another camp where Japs sat around and made jokes about us that we couldn't understand. They had a club and demanded that six of us nurses come along. We said no. They said they would starve us. We said we would prefer that, but we did go, all of us, instead of six of us there were about twenty-six and we looked absolutely awful. One wore a pair of football shorts. I was younger than the others, I didn't look so bad but I was asked not to go. One Jap wanted to kiss a girl and she pushed him over and fled, expecting him to kill her or something, but he must have been afraid he would look ridiculous in front of his peers. We managed to get word through to Japanese higher command about this business and were later moved into houses the Dutch had left behind, twenty-six in each little house. In the eight months we were in that camp we were allowed to write one card home. We didn't receive any mail until early 1945 and then very little. We didn't know how things were at home. Was Australia still free?

'We tried to get a bit of law and order in that camp, tried to control the hygiene. The lavatory was a hole in the ground and the Japs pumped it out when it was full and let it run down the gutter. Dysentery was rife. Dr McDowell was our camp commandant and he asked if some girls would volunteer for a hygiene squad. At night we had to bury excreta as best we could. The jungle at night was steamy, damp. We got bad tinea. Viv had it on her hands and feet. We were taken to hospital for treatment. Bad things happened. One civilian woman learned of her husband's fate when a bundle of his clothes was brought to her in camp. Women died one after another, I remember Mrs Jennings, Mrs Leyland. We didn't see the men from the other camp but one Christmas, going along the road, we women stopped near their camp and sang "Oh Come All Ye Faithful" to them. The next day as we went along we stopped and men's voices came to us "Oh Come All Ye Faithful". By such moments were we saved from despair.'

The degradation of prison life deprived the women of everything they had known. They were not only in a foreign land away from home and family but they were also bereft of the AIF, these men who had been their patients, companions and friends until near the last of the fighting on the Malay peninsula. 'We knew of the British surrender in Singapore', Iola Harper says. 'The Japs made sure we knew about that every day.' But they didn't know where their erstwhile comrades had been imprisoned or, indeed, which of the men or nurses were still alive.

A variety of deep emotions engulfed them. What was happening back home in Australia? Did anyone down there know about the prisoners? Know where they were? Barred windows and barbed wire were the extent of their parameters of information. Most of the nurses who had survived the sinking of the MV *Vyner Brooke* had little clothing, some had had what little they escaped in torn off by the strong currents in Banka Strait. Some had dragged themselves ashore in the mangroves. 'You can't walk through mangroves, or swim. They are not strong enough to support your body so you cannot rest. Thick grey mud, deep to your thighs, halts your progress.' Those who had duty uniforms on when captured, saved them for the day of deliverance and joined the majority of the women prisoners wearing shorts and tops made of any scrap of material they could find.

Postcards from some nurses got through, including one from Sister Mavis Hannah, at Sumatra, 1942:

Dear Mum, Dad, all the family and friends,
Here I am, well and unharmed, so don't worry please. There are thirty-two of us including Raymont, Parr Street, Largs Bay; Ashton, 57 Mary Street, Unley; Clancy, 40 Stanley Street, Nth Adelaide and Bullwinkel, King's Park. We comprise the only South Australians. Please communicate with their people. I'm wondering what has happened to you. As long distance breast-stroke does not permit baggage carrying, I now possess no worldly goods except very scanty attire. Please communicate with the Red Cross and try and send a letter, parcels and money if able to do so. If possible washing material, sewing cotton, serviceable shoes or sandshoes, 4½ size, toilet requisites, vitamin B tablets, sunglasses, dried fruits, vegetable seeds especially carrots, parsnips, lettuce, tomatoes, beans, peas, onions, etc., tinned goods, in fact anything edible or plain useful, wearable things, also books to read, sheets, towels, etc. Shakespeare, English History or something of interest which could be read and studied would be very useful beside novels. Rice is our staple diet and has its limitations. We have made cards and tiles and play contract bridge and mah jong. God bless you all, keep smiling, please don't worry. I'm OK. I hope and pray to see you soon. All my love to you.

There were not only army nurses (who, like the servicemen,

had volunteered for war service) but hundreds of civilian women who were swept into prison camps for the duration of the war. These were women who had lived in Asia, in the NEI and Singapore as well as Rabaul and other areas of New Britain; these women shared the prison experience along with the nurses, often with the added burden of not knowing in which prison camp their menfolk were suffering or if, indeed, they were alive.

Vivian Bullwinkel: 'When we came back to Australia, we all thought we were pretty normal but maybe we weren't. We missed each other tremendously to begin with. We were really lonely for the people we'd been with, and most of us had a special friend.'

Wilma Oram and Vivian were close friends. 'I went to Adelaide because mother was then living there and I was home about a week when Wilma rang from Victoria and said, "I'm coming over". Never mind about her family. I said to mum, "Wilma's coming to stay" and mother was absolutely horrified. She said, "But we've got nowhere to put her, we haven't got a spare bed". I said, "We don't need a bed. She can sleep on the floor", and mum said, "She cannot sleep on the floor!" And I said, "Well, she can have my bed and *I'll* sleep on the floor", because those things didn't matter any more. Mum insisted on getting a stretcher from somebody but to us it wasn't important.

'I used to take my washing with me when I had a bath and mother stood this for two or three days and she said, "Vivian, I'll do your washing", and I said, "No, there's no need mum, I'll be fine". "No", she said, "I'd like to do it". I said I would do it myself, and then she thumped the table and said, "Well, I'm not having the washing done in the bath!" And I said, "All that water going to waste!"

'Mother was very good and my brother was very understanding and so we had no problem there. But we nurses were lucky because we had a profession, we were trained and we had something to go to as soon as we got back, we didn't have to establish ourselves like the men did, some of them had just got married, had to come home and take on these responsibilities and those who hadn't married had to go and get a job to live, but nurses just went back and once you're on duty you haven't got time to think of anything else, and therefore we adjusted very quickly.'

Sister Jessie Symons wrote a book of these years, *While History Passed Us By*, a thoroughly appropriate title. These women missed out on years of history during their long imprisonment. 'Years later we were still catching up. You'd see newspaper articles or hear people speak and you didn't know anything about this thing, nothing. Where it struck us first was when they told us the war was over. We were still waiting in the camp to be found when five servicemen were parachuted in to take over the area and they went to the men's camp and the two Australians with them were told that there were Australian nurses here. Well, these two kids came over and asked for us and we rushed up and got hold of them and took them down to our hut and sat them down, some of us without hair and some with teeth and some without and we all looked ghastly and we bombarded them with all sorts of questions. We heard about the atomic bomb that ended the war, B24s, jeeps, and it was a new language to us, we really didn't know what they were talking about half the time. And to bring it back to our level, one of the girls said, "And what are they doing about permanent waves these days?" The boys said, "Oh yes, there's still permanent waves, and they've got cold ones now". After they went we said aren't they sweet, but they know nothing about permanent waves! They're just answering us because we asked all these questions. When we got out, the first thing we wanted was to have our hair done, and we had a *cold wave*. I remember those boys, Bates from Thornbury and Gillam from Perth. They tried to bridge the gap for us. But it couldn't ever be completely bridged.

'We hadn't any idea of anything that happened in Europe. We didn't know about the various battles that went on until somebody started talking about the landing in Normandy that went wrong, or Bader (who was well-known when we got out and we caught up with all his exploits) but it was years and we were still finding out bits and pieces of what happened. We didn't know about VE Day, didn't know about Victory in Europe.

'We had got one lot of mail and by everybody pooling their letters you found out that somebody's brother who had been in the Middle East when we went to Singapore was now up in New Guinea, so by that we realised that the AIF must have been brought home, but we didn't know what had happened in the Middle East. Had no idea how the war – or Australia – had gone.'

Vivian was called to the War Crimes Tribunal in Japan. 'They didn't say I *had* to go, but they asked me if I would go and I said I would like to think about it because I wasn't too sure how I'd react. Well, I tried to be sensible about it and decided I should go anyway because I owed it to the girls and that I would just play it by ear when I got there. I was glad I had because going to Japan gave me a slightly better understanding when I saw the way that they were treating their own women, women working out in the fields and carrying heavy loads while the men walked ahead empty-handed, and women road-mending down on their knees, and it was clear that nowhere did their women have the same freedom as we have. So I thought of that and it did make me understand a little of their treatment of us. But I found the first weeks hard, hearing raised Japanese voices or seeing them: they were still wearing their uniforms in those days because they had nothing else. Seeing a uniformed person coming along towards you, you just sort of, you tensed up, you just had no control over it. You tensed until he'd gone past and then relaxed.'

Less known than the nurses who had been captured ex-Singapore were the nineteen Australian women caught in New Britain. Along with the six army nurses were civilians, mostly missionaries, who, in July 1942, were shipped to Japan where they worked for the rest of the war, 30 kilometres from Yokohama. The winters were severe, no warm blankets or heating, no shoes, but they were given a 4-yard length of warm material, one pair of briefs, one pair of socks and a singlet. They dug air-raid shelters, carried and cut timber and felled trees. Some earned a little money to barter for food by knitting silk bags, even making paper envelopes for sale. Their food was poor, Red Cross parcels rare. They had no baths, only cold showers. With the women were Miss Joyce Olroyd-Harris, matron of the Rabaul Hospital, and Miss Dorothy Beale, another stalwart New Britain hand.

They survived imprisonment along with the other women, isolated from their homes, their own language, customs and security. Matron Olroyd-Harris later said, 'We knew what we took on when we went to outposts in those days, but who would have expected what happened to us?' Then, there were the very young.

A Time Apart

Edith Leemburger (Perth, WA) was 14 years old. 'It was a period when we were suspended in time. It's hard to relate to it now. It's a time apart. I like to think it helped me in my life. It prepared me for tragedies or anything that was to follow. I'm always optimistic, and I was always strong-willed and that helped.

'Grandad went down when our ship *Giangbee* was sunk. It was a small cargo freighter with eight cabins but there were over 300 of us on board, all over the decks and everywhere. On the night of 12 February when we left Singapore, they were bombing all around, we didn't even have time to get our luggage on board, just went on as we were. On the 13th we were shelled and bombed all day by Japanese ships and planes and six cruisers came around and they asked the captain whether there were any army soldiers or navy personnel on board (in the meantime the servicemen had thrown their uniforms overboard) and the Japanese said that they would come aboard and check and they lowered a boat from one of their cruisers and that little boat wasn't far away from us when two Dutch servicemen appeared on our deck and machine-gunned the people who were in the little boat. The Japs didn't bother to come aboard after that, they just turned back and said on the loud hailer, "Women and children off the ship, we're going to shell it". Only two of the lifeboats made it ashore out of the six on the *Giangbee*.

'My grandfather and grandmother were on either side of me holding my hands but when they were going to shell the ship a lot of people came up and somehow grandad's hand came out of mine and we spent a lot of time looking for him in the chaos and dark; we had no lighting on the ship because bombs had wrecked the engines and the generators, we were at a standstill. It was chaotic, a moonless night, pitch dark, and the only time we could even glimpse another's face was by the searchlights that the cruisers were playing around our ship. We were looking for grandad and my grandmother was absolutely frantic, she thought that I could have had a little more care in hanging on to him – I don't know whether she ever forgave me for this, they were very attached. Everything was so disorganised. I think I switched off to preserve my sanity, I felt that I was very apart from it all. I couldn't cry – there were people screaming and shouting because the lifeboat ropes had shrapnel through them and as a boat was lowered the ropes snapped and all the people just emptied out into the water and it was terrible. We were on the side of the ship where there were no more lifeboats and through a loud speaker the Japanese said they were now going to shell the ship and that we'd have to jump for it. Nan and I jumped into the water and a lifeboat came alongside and as the searchlights played across the water I heard someone say, "Oh, it's a very old lady and a young girl", and others said, "Well, there's definitely no way we can take any more on the boat" (there were fifty-six on the lifeboat that was built for twenty), but somehow we hung on the ropes, the lifelines on the side. There was another lifeboat near us and they started singing hymns. When I hear "Nearer my God to Thee" it always connects straight back to that time because that's what they were singing as they went down because of the shrapnel holes in the hull of their boat. From then on it got to a point where I felt it was unreal, it must surely be a dream. We had men hanging on to the lifelines around the lifeboat and the officer aboard said, "We have to make a decision because if we take them aboard we all sink". So they started to swing the oars and knock people away and my terrible concern was that one of them could be grandad and I remember starting to scream and scream and scream and call out for him, hoping that by my voice he would be attracted to where we were. Then the officer said we were to remain quiet, we were not to make a sound, and they even lifted the oars out of the water because the Japanese had started machine-gunning everyone in the water and lifeboats as well, and there was a time when we drifted right up to the hull of one of the Japanese ships but with the oars our men slowly pushed the boat away. We weren't even allowed to whisper and it's funny how in such a time one conforms. But there is also the terrible fear that someone will not. I remember at that time thinking oh well, if someone opens their mouth now that's going to be it.

'We drifted to sea, there was a storm. There was no sustenance on the lifeboat, no food, the water had gone putrid, it hadn't been checked for ages. Somebody had a tocologne cream jar (a great wrinkle cream it was!). Every time I see wrinkles I think of it. Well, they cleaned out that jar and rationed out the putrid water with the little tocologne jar which has more glass than the contents of the jar, so by the time we got our sip of water it was *just* a sip, which we treasured. I don't think the hunger worried me as much as the thirst. I didn't panic, but my tongue was swelling, my lips were swelling and we were getting very blistered with heat in the daytime. Although we were now on the boat there was no shelter. There was one person who said she was going to answer the telephone and got up and just walked off the boat.

'We were so crammed that I had my feet beneath me and couldn't move. No one spoke much. It was an eerie, eerie time.

When we saw the land you'd think that we'd be jubilant and shouting "land, land!" We were crazy for land, but it was a quiet time, perhaps because we were so hungry and thirsty. When we eventually landed on Banka Island on February the 15th, I had to roll myself off the lifeboat because of my cramped legs and when I hit the water in this position, I thought I was going to drown. But I crawled out on to the beach. We slept on the beach; I had slacks on and a long-sleeved silk blouse but the sandflies had bitten me everywhere, even my scalp was just a mass of sores. It's hard to look back in time, all I know is nothing was registering, not in a painful way. Can you understand what I am saying?

'Well, the fifty-six of us slept on that beach for about four days, then Malays took us for a bath with fresh water, the first for a long time. A Malay woman lent me a sarong. Then the Japanese came for us. Somebody had told them that we were there. They herded us into lorries and we were taken off. We didn't know where we were going. I'd never seen a Japanese before. I had studied about Japan in school, I thought it must be a beautiful place, Fujiyama and all those lovely places, but my first reaction was intense hate, because I made them responsible for my grandfather not being with us. I've never lost that feeling, I'm not proud of it, I think it's because one has to forget before one can forgive. I'm not able to forget. I have no control over that, there is nothing I can do about it. It gives me an emotion in which I can express myself. This is how I survived in camp.

'I became a loner and I've been a loner ever since those days. I still retreat from people simply because I feel I cannot relate. I can relate to music, to nature. Art gives me a lot of pleasure, but I'm still very suspicious of people because when I look back at man's inhumanity to man, you just can't believe the things they did. Even talking to you now I don't feel that I'm sharing anything with you because how can I tell you the smell of dying flesh, the stench of decaying dried blood, all the things that came on us. Death fascinated me in camp, we had a lot of that. I'd never seen death before. There was dry beriberi and wet beriberi. The wet beriberi bloated the body and when the body died I used to watch that water as it dripped through the bamboo slats we slept on and made a darker impression on the dirt floor and the body got thinner and thinner. It fascinated me, held my attention; if I knew there was a death I'd go and see what sort of death it was, what it was all about. No one knows the depth of mind of a child.

'The women started a choir later on and thought we children could contribute in some way and began teaching us the music, but we used to sing humpty-dumpty-dumpty-dump and they gave up on us. In fact, when we heard the older ones singing we used to go to where they were practising and we'd start humpty-dumpty-dump. I don't think we were serious about anything. That was a good time. Before we became very quiet. I had a little pair of shorts and a sun-top made out of an old flour bag.

'What did we do towards the end? I don't know what we did. I think we just sat and looked at each other, what was there to do? I'd walk along beside the barbed wire and put my hand outside the wire and look at my fingers and think gee, they're free. Silly things, but they meant something to me. I had malaria, all the different things that went around. That's how I met Viv Bullwinkel.

'Viv was on her rounds and told my grandmother that she would attend to the sores on my head. I liked Viv. I remember once her saying to look up at the stars and not down as prisoners tend to do. Whenever I'm down I always remember Viv and I go back to that time and I think, oh yes! One must look up at the stars.

'I knew of her situation, the wound, and the danger to her if the Japanese knew. I heard that she was very ill towards the end and it worried me. By then I was roaming around on my own because I couldn't relate to my grandmother. I'd grown lanky and had long thick hair. And the filth, the bugs, oh the rotting flesh, you couldn't be yourself and live with it. But I was never really there. Never. I wouldn't let myself be there.

'We suffered physically as well. I had to have a tooth out without an anaesthetic. The man was no dentist, just a carpenter with ordinary pliers and I think he fainted before I did. The root was left in the gum because he had cracked the tooth. I still have a gash right up into the palate of my mouth where he tried to remove the tooth. I learnt to bear pain, I've learnt a lot from it. I learnt to be patient, tolerant when things go wrong.

'In the beginning we children used to laugh and play and sing, and the adults initially treated us as children and took us under their wing, we had that little bit of protection. And then suddenly they were dissolving in front of us, they were dying, they were getting sick and it was hard for us to see that happen. In the beginning they used to say to us, now don't worry, you'll be alright, don't worry. At the end I can remember going to people I knew who were very ill or dying and saying, don't worry, it'll be alright, don't worry. The roles had reversed and this was hard. It was as though we had become the stronger, more protective. It was no longer, "Where are the children? How are the children?" It's not that they had no time for us, but they were exhausted and we lost that comfort of feeling protected.

'When the ship went down I had my period and I never had it again all during camp and for two years after that. I had to see a doctor. I think it was because I had malnutrition but in that sense I was fortunate because I saw how some of the others had to cope. But that again set me apart. I felt I was not relating because even that seemed unnatural.

'The truth is that when one goes through this sort of thing one doesn't want to be hurt again. I promised myself that one day I would end my years in a place that was beautiful and try and make up for everything that was so awful. I had a strong motive to have a lot of beauty around me towards the end. I don't know whether I hoped it would make up and take away the hate, the hurt, the anger. There is no bitterness now even when I see a Japanese; it's just that I can't relate and I know the feeling is hate – I'd rather be somewhere else – I don't want to be near.

'The adults seemed to fear hunger more than anything else, they said how hungry they were all the time and they were always talking about food, even fought over it. I was more afraid of being thirsty because of the experience I had when my tongue swelled up. I felt I couldn't swallow. For a year or so when I came out of camp I used to bring up my food, I couldn't retain it. I never thought when I came out of camp that food was important.

'The hustle, the bustle in Singapore, oh, I couldn't cope. I remember so clearly feeling that it wouldn't be too bad getting back to camp. I had been coping there and then suddenly I'm back again in a situation that I could not handle. The adults seemed to be pretty good at it, seemed to like it, to want it, they seemed to slip back into a social pattern, but I couldn't relate. I was nearly 18 when I came out of camp, and when they took us to Raffles Hotel I saw myself in a full-length mirror and I just couldn't relate to the image because I had not seen myself in a mirror as a grown person and for a long time after we came out of camp I used to just sit in front of a mirror and look and try to connect the image to the person I was in the prison.

'I didn't relate to the life that young girls were living at the time, it wasn't the life of boyfriends for me when I came out of camp. All I seemed to want was knowledge, I felt I'd missed out, I had to catch up on this. It was just wonderful, everything began to have meaning, a purpose.' (Edith Leemburger became a brilliant scholar, was awarded a US Information Scholarship to America and in New York got the cumulative score of 3.8 out of a possible 4 and a Fulbright Scholarship on top of that. Other honours followed.) 'I applied myself to study from the sheer love of knowledge and this is where I began to lose the hate in me: it turned to a love, but not to people, it was poured into learning.

'When I came out I couldn't relate – I didn't even recognise my mother or my young brother and sister when we were reunited. Of course they had grown up, but I couldn't remember names of friends, everything was just a total blank – it was a time apart. Some people say that the Japanese were kind to children, perhaps I never gave them that chance, but that was all I revelled in, just hating. Every time I saw them I just hated them. They were cruel, I saw some of the atrocities that happened in camp like when they booted our commandant; there was another lady that they hit with a rifle butt. I'd never seen aggression like that, I expected a reason for a happening.

'The Japanese used to tell us, "You're never going to get out of here. You're going to die and you can dig your graves." I suppose this propaganda got to us in the end and I began to value the moment, and this I have never lost. I have a past but I only know one thing: the future has got to be something beautiful – no way that I'm going to go through that again. No. I don't think about death. It's not worth thinking about, I've seen so much of it already. I don't think it will worry me, the howl of the wind will let us know when the time comes.'

She always knew she was going to get out. 'There was nothing surer than that, and I knew I was going to end up in something beautiful. [And her home is beautiful.] People say to me, "You'll get used to this view". But I never will. Never. I sometimes look at this and wonder if it will wipe out the rest. Perhaps it will. But barbed wire, oh, barbed wire . . . it is painful just to look out through barbed wire.

'As for today, I may not phone or see Viv or the others who were in camp with me for months and then – it's very settling, a very comfortable feeling this tie that binds us. We pick up conversation we left off months ago when we last met. It is a bond we will take to the grave with us. When you've been through the worst with people, words are not necessary any more. When I'm with other people I feel apart because there's something we've not shared. It was too real. Nothing before or after it was as intense.'

Henri Dunant's Cross

'Treat the captives and care for them.'

San Toyu, 4th century BC

'We live like kings on Red Cross things.'

Private E.V. Emerson, 2/3rd Battalion

IN NORMAL CIRCUMSTANCES IN the organised society in which he usually lives, man is protected by laws and finds sustenance close at hand. When wars throw society out of kilter laws are violated and chaos follows. War is said to be diplomacy continued by other means, the other means being the deaths, maiming and capture of young men. To succour the wounded and protect and care for captives in time of war is a relatively new concept dating only from the second half of the 19th century. Until that time the fate of the captive in wartime was, in the main, perilous. Rules governing prisoners were needed in an attempt to protect captives from worse excesses. The ordinary man at war has no means of exerting influence when the machine begins to roll. 'You and me are but ---ing cogs in this ---ing organisation' as the sergeant major said to Private Fitzroy MacLean when he joined the army.

It was not until Henri Dunant, a businessman from Geneva, accidentally stumbled on to the battlefield of Solferino on 24 June 1859 and subsequently founded an organisation to protect and assist mankind taken prisoner in war that captives had a champion. The heraldic device of a red cross on a white ground (the Swiss flag with colours reversed) was chosen, guaranteeing protection and assistance.

Dunant gathered philanthropists, medical men and crowned kings of the various empires of the day and gained their interest, sympathy and help. In 1863 Geneva, Switzerland, became the permanent headquarters of the International Red Cross. Geneva was the town of Calvin, the stronghold of the Reformation, and now also became the symbol of the greatest humanitarian movement of all time. An independent, humanitarian institute, the Red Cross is a neutral intermediary in case of armed conflicts or disturbances. It endeavours to protect and assist the victims of international and civil war and internal tensions. It has successfully had hospitals, medical staff, voluntary helpers and the wounded declared inviolate while under the distinctive sign, marking persons and objects to be protected. In two world wars when Australians like others have been taken prisoner, the wounded and sick regardless of nationality have been protected to a greater or lesser degree depending on which nation has captured them. In World War II, 3000 clerks were constantly employed on the card index in Geneva receiving and sending up to 60,000 messages a day. In the Red Cross Museum in Geneva is a large perspex case, a 3-metre squared block packed entirely with 7 million cards, each bearing the name and details of requests for news of lost daughters, mothers, sons, fathers and husbands listed for the 1939–45 war. It is a solid immensity of sorrow, more chilling than any words.

The men and women who lived through World War II were swept into the most destructive war in the history of mankind. There were weapons of destruction never before used on land, air or sea: all that went before it seemed as firm a dividing line as had been drawn between the bow and arrow and explosive devices. And most of all it destroyed much of the best of mankind; apart from lives lost, bodies broken, lives were destroyed by the disruption, the separation from families of young men and women, wives from husbands. It left a psychological legacy that will last to the death of all involved, including their children, and even these will be assisted by the International Red Cross Committee.

One part of Red Cross work that was most welcome and visible to POWs in both World War I and World War II was the food parcels sent to men once they were settled in a prison camp. Japan's delegates were signatories to the most recent Geneva Convention prior to World War II. However, their government did not ratify, thus gaining international recognition without any national obligation. Very few Red Cross parcels were issued to prisoners of this nation, although after the war, in Singapore for instance, warehouses of Red Cross food parcels were discovered which would have saved prisoners' lives.

Apart from unavoidable or understandable hold-ups, once the Red Cross parcels began to arrive at prison camps in Germany or Italy the supply continued, but the logistics were immense. The Red Cross fleet was the vital link in the route to the camps.

The transport of parcels and stores to enemy prison camps was, of necessity, a complicated procedure. Before France fell in June 1940 the journey was straightforward, as in World War I, across the channel and by rail across France to the German border. But since the Germans occupied the French coast all the way to the Spanish frontier the only available European port had been neutral Lisbon, Portugal.

At the Red Cross Packing Centres around the world the parcels were placed in post office bags and collected by the GPO in whose charge they remained until they reached Lisbon where warehouses were rented by the Red Cross and St John's War Organisation. The next stage of the journey was by sea past Gibraltar into the Mediterranean to Marseilles. Ships were specially chartered one by one for this service and because of the shortage of neutral shipping the negotiations were complex. Almost the only ships available were owned by companies from neutral Portugal and reciprocal arrangements had to be made, first with the owners and then with the Portuguese government to obtain the release of each ship.

That was only the beginning. The next step was to approach the belligerent powers, through the IRCC in Geneva, requesting them to grant safe conduct to the ship concerned through the dangerous waters from Lisbon to Marseilles – or Genoa, for some of the cargoes were landed there.

When at length safe conduct had been assured, the ship must be painted white with large red crosses and a green strip around the hull and, as well, special lighting equipment was installed to illuminate the signs by night. Six days' notice prior to sailing had to be given to the belligerent powers and if no objections were raised the ship sailed – in the charge of the IRCC.

The round journey to Marseilles and back took 23 days, and to Genoa and back 27 days. At Marseilles the cargo was handed over to the French postal authorities, but the IRCC did not regard its work as finished until transport to Switzerland had been provided.

In 1942 three ships were running from Lisbon, by 1943 there were seven and by 1944 two more were chartered. These ships carried a total capacity of over 737,000 standard food parcels, and each month the equivalent of 800,000 to 1 million parcels were forwarded from Lisbon, which included not only food but medical parcels, tobacco, books, next-of-kin permit parcels and many other stores. The hundredth voyage over the sea route was made in September 1943 by the merchant ship SS *Ambriz*.

To keep this fleet in constant operation and to avoid any hold-up when a ship arrived back at Lisbon for a cargo, a considerable stock of food parcels had to be maintained at Lisbon. The Red Cross ships were able to run to Marseilles on a fairly fixed timetable, as upwards of a million parcels were usually in the Lisbon warehouses to be cleared in rotation, thus minimising delays to individual parcels sent by the families – this route was the only way any parcels would be accepted in any of the belligerent countries.

Once the food parcels and general Red Cross stores arrived in Switzerland the IRCC took over full charge of them, its principal warehousing centre being at Vallorbe, over the France-Switzerland border. Here the large volume of parcels, clothing, books and comforts which were regularly distributed on behalf of the British Red Cross by the International Red Cross Committee were classified and sorted.

Regularly, fortnight after fortnight, the necessary supplies were forwarded to ensure that the prisoners in each camp – however many there were, and their numbers were constantly varying – received their parcels. And that was only one part of Red Cross work.

Red Cross has at times been labelled an exclusive organisation but once a man became a POW he quickly changed his opinion as these lines of doggerel tell us:

THANKS! TO THE RED CROSS

I'm only one of many
Who in the days gone by,
Refused to give Red Cross donations
But now I wonder why.

Even when the war news came,
My faith in them was poor,
I wouldn't give a copper when
They called round at the door.

We used to talk about them
When we were out at sea.
All you could hear from the men
Was, 'They've never done things for me'.

But later we learnt different,
When we were Prisoners of War.
For we were told there were parcels;
And we wondered who they were for.

They came in very handy,
We being hungry and without a smoke,
A parcel contained all we needed
Including a cake of soap.

There is no doubt about it,
They're the best friends a prisoner's got,
So when this war is over,
We'll help them quite a lot.

I'd like to tell the world,
Of the good turns they do
What they do for everyone
And not the favoured few.

Anon. World War II

Some Red Cross officers in the field were captured along with the men. Mr F.L. Wright, Australian Red Cross representative in Malaya, wrote about the *Last Nine Days* (in Singapore, February 1942) and thus leaves us an impression of his organisation. At that time the 2/9th and 2/10th Field Ambulances were at Roberts Barracks where men had retreated into Singapore and Red Cross was with them. It is a story reminiscent of books about the Indian mutiny we read when young. '7 February. Twenty-six Nipponese planes came over. A ripping, tearing sound began to creep towards us. We were enveloped in black smoke. A bomb had hit our mess, fuel dump and storeroom blew away. I'd not known anything so terrifying as the effect of that concentration of bombs. The patients needed cigarettes, even those who didn't smoke appreciated one now as a big gun, quite close, began firing. What a place for a hospital!

'8 February. The usual, twenty-seven bombers over this time; they dropped 200 large bombs. One dropped just outside matron's office and blasted everything to the other side of the building. A man at the place was killed instantly, everyone in the vicinity, including Colonel Hurdwood, was severely shaken by the intense power of the blast. Thirty personnel were killed or died of wounds, our cooking and dhobi (laundry) staff were wiped out.' At this stage the hospital was moved to the 52nd

Punjabi lines at Tyersall Park to where Wright, with his Red Cross flag, and young Captain Markowich MD trundled in the Red Cross truck and moved into an atap hut on a hillside to tend the wounded. And that is the story of only two days of Red Cross work in six years and in many countries at war.

The Healing Soldiers

A cohort of brave and tireless surgeons and physicians of every specialty and rank devoted their waking hours to the care of the men. These medical men, including the thirty-six doctors who went with the men to the Burma Railway, need no memorial of stone: 'Their crypt is within our loving hearts', wrote Donald Stuart, the wild poet of the outback, with no sense of a later generation finding his words effusive.

In Changi there was originally a surplus of medical personnel. Then, as the working parties left Changi, this surplus proved to be a boon, for almost without exception each working party was accompanied by trained medical personnel. As time elapsed the number of trained men decreased due to attrition. Orderlies trained in nursing techniques worked beside officers and tired, exhausted men worked in the hospitals. It is said by all who saw these men that it was amazing to see the devotion and sacrifice, especially those who volunteered to work in the cholera hospitals. In the larger hospitals, combatant officers were recruited as wardmasters. They were responsible to the medical officers for discipline and the general routine in the wards, for the supervision of patients, staff and nursing, the organisation of the supply of water in appropriate containers, for keeping the patients as clean as possible and for the keeping of records and running a canteen.

(It was usual for all ranks to contribute towards a canteen fund from their pay in order to buy extra food and medicines whenever possible. As a large portion of each officer's pay was banked by the Japanese, who also deducted his board and residence from his pay, by the time an officer contributed his share to the welfare fund he is said to have had little left.)

Surely if those who make the slaughter can claim a
place on the roll of honour, those who cure and are
often at the risk of their lives are entitled to their
due of esteem and gratitude.

Henri Dunant, Founder of the International
Red Cross Committee 1867

No one doctor can be chosen above another to feature in a story of the travail and glory of those medical officers who stood by their men. No doctor would wish it. All the men claim *their* doctor as the best, and he was. Only he, whoever he was, kept death and despair from the suffering patients. Here are a few, representative of all. 'The doctors from our State, Major Hobbs and Major Kranz among them, were looked upon as national heroes', say the South Australians.

'You must know of Claude Anderson', say the men of the 2/4th Machine Gun Battalion. Bert McKay says, 'He was a great doctor, a great man'. And the boys at Kilo 105 swore by doctors Hamilton and Higgins. 'In the monsoon period all was terrible. These two men had little to treat us with but they did everything they possibly could do for us.' 'And Doctor Ted Hunt of the 2/19th, don't forget him! He battled for us.' 'And what about the great Queenslander, Dr Burnett Clarke? He got Marmite into the men. Couldn't get hold of much but got it in for use against scurvy.' One could go on forever.

There were thirty-six doctors and surgeons caring for the men in thirteen camps and hospitals in the vicinity of the Burma railway line in 1943: each group of men claim that the one ministering to them was their saviour. But of the senior medical officer they reserved the brief but succinct praise: 'He was a man'.

'Albert Coates was our great hero', Lance-Corporal Syd Marshall, 8th Division Signals (NSW), says. 'At Kilo 55 this wonderful man did amazing work. A very human man. He never let us lose sight of the fact that discipline was the thing that would get us through. He had no affectation and we admired him for that. But I've seen him crying after leaving men he knew even he couldn't pull through. And later, when he left us we wept, he wept. A great man, a great surgeon.'

In interviews, Sir Albert 'Bertie' Coates was the most modest of men. When reminded of what the men called his 'miracle' cures in Thailand, he said, 'Any mug could have done that'. A country boy, he had left school aged 14 and matriculated while working in the Postal Department. When World War I broke out he joined up and sailed in the first convoy and worked much of the time at sea, assisting doctors inoculate the troops against typhoid. He was in the famous 7th Infantry Battalion that saw some of the worst of the fighting on Gallipoli and in France and knew the comradeship that soldiers have had since time immemorial. Enlisting again in World War II, he remained behind in Sumatra to care for the sick and wounded and was captured by the Japanese.

Private Bill Hood: 'The great doctor, Colonel Albert Coates was one of the finest men I have known in my life. All men who came in contact with Dr Coates believed that. He not only saved lives but saved reason. I had a tropical ulcer on my instep and it was thought the foot would have to be amputated. But Dr Coates told me he'd go on trying for a little while longer to see if he could arrest the gangrene, and nine days later I had begun to recover.'

Bill for a time worked in the theatre, where Doctor Coates was operating. 'I held men during the operations. Men were laid down on the table and were injected in the spine with diluted novocaine, the chemist had to make do with what he had to make it go around. It did not completely deaden but it eased the pain. I remember when Alan Banford had his leg off, we took the piece of rubber from inside the crown of a soldier's tin helmet and gave it to him to bite on, and another bloke and I each gave Alan our hand to hold. I couldn't close my hand properly for days after.

'I will never forget the burial of Tom Davison from Marble Bar, WA. Tom had an ulcer in the foot, similar to mine. He struggled with it and Dr Coates fought for him but eventually it had to come off; but he was too low, he died. He'd got a fixation about what little use it would be for him to go home to Marble Bar without a leg. He said, "You couldn't even kick anything".

'The men were sorry for Dr Coates because he had to work with a butcher's saw, chisels and that sort of thing for major operations. We could put ourselves in his position, day after day, knowing how he felt about his patients. I often thought what it must have done to Colonel Coates, on top of his surgical and medical roles he had all his administrative work to do. He was the senior man. He looked like an old farmer with rosy cheeks. But he couldn't save everyone and Tom Davison knew that. So, we put a rice bag over Tom's head and another over his remaining leg and dug a hole and he was buried.' Bill went to the funeral on bamboo crutches.

'We had several doctors with us, a good British MO, Dr Hamilton, and Dr Dunell and others, they were all good. But Coates stood out, he never then, or later (after the war), tried to make us feel obliged to see him as a hero, that wasn't a thing he would have liked for he was a man's man. But he must have known how we felt about him. I have nothing but sheer admiration for our medical officers, all of them, but Colonel Coates was a man among men.'

The English cricket commentator Jim Swanton was up the line. 'The people I first met among the Australians were the doctors who in camps disease-ridden, verminous and in every way generally appalling, were tending men in the last stages of weakness, and with virtually no drugs or equipment except what they contrived themselves. Whereas the RAMC [UK] perforce had to spread their talent over the whole theatre of war, the flower of the Australian medical service – volunteers all, of course – were recruited for their early formations (and many stayed with their battalion throughout the war). Such names as Corlette and Kranz, Dunlop, Moon and Coates will be readily remembered by all of us who lived and worked on the Burma-Siam Railway in the camps that followed the muddy waters of the River Me-Nam-Kwai-Noi. "Bertie" Coates was the senior medical officer in captivity and as such shouldered the permanently, indefinitely depressing job of negotiating with the Japs for medical supplies which they either did not have or refused to part with. Coates was a bluff, hard-bitten fellow to whom the Japs seemed to accord a grudging respect.'

For three and a half years the people back home in Australia knew almost nothing of this strange, shadowy world that had swallowed a whole division of their men.

Less than one in seven men of the captured 8th Division worked on the Burma Railway, and Changi was not the 'infamous hell-hole' it later was labelled, but it and the Burma Railway became catch-phrases for the Australian people, avid as they were for simple expressions with which to dress the war. This one-seventh of the division spent an average of eight months on the railway project, but this time was tattooed into the psyche of every man who laboured on the hurried construction of the miles of railway track that climbed through the jungle across the Burma-Thailand border. A smaller number worked on a stretch above the border in Burma where conditions were perhaps even more frightful.

Here Major Bruce Hunt captured the hearts of the men in his care by his skill as a doctor and his legendary stamina as a man. Men who knew him say, 'He had huge hairy shoulders, part covered with a haversack or two because he constantly foraged for life-saving food and drugs for us. Sometimes this meant a very long walk and once I saw him coming back after a day-long trudge to plead with the Jap Colonel Banno and he was mud from his waist down. He gave us some Marmite and stored his other spoils away and then went to report to the Nip commandant for the usual beating he got for leaving camp.' He was regularly beaten, slapped, forced to withstand disciplinary torture and constant harassment. He remains one of the memorable figures among the memorable doctors who went up the line with the AIF.

From the day of his departure from Changi in April until November 1943 when he was admitted to hospital at Kanburi suffering from acute cardiac beriberi brought on by excessive strain, Bruce Hunt worked tirelessly and unceasingly in an endeavour to save the lives of his men.

On occasions he walked great distances and returned with medical stores and special diet foods, heavy loads that he shouldered through the rain and mud. He had determination and physical capabilities far beyond the average man and his feats would have deterred any but the most dedicated. Assisting him during the cholera outbreak were Doctors John Taylor (RMO 2/30th Battalion) and L. Cahill (RMO 2/19th Battalion) who saw the desperate situation sweep into the camp and stepped forward with their leader. Hunt was always quick to praise and bring forward the names of others. 'Great courage and organising ability', said Hunt of the two younger men. 'They were praised and admired by the sick and dying men for their arduous and self-sacrificing work and their personal example.'

The first case of cholera among the Australians was diagnosed on the night of 15/16 May (Asian work camps nearby already held men dying of the scourge). Bruce Hunt and John Taylor arrived at this wretched camp having marched throughout the night after their ambulance was bogged in the jungle mud. After learning that there was an outbreak of cholera at Lower Sonkurai, some miles away, Hunt and Captain Cahill set off with seven AAMC men and eight British who volunteered to go with them.

Like most other MOs up the line, Bruce Hunt had no previous experience of treating cholera until it broke out in his camp. It was a disease little known in Australia. Bruce learned that the Japanese were terrified of it and he used this knowledge to the advantage of his men. He let the Japanese know that he understood how shameful it would be for them to lose face if all their slaves died and the railway building fell behind schedule. He arranged that his men should temporarily cease work on the railway and the Japanese send for a supply of cholera vaccine. He issued orders that all water must be boiled, all eating utensils seared each time they were used in the flames of fires that would be kept burning at every hut, and all food suspected of being contaminated by touch from a fly must be burned in the fire. He set them to work to scrape off the whole of the surface soil of the camp and burn this – a task planned as much to prevent the men dwelling on the dreadful death a cholera victim suffers as for hygiene. After three days the men were forced to resume work on the railway and the deaths came as Bruce knew they would, until so many died that the funeral fires were kept burning in the cholera pits.

Men working in quarries without boots had their feet badly cut and these cuts developed into tropical ulcers. Through incessant work in deep mud, trench feet became practically universal and rapidly developed into ulcers.

There were daily beatings of officers and men at work, some of them being beaten into unconsciousness. These beatings were not for disciplinary purposes but were intended to urge sick and enfeebled men to physical efforts beyond their remaining strength, or to punish officers for intervening on their behalf.

'Every morning the same grim spectacle was repeated in the camps: parading men for work at first light. Emerging from their crowded huts or leaky shelters in the pouring rain, even the fitter men appeared gaunt and starving, clad in rags or merely loincloths, most of them bootless and with cut and swollen feet. In addition, some fifty or sixty men from hospital, leaning on sticks or squatting in the mud would be paraded to complete the quota and would become the subject of a desperate argument between Bruce Hunt and the Japanese engineers. Sometimes all of these men, sometimes only a part would be taken out to work and would leave the camp hobbling on sticks or half-carried by their comrades. Many of the fitter men did not see their camp in daylight for weeks and had had no opportunity of washing either themselves or their rags of clothes.'

The attitude of the Japanese guards towards the sick was a mixture of callous indifference and active spite for, by their sickness, the men were regarded as impeding the Japanese war effort. Lieutenant Fukuda, commander of one of the camps, told Major Hunt, 'You are not our equals; you are our inferiors. Japanese soldiers are prepared to die, providing the job is done. Prisoners must have the same view. Some Japanese will die in the making of this railway. POWs will die also. You have spoken of the Geneva Convention and humanity. In present circumstances these things do not apply.'

Of the thirty-odd doctors who went up the Burma Railway for the eight months work on the line, there was scarcely a one who did not at the very least get 'a slapping'. Others were severely beaten, some were caged in tiny pens, cooped up in a tortuous position for days. And all had the horrible task of each day choosing which of their patients must go out to work.

In this era, preceding the 'wonder' drugs of later years (including penicillin, which did not reach the imprisoned men until war ended), diseases now considered serious but not necessarily fatal could be killers. Pneumonia, diphtheria, gross painful dermatitis, malaria were killers and other ailments now under control such as meningitis killed one in four who suffered from it.

At one of the staging camps Bruce Hunt was informed that all sick men had to be submitted for inspection to the IJA medical officer. There were twenty-seven with infected feet and ten with malaria or dysentery. The Japanese medical officer agreed that none of these men was fit to march, but the corporal of the guard only gave permission for the ten with malaria to remain. He even refused to accept a letter of instruction from the Japanese medical officer.

Bruce Hunt wrote, 'At the time scheduled for the parade I fell in the thirty-seven men apart from the main parade and Major Wild (an Indian army officer with us who acted as interpreter) and I stood in front of them. The corporal approached with a large bamboo in his hand and spoke menacingly to Major Wild who answered in a placatory fashion.

'The corporal's only reply was to hit Major Wild in the face. Another guard followed suit and as Major Wild staggered back the corporal thrust at him with his bamboo. I was left standing in front of the patients and was immediately set upon by the corporal and two other guards. After knocking me to the ground, they set about me with bamboos, causing considerable bruising and breaking a bone in my left hand. After I was disposed of, the corporal then made the majority of the sick men march with the rest of the troops. Most of these men, including an Australian chaplain, died during succeeding weeks, largely as the result of this calculated brutality.

'I never on any occasion asked for volunteers for nursing the sick without getting all the men I wanted, and those men from combatant units did a wonderful job. Twenty of them lost their lives from cholera during the epidemic, yet the supply of volunteers to fill the vacant places never failed.' At first the outbreak was mild, with just a few cases for the first four or five days. Then, suddenly, they had thirty-five cases in twenty-four hours.

'The men were out working all day on the railway and came back after dark soaked and exhausted, having done about twelve hours' work in the drenching rain. One night when they were on parade before being dismissed we asked for volunteers. We explained to them the nature and severity of cholera and pointed out the extreme danger anyone would face in nursing the sick cases: but men were urgently needed to start nursing that night. As soon as the parade was over we started enrolling volunteers. I stopped after I had taken the names of seventy-five men who were prepared to start straight away and there were then still between twenty and thirty men waiting to volunteer.'

Camp medical officers, NCOs and men also did 'wonderful' work. 'Sergeant A.J. Buttenshaw of Sydney was so competent that he was at one time placed in sole medical charge of 400 patients. Lance-Corporal K.R. Marshall of Sydney worked tirelessly and saved the lives of many men suffering from cholera; Sergeant J. Gorringe of Kondinin, WA, displayed outstanding nursing ability and others who worked untiringly and cheerfully amidst terrible difficulties included Privates G.

Nichol, D.E. Murray and A.E. Staff (all of NSW), and Sergeants A.R. Deans and C.H. Boan of Victoria. These nursing orderlies displayed courage of a high order in total disregard of personal danger. There is no doubt that their untiring and efficient work saved the lives of many men.' The men, in turn, had written of Hunt, 'He stood like an avenging angel between the Nips and us when we were sick. He was kicked regularly but still he stood between us and them. Later he made light of it, but we know what we saw.'

During the early months when the number of men in hospital rose to over 1000, the camp was without the services (through illness) of senior officers. This resulted in enormous additional responsibility being placed on Bruce Hunt who, according to Doctor Glyn White, 'Repeatedly and fearlessly approached the IJA authorities in attempts to obtain some alleviation of the conditions of the sick. He visited all British and AIF camps organising the cholera isolation hospitals and giving medical advice. His stirring addresses to the men and his own splendid example had an enormous effect on the morale of the force and gave many hundreds of sick men the will and desire to live, and at the same time inculcated in the minds of the fit men the necessary urge to perform greater efforts.'

From the first few weeks of the calvary they were to suffer, the Australians realised that the filth of all Japanese camps would be one of the major life-destroying problems they would meet. No camp had proper sanitary arrangements and one of the first efforts on arrival always was to dig latrines and cess pits and clear the area of excreta. 'Flies in large swarms covered all the camps.' In some camps, on arrival, the Australians had to scrape the whole of excreta-covered ground made available to them before falling in exhaustion to sleep.

Hunt's party arrived early one morning at yet another camp and set about inoculating 1400 men with vaccine brought forward in his medical kit from Changi. Within a few weeks the camp leader, Major Johnston, along with Bruce Hunt's ferocious energy, and his enthusiasm that encouraged exhausted men to work as a team, made the camp the most hygienic of all; because of the success of their endeavours the men's morale was uplifted to become an example to other groups in their fight for life.

But the exhausted condition of the men led to lack of resistance to all diseases. With no motor transport available, supplies must be brought from camps 16 miles away; for a time men had to drag ox-carts over the deplorable tracks; at other times they back-packed the great loads in. Although cholera had taken 47 per cent of victims, the work of Doctor Hunt had kept all other deaths down.

Hunt accepted no praise except that which reflected on his patients and his AAMC men and those who volunteered to nurse the sick men. He believed that the disparity between the deaths amongst the Australians and the British troops was a result of the general physical standard of the Australians being higher, 'because they had originally been selected more carefully than was the case with the British army, whole units or sections were sent away together when movement of troops was ordered, whereas the British selected the required number of bodies without worrying about units. The unit spirit amongst the Australians was thereby retained and assisted greatly in keeping up morale and an *esprit de corps* that showed in a unique manner when man cared for man in illness and death.'

Wherever he was sent, this humane and skilful medico changed everything for the betterment of the men's health. Hunt harassed, cajoled and wrote as obsequiously as he could bring himself to do to senior Japanese officers to gain assistance, not only for his patients, but for all men in the camp, as he knew they would all, in time, be his patients. When the men working on the line returned to camp exhausted, late in the dark of night, he would be waiting for them, to attend to cuts, scratches and anything that could cause ulcers in their debilitated, avitaminosis state, or dress wounds from beatings, then see them on their way to sterilise their mess gear before drawing their miserable rice and water meal. Early in the morning, when the Japanese came to demand workers from his hospital patients, Hunt was ready. To some hobbling, part-crippled men he would have to send out he would say a few words of encouragement. 'But', recalls Syd Marshall, 'when it would mean likely death for a man to leave the hut called a hospital, Bruce Hunt just said no, and awaited his punishment. Day by day.'

His constant recommendations to the Japanese led to the establishment of a hospital at Tanbaya, Burma, 50 miles north-west of Lower Songkurai. Hunt believed that if the more serious of the patients were transferred near a railhead they may get more, or better, rations and therefore may recover. Hunt took with him six doctors and 130 other ranks and 1900 patients, an example of his tenacity but, as well, his ability to get along well with Lieutenant Wakabyashi, one of the more sympathetic Japanese camp commanders they had yet met.

But when they eventually arrived at the site they found only a cookhouse and a few huts with roofs. 'Bruce Hunt got hold of our axe and, stripped to the waist as usual, he began on the trees for timber', his men recall. However, the move came too late for many men, twenty died en route and within a few weeks 282 British and sixty-four Australians had died at the new site, many with cardiac beriberi. Bruce Hunt believed the British died of starvation, partly caused through lack of knowl-edge of what foods would help them in this foreign environ-ment. (When Australian sick could not eat, they were force fed.) Most of the deaths had been from beriberi and Hunt begged and badgered until he got bags of beans, food that would have saved many of his patients and now prevented others from becoming ill.

His courage was legendary. As well as being a superb organ-iser and planner, he had a moral stance which all men admired and envied. 'He stood up to the Japanese on our behalf time and again, knowing he would be punished for it. Once they crushed his hand because he protested about his men being put into huts that cholera patients had been in. He was well built, medium height, broad shoulders and had the strength of a bull. The sight of him bred confidence in us, his energy was a by-word in the camps.'

When Alex Kelly, RAAF, was sent to the Burma Railway, he was told that he and others were going up to a rest camp. 'But it was a gruesome camp, the trees all around it full of buzzards staring down at us; looking very fiercesome, evil! We didn't know where we were going or what we were doing. It was as hot as hell. We marched during the night and slept during the day in amongst the trees and this went on for days along the track. Eventually we were halted, we were there. We had no idea what we were going to do, no idea what was happening. We'd hardly hit the place when cholera hit us. But we had this marvellous medical officer, Bruce Hunt. He took charge of the camp. (By and large the general officers weren't worth a bumper, they just disappeared into their huts and the whole place was run by the sergeant and the MO.)

'Bruce did his best to protect us in all ways, but the cholera raged through the camp; there was dysentery and God knows what. He slaved from daylight to dusk; half the blokes were in hospital, the other half out at daybreak and wouldn't be home till night. I can't describe the conditions, it was only the will to survive that kept you going. The blokes that relaxed at any stage were gone. I was probably at the ideal age, about 25, the younger blokes didn't have the mental balance to stand it and I think they were the worst hit, these very young fellows. And the older ones – 30 and over – they didn't have the physique. They just lived in a daze the whole time. Our particular section was the worst hit force on the line, mainly because we were right in the middle and of course when the rains came we had to pack in our provisions, and there you'd be walking up to your thighs in mud. We used to corduroy the road (with tree trunks laid sidewards as a base) but you'd do a length of corduroying and a couple of weeks later it would have sunk and you'd have to do it again.

'I suppose we did get a bit of pleasure, there was a bit of humour about occasionally, but there was a lot of death. Up on cholera hill, the fire burnt the whole time we were there, just burning the poor blokes who went down with cholera. They'd go straight to the fire.

'We came back to Kamburi and I nearly died there, and that was only because I relaxed. I was about 6½ stone at that stage, the heat was off there, the food was good – comparatively speaking. I was pretty anaemic; quite a few blokes got very serious burns from squatting down over the fire, then standing up quickly, they'd just faint and fall into the fire. I was in that sort of condition and one day I crawled under one of the huts, it was nice and cool, I curled up and relaxed. I was there about a day and all of a sudden I said to myself, you're going to die like a dog under here, and snapped out of it. I got out and didn't sit down for twenty-four hours and so it passed.'

Alex remembers the doctors. 'All our doctors were good; Weary Dunlop did a marvellous job up there, no question about that and there were so many others too. Bruce Hunt had as much form as any other doctor, probably more so because the heat was on much harder on his force than it was down in the railway cutting. You can see by the death ratio the amount of labour available was much more restricted up in the top end. Bruce had all that to go through to fill working parties, to stand over the Japs to get better conditions, all that sort of thing. When he got home Bruce Hunt faded out of the picture, you didn't hear any more of him, whereas Weary was continually in the public eye.

'The Cahill brothers, John and Frank, they were good medicos also. Conditions were crude, the doctors had to "make do". For instance, our force had to march 200 kilometres and everything we used we had to carry but you could only physically carry a certain amount; so our doctors carried the same as any other man. Where Weary's crowd were lucky, they could get down to Kamburi by river and market boats selling food could get up to them. Where we were we didn't see any of the local population.'

Many men remember Captain Lumkin (US army) and Commander Epstein (US navy). Ted Mooney, RAN, knew both. Captain S. Hugh Lumkin of the US army died up the line, and his death was undoubtedly brought about by his devotion to the sick at all times, especially during blitz periods when the Japanese would slap into him when he tried to protect a sick man whom they considered was fit to work.

'One of our own men, sick bay attendant Anderson from the *Perth*, though sick himself, was caring for and attending his patients' every want; he was as gentle and understanding as their own mother would have been.' This was at the 80K camp where conditions were appalling. 'Everything was tumbling down and some of my shipmates were so thin I didn't at first recognise them. But they still managed to smile even though one glance sufficed to see how ill they were.'

In this land accidents were as prevalent as illnesses, and the doctors helped all. RAAF Sergeant-Pilot Geoff Dewey, out on the railway, was cutting down a tree when the axe slipped and his foot was severely cut, the tendons on four toes being severed. 'Doctor Dunlop managed to get a vehicle and took me to Konyu where I was given an anaesthetic by Major Arthur Moon.' The men then devised a right-angled splint out of a kerosene tin and wire and borrowed two plaster bandages for binding and Dewey healed well, with almost full use of his foot.

The men working on the railway had no means of keeping a diary, so it was provident that Doctor Dunlop was in a position to keep a day-to-day account of his life in the jungle. From his daily entries about what happened to him personally, we learn something of what was happening to the men who were not able to write of it until later; and then in recall. Although, like all other doctors on the railway, he was in no way treated as badly as were the men, his description of a severe beating gives us a glimpse of the treatment the men suffered throughout.

His own worst punishment was for playing bridge after 'lights out'. Knowing he may be kicked, he 'ordered a pair of thick socks to help my shins and in due course reported to the guard well before time. I was ignored by the guard and remained rigidly to attention for some hours in the boiling sun ... one by one a long sequence of NCOs and guards marched up to me or rode up on their bikes, and kicked or struck me, wielding rifle butts and sticks.

'Finally I forsook my rigid position of attention and my stoicism broke. I waved my hands and yelled: "God Almighty, do you not think it punishment standing in this sun and being kicked and beaten by a pack of bandy legged baboons!" ... then all hell broke loose. With angry bellowing, the guard led by their commander fell upon me in a fashion recalling an otter hunt or the hounds cornering a fox. They belaboured me with rifle butts, chairs, boots, etc., whilst I rolled in the dust trying to keep in a ball, my elbows protectively over my large fragile spleen, face against chest.

'Eventually I was motionless beyond resistance, lying face down in the dust, conscious of broken ribs and blood from scalp wounds. I was gathered up, dazed, and rubber-limbed and trussed and roped backwards kneeling with a large log between my seat and knees. Breathing was sharply painful with fractured ribs. Slowly the pain ceased in my legs because they had no circulation. How long to gangrene in the tropical heat? Could I last four hours? I squared my shoulders and stared in disdain at the guard.

'At nightfall I was asked whether I would have hard feelings against the guard if the Japanese were so forgiving as to release me. Then I stood to attention, bowed and said, "And now, if you will excuse me, I shall amputate the Dutchman's arm who has been waiting all day".'

We are fortunate that this man was in a position to write daily; other doctors, alone in isolated camps with the whole responsibility of the working men on their hands, could scarcely spare paper or time to do so, and their sacrifice and labour for the men they loved have, to a degree, gone unrecorded.

There was the matter of receptacles. At all hospitals ordinary tins, pots, food holders were not available. The most mundane of daily living equipment was as scarce as was medical instruments. Doctor Dunlop had two 60-gallon drums for water. Then he had one only: a Japanese officer took the other to hold pig food. Dunlop says he thought that was 'a bit rich!'.

He knew where there were other drums but they were inside the Japanese lines. 'So this night I blackened my face and with a torch and a couple of chaps to help me, crept into the Jap lines and got hold of a couple of drums. We'd just got going when a Jap officer appeared; I knew him well, but being startled, like a fool I flicked my torch on and in the momentary flash I knew he'd recognised me so there was only one thing for it: I went bong! with the torch, right on his head and he fell over, we grabbed the drums and went for our lives back to our own lines. I leapt into my cot and feigned sleep. I knew he'd seen me. I was nearly shivering with fright.

'But no one came that night and next morning there was no sign of the officer nor was he on show the following morning. On the third day he turned up with a beautiful big lump on his head and – he said nothing. It was retrograde amnesia. He couldn't remember a thing about it. And we had the drums!'

The condition of tropical ulcer patients was pitiable, and the wards stank of the hospital gangrene of pre-Listerian days. Rags, paper, leaves and locally picked kapok and cotton were employed as dressings. The blowflies hanging in clouds about the patients produced maggot infections.

Friendly sources outside the camps (many of them Chinese) contributed 3000 dollars a month (60 dollars equalled one English pound) enabling drugs such as iodoform for tropical ulcers and some food to be bought.

Doctor Dunlop worked under Doctor Albert Coates at the large hospital at Nakom Paton, 20 miles from Bangkok, which contained up to 8000 men during its most active period. In an article published in the *Australian Medical Journal* after his return to Australia Doctor Dunlop wrote: 'Tropical ulcers were highly prevalent in jungle areas among famished, fever-ridden subjects exposed to blows and trauma. A distressing feature was massive spreading gangrene, frequently followed by gross involvement of bone, joint, muscle, tendon, vessels and nerves. The practice of flooding ill-equipped hovels with these patients was disastrous. The base hospital sections receiving them became cesspools of hospital gangrene. Waves of virulence spread about the wards, infecting other wounds. Ulcers were often multiple; at one time three men were dying in agony from large ulcers arising from minor skin lesions all over the body and limbs. The pain was very severe and caused muscle spasm, so that the lower limb frequently contracted with flexed knee and dropped foot. Natural healing, where the outcome was favourable, took months to years and often resulted in severe deformity.'

The best measure they found was removal of all gangrenous tissue by excision and curettage, followed by the application of pure phenol or lysol and a light sprinkle of iodoform powder. The Japanese did not supply iodoform, but it could be bought in small quantities at high prices from the Siamese. It was the most economical of all purchased drugs, 'and the sight of it brought a glad smile to sufferers', said Dunlop.

Many hundreds of men endured the agony of curettage of ulcers, necessarily without anaesthesia. 'Amputation was often necessary to save life, and some patients begged for it, despite the crude knives and butchers' saws employed.' Immediate mortality rates were surprisingly good – under 10 per cent – but there were associated gross nutritional disorders often evidenced by running diarrhoea and famine oedema. Ultimately about 50 per cent of amputation cases died, many of them after good healing. When hostilities ceased, 170 amputation cases surviving at Nakom Paton, including two with bilateral amputations, were already provided with useful artificial limbs 'made on the premises'.

Great originality was shown by men of all ranks in improvisation and every hospital had its home-made objects and remedies to do service for the lack of conventional equipment. Doctor Dunlop says that in the absence of strappings for extension, 'fractured femurs were best treated by driving the cleanest nail that could be found through the upper tibia'.

Lack of anaesthetic was the greatest difficulty, and most minor operations were performed in its absence. Minute amounts of chloroform were obtained from the Japanese and Siamese, and carefully conserved for special procedures.

Catgut and other suture materials were rarely supplied by the Japanese and silk was obtained by unlining the parachute cords carried by RAF personnel. The most useful product was a locally prepared 'catgut' from the peritoneum of pigs and cattle, first introduced by an ingenious Dutch chemist, Captain von Boxtel (working under Lieutenant Colonel Coates).

Major S. Krantz, AAMC, played an important role in the surgical work of the hospital, 'and there was plenty of that', Dunlop recalls. 'Excluding very minor procedures, 773 surgical interventions were carried out, including such varied operations as brain and spinal-cord surgery, thyroidectomy, gastrectomy, enterectomy and anastomosis, abdomino-perineal resection, cholecystectomy, thoracic surgery, splenectomy, nephrectomy, laryngectomy, orthopaedic measures, and nerve sutures.' All this with the minimum of orthodox equipment.

The men used bamboo to make brooms, brushes, baskets, containers, water-piping, tubing and splints. Solder was extracted from sardine tins, sources of hydrochloric acid included the human stomach. Sulphuric acid was stolen from the car batteries of the Japanese to manufacture flux, urinals, bed-pans, commodes, surgical beds and pulleys, feeding-cups, washbasins, irrigators, sterilisers, small portable charcoal stoves, disinfectors, stretchers and stretcher beds (with sack and bamboo), back-rests, leg-rests, oil-lamps, trays, tables, orthopaedic appliances, splints, surgical instruments and artificial limbs and eyes (from mah-jong pieces) were made. The artificial limbs made at Nakom Paton under the direction of Major F.A. Woods, AIF, were designed from crude timber, leather cured from buffalo or cow hide, thread from unravelled army packs, iron from retained portions of officers' stretchers, and oddments of sponge-rubber, elastic braces, etc.

The use of defibrinated blood for transfusion purposes, which was introduced by Major Reed, AAMC, and developed by Captain J. Markowich, RAMC, was a life-saving measure. Using soldiers trained as technicians, thousands of transfusions were carried out by simply collecting the blood of a suitable donor into a container while stirring continuously with a spatula or whisk. Vigorous stirring was carried on for five minutes after clotting commenced on the spatula. The blood was then filtered through many layers of gauze and administered by medical officers. Chemists, botanists and scientists helped in the preparation of drugs and chemicals. Another life-saving achievement was the production of emetine from a limited quantity of ipecacuanha by Captain von Boxtel at the 55-Kilo Camp with Sergeant A.J. Kosterman and Sergeant G.W. Chapman as assistants. Alcohol for surgical use was gained by the fermentation of rice with a suitable strain of fungus and distillation up to 90 per cent strength.

Venereal disease in these camps and hospitals was almost unknown although Doctor Dunlop has drawn the author's attention to one man he knew of in 1943 who was a VD patient. 'He had caught it in a Thai village he said. Sadly, he left the hospital area and decapitated himself by placing his neck on the railway line in front of an oncoming train.'

Men hasten to speak of their doctors: they want them recorded. Many speak of Dr Corlette and Dr Moon. 'Not only fine doctors but champions of the men as were most doctors. One day the Japs told Corlette they believed many Australians had escaped because there didn't seem to be as many around as usual. Corlette said, yes they had escaped, and pointed to the cemetery. "They've escaped alright!"'

Ivor Jones believes Australian doctors were much better than British. 'Whether ours were better trained or because of being descendants of pioneers – they cared more about people I think. Some of the regular British doctors didn't have a clue. They'd come out of India in the army, hadn't done a tap since the day they graduated. Aspros and iodine were about all they knew.'

Roy Mills was the first medical officer allotted to the first train-load of prisoner-troops to go to build the centre section of the Burma-Thailand Railway. Roy went by train to Bampong, Thailand. 'Five terrible days in steel trucks, hot as ovens – thirty men to a truck 16 feet 6 inches long by 7 feet –

we suffered great thirst. At Bampong we were herded into atap huts with central dirt floor and raised bamboo floors on each side to sleep on – unutterably filthy, human faeces everywhere on the dirt floor and on the bamboo.

'Then began the 270-kilometre march, each night for five nights, to Konkoita where Lieutenant Colonel Pond's party of 720 men was formed to do bridge building at Taimonta.' For much of the time on this dire task, he was the only doctor for these 700 men. He never considered he was alone: he had with him his medical orderlies who had fought with him down the Malayan peninsula to Singapore where the 2/10th Field Ambulance was taken prisoner while nursing the wounded.

'Captain Mills did outstanding work as RMO', according to Lieutenant Colonel S.A.F. Pond, 'Although working by himself he showed self-reliance, vision and medical knowledge to a remarkable degree in so young a doctor.

'He never spared himself though unwell for a considerable period; by his courage and sympathetic treatment of the sick he earned the respect and regard of every man in the party. No praise is too high for him. He would devote twenty-four hours at a time to save soldiers' lives.'

Mills had suffered a chest wound from a shell during the fighting in Malaya. (He later suffered with tuberculosis; twice he had lung collapse.) His time on the railway carrying stretchers and panniers have left their mark. Captain Adrian Curlewis, HQ 8th Division (later Sir Adrian and a distinguished judge), knew the spirit of this man. 'Roy Mills was the only medical officer in my party of 700-odd men on the railway. He was a big, upright, well-built man. I could carry a sick man's kitbag as well as my own gear but I've seen Mills put men over his shoulders on some of those marches.

'He'd never drilled before we were captured and because he stood to attention with his fists clenched the Japanese thought he was going to hit them. They ripped his badges of rank off and bashed him shockingly with a thick malacca stick, but he never batted an eye while they kept him kneeling all day.

'He had no weapons with which to contain cholera and was

severely hampered by lack of medical supplies: all he had was quinine and a few bandages that were used over and over again and the rubber piping of his stethoscope as a drainage tube on cholera patients. But there was absolutely no other thing with which to be innovative. His camp was miles away in the bush, it made base camps with their teams of surgeons and doctors and objects to turn into equipment seem like Guys Hospital, London. The ceaseless monsoonal deluge flooded the latrines washing effluent through the camp and the men in his care were too exhausted from working sixteen hours a day, almost all of them with one disease or another, to repair the damage: sick men were being made to work on the railway, those few exempt from labour because of the severity of their illness were starving because the food ration of men in hospital was cut to a daily bowl of watery gruel and a small quantity of rice. In this appalling, tormented camp, Roy Mills, often sick himself, fought to save men from death.'

Colonel Pond's party was to have had two medical officers, but Captain Peter Hendry was taken north and Mills was on his own for the next six months. 'We were starved and beaten. The monsoons broke. We all suffered malaria and for this we had about one-third as much quinine as needed. Dysentery was rife. Boots wore out and shale lacerated legs, causing ulcers. Cholera was treated by enormous infusions of saline into a vein through bamboo cannulas. The saline was made from fresh water gushing from the top of tents, mixed with kitchen salt, and boiled. We only had enough leaking old tents to cover half our numbers, the other half lay on mud under bamboo floors of tents elevated about 2 feet.

'After five weeks working on the bridge we had been building we were to move south – we anticipated better conditions. We felt we had triumphed. The morale of the men was simply magnificent. We set off carrying the sick on bamboo stretchers, as well as the wet tents, cooking gear and Japanese tools; mud was often knee deep. Our next camp was at Takanun on a piece of ground 50 yards by 120 yards, oozing water. On arrival, all men who could work were taken to a cutting;

"Speedo! Speedo" was the order of the day. We were surrounded by Asian slaves whose plight was worse than ours,
many dying, lying in their own faeces in the mud. In my flow
chart of diseases, written up in my "diary" I had written
"Hell" for the Taimonta period, "HELL" in capitals for the
Takanun period. Cholera broke out here again with 102 cases
all told.'

Although he was hard-pressed and young, his medical
school discipline never failed him. 'I had three books made. In
the first each illness a man suffered was written along a line
covering the double page. In the second book, a single page
was a summary of the first. A third, my work book, had thirty-
one vertical lines on each double page so that each man had
one square centimetre per day; entries were made in pencil (to
be rubbed out). Entries like hieroglyphics were made in this
small area so that good statistics could be kept and the inci-
dence of diseases charted. That's all the paper I had. Notes on
seriously ill patients in hospital tents were made on pages of
the book *Medical Diseases of War* which I carried with me.

'My day started one hour before dawn with a sick parade
by the light of a small oil flare. The men were forced to work
up to sixteen hours a day, sometimes more. Accordingly, my
day finished sixteen hours or more later with a final sick
parade. I would then write up my "diary" – a necessary part
of army existence. It was not a personal thing but the cold
record of diseases, deaths, etc. Through the day I would see
the sick in camp and one day I made notes on 464 men. Each
man seen on sick parade would be classified in descending
order of fitness: Light work one, Light work two, Light work
three, No work. The colonel and the adjutant would barter
with the Japanese as to how many would have to present for
work. If enough workers were not supplied, the guards would
grab any sick men and drive them out with sticks.

Mills and Captain B.A. Barnett, his adjutant, constantly
made spirited protests to Lieutenant Murayama against the
purposeful starvation of patients. So emphatic was Captain
Mills on one occasion that it called forth a challenge by

Murayama to a fight to the death with Japanese weapons to show, as he said, 'the superiority of the Japanese to the English'. Mills agreed to fight, but with fists, but Murayama withdrew. On another occasion, Mills was made to kneel for a long period before Murayama's sergeant and receive repeated blows on the head with a bamboo stick. Barnett (of 8th Division Signals) who carried out the duties of adjutant of the force of 700 for seven months says of Mills, 'He always faced the Japanese with tact, courage and determination and succeeded in gaining their confidence and respect. His administration within the unit left nothing to be desired.' After three more moves on later gangs on the railway, 'absolutely exhausted and seriously ill and useless for further work', the survivors rejoined the main body at Neiki and were taken south by train, then on to Singapore. Doctor Mills remains to this day modest about his own work, but full of praise for all other medical soldiers.

One of the most loved and gentle doctors was, and is, the New South Welshman Ian Duncan. He was 24 years old and a final-year medical student when the war started. He enlisted as soon as he graduated from Sydney University. 'I was terrified the war was going to finish before I got there. Everyone was the same.' He was sent to Malaya as a regimental medical officer in the 8th Division. 'The Malayan campaign lasted ten weeks.' (This was much longer than many battles in that war. Australia's battle casualties were among the highest per capita in World War II.)

'I was in Singapore when it fell to the Japanese on 15 February 1942. The din had been terrific while the battle was on. We were being bombed and shelled constantly. A hell of a mess. It went on day and night. Then suddenly it stopped.' He was posted KIA – killed in action. 'My people were notified.' But for the next three and a half years he was a prisoner of war, first in Singapore, then Thailand and finally in Japan.

'Being a doctor in the prison camps was a terrible responsibility. You played God.' Duncan, along with a handful of medicos, went 'the round trip' under the Japanese from Changi to the Burma Railway, Three Pagoda Pass, Thailand and to Japan, a long and hard odyssey that only a few doctors travelled. He saw only too clearly the effect of heavy work on men suffering from diseases that would have hospitalised men in civilian life. In a jungle camp near Three Pagoda Pass in Thailand, he was the only doctor for 250 prisoners helping to build the Burma-Thailand Railway. 'The Japanese insisted that 85 per cent of the men report for work each day. A few relatively healthy men had to stay behind to run the camp – cooks, medical orderlies and so on – which meant you were allowed only ten or fifteen blokes sick. Well, out of 250, 249 *were* sick.

'I had to decide which men were the sickest, who went to work and who stayed behind. Each morning before dawn I held a sick parade. The light of an oil lamp lit the faces of the working party lined up on one side, the sick on the other. Invariably some of the men in the working party were so ill that I knew they were going to die. The guards decided it was all my fault if the men were sick, so I got a belting every morning. But there was no option. My job was to protect my men, my patients. I held another sick parade by oil lamp in the dark of night when they came back from work. In the meantime, while they toiled on the railway during the day, I had to look after the hospital, check on the latrines and the cookhouse and the general hygiene of the camp, get wood for the cookhouse, and the medical officers in lonely jungle outposts were also expected to dig graves for the dead and bury them. About half the men in the group died, most of them from cholera. We had nothing to treat them with.'

Doctor Duncan was in jungle camps where ingenuity and compassion were the tools of trade. He later wrote a fine paper for the *Australian Medical Journal* titled 'Makeshift Medicine'. This doctor had been on the Burma Railway camps as well as the mines in Japan and had, therefore, seen and done much.

'The prisoner of war camps in Thailand were dotted along the Kwai Noi River like a string of beans', Dr Ian Duncan wrote. 'Some of the camps were in the hot, humid coastal plain, some in the foothills, others, like those in the Three Pagoda Pass area, were high in the mountains where winter temperatures dropped low at night. In the rainy season, this must be one of the wettest places on earth.

'We were told by the Japanese that, although their government had signed the Hague Convention, the Army had not and, therefore, the Army was not bound by its terms. Also, as we had dared to oppose the Imperial Japanese Army and had been defeated, so we must be punished. At first the men worked from daylight to dark, but later, shifts went on through the night with fires burning for light. Rest days were rare.

'Each area commander was responsible for food, clothing and medical supplies within his area. The typical monthly issue of medical supplies for 1000 men was six to twelve bandages, a small piece of gauze, 10 to 20 millilitres of tincture of iodine and a few dozen assorted tablets of dubious value. Almost all our own medical supplies and equipment had been confiscated after capture. The jungle camps I was in were built by the men themselves, usually after a long march on which they carried all their personal possessions, cooking gear and medical supplies. Accommodation consisted of leaky tents or flys or, if the camps became more permanent, huts of bamboo with atap roofing which were built in any spare time available. During the wet season, when cholera raged along the river, isolation hospitals had to be established and causeways had to be built to the cookhouse, latrines, and through the camp lines.

'Treatment of severe dehydration in some patients with dysentery and in most patients with cholera was a serious problem. In most camps, saline solution was made with rainwater, which was plentiful, or with strained river water. In the large, permanent camps water was distilled in improvised stills. In the more remote camps, salt was almost impossible to obtain and rock salt was used instead. What was estimated to be the correct amount was dissolved in water and the solution was boiled. Containers were made by removing the bottom from an empty Japanese wine or beer bottle and closing the neck with a wooden cork with a hole in it through which a piece of bamboo was inserted; this was then connected by stethoscope tubing to a cannula carved from a piece of bamboo. By this means, an intravenous infusion of saline could be given rapidly with hardly any side effects. If possible, saline was also administered per rectum.

'Amoebic dysentery was common in the jungle camps, and responded immediately to emetine injections when available but, for the most part, specific treatment was unavailable. Raw opium, obtained from friendly Thais, was valuable in treating the severe cramps and diarrhoea of patients with cholera and dysentery in that it at least relieved the pain and enabled the patient to rest. The doses were quite empirical. Everywhere men were suffering from pellagra as well as other vitamin deficiencies. Fractures were common and, of course, no x-rays were available. Bamboo splints were used extensively. Thomas splints were made from bamboo and heavily padded wire.

'Beds were made of bamboo slats and as a result, bed sores developed rapidly and were a constant worry. The usual treatment for ulcers were curettage with a sharpened spoon and carbolisation of the base, usually without anaesthesia. This arrested ulcers in most cases, but in Thailand and Burma, amputation was sometimes the only life-saving treatment. (In Japan where we later were sent, pinch grafts were used with success in the treatment of ulcers incurred by coal miners.) Most surgical instruments were improvised. Steel dinner knives were made into scalpels. Forks were made into retractors and haemostatic clips. Tenon saws were used for amputations and soldering irons for cautery. Early on, for sewing up wounds I used a darning needle and silk or cotton thread.

'Protoscopes were made from tin, the edges being turned in, and using a mirror in line with the sun was effective. In the larger camps, sigmoidoscopes which could be inflated were built, ileostomy bags were made from Dutch aluminium water-bottles and worked well. Surgical treatment of amoebic dysentery in the large hospitals such as Nakom Paton was of great value. Lieutenant Colonel Coates, AAMC, and other surgeons performed appendicostomy, ileostomy and caecostomy very successfully. In Changi and Nakom Paton artificial limbs were made using the ubiquitous bamboo as a pylon and sockets and corsets which were made with the help of skilled tradesmen in the camp. It is remarkable that major surgery was successfully undertaken on these emaciated, exhausted men: in Nakom Paton, cholecystectomy, drainage of hepatic abscess, nephrectomy, splenectomy for ruptured malarial spleen.'

In Burma the Dutch chemist Captain von Boxtel produced emetine from ipecacuanha, which was pure enough for injection and which often produced dramatic results in the treatment of amoebiasis. A microscope was constructed from bamboo and field-glass lenses, which enabled blood typing and recognition of malarial and amoebic parasites. 'Eye lesions were frequent in Burma and Thailand, and at the big hospital at Nakom Paton, Major Hazelton, AAMC, constructed an ingenious ophthalmoscope using an oil lamp burning coconut oil, parts of a Rolls razor, a metal concave mirror and some lenses.

'Ingenuity overcame some of the difficulties the prisoners faced in administering even rough and ready medicine. By distilling Burmese 'brandy', enough alcohol was made for use in surgery and to sterilise syringes. Intravenous tubes were fashioned from bamboo. In some camps artificial limbs were made complete with knee and ankle joints using bamboo, scraps of metal, wire, nails and screws salvaged by the men. Malaria was ever present, and at least 80 per cent of prisoners were infected. Quinine was rarely available, especially in the more remote camps; certainly there was never enough of it for treatment. Patients with blackwater fever were given fluids and bed rest and good results of this treatment were obtained. Cerebral malaria was usually fatal.

'Surgery in the jungle camps was done only as a last resort. Dental novocaine and diluted Japanese cocaine, when obtainable, were used almost universally for spinal anaesthesia. Instruments were scarce, most of them having been confiscated by the Japanese. Captain Boxtel, the Dutchman, made me needles from hardened copper wire or bamboo, and bored holes through thorns of bamboo for use in injections. You had to make do with what you could get. Catgut was made from the intestines of animals by peeling off the peritoneum, drying it, boiling it twice in saturated saline and storing it in alcohol. The theatre for surgery was an atap-covered hut with a bamboo operating table.

'Tropical ulcers were of great significance. The smallest wound or abrasion quickly turned into a rapidly expanding ulcer which, in some cases, exposed tendons and periosteum.

'Most parties were able to keep some records on scraps of paper or on bamboo strips. (Fortunately, on return at the end of the war, the Australian authorities accepted these records.)'

Dr Duncan was constantly beaten by guards wielding rifle butts, shovels and 'anything else to hand' because of his attempts to prevent sick men from having to join work parties.

Men try to forget, they try to make little of it, some try to speak just once of it in the hope of exorcising the memory. 'They brought out water. We were dying of thirst and they poured it out on the ground in front of us', says the young doctor who was sent with 500 men up the railway on flat-top wagons.

He had cholera, dysentery, beriberi, 'you name it I had it, and most of my men had these things, but we tried not to admit these things because it was tantamount to conceding defeat'. Some doctors were out in the jungle alone, with nothing but their own skills. When he was not too sick Doctor Duncan cleaned the latrines, or cut down trees to build a camp, but it was deep slush and men were up to their knees in mud and that made the work heavier.

Many patients suffered terrible rigours and some monks who had become friendly with Duncan told him where there was a salt lick in the jungle. He got lumps of this rock salt for saline drips and experimented by taste until he got the saline solution right. Unlike doctors in the big base camps, Duncan was in the jungle with nothing as a point of reference. 'Men would come to me and say, "Is this food alright to eat?" I'd say, "If you can keep it down it's OK".

'I'd do sick parade in the dark morning and night. Then tenko! Roll-call. Arguments always about which sick men must go to work. Then you'd go back and try to fix up the men left behind. Send someone to light duties, to chop wood, cart water, dig latrines, cut down trees for corduroy paths through mud to the knees, and the usual camp chores of hygiene of kitchen and latrines. The doctor had to do these things, there were not enough fit men. You insisted always that water must be boiled, and dixies washed in boiling water before meals to prevent cholera, etc. Then there was the doctoring, the dressing of ulcers, sickness, "wards" as we called the shelters of bedridden men.

'Three Pagoda Pass is at the tail-end of the Himalayas and winter can be 10 degrees below. All men, even those termed fit by the Japanese, were in a bad way and you watched for pneumonia and frost bite. Even summertime hit us. Many of these men had only a G-string, some had a hat. Sent off to walk 200 kilometres carrying everything to set up another camp. Disposed of everything not essential. Clothes disintegrated on the steaming walk. It was a strange time out of life. In "good" times little trading boats came up-river, once a fortnight, and the men bought bits of food with the few ticals they earned from labouring for the Japanese that worked out at about 5 cents for twelve hours of very hard work.

'A man could get three eggs with his money, if lucky, or some Modern Girls (dried fish slit down the middle, "Two faced, no guts" the men who'd had no luck with women called them). Out of the money the men earned a percentage was paid into a common fund to buy a bulk lot of food for the hospital. Men too sick to work were not paid at all. "Not worth feeding", the Japanese said.'

One of the few great joys that came from outside was the help and encouragement of the local Chinese. 'The Chinese were absolutely fantastic. Even on the march into Changi in the early days they brought water to us. They were belted unmercifully by the Japanese for this but still they came with fruit or food and water. Whenever they saw us, Chinese could pick Australians and waved or called out and brought water

...s. Girls from Lavender Street were the greatest of all. They risked their lives to help us with food and drink. I have great admiration for them.

'The Australian soldier is a remarkable man. We saw English and Dutch die alone without a friend but never an Australian. The Australian would wash friends, help them to the toilet, comfort them. They were ready to help strangers who were new in camp, and that didn't happen with other groups.

'We are talking here of man *in extremis*, when he may be expected to look out for himself, take no risks. But no, they risked all.'

Ian Duncan had a hand cart that he trundled 3 miles out and 3 back to pick up bodies. All dead. 'Dysentery, beriberi, cholera, you name it. Some bayoneted, some shot.' One day on his 'round', a man from the Free Thai army jumped out of the jungle. 'Scared me!' 'You want help?' the Thai asked. He was gathering ground food for his village. 'This bloke, Dibbawan, brought me raw opium in small capsules. Very useful, but I'd never used it before and didn't know how to administer it. Watered down you could give a dose before curetting ulcers. Blokes were going to die if you didn't do something. Anything!'

The Japanese sent this resourceful doctor out to treat villagers and make peace with 'primitives' who were still using bows and arrows (particularly on Japanese who took their women). Duncan was to learn what leaves, roots and berries could be eaten, and developed 'quite a flourishing practice in the village' and was paid in kind with chickens. Men claim that many times he supplied the whole hospital with food.

At the end of July the position of the force was desperate. Communication between the camps and with either Burma or Thailand had practically ceased owing to impassable roads and bridges; a large number of the force had died. In one camp alone there was cholera, typhus, spinal meningitis, smallpox, diphtheria, jaundice, pneumonia, pleurisy, malaria, dysentery, scabies, beriberi and tropical ulcers. With the exception of quinine there were very few drugs and no dressings available throughout the area. Severe tropical ulcers were dressed with banana leaves covered with the men's old army puttees, or with dressings improvised from old shorts and shirts. The result was that some seventy limbs were amputated. Deaths in one camp alone were averaging twelve a day.

Towards the end of November work at the labour camps ceased and most survivors were returned to Singapore by the end of December, except for 550 'desperately ill' cases and 150 medical staff at Kanburi in Thailand, and 320 including staff of about 100 at Tanbaya hospital camp in Burma. Of the 220 sick men in hospital in Burma, ninety-six died before the camp was evacuated down to Kanburi in February. In April 1944 both groups returned to Singapore.

On that 'health' trip up the Burma Railway, the force lost 3087 out of its total of 6998. The Australians, who had totalled 3662, lost 1058 men, while the British had lost 2029 out of a total of 3336.

The Burma Railroad was more than most men could bear, but Ian Duncan was now sent further. 'We were taken back to Singapore and crammed into the stinking hold of a ship bound for Japan. The night we arrived the first big air raid on Japan was taking place. Ships blowing up, ships on fire. A great sight! The Japanese put big hessian barriers up hoping we couldn't see. But we saw enough. There were bodies floating around the harbour.

'We were stripped naked and our clothes put in a heap to be disinfected after being on the stinking ship. Girls made fun of us as we were taken to the railway station at Moji Kyushi but we now knew for certain that the war had come to Japan and that buoyed us up. We went by train to the northern tip around Kyushu and there we were stoned and spat on by the Jap civilians as we were lined up outside Camp 17. Scotty Howe said, "We're going to march into this American camp as Australian soldiers", and we straightened ourselves up and marched in singing "Waltzing Matilda".' Professor, Doctor Thomas Hewlett, of Stanford University, California, told Ian that the previous day two of his men had been executed for

'Your men gave us the greatest lift! Marching in as if
re free men, not prisoners.'

wlett (a thoracic surgeon) was medical commander of the
p and Ian Duncan became second in command. He spoke
anese, had learnt it from an officer who had wanted to
rn English and had told Duncan that he was in line for a
nior post in Australia when Japan won the war!

Duncan was sent with 200 men to Omuta, a large POW
camp on Kyushu. Here the men worked down the coal face
along with American POWs. Starvation rations during the
bitter winter with the temperature well below zero day and
night caused the men to believe that this was harder than their
work on the Burma Railway; here they had no rest periods at
all whereas in the jungle they rested ten minutes every hour.
'An occasional Red Cross parcel was given out as a prize for
the section with the highest attendance figures as though it was
a gift from the Japanese.' Here Duncan was prisoner number
508. If absent from the hut the men must hang their wooden
number tags on nails at the door, red for camp, black for
outside work. 'Woe betide you if your wooden tag wasn't on
the right nail!' As winter drew on the cold was bitter. 'We all
had plumbing problems and the rice and water diet didn't help
in this minus-20 temperature. We'd make a rush for the latrine
and forget our tags. Always met a guard. Always made to
stand to attention while beaten. And bursting for the toilet.

'Of all places I was prisoner I think Japan was the worst.
Injuries were frequent. The men were taken as mine workers
and laboured in very confined spaces. When using the jack-
hammer one man had to go down on hands and knees and
another put the jack-hammer on his back to reach the coal
seam. (And the Repatriation Department now says there's
nothing wrong with this man's back!) Compound fractures
were common. The Allies were bombing Japan daily by this
time and we'd have to get everybody out of the bombed hospital, broken back and all.

'We landed in Japan on 9 June 1944. We had been captives
since February 1942. None of us were the fit men we had been

two years before. And now we had the most sadistic guards, men who had been wounded or were unfit for action. Japan was now being bombed as it had bombed others and they were bitter. More than ever Allied prisoners were looked on purely as labour, not as men, in our case to get the coal out for their war effort. The men were wearied, exhausted and sick beyond all telling. It was intensely cold, there was virtually a river running through the mine and men worked knee-deep in it.

'You did an awful lot of circumcisions in Japan. It was a life-saving operation. It meant ten days in camp for an exhausted body. We could always get away with it.'

Duncan knew two 'good' Japanese doctors. One of them, 'Doctor Marau did his utmost to help and was never obstructive. I remember one bitterly cold night we were cooking stolen potatoes in the steriliser in the hospital and there was this awful smell and the potatoes were bouncing around, bump, bump, bump, and in walked Marau wanting me to do a gastroscopy on one of his men and he huddled over the steriliser for warmth and the potatoes continued going bump, bump, bump. Finally he said, "They've got to be cooked by now!" And he ate them with us, all laughing together.

'But it was a hard war. For all of us. All personnel were young men at the start of the war. Doctors were young and inexperienced and our education had not prepared us for years in prison camps. There was no way of predicting the medical sequelae that might hound survivors to their graves. We did our best.

'In Camp 17, Omuta, a pericardium was drained; rib shears were made and thoracoplasties were performed on occasion. As well, a Dutch prisoner, Doctor Bras, constructed a microscope using bamboo and lenses from field glasses, and this instrument was good enough to enable blood typing and recognition of malarial and amoebic parasites. In Japan too we found that frequent small blood transfusions of about 200 mls were often life-saving in the treatment of pneumonia.'

At his camp on 16 August 1945, Ian Duncan saw Namaguchi, the Japanese camp interpreter read out the order that all POWs were to be executed. 'We saw machine guns being set up.' But it was too late. The Americans were on their way in and the young man who was admired by every man who came in contact with him was soon to be on his way home.

In the camp in Japan Ian Duncan attended the parade on 21 August 1945 when the Japanese officer read the Imperial Rescript at the end of the war, standing on a table in full ceremonial dress, white gloves and sword. 'Since you were interned in this camp, you doubtless have had to go through much trouble and agony. But you have overcome them. I sympathise with you who have been unable, due to illness or some other unfortunate reason, to greet this joyous day. We camp staff have done all in our power to protect you but owing to conditions this was not always possible.' Ian Duncan then, when it was all too late, discovered there were huge Red Cross crates stashed away in disused mines. 'There was enough to equip a hospital from 1942–45. Sulpha drugs, plaster of paris, all the things we needed and didn't have.'

Ian Duncan saw himself as a soldier doctoring, whereas some saw themselves as doctor-civilians in uniform. He is one of the most generous of men towards his fellows. 'All the doctors up the line were a credit to their profession. There were upwards of thirty-six doctors and surgeons went up the line, about fifteen of them were on the Burma side of the border. Men like Lloyd Kahl and Kevin Fagan could never be forgotten, and Euan Corlette, great blokes. Arthur Moon was one of my pin-up boys!' Men admired and respected Duncan not only for his medical practice but for the care and encouragement he gave to the boys. All these men, when they eventually got home into civilian, professional and home life, proved they had not sought adulation; they didn't need it, they were doctors and had cared for and treated their patients in the best way they could under the circumstances, innovative when need be but always professionally aware, and they would continue to be so in civilian life.

The revered Sydney doctor fights till this day for the men whose lives were in his hands. He, as much as anyone in

Australia, has encouraged research into the long-term effects of POW privation.

The war experiences of Doctor Rowland Richards have been fictionalised in a book. He had been a young militiaman before the war when he sailed with the 2/15th Field Regiment to Malaya. 'I wrote the book mainly for the medical orderlies, to give credit to them. Often there was little, or no time for medical officers to sit and talk with the patients. There's a lot more to medicine than just prescribing drugs, and that's where the orderlies performed such a splendid function.'

Doctor Richards has maintained close contact with his regiment as well as being active in community work. Although he is very much a man of today, he has not forgotten those three and a half years he spent with the Japanese almost half a century ago.

Like most other doctors he praises the other ranks, the ORs 'For every one doctor there were probably ten medical staff. They were dedicated, we needed volunteers for medical orderlies and never had any shortage. When we had the cholera epidemic, we had a few fellows who'd had no previous experience, they volunteered and a few of them died, but they knew that was a risk they'd taken.

'Up the railway, on 16 June 1943, Dr Kevin Fagan reported the grim news that cholera had broken out.' Richards called a parade of all men and tried to give them a picture of what was required of them on medical grounds and the strict hygiene to be carried out. He tried to cheer them up and extend some general advice, but all of this was ruined by the sudden hair-raising shrieks coming from the hospital area. Kevin Fagan called out, 'Don't take any notice of that, it's only a chap coming out of the anaesthetic I gave him!'

But it was the start of a trying and fearful period. The first death occurred on the same day and all were immediately inoculated, for it was the disease most feared by the Japanese. 'Seventy-two men died between 26 June and 4 July. The cholera isolation area was a horrible sight, with the dead and dying spread about. The tireless and unceasing efforts of Dr

Kevin Fagan and his medical orderlies were beyond comprehension in their devotion and dedication,' says Richards.
Those words could equally be said of himself.

'There was a lot that was positive, there was a great deal
one could do in the prevention area and in trying to educate
the men. For instance, there was no way the blokes I was with
would have a meal without putting their dixies in boiling water
afterwards. Even before we left Australia hygiene was a strong
subject in our unit; we started with a paddock and had to
create a whole drainage system there, grease traps, everything
improvised, which was very good training for all concerned.
They rapidly realised the differences between a well-planned
hygienic camp as distinct from some of the fly-ridden older
huts they'd seen where cleanliness hadn't been a discipline;
they realised by concentrating on hygiene you can reduce flies
and so defeat disease.'

The doctor sees the whole war experience as very positive,
not negative in any way, 'not the way you'd throw up your
hands and give in'. He had started off his military career in
peacetime as a gunner and gradually went up the ranks, was
commissioned and finished up as a battery commander.

'For every one doctor there were about ten medical staff and
they were the guys who did the work. In my group we didn't
have a single amputation whereas some of the others wrote
books on amputations necessitated by ulcers. We were strong
in prevention; our particular group had been trained to inspect
skin every day and the slightest scratch was treated, you did
something to clean it up even if only with boiled water. Instead
of the old traditional treatment of scooping it out with a
spoon, which destroys the granulating tissue, we used to spend
hours just taking the dead tissue out a bit at a time and leaving
the granulating tissue there. The fact that my group had no
amputations is no credit to me, it's a credit to these guys who
did all the work. They were dedicated, when the call went out
they volunteered as medical orderlies and some of them died,
but they knew that was a risk they'd taken. Our medical orderlies were the heroes, but they'll never admit it.'

Doctor Richards had vast admiration for other doctors, particularly (Sir) Albert Coates, the senior Australian medical man in the South-East Asia area. 'Bertie Coates was a magnificent bloke; he was a well-known character and deserved to be. He never became "a professional POW" (a term used by ex-POWs for men who use their past experiences to bolster their egos). Bertie quietly remained available to all who needed him. In our prison days, up in the rough stuff, he was magnificent.

'But it's quite wrong to discriminate one from the other. To my knowledge there's no doctor who didn't do a good job in the POW camps whether he was in Changi or at base camps such as Nakom Paton, or like others trudging along from makeshift to makeshift on the real hard slog.

'You hear comments and criticisms about some of the non-medical officers, most of which I think is probably justified, but I've never heard any criticisms about doctors, wherever they were. Arthur Moon was one I admired, he came back, and Euan Corlette came back, and they got straight back into business, they didn't bother getting involved in unit activities, they're examples of dozens of those fellows. Good doctors, they didn't seek fame. Their fame is in the memories of men they served.'

Richards accompanied the Australian prisoners to Sakata on the west coast of the island of Honshu, Japan, near the 39th Parallel. There he worked day and night to save lives.

He says, 'The men's physical state was one of extreme exhaustion aggravated by starvation and disease. Billeted in a rice store, sleeping on wooden floors or grass mats, trying to do the work of the coolies they replaced on 60 grams of rice, barley and beans, occasionally horse or pig offal. A diet grossly deficient in protein, fats and vitamins. Sometimes seaweed. No recreation. Eight men died of pneumonia during what we were told was the severest winter experienced in Japan for seventy years.'

'Whatever a medico was professionally or humanely before the war he had to be good to stick those years out', John Kennedy (Hobart, Tasmania) states. 'The doctor was all the men had between them and death; if he faltered the men were lost. Some were extroverts in civilian life and that streak in them showed in their army days. Some displayed or discussed the beatings they got during their battles with the Japanese over which patients should be kept in hospital and not be sent up the line. But that did not make them any more or less, not even any different than the quiet men who fought just as persistently and constantly and doggedly to keep their boys off the work list, and kept their scars and the cries of their own beatings to themselves. It merely demonstrates the greatness to which all mankind can rise in defence of the helpless. No doctor was greater or lesser than any other; each far transcended the oath they had taken and their mien ennobled their profession.'

David Hinder MD, with Major 'Roaring Reg' Newton, had one of the lowest mortality rates on the River (the Kwa Noi or any of the names men knew it by, including the fictitious one made famous by the film *Bridge on the River Kwai*). Hinder worked in the shadow of the Japanese Hiromatz, known as The Tiger. This man once reduced Hinder to the ranks because 'you no good doctor!' A 'no good doctor' was one who had sick men in his hospital. Presumably a good doctor was one with empty huts.

Hinder was with the men who worked down from the Burma end on the railway and who did the long hungry march in the mud of the monsoons. He accompanied the men on the 'hell' ship to Japan and never forgot their travail. A compassionate man, he has worked to gain recognition of their uniquely different health and life-threatening medical problems. He saw their brave stance in times so bad no young doctor today can envisage, and has continued his responsibility as a medico to care for them, and speak for them.

Doctor Hinder saw his patients labouring in three countries, but here he remembers Japan where he worked ten hours a day and, 'when the pressure was really on, for fourteen or sixteen hours a day, seven hours a day, seven days a week'. There were no holidays.

'For the first twelve months after capture, I was attached to a party that worked as wharf labourers in Singapore, for the second twelve months I was with a party working on the Burma-Thailand Railway; during the third year I was attached to a party which spent nine months in Japan working in an underground copper mine.

'Miners worked seventy hours a week on a diet of rice millet or barley and at times a little fish, the energy value of which was about 7500 kilojoules. This watery diet caused great frequency of micturition and disturbed sleep. I kept count one night, I made thirteen trips to the latrine between the hours of 8 p.m. and 6 a.m. This was usual. Some prisoners were too weak to move, with the obvious results.

'After about eight months the miners became too ill, exhausted and worn out to do the work down the mine. They were brought to the surface, to the daylight, where they worked in the factories. The hours of work remained the same but, since they were no longer working underground, their energy intake was reduced to 6300 kilojoules per day. At this time, towards the end of the war, some prisoners weighed only 20 or 30 kilograms. Many weighed only half their normal bodyweight. There were some whose weight was normal, but this was due to oedema from beriberi and malnutrition. These men could hardly shuffle their swollen legs and feet to work. Patients had tropical ulcers and on their return to Australia many were found to have intestinal parasites, including hookworm. For all these diseases there was no treatment, no rest, diet or drugs. Most prisoners, if not all, suffered from a combination of all of them. The only treatment was work and if any prisoner of war could not work he was of no use to the Japanese and was better out of the way dead. One in three prisoners perished from their privations.

'POWs were always hungry, under constant strain and stress, suffering from untreated diseases, at risk from physical violence from the Japanese and exposed to the possibility of injury at work. Miners from Western Australia, Broken Hill and the coalfields say that the conditions in the Japanese mines would never have been allowed in Australia. Towards the end of the war, there was the possibility of being blown up by our friends and Allies and, at the back of everybody's mind was the question of what the Japanese would do when the United States invaded Japan. The only thing we knew was that they were capable of anything. The atom bomb undoubtedly saved our lives.'

Doctor Hinder is adamant. 'Some of my civilian colleagues today are of the opinion that these untreated diseases (malnutrition, starvation and overwork) did not leave any permanent or lasting effects and that on return the treatment and diet of Western civilisation cured prisoners completely, without leaving any scars. I do not agree with them, for every system, every organ, tissue, cell, enzyme, hormone, must have been affected in some way by the privations of POW life and I cannot believe that any such living tissue could make a complete and unscarred recovery. Having seen it, it is my opinion that these experiences accelerated the onset of age and its complaints, as well as preparing the ground for other disabilities. My [civilian] colleagues do not agree with me and ask for scientific proof. There is no scientific proof for the privations of prisoners of war. They have never been recorded before and are unknown to science.

'Scientific colleagues remind me that exercise and starvation are good in the modern, affluent society. I agree with them, when one is in a position to cry "enough", but, in applying their scientific truth to the toiling, expendable slaves of the Japanese, they show their ignorance of the effect of seventy hours of labour a week on a 7500 kilojoule carbohydrate diet. The effects of this are worse when complicated by several untreated diseases and existing on the poverty line in an Eastern country whose code of honour was medieval and its own: the Japanese had never signed the Geneva Convention. To me, it is not scientific to compare and draw conclusions from a disease occurring in an individual living in the 20th century among his own people and having available proper hospitals, rest, diet, drugs and treatment, with the same disease occurring in a prisoner of war of a medieval, feudal people, who was denied proper hospitals, was overworked without rest, complicated by untreated diseases, suffering from extreme starvation and malnutrition and always subject to the possibility of violence and injury, either from his armed guards or from accidents at archaic working places. To me the treatment of ex-prisoners of war of the Japanese is a scandal and a disgrace to Australia.

'At the end of the war, United States bombers dropped all the wonderful things of Western civilisation into our camp and, at the time, they saved the lives of at least twelve men in our camp alone; if we had had to spend another winter in Japan, I expected at least 30 per cent would have perished.

'We were deluged with cartons of cigarettes, many men became chain smokers. We over-ate on butter, chocolate, full milk powder, pork meats, bully beef and cake; some men doubled their weight within a few months. Overnight we had passed out of Hell and into Heaven and we knew overnight that instead of dying in Japan we would be going home.

'Our own people, with the best of intentions, had put our feet firmly on the road to the diseases of an affluent Western society. Today nobody, under any circumstances, would be deluged with cartons of cigarettes or with untold packets of full-cream milk powder, butter, cheese, pork and beef.

'We had survived, more by good luck than anything else our period as POWs. It is a paradox that the atom bomb saved our lives while the ignorant benevolence of our own people showed us the way to those diseases, scientifically accepted as being caused by a modern Western civilised lifestyle.

'As for the brutal life our men had to endure, I can forgive the Japanese, for many of them had had a hard life and knew no better, but I cannot forgive our own people for their attitude to ex-prisoners of war and regard them with contempt.'

The Red Duster

'My Merchant Navy,'

> King George VI at war's end, 1945, when the distinctive flag of the
> Merchantmen, the Red Duster as it is known to seamen, was hauled aloft.

In FEBRUARY 1928 KING George V had appointed his son, the
then Prince of Wales, Master of the Merchant Navy 'as an
honour to all Merchant Seamen of the British Empire who
suffered so much during World War I.' This title is now held
by the Sovereign. At the close of World War II the King spoke
with affection of 'my Merchant Navy'. He said, 'The simple
words include the whole profession.'

As in World War I Britain's great weakness in World War
II was her dependence on imports – some 68 million tons
annually were needed, from food to raw materials for industry.
The needs of the navy, army and air force as well as of all
citizens depended on shipping. The men on these ships may
sound flippant when they describe their flag as 'the Red
Duster', but the sight of the Union Jack on the red background
brought honour and respect from all who knew this service.
On any given day there were 2500 British registered merchant
ships at sea (British denoting Empire at that time). Their cargo
was the life-blood of the country's existence. These ships and
the men who sailed them were the target the enemy must
destroy if they were to bring England and her empire down.
If enough of these cargo ships could be destroyed, the United
Kingdom's ability to wage war would be ended.

Early in August 1939 the German navy had its fleet at sea,
fully prepared for the disruption and destruction of enemy
merchant ships by all possible means. Across the North Sea,
in London, Whitehall issued 'Navigation Order No.1, 1939'
taking control of all merchant ships.

There may be lulls in fighting on land, but never on the sea. On any voyage there are the natural hazards of the sea, but added to these perils in time of war are mines, submarines, torpedoes, aerial bombs and shells from surface raiders. Merchantmen have never dallied in harbour because of the perils outside. Officers and men on deck, dressed like Arctic explorers on the winter convoys to Murmansk and Archangel, were attacked by U-boats on days almost perpetually dark, and on fine days torpedo bombers delivered in one convoy forty-two attacks in three days. At all times, with no ship lights showing, they sailed along the coasts with no navigational lights ashore to guide them. Applauding them at war's end, the Minister of War Transport said, 'Their duty has been to carry food, raw materials and armaments and take the troops to their appointed place to fight in foreign fields'. They had brought to Britain at least one-third of her meat, butter, cheese and wheat, as well as steel, timber, wool, cotton, iron ore, lead and oil. 'Every blow we deliver is firmly linked with the sea and seamen.' For a 500-bomber raid on Germany by four-engined aircraft, 750,000 gallons of fuel oil were needed, all brought in by sea by the men of the Merchant Navy who succoured a beleaguered nation.

You have seen him on the street rolling round on groggy feet,
You have seen him clutch a lamp post for support.
You have seen him arm in arm with a maid of doubtful charm
Who was leading Johnny safely back to port.

You have shuddered in disgust as he sometimes bit the dust,
You've ignored him when you've seen him on a spree.
But you've never seen the rip of his dark and lonely ship
Ploughing furrows through a sub-infested sea.

You have cheered our naval lads in their stately iron clads,
You have spared a cheer for Infantrymen too,
You have shuddered in a funk when you read 'big mail boat sunk'
Did you ever give a thought about the crew?

Yet he brings the wounded home through a mine-infested zone,
And he ferries all the troops across at night.
He belongs to no brigade, he's neglected, underpaid,
But he's always in the thickest of the fight.

And he fights the lurking Hun with his ancient 4-inch gun,
And he'll ruin Adolph Hitler's little plan.
He's a hero, he's a nut, he's the bloody limit (but)
He's just another Merchant Navy Man.

The Merchant Navy Man. Anon

At the beginning of this war the merchant vessels sailed totally unarmed because this navy was scattered to the four corners of the globe when war commenced and no neutral country would dare arm them; this could only be done in their own country and at selected ports. During the first six months many ships running the gauntlet unarmed used rifles and revolvers against aircraft, using skill and their ability to dodge bombs and bullets and hide when possible.

War had been declared on 3 September 1939 and in the previous month the German navy had prudently put sixteen U-boats on station in the North Sea and the North Atlantic, along with the most modern pocket battleships *Admiral Graf Spee* and the *Deutschland*. The *Athenia*, a British Merchant Navy ship, was sunk within hours of the outbreak of war.

Australian lives were lost on board thirty-seven vessels (Australian and foreign). Australian seamen were in twenty other vessels under attack but escaped casualties; twenty-six vessels went down, one was burned, one was beached and salvaged, and one was abandoned.

Send out your big warships to watch your big waters,
That no one may stop us from bringing you food.
For the bread that you eat and the biscuits you nibble,
The sweets that you suck and the joints that you carve,

They are all brought to you daily by all of us Big Steamers
And if anyone hinders our coming you'll starve.

'Big Steamers', Rudyard Kipling

There were, of course, doctors on the big merchant liners such as the *Queen Mary*, but there were no doctors on the average merchant ship. Those who escaped from sinking ships suffered in lifeboats and rafts from urgent need of medical attention, the main need being for third degree burns caused by steam pipes bursting, oil burning on the surface of the sea. They suffered exposure, thirst, starvation and sharks. 'Sharks swimming around a stricken ship give no quarter, no chance', as every seaman knows. Yet this fourth arm of the services in time of war has been almost totally ignored by the Australian government.

Noel Sligar, an Australian who served on American merchant ships during the war, has his Honourable Discharge from the Armed Services of the USA. He also served on Australian ships but this country does not give Honourable Discharges to merchant seamen as it does to other servicemen. A Merchant Navy medal was issued to World War I men, but not to those of World War II. (Noel Sligar has his Merchant Navy Emblem, but that was for his service in USA ships, not Australian.)

It becomes almost impossible to understand the lack of interest of the Australian government in these men who faced the enemy every time they left harbour.

As the late Hon. J.A. Beasley, Minister for Supply and Shipping, said on 6 March 1943, 'With due deference to the splendid other services, I would say that the recent operations around New Guinea would not have succeeded but for the magnificent work of the Merchant Navy'. And that could be said for every action because even the air force was dependent on the merchantmen to cross the seas with their fuel.

A uniqueness among Merchant Navy men was the extreme youth of many – 15, 15½, 16, 17 – in comparison to other Services. One was not legally able to join the army, navy or air force but one could join the Merchant Navy if over school age, which at that time was 14.

Alan Smith, who went to sea when aged 16, on the *River Burdekin*, was one of the first two cadets to sail away on the Government line. His only training was in the Merchant Navy Training Sea Corps and his first and only training in gunnery was when the ship reached Alexandria in the Mediterranean two months later.

'There was simulated practice on an Oerlikon gun while a shadow crossed a dome; for other guns wires were used, or a cut-out of a make-believe submarine. We all knew how stupid this was but it made no difference to our going to sea. Coming back from the Middle East the troops we were bringing home nearly died laughing at us. Our radio officer even shot his own wireless aerial down. There were no safety bars on the ship which meant you could, theoretically, blow the bridge away if you fired. Later we did get these bars and eventually we got a young naval gunner on board – and when it rained he stuffed cotton waste and oil down the Oerlikon gun to stop the rain from getting into it and when he fired the gun in practice, the whole barrel split in half and the mate was wounded with a bit of steel. That was the sort of protection we had on our ships. The naval officers that were put on board were questionable as to training.

'Some ships had one gun and this took at least four men bringing the shells up to fire them but there was only one RAN man. The RAN were ordered not to practise with real shells because they cost money! Merchant Navy officers and men went ashore and bought hand-held guns and rifles in the hope of defending themselves and their ship.'

Some Merchant Navy men were repatriated to Australia by means of an exchange of prisoners of war between Germany and Britain. The earliest to arrive home were 111 men who reached Sydney in October 1943.

Albert White (South Melbourne) had been captured when his ship the Norwegian tanker *Madrona* (5894 tons) was sunk in the Indian Ocean in 1942 when he was aged 16. Arthur

Wilson from Rosebery (NSW) was also 16 when he was captured by a German sea raider who shelled and sunk his ship the *Australind* (5020 tons) near the Panama Canal. He had spent nineteen months in a German prison camp and was now aged 18.

Able Seaman W.A. (Sid) Jones of Sydney was aged 20 when he sailed in the *Mareeba* (3472 tons, Australasian United Steam Navigation Co.) and was sunk by torpedo in the Bay of Bengal in June 1941. The *Mareeba*'s survivors were taken aboard the German raider *Kormoran* (9400 tons) for five months, and, after being transferred to a prison ship, they were torpedoed in the Atlantic. After three days in lifeboats, the survivors were picked up by a U-boat. 'After short rations on the prison ship, food on the U-boat was good scrambled eggs for breakfast and ham, soup and coffee for dinner', Sid remembered.

Many seamen were 'in the drink' more than once during those perilous years on enemy-ridden seas. Captain David Freeman, Master Mariner (at sea for forty-five years), holding a Master's certificate for square-rigged sailing ships (the huge barques that took our wheat to Europe in between the wars), went down twice. He was transferred to the SS *Mareeba* just before she sailed from Sydney, Captain Skinner in command, David Freeman second-in-command. 'Shortly after clearing the channel in the Andaman Islands we were stopped by the German raider, the *Kormoran* which shelled us and destroyed the amidships accommodation. Captain Skinner and I were on the bridge at the time, and he was so infuriated that he ordered "full speed" and said to me, "I'm going to ram the bugger". The *Kormoran* was a 20-knot ship and our best speed was 3½ knots in the weather we were experiencing, so there was not much chance of ramming her. We then decided to abandon ship.

'We launched the boats and were taken on the *Kormoran* without loss of life. Soon we were installed in our new home and settled down more or less comfortably. Conditions were not too bad on the raider which cruised around the Indian

Ocean for the next four months. Food was fair, our quarters in the bowels of the ship were complete with hammocks, we were allowed periods on deck during the day and occasionally we were allowed up to the cinema. Captain Detmers was a gentleman and I got on particularly well with the navigator, who was peacetime master of the ship.

'One morning we awoke to find another ship with us, the *Margaret Lunchenback* flying the US flag. She was really the German raider *Kalmerland*. We prisoners were transferred to this ship and she set off for the Pacific. We never saw the *Kormoran* again. [Ten days later, 19 November 1943, the raider *Kormoran* and HMAS *Sydney* sank each other off the coast of Western Australia. Captain Detmers of the German raider *Kormoran* was said to have staked everything on victory or total defeat.] There was little comfort in running and none in surrender. If discovered it would be a fight to the finish.

'The *Kalmerland* was south of Tasmania on Melbourne Cup day', Captain David Freeman wrote. 'A few days later another German supply ship that was en route from Japan to Bordeaux in France took us prisoners on board. This third ship we had been imprisoned on was the *Spreewald* and we settled down to a nice long voyage around Cape Horn in the Atlantic and then up north. We didn't sight anything all this time until 31 January 1944 when our German ship was torpedoed by mistake by a German submarine, U300.

'All hell broke out then; the ship was listing heavily to starboard. By the time I reached the deck I found one boat launched and towing by the falls. She swamped and they were busy lowering my boat on top of her. This was heading for disaster so I ordered the towing fall to be cut, and as the waterlogged boat slid astern, my boat successfully lowered into the sea. I ran aft and slid down a rope into the boat. There were fifteen men including some ships' masters in another boat, they had plenty of blankets and food but refused to take some of the men from our boat which was badly overloaded. There was a raft with about six men on it and also a dinghy with more aboard.

'It was unpleasant weather with choppy seas and fresh, cold winds. We had a very mixed crew aboard my boat, Germans, Scandinavians, Australians, English, Indians, Arabs, Italians, Yugoslavs and maybe a few more races.

'On the late afternoon of the third day, we sighted a big German submarine bearing down on us. They soon had us on board and proceeded to look for more survivors. None was found. The boat with the masters on it had hoisted a sail and sailed off into oblivion. About half the total complement of our ship was lost, and I was the senior man saved.

'The submariners were very good to us, they shared everything. A week later, on my birthday, we berthed at the German submarine base on the coast of France in the Bay of Biscay, and were marched ashore after nearly nine months at sea.' From there the seamen travelled by train to Bremen in Germany, en route for their prison, Milag, 'and years of boredom'.

Conditions differed on each ship. Keith Godridge, fourth engineer, and Percy Robinson, deck-hand (both of Melbourne), were among twelve survivors taken prisoner by the German raider *Orion* which sank the *Triastor* (6032 tons) off Nauru Island, on 8 December 1940 (along with her sister ship, *Triadic*). The men were captive on the raider for six weeks during which they lived on two slices of black bread a day, crowded into a cabin 12 foot by 15 foot. Twice, when the raider went into action, they were sent below decks at gun point and battened down.

'We were transferred to the *Ermlandt* (12,000 tons), sailed around Cape Horn under false flags and met a German fleet off Montevideo. In the fleet were the 26,000-ton battleships *Gneisenau* and *Scharnhorst*, the 10,000-ton pocket battleship *Admiral Scheer*, two other German ships and two U-boats.'

Eventually reaching occupied France, they were marched through the streets in scanty clothing to a temporary camp. 'Frenchwomen tried to help us by throwing food and clothing, but German soldiers stopped them and battered them with the butt ends of their guns', Godridge says. 'On a five-day train journey to Germany in horse-trucks we slept on straw previously used by horses.' Food was poor at Stalag 10B camp until September 1941, when each man received a British Red Cross food parcel and this continued weekly while the men were imprisoned there.

When the exchange of POWs took place in 1943 the men were taken to Lisbon, Portugal. 'German prisoners about to be repatriated in exchange for us told us they did not want to go home as they would be sent to the Russian front or placed in U-boats.'

Vaughan Richards went to sea in 1939 aged 15 years and 5 months, as deck-boy on the *Cycle*, an Australian coaster. On his first venture overseas in November 1940, he sailed on the *California Star* with a cargo of military supplies for Middle East ports – Alexandria, Suez, Port Said, Haifa. 'On the way over, south of Ceylon, enemy aircraft circled overhead and we went to battle stations with our one 4.7-inch gun, a quick firer. (Some of the guns they put on the ships were 1910 vintage, very slow; you put a projectile in, another person put cordite behind it, closed the breech and then put a firing cap in, a fairly messy procedure.)

'After discharge from the *California Star* in Sydney, I was on a few coastal vessels. There was quite a bit of activity around at that time, German raiders captured our ships and mined much of the Australian coast from north to south. An American ship was sunk near Gabo Island and another big ship, the *Cumberland*, struck a mine off Wilson's Promontory.'

Vaughan joined the motor vessel *Australind* in June 1941 and sailed for England via the Panama Canal, heavily loaded with zinc concentrates and dry foods. 'This vessel had no raised foc'sle head, but one deck right through; the accommodation was very old-fashioned, ten seamen sleeping in one room with a table in the middle with double bunks around it. There was no such thing as single cabins or two to a cabin. The only source of hot water was one steam geyser which was situated amidships. We had numerous stoppages with machinery breakdown. We wallowed for days at a time; then, after forty-two days, at a point near the Galapagos Islands, the 3000-ton German raider *Komet* came along (raiders having no registered name, she had been designated Ship 45 by the Imperial German Navy).

'It was 3.30 p.m.; I'd just had a call, as I was to go to the wheel at 4 p.m., when all of a sudden we heard loud explosions. We raced up on deck and what appeared to be a Japanese ship calling itself *Ryuku Maru* (a neutral) was looming out of the sun. In reality it was the *Komet* in disguise. The first shot was fired across our bow, the accepted signal from any aggressor to stop a vessel. When our wireless operator began to send out a message, as he was obliged to do by the British Admiralty, they opened up on us with intense fire. We were so close you could see the German gunners actually training the guns on us. After about ten minutes, the vessel was on fire, lifeboats were shot away; on the bridge the Master of the vessel, he was only 29, had half his head blown off. I and another boy went up to the bridge, and the Second Mate told us to carry him below. So we carried the Master down, laid him on the galley table, pulled his white coat up over his head and went out and locked the door after us.

'There was no doctor on board, no first aid at all. We went down to one of the working alleyways to alarm other personnel; things really started to happen, I went to wake the Fourth Engineer, tried to pull him out of his bunk and his arm came away, he was dead. The Third Engineer, he had his backside shot away and one arm just dangling on a sinew and we carried him out and laid him on the after-deck with a massive piece of cotton wool under the injury, he was losing blood at a rate of possibly half a gallon a minute, he died rapidly. The Second Mate, who was on the bridge, suffered severe injuries to the leg, ripped open. End result was three killed with eight injured.

'The Mate gave the orders when the Master was gone. We were ordered to action stations, I was in the gunners crew as the rammer, the bloke who has to ram the cordite up behind the projectile with a big mop; we trained the gun but immediately a projectile from the raider went past us. I saw it. It was every man for himself. All the life-saving appliances were gone, shot away or on fire, and a German crew came over in their boats and took us off the vessel along with the injured.' But the dead remained, the captain laid out as if for a Viking funeral.

'After boarding the raider, the injured were attended to in a very professional manner; the Second Mate recovered. The hospital and dental facilities were second to none and in all fairness I've got to say we were better treated there as far as food goes than on the ship we'd left. We weren't allowed to see our ship go down, they locked us down below straight away and she was sunk by demolition charges. That was 14 August 1941.'

The following week the *Komet* got her next victim, a British-India ship *Devon* with a large complement of Lascars with British officers. 'All prisoners were locked down in their quarters in No. 1 hold, no discrimination there, the officers were locked down as well; the Germans used to bolt the door and put an armed guard on. *Devon* was put down by gunfire and the prisoners brought aboard the *Komet*.'

Next, a Dutch vessel, *Kota Nopan*, en route from Java to the USA with rubber and tin, was captured intact. After two weeks of ferrying supplies back to the raider, a German prize crew was put on board and the prize was sent on her way with the Lascar prisoners to Bordeaux. The raider had to juggle both crew and captives to relieve crowding. 'By now, on the *Komet* we had the officers of the *Devon*, full crew of the *Australind* and some Dutch officers from the *Kota Nopan*.'

They cruised across the Pacific, rounded Cape Horn into the South Atlantic and sailed north. The ship changed colours, was disguised again, this time as a Portuguese vessel named the *St Hom*, 'and the German naval ratings were dressed in civilian gear as the raider proceeded up the neutral Portuguese coast'. Eventually they were escorted into German-occupied Le Havre by three German U-boats, and waited while preparations were made for a dash up the English Channel. 'We went at about eight o'clock at night – it was dark, you needed cover to go through the Channel unmolested.

'But about 11.30 p.m. action stations were sounded and they had a four-hour engagement with British motor torpedo boats, with shore batteries and some aircraft. A bomb went off on the starboard quarter of the raider and the vessel was lifted almost bodily out of the water and it took two days for minor repairs to be made before they continued on to Cuxhaven where all prisoners were put on shore and sent in motor lorries to the camp named Marlag und Milag Nord.'

By this time Vaughan Richards was aged 17. 'In the camp there were about thirty of that age or younger including little Albert White from Melbourne.' The vast sinkings of the early part of the war put pressure on the Germans, they must find quarters for merchant seamen. At first they put them in the concentration camp Sandbostel, later in Milag, a camp for Merchant Navy prisoners only. Most of the seamen held here were from England and Ireland; the second largest number were from Australia.

The last voyage of SS *British Corporal* gives some indication of the German control of the sea lanes, even to the mouth of the Thames. Dennis Sandford went to sea on 13 November 1939 at the age of 16 years and 9 months. On 20 June 1940 he sailed on SS *British Corporal* as Apprentice Deck Officer, his third voyage. The 10,000-ton ship had a complement of forty-five officers and men, including one gunner. She left Hull on 28 June 1940 at 1500 hours bound for New York.

'A convoy of twelve ships was formed at the mouth of the Humber for voyage to the Thames and was attacked by German E-boats (motor torpedo boats) on the night we left and twice by enemy aircraft during daylight next day. One coaster was sunk by bombs. The convoy arrived off Southend on 30 June and anchored awaiting additional vessels for a larger convoy down the English Channel. We sailed from Southend in the a.m. of 2 July 1940.

'Before the last vessel had taken up station in the convoy, large formations of German fighter-bombers were attacking.

Two vessels were damaged by the bombing which went on until dark by repeated waves of enemy aircraft. One ship in the convoy struck a mine off North Foreland. Daylight on 3 July saw the convoy clear of Dover and heading down the English Channel. Bombing and straffing of the convoy continued all day by wave upon wave of Junkers, Fokkers and Messerschmitts. Out of the convoy of twenty-eight ships which left Southend, nine were now damaged or sunk. No enemy attacks were made after dark that night, but repeated aircraft raids continued throughout daylight on 4 July – the convoy was now down towards Lands End.

'At 0100 hours on 5 July the convoy was attacked by a flotilla of enemy E-boats. The *Hartlepool*, a cargo ship, was torpedoed on our port beam and other vessels were seen to be hit. At 0230 hours our ship was hit by a torpedo in the starboard side of the engine room and started to go down by the stern. The captain sounded "Abandon ship" on the siren and all hands had to go to the amidship lifeboats because the after lifeboats had been destroyed by the explosion.

'We had just cast off and pulled clear of the ship's side when another torpoedo hit the vessel. We pulled around the stern of the sinking ship hoping to find the other boat and although we let off flares there was no sign of it.

'We headed for the English coast and partly rowed and sailed throughout the remainder of the night and the next day and night (6 July) until at about 0800 hours on 7 July we were sighted and rescued by the British frigate HMS *Ullswater* which landed us at Weymouth that evening. We later found that our starboard boat had overturned following the second torpedo and six men were lost. Eight men were lost in the engine room and aft accommodation when the first torpedo hit.'

Sandford had one month's 'torpedo' leave before joining SS *British Advocate* in August 1940 and sailed from Newport on 5 September 1940 for Cape Town and thence to Abadan in the Persian Gulf. The outward convoy in the North Atlantic was attacked by German aircraft first day out and twice by U-boats before the convoy dispersed in mid-Atlantic. *British*

Advocate did two voyages with aviation spirit from Abadan to Mombasa in East Africa. (Aviation spirit is high octane-rated gasoline for aircraft and highly explosive.) Then, sailing solo, the ship set off on a third trip from Abadan, this time bound for England.

Eleven days later, on 20 February 1941, Sandford's ship was sunk when the German pocket battleship *Admiral Scheer* attacked her off the Adabra Islands in the Indian Ocean. Sandford was taken on board the famous battleship, thus making him a prisoner before his 17th birthday. On 8 March 1941 the *Scheer* met the German prison ship *Ermlandt* cruising the South Atlantic and all POWs were transferred to her for a voyage to German-occupied France.

The camps for naval prisoners of the Germans were Marlag (for merchant seamen) and Milag. Both were divided into the groups O and M – officers and men. There were a greater number of nations represented among the internees in the merchant seamen's camp; and in Milag each hut had an individual character according to the national characteristics of its occupants. The men of both Marlag and Milag were great gardeners and brought in turf sods – under guard – to make garden beds. Seeds were sent to the camps by the Royal Horticultural Society in London and they grew vegetables as well as flowers (as did air force and army prisoners elsewhere).

Food parcels were received through the IRCC at Geneva as were uniforms, band instruments and games, books, cigarettes and tobacco. As well, the men received the necessary textbooks for the education programme run in each camp. Study courses for First Mate and Master and all grades of marine engineer and navigation were available, examinations held and officially recognised certificates awarded.

A Merchant Navy Comforts Service was formed in London and their packing centre helped relatives and friends with sending quarterly parcels to their prisoners – making up with their own funds items too expensive for poorer families to contribute, thus making sure all from captain to cabin boy received the best.

They had concerts, plays, pantomimes and sports meetings, five-day bridge tournaments as well as rugby and soccer matches between England, Scotland, Ireland, Australia, New Zealand and South Africa. Food was sufficient, and a British internee was in charge of the cooking for the whole camp; accommodation was eventually in good wooden barracks after a shaky start in shacks. There were delousing facilities and a hot shower per man per week.

At one time there were 2893 internees in Milag but altogether 4000 merchant seamen were held there. There was little to complain about, the Germans left both the naval and the merchant groups to administer their own camps. But time rolled on and the men's youth went with it.

'Settling into the camp was no drama, just a fact of life, you just accepted it', Vaughan Richards says. 'The officers and seniors didn't help us settle in, this is where the discrimination came in, they were all in a separate part of the camp. They didn't have to work.

'We had some good doctors and with their limited supplies they did a good job. Dr Sperber, a Czechoslovakian, was brilliant (after the war we saw him on TV in relation to Dachau and Auschwitz because that's where he ended up).'

Vaughan was an exchange prisoner in March 1943 in company with twenty-four other seamen. 'I was the only Australian. I think I was exchanged because we younger boys played up a lot and they wanted to get rid of us. We went from the camp to Bremen, Hanover, Munchen (Munich), on through the Alps down through Naples to the south of Italy by train, in proper carriages. We had three German guards and they hated the sight of the Italians, so the Italian fare-paying passengers were made to stand up and we sat down. When we got out of the train the Italians pelted us with rocks and house bricks and all sorts of things as we walked down the road.

'After a month we were put aboard an Italian hospital ship, the *Grapisca*. The exchange took place in Turkey. The British vessel *Talma* was laying a half mile away, so prisoners from both sides were mingling.'

The twenty-five seamen were taken to Alexandria. 'The British Consul wasn't concerned about our welfare or our lack of clothes, wasn't concerned about repatriation, his major concern was to get us back to sea as quickly as possible because there were ships in Alexandria yelling out for men; that was his first obligation. But I didn't go back for five months. Immediately I walked out of that Consul's office I was on my own. A long way from home.

'The air force (RAF) invited me to their camp and had a consultation with their adjutant and after that I was in the camp for five months. They clothed and fed me and generally accepted me as one of the lads. I helped where I could. Later I met some Australian seamen in Alexandria who said their ship was short of an AB, so I thought it was about time I made a move and I signed on a Norwegian tanker bound from Alexandria to Italian Somaliland, then to Bombay where we were paid off.' He got a berth on another Norwegian tanker, went back to Abadan, loaded with aviation fuel, to Portuguese East Africa, Madagascar. 'This time there was great German U-boat activity in the Mozambique Channel between Madagascar and the coast of Africa. But everything went all right and we made it back to Abadan where we got paid off.'

He was in Abadan three weeks before he joined a British tanker bound for Melbourne. 'After a voyage of thirty days we arrived at Williamstown, the end of the voyage. It had been fifteen months since I got out of the POW camp before I reached home. The authorities had to carry out an investigation to find out who I was. They didn't know. I lost all my discharges, haven't even got a discharge from the vessel I was sunk in. Companies didn't care for anyone. Every British vessel was operated by the British Ministry of Transport and the ships had their agents acting for them in various ports but they were all under that ministry. They made no effort to repatriate me, they just wiped me completely.'

After his ship disappeared, Vaughan's parents had received a cable from the vessel's owners, 'Please inform next of kin signed on *Australind* confidentially vessel seriously overdue presumed lost, no news present personnel. When we receive any further information we shall immediately advise you. Signed, the Traffic Manager, as agents for the company.'

In March 1943 J.F. Mackay, RAF chaplain, Middle East, wrote to Mrs Richards from Alexandria. 'I send to you hopes of some kind of personal assurances that your son Steve [Vaughan's nickname], whom I know well and whose friendship I value, is in excellent health and good spirits. I was very interested to meet Steve at one of our air force units. After all his experiences he is looking well again. He's very much at home among the RAF boys. I hope it is not too long before he is able to get on his way home, he certainly deserves it.' When he did get home Vaughan could have claimed the 39/45 star and ribbon but he has never bothered to pick it up.

Hugh Burgoyne was one of the four Australian merchant men from the motor tanker *Teddy* which had been sunk in the Indian Ocean in November 1940 by the German raider *Atlantis*. 'There was Don Dwyer, Bert Juniper, Charlie Lacey and me. The camp was constructed by a perimeter of barbed wire about 10 feet high on the outer of the area and 10 feet inside another similar fence was built. Then more of the same. We'd been made to construct it ourselves.

'Just before completion I made my escape, the first POW to escape from the camp. It was short-lived and I was in solitary confinement after a belting by German naval guards. I spent six weeks solitary in a military camp at Sandbostel and four months later was sent with other escapees to various punishment camps in Germany, finally returning to Milag in 1944 when the Russians were advancing through Poland.'

Charlie Lacey tells of the capture of the *Teddy*, a 6748-ton Norwegian tanker. 'We were steaming into the Gulf of Bengal when the German *Atlantis* sneaked up on us. Captain Rogge had made his ship look like a British ship, the *Antenor*, and her men were on board us before we knew. Some of the crew of *Atlantis* were under a tarpaulin in the bottom of their pinnace and leapt up on our deck as they came alongside.' The ship was taken unscathed. 'In a general sense I didn't mind leaving the ship', says Charlie. 'That line ran lousy, hungry ships. But we were being hurried (that was a busy sea lane in those days, lots of Allied shipping and lousy with U-boats), and Mervyn Ferguson shattered his leg as he came down on top of me. When we got on the German ship Captain Rogge gave Mervyn and me and other blokes a smoke.'

Captain Rogge didn't need the 10,000 tons of heating oil the *Teddy* carried as cargo and so the ship was sent to its last resting place 'in a funeral pyre so hot that it created rain clouds and showers', Rogge later wrote.

Men sailing beneath the Red Duster have a cocky attitude to their calling and they need this pluck in wartime. Merchant Navy man 'Sid' Jones, who was taken prisoner on board the German raider *Kormoran* says: 'If seamen were easily scared, they wouldn't be afloat in wartime'.

Ship 16, as the German raider *Atlantis* was listed on the German naval establishment, had left Germany in early 1940. Her charter was 'to lay mines and carry out warfare in the Indian Ocean'. Grand Admiral Raeder, chief of the German naval staff, had ordered his admirals and captains that their aim was to be 'the total annihilation of merchant shipping bound for Britain'.

The two-year cruise of the *Atlantis* was the longest of World War II; she had the highest score of all German raiders (the famous *Graf Spee* took only half the tonnage of this pirate). She belonged to the 'ghost fleet', one of the phantom raiders that terrorised merchant shipping in the Indian and Atlantic oceans. She captured twenty-two ships with her camouflaged guns and the tiny aircraft she carried on deck; yet perhaps the most remarkable thing about her was that her captives admired her, her captain and her crew, and were outspoken in their praise of the seamanship and raiding skills of their captor. Of her captured ships sixteen were sunk after their cargo was plundered, and six sent home to Germany as prizes.

There was very little bitterness felt by the victims. Charlie Lacey of Sydney says, 'We were cramped and crowded on board but always treated well, we were fed the food the German crew ate, had salt water baths once a week, competed with the German crew in sports including boxing. It was not until we were eventually put ashore into German prison camps we knew what being a Kriegsgefangener was really like.'

These ships were commerce-raiders, tracking the merchant ships that were the life-blood of the people and the war effort.

The young German sailor Wilhelm (Bill) Muller, from Hanover, had had only one voyage before the war, he then went on board the *Atlantis* and stayed at sea for her twenty-two months of life without respite. 'I was never sunk or captured until just before my 22nd birthday, and then I was sunk again a few weeks later.'

Every four weeks the outline of the ship was changed. Working from the Admiralty lists of registered ships, they could make-over their ship so skilfully that they confused most of their victims. 'We could work sixteen disguises and had flags of all nations ready to haul up.' The masts and funnel of *Atlantis* could be telescoped and the samson posts raised, the ship swiftly repainted to represent another vessel altogether. But when they went into combat they hoisted their own battle flag.

'The bloomin' war started with us', Bill Muller says. 'That idiot [Hitler] started it. We went on *Atlantis* into the Roaring Forties, six weeks of storms, we had to drop oil to calm the water and keep the ship afloat. I had never been sick but there I almost was. Then we came around Hobart to Sydney and there we got only one ship, a Norwegian, *Silverplatz*. Then into the South Seas. We had a desalination plant on board but fresh water was a problem. Only 2 litres of fresh water a day, all bathing, showers and washing up was with sea water, and sea-water soap. No greens at all in our food, only dried potatoes. One ship we captured gave us about 3000 eggs and then it was eggs, eggs, eggs! One time we got some stuff sent out from Japan – beer, pigs, vegetables.'

Wilhelm Muller (who migrated to Australia in 1960) was 19 when he went to sea. 'For 622 days we remained on *Atlantis*, never reaching a port. We got our first mail after fourteen months at sea. There were problems having 500–600 prisoners on board. We had a canvas swimming pool, we used it and they used it at different times. We made a little playground for the children captured with their parents. Our captain insisted the children must be free to play anywhere and they were under our feet all the time. They were on deck until teatime and only in the hold for the night. We didn't see any girls except when they were taken prisoner; had to have a special guard outside with guns so nobody could get in.'

After nine months at sea, and Christmas coming up, the captain gave the crew a holiday at Kerguelen Island in the Indian Ocean. 'Going in we hit a rock. For three days we stayed there and couldn't get off, then, full moon and a king tide came in the middle of the night and we ran from one side of the ship to the other to rock it, then it came off. We had six weeks for our holiday but we had to repair the ship and get water as we had none left. This we got out of a small waterfall with hoses some thousands of feet long.

'We spent December/January at Kerguelen and for a treat we were each handed a pudding which had all come on board from a captured ship. They had been meant for Australian soldiers. I didn't like the Christmas puddings!

'There was no dissatisfaction among the crew because of the long time at sea, we kept ourselves busy; the married men got homesick, but it didn't affect me at all, in fact I could have stayed another year or two out there. We couldn't contact our parents, but once a month they got a letter saying that we were well and couldn't get in touch with them for certain reasons.'

Then it was back to raiding. They caught a Yugoslav ship, and put some hundreds of prisoners on it and sent them to Mogadishu, Somaliland. 'When we captured a ship a boarding party was sent in', Wilhelm recalls. 'They were a specially trained group of ten men; each knew where to go, to the engine room, radio shack, the bridge (to seize papers), others to check the cargo and to see what could be used. Then they reported back to the captain. He would allow two hours to take what was there – foodstuffs, rice, tea, coffee, etc. One time we found about 250 cases of whisky, so took it over also! When the time was up the captain would signal with a flag: we used the radio as little as possible, that's why we survived so long. We had many frights.

'On 17 May, a full moon, clear night, midnight alarm, a report from the bridge that two ships were coming. They came closer and closer, were about 7000 metres away and were recognised as the British battleship HMS *Legal* and aircraft carrier HMS *Nelson*. We stood our ship so the enemy would be between us and the moon, and they didn't see us; everybody was praying that night. The next day was made a holiday. Just imagine if one of their 15 inch shells came over – there'd be nothing left of us, Australian prisoners as well as Germans.

Because of overcrowding on the *Atlantis*, Captain Rogge decided to land his prisoners in Abyssinia [Ethiopia] from where they could, hopefully, be repatriated by their own countries. Charlie Lacey: 'But two days sailing from Abyssinia, the *Stortap*, a Norwegian ship captured by the raider came alongside and took us twice-captured prisoners on board and delivered us to Bordeaux in German-occupied France on 8 March 1941.'

Atlantis was eventually sunk with the loss of seven crewmen's lives on 22 November 1941 by HMS *Devonshire* in the South Atlantic after 622 days at sea. *Devonshire* took the crew on board, but thirty-three days later a German submarine sunk the *Devonshire* and freed Captain Rogge and his crew. Bill Muller was on the submarine for four weeks. 'Then she was blown up by the British so, into the boats again. Rowed the boats for seven days and another two submarines were sent out to rescue us and scuttle all the boats and take us home to Germany.' To a heroes' welcome.

In October 1942 George Jackson wrote to his brother: 'Dear Steve, Just a line, hope it finds you in one lot. Had a letter from mother, tells me you are doing a lot of fishing, wish I was with you. I am 18 on 11th. Goodbye and remember me to others. George.'

This was his second birthday in prison camp. He was 15 when he first signed on as cabin boy in January 1940. 'My first ship was sunk after I signed off on sick leave and the whole crew machine-gunned. I survived another two ships before I was caught.

'At sea I'd got £1/4/6 per month and before capture sailed to Abadan and return, to Trinidad in the West Indies, the West Coast of Africa, Halifax, Nova Scotia (a four months trip). Went on the Danish ship *Dāgo II* to Newfoundland where we were in dry dock. No one spoke English, the food was all new to me, no freezer so the meat was rotten after two days. I was a galley boy.

'After two weeks in dry dock we got a convoy, lost it after two days because our old coal burner was too slow. Got to Scotland, ran over a vibration mine but it didn't do much damage. They fixed us up at Clyde. We were going to Rochester and were sunk by Stukas of the Italian air force, supposedly the first German/Italian raid on England. The navy came out and beached us, spent about two weeks on the mud, they pumped us out and salvaged the ship. The only time in my life I prayed was when the bombs came down.

'After that I joined the *San Roberto* taking fuel up the Firth of Forth from London. Did sixteen trips there to the end of 1941. (Got a bad discharge from the *San Roberto*, was going crazy from four months continuous runs.) After that I joined the *Tottenham* and that's when it happened. We went from Tilbury to Newcastle, loaded a complete air field. The amount of stuff that was lost when that ship was sunk!

'It was a brand new ship doing its second trip. Everyone was on their toes about the German *Bismark* being out, then we got the news it had been sunk, so the convoy broke up, and three days later we were prisoners of war on the *Atlantis*. It was nighttime. I was a galley hand and was taking dishes back to the galley from the petty officers who were sitting on the hatch and an American carpenter had a banjo and they were singing about "the banks of the Wabash far away"; I just got inside the galley door when the first shell hit. I came out and it was like daylight with star shells around us. The plane had apparently followed us all day, thinking we were a cruiser we were so low in the water; they stayed out of sight till nighttime. They were feeling us out with the first shell, when we didn't answer back they knew they had us. We had nothing to answer back with. We had got a radio message away but later learnt the raider's wireless operator had jammed it, so no one knew what happened or where we had got to. There were only twenty-seven of us picked up at first. A few more were picked up a week later in a lifeboat.

'Nine of us were on rafts, we still didn't know what had taken us, it was pitch dark, there were explosions, they were torpedoing our ship. This was off Freetown, Cape Verde Islands. We thought it was a warship, didn't know it was a raider. They lowered a motor boat and picked up the swimmers. I sat in the lifeboat with a young bloke who got his arm blown off. They shouted down, "Any wounded? Come round the stern". They lowered a stretcher, the lad went first then I was next. They gave us lime juice, searched us to see if we had knives or anything. They took us down in the hold, it was all rigged out and painted, very clean. We were issued with two sheets, a pillow case and two blankets, and allotted a bunk. It was built as a prison ship. Planned.'

Cabin boy, George Jackson, now learnt that he was a prisoner on the German raider *Atlantis*. 'We were kept in the hold, allowed up twice a day – an hour in the morning and an hour in the afternoon. We had table tennis, a big library, things they'd taken off captured ships. We made playing cards out of cigarette packets. We had enough to do to fill in time. We made wire brooms and wire brushes to remove the rust from the ship. We got extra cigarettes if we did these things. They gave us lengths of rope and canvas, we unplaited the rope and made our own shoes. I can say nothing against them on the raider. There were two surgeons; if you needed an operation you had it; if you wanted a tooth out you could get it out. Officers were put one side of the deck, we were on the other.

'Five days after she sunk us the *Atlantis* sunk another ship,

Balzac (Tosh Evans was on that). And then another was sunk. We went on deck one day and there were five ships gathered around – the *Kota Nopan*, a Dutch ship the *Kormoran* had captured, as well as a Norwegian and the raider itself and a Japanese ship supplying them all (and Japan wasn't officially in the war at that time).

'We didn't know where we were most of the time. We used to drop messages over the ship's side in tobacco tins, but no one came to rescue us. Captain Rogge of the *Atlantis* was reasonable, we used to get twenty-five Australian cigarettes each week, we had enough to eat. When we were put on *Kota Nopan*, the captured ship that took us to France, we were fed on dried bananas and raisins for about four weeks, only one bench to sit on, all mattresses on the floor together and when the sea came in, you were sharing one mattress with about four others. Got to Bordeaux the end of November. The SS were looking after us there but we thought we were in wonderland because the beds were from French whorehouses, silk bedspreads and pillow cases; but nothing to eat for nearly a fortnight, couldn't get a smoke or anything.

'Before they sent us on from Bordeaux we went in for interrogation. There was a German officer who spoke perfect English asking things like where I left from. I said I didn't know because I was only a deck boy. He went on, "You're a damned liar. And England can't win this war, it has no benzene". And as he said it, the air-raid siren went and I said, "Who's got no bloody benzene?"

'We were sent to Milag four days before Christmas. They gave me a Red Cross parcel and I had it all eaten the first day. This was when I met Vaughan Richards. A committee was set up in camp and they put groups of four men together, one was in charge and we shared the parcels, apart from the soap, chocolate and cigarettes. The idea was to try and save some for bad days as some weeks you got nothing. There were big notices up about fraternising with German frauleins, but we used to scream out "Hello darling" when they were going to work in the mornings and they'd wave back.'

In 1943 International Red Cross in Geneva arranged an exchange of prisoners and George, now 19, was on the list and so was young Vaughan Richards. Such exchange must be done via a neutral country and these boys were taken out through Turkey.

'You never forget having been a Kriegie', Charlie Lacey says. 'My number was 345 and sometimes I see a number plate on a car with those figures, in any order, and my mind flips over.'

On 17 April 1941 (following the sinking of the *British Corporal*), Dennis Sandford was put in a cattle-truck on a train for north-west Germany. 'We were given little food and no water on this four-day train journey and a petrol drum acted as our only toilet facility for over twenty men. On arrival we had to march the 15 kilometres to Sandbostel. It was a freezing cold morning and the tropical clothing most men wore did not help.

'Sandbostel was a hell camp and when captured by British forces in April 1945, they were appalled at the dead and dying. Over 2000 British Empire Merchant Navy prisoners were in this place and it was, as well, a death camp for Jews, Poles, Serbs and Russians. Daily we saw the carts carrying the dead and dying pass through our compound on the way to be burned. On war maps showing the location of prison camps in Germany, Sandbostel is shown as a hospital camp – the least like a hospital anyone could imagine!

'At Sandbostel at first there was no distinction made between officers and men and we were all made to work. I was cutting up tree roots for firewood for the German guards in bitter cold weather wearing only the shorts I was taken prisoner in, until being issued in June with old French army breeches and coat, also a pair of boots with wooden soles with a nail protruding into my foot (and that left me with a growth on the sole of my right foot). Merchant Navy prisoners were only moved out of this horrible camp into the special Merchant Navy camp, Milag Nord in February 1942, by a humane German navy captain.'

The first thing Charlie Lacey was told to do when he went

to sea was to shave. 'I said, "I've only got a bit of bum-fluff",
but the captain said to get it off.' He was aged 15½ and had
signed on the SS *Marrawah*. His mother didn't know he'd
signed on or left Australia. 'I couldn't write well, or at all I
suppose you would say. My writing was atrocious and so was
my spelling.

'The first time I saw a gun on a merchant ship I said,
"What's the gun for?" Nobody ever mentioned any fighting to
me!' There were four men 'tinkering around' with the gun on
the ship's bow. 'I was alright on it but the cook was the best
gunner of the lot of us.'

Life at sea was not what it was cracked up to be (but life at
sea never had been). 'On my first ship we put our lifeboat out
in the harbour and it sunk! The first time in twelve and a half
years since they'd been on the ship that the boats had been in
the water. But you saw a lot, the first time any of us saw
German torpedo boats we were stunned: 25 tonners, 60 feet
long, very narrow and very fast, two torpedoes ready.
Amazing.

'When my dad knew I was a POW on Christmas Eve 1940,
all the uniform I had left home he took down to the navy
office, dumped it on the counter and said, "He won't be
needing this again".'

Charlie's mother didn't learn of his whereabouts until he
had been a prisoner for some months. He wrote to her but she
did not believe the letters were written by him because she
thought he could not write. 'When I came home all the letters
were lined up on the mantelpiece in order of receipt. I
explained to her that when I reached Germany the captain had
got on my back and said I had to learn to write. I even went
through the navigation school. But until the day she died my
mother reckoned someone was writing my letters for me, and
when I got home and walked down the gangway, Dad was still
alive and the first thing he did was slap at my arm and he said,
"You haven't lost it!"'

These schools were tutored by ship's officers in Marlag, who
later signed as witness to the hours a boy had spent studying

under tuition. After release, other ranks could do the actual exams in London; apprentice officers were able to both study and receive certification while in the camp as their papers were sent through the Red Cross to London and results came back the same way.

'There was the officers' side of the wire and ours. I worked on a sewerage scheme and our boss said one day, "We'll fix these buggers" and when we finished our last inspection trap we didn't put the cover back over the hole and Lieutenant Ramsey DSM, off HMS *Glowworm*, fell down the hole. All the stuff had been there since 1914, and he was screaming his heart out and a big American coon walked up, looked down and said, "Boss, you sure am in big shit!" He dragged him out. Ramsey had no other gear, and on parade next morning he was standing over by himself like a country dunny. But Ramsey was a mighty bloke. He was so bloody harebrained, you'd talk to him and think he was a lah-de-dah, but he was so bloody brave I'd walk through hell for him.'

On 29 April 1945 when Allied tanks crashed through to their camp, Charlie Lacey remembered he was still a boy. 'I went out at 7.30 a.m. and borrowed a bloody Bren carrier. A mighty red-haired bloke got this thing to go and we tried to take it right through to the coast. Oh, it seemed a long time since we'd been larrikins.'

As the Allied armies pressed into Germany Allied prisoners began to 'make a run for our own lines'. One such was Reg Hutchinson from Port Melbourne who had been a prisoner in Germany for four and a half years. He escaped in 1944, was married in London and home in Australia by June 1945.

They may not have served on the same ships, may not have seen one another since prisoner-of-war days, but merchant seamen of war years keep in touch in a loose sort of way. And it's Merchant Navy and prison days they talk about.

Jimmy (Tosh) Evans of Whyalla (SA) to George Jackson, Kilsyth (Vic.): 'Do you remember Captain Lewis the camp captain? Had eye-brows like rain forests over his eyes.

'And of course you remember 4000 of us parading by barracks to be counted each day. When all were counted the barrack guards would then move to the middle of the square to the corporals who would turn round to the Ober Gefreiter (RSM) who would turn round to Sauerkraut and tell him all present and that stuff; but in the meantime the Smellie Nellie cart would have been filled up at that big shithouse – you would remember the little wooden walkways, half a plank for your arse and 10 foot of shit underneath if you fell. You gotta laugh now though, don't you. But that smelly cart, with about 250 gallons full of shit, would come through the middle of the parade from the corner by Barrack 3L (the Gangster Barrack) and always made it to the middle as the guards gave their count report. The cart was always chock-a-block to the top and on it reaching the guards, corporals, RSM and Sauerkraut, 4000 voices used to go Brrrr with their lips, the way you stopped horses in Germany. Being chock-a-block and the volume of 4000 Brrrrs! the horse would stop in its tracks immediately and shit would slop all over the inspection party, day after day; the bastards were too thick to order it to go around the back of the parade: always through the middle!

'Remember the wet and cold at sea? Remember rice and currants? We must have been at sea quite a few days, you from 17th, me 22nd of June to late November before we got to Bordeaux. And who else do you know who's been across the continent First Class in a cattle wagon with straw on the floor? Marvellous, eh?'

'My number was 379 and like you I'll never forget it. Do you remember Toni Funk (Gefreiter) corporal-interpreter, "You will keep your mouths shut yes?" ("Course I will you square-headed bastard!") When we got liberated by the Guards Armoured Brigade and the 51st Highland Division, we got our reward for our patience in the early days when we had taught Toni to say in good English, "give us a cigarette you big useless bastard". So now when war ended and the Krauts were rounded up and marched past the camp by a detachment of Jocks and a big one sergeant was in charge, we shouted,

"For Christ sake Toni, ask him for a smoke the way we taught you!" Well, if that Jock could have been signed up for Collingwood he would have been the greatest, he could have drop-kicked goals from 90 metres because when Toni said to him, "Give us a cigarette you big useless bastard", well, didn't that big boot get him square up the ring and shift him!

'As for old Sauerkraut, Captain Pruish, the day they brought me and Blondie Fowler back from our attempts, July 1942, I think everybody was by the wire at the gates. Sauerkraut was saying why did you etc. etc. and getting savage and he pulled out the revolver and I said to Blondie, "turn round and put your back to him" and we did, and the noise as 4000 blokes moved forward thinking he was going to shoot us was terrific: bet the guards in the pill-boxes were shitting themselves because if he had, the wire, the pill-boxes, everything else would have been pulled down and then who knows what might have happened?

'I got twenty-six days for that escape. There were only three cells and once a day, after the count parade, we would be escorted to the shit-house. We used to risk life and limb on the walkways and risked drowning in 10 feet of the proverbial because we used to dash in, straight down the middle to the last three seats on the right, where there was always a piece of bread or a couple of smokes left for us by our mates. In the cells there were wooden nuts holding the cell walls together and some had been loosened so you could pull one end back and play cards together. You would, of course, have to move your arse if you heard the guards coming to check cells.

'After that break we were sent to Upper Silesia near the Polish border to a pre-war lunatic asylum. Eighteen feet walls etc. etc., an escape-proof camp and special detention cells. Got three months special in there. We made an indescribable way to get out of there, we made ropes from bits of string and hung them from the window and put bunk boards on them to make a walkway to the walls and drop. Unfortunately in this place there were civvies there with British passports plus a lot of English professors working in German universities etc. who were interned, really smart blokes amongst them; unfortunately the night we were going over some bastard had shopped us. We had changed into the civvy clothes we'd had made and were standing ready, waiting for the space between searchlights to go when the fixed bayonets charged in and had us cold as a dog's nose. So eleven of us got special detention; you can imagine where that would be in a loony house, where they kept the real violent mad loonies: it has been said on occasion that we were in the right place anyway because in those days we were as mad as hatters. Young I suppose.

'Did another twenty days in another ex-loony bin; the boys tried to get out there but I couldn't get in on that one. Eventually I got back to Milag late 1944: they'd shifted us because the Russians were moving. I suppose they thought it was bad enough facing them let alone us.

'There were fifty prisoners and forty guards on that train and we were going to make a break for it as near to Switzerland as we could get, but we were dobbed again.

'Do you remember Bill Bailey and Andy Gray, the camp drunks? Petrol, metho, boot polish, anything with spirit in it. And the two navy sick-bay attendants Dave and George, big lads, who used to rush down with the hurry-up wagon made of two planks and two bike wheels to get them on the stomach pump before they killed themselves.

'When we came back on the Straffegang, any time the whistle went we had to report to the main camp gate and if we were late we were put in the cells. Two of us were sent back to the previous camp and with others sent to Katowice, Poland, for court martial for going over the roof and knocking off all the camp commandant's jewellery which they never proved. Bloody lucky again.'

Tosh is now a publican in Whyalla but says he is 'short of breath, short of time and bloody short of money', and tells George Jackson, 'Jacko, it was a good job I never sailed with you or we'd be bloody heroes or still locked up, possibly the second'.

On Monday 3 September 1989, Tosh 'put the flags out. Fifty

years. Seems not so long ago, eh? Blokes came in for their beer, "What's the flag out for Tosh?" I said, "You ignorant bastards!" "Sorry Tosh, never realised." Just bloody shows you.'

In 1989 when the Russian Medal was issued to those Australian merchant seamen who had sailed on the convoys to Russia in World War II, it served to remind men of the certain dangers men sailed into at that time. These vast armadas which took both food supplies and military weapons to that beleaguered ally were at all times within range of German bombers from the Norwegian coast, 15 flying miles away.

Convoy number PQ 17 is only one example of the volume of loss of ships and men on these perilous voyages. (PQ 13 and PQ 16 suffered similarly in the same period.) The famous German battleships *Tirpitz, Sheer* and *Hipper* were in the vicinity of Björnöya Island, Norway, but the urgency for the cargoes in these convoys was such that the British Admiralty and the USA Naval Board must risk all. Convoy PQ 17 was gathered together at Iceland.

Being so close to German-occupied Norway, the convoy was attacked immediately. Ten ships were sunk by U-boats and thirteen by aircraft. The Germans sent over twenty-nine reconnaissance planes, forty-three torpedo planes and 130 bombers. They lost no U-boats in the uneven sea battle and of their 202 aircraft sent over the convoy, only six were shot down. The courageous rescue ships *Zaafaran, Zamalek* and *Rathin* rescued 1300 seamen.

There was the loss of 100,000 tons of supplies for the Russians, 3350 vehicles, 430 tanks, 210 aircraft plus 99,316 tons of mixed cargo including ammunition. Of the eleven ships that eventually made port, three – *Ironclad, Silver Sword* and *Troubadour* – were guided by *Ayrshire*, a trawler, deep into the ice-floe where they were painted white and remained still and silent until they felt it was safe to make steam and continue to their destination with their cargo, as merchant ships do every day, every night around the world.

When the ships had left Hvalfiord at 4 p.m. on 27 June 1942, the film star Douglas Fairbanks Jnr who saw them said,

'They waddled like ducks past the submarine nets and out to sea. No honours or salutes were paid to them as they passed, as would be done for naval ships.' The original thirty-five ships were heavily laden with full holds of 156,000 tons of cargo and 297 crated aircraft, 594 tanks, 4246 trucks and gun carriers. This hundreds of millions of dollars worth of armaments was protected by twenty-seven Royal Naval vessels, some close to the convoy, others further back, waiting in calling distance.

But after more attacks, the British Admiralty ordered the protecting naval ships to withdraw and the merchant ships to scatter and continue through these heavily bombed waters, unprotected, until they reached the Russian ports. It was a death sentence for men and ships, a decision made by politicians that cost 153 seamen's lives and that of twenty-four ships. Only eleven ships reached Russian ports and three of these were badly damaged. 'We were left for dead', merchant mariner survivors said.

From the bridge to the lower deck there was disbelief that the Royal Navy would so desert them. German U-boat commanders, appalled at the abandonment of these brave men, showed great compassion to them floundering around in the freezing Arctic waters, clinging to any piece of wood that would float. They took ships' captains on board their overcrowded submarines and gave men in boats food as well as giving them bearings and course to reach land (even though it was German-held land where they would become prisoners of war).

Survivors were gathered in St Andrew's Hall, Glasgow, on 28 September 1942 for a memorial service and were addressed by the Minister for War Transport, Mr Philip Noel-Baker. 'We know what this convoy cost us', the minister said. 'But I want to tell you that whatever the cost, it was well worth it.' David Irving, the author, says, 'His speech was howled down by the weary and embittered seamen'.

In this convoy were two Australian naval ratings, Jack White and Philip Renton Power, who were to write an essay on their voyage as part of a naval officers' training course. Philip

Renton Power (who later served as a lieutenant in Tarakan and Borneo waters) wrote to the Naval Board. He stubbornly 'registered the disgust of all naval men on escort duty for having, under orders, left so many ships and their merchant seamen to the mercy of "wolf packs" and the Luftwaffe'. He asked, 'Why wasn't PQ 17 left to the professionals? The politicians should have kept out of it.' If medals were to be given where deserved, that young man deserved the highest award for initiative, courage and clear thinking followed by swift action. His letter, following the story of convoy PQ 17, is a clear indication of the perils merchant men faced, not only on the sea but from politicians and war lords on the distant shore.

FOR ALL SEAFARERS

Even in peace, scant quiet is at sea;
In war, each revolution of the screw,
Each breath of air that blows the colours free,
May be the last life movement known to you.

No rock, no danger, bears a warning sign,
No lighthouse scatters welcome through the dark;
Above the sea, the bomb; afloat, the mine;
Beneath, the gangs of the torpedo-shark.

Year after year, with insufficient guard,
Often with none, you have adventured thus;
Some, reaching harbour, maimed and battle-scarred,
Some, never more returning, lost to us.

But, if you escape, tomorrow, you will steer
To peril once again, to bring us bread,
To dare again, beneath the sky of fear,
The moon-moved graveyard of your brothers dead.

You were salvation to the army lost,
Trapped, but for you, upon the Dunkirk beach;

Death barred the way to Russia, but you crosst;
To Crete and Malta, but you succoured each.

Unrecognised, you put us in your debt;
Unthanked, you enter, or escape, the grave;
Whether your land remember or forget
You saved the land, or died to try to save.

John Masefield

The 'Rate of Effort'

'And there was the rub: the eternal dilemma of a small nation needing the protection of a large nation.'

Flight Sergeant Goeffrey Dewey, an Australian in No. 84 Squadron, RAF

SOME OF THE SADDEST and unnecessary deaths of very young Australian pilots occurred in 1945 when it was no longer of any tactical benefit to either Australia or the war effort to risk these men being killed or captured. This waste may well be laid at the feet of the American General Douglas MacArthur.

The war was coming to an end, the tide had turned and the Americans were on their way to Japan – alone. MacArthur did not intend any laurels to adorn the brows of any but himself and his own men, and so the Australian Allies were left behind to do 'intruder patrols' in the odd island outposts where the enemy still hung on. The pilots knew they had been assigned to an inferior role and were discontented. They knew they had been 'assigned to unspectacular drudgery' as the *Official History* states. They knew that pilots' lives were imperilled for little or no gain in the winning of the war: because the real enemy was away to the north, out of bounds to Australians. The gains were less than the losses, there were no strategic or tactical gains to be expected in these southern climes.

The airmen didn't need to be told that they were being left out of the important operations. When they had flown along the New Guinea coast in 1944 with their Kittyhawk squadrons in the van of operations they had been told they must 'maintain as high a rate of effort as the American squadrons'. They did maintain this 'rate of effort' but they did query the fact that 'the emphasis appeared to be on sorties and flying hours rather than results'. As Flight Sergeant Geoffrey Dewey remembered, it was all part of 'the eternal dilemma of a small nation needing the protection of a large nation'.

By 1945 the RAAF squadrons had been left behind the main battle yet the maximum flying hours must still be maintained: even though lucrative targets were no longer available. 'Some pilots were asking why they should be sent on missions where the results might mean loss of aircrew for very little damage to the enemy.' Their leader, Air Commodore Cobby, was unable to redress the position. It had been known for three years that the Americans were determined, that as they had lost the Philippines so ignominiously they would go back and win it, alone. And Cobby, like the other leaders of Australian services, had been ordered to cooperate with the American services. And there was the rub: the eternal dilemma of a small nation needing the assistance and protection of a powerful nation.

Group Captain Caldwell took twelve Spitfires from No.452 Squadron over Halmahera Island on 13 January 1945, damaged barges and strafed 'other targets' the same day. All returned safely to base, but on that afternoon Flight Sergeant Stevenson, a Dubbo boy aged 21, came down near the same beach. Overhead, Flying Officer Byrne saw the tail of Stevenson's plane sticking out of the water but couldn't see the young pilot. Later it was learnt from natives that he was unhurt when he hit the shallow water but the Japanese took him away. No more was heard of him except that he died 'while a prisoner'.

There was much activity that day. No.80 Squadron sent four pilots on a ferry flight to Morotai Island and they did not return. It was thought they may have run out of fuel as they carried no belly tank, leaving them limited time in the air. Searches were made of many islands, the men were not found, but natives told the searchers the Japanese had taken them prisoner. Of Flight Sergeant R.W. Parry (another 21 year old) it was later learnt that he was 'missing, presumed dead' on that day, 13 January 1945, whereas the other pilots, Officer F.L. Hamn, aged 26, Wireless Operator P. Waters, aged 23, and Flight Sergeant L.N. King, aged 22, were listed as 'killed while prisoner of war 23 March 1945'. During the war crimes trials held in Japan in 1946, a number of Japanese were tried and executed for complicity in these three deaths 'which occurred at a special ceremony'. In deference to the families of these men their files remain classified, available only to next-of-kin.

The deaths of the young pilots continued. Four young men, two pilots and two navigators, Taylor aged 25, Packham 22, McGuigan 21, and Lewis 20, were lost on 1 February 1945 in Beaufighters over Tomohon. By early February 1945, '193 Kittyhawks, twenty-four Spitfires and two Beaufighters attacked supply dumps, barges and buildings,' according to the *Official History*. 'On 3 February Nos.78 and 80 Squadrons sent fifty-three Kittyhawks to Halmahera; sixteen of them bombed Wasile Pier area and anti-aircraft positions at Lolobata. Squadron Leader J. Holloway was killed in action 27 February 1945.'

It rolls on in the most mind-crippling progression: all these brave, brilliant pilots, young men who spent their youth training to keep aircraft in the air, often out-gunned and out-manoeuvred by superior and newer planes, and dying for the cost of a sampan, or a jetty on islands of no strategic importance. And all the while the real air war was being fought hundreds of miles north of them, a war they were kept from by the greed of one man to gain *all* the fame, *all* the glory, and by the lack of courage of others to confront him and force the issue against all odds.

A Desperate, Lonely Time

'My little girl was screaming, "Who's that man in your bed, mummy?"'

Sheila Sinclair, on the return of her POW husband in 1944

IN 1915 DURING WORLD War I, Vera Deakin organised and administered the Wounded and Missing Inquiry Bureau in Cairo and London. This forthright, outspoken young woman was the daughter of Alfred Deakin, second Prime Minister of Australia, and she was not to be put down. She first cajoled and coaxed, but when this failed she could attack with verve, and in this way she enlisted young Australian women who had chosen to stay on in Egypt or London when war broke out. Working under the aegis of the Australian Red Cross, hers was the most effective search-and-report group in that war.

In World War II the Australian Central Army Records office was deluged with enquiries – and those striving to remain calm while hearing nothing relating to their missing men and women who had disappeared when the Japanese swept down to the north of Australia were aggravated by the seeming indifference to their enquiries. Relatives of men captured by the Italians and Germans had been notified as soon as it was possible (sometimes within weeks) by the enemy, and mail came, and was sent; but the Japanese government steadfastly remained silent, even though its delegates had attended the International Convention which covered this eventuality.

To obtain information regarding casualties, any and all letters arriving from Japanese-held areas were processed through the Chief Censor's Office. In this way the authorities learned that the Japanese were moving POWs around constantly but they could not learn for what reason or in what way this affected the prisoners or their lack of correspondence. The Records Office was roundly abused by many for not being able to give information of the whereabouts of the missing men: but it, in fact, was as ignorant of their whereabouts as were the civilians. All its efforts through the usual channels (such as those Germany and Italy did reply to) were fruitless and, indeed, the general position was obscure until the war ended and the various camps were discovered.

A few propaganda broadcasts were made giving the names of several POWs and around the world these were monitored by hundreds of people unknown to one another. 'I just did it thinking I may be able to phone someone and say I heard so-and-so's name mentioned', Betty Hart, Sydney, said. 'I switched on short-wave radio each night and I phoned people with the surnames of those from my State.' As well, of course, the broadcasts were officially monitored.

Later the Australian POW Relatives' Association along with the Australian Broadcasting Commission began a two-way short-wave message service. These were broadcast for one hour a day, twenty-five words being permitted each next-of-kin.

In January 1945 the Australian Red Cross Society arranged for each next-of-kin to send one telegram of ten words. Women waiting to hear news from the battlefronts have, throughout history, lived lonely hours. These days seem longer and lonelier when they read in newspapers of numbers of men being taken prisoner but no names given, and no official notification. Molly Deimel's husband Julius was in the city of Perth Regiment, the 2/11th Infantry Battalion, when they fought in Libya, mainland Greece, and Crete, where he was taken prisoner. Molly had stood her ground and refused to despair many times before he got back to Australia.

'All we knew was he may have been killed. Then I got a note and the "J" was below the line and I knew it was real, he was alive, as he always wrote below the line at the end of his letters. When I went to Crete in 1970, I looked at this little island and I thought there were not many places they could hide. Tears rolled down my cheeks then in a way they had never done when I was waiting to hear news of him. I never before let myself become emotional, I had thought if he was being strong and I was being strong, it might give him some chance.' (After his eventual return to Australia after Germany withdrew from the war, Julius was sent to fight in Wewak and Aitape in New Guinea.)

Elsie Morrison, married to Lieutenant John Morrison of the 2/4th Machine Gun Battalion, who had gone to war with Bernie O'Sullivan, hated the situation. 'I got an official notification telegram that he was a POW. In the three years until the end of the war I received cards of twenty-five words, all they were allowed to write. He received only two of the regular letters and cards I sent him. We had two girls before he left for the war and the baby came after he sailed. There were three of us wives of prisoners used to comfort one another.

'Brian Walton had sent a note to John by native, giving news of us. He pushed this in through the barbed wire. John was put in gaol when found with this letter and did a month in a rat-infested prison. He weighed 6 stone when he went back to the officers' quarters.

'Of course I was at the railway station when I was told the prisoners would be returned. John was pretty weak still, although after six weeks on Morotai getting set to come home he had put some weight on. He sent word to me, "Don't come to meet me". He thought I'd weep on the platform. Instead of being skinny he had put on, as I thought, weight, then I later learnt it was oedema. I put my finger on his cheek and the mark stayed in like a deep hollow. He had a sort of double chin of skin hanging down. I laughed, "If I'd known you were going to be like that, the kids could have come", I said.

'When we got home to our house, a big sign saying "Welcome Johnny Morrison" hung in the street and a big sign over our car, and all the way there was tooting by the trains, the cars, the neighbours and the neighbours' children welcoming him home.'

Mary Canty, whose husband enlisted in the 2/24th Battalion, was secretary to the association of the surviving members of the battalion. 'Many men were taken POW before they had time to prove themselves as soldiers. I thought that was one of the things that militated against them having any chance of picking up from their experience of being a prisoner. It was always in their mind. It was not only a lump of time, Lindsay was a prisoner for four years out of his young life, but it was the waste of all that splendid training they had had, and the lack of opportunity to put it into action for their country. We must remember that in those times we did have a great feeling about our country. They had all this preparation before the war and then they were taken before they had time to prove themselves.

'It's very hard for their wives, it's very hard for all ex-service people, those who have not been in the services can't understand what these people who go to war are caught up in. As for prisoners, it is not just a bad dream, yes they have them, they're non-stop. Even I, who am involved with the men today and lived the experience with my husband until he died, cannot describe it.

'The 2/24th lost three companies in one morning, they were men such as Lindsay had known in very close quarters for some years. It is often said that men who were prisoners of the Japanese feel that they may be considered by the population to have "given in too easily". (Even though the men themselves had nothing to do with the "giving in".)' Mary Canty says that even many prisoners taken by the Germans still have a problem about being taken prisoner. 'They feel they let the side down, although I can't see what else they thought they could do when their generals had arranged the capitulation.'

Women who had brought up their family of young children, some for almost six years, suddenly had not only a man overriding the authority they had had to exercise alone for up to six years but they had to assist the children to adjust to a new life. They had no way of anticipating the bewilderment of the child and of its sense of her abandoning them.

'My little girl came running in to my bedroom the day after my husband got home, and went hysterical. "Who's that man in your bed, mummy?" she was screaming.' And an ex-prisoner says his son did some horrific things. 'I just don't even know now how I didn't go out of my mind trying to cope. One time this child, who was only about 8, said to me, "Are you still here?"'

Sheila Sinclair (WA) received the issued card POWs were given from her husband Syd. 'I knew it wasn't a trick. It was his writing. So I went into Red Cross to tell them about it. Then I got a big seventy-word telegram from a man in the eastern States to say my husband was a prisoner of war. He had heard on short-wave radio that this was picked up by a private radio station in Switzerland and forwarded to Australia. Nobody believed it. Nobody knew who was living or how many had got taken prisoner.

'The army wrote me a letter "Your husband has been de-rated and who is going to pay, the soldier or you?" I said, "the soldier". I didn't know whether he was alive then. I said, "The soldier is missing", and I never heard another word about it.

'Mrs Myers in Perth started the prisoner-of-war information group. We used to meet every fortnight and exchange letters and information and we were able to meet other wives whose husbands were missing or prisoner and that made it easier for us. Mrs Myers ran her little office for many years. There was an afternoon every month and artists came and gave their time free. It was really wonderful. It made you feel a little bit better.

'It was a desperate, lonely time then. I never thought of him being gone. Something seemed to tell me he's not gone. In 1975 we went over to Crete and went to where he had been. I just stood and looked at that island and I thought, there's not many places they could hide, and the tears came in my eyes. The amount of men who were there, I suppose there were little caves and things they could get in but it wouldn't take them all so they got slaughtered.'

Censorship of mail from prisoners of the Germans had prevented those back home knowing *where* the men were, but some officers got word home (officers' mail was not censored).

'A Perth doctor used to write to his mother in a way that would let her know he was a prisoner on Crete. He'd name men he had been swimming with that day and his mother would let their families know. It was just six weeks later that I got a little card from Syd, "Just to say we are alive and well". Through these meetings arranged by Mrs Myers we gleaned a lot of information; you'd pick up little bits and pieces of news here and there and it kept your hope alive until you actually got your own message. There were some terrific ladies there, really lovely, and kind.

'Baby Dianne was 16 months old when Syd went to war. She was born in May of 1939, four months before war broke out. I was quite surprised really that he was allowed to join up because he was on essential service, fire brigade. His great cobber, Laurie Bell, he was going too. They were some of the last that got away before they clamped down on the essential services. But, he was only young and although I don't say it's a great adventure, that would be wrong, but men do sense an excitement when war comes. It beckons them.

'We had purchased a small house when we were first married and I lived there for about two years, and then my dad died so I went home to live with mum because she was on her own. When Syd went missing I went back and did part-time work at Wilson & Johns, a big florist shop, because the army cut your allotment back till they found exactly how long your man was missing, or dead. It was good for me to go back and mix amongst people because I was still only quite young, and mum said it gave her something to do to have little Dianne with her. There was sympathy for your child, everyone would know her daddy was away. But she didn't mind her daddy being away, after all, she didn't know him. But I could well imagine the shock to have this stranger walk in as though he owned both you, the child and the house. Also, the returning husband took so much of your time and your attention; and your behaviour towards him would be very odd to a child. She hadn't seen me behaving that way to another man.

'Dianne resented Syd very much when he came home. She loved him, but if we were out walking she would always walk between us and do silly things such as getting her foot caught in a fence or putting her foot under something just so that I would go back and get her and then she could be alone with me. Yes, she really resented him being home. I was still living with mum and Dianne was attached to her so that softened the betrayal she felt.

'When Syd was in prison Dianne used to sleep with me in the double bed. When he came home she was put into a single bed and she was quite indignant about it all. She would not keep away. She hated to share me. She used to give him some cheek and then run. Of course my mum would have a door open ready for her to run through. Syd was quite good with her, he was very patient with her really, but I'm afraid she did still resent him. As she grew a little older, and particularly when the next child arrived, it was a family again. At that time she was going to school and she accepted him, in fact, as part of the family.'

Some women are frank, and after half a century of experience are happy at last to speak out. 'The wives of prisoners of war have been prisoners for fifty years. A lifetime. Fifty years of watching war movies, of seeing the house full of books on war, of hearing talk of prisoner of war camps. Those years are the years that the men remember, relive. I for one am sick of it. I was sick of it right at the very beginning. I feel I've had no adult life, except for prisoner of war life.'

Another: 'I'm not a woman. I'm the wife of a prisoner of war.' Bill Hood's wife had her husband's admiration, as most prisoner's wives do. 'Wives are the ones who really have to put up with a heck of a lot ... they know it all.'

Cecile, his wife, was in the Wives POW Association during the war, and when he came home Bill worked for wives at the Pensions Tribunal. 'A wife has to live with the man all those years after he has returned from the war. She knows the traumas of nighttime when the light of day ends and memories take over.' Cecile said of Bill, 'We shared the traumas, everything fitted with us, I became a part of his post-war problems. He had nightmares when he came home, he was fighting the Japanese. I had to move out to another bedroom. The mind takes over, the past cannot be removed from the body as a disease can be removed.'

Bill Jinkins and his wife Gwen met during the war. She was a special driver in the army car pool and drove him during his brief journeys back to Melbourne from his clandestine forays behind the lines. Gwen was circumspect as her position demanded. 'No, I had no idea what he was up to. Suddenly he and others would be there in the car, then they would disappear. We didn't talk ... not about his work, there was no way we could. We were just special drivers ...'

Janet Lim had been a prisoner and her story was this: she and another young Chinese girl who were both trainee nurses had been captured by the Japanese and locked into a room. There they barricaded themselves against the advances of the Japanese guards and through a window at the back of their room which could only be opened from the inside, they had once escaped when the importunate guards broke down the door. The girls lay in a ditch, 'Soldiers passing by on their way to work saw us and said, "You're doing very well girls". We knew by their hats they were Australian.'

A year later she was on a ship being transported to Japan and was ill. She had previously been on a ship which had been sunk and she had jumped from the top deck and hit the water hard and had what she termed 'busted' her stomach. Now she lay semi-conscious in the hold in her second prison ship, on floor level with two bunks above her, the three bolted together. The sick prisoner on the top bunk was shaking uncontrollably from malaria and thus rattling the bunks beneath him. Her main memory of that time is of an Australian doctor coming and saying to the man, 'Try to be still. There's a little Chinese girl dying on the bottom bunk. Let her go in peace.' Squatting down beside Janet the doctor said, 'I know you are very sick but we don't know what's wrong with you and if we did we have nothing with which to help you.' She said, 'Here', and put his hand on her abdomen. 'This good man sat and gently stroked my abdomen until I went off to sleep.'

Many years later Janet was in Melbourne and saw a notice

regarding a POW meeting. 'This sent me off without thinking whether I would know anyone. It was just that this talk of prisoners sent my mind back to those days. I sat alone and was feeling very uncomfortable until a kindly elderly man came and said, "Were you a prisoner dear?" "Yes", I said. He said, "I saw some Chinese girls in a prison camp I was in. They were very brave. And I once sat with a little girl in a ship while she was dying." I said, "I was very sick on a ship, my abdomen had been ruptured, and an Australian doctor helped me all he could", and she told her story. "Oh", said the now Sir Albert Coates, "that must have been me". And it had been. We talked and talked.'

The effect on the homeland was similar in one sense to that on the men: a whorl of emotions, none of which could be resolved. While the prisoners of war may have had feelings of guilt (and most prisoners did, even though the facts constantly reminded them that they had had no option), the families back home in Australia had no blueprint from history to advise them on what their emotions may be in their lonely, confused vigils. They wrote to 'the army', the Red Cross, their church; they moved around like bewildered wraiths, smiling in an attempt to appear unconcerned.

'Aunty Gert Jackson' of the little town of Lang Lang (Vic.), whose two sons, Privates Pompey (Stanley) and Doug Jackson, 2/21st Battalion, were reported missing in 1942 always asked anyone she met in uniform if they 'knew anything'. When her niece, Driver Sheila Adams, AWAS, visited her she asked, 'Do you know if it's like a gaol? Are they shut in somewhere?' But Pompey and Doug had not been reported prisoners of war: they were missing, an even more mysterious, eerie state. 'They wouldn't have run away?' 'No', said Sheila, 'they wouldn't have run away. They were on Ambon, an island, and no one has heard a word from that island since the Japanese landed.'

Much has been said, and written, of the Malayan campaign. Briefly it can be summed up thus: well-trained men with suitable arms and good leaders fought well. The young untrained reinforcements, some with defective rifles, fought as one may imagine men facing a tough, experienced enemy would do. To defect in these latter circumstances would appear understandable to any reasonable person. But there is no reason in war and many a parent or wife must still, fifty years on, bleed tears for the son or husband who is mateless, mute, unable to join comrades for a drink.

'Service Casualty' lists were filling the columns of major newspapers and behind the cold, formal release of names those down south could sense the tragic and huge disasters that had swept over their nation.

The members of the AANS who were 'missing' later were listed as 'Missing, believed prisoner'. 'It was a long war for loved ones back home', says Sister Betty Jeffrey, one of those 'Missing, believed prisoner', for three and half years. 'Not a word', repeated Mrs Jackson. It was, to a mother, as if a child had failed to come home after being sent out to buy a loaf of bread.

We must walk our minds back to those much simpler times when fewer people had cars, few travelled far from their own district and only the very privileged few went 'abroad'. And even these privileged travellers would scarcely have heard of Ambon, and if any knew of Timor it was likely to be because there were stories in print of the little Timor ponies being brought into Northern Australia. Java, Sumatra, New Britain, New Ireland, New Guinea, Borneo and Singapore were, to the average Australian, spice-scented, romantic outposts of Empire. That many a young man, some merely boys, would disappear forever on these outlandish places was beyond the comprehension of many much more sophisticated than Aunty Gert Jackson.

It was as though the Pied Piper of Hamlyn had returned from his unknown world where he had once taken children and now had replenished his tribe and disappeared, with 'noisy, naughty, laughing boys'. The mother of young Jacky Page (Penshurst, Vic.) said it felt 'as though someone had put a hand over Jacky's mouth and led him secretly away'. We had read that mothers in ancient times farewelled their sons thus:

'Come home with your shield or on it'. But Australian mothers knew not such sophistry. 'Now you look after yourself!' was the common farewell of an Australian mother. Private Arthur Simpson, 2/29th Battalion, who enlisted with his brother Harry, wrote in January 1942 from Malaya to his cousin Jean Smith, 'Mum told me not to get into mischief but so little happens here a bloke hardly has the energy to get into a bath.'

Later, when the official notification arrived to say that the men were prisoners, or 'missing, believed prisoner', we were as mystified as were the mothers of the children the Pied Piper had led away, and Jean Smith waited until 1985 to search for Arthur Simpson's grave. As for Pompey and Doug Jackson there was no grave to search for, none but an unidentifiable jumble of bones in a pit on Ambon Island.

Letters from men held prisoners in the European sector of the war often arrived within two months of the notice of their capture, but some families did not receive any of the few letter-cards sent from Japanese camps, and their prisoner-sons received very few from home, and for some, no mail at all was received for the whole three and a half years of their incarceration.

There were now, in the 20th century, international rules to cover such exigencies as the taking and protection of prisoners and therefore no one could have anticipated what happened in World War II.

Deliverance

'Let not them that are mine enemies wrongfully rejoice over me: *neither* let them wink with the eye that hate me without a cause.'

Psalms 35:19

THEY RANG OUT JOY in victory, not over the enemy, but over their own afflictions; 'they had not been false to their covenant. In the days of their greatest distress, they had still believed their enemy would be forced back to his own land. We never doubted it', Leslie Greener said in 1945. 'And now it was done we could speak. "Now O Kings, understand; take warning rulers of the earth. You have uprooted nations, made homeless mankind. Let there be an end."'

When the day came that Lionel Jones, the gentle flower gardener, could surrender his évade document to the Swiss authorities he received a note. 'My dear Australian boy, my dear Lionel. The last day you are in this country. I cannot believe it. I wish you all the bests and happiness possible. Your Swiss girl Antoinette.' And so he set off for home. When his ship docked in Colombo a letter was waiting to tell him his mother had died. She had waited and watched for word of him for three years and now she heard he was safe and on his way back she died as he set off for home.

His last diary entry, written on board ship, is, 'Can see the west coast of Australia'. He was home. He never wore his medals. 'I didn't win them, I was out of much of the fighting.' He went to reunions only 'to see how my mates are getting on'.

Alice Hempel tried for many years to get a photograph of the grave of Alan, the brother that had teased her about 'lairing around'. Eventually one was sent from the British War Memorials Committee. Alice was distressed, disappointed at the shabby condition of the graves and grounds at Tobruk in Gaddafi's country. 'It made you feel that it was all wasted, all those boys. I wish I hadn't seen the awful state where they rest.'

In 1943 when Bill Gamble arrived home as an exchanged POW, the effect of war was noticeable in Australia. 'There were so many girls who lost their young husbands and their fiancés. You lived from day to day to see what tomorrow brought. One day was all we had.

'My brother was doing medicine at Sydney University. When I left for the war we were terribly close, thirteen months difference in age, and when I was caught, he found that he just couldn't study. His mind went right off it, so he joined the air force on Lancasters, and he was killed. So I never saw him again. Yes, a long time ago.'

Ken Watts recalled: 'War is deception and lies. If you get back to the squadron base from an operation, the Intelligence Officer debriefs you, sends the squadron's doings for the day to Wing Ops who, in turn, send them to the Air Ministry, London, and at night the BBC's Richard Dimbleby broadcasting to the nation, says: "From all our operations only two of our aircraft are missing". Like hell! We knew from our own 244 Wing and the 239 Wing that we lost five, and I'm just referring to the fighter squadrons. What about the bomber boys? How many of our bombers are missing? And that was any day.'

The bashing from a rifle butt about his head in Verona in 1944 has resulted in this dashing, handsome, debonair, daring young air ace being in a wheelchair since 1973, although the zest for living has never diminished. 'For me the war was a tremendous experience. I just loved to fly. I was free up there. It being a war I had a licence to kill. I was too young then to be bothered with moral issues. Now I am pacifist and agnostic. It is not so important what happens to you but how you adjust to the happening. I cannot blame the Germans. I willingly joined the RAAF and, when trained, I dished it out to our enemies of that time. Consequently, I had the attitude of *when*

694 PRISONERS OF WAR

or *if* I was clobbered I would take what they dished out.'

Even after fifty years few servicemen are unscarred either physically or, more importantly, psychologically. After five or six adrenalin-charged years away from loved ones and home, major changes are brought about in one's attitudes to life and in personality.

General Patton arrived in the German camp where John Fitzhardinge was a prisoner. 'With two pearl-handled revolvers sticking out of his pockets. He liberated us, as well as British prisoners who had been there since Dunkirk. Six years. The men had got to be in a very poor state.' John loved music. 'The most satisfying thing I have known in life is after I got out of prison and I heard the Mozart String Quartet in D Minor being played by four good musicians in a potato cellar near my camp in Germany.

'We were flown from Paris on VE [Victory in Europe] night. As soon as we landed they deloused us and all that, gave us the works. We were near a big town and they had the pubs open and the beer was really flowing and the lights were on. It was the first night the lights had been on in England since the war began. We were all staring in wonder.'

Sam Stratton: 'Being a POW is about the last card in the pack, because you've got no rights, you can be humiliated and degraded, spat at, sworn at, but you can't retaliate. It's a pretty grim business. You used to always keep cigarette butts, put them in your pocket. And for a couple of years after I got home I couldn't stop butting them out and putting them in my pocket. My wife used to go mad, she used to go through all my pockets but I couldn't stop doing it.

'I joined up when I turned 21; when I came home I was 27. That's a hell of a slice out of your life, and one of the main things being a prisoner did to me was to send me home still 21 years of age. I hadn't matured naturally. When I first started back with the railways I had a bit of a battle to cope with the job, but after a while it went away. But I was a bloody nervous wreck.'

Reg King: 'I remember the day the tanks rolled into our

camp to liberate us. In the hospital we had made knee-pads
for our two amputee patients, and each had two walking sticks
about a foot high, and they were coming out walking on their
knee-pads and they were crying like children, the tears streaming down their faces.'

In 1965 Reg, his wife Lois and his mother, 'saved our
money' and returned to Germany to visit Hedwig as Reg had
promised. 'When the train arrived at the little siding, there she
was with a wooden wheelbarrow, all ready to carry our
luggage. She wouldn't allow me to push it, she herself would
push it and as we went down from the station towards the
village everybody came out to their gates or to the windows
to say hullo to Digger, because it had been announced in the
local paper that I was coming back. We were still friends.' Fritz
Heinz, the friendly German guard, was there. 'We had a great
chin wag.'

Reg returned to Crete for a day in 1980. 'I wanted to see
my mate's grave, Alan's buried there. I just needed to go.' A
publican on Crete said a taxi would be expensive. ' "Take my
car and driver for the day", he said. I wasn't sure of the place
where we fought and my mate had been killed so I asked an
elderly Greek coming down the road astride a donkey, "Were
you here during the war? We're Australians." The man jumped
off the donkey, raced over, hugged me, tears rolling from his
eyes. "Australians!" ' And yes, right there exactly where Reg
stood was where the short sharp battle had taken place, and
Alan had been killed. As for religion, Reg says, 'No, no, religion didn't affect me there, all the things I saw only made me
think what's it all about, *what is it all about?*'

John Goodelich (a pharmacist with 8th Division) says, 'I
don't believe that any psychiatrist or psychologist could ever
have got from any of us what it is all about. When you were
in the camps you didn't have time, or energy to spend on anal-
ysis. Afterwards, it was too late. It had grown into you.' Now,
fifty years later, it is different again. 'A deep thing.'

Doctor Rowland Richards: 'Most of us felt we shouldn't
have capitulated. I thought at the time we should have fought

on to the end, even to death, though one realises that we wouldn't have achieved anything. A sense of guilt? It has worried some people, but I think the majority of us thought it was all out of our control, it wasn't anything we did that caused it. Where there was a sense of guilt perhaps was after we got back and sat talking to the relatives of those who didn't come back and you'd feel, "Why me? Why should he die and not me?"

'I was the only officer to survive the sinking of the ship we were on. When I got home I had interviews with lots of relatives, it was a very trying period and some of them made it very clear to me that they thought, "Why should you be here and my lad isn't?" I'd take a room in a hotel and have an appointment at nine o'clock, another at ten, someone for morning tea, someone for lunch, someone in the afternoon. This went on for a fortnight. And I visited people. At one home, if I'd been the King of England I couldn't have been given a better welcome. Out came the champagne and everything else, and in those days champagne just wasn't available. But this was a major thing for this woman, she was seeing someone who was the last person to see her husband alive. The champagne had been saved up for his home-coming. After that I spent quite a bit of time, and have over the years, keeping in contact with widows and relatives.'

Colonel Tom Hamilton, 2/4th CCS, wrote, 'In 1940 when Colonel Mac Sheppard asked my permission to ask some of my NCOs to enlist in Mac's new 2/10th Field Ambulance I gladly assented and ten of my NCOs volunteered and went overseas with him. After the war I was saddened to find that eight of these NCOs had died in Borneo, in the Sandakan death march.'

The two leaders had seen one another briefly during the battle of Johore. 'My casualty clearing station, the 2/4th, served behind the 2/10th and I saw the efficiency with which its personnel brought in the wounded soldiers from the front lines. Their memory will live.' This unit set off to war with 292 members; 131 returned. Of the originals 161 were killed in action, or killed by disease and starvation as prisoners, a death rate of 55 per cent. 'Of the 131 who survived, 50 per cent are now dead.'

Reg Holloway wrote home after liberation: 'I have watched and held my best friends and companions while they faded away and died beside me, with absolutely nothing the doctors or myself could do to relieve or help them. This has been such an everyday occurrence that my feelings are now cast iron. Thousands of incidents in this life will never be published as the public would not believe them possible. But perhaps books will eventually be written. I hope so.

'All that us survivors want in the next few months is home, sweet home, an armchair, and all the newspapers dating from February 1942. And good food. You cannot imagine how strange it is to change back to Western civilisation, wearing boots and socks, respectable clothes; to shave, clean our teeth and wash with soap, and to use a knife and fork and grow hair on our heads again. We are slowly slipping back to civilisation and taking a childlike delight in doing so. Reg.'

The Roediger brothers were taken off Japan in a US hospital ship. 'We got our first letter from home when we reached Manila. They had been advised that we were safe and they wrote to bring us up to date with the situation at home. I said to Eric, "Funny thing, mum never mentioned dad". Then we read the letter again. Claude said, "She didn't mention him". Next day we got what should have been the first letter ... which told us that our father had died ten months earlier.

'On the way home they played "Give me land, lots of land and the starry skies above, don't fence me in", that was the song that we had going all day and all night. When you came into Sydney Harbour you nearly burst out crying. A whole lot of little boats came out to meet us, and little kids, all waving flags and cheering us and we were lined up and everybody is just about crying. It was tremendous, the emotional thing that happened to us, no doubt about that.

'We got home to the west and brother Keith, a pilot, landed

home a few days after us from England. It was some years later I learnt from a magazine that he had shot down more flying bombers than any other Australian airman.'

When he got home, Jim Steven was lonely for Changi. 'We had lived there for so long. Even when war ended and we were free and we'd go down to the wharf every time a Changi vehicle came by we cheered it as if it were a sign from home.'

He has no feeling about the Japanese. 'No longer can I remember the bad things. At first I could, but I longed in some strange way for Changi, so I called there on the way on a trip to England and laid that ghost for all time. But I can't remember the Burma Railway. I can't remember it at all.'

'A man doesn't know how he will perform until he faces a thing. The first shot distressed one and so did the last.' Signaller Syd Marshall (8th Division Signals) had two brothers overseas, 'All three of us. My parents got two cards from me in 1944 and nothing more until the war ended. My father and his two brothers had been at World War I, dad, a signaller with the 55th Battalion was taken prisoner at Fromelles so knew what it was all about, and Uncle Tom got an MM advancing with the 13th. But I don't think all that experience makes any difference to the family reaction when their sons go to war.'

Like many other men, William Dodds had expected to recover quickly. 'I thought I'd be alright when I got home.' But he was burnt out. 'I only stayed a few years down south and then I moved north to Darwin to pick up my health. And there I stayed.'

Private Gordon Mountford had fought down the peninsula with the 2/29th Battalion, also surviving the Burma Railway and three and a half years of imprisonment. 'Sometimes, always perhaps, I wonder if it really was me there, I wonder if it really happened, perhaps it didn't happen at all, perhaps it was only a bad dream. But then I know no dream could be as bad as this.'

The doctor Edward ('Weary') Dunlop did not attend the War Crimes Trials when many such as Hiramata the Tiger were arraigned. 'They hanged Abana. The men hated him. Called him the Colonel of Death. He was rather ubiquitous I thought, on the edge of things. I could have spoken for him had I gone to the War Crimes Trials in Tokyo as I was asked, but I'd been away from home for eight years and had to get on with things.'

All men claim they would not have got home but for the help of others. Privates Bill Thomas and Mel Lane, 2/3rd Motor Transport: 'None of us would have got home from Burma or Japan if we hadn't had three good men with us. Padre Mathieson inspired us to stay alive no matter what indignities were put upon us; Colonel Jack Williams was No. 1 in our eyes: when the Japs would begin to beat one of us he'd step forward and say, "Belt me in his place". And Doctor Higgins, well, he got us home. When we were too sick to eat he'd say: "The bottom of your dixie is your return ticket home".'

'We didn't know the war had ended', Private Horrie Brown, Royal Australian Engineers, remembers. 'We were being brought back into camp and going through Singapore the Chinese were lining the street and giving us the thumbs-up sign. They were calling out to us that the war was over.'

Alex Kelly, RAAF: 'I was lucky because I was in Changi when the war ended and the air force sent in half a dozen Catalinas to Singapore. We were the first POWs back into Melbourne. There was Mick Moritz, myself and Noel Quinn.'

Ivor Hanger MBE, General Secretary YMCA Perth, remembers the gramophone pick-up affectionately known as the Pan-atrope. 'What a grand job it did! Day after day, week after week, year after year it entertained us and took our minds off the futility and despair of our situation. Tuesday nights, programmes of light music; Thursday nights, jazz; come Saturday and George McNeilly would provide a classical programme for highbrows. It also served well the men in hospital wards. That old faithful gramophone came back home with us in 1945.'

Ivor's other memory is the official surrender of Singapore by the Japanese, 6 September 1945. 'Until the day I die I shall be able to remember my feelings as I stood watching the Rising Sun going down and the Union Jack going up to the top of the flag mast over Changi Gaol. For years we had watched the "Hard Boiled Egg" as we called it, flying over us, always reminding us of our captivity. I suppose it is impossible to recapture one's feelings completely, but I know I was brimming over and tears refused to stop.'

Men learned to know one another's qualities in a way few do in civilian life. When Leslie Greener died in Hobart in 1975, Sir David Griffin described him as 'Captain, 2nd AIF, OIC Education Centre, Changi POW Camp; artist, author, poet, gentleman. One of the most fascinating people I have ever known.'

Bill Jinkins, who had successfully made one of the most daring escapes in the war, learned of Peter, the young Ambonese who had helped him. In appreciation Jinkins had given the boy Peter a sailing boat, a sad mistake as it turned out, because on his return to Ambon the men of the next village, envious of the gift to the boy, 'dobbed him in' to the Japanese. He was put in a cell (Bill Gaspersz, another of Jinkins's friends, was also in the cell because of 'non-cooperation'), then taken out and beheaded. On release, Gaspersz had the boy's body buried in his garden. Gaspersz was gaoled three times but continued to refuse to cooperate. (Jinkins has visited Ambon several times since 1945 to renew that wartime comradeship.)

Ivor Jones, RAAF: 'When the war ended I was stunned, I couldn't believe it. We took it quietly, we were fairly isolated, until a couple of Americans parachuted into the camp from a transport plane and others dropped supplies. Our blokes grabbed the parachutes, nicked into the village and sold them to the Thais. Lovely material. My family knew I was a prisoner, they had received a message in 1944 over the radio. In that same year, 1944, my mate had told me that my mother was dead, he had got the information in a letter. We had time to think in those days, at night we'd look at the Southern Cross, it would seem so far away; but we were like dirty natives sitting on the ground in our scanty clothes, looking up at the stars.

'At the end of the war I got a letter from one of my brothers, there were seven of us in the family, we had all joined up and I wondered who was alive. The brother next to me, a Lieutenant Colonel commanding an infantry battalion, wrote and said, "Mum's very well." The earlier message had been a mistake. And all the boys were okay, they'd been at Tobruk and Alamein, all over the place, all got through. My sister was in the AWAS in signals. We could all go home now.

'But the end was a bit of an anti-climax. As soon as the first meeting of the family was over, we each found we had to go back and see our mates again, you missed them. People would come up and say, "Oh, you've been a prisoner of war, was it terrible?" Then they'd look away and that was it.

'It's only in the last few years that we've talked about it, but we've thought about it every day. I'm a better person from being a POW. I'm glad I had the experience, glad that I've got friends I can talk to, be proud to know, it gives you something to hold on to. Even though our numbers are dwindling, we feel a security having these blokes around us.'

The men may have been down, but not out. When they arrived in Sydney, the West Australians had learned they were to be shipped home to Perth, a slow, long voyage.

Bill Monks: 'The little ship was already crowded with English soldiers going home to England with their Aussie wives. Cramped. Like we'd travelled before, conditions were exactly the same. Twelve us walked off the ship, and with one or two exceptions these were the best behaved men in the whole unit: the two Roediger brothers for instance had never stepped out of line during the whole war; and Sergeant Norm Hurley, he'd never done anything wrong in his whole life; but this was a wrong thing they were trying to do to us and we knew it. We were the first to walk off and after twelve of us got off they stopped others following us by pulling the gangplank up. They flew us twelve home.' The first thing Bill's mother said was, 'Are you whole son? Have you got your legs and arms?'

'I was the eldest in the family. When I'd gone away my sister was about fifteen, but when I came back she was a nursing sister. I'd missed nearly six years out of my family's life.

'I can imagine a mother waiting for a son. We would have changed so much, apart from hardship, we were six years on. Different people. At first I was lucky, got back into ordinary life, mixed and talked with people, got it out of me; I could talk about it then. But a year or two later it fell on me. I got worse. They had sold the farm after I went to war – I was the eldest child. My future was going to have been a farmer. I got much worse, got to the stage where I didn't want to talk. After that I would meet some of the chaps, they'd talk and I'd talk, but I'd shut it out of my other life. I wanted to get on with my life and just shut the past right out. It hits you.' Later he went back to the graveyard near the river Kwai Noi. 'Here was a part of our lives we can never forget but don't want to remember. I saw a lot of names of the chaps that we'd buried and put in the hole, they'd been burnt, whatever, and I got thoroughly depressed.

'I got married and everything, I thought I was right. But then, I suppose you call it a nervous breakdown, I went into the military hospital to get some treatment.' Later a large piece of bamboo was found rotting in his leg. 'It had dragged me down. I had been playing football with this thing, stupid really. My health came good after that.

'I think it's hard for a lot of the younger ones to understand. I have children. I think my daughter understands, but she reads more than the boys. I think they're understanding a little, but they're grown up now. I still think about some things a lot. In 1944, we sailed from Singapore to Japan. I remember it was the 1st July because it was my sister's birthday and when we were marching down to the wharf I said, "It's Connie's birthday, 1st July".'

All the ex-prisoners remember the welcome they received on their way home when the ship *Oranje* berthed at Darwin. 'A banner read, "We are Australians, we never forgot you". Gosh, we'll never forget that welcome. They turned it on properly. We never dreamed it would be like that. Darwin had said, "We are the front door to Australia. Enter in veterans of a terrible war. We have not forgotten you." Notes they sent aboard said, "Men of the *Oranje*, we salute you". That is why we will always love Darwin and the valiant garrison that guards her dry sand and beautiful shores.' The men then went south 'to home sweet home'.

Colin Gooch was in an isolated group in a working camp on the Cambodian/Laos border. 'First we heard a little boy out on the sidelines saying something about "finished".

'We didn't know what that meant. Then a Korean who thought a lot of King George, as all Koreans did at that stage, came up and said, "King George!" (If it was "King George" it was number one!) No one took any notice of him. But soon after that they took us working parties back to camp. Nobody went out for two or three days and we started to think, something's different. Everybody said it must be finished. Go and ask, we kept saying. We didn't have any officers. Anyhow, Sergeant Frank Creedy went up to the Japs and they said yes, the war is finished.

'The Japanese stayed pretty quiet, they kept away. A week went by, nothing. Then Pluto, from the Thai underground, led two officers in, an American and an Englishman, and they said we'd be released in time, when the authorities could get up to us. Pluto had been out in the hills for quite a while, he knew about us being here, what we did, everything. But it was the first we knew of the Thai underground.'

Colin returned to Australia by ship. 'We got off the boat in Melbourne. That was pretty exciting because they put us on coaches out at Port Melbourne and people lined the route all the way in to the city.

'Perhaps people thought it surprising that we didn't do something about the Japanese when we were freed, but I think we were happy just to be alive at this stage; and it's not part of Australians' nature anyhow. No one thought of taking spite out on the Japanese. You need quite a lot of energy for spite.'

Ordinary Seaman Fred Skeels, ex-HMAS *Perth*, was down to 99 pounds in weight when the war ended. For two years his parents hadn't heard anything of him and then, 'there was a whisper that I was a prisoner of war'. But there was nothing official. They later received a twenty-five word letter from Fred and later again they received a batch of letters. 'It took a while to settle down after we got home. I neglected my parents and my home. Each day you'd go into town and meet cobbers you'd been away with. It seemed the only way you could survive, it wasn't that you wanted to talk about what had happened, it was that you didn't know what to talk about at home. I still don't like crowds, noise, people, I don't go to football matches, I still don't like things like that.'

Geoff Dewey, the pilot, was, like many other ex-prisoners, unable to recall his life in prison camps. 'I had forgotten the date we were captured. Just one of those things a bloke should remember for the rest of his life and I'd forgotten until I rang Al, my old air force mate one day, after forty years, and said, "Voice out of the past". He said, "Hi, how are you going?" That's one of the lovely things about him. Easy going. He said, "Do you remember?" and I said no. He said, "I go out under the stars every 21st of April and have a little drink and remember". And I thought that was lovely because I wasn't remembering anything. We were close friends on 84 Squadron RAF and there's only four of us to my knowledge in Australia, so now we meet once a year and have a little reunion on that date, the anniversary of our capture.'

Alan Davies now runs a caravan park in isolated Halls Creek, north-west Australia. 'My feelings towards the Japanese are pretty hard to define. I have Japanese coming here to my caravan park and they camp and I talk to them. They are mostly young people. But when I see them, something tightens up inside me, but I don't ever let it get the better of me, because I think if you did it would destroy you. And I've never, ever since I've come home, talked about it. You'd be the first person I've spoken to in bloody all the time I've been home about all this stuff. I never talk about it, I might relate little incidents, funny things that happened. And I think through this I've lost a lot of hatred, a lot of bad feelings, but I would never, never trust them or never in any way like them, it wouldn't matter how bloody close they ever became.

'It destroyed a lot of men this hatred they had for them. It destroyed them completely. Some drank themselves to death. They had a thing about it. Some very good friends of mine ...

'The Japs came into Cairns in a boat after the war, swaggered ashore. It surprised me that they were so thick of hide that they thought they could come here as though we would be pleased to see them. What a cheek! MacArthur turned himself inside out to make them feel OK. He thought that would stabilise the country, build it up. And their kids have never read about it because it's never been in their history books. So how can they change?'

Petty Officer Tom Mooney: 'When they learnt that the war was over the naval men set to and made up the White Ensign. We rigged up a mast and jack staff out of bamboo, had a colour party and bugler to "sound off colours" and hoisted our White Ensign to the cheers of all in the camp; the navy had come into its own again and I was proud to have been a member of the *Perth's* crew, as these surviving crew members had stuck together and always helped one another and had never during the three years and eight months forgotten that they were Royal Australian Navy men.'

William 'Buzzer' Bee from HMAS *Perth* was twelve months in Burma, building the line. 'Then, the healthiest of us were picked to go on this Japanese party, and I'm really not sorry now, because I did come through it. I was only 30 miles from Nagasaki when the atomic bomb went off. We were able to go home then.'

After the sailor Arthur Bancroft returned home to Perth, he went with his mother to meet with the POW Relatives and Friends Association there. 'I had had to reply to over 300 letters from all over Australia from parents asking for news of their boys. The RAN had given us strict instructions not to talk but I felt I must be frank with these people, they were in such distress. It was most difficult to go to visit some, they always wanted to know how their boys died and I felt I owed it to them to tell them. I took my mother with me when I went to break the news. One woman that we visited hadn't heard from her son and I told her he was indeed dead and I had seen it happen. A few months later she got a card from him, it had been delayed like anything the Japanese did, it was most distressing for her.'

Arthur, who had been rescued by USS *Queenfish*, travels to the USA for reunions with the mariners. Several of the Americans from USS *Houston* have come to Australia for reunions with Australians they were imprisoned with, and Australian sailors from HMAS *Perth* have returned the compliment.

Peter Oates had been a fit young man pre-war. But his heart and lungs were damaged. 'That life in dungeons, in cells and cold places, with malnutrition and beatings and all sorts of strange things is now having an effect on me. I have vascular disease, I have chain-smoked ever since prison days. My doctor believes that everything that's wrong with me is caused by the whack on my skull.' He cannot sit or stand still.

Sapper Pat Reid, 26th Engineers, works today with his wife Rose to help other ex-prisoners. 'The men of that war were boys of the Great Depression, poor, some almost illiterate. They were thankful to get back to Australia, they didn't apply for a pension, they just went their own way, tried to battle on as they had pre-war, but they weren't the same men as went away and never would regain that stamina. When middle age hit them they were burnt out, but by then they had been forgotten and, unfortunately for them, the attitude was that if they'd managed to toil until they were 55 or 60, then there couldn't be much need for a service pension.

'Advocates find it difficult to help them. These men find phrases and words on application forms beyond them. "Hypothesis" is one that constantly worries them, and "normed". Some are men who carry disappointments about what has been dealt out to them in life.'

(Pat's brother, Doctor Harry Reid, 2/4th Infantry Battalion, served as chaplain in the Middle East and the Pacific. When the war ended he chose to serve as a missionary in Japan and then as Chaplain General in Korea.)

Flight Sergeant Bert McKay: 'You see photos of people

jumping for joy and shouting when the war ended. There was none of that, I think we were so exhausted. Psychologically I think I needed some treatment, I cracked up, just couldn't take it. But I was just depressed. You'd think going through all that there'd be nothing that could in any way affect you but it didn't work out like that. I gradually came back to reason but I've had several bouts of depression. I've seen American blokes that were taken hostage and had been incarcerated for only twelve months; they had psychological treatment for about twelve months after they arrived home and they looked as though they were in reasonable condition and health. I've thought Australia should have learnt after the First World War, but there was nothing set up at all for us.'

Bernie O'Sullivan, the machine gun officer, had collapsed and Major Fortune nursed him in Singapore. At that time the Duke of Gloucester was Governor-General of Australia and his Avro York airplane came to Singapore and brought a load of sick men direct to Perth in one day. The courageous Major Saggers was on the plane, as was Vic Mentiplay (a survivor of the battle against the Japanese in Malaya) and Bernie O'Sullivan. They landed at Guildford in Western Australia. Bernie remembers: 'We came in in the blackout to Perth. I didn't know they had blackouts or rationing at home, I didn't know anything that happened to Australia for all these years. But there was no trouble finding my way around town, nothing had changed, no building had gone on, everything had stopped, all energy had gone to the war effort.' But there was change. Bernie's family was sadly depleted. His father had died of gas gangrene during the World War I, now he learnt that his brother, a flight lieutenant in the RAAF, had been killed in action and another brother invalided out of the army. But his mother was waiting, and Val, his fiancée. He was married four days after discharge from the army. Val had been at work every day during the war, but at nighttime had sat down and taken by shorthand every message that came through from Japanese radio. She would then phone the families to whom messages had been sent and she did this for the whole war period. There were many nights when she sat waiting and nothing came through, but she persevered.

Geoff Breaden, the air navigator, went back home to Hobart. 'You can't snap fingers and forget the training to kill scientifically. No one at home knows that. People said, "Why don't you settle down, forget it!"'

The world had indeed changed. The life they knew before the war was no longer viable. Youngsters were about to sing 'The times they are a-changin'. There was no longer a clear path, the lines no longer held firm, sometimes they were sharp, at other times blurred. But the constants remained.

Tommy Taylor, the young boy from the Gippsland hills who escaped to Russia in 1918, had fallen on hard times like many of his mates during the Great Depression. The price of the little book he'd written about his adventures and escape to Moscow during World War I had fallen from threepence to one penny a copy by 1930. 'A comment on "Yesterday's Heroes!"' he said in 1970. His mother, who had waited for him in the mountains, treasured a letter she had from the woman on whose farm Tommy had worked in Austria. After Tommy headed off with the Russian prisoners the woman, her own sons and husband still away at the war, wrote Mrs Taylor telling her Tommy no longer worked on her farm and she imagined the mother 'would see him soon'. A touching gesture from one side of the war to the other. Tommy 'felt bad' at home in Australia during World War II. 'You remember how it felt.'

When World War II ended in the Pacific, there were over 14,000 Australian men to be brought back from Japanese prison camps stretching in a great triangle from Rabaul in the east across to Ambon in the west, completing the triangle in the north in Japan itself. Much of the recovery was done by RAAF transport pilots in under two months of non-stop flying. Nursing sisters of the RAAF accompanied many of the planes attending to the very ill.

A massive work of investigation of missing POWs not listed among the dead in camps began simultaneously with the evacuation of the living. 'The customs of the Japanese', wrote

MacArthur's general staff report, 'did not allow for the proper burial of the dead, consequently the problems were much greater than anticipated'.

If Australia had not ceded control of its armed services to America, would things have been different for our POWs? Would there have been an attempt to rescue our enslaved men so little distance from our northern shores? It certainly was thought of by men such as Bill Jinkins and others but never widely acted on, seemingly because MacArthur did not wish it. At the end of the war almost 6000 Japanese were brought to trial, and of these many were given terms of imprisonment and over 800 were sentenced to death. It was stated and accepted at the trials that many more cases had been reported but it had been impossible to identify the perpetrators. Often the victims knew only the camp name given to a Japanese by the prisoners themselves. Figures produced by senior observers indicated that the Japanese had killed or caused the deaths of over 1 million captives in the Pacific region. This figure appeared to be inflated until evidence was given of 302,000 specified instances of brutality that caused death.

Donald Stuart: 'The thing we all disdained in the Japanese was his universal lack of honour. What passed for him as honour was the mystification of brutish rites and the habits of centuries, blindly forged by their seclusion from the advancement of thought in the world outside their own backwater.'

Many of the young saplings had not yet filled out when they had left home to go to war. Now they staggered on to ships, some reeled like drunkards, others had to be helped, some were carried up the gangway. They were too weak to seek retribution for the aberrations of the spirit of their captors, and too proud. The pharmacist George Copland had 'wanted to rise up in my anger against the fury of my foes. But we just couldn't be bothered. It was all over and I was going to my home at lovely Ulverstone by the sea in Tasmania. Men had said they would exact vengeance as the actions of our tormentors deserved, for the malice of their deeds. But when the Japanese were humbled, they were abject, and men thought it beneath them to recognise their erstwhile gaolers.'

War and battle is the ultimate testing time and so is the humility of defeat and imprisonment. In a world at war many sparrows do fall, but the ordinary man is not amongst them: his spirit triumphs over all. He may not make learned statements as to how the war ended or indeed how it began or who began it, he only knows how he himself stood in that worst of times. Such self-knowledge is enough and is given to few.

Donald Stuart: 'Sometimes, out of nowhere, you hear the thin, silver notes of the bugle; I've heard that phantom bugle crying the "Last Post" through the silky whisper of the she-oaks in the bush and I've stood still, alone, not thinking of men I've seen buried, or helped bury, just standing, listening, but I don't know where the music comes from. I don't know who sounds the bugle.'

The Korean War
1950–1953

And Yet – Korea

'I was very proud to be accepted among all those veteran diggers.'

Keith ('Mo') Gwyther when enlisting for Korea

AND YET. AT FIRST light on the winter morning of 8 July 1950, five years after this last devastating war ended, a young man from a country farm was waiting at the army recruiting office to enlist for another war. He was Mo (Keith) Gwyther of Leongatha (Vic.), the twenty-fourth man in his State to enlist for the war in Korea. 'I had always been disappointed to have missed the fighting in World War II. I was sweating it out that morning waiting for the army office to open, afraid I may not be accepted because thousands of veterans of World War II were volunteering.' This was the first intake although the war had been declared on 25 January of that year. This 23-year-old had missed out on World War II because of his youthful age. But he had seen veterans return home, even in his quiet bush town; from that area boys still in their teens had rushed to the last war and at least one had been a POW (and caught up in the grisly Tol massacre on New Britain).

Along the line with Mo that winter morning were men as old as his father, men who had fought five years before in World War II and were anxious to be back in the fray. 'I was very proud to be accepted among all those veteran Diggers.' Mo wanted to be 'first into camp and first over to Korea'.

'I didn't play up or anything during training in case I missed the draft. We all wanted to be in it.' He had three weeks training in Australia then three weeks in Japan at the Japanese traditional training ground, Haramure. 'And then, all aboard for Korea.'

What will humanity a hundred years from now say about this? They will know of the treatment of the Koreans by the

Japanese who forcibly annexed their country in 1910 and remained in power until World War II; they will know about the vicious war fought by the Japanese in 1941–45 and then, only five years after their countrymen had returned to Australia from that war, they will find Australians proudly training, as guests in Japan, on the field of their recent enemy whilst on their way to fight Koreans and Chinese (one of our Allies of World War II).

But, the fashion had changed and ushered in the years of 'Commies', 'Reds under the bed', and the nearest Reds seemed to be in Korea, and Korea was near Japan who would benefit enough by supplying Allied needs for this war to put her back on her feet. Later it would be 'forgive and forget' time and 'remember our balance of trade'.

The Korean War was, in origin, a civil war between rival Korean regimes, encouraged by nations other than their own. At the end of World War II China, with the zeal created by its new political regime, saw its chance to move in and threw in her lot with the North Koreans. America intervened, justifying the intrusion as being a means of halting the spread of Communism; Australia followed as a means of retaining status with America. Troops were sent in as United Nations forces although the United Nations Charter (of which both America and Australia are signatories) does not sanction involvement in a civil war.

Mo Gwyther played his role as soldier well. His father, Captain L.T. Gwyther, had been awarded the MC and Bar in World War II. His family had farmed in Gippsland on the pioneer road simply called Gwyther's Track. His father, according to Mo, was 'a hard man' and the boy, like most Australian dairy farm boys of that era, had had a tough life. 'I wouldn't wish it on a dog', he once said. 'But I wouldn't want any other life than farming.' He could ride, shoot, take orders, use his initiative and rough it with the best. In short, he was an ideal model for a foot soldier.

He was in action almost from the day he landed. 'We were sent off in a box-car type of plane, no seats, had to strap parachutes on before we boarded. I was carrying a Bren gun and a rifle and I was worried because I didn't know if I had to drop the Bren if we were forced to jump out and I didn't want to do the wrong thing. The plane landed us alright but it gave us an idea of how things could be.' Then there came the time he was firing at what he thought was a foxhole camouflaged with branches of trees only to see it open up and big guns swing down towards him. 'It was a tank, camouflaged, I thought they'd blow my head off, the shells went over about 3 feet above my head and I flattened down into the ground.

'The Gooks were everywhere. You can't imagine what a war it was with us and them all over the countryside, fighting to kill. There's no quarter given in a place like Korea. It was kill or be killed.' It was a war with new terminology. Gwyther speaks of Gooks (the enemy), Burp guns ('most effective in Korea'). On 24 October 1950 'a Gook got me in the shoulder with a Burp and Paddy Trump from Sydney got a burst in the feet from a Burp when he clambered down to get my Bren because I couldn't lift it with me being winged and all. Then another Burp got Ossie Osborne from Perth WA in the shoulder.'

On this, his first journey away from home, the thought of becoming a prisoner 'never entered my mind', yet he was to spend more time as a captive across the 38th Parallel that divided North from South Korea than he did fighting. On Anzac Day 1951, nine months after enlisting, seven months after arriving in Korea, he was taken prisoner at Kapyong. The Australian newspapers reported the battle he had fought in as having the highest enemy casualty rate any Commonwealth Unit has claimed in a single day.

'Their stand will be remembered as one of the finest of the war. They ripped a Chinese attacking force to pieces, and when the sun went down on Anzac night, 500 Chinese lay dead on the shell-cratered hillsides.' And, unknown to his mates, Mo Gwyther lay there with the Chinese, buried almost to his neck in clods of dirt from a bomb blast on the foxhole he had been firing from.

'My mob, D Company, the Third Battalion, Royal Australian Regiment had moved up towards the Yalu River, on Hill 504 near the Parallel and in the morning the Chinese started attacking our positions. It was a mixed up fight. I had a Bren gun, then in came Chinese mortars. We withdrew up a slope. No one needed to tell us the drill, we took our own initiative and dug in. During a break in firing my mate on the Bren gun went up to the top of the slope to where the others had dug in and while he was away I saw four planes coming in at eye level towards our hill slope, their big napalm containers under each wing beginning to fall.

'They burst so close they shrivelled the dry leaves I'd used to camouflage my foxhole. I wasn't burnt, but I could see our guys up the hill waving desperately, signalling to the planes – because they were our planes firing mistakenly on *us*.'

Half buried by the clods of clay dislodged by the bombing, he was later dug out by the Chinese who were searching for their own wounded amongst the dead. 'I was concussed by the bombing and was unconscious. When I came to I was surrounded by Chinese. I called out and they saw me.' The battle was at its height and the Chinese dug a small pit for Gwyther and covered him with branches while they went on with the battle. 'I thought they'd left me but later they came back and took me to their dugout where they were putting bits of rags on to their wounded.'

That night the Chinese began to move back, carrying their wounded, as reinforcements took their place, and Mo Gwyther was taken along with them. 'We went at a fast trot, I thought I'd die from the pace or the shells bursting around us. We got to a village and every house there had wounded men, and others were digging graves for dead men being carried out of the houses. There were arm stumps and legs hanging off, no medicine, nothing, only water.'

Mo met another Australian prisoner, Private Bob Parker. 'He was a Don R [Despatch Rider] and had been caught while trying to get back to HQ. He had a wound in the hip but could get around and had fought like hell to escape being captured, but they got him and made him collect their wounded off the battleground. (Bob didn't get anything done to his hip until we were repatriated in 1953.) We saw many things. One day they lined us up and said an American had murdered a Chinese soldier. They took him, led him off and shot him slowly, seven shots it took. But one thing we learned was that the man who has been a front-line soldier is less bitter towards you than a man who has never seen action. We went up a peak where mules with Chinese drivers were bringing down ammunition on a terrible mountain track and hanging up in the trees were rotting lumps of mules and drivers that our air force had bombed. We marched by night, sometimes up to 37 miles a night. We were forever being asked questions, interrogated, but we played dumb. We didn't know why, but they took Bob's Digger hat and my identity disc.

'The greatest Australian I knew over there was Sergeant Don Buck. He was a great one for escaping and he and Parker were out for eleven days once. The three of us had met at Bean Camp (you only got beans there, that's where it got its name) and we stuck together. Later we were being marched off to Camp Five and my two mates Parker and Buck sloped off and were on the run for eleven days. A Korean who hated Chinese helped them but eventually they were caught by North Koreans and tied up with wire and given the treatment. We didn't see them again until they were brought back to Camp Five near Christmas Day 1951. The Chinese had rescued them from the Gooks or they would have been killed. Bob Parker and Don Buck had spent six months in Camp Twelve, an indoctrination school. These schools took in many United Nations prisoners and attempted to convert them to Communism. Because of their need to ingratiate themselves with their captives, the Chinese forbade any punishment to be meted out to the two Australians for their having escaped.'

Mo Gwyther had also attempted escape. 'I went with an American just after Bob Parker and Don Buck lit out. We were east of Pyongyang when we found a small boat near the Taedong River and set off, but got stuck on an island, swam ashore and were picked up.' Mo and his American co-escapee were handed over to an unexpectedly benign bunch of men, a group of Chinese whose main object was to practise their English. 'Once they gave up trying to convert us they'd come in and talk about anything at all, and their lingo improved no end!' These captors fed the men and cared for them for three months until they were handed back to Camp Five.

'At Camp Five I met Tom Hollis, the only other Australian there at the time. He stalked across to me, 6 foot 3 of him, put his hand out and we shook hands and grinned at each other. It was a good feeling. He was a cobber of Don Buck who, with Bob Parker, joined us later. Buck and Parker had had a heavy time at the indoctrination school but hadn't given an inch. Not one Australian fell for this stuff they tried to feed us. We were the first Australians in any war to have to stand up to brain washing. But generally speaking Camp Five was bad. They said we were reactionaries. Put us in a little cell with us all crowded in, called it the Sweat Box. We had to stand, or sit with our legs outstretched, at attention and not speak, no sound, from 4.30 in the morning until 11 p.m. Even then there was no rest for us. They wakened us often and sometimes Tong, the Provost-Marshal, and his larrikins beat us up with their rifle butts, clubs, even pistol butts, and sometimes did this until we were unconscious. We were starved, could only go to the lavatory once a day, even then the guards decided the time and that was bad because we all had dysentery. Often we had no water to drink and rarely had water to wash with.

'Tong had a long thin stick pushed through a hole in the door and you had to hang on to this with your teeth, and the idea was that the sentry outside would take you unawares and knock the stick sideways. A couple had teeth knocked out this way, all of us got cuts inside our mouths, but the worst was when they'd whip it down your throat. They had some outlandish tricks. They tied blokes up by the wrists on to the roof, feet barely touching the ground. This is a terrible torture for a man to go through, but just as bad was one I saw with the rope from his neck to his ankles, then hoisted up so that if he let his heels down he would hang himself. They'd call it suicide then.'

In June 1952 Don Buck led an escape of twenty-four men in small groups from this prison. 'For this break-out I made some pretty good compasses. I got a piece of cable from a loud speaker and made a coil with the copper strands. There weren't many electric lights in the camp but I connected to one and magnetised steel wires off the cables. The magnetism would last for a few months. It was simple to cut the wires into short lengths and pin each through the centre so it could swing and there were our compasses!' Unknown to them, an American who had learnt of this break-out now informed on them and they were recaptured and punished severely. 'There is no man in the world I admire as much as Sergeant Buck', Mo said. 'He was the greatest. He took all the beatings but never once gave in to tell them anything about our break-out.

'Another brave man I knew was Slim Madden. We'd been together from the time we were taken in April 1951. But he was in a bad way, been badly treated, and when we left Bean Camp he was too sick to move. They left him behind. He was later awarded the George Cross because of the many courageous stands he took against the enemy.'

At Camp Five, Mo was issued with the Korean wool-padded suit, warm and comfortable, as well as a blanket. 'Here we had soup made by a big negro who used to toss in a pig, guts and everything, enough to last us for a week. Here I also cooked and I turned out decent enough bread. We didn't have much work to do except to dig out and shift 2000 tons of clay on Chinese-type baskets to make a parade ground, and carry rocks to build a lecture hall for their darned Commie speeches. These Commie talks could get a man into a lot of trouble. I had to back down once and end up half agreeing with them to get myself out of a mess after I'd started arguing with a lecturer who had got his degree from an American university. And Tom Hollis got into trouble too, but luckily when Spiti Itchi, as we called the commander, spat in Tom's face and said

"I'll see you starve!" an interpreter hopped in and separated them. I thought Tom would be shot for this.'

From here, Mo, Bob Parker and Don Buck tried their next escape but were recaptured the following day and now 'it was back into the Sweat Box'. This room was 10 feet by 8 feet, the floor a raised platform of pine poles 'with the knots left on'.

'If they caught you talking they made you squat on one of the round poles like a chook. If you stretched your legs they shouted at you and they'd make you take the stick in your teeth again while they jabbed it through a hole in the door. You just had to take it easy, try not to let them rattle you because that's what they wanted, the excuse to use the bayonet. We were ten days in the Sweat Box but there was a Yank who had been there for fifty-seven days. We heard men getting beaten in the box next to us but we'd whisper to one another, "Take it easy", the only way to survive. Tong the bastard was going round bashing everyone he could get at. I kept my eyes down so as not to provoke him.'

When they were released from the 'Box' they were ordered to write a confession, 'a self-criticism' for attempting to escape. 'If it wasn't good it was "back in the Sweat Box" for us. Buck told us to do this confession as it was done under duress and wouldn't count against us.' At this time the men met Wilfred Burchett, an Australian whose attitudes had him branded as a traitor by the Australian populace, although he always denied any traitorous behaviour, declaring that he wrote, as he believed, honestly.

'Burchett came from Gippsland, as I did', Mo Gwyther said. 'He was no ornament to us, he was nothing for us to be proud of. He came and went as he pleased in North Korea. That's enough to let any man know what he was.' To a man, the Australian prisoners rejected his blandishments and refused to discuss politics with him. 'He told us he was an Australian newspaper correspondent and wanted to talk with us four Australian prisoners in Camp Five. When we were taken in to his hut he wanted to shake hands with us but none of us put out our hand so he eventually had to drop his. He said to write our names and addresses in his notebook so he could contact our parents, but we wouldn't do this. He knew then we were a wake-up to him. He tried to tell us about North Korean kids being killed by United Nations aircraft, he said we couldn't imagine the napalm bombing so we said yes we could, we'd seen plenty of it from the North Koreans. We were only with him about two minutes and then he opened the door and we left him.'

The months rolled on and these young men were succumbing to more illnesses but remarkably, although they received little mail, and that censored, they never thought they would not survive. 'No, we knew it was just a matter of keeping cool, never get hot under the collar, never give them an excuse to shoot you or beat you up too badly and things would work out. Don Buck always said that, "Keep cool, give in to them if there is no other way out, but only in things that don't matter. Just hang on."' It was this advice that led to these four Australians each being mentioned in Despatches at the end of war, when news of their 'outstanding conduct' became known.

Gwyther later heard what happened to Madden GC. 'He was the only one of us POWs in Korea who didn't get home. He was left behind, too ill to continue when we were marched to Camp Five. We later learnt he was taken to Caves Camp, Kangdong, where not one man was fit to march but nevertheless were sent off on a 220-mile march to the Yalu River. There was a cartload who couldn't walk at all and Madden was in this with seven others. Only five survived the journey and Madden died shortly after. He'd been beaten, they'd done bad things to him but he stayed his cheerful self. He never gave in and that was a real inspiration to all prisoners. He deserved the George Cross that was awarded him posthumously.'

Of the twenty-nine Australian soldiers taken prisoner, only one, Madden, died. The rest were repatriated home.

The official history of the Korean War listed thirty-one members of No.77 Squadron RAAF posted Missing. Of these only seven were repatriated. (Six of these missing men were RAF serving with the Australian Squadron.) The treatment of

most of the captured airmen was as violent as that of the prisoners of the Japanese in World War II. Some had been in
camps where Mo Gwyther had been imprisoned, in particular
many had been in 'Paks Palace' after being recaptured when
attempting escape. For all that, of the few men repatriated,
three continued flying. Two of these survivors of the North
Korean prison camps and treks across snow and iced-over
rivers were eventually to die in air crashes and one in a road
accident in peacetime.

On 19 January 1951 Flight Lieutenant G.R. Harvey had
became the first Australian to become a prisoner in the Korean
War. His Mustang aircraft was hit by ground fire as he was
attacking a 'suspected' Chinese headquarters in Pyongyang.
With smoke and oil obscuring his vision, Harvey crash-landed
on a sand bank outside the city. Shots ricocheted around him,
and, having no cover in the frozen landscape, he had to surrender. For twelve weeks he underwent periodic interrogation.
The principal North Korean interrogators were named Pak
and Lee, the men who later conducted the notorious interrogation centre known as Pak's Palace, to which Harvey was
committed on 7 April 1951. At one period, Harvey and two
other pilots were put in a totally dark tunnel 2 metres high
and 2 wide, 10 long, where prisoners sat side by side in the
stench of an open-hole toilet.

At Pak's Palace the three pilots were beaten and punched
before spending forty-five days in a metre square, 2 metres
deep hole in the ground. Two days after removal to Pyoktong
one of the pilots, Simpson, died.

After 958 days as a prisoner, Harvey was repatriated on 29
August 1953 in the operation 'Big Switch' when prisoners were
exchanged.

It was a different war from any other that had taken prisoners. In this, the captives were exposed to 'brain washing' for
the first time, and the temptation in the face of beatings and
hunger was fierce. Their enemy attempted to indoctrinate with
a philosophy foreign to their own, it was a war of propaganda.
There were 'corrective camps', 're-education programmes'.

They were offered baits to show 'the correct attitude' and to admit they had been 'duped' by their own country. If they agreed to all this they could be invited to 'fight the forces of reaction', that is to change sides. It was also the height – or the depth – of anti-Communism in Australia and ushered in a peculiar period of politics and of war. It was a war that never grabbed the imagination or the troubled hearts of the people back home. It was the last war we were likely to see with Australian volunteers rushing to join the colours.

Epilogue: The Pity of War

Let them in, Peter, they are very tired
Give them the couches where the angels sleep.
Let them wake whole again to the new dawn fired
With sun – not war, and may their peace be deep.

A soldier's prayer for his friends

THE PITY OF WAR is that it brings out all that is noblest in man – while at the same time all the brain-spattering arts that peacetime would never countenance are perfected and practised openly. None but the ordinary man who does what he is ordered to do are innocent.

During the trial of the American Lieutenant Calley, charged for his part in the massacre at My Lei, Vietnam, in 1967, it was said, 'What was done at My Lei was outside all the rules and laws of war. It was cold-blooded killing.' Yes, but how else is a soldier to kill if not in cold blood? And is there anything more chilling than the statement, 'the rules and laws of war'?

Lieutenant Calley, found guilty of the murder of 102 innocents, said he didn't know who the enemy were. 'All I was told was that the enemy was Communism, an ideology, a philosophy in a man's mind. That was the enemy I was told to kill.' Calley had forgotten the major rule in war or peace – not to be caught. Civilians are very touchy about such things. They respect the laws of war and even the bloodiest war if run by rules, that is, women and children are usually protected even in what is strangely termed 'total war'.

Hence the Hague and Geneva Conventions and the International Laws of War and other such do's and don'ts for the waging of war give rise to the question Why? Why are some acts outlawed in war? Wars are notorious for their constant

723

savagery. 'Thousands slaughtered', we read. 'No front line', 'no granting status of POW to captives'. Military hierarchy itself begs the question 'How can a chief of an army be acquitted and his men convicted?' 'Civilised' folk don't hold with a lynching. They speak of 'levels of barbarism'. What levels are there in barbarism? Surely barbarism is absolute? We can't make rules for it.

Our sin is the sin of our forebears and our children's sin will be the sin of their forebears unless we devise an end to the madness. 'Lord of Hosts be with us yet', the soldiers sing. 'Lest we forget, lest we forget.'

We know that if we forget we endow our children with the legacy of war but how can we tell the generations to come that we have found the way, have surveyed a safe path that would lead them to sweet, merry, boisterous peace? For in our going we will not have discovered that most mighty and powerful weapon ever made, the arms that will make peace victorious. Had we done this seemingly impossible thing, our lives and the pain we have known in wars would perhaps have some reason. But as we move towards the year 2000 AD we know we have no more defence against war than did men in the dawn of time.

If there is no alternative, let's break out the pennants once again, polish the trumpet and hear the silver cry come down from the hills to the city streets, thrill to the blood-bumping tarroom, tarroom of the slow march on the bass drum; let the young men swing in mesmeric rhythm down the streets, the young girls line the footpaths and throw kisses to one and all. Let's do it well and make the most of it. Let's stop this genteel posturing.

Hopefully our descendants will see some of our reasoning and remember it is easy to be wise in retrospect. And will they do any better? All the peace marches and peace talks since the end of World War II do not give us great hope. Certainly many young Australian men were none too willing to be conscripted for Vietnam and many of the World War II generation agreed with them. But the crux, the moment of truth, may come if we have an enemy come against our own homeland. Remembering that up until now we have only fought on other people's lands, we have no knowledge of how a generation might act if the Australian continent were to be invaded. Some believe the young men and women would rush to the barricades to save their country. Some say no, that peace marches and total antipathy to war would stop most from repelling an enemy. They will say, 'No country is worth the spilling of one drop of blood of young Australian men. If I must, I will live under a foreign invader and come what may, take my chance.' Or they will vote: 'I am willing, if necessary, to die in an attempt to repel a regime not of my choosing'. There is no other choice, just one of the two. And when this question is asked, it should be perfectly clear that no woman or man should look askance at any who votes differently from him, for both should act responsibly with honourable intention, both under sincere belief and the wisdom of deep folk memory. Each is simply and coldly final, and as history has taught us, each holds terrifying possibilities. As well, history has taught us we cannot live without fear of invasion unless we direct great energy towards achieving peace.

Wars were once not seen as abominations against humanity or as an obscenity. Australian settlers brought all the mores of the old world across the oceans with them and old mores die hard. Heroes belong to our youthful dreams and fancies, warriors lost in time haunt our later years. But to understand a nation you must know its memories. What can they tell us, what can we learn from them about the kind of people our country has bred, what can they give us to take into the future, these men who were prisoners but had committed no crime?

They walked a strange, eerie trail with dead men for company almost the whole of the years that should have been the liveliest and best of their young manhood. That will always set them apart. It is a further edge of that mateship that all soldiers experience, and if we ridicule this it is only because we envy them this rare oneness with each other. They walked a dozen calvaries that belonged to the barbarian times we thought were past, and it is we who should shoulder a communal guilt that we placed our men in this position.

When they come, let them in, Peter, they are very tired. Give them the couches where the angels sleep.

List of Abbreviations

AAMC	Australian Army Medical Corps	EST	Eastern Standard Time
AANS	Australian Army Nursing Service	GC	George Cross
		GPO	General Post Office
AASC	Australian Army Service Corps	HMAS	His Majesty's Australian Ship
AB	Able Bodied [Seaman]	HQ	Headquarters
ABDA	American, British, Dutch and Australian	IFF	Identification Friend or Foe
A/c	Aircraft	IJA	Imperial Japanese Army
ADS	Advanced Dressing Station	IRCC	International Red Cross Committee
AFC	Australian Flying Corps	ISO	(Companion of the) Imperial Service Order
AGH	Australian General Hospital	KIA	Killed in Action
AIB	Allied Intelligence Bureau	MAC	Motor Ambulance Convoy
AIF	Australian Imperial Force	MBE	Member of the Order of the British Empire
ALG	Advance Landing Group		
ARCS	Australian Red Cross Service	MC	Military Cross
		MM	Military Medal
AWAS	Australian Women's Army Service	MO	Medical Officer
		MV	Motor Vessel
CCS	Casualty Clearing Station	NCO	Non-commissioned Officer
CO	Commanding Officer		
CPO	Chief Petty Officer	NEI	Netherlands East Indies
DFC	Distinguished Flying Cross	NGVR	New Guinea Volunteer Rifles
DR	Despatch Rider (commonly known as Don R)	OBE	Order of the British Empire
		OC	Officer in Command
DSC	Distinguished Service Cross	OP	Observation Post
		ORs	Other Ranks (that is, neither officers nor NCOs)
DSO	Distinguished Service Order		
ED	Efficiency Decoration	OS	Ordinary Seaman

PO	Petty Officer	SOA	Special Operations Australia
POW	Prisoner of War		
PRU	Photo Reconnaissance Unit	SOE	Special Operations Executive
PT	Physical Training	SS	Schutzstaffel (Nazi elite corps); Steamship
RAAF	Royal Australian Air Force	TB	tuberculosis (tubercle bacillus)
RAF	Royal Air Force [UK]		
RAMC	Royal Army Medical Corps [UK]	USAAF	United States of America Air Force
RAN	Royal Australian Navy	USFIP	United States Forces in the Philippines
RANVR	Royal Australian Navy Volunteer Reserve		
RAP	Regimental Aid Post	USS	United States Ship
RASC	Royal Army Service Corps	VAD	Voluntary Aid Detachment [nursing staff]
RC	Roman Catholic	VC	Victoria Cross
RMO	Resident Medical Officer	VE	Victory in Europe
RSL	Returned Servicemen's League	VP	Victory in Pacific
		WO	Warrant Officer
RSM	Regimental Sergeant Major	YMCA	Young Men's Christian Association
SBO	Senior British Officer	2IC	2nd-in-command

Further Reading

Arneil, Stan. *Black Jack. The Life and Times of Brigadier Sir Frederick Galleghan*. Macmillan, South Melbourne, 1983.

Bean, C.E.W. (ed.) *Official History of Australia in the War of 1914–18*. 12 Volumes. Angus & Robertson, Sydney, 1934.

Butler, Col. A.G., DSO, VD, AAMC (ed.) *Official History of the Australian Army Medical Services, 1914–18*. Volumes 1 & 2.

Barber, Noel. *Sinister Twilight* (Singapore pre-1942). Collins, London, 1968.

Blair, Joan & Clay Jr. *Return from the River Kwai*. Simon & Schuster, New York, 1979.

Chiron. *Journal of the University of Melbourne Medical Society*. Vol. 2, No. 1, April 1988.

Connelly, Roy & Wilson, B. (co-ed.) *Medical Soldiers*. Pub. 2/10 A.F.A., Kingsgrove, Australia, 1985.

Callinan, Bernard. *Independent Company. The Australian Army in Portuguese Timor 1941–43*. William Heinemann, Australia, 1953.

Cooper, Alan. *Free to Fight Again*. Kimber Press, London, 1988.

Churchill, Winston. *The Second World War*. Volumes I–IV. Cassell & Co. Ltd., London, 1948.

Farrar-Hockley, Anthony. *The Edge of the Sword*. Frederick Muller, London, 1954.

Greener, L. *No Time to Look Back*. Gollancz, London, 1951.

Hamilton, Col. T. *Soldier Surgeon in Malaya*. Angus & Robertson, Sydney, 1957.

Hardie, Dr Robert. *The Burma–Siam Railway. The Secret Diary of Dr Robert Hardie.* London War Museum. Colliers, Sydney, 1983.

Irving, David. *The Destruction of Convoy PQ17.* Cassell, London, 1968.

Kent Hughes, W.S. *Slaves of the Samurai.* Oxford University Press, Melbourne, 1946.

Le Souef, Leslie. *To War Without a Gun.* Artlook, Perth, 1980.

Lane, John. *Summer Will Come Again.* Fremantle Arts Centre Press, Fremantle, 1987.

Long, Gavin. *Greece, Crete and Syria.* Australian War Memorial, Canberra, 1953.

Legg, Frank. *The Gordon Bennett Story.* Angus & Robertson, Sydney, 1965.

Lowenthal, David. *The Past is a Foreign Country.* Cambridge University Press, Melbourne, 1985.

Moffit, Athol. *Project Kingfisher.* Angus & Robertson, Sydney, 1989.

Morris Dictionary of Word and Phrase Origins. 2nd edn. Harper & Row, New York, 1971.

Muggenthaler, August Karl. *German Raiders of World War II.* (Published USA, 1977) English edn. 1978.

Ministry of War Transport. *Merchantmen at War. The Official Story of the Merchant Navy: 1939–1944.* His Majesty's Stationery Office, London, 1944.

Newton, R.W. *The Grim Story of the 2/19th Battalion AIF.* 2/19th Battalion, 1976.

O'Neill, Robert. *Australia in the Korean War 1950–53.* Australian War Memorial & Australian Government Publishing Service, Canberra, 1985. Vol. II. Combat Operations.

Page, Sergeant Major Martin. *Kiss Me Goodnight Sergeant-Major – Songs & Ballads of World War II.* Hart-Davis, London, 1973.

Rudyard Kipling's Verse. Def. edn. Hodder & Stoughton, London, 1940.

Stand-To. Vol. 3, No. 2. February 1952.

Spur, Russell. *A Glorious Way to Die*. London, 1982.

Simons, Jessie. *While History Passed*. William Heinemann, Melbourne, 1954.

Strange, Louis Arbon. *Recollections of an Airman*. John Hamilton, London, 1933.

Walker, A.S. *Clinical Problems of War*. Australian War Memorial, Canberra, 1952. (Australia in the war of 1939 to 1945; series 5 (medical); vol. 1 and vol. 2.)

Wigmore, L. *The Japanese Thrust*. Australian War Memorial, Canberra, 1952. (Australia in the war of 1939 to 1945; series 1 (army); vol. 2.)

White, Thomas Walter, Lt. Colonel DFC, VD. *Guests of the Unspeakable*. John Hamilton, London, 1928.

Acknowledgements

This book had its genesis in a discussion over lunch in 1978 with Nick Hudson, then Managing Director of Heinemann, Australia. He, being English, thought of the title *In The Bag*, but I assured him it was not a term commonly used by Australians except those who had been taken prisoner by the Germans, and even there not universally used. Men incarcerated by the Japanese did not use it at all. However, it was Nick's idea in the first place for me to write this book.

I acknowledge the assistance of the Australian War Memorial Research Grants. Also, ex-prisoners of World War I, World War II and Korea who lent personal and family diaries and letters; the Mitchell Library, NSW; La Trobe Library, Vic.; Oxley Library, Qld; State Library of Tasmania; Battye Library, WA, and staff of the Darwin Public Library; International Red Cross Committee, Geneva, Switzerland (in particular Mrs P. Troya); Australian Red Cross Society (Vic. branch); the Commanding Officer, Officers and men, 8/7th Battalion; Ranger Museum, the Royal Victoria Regiment, Ballarat (Vic.); Sapper Pat Reid, 2/6th Field Company for help and advice; Squadron Leader Ernie Stanton, Air Force Association, NSW; Captain Alan Smith, MN, and Mrs Olive Smith, for their generous help; Mick Toohey, RAN; HMAS *Tingira* Old Boys' Association; Ray Parkin; Doctor Ian Duncan, NSW ex-Prisoners of War Association; Robert Freeman, Mackay, Qld, for material of his late father, Captain David Freeman, MN; men of the 2/6th Field Company for permission to cite their unpublished book *The Gap*; Len Blease AM, MBE, National President, Merchant Navy War Service League; Captain K. A. Brumpton,

ACKNOWLEDGEMENTS 733

RACT; Colonel J. P. Buckley OBE, ED; Brigadier Keith Colwill; Brigadier John Deighton SM; Len Hansen; Lieutenant Colonel Harry Jackson and Captain Bill Jinkins for assistance with the Borneo chapter; Joyce Ancliffe and Ken Gaunt of Perth; Bert Beros, Peter Coverdale, Sergeant Brand, Claude Mawby, Joe Kingston, Bob Read, Paddy Birmingham and Maureen Quigley for their verses; Mrs Betty Van Nooten; Private C. (Bill) Harry for sharing his incomparable knowledge of the 2/22nd Battalion with me; Roy Connelly and Bob Wilson, editors of *Medical Soldiers*, for permission to quote; WOII David Elder who has been most generous in sharing his own work with me; Bob Nelson of Newcastle; Colonel Wheeler; Tony Roe; F. S. (Sep) Owen for permission to quote his writings on the 2/10th Field Ambulance; Private W. 'Bill' Cook, 2/10th Field Ambulance, for help long ago; Brigadier Keith Rossi OBE, ED, RFD; Flying Officer Alan Fraser assisted with research as did Jenny Carew; Dianne Ellis and Maureen Sheehan typed the manuscript during its six drafts and got to know many of the warriors in this book. Thanks, too, are due to the physician who made it all possible.

Every attempt has been made to credit correctly the many illustrations and information sent to me. For any error in such crediting I apologise.

I have made no effort to alter the expressions the men use: they were of the period now fifty years past and as such they bear no more malice than today's expressions will appear to our grandchildren.

It should be noted that Australians, as did other 'colonials' in the wars covered in this book, often referred to themselves as British, meaning Allied, troops.

Index

561, 562, 563, 564, 574, 575, 583, 585 587, 594, 601, 625, 633
Singora 273
Skeels, Fred 340, 341, 703, 704
Skeles Prison Camp 206
Skinner, Captain 649
Slessor, Kenneth 112
Sligar, Noel 647
Sloss, J. 89
Small, Corporal 464, 465
Smith, Alan 648
Smith, C.R. 456
Smith, F.R. 96
Smith, George 377
Smith, Jean 389, 416, 691
Smith, L.H. 92
Smith, Ross 92
Smith, R.W. 560
Smolensk 65
Socfin 281
Soley, Corporal 89
Solferino 596
Solomons 383
Sora Valley 140
Sourabaya 428
South Africa 28
South Africans 188, 197
Southern Cross, MV 405, 406
Sowacoad 412
Sparkes, Ron 343, 557
Sparrow Force 389
Special Operations Australia 408
Sperber, Dr 658
Sphakia 205
Spowers, Colonel 126
Spreewald 650
Spurgeon, 'Spud' 355, 356
St Andrews Cathedral 286, 575
St Hom 654
St Petersburg 68
Staff, A.E. 611
Stalag III 173, 204

Stalag VIIA 146, 172
Stalag VIIIA 162
Stalag VIIIB 147, 173
Stalag Luft I 262, 263
Stalag 383 227, 238
Stark, Sergeant 278
Stayt, Butch 333
Steele, Ray 457, 459, 460, 462
Stephen, Jock 352
Steven, Jim 698
Stevens, Major 425
Stevenson, Flight Sergeant 679
Sticpewich, William 469, 470, 471, 475, 477, 480, 481, 482, 483, 484, 485, 487
Stirling Castle 157
Stoker, Captain 13, 14, 19
Stortap 664
Strange, L.A. 97
Strathmore Prison 207
Strathnaver 345
Stratton, Sam 191–7, 198, 199, 694
Strickland, Wally 212
Stuart, Charles 293, 296
Stuart, Donald 2, 3, 7, 314, 325, 528, 531, 602, 710
Stuart, HMAS 144, 147, 223
Sturdee, General 390, 404
Sturgeon, USS 386
Suarez, Allessandro 459, 461
Suda Bay 144, 169, 171, 177, 203, 205
Sue, Jack 470
Suez 439
Suez Canal 34
Suga, Lieutenant Colonel 494
Sumatra 249, 317, 329, 346, 351, 357, 435, 436, 437 445, 496, 564, 577
Summons, Hedley 306
Sunda Strait 148, 328, 330, 333, 334, 340, 343